Ziegfeld
and His Follies

ZIEGFELD
AND HIS
FOLLIES

A BIOGRAPHY
OF BROADWAY'S
GREATEST PRODUCER

CYNTHIA BRIDESON
and
SARA BRIDESON

UNIVERSITY PRESS OF KENTUCKY

Scholarly publisher for the Commonwealth,
serving Bellarmine University, Berea College, Centre College of Kentucky,
Eastern Kentucky University, The Filson Historical Society, Georgetown College,
Kentucky Historical Society, Kentucky State University, Morehead State
University, Murray State University, Northern Kentucky University, Transylvania
University, University of Kentucky, University of Louisville, and Western
Kentucky University.

Editorial and Sales Offices: The University Press of Kentucky
663 South Limestone Street, Lexington, Kentucky 40508-4008
www.kentuckypress.com

Library of Congress Cataloging-in-Publication Data

Brideson, Cynthia.
  Ziegfeld and his follies : a biography of Broadway's greatest producer / Cynthia
Brideson and Sara Brideson.
      pages cm — (Screen classics)
  Includes bibliographical references and index.
  ISBN 978-0-8131-6088-7 (hardcover : alk. paper) —
  ISBN 978-0-8131-6090-0 (pdf) — ISBN 978-0-8131-6089-4 (epub)
  1. Ziegfeld, Flo, 1869-1932. 2. Theatrical producers and directors—United
States—Biography. I. Brideson, Sara. II. Title.
  PN2287.Z5B75 2015
  792.02'32092—dc23
  [B]   2015006372

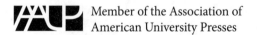 Member of the Association of
American University Presses

To our parents, Amelia and Mark Brideson, who, when we were children, endured watching *The Wizard of Oz* over and over again with us and who patiently chauffeured us to library after library in our insatiable quest for knowledge about all things Ziegfeld and Billie Burke. Thank you too, Mamma and Daddy, for never doubting our abilities to reach our goals.

And to the memory of our grandpa, David Nolan Salter, who always had an excellent appreciation of what Ziegfeld's shows presented best: good music and storytelling.

Contents

Photographs follow pages 168 and 328

Introduction

"A Man of Triple and Quadruple Personalities"

Florenz Ziegfeld, Jr. does not seem to be acquainted with himself.
He thinks he is a person. He doesn't know that he is an institution.
—*"The Follies of Florenz Ziegfeld," New Yorker, March 14, 1925*

Before and after his death in 1932, Florenz Ziegfeld's friends, employees, and lovers, as well as critics, historians, and screenwriters, have conjectured and written exhaustively about him—as an institution, that is. There has been far less written about the man behind the institution. The elusive Broadway producer was, in the words of his second wife, Billie Burke, a man of "triple and quadruple personalities."[1] If one were to read every bit of literature available on the man, one would find him to be a mass of contradictions.

His press agent, Bernard Sobel, wrote, "In dealing with his girls, stars, friends, and newspaper men, he was gentle, but he was also frequently cruel, sarcastic, never satisfied and seldom grateful."[2] Burke bemoaned Ziegfeld's infidelities and called him "cool, aloof, and difficult," yet at the same time she professed him to be a loving husband and adoring father.[3] In a posthumous article about Ziegfeld, a writer for *Time* quoted drama critic Percy Hammond, who condemned Ziegfeld's 1907 productions as "loud, leering orgies of indelicacy and suggestiveness."[4] Another critic at the *New Yorker* called him "the greatest moral influence in New York City."[5] Songwriter Richard Rodgers saw the producer as a "slippery piece of showmanship"; Sobel saw him as "the living measure of high theatrical achievement" and stated, "The words 'Ziegfeld's out front' put every member of the cast on the alert; and the mention of his name in rival theatres, whether they were musicals or dramas, had the same effect on every company."[6] Ziegfeld star Eddie Cantor concurred with Sobel's estimation, describing his employer as "all the gods rolled into one. The greatest name in show business!"[7] In addition to being Ziegfeld's star, Cantor was his friend, surrogate son, and enemy. He knew his boss's many sides better than most. Yet even he saw Ziegfeld as more of an icon than a man. The conception of Ziegfeld as mythical rather than mortal is most obvious in Hollywood's depictions of him. In *The Great Ziegfeld* (1936), MGM's lavish biopic, William Powell portrays a brash, confident Ziegfeld who, in terms of looks and manner, does not resemble the real producer at all. The film gives viewers no glimpse into his human flaws, thus perpetuating the idea of Ziegfeld as an untouchable god of theater for each new generation of viewers. Most other films involving Ziegfeld, such as *Ziegfeld Girl* (1941), do not even show him onscreen; they merely mention him as an unseen but all-important presence. Unfortunately, it is these films, with their faulty depictions of Ziegfeld, that keep his name known to modern audiences

In his own time, the shows that made Ziegfeld a symbol were his *Follies*. Though the *Follies* are synonymous with their producer, they reflect only a part of his character. The popularity of Ziegfeld's shows relied heavily on comedy, yet Ziegfeld admitted to having a limited sense of humor and little fondness for comedians. Pushing his personal opinions aside, Ziegfeld tapped into precisely what the public wanted, thus creating a musical mirror of his times and satisfying audiences' every craving for the first third of the twentieth century.

The *Ziegfeld Follies*. The name alone conjures a flood of impressions: gorgeous women garbed in outrageous and dreamlike costumes; street-smart humor by Eddie Cantor; homespun musings by Will Rogers; clumsy Yiddish ballerinas played by Fanny Brice; graceful and spritely ballerinas played by Marilyn Miller; darkly humorous tunes sung by Bert Williams; caustic barbs by W. C. Fields; clever lyrics, ragtime, and jazz by Irving Berlin or the Gershwins; haunting ballads by Jerome Kern; ethereal ballets by Victor Herbert. Each summer, New Yorkers came to anticipate the *Follies* as more than entertainment. Indeed, the *Follies* were an event. The revues became so much a part of the metropolis that one critic for the *New Yorker* observed: "As a barometer of New York, it [the *Follies*] cannot be excelled. . . . Mr. Ziegfeld seems to imagine . . . that New Yorkers go to the *Follies* to be entertained. They don't. They go there to worship—and to discover where the exact limit of propriety has moved."[8]

The *Follies* reflected the swiftly changing world of the early twentieth century, a world in which a new middle class had emerged. This new middle class saw "thrift as socially harmful and spending a virtue."[9] If spending was a virtue, Ziegfeld was the most virtuous man in New York. A look at his most costly production numbers provides a glimpse of his essence. According to Burke, the "things he cherished most as a showman" were "color, music, and spectacle."[10] The *Follies* certainly had these elements, plus the speed that modern audiences demanded. Ziegfeld's musical comedies—*Sally* (1920) and *Show Boat* (1927)—also kept in step with audiences' changing tastes. His musicals revolutionized the genre by flawlessly blending music and action with theme. The plots often told rags-to-riches stories reflective of the American Dream, yet the shows pleased audiences outside of America and remain universally appealing.

Though Ziegfeld's innovative work in revues and musical comedies made him a legend in his own time, he did not see himself as infallible. On each of his opening nights, he was certain he had produced a flop. The very shows that were his greatest hits might have been failures if any other producer had staged them. But Ziegfeld's gloomy outlook worked in his favor; it drove him to experiment until he created a perfect product. Sobel commented, "To work for Ziggy meant living up to full responsibility in every department, for the producer might, at any minute, find fault."[11] Ziegfeld demanded the same perfection from himself that he demanded from all those around him, even at the cost of his health and the well-being of those he loved. His perfectionism was well worth the effort. Modern historians now credit Ziegfeld with inventing the American musical as it exists today and describe musical theater in terms of pre–*Show Boat* and post–*Show Boat*.

"Magic there was in the Ziegfeld touch. Magic that no other man has ever had," columnist Adela Rogers St. Johns commented.[12] One writer for the *New Yorker* went further, crediting Ziegfeld not only with a magic touch but also with the power to shape and sway public taste: "It is preordained that his [Ziegfeld's] show must be absolutely correct. If he puts it on, of course, it becomes correct forthwith . . . not that Mr. Ziegfeld set the styles in either morals or esthetics. But he *registers* them, which is a much more responsible job. . . . A style isn't a style until he approves it, but he cannot approve a style until it has become stylish."[13]

The most conspicuous moral and aesthetic styles Ziegfeld created were those involving the showgirl. Ziegfeld invested his personal taste and tremendous energy and love in numbers that did little more than present exquisite girls. These girls, in living tableaux, were flesh made into art. Ziegfeld was so closely involved in every aspect of producing such numbers that he frequently fell in and out of passionate love with many chorines—some he loved as mistresses, while others he loved like daughters. And his girls deserved nothing but the best. Sobel stated, "In perfecting the American revue, Ziegfeld glorified the American girl. He gave his showgirls salaries as large as those the principals received . . . more important, he exploited them as personalities [and] listed them in the program."[14]

Ziegfeld was in his element when selecting girls for his choruses; each year, the number of chorines seemed to grow. They came from all over the world and from every class. Short, tall, buxom, lithe, blonde, brunette, redhead—every type of girl had her place in the Ziegfeld ranks. Searching for raw talent waiting to be shaped and exploited filled him with the same exhilaration he felt when on a lucky gambling streak. Once his girls were dressed in "silks and paints and powder and lighting," their beauty trumped any deficiencies the actresses may have had, be it a poor singing voice, limited acting talent, or little dancing ability.[15]

Many critics have called Ziegfeld a womanizer; however, the most important women in his life—his first wife, Anna Held; his brightest female star, Marilyn Miller; and Billie Burke—were powerful, individual personalities. Ziegfeld gave women an indomitable presence in a male-centric era; biographer Charles Higham went so far as to call him an "iconolater of women with power."[16] Ziegfeld sought powerful women; even his mistresses were fiery and volatile. His relationships with women and his behavior toward his showgirls were alternately thoughtless and attentive, but his cousin and biographer Richard Ziegfeld wrote, "He respected women and was deeply concerned with the individual woman's welfare . . . Ziegfeld seemed more comfortable with women than with men."[17] Marilyn Miller and another of Ziegfeld's greatest stars, Fanny Brice, considered him one of the most outstanding men they had ever known.[18] His wives and stars quarreled furiously with him, but at the end of his life, they spoke of him with fondness and remained protective of and loyal to his memory. His love for women and beauty was authentic and required no pushing aside of his personal tastes.

"He . . . is the greatest manager for girls America has ever had," Cantor asserted. "As far as actors are concerned, a man to Zieggy [Cantor's spell-

4

ing of Ziegfeld's nickname] means nothing, but girls!—he had made many girls and girls have made him, and on that principle is based his chivalry, theatrical display, and success."[19]

Considering his impeccable showmanship and conspicuous attention to women, one would expect Ziegfeld to be confident, outgoing, and flamboyant. Although he did dress in a foppish manner, this did not reflect his personality. He was shy, preferred to communicate through telegrams, and did not possess any stage presence of his own. He made up for his lack of command before an audience by finding those who had it. The producer summarized his gift with this statement: "I *make* talent."[20]

An examination of Ziegfeld's multilayered relationships with his stars, his friends, and his lovers, paired with an examination of his productions' innovations and content, comes as close as possible to revealing Ziegfeld the man. In endeavoring to uncover the true Ziegfeld, we used all the literature available on him and on those to whom he was closest. We also made generous use of rare interviews and previously unpublished correspondence. After closely reviewing these resources, we discovered new contradictions about Ziegfeld and new facets of his personality at every turn. Ziegfeld is still somewhat of an enigma. Though he seems virtually unknowable, we hope this book helps readers become better acquainted with the great producer through our balanced account of the facts of his life, his work, and his relationships with family and associates. His life was so flamboyant that, at times, it seemed he planned it that way to avoid examining himself, his life choices, and the world around him. His shows were escapist and full of contradictions—blending old with new and drama with comedy. The contradictions of Ziegfeld's work mirror the contradictions in his own character, and thus the producer and his work are inextricably linked.

This book is primarily the story of Ziegfeld's personal follies, but because his work was so much a part of him, we intertwine the follies and triumphs of his private life with those of his professional life. We begin with his first show business enterprise at the 1893 Chicago World's Fair and end with the ongoing influence of his inimitable touch in both film and theater after his death. Separating the man from the institution is almost impossible. But that is precisely what Ziegfeld wanted—to make his name a brand that would endure forever.

PART 1

Anna and Flo ... and Lillian, 1867–1913

Shine on harvest moon, for me and my gal.
—*Jack Norworth, "Shine on, Harvest Moon" (1908)*

I

The Showman, the Strongman, and the Girl with the Eyes

In 1867 a man with the impressive title of Herr Doktor Florenz Ziegfeld Sr. opened the Chicago Musical College. If one were to step into the professor's hall at any time of the day—morning, afternoon, or night—one would hear young pupils tapping out the melodies of Beethoven, Mozart, and Schubert. Herr Doktor would be standing behind his students at the piano, beaming with pride that the compositions the students were playing had been written by grand maestros from his native Germany. The classical tunes rang out in stark contrast to the city noise outside: the roar of intersecting railroad lines, the clip-clop of horse-drawn cabs, the shouts of newsboys reporting the latest headlines.

By the 1880s, one member of Professor Ziegfeld's college was as incongruous to the institution as the racket of the city. He bore the same name as the professor, but their similarities ended there. At age sixteen, Florenz Ziegfeld Jr. was a slightly built young man with a face that was both sensitive and sardonic. Journalist Djuna Barnes later called him "close-mouthed and satirical-eyed," but this description was applicable even in his teen years.[1] Sometimes he wore a smirk on his lips, but more often, even when he seemed to be enjoying himself, he wore an expression of funereal solemnity. Young Ziegfeld spent his afternoons studying not the compositions of Mozart or Beethoven but the throbbing urban life of Chicago.

Professor Ziegfeld saw his son's interests as a snubbing of the traditions he had shared with all his children. Ziegfeld's three younger siblings

(Carl, William, and Louise) all attended the musical college and eventually worked there, but for Junior, sitting for hours learning a foreign language composed of sharps, flats, A notes, and G notes spelled drudgery. He was the eldest son in the family, but he had the impetuosity and lack of patience for anything passé that is more characteristic of a younger sibling. According to Ziegfeld's daughter, Patricia, "From the moment that Daddy was old enough to be coaxed over to the piano, it was painfully obvious that he was tone-deaf and had absolutely no aptitude in the performing arts. He also failed to exhibit even the faintest interest as he grew older in mastering the intricacies of college administration."[2] Young Ziegfeld intuitively knew that the classical works of Schubert and Mozart were not going to win mass audiences' attention in post–Civil War America, even if his father made the opposite argument.

Ziegfeld's complete lack of interest in the musical college was, to say the least, a difficult fact for his father to face. The professor prized the reputation he had earned among the crème de la crème of Chicago's first families; they all sent their children to him for music lessons. He felt comfortable consorting with the city's finest families, for as a child prodigy, he had been trained at the Leipzig, the most famous conservatory in Germany. Following graduation, Ziegfeld had been in high demand and received offers to teach music and give concerts in various countries in the Western Hemisphere, from Russia to the United States. Professor Ziegfeld chose to move to New York, where he partnered with famed piano salesman W. W. Kimball and music publisher George Root to sell instruments and sheet music. He relocated to Chicago in 1863, but his early attempts at entrepreneurship failed.

Professor Ziegfeld found more success in his personal life; on May 17, 1865, he married Belgian immigrant Rosalie de Hez. Rosalie's background was as illustrious as that of her husband. She was the grandniece of General Etienne Gerard, Napoleon's marshal. Their first child, Florenz Ziegfeld Jr., was born on March 21, 1867. Two more sons, Carl (born in 1869) and William (born in 1873), and one daughter, Louise (born in 1875), followed. The Ziegfelds' lack of formal religious affiliation is proved by the fact that their children were baptized under different faiths. Florenz was baptized Catholic, his brothers Lutheran, and his sister Methodist. Rosalie herself was Catholic, and her husband was Lutheran.

With a wife and newborn son to provide for, Professor Ziegfeld resurrected his musical conservatory in the year of Ziegfeld Jr.'s birth. The college struggled for the next five years and, remarkably, survived the Great Fire of 1871, although the blaze destroyed its structure and instruments. The professor, however, was not deterred; he posted signs amid the ruins of Chicago only days after the fire, announcing the reopening of the school. As the institution was being rebuilt, Ziegfeld took eleven of his pupils to Germany, where composer Franz Liszt planned a dinner in their honor. Ziegfeld's relationship with one of the most highly regarded European composers greatly contributed to making him a confident, self-sufficient entrepreneur who was as resilient as Chicago itself.

The Chicago Musical College reopened and subsequently moved to various locations, ending up at 1448 West Addams Street in 1882. The final locale was a tall brownstone building that served the dual purpose of conservatory and family home. West Addams Street was not where the richest Chicagoans lived; nor was it in a family-friendly suburb. Though maintaining a close rapport with the upper crust was necessary to gain patrons to support his academy, Ziegfeld was more like his eldest son than he may have realized. His conservatory was located in the Loop, Chicago's business district. Professor Ziegfeld (like Florenz, years later) enjoyed being in the center of a city that was booming both literally and figuratively. Between 1865 and 1871, the city's population exploded from 179,000 to 334,000.[3] Its flourishing economy made it a Mecca for upper-class families, most of whom could afford to have a piano in the house and were willing to pay for their children to be instructed at institutions such as the Chicago Musical College. What allowed many of these families to be upwardly mobile was entrepreneurship, and arguably, the most ambitious entrepreneurs were German immigrants who, like Ziegfeld, were well established in their home countries and came to America with the hope of using their talents to the greatest advantage—and profit.

Nowhere was the country's, and Chicago's, boom more apparent than in the entertainment industry. Some deemed the industry immoral because it pulsated with a sensual vitality. On the higher end of the entertainment spectrum was classic theater, including opera; in the middle was the circus; and on the lower end was minstrelsy, melodrama, and burlesque, a form of entertainment that had originated in London. The bulk of Chicago audiences fell outside the highbrow category and preferred burlesque. In burlesque houses, the shows were irreverent satires of classics: Shakespeare's *The Merchant of Venice* was made into *Shylock: A Jerusalem Hearty Joke,* and Verdi's *Il Trovatore* became *Kill Trovatore!* More offensive was the brazen flouting of decency. Women played sexually aggressive characters and wore clothes that left little to the imagination. Historian Robert G. Allen offered a more favorable interpretation of burlesque's place in society: "Without question . . . burlesque's principal legacy as a cultural form was its establishment of patterns of gender representation that forever changed the role of the woman on the American stage . . . it playfully called attention to the entire question of the 'place' of woman in American society."[4] Not surprisingly, editorials condemning burlesque only made it more popular.

Not a mile from the Ziegfeld home were establishments as lowbrow and popular as burlesque theaters: houses of gambling and prostitution. The popular music of the era reflected the warring lowbrow and highbrow cultures—temperance songs competed with drinking songs or tunes about "swells" (men who appreciated good drink and good living). Young Ziegfeld may have heard the music of Franz Liszt and Johann Strauss in the confines of his home, but on the steps of his family's brownstone, he was more enticed by tunes that rebelled against the traditions of his father.

British journalist George W. Stevens aptly described the different realms in which Chicagoans lived. He called the city "the most beautiful and the most squalid, girdled with a twofold zone of parks and slums . . . where women ride straddle-wise and millionaires dine at midday on the Sabbath. . . . Where in all the world can words be found for this miracle of paradox and incongruity?"[5] The paradox of Chicago made it ripe territory for a future showman, a boy who longed to break from his father's traditionalism and explore the lives and tastes of the rich, the poor, the lowbrow, the highbrow—and always the unique.

Dissociating himself from his father was not an easy task for young Florenz. In their biography of Ziegfeld Jr., Richard and Paulette Ziegfeld describe the professor as being a sort of caricature of a "Prussian autocrat," complete with "booming voice and commanding presence."[6] He was rather intimidating, but not intimidating enough to keep young Ziegfeld out of trouble. By 1883 Ziegfeld had succeeded in making the Chicago Musical College a small but well-respected player in Chicago's eclectic entertainment culture. The conservatory enjoyed a steady stream of up to 900 students from society families. The school had broadened its offerings beyond music to elocution, languages (German, French, and Italian), and dance instruction. Since his recognition by Liszt, Ziegfeld had established ties with the conductor of the Chicago Orchestra and Johann Strauss. In 1872 he even convinced Strauss to participate in the Boston Peace Jubilee. His father's ability to persuade great celebrities to come to America impressed Ziegfeld Jr. more than the professor's musical acumen.

However, Ziegfeld Jr. still showed no signs of emulating even the characteristics he admired in his father. He spent his spare time honing his skills as a sharpshooter rather than as a classical musician. The conservatory's small attic, according to Ziegfeld's daughter, had bullet holes in the wall as evidence of the boy's target practice. But whether he knew it or not, his marksmanship was a talent he had inherited from his father. The professor was a member of the Illinois National Guard.

Sharpshooting was of much more interest to Ziegfeld Jr. than any scholastic pursuits at either Brown Elementary School or Ogden High School. Despite Brown's reputation for a strong academic regimen, its stringent curriculum did not reform Ziegfeld or its other well-known alumni, Eddie Foy and Lillian Russell. Billie Burke recalled, "He always flattered himself that he never even went to school, but bless his heart, if he didn't he was pretty well self-educated. I remember his father used to lock him in to make him practice piano, but even then he found his way out, through making up to the cook I believe."[7]

Ziegfeld's parents decided a summer spent on a cattle ranch in Wyoming would fulfill the boy's thirst for independence and all-American adventure. According to Patricia Ziegfeld, "Grandma and Grandpa Ziegfeld tried in vain to discover exactly what their oldest son *was* interested in."[8] Contrary to his parents' expectations, Ziegfeld's time in Wyoming made an impression on him that only increased his interest in showmanship. Gilbert Seldes of the *New Yorker* wrote in 1931: "His pleasures to this day are traceable to this experience. He is an excellent rider, a remarkable shot, and a passionate fisherman. A few years ago, when a *Follies* was opening in Atlantic City, he startled his associates by breaking innumerable clay pigeons with shots over his shoulder and without altering his funereal expression, doing trick riding . . . on the placid sands in front of the theater."[9]

Ziegfeld honed these skills in the hope of becoming like his new idol: Buffalo Bill Cody. While in Wyoming, Ziegfeld had caught a glimpse of

Cody's Wild West Show as it was passing through the state. Cody was unlike any man Ziegfeld had ever seen. He did everything in a big way—he dressed loudly, he staged his shows elaborately, and he promoted them sensationally. He once attracted audiences by claiming he could scalp an Indian in five seconds. Cody's technique was the complete opposite of the subtle showmanship employed by Ziegfeld's father. The professor hosted small after-hours dinner parties for Chicago's dominant musical figures, rewarded his best students with diamond pins donated by wealthy patrons, and employed a hansom cab to pick up arriving students at the train station. Ziegfeld was absorbing his father's technique, but he yearned to combine his father's tastefulness with Buffalo Bill's flamboyance.

Once he was back in Chicago, Ziegfeld could not believe his luck when Buffalo Bill Cody's show came to town. Several tall tales exist about what happened next. Some claim that Cody picked Ziegfeld out of the audience to engage in a shooting match with Annie Oakley, which the boy won, and Cody subsequently hired him to be part of the entertainment. No evidence exists that such a contest ever took place. In fact, Annie Oakley did not join Buffalo Bill's show until 1885, two years after the supposed match with Ziegfeld. According to Patricia, Ziegfeld snuck away to see the show and followed it as it traveled through the Midwest. But her father's caprice didn't last long: "The runaway was caught up with at the next town and brought home again, but the damage had been done. Daddy had experienced show business and independence in one heady draught, and though he returned home outwardly docile he was only biding his time until his big chance came again."[10]

The outwardly docile Ziegfeld continued to work for his father until 1893, advancing from assistant treasurer to treasurer and finally to general manager at the conservatory. Despite his conventional occupation, Ziegfeld still managed to find excitement. His tall stature, Roman nose, thoughtful eyes, and dapper attire made the young man popular. Billie Burke stated, "He was a great favorite in Chicago society in his twenties, squiring among others the daughters of the fabulously wealthy Pullman family."[11] He often hosted Chicago cotillions during the day, while at night he perfected his favorite hobby: dancing. He won numerous local dance contests, and for the rest of his life, he helped set trends in dance. In the early 1900s he played no small part in the national dance craze—the turkey trot. Gilbert

Seldes called Ziegfeld "a fanatical turkey trotter,"[12] and Rennold Wolf, who wrote sketches for the *Follies,* claimed that all the champion trotters followed Ziegfeld from restaurant to restaurant or from cabaret to cabaret.

Dancing was more than a hobby to Ziegfeld; it was an art in which he wanted to become a master. Seldes noted, "He was always interested in dancing and theatricals—his passion for the theater is not a passion for money as much as it is a genuine development of all the major interests of his life."[13] His interests in life—dancing, girls, and theater—wove together perfectly. In the exclusive clubs where he danced, he found ample audiences on which to test his business ventures. He managed amateur shows at the Farragut Boat Club with some success but ran into some trouble when the SPCA stopped his ill-conceived act titled "The Dancing Ducks of Denmark." The ducks would hop about the stage rhythmically, but not because they had been trained to do so. A hot flame under the stage induced the unfortunate ducks to "dance" to avoid burning their feet.

Despite his occasional forays into show business and showmanship, Ziegfeld found that his most promising work was performed under his father's employ. The musical college gained more prestige when Professor Ziegfeld, along with Theodore Thomas (the man responsible for creating the New York Philharmonic) organized the Chicago Symphony Orchestra. The elder Ziegfeld's involvement with the orchestra increased the Chicago Musical College's clientele and, in turn, resulted in a bigger salary for young Ziegfeld. When his father was elected to the board of commissioners for the International Congress of Musicians, Ziegfeld Jr. encountered his most promising opportunity yet to become involved in show business. The board of commissioners was in charge of producing the musical portion of the upcoming 1893 World's Fair, which was to be held in Chicago.

Professor Ziegfeld and Theodore Thomas worked to create an epic, lush musical program for the fair. They felt confident that their program would make Europe take notice of the talent and high culture of Chicago and its premier musical college. They planned to offer traditional European masterpieces from Wagner and Handel, most of which would be sung by American choral groups. Ziegfeld entrusted his eldest son with the task of seeking performers in Europe, and Ziegfeld Jr. brought back an eclectic mix of musicians that reflected his father's tastes rather than his own, including the Hamburg Bulow Orchestra and Iwanoff's Russian Singers and Dancers. The only entertainer who was more to young Ziegfeld's liking was Cyrene, an eccentric female dancer from England. The orchestras played selections from Strauss's *Blue Danube Waltz* and Gounod's *Faust*. Sadly, the expensive program was not popular, except for the pop concerts and the children's choruses included in the mix. Audiences seemed to prefer the fair's less cultured offerings, such as the exotic replicas of Cairo, a Bedouin village, and the Temple of Luxor. Ziegfeld Jr. was the first to notice the fairgoers' preferences, and he sought to satisfy them with his own idea of lowbrow entertainment. Though he was not a performer, he possessed a performer's charisma and was able to attract customers. At his stall, he employed the philosophy of P. T. Barnum, one of Ziegfeld's heroes and role models, to outdraw his competitors: "There's a sucker born every minute."

"Come and see the magical invisible fish! Yes, ladies and gents, an invisible fish from Brazil! I fool you not!" Ziegfeld called out in a voice that has been variously described as whiny, nasal, twangy, murmuring, and forceful. A group of curious passersby clustered about him and eagerly bought tickets. The young man's smirk grew closer to a smile as he swept aside a cloth to reveal a glass bowl on the platform before him. The customers nearly dropped to their knees; their eyes widened as they stared expectantly into the empty bowl of water. Ziegfeld's inability to prove or disprove the fish's existence slowly dawned on the crowd, and color rose in their cheeks. Before a riot began, the mischievous showman refunded his unhappy customers' money. Ziegfeld's failures, first with the dancing ducks and then with the invisible fish, did not diminish his ambition. He continued to search for a form of entertainment that would please audiences from all classes. And he had only six months to do so, since the fair, which had opened in May, would close in October.

The elder Ziegfeld was just as ambitious as his son, and like his son, the professor had noted the popularity of less refined entertainment. Consequently, he decided to open a nightclub that would offer a mix of classical and modern music, as well as variety acts. The club, originally called the International Temple of Music, was renamed the Trocadero when it moved downtown near the Loop (on the opposite end of the city from the World's Fair). The club attracted few patrons at first. It was competing not only with the fair but also with other performers who had erected exhibits outside the fairgrounds. The stiffest competition came from Lillian Russell and Buffalo Bill, whose exciting offerings outshone any of those at the fair.

When Ziegfeld Jr. became manager of the nightclub, he was determined to make it a success—even if it meant bringing in acts his father wouldn't have considered or condoned. Ziegfeld "decided to try his hand at fixing whatever was wrong—if he could discover what it was, that is," according to Patricia Ziegfeld. "He took a long look at the empty auditorium of the Trocadero, and then he walked across the Fairgrounds and took an even longer look at the crowds strolling happily up and down the Midway eating hotdogs, buying souvenirs, and crowding eagerly in to see Little Egypt do her scandalous belly dance."[14] Audiences laughed and gasped as Little Egypt introduced the "cooch" dance to America.[15]

Ziegfeld knew people craved the exotic, but the exotic was not exclusively foreign. It *could* be found in America. Thus, he went to New York to scout for talent and found the ideal place to search: Manhattan's Casino Theatre. The theater offered rooftop shows featuring European-inspired entertainment forms, including burlesque and light opera, as well as newer forms of entertainment such as vaudeville and musical comedy. The Casino Theatre, opened in 1882, was the first establishment designed specifically for musicals. However, it was not a musical performer that Ziegfeld brought back to Chicago as a headliner for his father's club.

At the Casino, Ziegfeld attended a burlesque musical entitled *Adonis*. He was prepared to be bored until he noticed that the two girls sitting in front of him begin to giggle and clutch each other's arms with anticipation. At the same time, a "middle-aged matron at his left . . . a chocolate bon bon half way to her mouth . . . gazed adoringly at the stage."[16] Ziegfeld immediately turned his eyes to the stage to see what was causing such a commotion. In the spotlight was a diminutive but robust young man with blond hair lifting a barbell from the floor. Turning in profile, he flexed his biceps to show the audience. Ziegfeld looked down at his program to discover this live Adonis's name. He was Eugen Sandow (born Muller), a Prussian immigrant and, though it was not publicized, a Jew. Photographs show him dressed in his scanty gymnastics costume with a large Star of David hanging from a chain around his neck. In part because of his Jewishness and in part because Sandow had been a frail and delicate youth, he was determined to prove he could be a great star despite the odds against him. By the time Sandow was eighteen, he had turned himself into the perfect specimen of health and strength through an intense exercise regimen. Yet he still retained a shy and gentle nature. His face, in the words of one reporter, was "little more than a boy's" and stood in stark contrast to a "neck that was massive and shoulders that seemed a yard apart."[17]

Despite Sandow's ability to stir women in the audience, the strongman did not bring significant revenue to his managers. This did not stop him from demanding double the salary they had been paying him. Ziegfeld stepped in at precisely the right moment. He offered Sandow 10 percent of the gross to play at the Trocadero. Patricia Ziegfeld later commented, "Daddy realized that Sandow's appeal lay in this contrast between his gentleness and his strength, and he set out to capitalize on it."[18] Professor Ziegfeld had given his son $5,000 to use in his talent search, and the young Ziegfeld spent every penny of it on Sandow's publicity campaign. To create interest in his new star, Ziegfeld developed an early glorification formula of "one-third glamour, one-third merit, and one-third advertising."[19]

When Ziegfeld returned to Chicago, he papered "the town with posters of the scantily clad muscleman and placed rather lurid advertisements in local theatre programs to tantalize the public." He also created "highly romanticized . . . biographies of Sandow to catch the media's eye."[20] One particularly eye-catching advertisement planted by Ziegfeld read: "Sandow! The monarch of muscle. The world's greatest acrobats have found it almost impossible to turn somersaults landing on the same spot they spring from and only a few have accomplished it and to perform this feat with weights has never been attempted. Mr. Sandow stands alone in accomplishing this feat with fifty-six pounds in each hand."[21]

To build even more public interest, Ziegfeld invited doctors to examine Sandow and declare him the perfect example of male physicality—a flesh-and-blood Grecian "discus thrower." Sandow was "only 5' 8" tall, it's true, but what six foot man could expand his chest to fifty-eight inches? Fifty-eight inches is a low figure, mind you," Ziegfeld argued with the physicians. "He can wrestle three men at once . . . better yet, untie the horses from your carriages outside. Three of them can walk across a plank on Mr. Sandow's chest and he will not feel the slightest pressure!" After witnessing Sandow's feats, the doctors were convinced and agreed that he was the perfect physical specimen.[22]

With the hype Ziegfeld created for Sandow, he had little difficulty convincing Chicago's most prominent society ladies to accept his invitations to the Trocadero. One invitee, Mrs. Potter Palmer, "allowed herself to be photographed while artistically fingering Sandow's biceps."[23] Thanks to

Sandow's reputation, the Trocadero was grossing $30,000 a week during his engagement there (comparable to $766,226 in 2013).[24] Interspersed with Sandow's appearances onstage were performances by "The Trocadero Vaudevilles," which included trapeze artists, clowns, and vocalists. This mélange of entertainment offered a circus atmosphere with a touch of class. For the first time in the Trocadero's history, its performers played to packed houses. One reporter for the *Chicago Tribune* wrote, "Under manager F. Ziegfeld Jr. the Trocadero has accomplished in a comparatively short space of time what it has taken New York . . . many years to achieve— namely: the securing of a high class of patronage for a refined vaudeville and music hall enterprise."[25]

The packed houses emptied all too quickly when Sandow took an abrupt trip to Europe. Professor Ziegfeld was desperate. Even the hefty fifty-cent admission fee was not enough to keep the Trocadero profitable. Those who had invested stock in the club lost $40,000 and accused the elder Ziegfeld of mismanagement, extravagance, and neglect. He lost the lease to the Trocadero and, as a result, also experienced a 50 percent drop in his income at the conservatory.

Ziegfeld Jr. was undaunted by the club's failure. Even though the Trocadero was now closed, Sandow could still draw crowds. When the strongman returned from Europe in January 1894, he signed a contract with Ziegfeld Jr. for a cross-country road tour with other audience favorites at the Trocadero. The responsibility of assisting the professor in managing the musical college fell to Ziegfeld's younger brothers, and by the following year, the conservatory was prospering again. Professor Ziegfeld did not completely understand his eldest son's vague plans or his questionable taste in entertainment. However, the fact that he had made a society-approved celebrity out of a circus performer showed that the boy had something. Ziegfeld hoped his son would use his talents to the conservatory's advantage, and, because Florenz was the eldest son, his father assumed he would carry on the family business and put its interests before his own ambition.

Ziegfeld Jr.'s dilemma of fulfilling his familial duty versus making a name for himself was a problem faced by many first-generation Americans. The children of immigrants had no memories of life in their parents' homelands and thus possessed no strong allegiances to those lands. Despite Ziegfeld Jr.'s decidedly American tastes, he learned valuable lessons from the professor that he used in his own business, including how to make a client feel special. Richard Ziegfeld has pointed out that the professor's obsessive passion to make his musical college the best in the United States was mirrored by Ziegfeld Jr.'s ambition to create the best artistic visions in theater. Ziegfeld recognized himself in Florenz's ambitious, stubborn nature and saw that there would be no changing his son's mind about his chosen path.

In 1894 Professor Ziegfeld and his wife gave their eldest son their blessing to break from tradition. Ziegfeld packed up his troupe, and they headed off together with dreams of conquering entertainment circuits from New York to San Francisco. They succeeded in conquering New York, where Sandow drew massive crowds, thanks to Ziegfeld's publicity machine and his gasp-worthy choice of costume for the strongman. The Gilded Age was in full bloom, and society was becoming less tight-lipped about sex. But Ziegfeld did not transition slowly into the new era; he jumped one step ahead of it. He changed Sandow's costume from a modest blue top and pink tights to just a pair of silk shorts. Sandow also posed for photographers wearing nothing but a leaf covering his front. Victorians condemned such immodesty, claiming it was found only in "infamous resorts,"[26] but in the 1890s more and more Americans were traveling abroad and bringing home classically modeled photographs of tasteful nudity. Ziegfeld played no small part in making Sandow one of the first sex symbols about whom adolescent girls (and adult women) dreamed. Many daughters of the most aristocratic families had Sandow's photo hung in their bedrooms.[27] Ziegfeld is best known for using the classical seminude style with his legendary glorified showgirls; it is ironic that his first star was a glorified boy.

Ziegfeld continued his mission to make Sandow a national icon. Predating Hedda Hopper, he planted juicy pieces of gossip in newspaper columns just to create a buzz, including Sandow's fabricated love affair with Lillian Russell. But a story that had nothing to do with romance proved to be the most sensational. Ziegfeld's inspiration came while he and his troupe were in New York and he noticed a mammoth crowd waiting to pay $50 a seat to witness a fight between a lion and a bear. The police ultimately stopped the fight from taking place, but after they left, Ziegfeld approached the owner of Parnell, the big cat. "What would you think of a man fighting this beast?" he asked. The lion's owner agreed only after

Ziegfeld assured him that Sandow would not harm the lion and the lion would not harm Sandow.

Parnell, Ziegfeld, and Sandow traveled to San Francisco in April 1894 to enact their battle, which the press hyped as the event of the century. Ziegfeld listened to the crowd at Golden Gate Park shriek gleefully as they heard Parnell roaring in his cage. The cat bared its fangs, revealing them to be larger than a child's hand. The audience paid a dollar a ticket and stepped inside a tent that had been erected for the fight. As they watched the lion, attired in a muzzle and leather mittens, being carried inside the ring, murmurs spread through the crowd: "It's not a fair fight. Look at the size of those mittens. The animal won't even be able to lift a paw." Sandow stepped inside the ring and bowed to the society ladies sitting in the front row. They were impressed by his looks alone, but the disgruntled men in the audience were less so, especially when they noticed that the lion suddenly seemed to be lethargic. Sandow put up his fists as if preparing to box another man. The lion yawned at him. Sandow pulled at the big cat's whiskers to rouse him. The lion half rose but then lay down again. Sandow then grabbed the lion's mane, but the cat did nothing more than flick sawdust in the strongman's face with his tail. "Throw in the box and let 'im wrestle that!" one man yelled from the crowd, nodding to the now empty box Parnell had occupied. In an attempt to salvage the evening, Sandow lifted the lion as if it were a house cat and carried it around the ring. The lion seemed to enjoy being carried, which only angered the crowd more. Although Sandow was named victor, he left the ring humiliated and vowed he would have a rematch when the lion was less frightened.

Ziegfeld grabbed the $3,000 profit from the match and spent the night safely in Oakland until the uproar died down in San Francisco. The audience's anger was not quelled when they learned that the vicious Parnell had been replaced with Commodore, an old, tired lion from the same menagerie as Parnell. Nearly twenty years later, when Ziegfeld brought his *Follies* to San Francisco, he found that the city's inhabitants had long memories. Audiences received him coldly, and newspapers reminded citizens that this was the same man who had staged that debacle of a fight between a strongman and a supposed beast.

After the fiasco in San Francisco, Ziegfeld, Sandow, and the troupe went on an extended tour of the major vaudeville circuit (there is no concrete information as to the locations of their stops). The embarrassing match with the lion, contrary to legend, did not spoil Sandow's career; his glorious appearance and strength more than overshadowed this one humiliation. The *Cleveland Plain Dealer* declared: "Probably no man of our times has been so much talked and written about."[28] Thomas Edison did not want to miss out on the Sandow craze and wrote Ziegfeld a letter proposing that Sandow appear in one of the first silent films to be exhibited. The short film showed Sandow flexing his muscles with elegant synchronization. Ziegfeld did not pursue the new silent film medium even after its popularity exploded in the 1910s. He depended on song, color, and spectacle—things early films did not offer. However, the Sandow film garnered much attention and helped make the Trocadero troupe's tour very profitable. With an abundance of money on his hands, Ziegfeld was lured to the gambling tables and ultimately lost the bulk of his profits on this spree. The only positive aspect of his penchant for gambling was that it forced him to seek other artists on which to gamble and make into lucrative sensations, as he had with Sandow.

Ziegfeld still had much to learn about show business, as proved by the botched boxing match and the gambling losses. Despite the considerable dent in Ziegfeld's bank account, he did not choose to stop gambling. Rather, his experience at the casino taught him that show business is a gamble and it's worth the risk, even if it means a few failures before hitting on a winner. Ziegfeld knew he had a winner in Sandow, but he was ready to take another chance. Ziegfeld knew that the prospect of a man fighting a lion could fill auditorium seats, but now he also knew that he had to deliver on his promises to patrons. Ziegfeld realized that the one aspect of the boxing match that had gone right was the women's reaction to Sandow's good looks. Ziegfeld's talent lay not in being a Barnum or a Bailey but in being an exploiter of rare beauty. What he needed was someone to help him embrace his appreciation for dance and music as well as appeal to his eye for beauty. Sandow's attractiveness was purely visual, thus limiting Ziegfeld's scope as a manager. Although he remained Sandow's manager for two more years, his thoughts turned increasingly toward the musical stages of Broadway.

Meanwhile, in the midst of one of his tours, Sandow made another sudden trip to Europe. As it turned out, he had met a girl in Manchester, England, and went back to marry her. Because he was no longer a bachelor, his appeal to female audiences diminished. He left show business when his wife expressed her displeasure at his being on the road for most of the year. In 1897 Sandow founded an early gymnasium for bodybuilders, the Institute of Physical Culture at 32 St. James Street in London. He went on to participate in and judge bodybuilding contests at the Royal Albert Hall. Thus, although they had gone their separate ways, Ziegfeld and Sandow both found themselves in England as they took the next step in their careers. Sandow may have lost his celebrity status, but Florenz Ziegfeld Jr. was not prepared to retreat from the public's consciousness. He was ready to make his name not just a moniker but an adjective.

At Broadway and Forty-Eighth Street, in the plush dining room of Rector's Restaurant, one could find the most respected businessmen and theater personalities dining alongside chorus girls and gamblers. The line between the two castes of society fell away as Fifth Avenue stockbrokers slipped into back rooms to play poker and drink liquor with their mistresses. The decadent establishment was baroque in theme, with white cherubs beckoning at the entrance and a gold-domed ceiling. The interior also resembled a resort; palm trees lined its walls, and the smell of fresh lobster wafted from customers' plates. Rector's retained an air of tradition while also being innovative and a touch risqué—precisely the mixture Ziegfeld was looking for in his next venture.

Establishments such as Rector's or the Casino Theatre, where Ziegfeld had discovered Sandow, were among the first institutions to elevate Broadway's reputation. However, in 1896, Broadway was not yet considered the crossroads of the show business world. Broadway in the early 1890s was dominated by burlesque and farcical productions, interspersed with specialty musical numbers. Nearly all the shows were produced by Jewish entrepreneurs. Ziegfeld's meeting with Sandow, a Jewish immigrant, had given him his first real success; likewise, his meeting with the most powerful theater owners of Broadway, most of whom were Jewish, led to his first hit show. The six men who controlled Broadway at the beginning of Ziegfeld's New York career were Charles Frohman, Alf Hayman, Samuel Nixon, J. Fred Zimmerman, Marc Klaw, and Abraham Erlanger. They were known as the Syndicate, and they reformed Broadway by introducing the cohesion and efficiency that show business lacked in the 1890s. According to historian Robert Ruise, "without an association with the Syndicate, it was difficult or impossible to book a show or find employment as an actor."[29] Anyone who went against the Syndicate was virtually blacklisted. However, two brothers, Daniel and Lee Shubert (founders of the Shubert Theatre), succeeded in rising against the Syndicate and thus started a war of managers. The *Dramatic Mirror* tactlessly called the six men in the Syndicate "a Shylock combination."[30]

The Jews' rapid ascendance on Broadway was no coincidence. Show business became the "ultimate meritocracy" for ambitious Jews like Frohman and Erlanger. The Jewish residents of New York made up half the audiences on Broadway. Most of the Jewish performers on Broadway had started in Yiddish theater on the east side of New York City and moved their way up to mainstream New York stages. One of the most popular Broadway teams at the time was the vaudeville pair Lew Fields (born Moses Schoenfeld) and Joe Weber, both Jewish immigrants from Poland. Jews were most prolific in their production of musical comedy. Popular songs were placed in the midst of a show's action, and even dramatic plays tried to incorporate music in a more subtle way. As he had been in Chicago, Ziegfeld was most attracted to entertainment that was neither highbrow nor completely mainstream. He was aware of what was happening on the Lower East Side, and he had the foresight to observe that trends most often begin on the outskirts of town. As James Traub, a New York historian, wrote: "What Broadway lacked at the turn of the century [including the five years preceding it] was a figure who could fuse naughty sexuality of the streets and the saloons and the burlesque show with the savoir-faire of lobster-palace society—someone who could make sex delightful and amusing. What it lacked was Florenz Ziegfeld."[31]

It was in lobster-palace society that Ziegfeld found his first opportunity to move theater into the modern era and tastefully meld elements of burlesque, melodrama, and Yiddish theater. At Rector's, he met two men who would help him make this fusion possible: Diamond Jim Brady and Charles Evans. James Brady was a fabulously wealthy railroad tycoon who spent his money on what pleased him most: food, women, and entertainment. Ziegfeld shrewdly became Diamond Jim's friend, and in turn, Diamond Jim became a willing backer of Ziegfeld's theatrical endeavors. Like Brady, Charles Evans was a millionaire. He had made his fortune during the 1893 Chicago World's Fair, when he teamed with fellow thespian William Hoey to stage the hit musical comedy *A Parlor Match*. Ziegfeld saw endless possibilities in the show. The play was a satire on Spiritualism, and its climax came during a séance scene in which one ghost after another—each with his or her own special talent—emerged from a large cabinet. The séance scene alone made the production ripe for new musical acts or comedic performers to join the cast each season. Ziegfeld saw the show as the ideal place to introduce his next new star—whoever he or she might be. *A Parlor Match* was tried and true, but it needed a touch of innovation that only Ziegfeld could bring to it.

Ziegfeld was twenty-seven years old and broke, having just spent his last cent on a sumptuous dinner with his potential new partner, Evans. He had needed every bit of his salesmanship skill to sell the idea of reviving *A Parlor Match* to Evans. First, he promised Evans that he would secure exciting new talent for the cabinet scene. Then Ziegfeld presented a sheaf of new songs to Evans. One of the tunes, "Daisy Belle," capitalized on the latest craze: bicycles. In his "rather high pitched, acid voice," Ziegfeld sang the tune: "Daisy, Daisy give me your answer do . . . it won't be a stylish marriage, I can't afford a carriage. But you look sweet on the seat of a bicycle built for two."[32] Despite Ziegfeld's limited singing talents, Evans loved the song. However, he was still not fully convinced about reviving the show. It needed a new star who could draw in old and new audiences alike. Ziegfeld knew that if he could find the right talent, he could make that individual a household name before the show even opened. He had done it with Sandow, and he could do it again. Evans paused. Like Ziegfeld, he was a gambler. Perhaps this was a risk worth taking. "All right," he agreed. "Where do we start?"

London was Ziegfeld's answer. London was the location of the predecessors of the *Ziegfeld Follies: The Gaiety Girl* and *The Belle of New York* (the former show opened in 1894, and the latter show opened in 1897, shortly after Ziegfeld returned to New York). Both shows were comedies with very thin plots involving working girls ignored by high society until they proved themselves on the stage, regained lost inheritances, or married rich young men. Theater historian John Kendrick elaborated: "*The Belle of New York* . . . was a lighthearted musical comedy with a touch of innocent romance, all designed to showcase lovely young women in lavish but moderately immodest outfits."[33]

When shows like *The Belle of New York* and *The Gaeity Girl* came to America, they became part of the first golden age of Broadway—an era fondly called the Gay Nineties. The 1890s saw more musicals produced than ever before, sometimes up to fifty per season. Musical comedies as well as musical revues were maturing into legitimate stage productions in London. Historian Lee Allyn Davis wrote of the British revue: "Variety was its identity and a third of its ancestry. Humor was its staple, music its underpinning, spectacle its clothing . . . [a revue was] a musical mirror of its time."[34]

Producer George Lederer pioneered the revue in America. To the series of unrelated acts that constituted his shows he added lush settings, costumes, and burlesque or modern songs. The most impressive Lederer production numbers were his "living picture" skits that showed lovely women posing in various costumes. Lederer's revue was also different in that it used songs written specifically for the show rather than popular songs of the times. His first revue, *The Passing Show*, was a sensation at New York's Casino Theatre in 1894 and spawned many imitators. Despite Lederer's strides in American theater, London was still the musical comedy capital. This was something Ziegfeld sought to change.

As Evans and Ziegfeld entered London's Palace Music Hall, Ziegfeld was yawning before he even reached his seat. Eddie Cantor recalled that Ziegfeld told him "the show was dreary, the settings poor, and the acts humdrum. Then suddenly the stage was transformed."[35] A petite young woman with soft features, thick brown hair, and round, soulful eyes stepped onto the stage, demurely singing these sexually charged lyrics: "I wish you'd come and play with me, / For I have such a way with me . . . / Do not think it wrong."[36] Perfectly timing her movements to the songs' lyrics, she shrugged, wiggled, or let out a small erotic laugh after each stanza.[37]

"That's her," Ziegfeld said, finding the performer's name on the program. "Anna Held. That's our new star." Leaping from his seat, he pushed past the stage door Johnnies and bribed his way into the young actress's dressing room. He lost no time in offering her a contract to appear in *A Parlor Match*. She coolly told him that she had already signed a contract with the *Folies Bergère*. Ziegfeld insisted that if she broke that contract, he would give her the New World "on a silver platter," and he assured Anna that she would be famous before she even reached Broadway.[38] She hesitated, but Anna was eager to be free of her husband's gambling debts, and Ziegfeld's offer of $1,500 a week for twenty weeks gave her the perfect escape route (Ziegfeld had acquired her salary from Diamond Jim Brady). Anna could not have guessed that Ziegfeld had no money of his own.

On Brady and Evans's dime, Ziegfeld sent Anna lengthy telegrams articulating the wonders that awaited her in America, tucked jewelry into her corsages, and had bouquets delivered to her dressing room. Anna decided to take a chance with the fledgling producer from America. She later commented that, because Ziegfeld had risen from relative obscurity like herself, his success offered "an illusion of security amid the uncertainties of show business—a world where only ants endowed with the singing talents of the grasshopper in the fable can hope not to end up in the poorhouse."[39]

Anna Held called herself a Catholic *Parisienne*, hoping these affiliations would give her the security she craved. In reality, she was a Jewish orphan from Poland. Officially, her birth date was March 18, 1873, although new sources suggest it was 1876.[40] That she was born in Warsaw is not a matter of debate, but Anna made it one during an interview in 1909. "No, no, no. I was not born in Belgium nor in Indiana," she stated. "My father and mother were living in Paris. I was born in Paris. Voila! That is settled."[41] Anna's insistence that her place of birth was France was meant to reinforce her stage persona as a "naughty" *Parisienne*, but a deeper reason was to avoid the anti-Semitism that had driven her family from Warsaw. The Helds sought refuge in Paris, which, during the 1880s, offered lucrative opportunities for immigrants. Young Anna immediately fell in love with the city, and she was certain that if she worked hard enough, her dreams of wearing exquisite fashions and living in luxurious hotels would come true.

When her father died in 1884, Anna needed all the ambition she could summon. "We became poorer than ever. My mother became an invalid," Anna explained.[42] The girl and her mother moved near family in London, and Anna took degrading factory jobs that could have sprung from the pages of a Dickens novel. However, because of her fluency in Yiddish and the popularity of Yiddish theater in London at the time, Anna moved from factory work to stage work. She was employed by some of the best managers of Yiddish theater, including the legendary Avram Goldfaden and Jacob Adler.[43] The death of Anna's mother (sometime in 1885 or 1886) coincided with the waning popularity of Yiddish plays in London. Anna was thus forced to master new forms of entertainment. Audiences were now attracted by the aforementioned *Gaiety* girls, but for actresses who had not yet risen to such glamorous ranks, risqué music-hall song and dance routines were their bread and butter. In this milieu, Anna created an entirely new persona and lifestyle full of "gaiety, champagne, naughtiness, and high kicks."[44] Anna had an advantage over the more seasoned dance-hall girls: she exuded ingenuousness along with the sexuality of a sophisticated, worldly-wise woman. This duality made her songs, which were filled with double entendres, irresistible to audiences.

Her physical appearance increased her sex appeal. The London orphan had grown into a stunning young woman with a waist that was an impossibly small eighteen inches—its minuteness accentuated by the padding Anna wore on her hips. A writer for the *New York Times* later described her "chiefest charm" as her "great, hazel eyes, over which hang long curtains, deeply fringed. With her eyes she talks as much as her lips, and the combination of both cannot fail to be effective with an audience."[45] The reporter's words were no exaggeration. Anna was indeed a hit with audiences, and she was engaged at the finest Parisian cafés such as the El Dorado and La Scala.

Anna began to take note of the admirers who lined up outside her dressing room after each performance. One suitor was particularly attentive. His name was Maximo Carrera, a South American playboy and gambler thirty years her senior. His wealth and lavish attention won Anna's affection, and she became his mistress. They had no intention of marrying until Anna became pregnant, and in 1895 they arranged a hasty marriage to legitimize the birth of their daughter, Liane. She was an unwanted child and was sent to a convent at a young age and later to a boarding school. Anna's own youth and tumultuous upbringing contributed to her inability to be a mother to Liane. Because she became her family's breadwinner at an early age, Anna was accustomed to work being the center of her life. In 1908 Anna made no mention of either her marriage or her daughter when relating her life story to a reporter. "Everywhere the world was at her feet. Why should an old man or an insignificant child intrude?" a wounded Liane later asked.[46] With no real familial bonds holding her back, Anna resumed her career. Her short absence from the stage had only made her more popular. Audiences clamored for her in Germany and England, where she toured with great success. It was at this stage in her career that Florenz Ziegfeld materialized and promised to make her a big star in America as well.

Anna inspired Ziegfeld to build on Lederer's format for revue shows.

Through her, he saw the merit of inserting aspects of broad comedy (similar to that of Weber and Fields) plus the sensuality of French revues at the *Folies Bergère*. Staying true to his promise that Anna would be famous before she set foot in America, Ziegfeld posted tantalizing headlines (e.g., "Go to Held!") and photographs in windows of heavily trafficked shops. His most effective method was inserting exaggerated stories about her in major newspapers.

Before Anna arrived in New York, Americans were already enthralled with her. According to reports Ziegfeld had given the newspapers, she had endured an epic ocean voyage from London, allegedly surviving threats from a crazed jewel robber found in the baggage room. Even after this traumatic experience, she had arranged a ship's concert to aid the widow and children of a deck steward who happened to fall overboard. All this publicity was necessary if Ziegfeld wanted Anna to outshine the already established dramatic, musical, and comedy stars of the New York stage, including the popular Mrs. Leslie Carter, Mrs. Minnie Maddern Fiske, and Lillian Russell. Her fiercest rival was Russell, whose clear soprano voice was much more accessible to audiences than Anna's heavily accented, untrained one. However, the show Ziegfeld planned for Anna worked in favor of her accent. He had witnessed the popularity of foreign entertainment at the 1893 World's Fair. Exotic was what audiences wanted.

On the day of Anna's arrival, Ziegfeld chartered a yacht to meet her boat. On board the yacht were the elite of theater society—Diamond Jim Brady and Lillian Russell.[47] (The women, ironically, took an instant liking to each other.) A swarm of newspapermen and photographers awaited as Anna stepped onto American soil. They were enamored with her charming, broken English and her candid words against the sensible Gibson girl image: "Well, most of us prefer not to be sensible," she said.[48]

Anna later increased her saucy image during a *New York Times* interview in September 1896. Among other things, she discussed her bicycle-riding garb, blushing when she admitted she had once ridden in her knickers. They were, in her words, "Oh, so shocking. I shall never try them again. I wear now a short—not too short—skirt with leggings." What most charmed reporters and readers alike was Anna's naiveté. "Are you going to Chicago?" one reporter asked. "Chee-cago? Chee-cago?" Anna replied. "Oh yes. I heard of Chee-cago. . . . They had an exposition in Chicago." At one point in the interview, Anna turned "imploring eyes" to her agent, Ted

Marks, and asked him: "What is a cocktail? I heard you say on the boat that you were going to get a cocktail. I must have one soon just to know what it is." She concluded the interview by singing two of her songs, and although their words were "as innocent as childhood," the "rare command" she had over her facial expressions imbued them with meaning "that cannot be found in a cursory reading."[49]

After leaving the enthusiastic crowd at the docks, Anna went with Ziegfeld to the Hotel Netherland, located at Fifth Avenue and East Fifty-Ninth Street, where she could have as many cocktails as she wished. Much like the helter-skelter atmosphere of Chicago, New York in 1896 was, according to Anna's biographer Eve Golden, "quaint and picturesque," but it was also a city undergoing "upheaval and change."[50] The city was in transition between its simple, preindustrial past and its future as a modern, world-class, industrialized metropolis. Compared with the Paris that Anna knew, New York seemed more quaint and picturesque than modern and cosmopolitan. Ziegfeld exposed her to the best restaurants the city had to offer, such as Rector's and DelMonico's, and to the best hotels, including the Netherland and the Savoy. Both sported Romanesque facades and lavish suites with furnishings tailored to each new tenant.

The Theater District, though not yet cohesive, was among the most exciting locales in New York. Before Broadway and Times Square became synonymous with theater, Union Square, Madison Square, and Herald Square boasted clusters of theaters that stretched along Broadway from West Thirty-Seventh Street to Fortieth Street. In 1882 journalist James D. McCabe Jr. described Broadway so vividly that it might be mistaken for a living entity: "Broadway . . . the great thoroughfare is ablaze with the electric light, which illuminates it with the radiance of day. . . . The crowd is out for pleasure at night, and many varied are the forms which the pursuit of it takes. Then the theaters pour out their audiences to join it in an hour or more . . . as midnight comes, the streets become quieter and more deserted . . . only to begin at daybreak a repetition of the scenes from the previous day."[51]

The world of Broadway and high society was a stark contrast to the Lower East Side, where people lived not in hotels but in tenements. The seedy area west of Broadway, called the Tenderloin, was known for prostitution and vice.[52] Nevertheless, it was from these unsavory areas that most of Ziegfeld's future stars emerged.

The Anna Held that Ziegfeld introduced to America in 1896 felt no connection with the Jewish population struggling on the Lower East Side. She was far removed from her poverty-stricken Jewish roots, and she intended to keep it that way. As much as she fought to conceal her heritage, the *New York Times* reported in 1897, "Miss Held is of Polish Jewish parentage."[53] The report was truthful in this respect, but it perpetuated the falsehood that Anna had been born in Paris. Thus, it preserved her carefully fostered image of a carefree *Parisienne*. Although anti-Semitism was present in America, the threat of expulsion or persecution was not. Thanks to Ziegfeld, Anna became like the women she used to admire in Paris— living in a fancy hotel and adorning herself in fine clothes. Anna had become a flesh-and-blood Cinderella.

Despite Anna's popularity, her debut in *A Parlor Match* (1896) did not initially impress audiences, but that changed with a bit of clever restaging. Charles Evans recalled in a 1907 interview: "We opened to a packed house and Anna's first song fell rather flat . . . and her second song did not go much better and we were all feeling rather blue when [William] Hoey saved the day."[54] When the audience failed to respond to Anna's appeal to "come and play" with her, she turned to Hoey, who was playing a tramp looking through Anna's window. "Won't you come and play with me?" she sang. "In a minute, sis!" Hoey ad-libbed, as he drew the window blind and came around to the front with outstretched arms. "That broke the ice," Evans recalled. "The house screamed as the tattered tramp pursued the daintily-clad chanteuse."[55]

Anna appeared in just this one scene, but the show belonged to her. Ziegfeld had planted someone in the audience to call for encores, but that proved to be unnecessary after Hoey's ad-lib. Audiences could not get enough of Anna's "charming, suggestive" delivery of "Won't You Come and Play with Me?" in an exaggerated French accent (she pronounced *with* as *wiz*).[56] Anna's new fans were blind to the lukewarm critical reviews stating that Anna's voice would simply "do."[57] They hardly noticed any imperfection in her singing when she rolled her eyes and fluttered her lashes to increase the song's thinly veiled naughtiness.

According to Ziegfeld historian John Kendrick, after the closing curtain and Anna's exit from the theater on opening night, "a wild group of admirers (possibly paid for by Ziegfeld) unhooked Held's carriage from its horses and pulled her through the streets."[58] Ziegfeld had succeeded in introducing Anna as a new and exotic talent to American audiences. Dressing her in an innocent pink and blue dress and having her sing a risqué French song was so oxymoronic that it added an innovative, unexpected flavor to an old show. No one could argue that Anna did not stand out from her rivals. Ziegfeld had transformed Sandow from a novelty player into a headliner, but he did not have to transform Anna. As Golden explained, "Ziegfeld did not mold Anna Held—her act and her persona were fully formed when they met, and he exploited her brilliantly."[59]

With Anna, Ziegfeld had found a star who fulfilled his desire to combine music, dance, and beauty in one unique package. He had far surpassed any level of success foreseen by Professor Ziegfeld when young Florenz chose to abandon the musical college. He had gone from being a sort of snake-oil salesman at the Chicago World's Fair to being the manager of the most talked-about man in the world. And now he was the manager of the most talked-about woman in the world. Ziegfeld did not want Anna's status to be temporary. He needed a story that would make people remember her for generations to come. He found that story sooner than he expected—one that created such a stir that the *New York World* observed: "The name of the young woman became as well-known in this country as the name of the President."[60]

2

Gloomy Gus and the Petit Bourgeois

Thanks to Ziegfeld, the dairy business was booming in the fall of 1896. But what possible connection could there be between the showman and milk?

Ziegfeld, though an ingenious promoter, needed help coming up with a publicity stunt that would make Anna as well known as the president of the United States. He offered a handsome sum to the individual who presented him with the most tantalizing promotional idea. A man named Max Marcin was the lucky recipient of that reward. At Marcin's suggestion, Ziegfeld announced to the press that Anna had forty gallons of milk delivered to her suite every day—to use as bathwater. Ziegfeld added scandal to the story by deliberately defaulting on a payment for the milk, claiming it was sour.[1] As he expected, the press swarmed outside Anna's apartment to see the furious milkman demand payment. Anna was ready for both the reporters and the milkman. "It is, you see, to take zee beauty bath," she explained to the eager reporters. "The milk, she preserve the creamy complexion."[2] Her explanation did little to assuage the milkman's indignation. He sued Anna for the $64 owed to him. In the end, the debt was settled out of court, "as milk baths were too peculiar to be discussed in public."[3]

Ziegfeld's hoax and the ensuing hoopla in court catapulted Anna to nationwide celebrity status; she was America's first "It" girl. Anna could no longer ride her bicycle in Central Park without having 300 men follow her. Her name was used to endorse everything from corsets to cosmetics. Seemingly no one could resist talking about the unbelievable decadence of twenty-three-year-old Anna's lifestyle. It shocked and even angered the public, yet at the same time, women wanted to imitate her. According to one reporter for the *San Francisco Call,* the dairy business was enjoying healthier revenue than ever because "fool women all over the country began taking milk baths."[4] Biographer Ethan Mordden explained the phenomenon, asserting that Ziegfeld had anticipated that "modern American culture" was turning "all public life [into] a form of theater. If it's news, it's true, whether it's true or not."[5]

Anna was as appealing to Ziegfeld as she was to audiences and critics. By the time *A Parlor Match* closed for the season on October 31, 1896, he had moved into Anna's suite at the Hotel Netherland. Ziegfeld and Anna were no longer just a manager and a star; they were companions who sincerely enjoyed each other's company. They often went on youthful larks together, such as bicycle rides around Coney Island during which they gaily sang "Daisy Belle."[6] Anna had been infatuated with Ziegfeld since their first dinner together. Unlike his detractors, she even found his high-pitched voice charming. Ziegfeld continued to be fascinated by Anna's beauty and sent her fresh flowers each day and jewels on a regular basis.

"To him no idea seemed too fantastic if he found in it the germ of some kind of grandeur. What he wanted, he said, was to do away with all the old tricks of the stage and infuse it with new life—to carry it as far as dreams could go. His creations would make of musical comedy something entirely new and different," Anna stated.[7] Ziegfeld convinced Anna that she was the "new life" that would transform musical comedy into "something entirely . . . different." Anna admitted that after only two days with him, she planned to divorce Maximo Carrera. "There was already something between us," she said. "Without one tender word between us we were bound by a thread."[8]

At the beginning of all Ziegfeld's courtships, the objects of his affection invariably felt the same silent bond that Anna described. He was a man of few words but many gestures. He showed his love by making his women into queens. However, he was equally talented at displeasing his lovers. As Billie Burke explained, he was "a bewitching person when he wanted to be, a troublesome, fascinating lover, but he possessed a world of his own to which he could and to which he often did retire."[9] His restlessness and taciturnity were sources of great displeasure to both women. Anna worked hard to keep Ziegfeld from retreating into his own world, preferring that he stay in the real world with her.

After an evening performance of *A Parlor Match* at Gilmore's Auditorium on January 7, 1897, a swarm of journalists surrounded Ziegfeld and Anna.

The manager and his star were buttoning their fur coats, bracing themselves against the snowfall outside.

"When will the happy occasion take place, Miss Held?"

"How soon will you be married?"

"Miss Held and I are not granting interviews now," Ziegfeld said, scowling.

Ziegfeld's carriage awaited them at the curb, and he ushered Anna into it, leaving behind a group of frustrated reporters.

"You are ashamed to be my husband?" Anna teased him.

"If those hounds ever find out you're still married to Carrera, your career is finished. I'll speak to the press after we announce our marriage to the company," Ziegfeld told her.

Anna did not argue. She was still a married woman, though estranged from her husband. Divorce was nearly impossible, however, due to the stringent laws in France. But no foreign laws could daunt Ziegfeld. He was a genius at making dreams into reality.

On March 26, 1897, in their suite at the Hotel Netherland, Ziegfeld declared that he and Anna were husband and wife. Most historians agree that the proclamation was a spontaneous decision on Ziegfeld's part. Yet the party he arranged for Anna that day certainly looked like a wedding celebration. Only the couple's most intimate friends, including Diamond Jim Brady and Lillian Russell, were invited to the gathering. Ziegfeld served vintage wine and hired a stringed orchestra to play Viennese music in the background. When Anna arrived, she could not have made a more glamorous entrance. She stepped through the door draped in sable and, upon removing her coat, revealed a white gown embroidered with long-stemmed lilies and a $15,000 pearl pendant at her throat. Unbeknownst to the other guests, she also wore a diamond garter on her right leg. A silence fell upon the room; she did indeed look like a bride. Ziegfeld began to speak in an uncharacteristically soft voice: "I Florenz take thee Anna . . . ," to which Anna replied in an equally soft voice, "I Anna take thee Florenz . . ."[10] The guests were quiet until the couple had completed their vows. Then Ziegfeld uncorked a fresh bottle of wine and raised his glass to Anna. Hearty handshakes and congratulations followed. Neither of them told their guests that the declaration of marriage was as exaggerated as one of Ziegfeld's sensational newspaper stories. Only those closest to the Ziegfelds knew their marriage was not legal. However, New York law dictated that if a man and woman lived together for seven years, they were a legitimately married couple. Anna could only hope that her union with Carrera remained secret.

Ziegfeld and Anna chose Paris for their honeymoon, not only because of the city's romantic reputation but also because Anna was homesick. In addition, she and Ziegfeld were confident that Paris was the place to find inspiration for a new show. However, the honeymoon was not the ideal beginning to their marriage they had hoped for. As liberal as Ziegfeld was concerning Anna's marriage to Carrera, he was less understanding about her daughter, three-year-old Liane. Nevertheless, Anna introduced him to the child upon their arrival in France.

During their "marriage," Anna and Ziegfeld took trips to Europe each summer, but they spent little time visiting with Liane and more time frequenting cafés, theaters, and, to Anna's distress, casinos. Ziegfeld kept his involvement with mother and daughter to a minimum while abroad, and business matters occupied the bulk of his time. Still, Liane saw Ziegfeld as the villain of her life; she blamed him for keeping Anna from her and for thwarting her own desire to become an actress later in life. Liane's father still lived in France, and she spent far more time with him than with Anna and Ziegfeld. She naturally preferred Carrera to her stepfather and considered Carrera her primary guardian. But there is no evidence that Ziegfeld ever discouraged or mistreated the girl. He never dissuaded Anna from visiting Liane or objected to having Liane come and stay with them in New York. Nevertheless, Liane never let go of her antipathy toward Ziegfeld. She even invented a story that, to this day, is largely believed to be true: she claimed that Ziegfeld forced Anna to have an abortion in 1908. But according to Anna's biographer Eve Golden, "the parental instincts of the couple suggest that Anna, rather than Ziegfeld, would have been more likely to rush to the abortionist's office. She never had an ounce of maternal feelings for Liane."[11] If Golden's assertion is true, Anna possessed a callous side that audiences never saw. Given that Anna and her own mother were close, it is regrettable she did not forge the same bond with Liane.

Strolling along the boulevards of Paris while on his honeymoon, Ziegfeld found himself increasingly enamored with the city's revues. The shows included tasteful nudity and a joie de vivre that electrified audiences. Ziegfeld decided that Anna's next vehicle must be a French one. The property on which he settled was not a revue but a comic opera called *La Poupee* (The Doll). The plot involves a young monk who will inherit

100,000 francs only if he marries. To solve the problem, he makes a doll that looks like a real woman. However, the doll breaks, and a real girl takes its place without the monk's knowledge. Comedy ensues when the monk awakes to find himself married to a flesh-and-blood girl. After Ziegfeld and Anna returned from their honeymoon trip, the play went into production.

As amusing as the plot may have been, *La Poupee* failed. None of Anna's liveliness and charm came through in her scenes as a stiff, lifeless doll, and her scenes as a living girl drew only enough audiences to keep the show running for fourteen performances during the week of October 21, 1897.[12] Anna's charm and pleasing appearance were not enough to carry the show. Her singing abilities were limited, so it is curious that Ziegfeld chose an operetta for her. The ill-conceived show brought more misfortune when Oscar Hammerstein, whose Lyric Theatre Ziegfeld had rented, sued Ziegfeld for breach of contract. The issue involved Anna's decision to leave the show after two weeks. She claimed she was ill, but the truth was that she was accustomed to singing in intimate music halls and cafés and found it difficult to project her voice across the Lyric's 1,700-seat auditorium. Ziegfeld countersued Hammerstein, accusing the theater owner of dismissing Anna for the sole purpose of replacing her with his mistress, Alice Rose. The ballyhoo continued, as evidenced by a piece in the *New York Times* (which amusingly referred to Ziegfeld as "Florence"). The article reported that Ziegfeld "has changed his mind about suing Mr. Hammerstein for $20,000 and will only sue for one week's salary, amounting to $1,000."[13] Eventually, the various suits and countersuits were dropped. Ziegfeld could not afford the legal fees.

The dispute with Hammerstein was the first of many between Ziegfeld and well-established producers, most of whom belonged to the Syndicate. Ziegfeld had scoffed at authority from the time he was a boy. *He* was the leader; *he* was in charge of his productions. He could produce better shows with his little finger than Hammerstein could with his entire hand. The same kind of comparisons applied to Anna. Among the reasons for *La Poupee*'s failure was that she was performing someone else's material; it had not been tailored to her nuances and charms. What Ziegfeld and Anna needed was another vehicle like *A Parlor Match* that allowed originality and flexibility. But while Ziegfeld searched for the right vehicle, he had to keep Anna's name in the papers. Ziegfeld's next publicity stunt was a kissing marathon at New York's Hotel Martin. During the event Anna reportedly received 156 kisses, after which she was "overwhelmed with such inertia" that she had to lie down.[14]

Ziegfeld also found a way to keep Anna on the stage—though not in a legitimate theater production. He signed her to a contract with Koster and Bial's Music Hall, one of the foremost vaudeville venues. Her act consisted of singing "coon" songs. These songs, which were most often delivered in a southern drawl by a performer with a blackened face, were a mainstay for vaudevillians through the 1920s. Though blackface is offensive by modern standards, in the early twentieth century many Jews (including Sophie Tucker, Al Jolson, and Eddie Cantor) used blackface as a reliable method of assimilating into the mainstream entertainment world.

Audiences were tickled to see Anna, the quintessential French girl, singing in the American tradition of minstrelsy. But Ziegfeld saw to it that Anna put a unique, modern stamp on the old theater tradition. She spoke in a drawl (mixed with a French accent) but did not blacken her face. Thus, she conveyed the spirit if not the image of a minstrel. A chorus of thirty boys with charcoaled faces danced behind her, which made her stand out even more. Anna drew standing-room-only crowds. Ziegfeld was so enthused by Anna's success that he suggested she go on a countrywide tour. Anna rejected the proposal; she did not relish the idea of riding all night in trains and inhaling their unpleasant odors. Ziegfeld remained impassive, with only the trace of a smirk on his lips, as Anna complained. "You won't sleep standing up and you will not inhale gases. You'll have your own private car, better than our room at the hotel," he explained. "You'll have a state room, dining room, parlor, a cook, a kitchen, and you may even bring your piano." After Ziegfeld promised that she could also take Chico, Nellie, and Tiger, her Mexican hairless dogs, Anna agreed to the tour.

Before Anna embarked on her trip, she and Ziegfeld enjoyed one more lark together. This time, they visited the circus, one of the earliest sources of inspiration for the young Florenz. Anna and Ziegfeld discovered they shared a love of elephants. Anna even climbed atop one and slid down its long trunk to the ground. "It is great fun! I am Queen of India!" Anna laughed. "I should so love to have a menagerie of my own." Not one to take even such an extravagant wish lightly, Ziegfeld gave her a pet befitting the queen of India as a going-away present: a tiger cub (with its claws carefully shaved). He had recently given Anna a bear cub from the New York Zoo, and he later added two pug dogs to the mix. The entire menagerie was herded into a specially built addition to the $22,000 private railway car he had bought for Anna. The car had once belonged to actress Lillie Langtry, mistress to the Prince of Wales (Edward VII). Anna was delighted and felt less lonely on the tour with her pets to divert her.[15] The tour, which covered the West (including San Francisco) and the South, lasted from February to June 1898. It proved to be very profitable but extremely taxing for Anna. "I do not like vaudeville, but what can I say? It likes me," she stated.[16]

As attentive as he was to his wife's wishes and comforts, Ziegfeld became less engrossed in furthering Anna's career while she was away. He began to funnel more attention toward his own career and on making a name as someone other than Anna Held's manager. One of the many reasons for Ziegfeld's clash with Hammerstein had been his own feelings of inadequacy—Hammerstein's name was well known on Broadway, while Ziegfeld's was not. Hammerstein had built his reputation by acquiring his own theater, but Ziegfeld did not have the money to lease one. Although he frequently borrowed funds from Anna to invest in his business ventures, he was not desperate enough to ask his wife to be his benefactor. As Anna became more and more well known in vaudeville, Ziegfeld struggled.

In the winter of 1898 Ziegfeld finally found a backer: William Anthony Brady, a successful, twenty-five-year-old manager. The fact that Brady was Ziegfeld's junior and was not well known prevented the two men from quarreling. They bought a recently renovated theater between Thirty-Second and Thirty-Third Streets, close to the wealthy inhabitants of Fifth and Madison Avenues. Ziegfeld and Brady chose a dramatic play, *Way Down East,* as the premier production for their theater, which they named the Manhattan. The show relied heavily on Victorian melodramatic devices for its plot, but it also dealt with controversial issues (such as premarital sex and illegitimate children), which prevented it from seeming dated. The show ran for 152 performances beginning on February 7, 1898, and is considered one of the most popular plays of its era.

Ziegfeld had become so involved with his own business ventures that when Anna returned to New York, he had no starring vehicle to offer her. The only part he could give her was a specialty number in his and Brady's next show, *A Gay Deceiver.* Staged at the Harlem Opera House in February 1898, the show consisted of three acts, one of which featured Anna in an "animated song sheet." The act included one of Ziegfeld's first innovations onstage: from the larger-than-life musical notes behind Anna, minstrels poked their heads out and sang along with her. Ziegfeld and Anna were separated once again when that show went on tour. Anna's act was the only one to draw attention from critics—even if their reviews were not always complimentary. The tour closed in San Francisco, and the city's reporters apparently still bore a grudge over the Sandow versus man-eating lion debacle. The unforgiving press wrote that Ziegfeld's new star "did not smoke and melt and sizzle"; she had a "roly poly figure" and "a too emphatic nose." The reviewer concluded that "Mlle. Held does nothing so cleverly that you can forget that her talents are all centered below the brow."[17] As had been the case with A Parlor Match, audiences largely ignored Anna's critics and kept paying to see the woman who was the epitome of chic Parisian entertainment.

Anna had no chance to rest after her vaudeville tour ended; her old employer, Edoard Marchand, demanded that she fulfill the vestiges of her Folies Bergère contract. Ziegfeld, who accompanied Anna to France in the summer of 1898, fought Marchand's request, but the courts ultimately sided with Marchand. Finally, a compromise was reached: rather than paying Marchand the $5,000 she owed for breach of contract, Anna would perform at the Folies Bergère without salary during June 1898. While Anna fulfilled her obligations, Ziegfeld traveled to London and reteamed with Charles Evans to bring the 1897 smash hit The French Maid to America. With his confidence high, Ziegfeld was certain The French Maid would be another step toward elevating his reputation to the level of men like Oscar Hammerstein or J. J. and Lee Shubert. Ziegfeld assumed that since the show was based on an established hit and tailored for Anna's talents, it could not miss. Upon returning to the States, he also made plans with William Brady to produce another show at the Manhattan Theatre, a marital farce entitled The Turtle, which proved to be nearly as successful as Way Down East.

The French Maid opened at the Herald Square Theatre on September 26, 1898. From the show's title, one might assume that Anna portrayed the French maid, but this was not the case. Ziegfeld used the production as a vehicle for Anna to perfect her English-speaking skills. As in A Gay Deceiver, she merely performed specialty numbers. Ziegfeld was crushed when the play ended its New York run after only five days. He hoped the tour of The French Maid would be more successful, and he promoted Anna to the leading role, but critics were still nonplussed. However, Ziegfeld's goal was to please the average theatergoer, not critics. He found encouragement in the wild applause Anna received from her audiences. Her lack of pretension as well as the novelty of her being French won them over. Even though she had her own private railroad car and a suite at the Hotel Netherland, she never asked for a star's dressing room or top billing in vaudeville. Her coworkers and interviewers found her to be "charming and unaffected."[18] On one occasion, Anna called herself a member of the petite bourgeoisie (the lower middle class).

As much as she fancied herself a humble member of the middle class and spoke out against her husband's gambling, Anna was not above reproach when it came to money. She hosted more than a few supper parties in her private car while touring the West Coast with *The French Maid*. One of her guests was Tod Sloane, a jockey in the California Derby. She expressed a great desire to see him ride in the race, but a matinee performance made her attendance nearly impossible. Enter George M. Bowles, who told Anna that he could charter a railway car for $60, and if she hurried her performance, the train could get her to the racetrack in time to see Sloane ride. Anna accepted his offer, Bowles fronted the money, and Anna made it to the race, where she lost $1,000 betting on a tip. This considerable loss made her forget about the $60 she owed Bowles. "She kept on forgetting it ever since and was not reminded of the fact until it was called to her attention yesterday afternoon by the Deputy Sheriff," a writer for the *New York Times* reported on October 28, 1898. Anna was confronted with Bowles's charges against her and documents that could have resulted in a warrant for her arrest. She was in a state of near hysteria until Ziegfeld stepped in. "If anyone owes money to Bowles it's me," he said. "I'll fight this case to the end."[19] How the case concluded is unclear, but Ziegfeld most likely paid the debt.

Ziegfeld's next show for Anna, *Mlle. Fifi*, was a slight improvement over *The French Maid*. Anna had no brushes with the law during its run, which was considerably longer than *The French Maid*'s five days. *Mlle. Fifi* played for three months at the Manhattan Theatre beginning on February 1, 1899, and then for a week at the Harlem Opera House. Despite its respectable run and the audience's enthusiasm, it failed to impress critics. The show remains noteworthy because Ziegfeld honed techniques that later became trademarks in the *Follies*. According to his cousin Richard, Ziegfeld "spiced . . . up" the show's lifeless plot by adding scenes that allowed the actresses to show a bit of skin. He developed the credo he applied to each successive show: "Beauty in the flesh will continue to rule the world."[20] In one particularly daring scene, Fifi tempts her former beau by lying on a sofa and exposing her legs, which are covered only by black tights. Ziegfeld also relied on his typical technique of using flashy posters to publicize the show. One such poster pictured a young girl sobbing on her indignant mother's shoulder as a foppish young man stood with his back to them. Across the top of the picture was the racy tagline: "He has deceived me, Mamma!!! With a woman named 'Fifi'!" Critics deemed the show indecent, but it was this "indecent" dash of flavor that prevented *Mlle. Fifi* from being a complete box-office failure. Ziegfeld had not yet learned how to craft the licentious scenes in his shows into artistic ones featuring women who were more reminiscent of a Venus de Milo than a can-can dancer.

In April 1899 Ziegfeld produced yet another show for Anna, *The Manicure.* Though it lacked the spice of *Mlle. Fifi,* it possessed the same "latent French taste in both themes and approach" that Ziegfeld had been exploring since he met Anna.[21] *The Manicure* was Ziegfeld's largest failure yet; it ran for only one performance at the Manhattan Theatre on April 24, 1899. Increasingly, it seemed as if Anna's shows were cursed; however, Ziegfeld made one more attempt to find a hit for his wife. He loaned Anna out to perform a specialty number in the unsophisticated farce *By the Sad Sea Waves,* which had been brought in to replace *The Manicure.* The show had been playing at another theater since February, but once it came to the Manhattan, it died within a week.

Though it seemed as if Anna would be as broke as her husband after their marathon of failed shows, she had developed more sense when it came to money, especially after her near arrest. She ensured that her bank account (separate from Ziegfeld's) was well stocked and safe from both lawsuits and Ziegfeld's gambling habit. One reporter wrote, "Anna loves the American dollar five times better than she does the franc of her native land," and it caused her "a severe spasm of anguish" to part with her dollars. But she, like Ziegfeld, suffered no anguish when using her money to acquire beautiful things. After an auction held in March 1900, a *New York Times* reporter observed: "More than one piano was sold, Anna Held buying the most expensive one ... she paid $140 for it, but could have obtained it for less had she not in her eagerness insisted on bidding against herself. Miss Held also secured a pretty window seat, upholstered in Spanish leather, for $17."[22]

Anna's acquisitions were meant for the home she hoped to create with

Ziegfeld. During the rare opportunities they had to be husband and wife rather than manager and star, they tried to build the semblance of a normal married life. In 1898 they bought the modestly sized Prey Farm outside Belgrade Lakes in Maine. Ziegfeld announced the purchase to the press with this tongue-in-cheek statement: "Miss Anna Held has purchased the farm of Prey, and guests are invited to come and inspect her calves."[23] But neither guests nor the Ziegfelds had much time to inspect any calves, animal or human. Indeed, Anna and Ziegfeld spent little time at Prey. Anna may have done this on purpose; having grown up in cities, she disliked country living and found the mosquitoes and the lack of luxury at the farm especially repulsive. Ziegfeld, in contrast, relished a rustic existence. Ever since his trip to Wyoming as a teen, wide-open spaces had captured his imagination. His laconic and withdrawn nature was a perfect match for the silence of the woods. He spent hours stalking through the forest, enjoying every moment without the telephone ringing or telegrams being slipped under the door. But maintaining both the farm and the hotel suite where he and Anna lived required money. And with no new shows in their immediate future, money would not be forthcoming.

With or without money, Ziegfeld and Anna traveled to France for the summer. Parisians had not forgotten Anna; in June 1899 she won first prize in Paris's annual *Fete de Fleurs*. Dressed in pink and white and wearing a hat of lavender orchids, Anna drew the loudest cheers. Among her most ardent supporters was Ziegfeld, who stood on the sidelines and tossed her a five-pound bouquet as she passed by. Laughter ensued when she failed to catch the bouquet and it knocked off her hat.

Strolling down the flower-laden boulevards later that evening, Anna sighed at the thought of returning to America and suggested they remain in Paris. Ziegfeld assured her that they would return each summer, but he was not willing to give up his life in New York and his lease on the Manhattan Theatre. "And you need to learn more English," Ziegfeld argued. "Not too much—audiences don't understand a word of French, but they still want anything Parisian. I know that if we find the right show for you, you'll be a great actress. Better than Lillian Russell." Anna asked if she should hire a tutor, but Ziegfeld shook his head. What she needed was total immersion—no French spoken by her or to her, for a time at least. "I will become like your American girls, Gussy Gloom," Anna agreed, unknowingly flubbing his nickname. But there was no laughter from Ziegfeld, who remained withdrawn and thoughtful. Ziegfeld's countenance, as Eddie Cantor later wrote, seldom changed. "He has a real poker face, something he had acquired years before playing poker, roulette."[24]

Unlike Ziegfeld, who was willing to change with every new trend or preference of the times, Anna did not want to change her carefully created persona. If Anna wished to remain as she was, Ziegfeld would not hesitate to move forward without her. But for the time being, Ziegfeld was pleased that Anna had agreed to follow his lead and evolve with him—at least to a small degree.

Ziegfeld did everything in an exaggerated fashion, and immersing Anna in learning the English language was no exception. Once they were back in New York, he hired all English-speaking servants, but their brands of English varied; thus, Anna's accent was a bit eccentric. For instance, she pronounced some words with a hint of Cockney she had picked up from her chauffeur. In any case, Ziegfeld was certain that perfecting Anna's English was the key to making their show for the 1899–1900 season a hit.

While searching for a vehicle that would pull them both out of their slump, Ziegfeld kept Americans interested in Anna by publicizing news-worthy tales about her. His latest outlandish story was actually based in reality. Anna had taken a liking to automobiles, despite the fact that they were smelly, rickety, and difficult to operate. Ziegfeld latched onto Anna's love of the horseless carriage and encouraged her to publish an announce-ment challenging any female driver to race her from New York to Philadelphia. The proclamation served its purpose, bringing some chuck-les and a renewed interest in the hedonistic French actress. It appears that no one accepted the challenge, which was not surprising, given that most cars of the era were considered to be speeding if they went over twelve miles per hour.

Before long, the sensational stories became unnecessary because Anna and Ziegfeld found a play. Although Ziegfeld is most often credited as being the brains behind his shows, he admitted that Anna was often the inspiration and adviser for his productions. Anna suggested that a French musical comedy, *La Femme a Papa* (Papa's Wife), be translated for her to perform on Broadway. The piece cast her as a young wife thrown into the company of soubrettes. This show would be the first to give Anna star bill-ing. To add prestige to the play, Ziegfeld hired the most innovative musi-cal-comedy writers of the era: Harry B. Smith and Reginald DeKoven. According to Ziegfeld historian Ethan Mordden, Smith and DeKoven's show *Robin Hood* (1891) was "the launching title in the . . . classic line of comic/opera/operetta/musical play, in which the score is the work of a single writing team."[25] Such vehicles did not rely on specialty numbers but instead used the score to further the plot.

Harry B. Smith was a former Chicagoan (though he was born in New York) and a friend of the Ziegfelds. Smith first met Ziegfeld when Smith's sister was receiving piano instruction from Professor Ziegfeld and Smith was working as a public-relations man for the musical college. Smith and Ziegfeld reconnected in New York, and Smith's wife and Anna quickly became close friends. The two couples traveled through Europe each summer, and it was during one of these trips that the idea for *Papa's Wife* came to Anna.

Because Anna was the star of the show, its success or failure depended largely on her. Such pressure caused her severe anxiety, for more reasons than one. According to her biographer, "She knew if she wasn't a success in *Papa's Wife,* her marriage might be doomed as well."[26] Anna followed Ziegfeld's advice without complaint, dealt with her homesickness, was flexible about her plans and schedules as they related to her husband, and pulled him out of his withdrawn moods. Anna and Ziegfeld loved each other, but theater was such a big part of their relationship that if Anna failed, it would be as if she had dropped out of Ziegfeld's world.

Ziegfeld had as many anxieties as Anna did. He worried not only about her ability to carry the show but also about every mechanical intricacy of the production, which was more complicated than any other show he had staged. *Papa's Wife* helped make Ziegfeld's name synonymous with glorified girls, lavish costumes and sets, and a rich supply of comedy and song. Harry B. Smith asserted: "It was with this play that Mr. Ziegfeld first revealed himself as a connoisseur of pulchritude. There were only sixteen girls in *Papa's Wife,* but they were all highly decorative and in their costuming economy was not considered."[27] Ziegfeld fully invested himself in the glamorous numbers featuring chorines, but when it came to dialogue or comedy bits, he did not interfere. "Gloomy Gus" admitted he had no sense of what audiences would find humorous. He let public reaction be his guide.

Eddie Cantor aptly described Ziegfeld's intimidating presence during rehearsals: "Ziegfeld removed his coat, and when Ziegfeld removes his coat the serious part of show business begins. He has often worked through a dress rehearsal for a span of twenty hours, starting at two and still going strong in the morning. The theater is empty and a solemn air pervades the darkened orchestra where only the glow of a lighted cigar betrays his presence." When he emerged, no one could miss him. He most often wore a flamboyantly colored shirt and a suit jacket with a bright, printed handkerchief poking from the breast pocket and smelling faintly of perfume. Then, according to Cantor, he would begin his critique: "The finale is too drawn out. . . . the first specialty number needs to be moved, too rushed the way it is now. Costumes don't go with the scene. Throw them out, get new ones," he rat-tatted, his voice alternating between mumbling and shouting.[28]

Ziegfeld's anxiety was heightened after the illustrious producer David Belasco visited a rehearsal of *Papa's Wife*, pointed to Anna, and declared, "I can't understand a word she's saying!"[29] But even if Anna failed, Ziegfeld was sure that critics would compliment the show's visual beauty. He bombarded the musical director with suggestions for production numbers and oversaw costume and set designs in painstaking detail. "He begins to give instructions for the lighting of every scene and most of it sounds like deep Greek," Cantor observed.[30] There was certainly no shortage of gorgeousness; one production number included sixteen fetching chorus girls, with Anna front and center. Her gowns alone, designed by Mme. Landorff of Paris, were enough to draw audiences. For one elaborate costume, Anna's hair was piled into a pompadour made even more voluminous by a wreath of roses and myrtle branches entwined about it. She wore two pearl chokers, and her white lace gown was encrusted with jewels.

Even after he had seen to every conceivable detail, Ziegfeld still had a pessimistic outlook about the show's opening night tryout in Boston. For all his shows, Ziegfeld stayed in the lobby on opening night, rather than sit in the auditorium. As he paced back and forth he murmured, "Let's burn the show up" or "I think it's a sure flop!" Only if the cast received numerous curtain calls and standing ovations would his anxiety abate.

Ziegfeld was more than pleased by audiences' and critics' reactions to *Papa's Wife*. Anna had perfected her English as much as humanly possible, and she won praise for her reading of "suggestive lines in a way that is not suggestive."[31] Her gowns played no small part in making the show a hit as well. Even one slight mishap during a Philadelphia tryout did not dampen audiences' enthusiasm. To play on Anna's love of the automobile, Ziegfeld had added a number in which she was supposed to drive offstage amidst the dancing chorus girls. However, that night, when the time came for the car to roll onstage, it failed to appear. Peering through the lobby curtains,

Ziegfeld bit down on his cigar. "What's wrong? Where's the damned thing?" he muttered. "It won't start, Mr. Ziegfeld," a stagehand told him. Anna continued to dance and smile while anxiously glancing into the wings, looking for the car. Ziegfeld, in what was the closest he had come to an onstage performance up to that time, ran backstage, leaped into the car, and managed to get it to Anna in time for her cue.

Despite the fact that he was "as vain as a peacock," and despite his unquenchable thirst for publicity, Ziegfeld preferred that all his interactions with the public be through print. According to a 1931 spread about Ziegfeld in the *New Yorker*, on one occasion when he was "dragged out onto the stage on opening night, he [was] not shamming stage fright—it [was] real and he suffer[ed] for days after."[32] Once Ziegfeld had a show polished and running smoothly, he often retreated to the farm or the hotel suite. His lack of sociability and his dislike of making personal appearances added to his reputation for elusiveness and accounted for a new nickname given to him by his colleagues: "Mr. Ice Water."

Even after the successful tryouts of *Papa's Wife,* Ziegfeld's relentless doubts continued. However, each successive out-of-town opening leading up to New York helped convince him of the production's value. In Boston, reviewers declared that Anna was no longer "a fad" but "worthy of serious critical consideration."[33] Yet some critics thought the show was too racy. Ziegfeld and Smith attempted to tone it down to attract a family crowd and were rewarded by a sizable number of women and children in the audience. Toned down or not, the initial condemnation of the show only increased ticket sales. About the women who came to see the show, one observer wrote that Anna provided a release for the generation preceding the liberated, "new woman" of the 1910s and 1920s. These "unliberated" women flocked to Anna's shows, longing "to gaze, just once a season, on vice, when it is well-dressed and glitters."[34]

Anna's mastery of English allowed the women in the audience to relate to her more easily, and as Ziegfeld had predicted, it was what she needed to become an actress in her own right. Anna ruefully said, "I speak English so well, I am no longer cute."[35] Audiences did not agree with her. Cute, beautiful, or charming, she was now on a par with Lillian Russell and Mrs. Leslie Carter. Indeed, Carter now found that Anna was a legitimate rival. In a review of Carter's hit *Zaza,* a critic stated, "It verges upon the vaudeville when, in the costume of an Anna Held—which by the by, this actress [Carter] did not know how to hitch up Frenchily—Mrs. Carter burst into song."[36] Anna still had a corner on all things French, even if she thought she was becoming "too English." Anna had gained such prestige that Admiral George Dewey, fresh from his victory in the Spanish-American War, attended *Papa's Wife* during his trip to New York with Mrs. Dewey.

The phenomenon of *Papa's Wife* continued to spread. The downside to its success was that Anna had to endure a four-month road tour beginning in April 1900. Theatergoers in big cities like Chicago and San Francisco and smaller locales such as Chattanooga and East Saginaw were thrilled to get a taste of the Broadway sensation. The tour of *Papa's Wife* ultimately chalked up a near-record 500 performances. The show stood up well against the stiff competition from other productions opening during the same theater season. The hit of the decade, comparable only to *The Belle of New York* in terms of defining its era, was the British import *Florodora*. *Florodora* was a smash hit on Broadway in 1900, and Ziegfeld took note of its exultation of chorus girls. The chorines became celebrities and garnered attention comparable to that given to Anna. The plot of *Florodora* was almost nonexistent, as was the case with most shows of the day. Simply put, the story involved heiresses and soldiers, comedy and romance.

Less reliant on spectacle and more reliant on plot was *The Governor's Son,* George M. Cohan's first production, about the "comic misadventures of several guests at a country resort." It was the first of many "Yankee know-how" shows that preached there was nothing "a dash of common American decency couldn't fix." Critics described the show as a "near miss." For now, European locales, beautiful girls, and spectacles were the victors at the box office; *Papa's Wife* contained all three elements.

Ziegfeld and Anna returned to Paris after the first season of *Papa's Wife.* This time, they were not desperately seeking inspiration, and Ziegfeld did not frequent the casinos as often as was his custom. Golden wrote that during this particular summer, "Ziegfeld did not fall prey to his dreaded dark moods."[37] Anna visited Liane and gave her an enormous pile of toys before returning to New York. Liane, as usual, was not overly happy to see her stepfather. Her resentment grew each time her mother left her and returned to New York with him. In her heart, Anna did not have what it takes to be domestic, and truth be told, nothing gave her a greater thrill than seeing her name in the paper. Nevertheless, the twenty-seven-year-old actress admitted that she was tired of living up to the image of the naughty French girl that had made her famous. "I like to be natural, and myself," she said.[38]

In New York, Ziegfeld met again with Smith and DeKoven to discuss Anna's new show—one that would do nothing to diminish her naughty French girl image. That personality had served both Anna and Ziegfeld well. They now had enough funds to relocate to an even finer suite at a newer hotel, the Savoy, at the corner of Fifth Avenue and Fifty-Ninth Street. Anna did not have much time to acquaint herself with her new lodgings before she returned to Paris to be fitted for the wardrobe she would wear in her next production.

The new show, entitled *The Little Duchess,* had no shortage of numbers intended to showcase Anna's best attributes. Smith and DeKoven wrote six fresh acts for her that ranged from coon songs to Irish ditties. Because they had become her trademark, Anna sang two songs written to highlight her expressive eyes: "The Maiden with the Dreamy Eyes" and "Those Great Big Eyes." *The Little Duchess* was ostensibly about a destitute actress who poses as a duchess to dodge her creditors, but with all the new material added by Smith and DeKoven, the plot was unnoticeable; the costumes and settings dominated. A critic for the *New York Times* derided the show with this statement: "For a definition [of the plot] just consult any dictionary that happens to be at hand, and run down the page until the finger touches the word 'inane.' For a description of the dialogue, the same book of words and the one spelled 'vacuous' will answer." Smith, as if expecting such a negative review, inserted a droll addendum in the show's program: "Owing to the length of this performance the plot has been eliminated."[39] Ziegfeld's early successes were basically revues under the guise of musical comedy. Reviewers failed to realize that his goal was not to find original or intellectual plots but to create breathtaking spectacle accompanied by original music.

Critics again berated Anna's acting style and called her wardrobe "garish," but even the harshest reviewer conceded that the show boasted "really pretty stage pictures" and "a setting that is pleasing."[40] Ziegfeld spent more than $50,000 on scenery and costumes (equivalent to more than $1.3 million in 2013)—double what any other producer would have considered acceptable. Cantor remarked, "Money meant nothing to him; it was to spend, and with the taste to spend it, he introduced into the American theater an era of lavishness and glamour that has never been surpassed."[41]

Like *Papa's Wife,* the new show pushed the era's moral guidelines to their limits, particularly when it came to costumes. One scene had Anna wearing pants, something other producers had already tried to convince their female stars to do purely for the shock value. However, trousers did not suit the voluptuous Anna; critics went so far as to say she looked overweight in them. Ziegfeld insisted that she wore them only to satisfy the audience's desire to see the elegant Anna Held out of her customary extravagant gowns. Anna stated that she felt like she had been "assassinated" by the number of costume changes required for *The Little Duchess*. Another controversial scene had six girls peeling off their stockings, and yet another had a group of girls dressed in swimming attire. One critic for the *New York Times* asserted that the stockings scene was "an innocuous exhibition, though tastes will differ as to just the degree of vulgarity."[42] That critic seemed bored by the show, but others who objected to it thought the sensuality was anything but innocuous. "What is there to object to?" Anna asked an interviewer after the show. "The girls are all good, nice girls."[43]

Good and nice was precisely how Ziegfeld wanted to present his chorus girls—onstage and off. Anna's naiveté ("What is there to object to?") only sealed the impression. According to Bernard Sobel, the chorines' "backstage conduct was exemplary. Whenever an emergency did arise, the girls solved it in their own way."[44] Whatever the public thought of Ziegfeld, his girls, or Anna, audiences lapped up everything he had to offer. Critics who used harsh words to describe Anna's performances were in the minority. Most considered her a true comedic artist who had noticeably improved her talents.

The Little Duchess played for two full seasons, first at the Casino Theatre and then at the Grand Opera House. The production broke box-office records at the Casino, outgrossing even *Florodora* and Lillian Russell's new show, *Hoity Toity*. Ziegfeld hoped the artistry and success of *The Little Duchess* would finally bring him some fame. He had produced the show under the illustrious title "F. Ziegfeld, Jr. Musical Company." However, F. Ziegfeld Jr. was barely acknowledged in reviews, and when he was, he was often referred to as "Mr. Held." Ziegfeld's fiercest rivals, the Shuberts, later claimed that Anna Held was "Ziegfeld's one excuse for his managerial existence" and "his meal ticket."[45] Tactless as such statements were, it was hard to argue with them, since the majority of Ziegfeld's shows thus far had depended on Anna's star power. According to a story Anna related to the *San Francisco Call*, her importance to Ziegfeld sometimes made her feel like a commodity. After one performance of *The Little Duchess*, she had felt very warm in the railway car. When she stepped outside for some fresh air, Ziegfeld raced after her and cried, "You'll get ill and ruin me!"

"I have never been ill," Anna replied.

Ziegfeld's face grew unduly sober, and he knelt down beside her. "I want you to knock on wood," he said.

Anna burst out laughing. "I believe not in such things," she said. "And it is Friday, my particular day of luck. So bah!"

Ziegfeld was still perturbed and would not stop pacing until Anna knocked on wood to placate him.[46]

Knocking on wood was not Ziegfeld's only superstition. In his bedroom and on his desk were dozens of carved elephants with their trunks raised, which he considered a sign of good luck. Ziegfeld even kept a crystal ball handy to stare into before opening nights.

Whether it was due to knocking on wood or Anna's excellent immune system, she did not become ill during the long run of *The Little Duchess*. The play's triumph allowed Ziegfeld and Anna to relax in the 1902 season and mull over what their next venture should be. Anna had grown so confident of her mastery of musical comedy that she now expressed the ambition to make her audiences cry. This idea left Ziegfeld nonplussed. Anna was annoyed by his lack of enthusiasm, but, as was her fashion, she did not chastise him. Instead, she took a stroll up Fifth Avenue and treated herself to a new wardrobe. When not using material delights as a balm, she most often lamented to her female friends over the telephone or hinted at her dissatisfaction to interviewers. "I can bring tears to the eyes of the people . . . they listened to me as in a church in *Papa's Wife* . . . I have some sentiment, I know, but people like best to see things like *The Little Duchess*," she told one newspaperman.[47]

Although Ziegfeld and Anna disagreed on which direction their next show should take, their free summer gave them some much-needed time to become reacquainted on a nonprofessional level. Anna, though "naughty" onstage, was routine oriented and very much a housewife offstage. Each morning she made Ziegfeld breakfast, returned to bed for an hour or two, and then went out for a drive, during which she attended to shopping and other errands. She and Ziegfeld then lunched together. Later, Anna took another drive, this time to the country or to the park to relax before her evening performance (during the theater season, that is). After a quick nap, Anna put on her makeup and costume before starting rehearsals, "already humming my songs or going over a few other lines."[48] Anna was predictable and good-natured, but she was not deaf to the rumors that Ziegfeld flirted with the chorus girls he employed. There is no proof that he actually had affairs with any of the girls, but his growing obsession with glorifying the ladies of the chorus was enough to make any wife suspicious. Still, Anna never flew into jealous rages or threatened to carry on affairs of her own. Faithful or not, Ziegfeld was a gentle and generous partner. He seldom lost his temper with Anna—even when it came to Carrera and Liane.

One morning, Ziegfeld emerged from his room dressed in his coral satin bathrobe. Anna poured a cup of coffee and sat beside him at the breakfast table. She stared at him pensively before telling him that Maximo Carrera was suing her for some bonds and for custody of Liane. "That's absurd," Ziegfeld declared. "Carrera hasn't any money of his own. The man lives with his sisters and gambles everything he has." Anna did not bring up the fact that Ziegfeld gambled with equal excess. She told him she was going to fight for Liane, and Ziegfeld nodded without argument. The Ziegfelds' scheduled departure for their annual trip to France was only days away, but Anna decided to sail early.

On his way to see Anna off at the dock, Ziegfeld passed by a telephone booth and stepped inside. According to Cantor, he "could never pass a phone booth without going in to call up the world."[49] Whoever he called, he became so engrossed that he forgot where he was going and missed the chance to say good-bye to his wife, but as usual, Anna did not chastise him. He joined her in France in July, during which time Anna won custody of Liane.

Little documentation exists to illuminate Ziegfeld's feelings about becoming a true stepfather to Liane and having the girl live with him and Anna. Ziegfeld kept Anna so busy upon her return to New York that it seems Liane's care was not on his mind at all. He showered Anna with a new wardrobe for the second season of *The Little Duchess* that was even more ornate than the first. Anna reciprocated her husband's lavishness by buying him a new car worth $1,400. She confided to a curious journalist that such an extravagant act would make Ziegfeld furious. But there was money aplenty; *The Little Duchess* continued to break records at the box office and made a tidy profit of $142,000 during its second season. Anna deposited her salary into her Paris bank account, but Ziegfeld was not so frugal. He spent $100 a day on Anna's private railway car, not to mention the salaries of her entourage of servants.

Ziegfeld would have done well to deposit his profits in the bank with Anna's. He knew that success was often temporary and that the next theater season could find him penniless and at the mercy of the almighty Syndicate. But receipts from *The Little Duchess* kept Ziegfeld's pessimism at bay. He saw only more success in his future and even considered building his own theater. Several palatial playhouses were opening on Forty-Second Street, including Klaw and Erlanger's New Amsterdam and Knickerbocker. The Lyric, which DeKoven leased to the Shuberts, was directly across the street from Syndicate theaters and was struggling to compete.

DeKoven agreed to back Ziegfeld's next show, given their positive history. This production did not include Anna; Ziegfeld saw it as an opportunity to prove he did not need her as a "meal ticket." Entitled *The Red Feather,* the play tells the story of a countess who lives a double life as a bandit. It boasted thirty musical numbers and no shortage of the Ziegfeldian standard of beauty. The show was a critical success, but its run at the Lyric Theatre in November was short, as was its second season at the Grand Opera House in April 1904. In total, there were only sixty-eight performances. Ziegfeld had assumed a musical comedy with pretty girls would be a sure hit, but somehow, *The Red Feather* did not click with audiences.

After *The Red Feather* closed, Ziegfeld arrived home at the Savoy. His solemn face was more dour than usual. He had begun to believe his detractors' opinion that he was incapable of producing a hit without Anna. However, she was not agreeable to taking just any role for his sake. Again, she brought up the possibility of playing a serious part. "I want to please the audiences, but why can I not do that by making them cry?" Anna asked.

Ziegfeld shook his head. "We don't know if anyone will come to see you in a Sarah Bernhardt role," he said. He then retreated to his room to avoid further discussion.

In later years Ziegfeld was quoted as saying that "it was all delusion and folly" that he enjoyed "musical comedy." In truth, he enjoyed the more dramatic plays that Anna was attracted to. "I like to laugh, but I enjoy musical comedy only as a money-getter," Ziegfeld admitted.[50]

Anna had been right in the past when it came to choosing her vehicles, and she was sure she was right again. While vacationing in Paris, Anna and Ziegfeld had attended *Mlle. Mars,* the romantic story of an actress who saves her lover, an imperial guard, from Napoleon Bonaparte. Anna saw herself in the role of the actress in a musical adaptation of the play. The show would blend Anna's desire for pathos with Ziegfeld's desire to capitalize on her tried-and-true musical talents. *New Yorker* essayist Gilbert Seldes later commented that Anna "had ambitions to surpass Bernhardt in tragedy . . . and used to visit hospitals and feed on horrors in order to approach tragedy." As it turned out, these alleged pilgrimages to hospitals were fictional. "The hand of the press agent is as obvious in Paris as [it] is in New York," Seldes observed.[51]

Though he was wary of *Mlle. Mars*, Ziegfeld agreed to produce the show. He put his own stamp on the production by renaming it *Mam'selle Napoleon*. He also resurrected Anna's original hit song, "Won't You Come and Play with Me?" as a foolproof audience pleaser. To further ensure the audience's approval, Ziegfeld sent Anna to Paris to acquire a new wardrobe that would outdo all her previous gowns; she and a bevy of models employed in the show all sailed across the ocean for clothes fittings. Ziegfeld remained behind to explain his visions for the show to the set designers: "Act one takes place at the *Comédie-Française*. I want you to reconstruct it as exactly as possible—spare no expense. Act two is Napoleon's residence. . . . I need the best costumers. There will be not one but two costume balls . . . and I need a copy of Gainsborough's 'Blue Boy' made for Miss Held," Ziegfeld instructed his production crew.

The show opened on December 8, 1903, at the Knickerbocker, a Syndicate-owned theater. Ziegfeld no longer believed he could make a profit without the help of the established Syndicate producers Klaw and Erlanger. Ziegfeld had spent $100,000 on the production and could not afford for it to fail. But even the Syndicate could not force audiences or critics to enjoy the show, which ran for only forty-three performances, ending on January 16. One reviewer called the play "coarse and infantile" and belittled the lavish ball scene that Ziegfeld had planned so meticulously, claiming it was irrelevant to the plot.[52] However, there were just enough good reviews to keep Ziegfeld hopeful that the show would catch on during its tour.

"*Mam'selle Napoleon* is one of the most artistic productions of its kind . . . Anna Held's manager, Florenz Ziegfeld, Jr., has staged this production gloriously and with an eye to artistic detail which lifts it out of the usual rut of . . . musical plays," a critic for the *San Francisco Call* wrote. But such accolades, even on tour, were exceptions. The reviews became more caustic. One critic, Rodney Lee, called the play "the worst yet; the season's most colossal failure." Nor was Lee charmed by Anna's flirtatious eye-rolling; it only exasperated him and made him wish to "throw things."[53] Ziegfeld defiantly ordered the tour to continue for the first half of 1904. *Mam'selle Napoleon* would have had to close if not for wealthy Wall Street financier Jake Fields, who gave Ziegfeld $20,000 to keep it going. The $20,000 soon ran out, however, and each month brought more critical blows until the show was finally bludgeoned to death in April. Ziegfeld was now deeply in debt.

"Every generation seems to have one or two showmen who were always larger than life," television director Buzz Kulick stated in 1978. "They fly by the seat of their pants and they're always broke. That was Ziegfeld."[54]

Ziegfeld could have said "I told you so" to Anna after her failure at drama, but he took the blame himself. In 1931 Seldes quoted Ziegfeld as saying about *Mam'selle Napoleon:* "It serves me right for trying to be artistic."[55] Anna had no further desire to pursue drama and resigned herself to her established shtick; even if certain critics felt like throwing things when Anna sang and rolled her eyes, audiences felt like throwing her bouquets of roses. Anna told one reporter that her comedies were "the best thing for people. There is so much trouble in life."[56]

Rumors abounded that there was trouble in "Annie and Flo's" union, but they both denied it. Their relationship was not perfect, but they had not yet considered a separation. They seemed to enjoy each other's company during their usual summer trips to Paris. Much like Anna, Ziegfeld had taken a liking to automobiles. They zipped about Europe, and Anna declared him a "chauffeur sublime."[57] They tried to forget their failed theater season through such escapades. But Ziegfeld's preferred escape was gambling or purchasing expensive cars and clothes, while Anna stayed in their hotel room, wringing her hands each time he went to the casino.

Broke or not, when Ziegfeld and Anna returned to New York they moved from the Savoy to an even newer establishment, the Ansonia, located at 2109 Broadway between West Seventy-Third and West Seventy-Fourth Streets. The Beaux-Arts luxury apartment house featured an impressive 2,500 rooms and sixteen floors. The staircases were made of green marble. Residents lived in decadent apartments with multiple bedrooms, parlors, libraries, and formal dining rooms that were usually round or oval. There were private or serving kitchens on every floor, so the residents could employ the services of professional chefs while dining in their private apartments. The hotel also included tearooms, restaurants, a grand ballroom, Turkish baths, and a lobby fountain with live seals.[58]

Room 8-41, the Ziegfelds' suite, was filled with their Louis XIV furniture from the Savoy, including Anna's gold-embossed piano with mother-of-pearl keys. The entry was pure white with a frescoed, domed ceiling supported by six Ionic columns. Five paneled doors led from the entryway into a luxurious penthouse with a private bedroom, parlor, salon, music room, and wood-paneled library. The kitchen and sizable butler's pantry were more than adequate for Anna's increasingly popular dinner parties, where the guests included luminaries such as Victor Herbert. Anna's cooking led Herbert to claim he wished to put her recipes to music. Ziegfeld's lanky frame became fuller as he ingested more of Anna's cooking.[59]

The Ziegfelds' opulent abode proved once again that they were masters at making dreams into reality. But their glittering life was only a facade. The reality was that the Ziegfelds were living in genteel poverty, and Ziegfeld was having difficulty holding on to the title of producer. As the 1904 theater season approached, he was reduced to partnering with better-established Broadway names. Joe Weber and Lew Fields, the popular burlesque comedians, had recently split up their act, and Weber was in search of a new format as an individual entertainer. He and Ziegfeld teamed to create the Weber and Ziegfeld Stock Company. The two men made an odd pair, for their styles were in complete juxtaposition. Weber was a "hokum" artist—a low comedian like those Ziegfeld might have seen at the circus in Chicago. Ziegfeld, with his admitted lack of a sense of humor, was an artist in the most aesthetic sense—or, as his new business cards boasted, an "impresario extraordinaire." However, the aspiring impresario was desperate and needed a partner—any partner. According to biographer Ethan Mordden, another motive may have been that he "wanted to get in on the entertainment business' story of the decade: Weber and Fields had broken up their act."[60]

The comedy duo's split may have made an interesting story, but it did not compensate for the series of disappointments Ziegfeld and Anna suffered during the production of Weber's show. It bore the undignified title of *Higgledy-Piggledy* and had a very stale story line involving an American touring in Europe and the unmarriageable daughter of a business magnate. Anna portrayed Mimi de Chartreuse, who is the object of interest for the "Fields" character in the Paris-set section of the show. The production claimed to bear no resemblance to burlesque, but it did, and Ziegfeld squirmed at the sight of it. The first targets of his ire were the sets: what was supposed to look like a pavilion in Armenonville looked like Hoboken, New Jersey. Weber gritted his teeth and agreed to redo the set, but he did not understand why it mattered so much. According to him, comedy was more important.

Comedy was what prevented the show from being a debacle on a par with *Mam'selle Napoleon*. Thirty-five-year-old Marie Dressler portrayed the unmarriageable daughter (a part larger than Anna's). Dressler, whose homely mug, stocky build, and bold tongue made her a vaudeville favorite, was the uncontested star of *Higgledy-Piggledy* when it opened on October 20, 1904, at Weber and Fields' Broadway Music Hall. Reviewers called Dressler "festive" and "the only genuine funmaker in the show."[61] Anna received tepid reviews, most of which claimed she had not broken any new ground with songs like "Gay Paree." On an even less flattering note, one critic said she was developing wrinkles around her mouth. Ziegfeld's impeccable aesthetics, however, did not go unnoticed. A *New York Times* reporter observed that "the costumes were gorgeous and the chorus was a feature."[62]

Since Dressler was the biggest hit of the show, she demanded that her name, not Anna's, be emblazoned on the electric sign outside the theater. The *Evening World* quipped that Dressler's friends and followers "regard it as singularly appropriate that the Parisienne's name should be in the past tense of the verb 'to hold.'"[63] Weber had agreed that his stock company would share equal billing, but Ziegfeld had made his success with "names," and he was not about to relinquish Anna's star power. The *Evening World* noted: "Weber's position is unenviable, for, whatever his inclination might be, he has as his partner the husband of the 'star.'"[64]

Weber somehow managed to calm Dressler and convince her not to leave the show over marquee issues. Still, Dressler was not enough to make the show a true hit. There was stiff competition on the New York stage. Most notable was George M. Cohan's all-American *Little Johnny Jones*, which introduced the now classic "Yankee Doodle Boy." Was all-American what audiences now wanted? If so, Anna was at a disadvantage. Despite ongoing remarks in more than one newspaper that Anna was a "Jewess," she continued to deny it. Regardless of whether audiences knew or cared if Anna was Jewish, they certainly knew she was European. Ziegfeld sensed that the Eurocentrism that had dominated Broadway for years was losing steam. But the European-influenced operettas and musical comedies did not fade away without a fight from their writers and producers.

By February 1905, it was clear to the Weber and Ziegfeld Stock

Company that *Higgledy-Piggledy* was a losing battle. Ziegfeld attempted one more ploy to increase ticket sales. The *New York Sun* ran a tantalizing advertisement offering a $500 prize for "the person suggesting the most feasible plan to enable them [Ziegfeld and Weber] to dispose of seats and boxes . . . and to prevent tickets from falling into the hands of speculators."[65] The winner of the contest was promised an informal reception with Anna Held and the "Ziegfeld All Star Company." The challenge stirred little interest. The next year, *Higgledy-Piggledy* went on tour without Anna (but with Dressler) and with Weber as the sole producer; the Weber-Ziegfeld partnership seemed to be at an end. They had planned to produce *The College Widow* in January, but Anna quit because Weber had reduced her part to twenty lines.

However, as usual, Ziegfeld ensured that Anna's name was not out of print long enough for audiences to forget her. In February 1905 he ran an advertisement in the *New York Tribune* offering $2,500 in gold to anyone who could compose a "topical song particularly adapted to the methods of Miss Anna Held."[66] The song was supposed to be included in a show written by Harry B. Smith entitled *Papa's Duchess.* Such a show never came to fruition, but Smith was indeed creating a new show that both the Shuberts and the Syndicate wanted. At this time, Ziegfeld found himself an outcast from both groups. When he had partnered with Weber, the Shuberts and the Syndicate had seen this as Ziegfeld thumbing his nose at them. Weber, as an independent producer, did not do business with either one. In March 1905 Ziegfeld gave in to the Shuberts and signed a contract for an equal partnership in the production of *La Belle Marseille.* The Shuberts agreed to fund his annual trip to Europe if he would spend part of his time recruiting performers for the cast.

When Anna learned about the deal, she objected: "We need to spend the summer relaxing," she argued. "I don't want to rush into another show . . . perhaps America is tired of me." Meanwhile, Ziegfeld sat at his desk writing three telegrams at once: one to the Shuberts, one to Klaw and Erlanger, and one to his father in Chicago. Despite his contract with the Shuberts, he was not averse to seeking better offers from the Syndicate. Still, "Gloomy Gus" did not trust his prospects and, as a backup, wrote to his father explaining that he might have to rejoin the faculty at the musical college. Ultimately, Ziegfeld admitted, "Wanderlust got me."[67] He returned to Europe, as he usually did when he needed money, new performers, or an idea for a hit.

Once in Europe, Ziegfeld wasted no time in maximizing the money he had left. He and composer Gustave Kerker wagered the last of their cash at a French casino and came away with massive winnings. A gleeful Ziegfeld arrived back at the hotel with his pockets full of coins. Anna met him with the usual dread in her eyes that appeared when he was gambling, but Ziegfeld surprised her by lining the entire bed with gold coins. Despite her misgivings about gambling, Anna was cajoled into trying her own luck, and the self-described petit bourgeois appeared in a different light in a headline shouting: "Fair Actress Is a Lucky Gambler: Anna Held Is Fortunate at Monte Carlo. Noted Parisian Beauty Plays Almost Nightly and Wins with Remarkable Frequency—Husband Is with Her." Anna's winnings amounted to $60,000.[68]

Both Anna and Ziegfeld had been lucky, but the difference was that she could stop when she was ahead. Ziegfeld could not. During the same vacation, on a stop in Biarritz, Ziegfeld lost 2.5 million francs at baccarat (the equivalent to nearly $500,000 in modern currency). It was more than he could ever repay. "The game was rigged," Ziegfeld grumbled. After signing a promissory note, Ziegfeld fled the gambling table.

Upon his return to Paris, he found a telegram from the Shuberts stating that they had reserved the Casino Theatre for *The Motor Girl,* another show Ziegfeld had in mind for Anna. Ziegfeld cabled back asking for $1,000 in traveling expenses. Lee Shubert shot back: "I'll cable you a few hundred, but not a thousand!" Ziegfeld continued to argue for his $1,000 before sailing for New York, and Shubert gave in, also agreeing that Ziegfeld would get 50 percent of the show's profits but Shubert would be in charge of production.

Alfred Baulant from the casino had been shadowing Ziegfeld for the payment of his debt, and he did not escape the country with no consequences. The French authorities placed a lien on Anna's property, since under French law, a husband's debt was also his wife's debt. "That is silly. We are not man and wife legally," Anna argued. Because France did not recognize common-law marriage, Anna was cleared of responsibility for Ziegfeld's carelessness. The Biarritz debacle was not resolved until 1910, at which point Ziegfeld was plunged into virtual bankruptcy.

Such swings between riches and genteel poverty were the norm for Ziegfeld. Money was an afterthought when he was in the middle of a production. But Anna could not reconcile herself to seeing riches lost and gained in the course of one evening. She knew Ziegfeld could regain all his losses, and more, with another hit show. Her confidence in him was severely shaken, but she could not ignore the fact that he had made her a transcontinental star. And Ziegfeld could not deny that Anna had made him a producer that both the Syndicate and the Shuberts now considered a worthy colleague. Anna and Ziegfeld were a team. All they needed was trust in each other, but trust was harder to come by with each passing year of their marriage.

3

"It's Delightful to Be Married"

Like Anna, the Shubert brothers had lost trust in Ziegfeld. When Ziegfeld returned to New York from his excursion to Paris in the summer of 1906, he brought with him none of the new talent he had promised to recruit. This was not the only way he double-crossed the brothers. Despite having an unofficial agreement with the Shuberts to book his next show, he went directly to Klaw and Erlanger with a proposal for a different production. Klaw and Erlanger, along with other powerful men of the Broadway Syndicate, including Charles Frohman and Alf Hayman, had recently formed the Theatre Trust, which controlled bookings, stars, scripts, and theaters. The Shuberts were not a part of the trust and were still warring with the Syndicate for control of Broadway. But the Syndicate had the upper hand; all the top stars had to go through the Theatre Trust if they wanted to perform in major American theaters. Ziegfeld saw the advantage of signing with the more powerful men, so he turned his back on the Shuberts and partnered with Klaw and Erlanger. The apoplectic Lee Shubert sued the slippery Ziegfeld for the $1,000 he had cabled him in Paris. Ziegfeld disputed the debt, but three years later the Appellate Division court found that Ziegfeld owed $1,299 to Shubert. Shubert was heard vowing on his way out of court, "No Ziegfeld show will ever play a Shubert house!"[1] "They all hope I will go broke and I wouldn't like to cause them displeasure," Ziegfeld wryly observed to an exasperated Anna, who was now describing her husband as "profligacy incarnate."[2]

Though reneging on his agreement with the Shuberts was dishonorable, to say the least, Ziegfeld and the brothers were polar opposites when it came to styles of producing; they never would have been able to work together amicably. The Shubert brothers defined theater as "a machine that makes dollars."[3] In contrast, Klaw was willing to take chances in a show and give liberal artistic license to creative associates.[4] He was also more receptive to European entertainment and performers, often traveling to England, Germany, and France to seek novelties to import to New York City. Another shared characteristic between Ziegfeld and Klaw was that they were both gamblers—they gambled on shows, on new talent, and, naturally, on games of chance. However, when asked the secret of his success at the roulette table, Klaw's answer was more reflective of Anna's sensibilities than Ziegfeld's: "Make it your rule to always quit when you're well ahead."[5]

By the fall of 1906, no one could say that Ziegfeld and Anna were well ahead. Without the Shuberts as fallbacks, they knew that unless their partnership with Klaw and Erlanger was a success, they would be ostracized from any legitimate Broadway stage. Fortunately, their new show had all the earmarks of a hit (though, as usual, Ziegfeld thought it was a flop before rehearsals even began). The play, titled *The Parisian Model,* sounded as if it had been tailor-made for Anna; the title character was even named Anna. The plot centers on a Paris fashion model who is also an heiress. When her boyfriend (an artist) presumes that she makes her money through unsavory means, the infuriated Anna acts out. She emerges as the heroine at the close of the show, however: after her boyfriend's artwork is stolen, she poses inside the frames as "living paintings" for the critics.[6] Charles Bigelow, who also appeared with Anna in *Papa's Wife* and *Higgledy-Piggledy,* offered comic relief in his role as a zany millionaire. Chorus girl Gertrude Hoffman provided more laughs with her mimicry; she even did a humorous imitation of Anna. Anna was so amused by Gertrude's impersonations that she asked Ziegfeld to showcase the comedienne's talent in their production. Ziegfeld acted on Anna's suggestion, again grateful to have an outside opinion on the comedic aspects of the show.

Ziegfeld knew that comedy had been an important element in each of his hits to date, but equally important had been a touch of the risqué paired with lavish spectacle. Biographer Ethan Mordden asserts that *The Parisian Model* was "a little crash course in Ziegfeld 101."[7] All the essential ingredients of the Ziegfeld formula were there: catchy tunes, clever comedy, elaborate costumes, and inventive production numbers. "The entire show was extravagant, with each scene seeming to outdo the last," Richard Ziegfeld observed.[8]

For *The Parisian Model*, Ziegfeld gathered cutting-edge backstage talents to create the spectacles he had in mind. Among the brightest talents was choreographer Julian Mitchell, who was most famous for his work in *The Wizard of Oz* (1903) and *Babes in Toyland* (1903). The eccentric Mitchell was deaf, but he placed his head against a piano to feel the rhythms to teach the chorus girls. Another important member of Ziegfeld's team was Gus Edwards, a vaudevillian and a songwriter. Edwards was later dubbed "the star maker" for his knack at discovering many of Broadway's future stars, including Eddie Cantor, George Jessel, the Marx Brothers, and Eleanor Powell. Edwards was the second composer (the first was Harry B. Smith) with whom Ziegfeld had a fruitful association. Edwards was responsible for writing the song that replaced "Won't You Come and Play with Me?" as Anna's signature tune. During preproduction for *The Parisian Model*, Edwards approached Anna with a pile of his recent compositions. She flipped through the songs and then challenged him to write an "eyes" song to end all eyes songs. Edwards appeared at Anna's hotel suite later the same day. Sitting down at her golden piano, he ran his fingers over the pearl keys. It must have been comical to hear Edwards's masculine voice singing a woman's flirty ditty: "I just can't make my eyes behave / Two bad brown eyes / I am their slave. / My lips may say / Run away from me! / But my eyes say come and play with me."[9] Anna clapped her hands and took over for Edwards, singing the rest of the tune. When Ziegfeld heard the song, he gave it his full approval. A touch of the risqué had worked in previous shows, and in that respect, Edwards's song left nothing to be desired.

To balance the suggestive Edwards tune was a song based on a composition by Henri Christine and Vincent Scotto. The song, entitled "It's Delightful to Be Married," contained surprisingly innocent lyrics written by Anna herself. Despite the couple's recent discord over Ziegfeld's gambling disaster, Anna's lyrics revealed that she was trying to maintain an unjaded view of marriage: "It's delightful to be married / To be, be, be, be, be, be, be, be, be married / With a house, a man, a family / You should be happy like a bumblebee . . . / There is nothing half so jolly as / A jolly married life."[10]

With music taken care of, Ziegfeld now honed the visual aesthetics of the show. One of the most inventive numbers was the opening scene, which set the standard for countless classic musicals to follow. Mordden describes the opening, set at "Callot's Dressmaking Establishment," as an early example of the "Heroine's Wanting Song."[11] Other versions would be seen decades later in *My Fair Lady* ("All I Want Is a Room Somewhere") and *The Wizard of Oz* ("Somewhere over the Rainbow"). As Anna sang "Trying on Dresses," her dancing related to its lyrics; matching a song and a dance was unprecedented in 1906. The concept was not fully perfected until the 1930s and 1940s by such dancers as Fred Astaire and Gene Kelly.

Following the opening scene, Ziegfeld showed more inventiveness in dance—and more audacity. In "La Mattiche," Anna danced a tango in two-step time not with a man but with Gertrude Hoffman dressed as a man. Historian John Kendrick described another shocking scene: "The song 'I'd Like to See a Little More of You' had the female chorus seemingly undress while modeling behind easels in an artist's studio, only to have the girls step forward to reveal they were wearing strapless gowns that reached down to their knees."[12] Another number in the first act, "A Gown for Every Hour," had its own bit of raciness as Anna undressed onstage (behind a screen, of course). That number also reached the highest pinnacle of beauty and splendor achieved in a Broadway production up to that time. After posing in several dresses of escalating brilliance, Anna appeared in the final scene standing immobile in a frame, looking like a masterpiece by Rossetti. Pretty girls posing in frames was another device that, in years to come, would be replicated by both theater and film producers.

The Parisian Model succeeded not just at the aesthetic level. It also succeeded in making scantily clad women into art—in stark contrast to a girlie show at a cheap burlesque house. Ziegfeld girl Doris Eaton later wrote: "Mr. Ziegfeld loved beautiful girls and he didn't object to presenting the girls in a sensuous manner—but not a vulgar manner. His sensuousness was like a painting of the Renaissance period. You couldn't take offense; it was beauty and that was the way that he presented his girls. They may have had some scant costumes on, but they moved beautifully and they looked beautiful, not vulgar."[13]

Though the costumes were innovative and beautiful, Anna had misgivings about them. Perhaps they were too avant-garde. She begged Ziegfeld to put her in the low-cut, gaudy gowns she had seen Lillian Russell wear onstage, but Ziegfeld insisted that Anna wear understated finery while the chorus girls behind her were attired in Russell-inspired costumes. In the partly fictionalized biopic *The Great Ziegfeld* (1936), screenwriter William Anthony McGuire accurately captured Ziegfeld's eye for women's clothes. One scene shows Ziegfeld advising a society woman to tone down her garish clothing in favor of something more refined. "Do you always check up on the combinations of women?" the lady asks. "Only beautiful women," Ziegfeld answers.

Ziegfeld's costume choice made Anna appear more polished and delicate: the single white rose in a bouquet of red ones, so to speak. But Ziegfeld's image of the ideal girl was changing. In contrast to the Gibson or Florodora girls dressed in stiffly corseted gowns that reached the floor, Ziegfeld was beginning to shape a less inhibited, more modern image of the young American woman. In *The Parisian Model,* Anna certainly fit Ziegfeld's evolving concept of beauty, but some critics saw his ideas as a devolution instead. "*A Parisian Model* should not be permitted even in a men-only burlesque house!" "It's vulgar, it's rubbish!"[14] These were the first reviews Ziegfeld and Anna read after their show opened on November 27, 1906, at the Broadway Theatre at Broadway and West Forty-First Street. Anna fretted and declared she should go back to Paris and stay there; Ziegfeld calmly puffed on his cigar and read on. The scene that spurred the most scorn was the suggestive "La Mattiche" dance between Anna and Gertrude Hoffman. "Rubbish, vulgar . . . so much the better," Ziegfeld mumbled. "The more the show's condemned, the more people will buy tickets." In particular, a condemnation by the Reverend Dr. Madison J. Peters convinced Ziegfeld of the accuracy of his prediction.

Ziegfeld was indeed correct; the show ran for eight months and carried over into the next season after the summer hiatus. It attracted standing-room-only crowds. Sex had sold the show, but what had truly elevated it was its sheer opulence and beauty. Contrary to the initial condemnatory reviews, the *New York Times* theater critic had only praise. Another reviewer described it as "bewildering glitter . . . a pungent show with a great amount of feminine spice attractively attired. . . . Miss Held would put a chameleon to shame by the variety of colors she displays while wearing specimens of what seemed . . . to be an absolutely unlimited wardrobe. . . . The plot, as one catches glimpses of it from time to time through mazes of scenery, costuming, and 'specialties' is a very small plot indeed . . . but, so to speak, has the virtue of being delicately attenuated."[15]

Gertrude Hoffman was singled out and received special praise for her imitations, but Anna got gracious notices as well. The *New York Times* critic deemed her songs "contagious" and expressed admiration for her ability to still enchant audiences as she had been doing for years. More than any other show staged by Ziegfeld, this one reflected the dream he had discussed long ago with Anna of a new and different type of musical devoid of old stage tricks.

New Yorkers, particularly those who patronized the theater, were ready for a fresh and innovative producer who could bring sweeping changes to the stage to match those happening in their own city. In 1904 New York had opened its underground subway system. This new method of mass transit gave people from the city's outlying boroughs, such as Brooklyn and the Bronx, an opportunity to experience Broadway shows. The subway democratized Broadway. The rich and poor, old money and new, immigrants and native-born Americans all had easy access to New York City now. The place where the most varied crowds of people brushed shoulders was the newly built Grand Central Terminal at Park Avenue and Forty-Second Street. Within walking distance of the train station was the triangular Long Acre Square, and standing at its center was the Times Tower (home to the *New York Times*). The publishers of the newspaper convinced city officials to rename Long Acre Square—thus it became known as Times Square. But newspaper reporting was not what made Times Square famous; it was theater, grander and more extravagant than it had ever been. And Ziegfeld was determined to make his name synonymous with everything that modern Broadway had come to symbolize.

"Abundance of talent, abundance of design . . . everything was absolutely the best that money could buy, and that's what he sold. The joy of Ziegfeld is that he's his own best creation. Florenz Ziegfeld, impresario extraordinaire," drama critic John Lahr stated.[16] Yet Ziegfeld still did not receive the recognition due an impresario extraordinaire. His name was still misspelled in newspapers or he was not referred to by name at all, even in reviews for *The Parisian Model*, his greatest creation. "She [Anna] was at the top and had taken Ziegfeld there with her as a kind of prince consort, walking a few paces behind," Mordden observed.[17] He had done well in making Anna a star, but he had been less successful in his own quest for fame. Despite his stage fright, he too wanted to be a star—a mysterious one that everyone knows but who is rarely seen.

The fact that Anna outshone Ziegfeld exacerbated the tensions between them. They may have been the golden couple of Broadway after the success of *The Parisian Model*, but calling their union a happy one would be an overstatement. They still lived a seemingly fairy-tale existence. Both were flush with success and lived like royals in their sumptuous suite at the

Ansonia. But problems began when Ziegfeld, realizing that Anna had reached the zenith of her success, began to look for the next "big thing." Though aloof and laconic, he never missed a trend. Richard Ziegfeld observed, "He rarely read fiction. . . . He stayed abreast of current events and gleaned ideas for his shows by reading six daily newspapers."[18] Ziegfeld was losing interest in producing Anna Held shows. He needed something fresh, and the show brewing in his mind for 1907 did not involve Anna at all.

His new endeavor would require funding, however, and money was something Ziegfeld did not have. For weeks at a time he would be absent on gambling sprees, hoping to win enough to produce his show. Anna was left alone, oblivious as to his whereabouts. When he returned with no money in his pockets, Anna knew he had been gambling and womanizing. She had been desperate to escape her first husband for similar reasons, and now it seemed that the past was repeating itself.

"Money was always the starting point for our daily quarrel," Anna commented. "An habitué of casinos, racetracks, and even the kind of gambling dens found in bawdy houses, wherever he went he gambled like a fiend—losing everywhere, of course, and borrowing from everyone."[19] During one disastrous spree, Ziegfeld lost such an enormous sum that he bet his automobile and Anna's jewels. Anna traveled to Paris alone after this incident, leaving him to sort out his debts. "My patience was exhausted. The gambling had destroyed what trust I had left for my husband. . . . For the first time, I considered the possibility of a separation," she admitted.[20] What prevented her from actually leaving Ziegfeld was the fact that she still loved him and the fact that she kept her money in a separate bank account. Thus, she knew that no matter how much Ziegfeld gambled, she would still have her savings as security. With her money safe from Ziegfeld's irresponsible hands, Anna was able to "understand everything in my heart. I had always loved that . . . boy."[21] Ziegfeld did not see Anna's financial arrangements as a solution to their problems. Instead, he viewed it as Anna's way of cutting him out of her life.

Ziegfeld funneled more attention into his next production than into his marriage. The structure of the show was still abstract, but he knew he wanted it to possess the opulence of his greatest hits. *The Great Ziegfeld* contains an accurate bit of dialogue in which Ziegfeld articulates his vision: "I want a show with silk drapes, with lace, with beautiful girls. . . . I want to dress them [the girls] not for the bald heads in the front row but the women in the back row." Ziegfeld may have been having difficulty pleasing Anna, but at least he knew how to please female theatergoers. But how could he bring "silk drapes" and "lace" to the stage with so many unpaid debts? The story of how he acquired the money is arguably the most infamous episode in his and Anna's marriage.

The saga began while Ziegfeld and Anna were touring with the *Parisian Model* company. As she slept in her train compartment, Anna's bag containing her jewelry, a large portion of her savings, and about $250,000 worth of other valuables (including one of Ziegfeld's lucky elephant statues) was stolen. "Nearly all my life's earnings, everything I made since I was a girl is in those jewels!" Anna wept. Ziegfeld remained strangely calm about the fiasco. "Why don't you do something, Flo? Did you see anyone come by my compartment last night? Did you see anyone suspicious? Try to remember, Flo!" she cried. "Weren't there two seedy-looking men last night?" she asked. "I would remember their faces."

The policemen at the crime scene eyed Ziegfeld suspiciously. "This could be a publicity stunt, and if it is, Mr. Ziegfeld, we won't hesitate to prosecute," one officer warned. Ziegfeld's cool exterior finally broke at this accusation. His voice was as near to a shout as it ever came. "We don't have to stoop to such things," he said. "Look at Miss Held—that ought to tell you whether it is true or not." He motioned toward the tear-soaked, hysterical Anna. Ziegfeld took Anna to the police station, and she identified the possible thieves from an assortment of mug shots. According to witnesses on the train, one of them looked like a ferret, and the other was a bearded older man. The ferret look-alike and the bearded man were never identified and possibly never existed.

The night after the robbery, Anna announced that she could not go onstage. She had not slept for twenty-four hours and her eyes were puffy from crying. But she had no understudy. Her doctor administered sedation, and Ziegfeld told reporters, "She will surely go on with her part." Anna stayed with the tour but became "nearly insane" as days passed with no sign of her stolen jewels or money.[22]

Reporters from the *New York Times* recounted the following succession of events, which sound like the plot of a cheap mystery novel. Two men with a suitcase allegedly disembarked from a train in Painesville, Ohio, and were apprehended by two "detectives." The detectives and the prisoners then departed on another train and were not seen again. The detectives were not lawmen at all but associates of the thieves. The following afternoon, a police captain in Toledo received a mysterious phone call (from one of the four men) telling him that the suitcase contained Anna's jewels. The story was a ruse to confuse the real detectives on Anna's case. "It's a lie. The jewels have not been recovered!" Anna told eager reporters.[23]

The affair of the stolen jewels soon reached its climax. One night, a breathless Ziegfeld came home and told Anna of a bizarre development. He had received a message instructing him to go to a certain hotel and place a set amount of money in a specific room. If he did, Anna's jewels would be returned. Ziegfeld obeyed, although he carried a gun for his protection. He waited in an adjacent room until he heard a door shut, signaling that the thief had taken his ransom. Ziegfeld then slipped back into the room, his hand on his gun, and found a black satchel in place of the money he had left. Anna's jewels were inside, but the money stolen from her bag was never returned.[24]

Anna did not believe Ziegfeld's wild ransom story. She assumed it was another hoax—an elaborate attempt to keep her name in the papers while also providing a convenient excuse for the missing money. Anna did not know whether Ziegfeld had gambled it away, used it to fund his new show, or a little of both. Luise Rainier, playing Anna in *The Great Ziegfeld*, asks, "How can I love someone who plays tricks on me, who puts terrible things in the newspaper, and who had millions of reporters annoying me?" These may not have been the real Anna's exact words, but the sentiment is authentic.

Whether or not the jewel robbery was a swindle remains unclear. In the memoir that Liane Carrera ghostwrote under Anna's name, she claimed it was a fraud. But given her strong dislike of her stepfather, the validity of her assumptions must be viewed warily. Ziegfeld may have become an increasingly "opulent individualist," but he still cared for Anna, just as she still cared for him.[25] It seems unlikely that he would play such a cruel trick on her. But if he did indeed fabricate the robbery, he did so out of desperation, not malice. Ziegfeld was an artistic genius but lacked people skills. To his way of thinking, money existed only to spend, and he found it impossible to comprehend Anna's concern, since the lost funds could be replaced with her next show's receipts. All Anna knew was that the robbery had dealt another blow to her virtually nonexistent trust in Ziegfeld.

Following the robbery, Anna's costars noticed that she became moody backstage, whereas she had been a delight to work with in the past. Though she was still like a mother to the chorus girls, she and comedian Charles

Bigelow had no camaraderie. Anna redirected her anger toward Ziegfeld at the actor, who was often late for rehearsals due to rendezvous in bars. She told him: "You couldn't become a star if you stayed in the business 5,000 years!" Bigelow ultimately left the show after the Shuberts offered him a contract, but the main reason for his departure, he claimed, was Anna's meanness. Ziegfeld was upset at the unprofessionalism exhibited by Bigelow, the Shuberts, and even Anna. However, for the most part, he was able to keep his company happy. The chorus girls took a genuine interest in their work, thanks in part to Anna. As had been the case with Gertrude Hoffman, she often thought of ways to make the girls more prominent onstage, even at her own expense. Ziegfeld increased the girls' satisfaction by leaving large-denomination bills in their dressing rooms or tucked in bouquets. One reviewer remarked, "The fact that Mr. Ziegfeld can maintain such enthusiasm among his people speaks volumes for his sagacity and tact."[26]

Ziegfeld kept not only his company but also theatergoers happy. He added new musical numbers in each season of *The Parisian Model*, which kept audiences coming back even if they had already seen the show. One new number capitalized on the teddy bear craze, which began after President Theodore Roosevelt refused to shoot a bear his colleagues had caught and tied to a tree. Roosevelt, incidentally, was a frequent patron of Ziegfeld shows and even invited Anna and Ziegfeld out to dinner on several occasions. The song was entitled "Won't You Be My Teddy Bear?" and featured two children dressed as bears and six chorus girls sitting atop fake bears. It was a wholesome act in the midst of a risqué show that, as one reviewer put it, "smelled vilely."[27]

Ziegfeld could no longer afford to ignore his critics. In acknowledgment of the families who now came to Broadway on the subway each weekend, Ziegfeld cleaned up *The Parisian Model* for the new season—but not so clean that it smelled of bleach. In any case, the show must have been wholesome enough for young girls to see, for a girls' chorus sang the teddy bear song for their 1907 graduation exercises at the First Reformed Church in Hackensack, New Jersey. According to a writer for the *New York Tribune*, "There were many who couldn't see the harm in it but the church trustees are said to be indignant, and one of them said this afternoon that it would be the last year for the public exercises in the church. The song was encored and the girls repeated it."[28] In spite of the hoopla still sparked by *The Parisian Model*, Ziegfeld was growing increasingly restless and did not travel with Anna to every stop on the show's tour, which ran from the winter of 1907 to the summer of 1908. He was spending more time in talks with Abe Erlanger about his next production, which would be staged in Erlanger's roof garden atop the New York Theatre at Broadway and Forty-Fourth Street.

Now that he had a backer and a firm plan for his next show, Ziegfeld found time to catch up with Anna when the *Parisian Model* company stopped in his hometown of Chicago. Anna and Ziegfeld put their tensions and distrust aside and enjoyed a long visit, during which Professor Ziegfeld invited his daughter-in-law to give a lecture to his students. Ziegfeld had his doubts that Anna was the ideal speaker for a class of acting hopefuls. He had a sixth sense when it came to theater and could foresee when a certain style was on its way out. He knew that Anna's style of acting was becoming old-fashioned. Several times after her curtain calls, Ziegfeld had stood backstage with a pensive look on his face and warned the thirty-five-year-old actress not to be a caricature of herself. "If I am a caricature, you make it no better," Anna retorted. Ziegfeld could not argue, for he played up the very attributes that made Anna a caricature. Most obviously, Ziegfeld had commissioned an illuminated electric sign—in the shape of two huge eyes that rolled flirtatiously—to be erected in front of the Broadway Theatre for the new season of *The Parisian Model*. He was trying to outdo the sign that had advertised *Florodora,* which sported a line of chorus girls whose legs rose up and down. But the superstitious Ziegfeld took it as a warning against caricature when his sign began to malfunction. Although an electrician attempted to rewire it, the sign never worked correctly and was more of an embarrassment than a drawing point.

Anna did not fear becoming a caricature of herself. She had long abandoned her ambition to become a dramatic actress and was now very comfortable in the persona she had created. However, that persona was always in danger of being proved false. She spent much of 1906 and 1907 denying rumors that Liane was her daughter. At the turn of the twentieth century, actresses seldom had children because it made them less appealing to audiences. When she was unable to explain her relationship to Liane in any other way, Anna placated reporters by claiming that Liane was an orphan girl she had adopted in France. This falsehood did nothing to make Liane feel more kindly toward her mother or stepfather.

Anna may have feared the exposure of her past, but her fears about her marriage had temporarily lessened. Despite her misgivings about Ziegfeld, she wanted to take care of him and do whatever she could to save their marriage. Ziegfeld made his own efforts to keep the union intact. When Marshall Field and Company sued Anna, claiming she had failed to pay for thousands of dollars worth of hats and lingerie, Ziegfeld filed a countersuit claiming that the company had defamed his wife's character. The case was settled out of court. The fact that Ziegfeld came to Anna's defense proved he still possessed the gallantry she loved, but Ziegfeld could be doting one day and faraway the next.

"Sensing the danger that was threatening our marriage," she wrote, "I tried to save Flo the gambler and skirt chaser by orienting his destructive anxiety toward constructive work."[29] The "constructive work" Anna suggested for her husband was creating a revue show in America like the ones staged in France. Anna had made her start in Paris revues that displayed beautiful young girls in lavish costumes. "But you will do better," she told her husband. "The American girls are so much prettier."[30] Anna's words are somewhat surprising, as they opened up the opportunity for Ziegfeld to grow more distant as he pursued beautiful young girls who were ripe for shaping.

Ziegfeld accepted the idea, even though he later whispered to playwright-composer Harry B. Smith that he considered French revues "rather stupid affairs."[31] Ziegfeld's revue would not be "stupid." Since it would bear his stamp, it would have to carry his trademark mixture of the traditional and the original. And of course, there would have to be a surplus of glamour and spectacle, a touch of the risqué, and carefully selected comedic bits. If the show was to be truly American, Ziegfeld decided that its title could not have a French flavor. It had to be American—and it had to be lucky. "Thirteen letters, preferably. I want a title with thirteen letters," Ziegfeld told Smith, whom he approached with a request to write a script for the revue.

"Why thirteen? Isn't thirteen an unlucky number?" Smith asked.

"No. Not to me," Ziegfeld said as he rubbed the miniature jade elephant in his pocket. Smith and Ziegfeld crossed their arms and paced the floor of Erlanger's roof garden at the New York Theatre, where the new revue would be presented. They would certainly need luck to make the show a success. The roof garden's stage was rather small and close to the ground, but the most foreboding aspect was the heat. As historian Marjorie Farnsworth observed, the "little, listless breeze that occasionally drifted across the roof of the New York Theatre" did not help; it "was like a dank and wilted caress."[32] The glass dome covering the roof only intensified the sun's rays, and it would not keep the rain out if there was a summer shower. Air-conditioning had not yet been invented, so opening a show in the midst of summer was unthinkable. And the production would have to be spectacular to lure potential audiences out of their homes and into the summer night. But Ziegfeld was not unduly worried about audiences. He knew how to make the most unappealing places appealing. Ziegfeld arranged with Klaw and Erlanger to reconstruct the roof to resemble a Parisian garden. Although the show's title and material would have to be all-American, Ziegfeld still felt it needed a hint of the exotic to pay homage to the *Folies Bergère*. In 1912 he wrote, "To give a foreign atmosphere to the place, I christened it the *Jardin de Paris*."[33] Now all he needed was a lucky title as tantalizing as the name of the rooftop.

"What about the *Follies of the Year*?" Smith asked. Ziegfeld stopped pacing and uncrossed his arms. In his mind he counted the letters. "I used to write a newspaper column—'Follies of the Day.' What do you think?" Smith persisted.

"It's sixteen letters," Ziegfeld told him. "What about . . . *Follies of . . . 1907*?" he suggested. Smith nodded, and the title was set. Ziegfeld had not yet considered putting his name in the title. If the show was a flop, it would not be immediately apparent who was responsible for the disaster. If it was a hit, then his name could stand alone—independent of the Shuberts, the Syndicate, and Anna Held.

4

A Maelstrom of Mirth

Ziegfeld knew he needed more than a thirteen-letter title to ensure that the *Follies of 1907* was a lucky endeavor. To increase the likelihood of the show's success, he gathered as much backstage talent as his wallet allowed. He assigned Julian Mitchell (director of *The Parisian Model*) plus three other colleagues, John O'Neill, Herbert Gresham, and Joe Smith, to direct. He employed so many songwriters to create the eighteen numbers in the show that the program ultimately read: "Music by Everyone."[1] The best-known songwriter of the bunch was Gus Edwards, the mind behind "I Just Can't Make My Eyes Behave." The reliable Harry B. Smith developed the nonmusical portion of the show, built around the 300th anniversary of the Jamestown Colony, which was a popular news topic in 1906. Smith wrote in his autobiography, "There was just enough story to hold the scenes together, the theme being the introduction of Pocahontas and Captain John Smith . . . to the modern life."[2] Among the modern scenes witnessed by the colonial sweethearts on their trip to New York were Gibson girls, *Salome* at the Metropolitan Opera House, Enrico Caruso's trial (for molesting a woman in Central Park), and the beach.

Ziegfeld disliked Smith's plot structure for the show; he believed that in musical theater, plots were always the same and thus useless. "For this reason, I boldly disregarded every pretense of plot," Ziegfeld later stated.[3] Despite its lack of a recognizable plot, the *Follies of 1907* retained a unifying theme that many argued was a pretense of plot. However, one thing was inarguable: the *Follies of 1907* was unlike any other entertainment in America. It was simultaneously modern, old-fashioned, fast-paced, gorgeous, and hilarious. "*The Ziegfeld Follies* were really an amalgamation of everything that was happening in New York at that time. This was an age when all these different ethnic communities were coming together and different kinds of music and ethnic comedy routines. He [Ziegfeld] wedded them together," historian Phil Furia explained.[4]

The first *Follies* was not as diverse as later editions in the series. But the onstage talent was drawn primarily from vaudeville, which was the most diverse entertainment community at the turn of the century. One theater critic stated that vaudeville offered an opportunity for everyone and consequently provided satisfaction to everyone. The "amalgamation" the *Follies* presented certainly offered something to suit all tastes and gave opportunities to all types of entertainers. "Vaudeville was essentially about the individual performer in the individual act," Furia explained. "You came on, you did your act," and "the focus [was] on the individual performer."[5] Showcasing unique, individual talents had been Ziegfeld's forte beginning with Sandow and continuing with Anna. Now, in his own revue show, he could showcase not just one unique talent but three, four, five, or more. Yet early critics of the *Follies* did not fully appreciate the difference between vaudeville and Ziegfeld's revue. Almost unanimously, New York theatergoers called it a vaudeville show made up of specialties, or one "of those things in thirteen acts."[6] The distinction between vaudeville and the *Follies* was that Ziegfeld's shows were frequented by the higher echelons of society rather than working-class Americans or immigrants living in Brooklyn and the Bowery. The *Follies* did not forget members of the lower classes, however; Ziegfeld hired them as performers and gave them star billing. They performed topical humor and, according to Ethan Mordden, gave wealthy audiences "a sophisticated view of man's appetites." Ziegfeld presented vaudeville, a pedestrian form of entertainment, in a legitimate Broadway setting. As Mordden observed, the *Follies* were "vaudeville meeting you with bells and spangles on."[7]

As usual, despite his bold ambition and bravado, Ziegfeld was sure his new endeavor was destined to fail. The dress rehearsal for the first *Follies* looked so bad that its backers shook their heads in sorrow and Ziegfeld let out his customary exclamation, "Let's burn it up!" Why Ziegfeld and his backers were so pessimistic is anyone's guess. The topical humor in Harry B. Smith's script and the musical acts showcasing vivacious chorus girls were guaranteed audience pleasers. Ticket sales were high, despite the sweltering heat in the Jardin de Paris.

But New York society was in for a surprise, because Ziegfeld was brave enough to poke fun at millionaires, even if they were his primary patrons. Among the most popular and timely skits in the show was one that made fun of Andrew Carnegie's Scottish accent. The skit used the type of ethnic comedy that was popular in vaudeville, and it remains a relevant and hilarious spoof, even in the twenty-first century. Following is a sample of the dialogue between Carnegie (Andy) and John D. Rockefeller, set at one of the hundreds of libraries Carnegie had opened throughout the world since 1883:

Setting: The New Library
(Enter JOHN D. and ANDY C. JOHN has wings sprouting and wears a halo. ANDY is dressed in Scotch costume. They enter Right and Left. "The Sweet By and By" is played for JOHN D. to enter; he comes on singing from a hymn book. "Highland Fling" music for ANDY's entrance. He dances on.)

JOHN D.: (Shocked) What! Andy, my dear friend—dancing?
ANDY: (Broad Scotch dialect) Hoot mon, sure! I dance every time I open a new library.
JOHN D.: Very wrong, my dear friend! I never dance!
ANDY: Vura true, mon, vurra true; but ye mak the public dance.
JOHN D.: Did you ever think, Andy, what a wicked world this would be if it wasn't for us?
ANDY: Ay, John, ay. We're a couple of braw and bonnie laddies and good golf players.
(Enter a BEGGAR.)
BEGGAR: Say, gents, would you give a fellow a nickel for a cup of coffee?
ANDY & JOHN: (Shocked) Oh! Money! Always money!
BEGGAR: I'm hungry, boss. For three days nothing has passed my lips but my breath.
JOHN D.: Hungry, eh? Well, here my poor man. (Gives BEGGAR a hymn book.) There's a very sweet hymn there called "In Thee I Put My Trust."
ANDY: Hungry, are you? Well, here's a copper. Go into the library and weigh yourself.
BEGGAR: (Going, crying.) Say, gents, I'll never forget your kindness. (Bites piece out of the hymn book and exits.). . . .
JOHN D.: Oh, I do love to do the people good.
ANDY & JOHN: (Both sing, to the tune of "Mary and John.")
"I do 'em all good," says ANDY.

"I do 'em too," says JOHN.
"I take all there is," says ANDY.
"I take the same," says JOHN.
"You mustn't die rich," says ANDY.
"I'll make you die poor, you bet.
It's really unhealthy
to be very wealthy
so spend all you get."

(They do an eccentric dance to make music with the chink of money. The audience throws money on the stage. John and Andy scramble for it.)[8]

"Spend all you get" is a particularly humorous line, as it could have been the title of Ziegfeld's life story. Indeed, the show cost $13,000 to produce and spurred one critic to observe that Ziegfeld "has spent money like water. . . . No man can put on a show like the *Follies* and be a piker."[9]

Interspersed between the satires of public figures such as Caruso, Carnegie, and Rockefeller were the numbers featuring the performers Ziegfeld saw as the true stars of the show (and on whom he spent the most money): the chorines. According to Richard Ziegfeld, these young women were so prominent on Ziegfeld's agenda because "he considered himself above all an artist whose goal in life was to produce as much beauty as possible."[10] In the first *Follies*, Ziegfeld billed the attractively clad chorines as the "Anna Held Girls." In one number they paraded about as bathing Gibson girls. Their rosebud mouths, heart-shaped faces, and pleasantly plump figures accented by tiny waists clearly mimicked Anna's appearance. The name of the chorus line was a thoughtful tribute to the woman whose talents and shrewd suggestions had made Ziegfeld a success.[11] Part of Ziegfeld's motive in naming the chorus after Anna was to make amends, but an even greater reason was that, despite the ever-present threat that she would become outmoded, Anna was still the ideal girl to Ziegfeld and to theatergoers.

Because he put the most personal effort into the numbers featuring the girls, Ziegfeld did not acknowledge that the comedic bits were actually the best-received parts of the show. To him, they were more or less fillers that gave the chorines time to change costumes. In 1931 Gilbert Seldes of the *New Yorker* wrote about Ziegfeld's focus on the girls and his conviction that they were what audiences came to see: "In the background of his mind, perpetually brushed away like a persistent mosquito, is a comedian with a sketch. . . . In the midst of a thousand demands for his time and attention, he will spend half an hour changing the position of a rosette on a chorus girl's costume and refuse two minutes for the discussion of a gag or a blackout."[12]

As much as Ziegfeld disliked comedy, he managed to meld it with a "girlie" number in one particularly memorable routine. During the show, a man ran in from the back of the theater yelling, "Raid! The theater's about to be raided!" A flock of men in policemen's uniforms swarmed in after him, blowing whistles. But rather than carting the actors and the frightened audience members off to headquarters, the policemen jumped onstage and joined the chorines in a jaunty dance. In the finale, Ziegfeld also included a surprise: "to the astonishment of the audience," sixty-four chorus girls beating snare drums "marched down a flight of steps from the right hand of the stage, up the right aisle to the rear of the auditorium, across the rear of the theater, and down the other aisle to another flight of steps, and thence to the stage." Having the performers interact with the audience in such a way was unprecedented. Ziegfeld later noted that it "was an innovation and it made a great hit with the audience. The drummer girls were the big feature of the *Follies of 1907*."[13]

Though such stunts thrilled audiences, critics were less amused. "A loud leering orgy of indelicacy and suggestiveness . . . a vulgar catering to garter immorality," theater critic Percy Hammond wrote in condemnation of the *Follies*.[14] As had been the case with Anna's most popular shows, bad press only boosted ticket sales. Another booster was Ziegfeld's plan to keep the *Follies* fresh by introducing new acts each week. These newly discovered talents did not have to be polished or experienced. If Ziegfeld found a beautiful girl but she was not particularly talented in singing, dancing, or acting, it did not matter. "Glorifying the American Girl . . . was an actual process invented by Zieggy," Eddie Cantor later wrote. "And it worked so faultlessly and amazingly that even homely-looking comediennes and burlesque clowns took on an aura of grandeur on his stage that they never had before."[15]

The first glorified star of the *Follies* was Eleanor "Dora" Goldberg, a Jewish girl from Ziegfeld's home state of Illinois. Her stage name was Nora Bayes, and in Ziegfeld's show she truly put bells and spangles on vaudeville with the appropriately titled song "Meet Me with Bells and Spangles On."

Nora became an overnight celebrity despite her top-heavy figure and large, protruding eyes. Her soulful expression and unpretentious personality gave her a unique attractiveness. But Nora's personality alone did not make her a star. As he had done to stir public interest in Anna, Ziegfeld planted fantastic tales in the papers about Nora, the most famous one being that she sucked down lollipops every hour. "Miss Bayes does not eat lollipops simply to boost her energy," Ziegfeld told the press. The reporters turned to Nora, who stood beside her producer, lollipop in hand. "I eat them before each meal to cut down my appetite. How else could I maintain my figure?" Nora declared. Just as milk sales had skyrocketed after the rumor about Anna's milk baths, lollipop sales shot up. Society women began to display the candies in expensive, cut-glass bonbon dishes.

Another story involving the *Follies of 1907* was not a preplanned publicity stunt. During the last New York performance of the *Follies* on September 14, 1907, Ziegfeld arrived flamboyantly dressed in a broad-striped suit, a pink shirt, and diamond cufflinks. From backstage he observed the bathing Gibson girl number, mopping his brow and fanning himself with a newspaper to dissipate the heat. He barely noticed comedian Billy Reeves standing next to him until Reeves said, "Come on in to the tank. It'll cool ya off," nodding toward the authentic swimming tank the Gibson girl number utilized. "I had a bath—yesterday that is. The tank's not for me," Ziegfeld said. Three nearby bathers cajoled him as well, but he could not be moved. Reeves heard his cue to make a high dive into the tank, but he decided to add a new cast member to the number. Dragging Ziegfeld onstage, he threw the elegantly dressed man into the tank. The audience went wild. The *New York Telegraph* declared that Ziegfeld looked like "the sorriest spectacle that has ever been permitted on the New York roof" as he climbed out of the tank. Julian Mitchell, who was onstage, provoked more laughs from the audience when he said: "When he's all wetted up like that, he doesn't look like a human being at all but more like a pickled string bean."[16] Ziegfeld was the only member of New York society who found no humor in the incident. Though the ad-lib got more laughs than any other act in the show, Ziegfeld did not keep the stunt as a regular attraction.

Ziegfeld's revue was the only rooftop show to date to run for more than three months (June 8–September 14). Because the show had opened in the summer, it was not regarded as part of the Broadway season, which began in early fall. Ziegfeld persuaded Klaw and Erlanger to move the

Follies inside, to the Liberty Theatre, for the Broadway season, but New York audiences "ignored it absolutely as the attraction at a regular theater."[17] Ziegfeld and his associates were dismayed at this turn of events until Erlanger, undefeated, suggested that they try the show at a theater outside of New York. His suggestion paid off: out-of-town audiences in Washington DC, Baltimore, and Boston deemed the *Follies* a legitimate attraction in any season and at any theater. Ziegfeld had not yet conquered New York, but he was determined to prove that his revue was more than light vaudevillian rooftop entertainment. All he had to do was convince New York audiences to agree with him.

According to Richard Ziegfeld, the *Follies* was "a lark to begin with . . . [it] started as a summer experiment."[18] Neither Ziegfeld nor Erlanger could have known that their little summer experiment was on its way to becoming "better known than any other American entertainment except the minstrel show."[19]

Critics and New York audiences may have considered the *Follies* nothing but a summer "lark," but this in no way diminished the fact that 1907 had been a banner year for Ziegfeld. The *Follies* became the only revue on Broadway to run for an entire summer, and *The Parisian Model* was having a record-breaking run in its second season; it was the highest-grossing musical to star a woman.

Ziegfeld and Anna, both swamped with work, rarely saw each other during 1907. Anna was feeling the strain of the seemingly endless run of *The Parisian Model*. She vetoed an offer for a vaudeville tour between seasons after falling ill with the flu and missing several performances of the show during its Philadelphia tour. Ziegfeld spent weeks running between the theater and the suite at the Ansonia, anxiously awaiting signs that Anna's health was improving. Having spent tens of thousands of dollars on publicity and production, he was aggrieved that each performance she missed meant greatly diminished profits. However, he did not chastise Anna for this inadvertent loss of money. She was his wife first and a star second. He lavished her room with violets and roses, which she removed after he left because their pungent scent made her sneezing and coughing fits worse.

After two weeks, Anna returned to the stage. She and Ziegfeld did not see each other again until the *Follies of 1907* and *The Parisian Model* were both playing in Cleveland on New Year's Eve. Ziegfeld was in the midst of preparing a new show by Harry B. Smith, *The Soul Kiss*. The show, which opened on January 28, 1908, at the New York Theatre, continued Ziegfeld's winning streak. *The Soul Kiss* was neither groundbreaking nor an integrated musical, but it ran for 122 performances and cemented Ziegfeld's reputation for extravagance through its lavish costumes and sets.

Anna was unable to keep up with her husband's tireless pace and was not particularly interested in committing to a new production for herself. She was not sorry that a plan to bring *The Parisian Model* to London for the summer of 1908 was never realized. "I'm exhausted, Flo," she sighed, rubbing her shoulder, which had been stricken with rheumatism. "I think I shall take a holiday at our cottage." They still had their Maine getaway, though they seldom spent any time there. Maine was a good place for Anna to rest, but the place she truly wished to be was Paris. By the late spring of 1908, Ziegfeld was engrossed in preparing for the second edition of his "summer experiment." Thus, he would not accompany Anna on their customary summer excursion to Europe.

Ziegfeld thought that Anna should stay in Maine; he did not see how she could possibly get any rest in the nightclubs of Paris. She did not elaborate on the reasons for her wish to go to France. Maximo Carrera had died on April 23, 1908, and she had to settle details concerning thirteen-year-old Liane's upbringing. In addition, the French climate was better for her rheumatism than the damp Maine air. Rheumatism and motherhood were both signs of age, whereas Ziegfeld was increasingly concerned with keeping himself young by producing youth-centered shows. The *Follies*, which he called "one continuous maelstrom of mirth," were made more ebullient by the abundance of young talent onstage.[20] The performers were members of a new generation of actresses who had been children when Anna first played on Broadway.

Other changes on Broadway were beginning to make the generation gap between Anna and these new stars more evident. George M. Cohan had started a trend in musical theater with his first integrated book musical in 1904, *Little Johnny Jones*. In the 1907–1908 season he opened three new shows on Broadway: *The Honeymooners, The Talk of New York,* and *Fifty Miles from Boston*. Like his first show, these new productions were decidedly American and employed musical and dance routines that arose naturally from characters and plot points. Cohan's plays were snappy and fast, as were the *Follies*. His philosophy for wowing an audience was "speed, speed—and lots of it! That's my idea of the thing."[21] Critics initially condemned Cohan for using contemporary, slangy dialogue, but at the same time, audiences and critics alike were tired of "the talk in most musicals [that was] absolutely stilted."[22] Modern musicals like Cohan's, because of their reliance on plot, were not star vehicles and could be revived and appreciated by more than one generation.[23] Anna's shows, though enormously popular, were tailored specifically to her and could not be adapted for any other actress.

Ziegfeld still believed in building a show around a particular star's talents, but he did not think star vehicles had to be old-fashioned. Ziegfeld was adapting well to the modern theater, and he refused to let Anna fall out of step with it. Using his formula of fusing old and new production styles, he planned to bring audiences a view of Anna Held that was as fresh and exciting as his *Follies*.

Despite Anna's wariness about plunging into another production, Ziegfeld spent the summer of 1908 preparing not only the *Follies* but also a new show for her. Meanwhile, her trip to Paris, as Ziegfeld had foreseen, was not a restful one. Anna spent most of her time attempting to be a mother to Liane while also trying to ward off reporters, who had grown wise to the fact that the girl was not adopted. For the first time in their lives, Liane and Anna shared a house and engaged in normal mother-daughter activities, including going out to dinner, seeing shows, and strolling the boulevards in search of new wardrobes. By the end of the summer, Ziegfeld had joined Anna and Liane in Paris. Under his arm, he carried a script for Anna's new show.

"What about your *Follies*?" Anna asked her husband when he arrived. "I thought you would not be able to get away."

"I want to get your new show under way first. Harry's written one that's perfect for you: *Miss Innocence*," Ziegfeld explained. Even he must have been amused at the irony of the title, given Anna's manufactured reputation for being anything but innocent.

Though Ziegfeld was no less exhausted than Anna, he had only the next show on his mind. However, while in Paris, he was forced to acknowledge both the troubles in his marriage and his own precarious state of health. He was a sick man when he first arrived; he had somehow contracted a tapeworm. His ailment did not make him the best of company for anyone—especially for the teenaged Liane. Oddly, Anna insisted on having her own bathroom in their Paris hotel suite, which meant that Ziegfeld and Liane had to share the second one. This could not have been easy for either of them. Liane was revolted by his illness and the smell of his medicine. And for a man who had built his reputation on immaculate taste and sophistication, the indignity of having a tapeworm must have been humiliating for Ziegfeld. But Anna attended to him, and he was soon back to his normal, enterprising self. He bustled about town making color-ful new acquisitions for his shows, including a performing police dog, a Spanish dancer, and a group of showgirls. By the end of the summer, Anna's interest in her professional life was once again piqued, largely because *Miss Innocence* was different from her customary risqué shows.

"We don't need the raciness in this one," Ziegfeld explained. "It's become a custom for critics to find fault with my productions, but this hasn't affected attendance in the least. I produce these shows for the public and it seems the public has a mass wish to return to childhood. *The Wizard of Oz, Babes in Toyland* . . . these are what are selling tickets now. What do you think of a fairy-tale theme to the show? Something new for you?" Ziegfeld asked Anna during a late dinner at a Paris restaurant. Anna was enthusiastic. The play's whimsical plot had the heroine, again named Anna, leaving the fantastical School of Innocence on the Isle of Innocence, located somewhere in the Mediterranean Sea. Left to wander, Anna travels across Europe with a detective (ironically, played by her nemesis Charles Bigelow) in search of her parents. During the course of events she falls in love with Captain Mountjoy and, in the end, flies with him over Paris to a "Land of Peach Blossoms." Ziegfeld planned for *Miss Innocence* to outdo *The Parisian Model* in lavishness, so it would require considerable funding.

The *Follies of 1908* required money as well. Klaw and Erlanger would back the show, but the two managers would also take the majority of the profits, and Ziegfeld would emerge again as the penniless millionaire. The newspapers delighted in spreading rumors that Anna was selling her furs to fill the bank account Ziegfeld had emptied. The truth was that Anna's bank account was robust and healthy. "I wish I were no nearer being broke than Miss Held," Ziegfeld told the press in September 1908.[24] Anna remained firm about keeping her money separate from his, which drove them further apart. Ziegfeld would simply have to accept funding from the Syndicate, or there would be no shows.

With preparations for *Miss Innocence* completed, Anna, Ziegfeld, and Liane packed their bags, ready to begin life as a supposedly close-knit fam-ily in America. To reporters, Anna exaggerated their unity, claiming it had been Ziegfeld's idea for Liane to come and live with them. Those who knew the sober-faced Ziegfeld would not have believed Anna's concluding statement for a moment: "Now he is happy. He smiles. He knows I will not have to leave him when the season is over."[25] In reality, the only time the family was together was on Sundays, when Liane came home from her New York boarding school. The girl had been raised in a convent and claimed to be ashamed of her mother's connection to the stage. Her disapproval of Anna's career was peculiar, however, given that she would later castigate Ziegfeld for discouraging her own pursuit of a stage career. Though the sincerity of Liane's interest in the theater was questionable, there is little doubt that she used it as a way to grow closer to her mother. However, in 1908 the threesome was "less a family than a bohemian couple with a resentful child in tow."[26]

Though Ziegfeld and Anna seemed to be reconciled, Ziegfeld was no more committed to family life. Work was still his preoccupation, and it was becoming increasingly more pleasurable for reasons other than profits or creativity. Ziegfeld had met a certain "slender slip of a girl" while Anna was touring in November 1907. He had first seen the girl when he attended a Shubert show called *The Tourists,* hoping to snatch talent from his competitors. He felt such thievery would be justified, as the Shuberts' show was an obvious copy of the *Follies. The Tourists* could easily be mistaken for a Ziegfeld production. It was described as "a mystic maze of brilliant color, popular melody, obvious comicality, with the inevitable girls, girls, girls."[27] Sitting in the third row center, Ziegfeld watched one of the girls in the chorus, noting her "traces of peculiar beauty."[28] She was only fifteen years old, but Ziegfeld saw her as a potential new star. Her name was Lillian Lorraine. Biographer Nils Hanson called her a painter's dream, an "exquisitely beautiful young woman with wide-set eyes, sculpted cheek bones, and sensuously shaped lips." Her eyes were "sapphire blue," and her hair was "dark with auburn tints framing a flawless peaches and cream complexion that complement[ed] her quick wit and outgoing personality."[29] One of her greatest assets was her smile, which hypnotized Ziegfeld as it had her many other admirers. Ziegfeld took note of the girl's name, with the intention of offering her a contract. Ziegfeld's interest in his work thus became passionate not only on a professional level but also on a personal one.

Lillian Lorraine was born in 1892 as Mary Ann Brennan, and she was forced to grow up much too quickly. Raised in an abusive household, she struck out on her own at an early age. According to her own admission, she "devoted a considerable amount of time to devising means of escape and just generally getting into trouble."[30] Her life inspired many wild tales and much speculation that history has neither proved nor disproved. Among the most disturbing stories is that Lillian lost her virginity at age thirteen in order to make enough money to leave home. Her seedy existence led her to be impetuous in her relationships yet willful in her determination to be a success on the stage. Her story was, like Anna's, one of rags to riches. However, unlike Anna, Lillian made it on Broadway based solely on her looks. Before she became a chorus girl, she worked as a photographer's model, and her face became so well known that she was hailed as "the girl who possesses the ideal American face."[31] Ziegfeld, however, had never heard of her until he saw her in *The Tourists*. She presented an even more exciting prospect than Anna had; Lillian was a blank slate, so to speak. Despite her beauty and personality, she had no particular talent to speak of, whereas Anna had possessed an adequate singing voice, acting ability, and a distinct persona. Lillian looked like an actress, but her qualifications for the stage ended there.

Lillian had one asset other than her looks, and it had nothing to do with acting: she was American. As Cohan's shows had proved, Americans were becoming more interested in their fellow countrymen than in European imports. Partly due to the large influx of immigrants at the turn of the century, Americans were no longer entranced by the exotic. Ziegfeld saw in Lillian a potential "next big thing." He could see the headlines blaring, "Florenz Ziegfeld Jr.'s First All-American Discovery!" In her, he saw the American Dream incarnate. Because Lillian would still be engaged with the Shuberts for several months, Ziegfeld was disappointed that he could not secure her for the 1908 *Follies*.

Fortunately, the *Follies of 1908* was a success even without Lillian. It outran the 1907 edition, with a total of 120 performances. The chorines still bore a resemblance to Gibson girls, and the show's format followed that of the 1907 edition. But instead of John Smith and Pocahontas taking a trip through modern New York, the 1908 version had Adam and Eve viewing the accomplishments of their progeny.[32] The most memorable production number showcased chorines dressed as giant mosquitoes flying through the newly built Holland Tunnel between New York and New Jersey. However, there were two noteworthy differences between the first and second *Follies*. First, theatergoers were not subjected to scandalous stories planted in newspapers or bawdy lyrics smacking of burlesque and vaudeville. Second, and more important, the show introduced an element that would characterize every *Follies* afterward: a big hit song.[33] The hit song in 1908 was written and performed by Ziegfeld's first *Follies* star, Nora Bayes, and her husband, Jack Norworth. Earlier that year, Norworth had enjoyed a hit as the lyricist for "Take Me Out to the Ball Game." His next tune, "Shine on, Harvest Moon," became the *Follies'* theme for the next eleven years. It was not naughty like Anna's songs; rather, the lyrics brought to mind small-town, all-American youths speaking all-American slang: "Oh, Shine on, shine on, harvest moon / Up in the sky; / I ain't had no lovin' / Since April, January, June or July. / Snow time ain't no time to stay / Outdoors and spoon; / So shine on, shine on, harvest moon, / For me and my gal."[34] "Shine on, Harvest Moon" became the first classic to emerge from a Ziegfeld show—something that even Anna's most lauded productions had not achieved.

Owing to its popularity, Ziegfeld decided to use "Shine on, Harvest Moon" in *Miss Innocence.* He saw it as the perfect song to introduce Lillian Lorraine, who was now free from her Shubert contract and ready to enter Ziegfeld's world. He had promised Anna that the show would give audiences a modern, fresh view of her, but the fact that he gave the song to Lillian proves the extent of his infatuation with the young woman. Anna's role, though more whimsical than her former parts, included little new material. She sang the expected "eyes" and "coon" songs and also appeased those who craved a hint of raciness in the more ribald scenes set in what one critic called "the atmosphere of the Tenderloin." Even the publicity Ziegfeld created for the show did not fulfill his promise to present a modernized Anna Held. Ziegfeld tried his luck again with an eye-catching marquee, but this time he ordered lightning bolts to be lit around Anna's name. He also inserted a story in the newspapers singing Anna's praises for heroically putting out a fire in the dressing rooms of the theater. But the story did not produce the lightning-bolt reaction Ziegfeld expected. Audiences, he was discovering, were becoming weary of blatantly fictitious stories.

Even if Ziegfeld's over-the-top publicity left audiences unenthused, *Miss Innocence* itself did not. Opening at the New York Theatre on November 30, 1908, after the *Follies* had closed, *Miss Innocence* proved to be a hit, particularly after Ziegfeld added "Harvest Moon" and other songs that gave it a contemporary feel. Several ragtime tunes, such as "Yankiana Rag," and one that acknowledged the most exciting new invention of the era, "We Two in an Aeroplane" (sung by Anna), were among the best-received musical numbers in the show. Anna's and the chorus girls' costumes also won praise. Anna's most exquisite gown was adorned with 3,000 genuine diamonds. Only slightly less ornate was an intricate lace gown and a sable coat made of more than 100 pelts.

Ziegfeld was as fastidious about his stars' wardrobe as he was about his own. "He takes pleasure in the excessive and the rare. . . . His lavender shirts are countless and he certainly never wears the same suit of clothes twice in succession, so dazzling his associates that they are under the impression that once he has worn a suit it disappears from his wardrobe," Seldes wrote in the *New Yorker*.[35] Just as Ziegfeld never seemed to wear the same outfit twice, he never recycled a costume from one show to the next. His girls' clothing had to be the envy of every woman in the audience. Ziegfeld, according to biographer John Kendrick, could not "write, compose, design, or direct. But he knew how to showcase the female form to its best advantage."[36] Most of his producing was done with his eyes.

"I want the girls bathed in pink, silver, and white. Bright white, as bright as possible," Ziegfeld explained during rehearsals.

Julian Mitchell, again in charge of staging, suggested, "What about purple, Zieggy? I think it would . . . "

"No. No purple. I don't want any shade of purple light on those girls," Ziegfeld interrupted. His favorite dress shirts may have been lavender, but that is where his fondness for purple ended.

Ziegfeld had ordered the musical numbers to be built around the costume sketches. Clothing would make or break the show. His attention to visual details paid off with the critics. *Miss Innocence* was heralded as Ziegfeld's "most elaborate production."[37] One reviewer wrote that "the eye is constantly feasted with a vision of beautiful girls handsomely gowned and scenery that reaches the highest pinnacle of the scene painter's art."[38] Among the beautiful girls was, of course, Lillian Lorraine—one of the few chorines that Anna had not helped select.

As had been the case with the company of *The Little Duchess* and *The Parisian Model*, Anna and the ladies of the chorus were a close-knit group. Anna readily took part in the showgirls' conviviality. She joined them at a "Salome Ball" in early January 1909, even though it meant lifting the curtain for *Miss Innocence* fifteen minutes early. Anna used her charm and wiles to convince Ziegfeld to agree to the earlier start time. Anna also participated in a plan hatched by one of the chorines, Eunice McKay. McKay, a baseball enthusiast, took up a collection backstage to purchase a loving cup that she planned to present to either the Giants or the Yankees (both New York teams), depending on which one emerged as the victor at the end of the season. Ziegfeld announced to the press that Anna would head the contribution list with $100 and would have the cup engraved "From the Broadway Showgirls."[39]

Anna's happiness with the company of *Miss Innocence* did not extend to her married life. She began to take notice of her husband's special interest in Lillian Lorraine, especially when he gave her another obviously superior song in the show. After the summer hiatus, Lillian switched from singing "Shine on, Harvest Moon" to "By the Light of the Silvery Moon," a tune introduced by Gus Edwards in vaudeville. As he did in the *Follies,* Ziegfeld continually added and removed tunes to keep the show fresh. Similar to "Harvest Moon," "Silvery Moon" was another song of young America, complete with the romantic slang of the day: "By the light of the silvery moon, / I want to spoon, to my honey I'll croon love's tune."[40] On top of winning the show's best song, Lillian received six costume changes— almost as many as Anna.

When reporters flocked to the stage door to interview the chorus girls, one of Ziegfeld's press agents stood guard in front of Lillian's dressing room and shook his head. "Miss Lorraine is to be interviewed separately from the supporting cast," he said. "*Supporting* cast?" the other showgirls grumbled. By this time, they had formed the opinion that Lillian was the equivalent of a teacher's pet.

At first, Anna feigned ignorance of the affair between her husband and Lillian, but his increasing displays of favoritism could not be ignored. She knew that she was becoming passé, and she realized that Lillian's hit songs did not "comfortably fit into her French-accented repertoire."[41] With her jealousy aroused and her patience spent, Anna could no longer hold her tongue: "Either she goes or I go!" she cried. Ziegfeld removed Lillian from the cast of the show. But unbeknownst to Anna, he was grooming Lillian for his next show, the *Follies of 1909.*

Despite Lillian's dismissal from *Miss Innocence,* it enjoyed a record-breaking run at the New York Theatre and played to packed houses until the end of the season on May 1, 1909. Why, then, did Ziegfeld decide not to extend it for another full season in New York, as he had done with Anna's previous hits? He agreed only to a fall revival and a tour of the East Coast and selected midwestern cities such as Cincinnati and Indianapolis.

The tour would run for as long as tickets sold. Ziegfeld's reason for cutting short his greatest success to date was simple: he was now more interested in the *Follies* and Lillian.

Anna was in danger of losing not only Ziegfeld but also her status as Broadway's most influential "clothes horse." She became perturbed when, strolling along Fifth Avenue, she saw Paul Poiret's new gowns in every shop window. Almost overnight, his style had grabbed hold of New York, rendering Anna's hourglass look old-fashioned. Poiret's waistlines came up beneath the chest, emphasizing the bust. Corsets were abandoned for flat-fronted waist cinchers. Skirts were slim and straight, with none of the frills that had become Anna's trademark. The new style of dress did not flatter Anna's figure. Because she was short (only five feet tall), with a round face and a large chest, Poiret's gowns made her appear top-heavy. Biographer Eve Golden observed, "Anna showed her age by complaining about the crazy new fashions young people were wearing." Anna claimed, "The poor women are falling and tumbling around because they cannot move in the tight skirts."[42] However, to satisfy audiences' eagerness to see her display the new fashions, Anna wore Poiret gowns no matter how much she despised them.

Anna could update her look simply by changing clothes; changing her acting technique was not as easy. With the advent of the modern Broadway musical, her style became a relic of the Gay Nineties. Critics now found her acting too calculated and precious. Anna was influenced by the school of Delsarte acting, which taught specific poses and gestures for every conceivable emotion, from hope to horror.[43] This was the style that Ziegfeld had predicted would make Anna a caricature of herself.

Despite Anna's fear of losing her place of prominence on the stage, she told the press she did not mind stepping from the limelight for the next generation. "There will be no more Anna Held behind the footlights," she told the press after *Miss Innocence* closed in New York. "I have lasted longer than most women on Broadway."[44] She had millions in savings and ambitions to purchase an estate in France where she could entertain friends, drink champagne, and learn to love leisure.

Other interviews hinted that she was less content with her abrupt retirement. "I hate to acknowledge that I am near the end," Anna said. "But I must obey Mr. Ziegfeld, and he says that next year is the last."[45] In MGM's 1936 biopic of Florenz, *The Great Ziegfeld*, screenwriter William Anthony McGuire portrayed Anna as much more histrionic about her loss of status in Ziegfeld's life and on the stage: "I thought you loved me more than anything in the world. I thought I was your one ideal, your ambition . . . [now] you have big plans for [a] big show without me."

Though Ziegfeld's actions indicated otherwise, he had not given up on his and Anna's union. He made an effort to be a family man and spent the summer of 1909 with Anna. Perhaps with future vacations in mind, and driven by his fascination with the rustic life, he purchased a secluded campsite in New Brunswick, Canada, that summer. The idea for such a retreat came from being a frequent guest at May Erwin's Canadian hideaway. May was one of Ziegfeld's few female acquaintances who was not a potential romantic conquest. A popular stage comedienne in the 1890s and early 1900s, she was strictly fun company, a confidante, and a mother figure. However, given Anna's known dislike for roughing it, the New Brunswick cabin was not much of a gift to her at all. The camp ultimately served as a convenient spot for Ziegfeld's friends and lovers to stay, rather than a place to bond with his family.

Anna found considerably more enjoyment touring the French countryside with Ziegfeld and Liane for the rest of the summer. Anna spent much of her time teaching the awkward teen how to be a lady. In Paris, the family stayed with Ziegfeld's sister, Lulu, and her son, Teddy, whom Liane despised for being what she deemed a perfect child. Anna, in contrast, adored the Ziegfeld family: "I love them so much, the dear people."[46] Ziegfeld and his parents were still in close contact, despite the distance between them. He and his father exchanged many telegrams to tell each other even the most innocuous bits of news.

Ziegfeld managed to fit in a talent-scouting trip with Harry B. Smith during his time in Europe, but they failed to find any artists who stirred their interest. Ziegfeld returned to New York to prepare for the fall opening of the 1909 edition of the *Follies,* undaunted by the lackluster European trip. After all, he had Lillian Lorraine signed for the show, and her presence alone would make it exciting. Anna remained in France with Liane for the time being, but she was fully aware of Ziegfeld's nights on the town accompanied by the girl with the ideal American face.

By 1909, Ziegfeld had moved past planting outrageous stories for publicity, but juicy headlines seemed to follow him. The *Follies of 1909* gave reporters plenty to write about, especially the dramatic goings-on backstage. However, the press did not have anything scandalous to print about Lillian Lorraine—yet.

For a change, one of the first headlines after the *Follies'* premiere involved Ziegfeld himself. The incident occurred during the show's Atlantic City opening on June 12, 1909, at the Apollo Theatre. In the audience were Lew Fields (now a theatrical manager after parting with Joe Weber), Ziegfeld's competitor Lee Shubert, and Shubert's representative with the villainous name of A. Toxen Worm. Ziegfeld, standing behind the stage curtain, caught sight of the three men. He was sure they were planning to try to entice talent away from him. And although Ziegfeld had stolen many a star from other producers, he would not let the same thing happen to him. He motioned to the special officer of the house. "I want those three men ejected immediately," he demanded.

"Yes, Mr. Ziegfeld," the officer said. He strode down the theater aisle and approached the astonished Fields, Shubert, and Worm. "I'm going to have to ask you gentlemen to leave," he said.

"We're paying customers. We're not going anywhere," Fields retorted.

The officer turned and left, returning to an enraged Ziegfeld backstage. Ziegfeld stamped out his cigar and gathered his stage manager, his business manager, and two stagehands as reinforcements. Heading the posse, Ziegfeld approached his rivals. By now, several members of the audience had taken notice and turned in their seats to watch what might prove to be an exciting confrontation. Some assumed it was part of the show.

"Please leave this theater. Now," Ziegfeld said. His voice remained calm and cool—more a threat than a shout. Fields and Shubert turned to their wives, who were now flustered and in need of smelling salts. Out of consideration for the women, the men acquiesced, and the party exited the theater amid much whispering from the audience.

To the press, Fields declared: "I know that Mr. Shubert never barred Mr. Ziegfeld from any of the theatres in New York, and never has had him stopped at the door or refused him admittance thereto."

Later the same evening, Ziegfeld caught up with Fields in the lobby of his hotel and approached him with an amicable smile on his face. He tried to explain what had happened earlier, but without a word, Fields turned on his heel, "refusing to entertain any offers of apology or any explanation of the humiliation to which Mrs. Fields had been subjected by the conduct of Mr. Ziegfeld."[47] The dislike between Ziegfeld and the Shuberts and their associates was only enhanced after this confrontation.

The next scandal associated with the 1909 *Follies* occurred backstage and involved not rival producers but rival stars. Nora Bayes did not want to share accolades with *Follies* newcomer Sophie Tucker. Like Nora, Sophie was a popular vaudeville entertainer, but her trademark was belting out soulful songs of lament or bawdy love songs while dressed in blackface. By the time she joined the *Follies*, she had abandoned blackface but not her singing style. Nora threatened to walk out of the *Follies* if Sophie's part was not reduced. Sophie was a scene stealer, and Nora knew it. Ziegfeld placated Nora by cutting Sophie's part down to one song, but ironically, Sophie's song was the most successful in the show. The tune, "Moving Day in Jungle Town," was a parody of Theodore Roosevelt's hunting expeditions written by Harry B. Smith and Maurice Levi. The success of the number only incensed Nora more. In an attempt to maintain peace among the company, Ziegfeld dismissed Sophie and replaced her with the exuberant Eva Tanguay. Eva was a physical singer; she pranced and whirled about the stage, whereas Nora remained fairly still. Their styles were different enough so as not to threaten each other. Eva sang the popular "I Don't Care," to the delight of audiences. Though Ziegfeld had appeased Nora, her contentment was only temporary.

"Miss Bayes, I'd like you to appear in the jungle song," Ziegfeld said after Sophie's departure, assuming the assignment would please Nora. "Here's your costume." He handed her a pair of tights. She held them between her thumb and forefinger with an air of revulsion. "You'll ride atop an elephant—it will give the number a circus feel," Ziegfeld explained.

"I have never worn tights, Mr. Ziegfeld, and I do not intend to do so while on an elephant's back or anywhere else!" Nora declared.

Ziegfeld remained cool and offered her another option: singing "Shine on, Harvest Moon." It was still an audience favorite, even though it was a year old and had already been used in two previous shows. After consulting with her husband, Nora informed Ziegfeld, "I'll sing no more than one verse. No more." She then turned and joined her husband in the wings, making it clear that they would seek a new manager if their wishes were not granted.[48] Ziegfeld did not acquiesce, and when they left the show, he filed suit against them for breach of contract. According to Richard Ziegfeld, "The circumstances that usually promoted Ziegfeld to take someone to court . . . was seldom money [but] artistic control over the production."[49]

Nora's prima donna behavior confused Ziegfeld, and he was always shocked when anyone left his employ. His employees attested that it was "nearly impossible to break away" from him. "He is known as an easy boss, and at the same time secretaries and assistants testify to the fury which overcomes them at Ziegfeld's amazing fickleness and irresponsibility," Seldes wrote. These same secretaries and assistants invariably contradicted themselves moments later by saying, "But I'd never want to work for anyone else."[50] Nora was not of the same mind-set. This was partly due to Sophie Tucker and the tights fiasco, but a larger reason for her dissatisfaction with Ziegfeld was Lillian Lorraine. Ziegfeld discovered how Lillian fit into the equation during the trial addressing his suit against Nora Bayes and Jack Norworth.

"What displeases you about Mr. Ziegfeld's employ?" the cross-examiner asked Nora.

"The whir of electric fans on the Rooftop Garden disrupts my singing and then there's the constant circulation of waiters and customers calling for drinks. It makes me nervous. I'm accustomed to performing with dim lights and fans shut off during my performances," she explained.

The lawyer then called Ziegfeld to the stand and demanded: "Did you not come into Miss Bayes's dressing room on the opening night of the *Follies* in Atlantic City and tell her: 'The play was rotten, you looked rotten, and sang rotten'?"

Ziegfeld's face remained impassive except for a slight deepening of his frown. "No," he said.

"On that same night, did you not say to Miss Lillian Lorraine, an actress in the company, 'You were the prettiest little thing I ever saw'?"

"I may have," Ziegfeld admitted. "Because you know it's true."[51]

Lillian was present at the proceedings, dressed conservatively in a "highly stylized navy blue suit."[52] She was never called to the stand.

Admitting to such a flirtatious statement did not help Ziegfeld's case, but it had nothing to do with the breach of contract in question. Ziegfeld won the case, and Nora Bayes and Jack Norworth were banned from performing until their contract with Ziegfeld ended in 1911.

Ziegfeld had no arguments from Lillian Lorraine regarding either costumes or song choices. Ziegfeld placed her in three artistically pleasing sequences that, though delightful to the eye, were not as pleasing to the ear. One act had Lillian posing as a *Life* magazine cover girl, singing "Nothing but a Bubble" while dancing in an actual bubble bath. *Variety* quipped, "Perchance a librettist had named the song with an eye to sarcasm." This observation did nothing to dispel the impression that Lillian was beautiful but untalented and empty-headed.[53] Later in the show, Lillian was suspended above the audience in a model of the Wright brothers' plane, dropping American Beauty roses while singing "Up, Up, Up in My Aeroplane." In her next scene, Lillian sang a baseball-themed tune by Gus Edwards, "Come On, Play Ball with Me Dearie." It was a suggestive song that boldly stated: "I know lots of places where we can 'run bases.'" Following the baseball number, Lillian rode onstage astride a prize pony and tossed 500 multicolored balls into the audience. Theatergoers, if not critics, were charmed by Lillian's beauty and her evocativeness. Both attributes had made Anna Held a star a decade before. However, Lillian's boldness was different from Anna's. Anna was the innocent playing at being risqué; Lillian did not pretend to be innocent. According to historian Ann Ommen van der Merwe, in 1909 society, most people accepted that theater folk, especially chorus girls, "shunned the traditional role of women in society."[54] Lillian was the tangible image of the modern, independent showgirl who was not ashamed to accept advances from a "stage door Johnnie" or show off "what her body exemplified . . . the epitome of womanhood."[55]

The Ziegfeld girl suggested sex and daring, but it remained just that: a suggestion. Many Ziegfeld girls were inexperienced in matters of romance and came from provincial towns and traditional households. According to writer Lewis Erenberg, "Some of the girls lived with families or sent their salaries home, but some managed to live single, independent lives with money for personal exploration outside the homes of their fathers and husbands."[56] The latter description fit Lillian Lorraine. The liberated woman became synonymous with all Ziegfeld girls—but Ziegfeld sought to meld the liberated woman and the old-fashioned girl. His ideal woman could be alluring but still go home at night. Unlike many other producers, Ziegfeld did not fire girls for marrying or for having children, even if that choice interfered with their ability to put in as many hours for rehearsal. He thought a girl who had settled down made a better employee than a single girl who led a pleasure-seeking lifestyle like Lillian. Those who worked for Ziegfeld knew they would lose their jobs if they drank excessively, took drugs, or engaged in generally hedonistic behavior. Some employees he gave a second chance; some he did not. He gave Lillian more than one chance during her time in the *Follies*.

Despite Ziegfeld's insistence on the morality of his showgirls, he helped many of them engage in "personal explorations" outside their homes. He carried on his affairs with the type of sophistication he expected from his chorines. He treated his lovers like queens, and the ones he was not romancing, he treated like beloved princesses. Lillian was one of the first of his female stars to receive a queenly level of treatment, and all of Broadway knew it. A writer for *Time* magazine commented on Ziegfeld's generosity, noting that "Ziegfeld chorus girls . . . dress not in large, damp rooms but in small, cozy ones, with walls covered in photographs and curious trophies."[57] Among the most common "trophies" Ziegfeld gave to his chorus girls were gold coins. He never wrapped the lavish presents he pulled from his pockets; each gift seemed to be a spur-of-the-moment idea. "He didn't want to be kept waiting while his beneficiary tore the paper," Ziegfeld's second wife, Billie Burke, later revealed. "He wanted to enjoy the surprise instantly."[58] At Christmastime he doubled all his employees' salaries, including the scrubwomen.

Ziegfeld no longer had the anonymity that had so irritated him two years before. He had created a revue with a "magic connotation" that no other form of American entertainment possessed. Eddie Cantor observed that when someone mentioned the *Follies*, "you expected the Seven Wonders of the World to stand to attention and say, 'Yessir!'"[59] Ziegfeld could not expect to be responsible for such a phenomenon and have his personal life remain free from public scrutiny.

5

Entrances and Exits

"Anna, I thought you should know . . . most every night Flo and that Lorraine girl dine at Rector's or Delmonico's . . . together." While in Paris in June 1909, Anna heard little else but this kind of news from numerous friends, including Lillian Russell and Harry B. Smith and his wife, Irene. Another reported, "I don't know what it will do to Flo's name if he remains involved with Lorraine. Have you heard the latest? She and her chauffeur have been carrying on and she's accusing him of taking her $3,000 necklace and now he's in jail. It's in all the New York papers." Anna knew her friends meant well, but she did not believe that Ziegfeld's affair with Lillian had gone as far as the gossip columns implied. After all, Ziegfeld had fired Lillian from *Miss Innocence* and had assured Anna that his personal interest in the girl was over. Nevertheless, Anna sent an increasing number of telegrams and letters to Ziegfeld, voicing her dismay at the rumors surrounding him and Lillian.

Ziegfeld set out to reassure Anna of his loyalty in his customary, over-the-top way. He planted a dramatic story in the newspapers that had Ziegfeld knocking a man named Charles Alexander flat on his back outside the Apollo Theatre for soiling Anna's name. According to the story, the fictitious Alexander had been showing a scar on his wrist and claiming it was from a shot Ziegfeld had fired in a duel over Anna's love. Ziegfeld clipped the stories from the papers and proudly sent them to Anna as evidence of his devotion. Clearly, the stories were less a display of love for Anna and more a reflection of Ziegfeld's increasing narcissism. He found it hard to fathom why a woman would leave him, just as he failed to understand why an employee would quit working for him. Even if he lost interest in a woman, she should not lose interest in him. He wanted an excess of everything in his shows, and he carried the same philosophy into his personal life. Such behavior was partly due to the chauvinistic era he lived in and partly due to his indulgent upbringing. Deeper driving forces behind his actions are debatable. Why he chose to romance a girl barely eighteen years old reflects his inability to accept his age in an increasingly youth-centered era. Anna, in contrast, was eager for retirement. She was not fooled by Ziegfeld's false stories of devotion, especially when she discovered that he had engaged Lillian Lorraine for the *Follies of 1910*. In his biography of Florenz, Richard Ziegfeld explained, "Ziegfeld never said publicly why he did something so risky and hurtful [to Anna]. It certainly fit a larger pattern in his life."[1] Billie Burke elaborated on Ziegfeld's risky behavior: "When asked why he gambled so recklessly, he once explained that he needed the thrill of danger and went on to draw a connection between gambling and the . . . mounting of a show on Broadway, which he said was as chancy as rolling the dice."[2] Lillian certainly gave Ziegfeld the thrill of danger, but at some point, danger stopped being an attraction and became a source of frustration and destruction.

In May 1910 Ziegfeld made the most reckless decision yet in his relationship with Lillian: he reserved a room for her two floors above his and Anna's at the Ansonia. The suite was both a love nest and a way to keep Lillian away from unsavory characters. May Irwin, Ziegfeld's confidante, suggested that he hire a maid for Lillian, and May had a girl in mind. She was a Swedish immigrant named Nanny Johnson who would act as a chaperone and a steadying influence on Lillian. The two women met at Lillian's Ansonia apartment and, according to Nanny's son, Nils Hanson, "hit it off immediately . . . [and] became close as sisters. First as a maid, then as a secretary, and then as confidante and best friend."[3]

Though Nanny Johnson was a positive influence on Lillian, she could not control the actress's impulsivity. Ziegfeld was not accustomed to having a volatile lover, and he did not expect Lillian to be such a handful. One of the reasons their relationship was common knowledge was that they often fought in public, with "violent exchange[s] of epithets."[4] After one particularly heated argument, Lillian ran away with an ex–society woman whom Ziegfeld had briefly employed as a companion for Lillian. Upon finding that Lillian had fled, Ziegfeld called Nanny and asked, "Miss Johnson, do you know where Miss Lorraine has gone? She's not in her suite."

"I believe she's in Boston, Mr. Ziegfeld."

"I need you to go to the train station, buy a ticket to Boston, and bring her back. I'll wire you the money for the tickets."

Nanny dutifully went to the station and, seven hours later, disembarked from the train and took a taxi to Lillian's hotel. In Nanny's words, "Lillian's so-called chaperone was drunk and after a lot of cajoling on my part, Lillian agreed to return with me to New York. Flo sent the chaperone packing and I ended up with one more job title."[5]

During this time, Anna reluctantly returned to America for a second tour of *Miss Innocence* and left Liane behind at a school in Versailles. She was oblivious to the fact that Lillian lived two floors above her. Anna acted blasé when the press asked for her views on Ziegfeld's alleged affair: "If [he] wants to marry Miss Lorraine, I will say 'so sorry,' but he can have his divorce . . . he is a fine, splendid fellow. I know him, and there is no truth in these rumors about another woman. He is not that kind."[6] Anna's certainty about her husband's fidelity seems exaggerated, given that she had admittedly lost virtually all faith in him after the 1907 jewel robbery. After her second tour of *Miss Innocence* ended, Anna went back to Paris. She used that time away from Ziegfeld as a sort of test to see whether he could remain loyal to her. But the test seemed destined to fail. Anna admitted that she and Ziegfeld lived apart for most of the time now. She was no longer the only star under his management; every day he was surrounded by dozens of budding leading ladies. She was well aware of how successful Ziegfeld's *Follies* had become, largely due to these women. Though she knew it was unlikely that Ziegfeld would want to live in Paris for half the year, she defiantly stated to the press: "I love Paris. It's my home and I want to live here and enjoy myself. But I can't do this alone. I'm serious. You can tell Mr. Ziegfeld he better come to Paris."[7]

Ziegfeld, who read the paper every morning, saw Anna's words, but they did not prompt him to leave New York. The newspaper also revealed that the entire theater world was taking sides between him and Anna. The *Cincinnati Commercial* was on Ziegfeld's side, even if it was still misspelling his name as "Florence." One of its reporters claimed that Ziegfeld was running himself ragged for Anna's sake and that she would be nothing without him. A Shubert-owned publication, the *New York Review,* printed an opposing viewpoint: Ziegfeld would be nothing without Anna. "It is not to be wondered that at last she [Anna] has rebelled and refuses to permit herself to be so used," the journalist stated.[8]

Anna's New York friends watched Ziegfeld's behavior as closely as the Shuberts' reporters did. They still faithfully reported his doings to her while she was in Paris. Journalist Amy Leslie, one of Anna's closest companions, confronted Ziegfeld about his relationship with Lillian. "I know that there is something between you and Lillian Lorraine and I think Anna is beginning to believe it, too," she told him backstage during a performance of the *Follies of 1909*.

"The Shuberts will do anything to discredit me; handing out all that Lorraine stuff is just one of their tactics. I *am* interested in Miss Lorraine. I think I can make a paying star out of her as long as she listens to me and doesn't marry the first millionaire to give her a ring before I get her ready for a star role," Ziegfeld explained.

"Then why don't you go to Paris and tell Anna that?" Amy asked.

"I can't leave my business right now," Ziegfeld said. "And I know this puts her into a pet [slang for temper]. I can tell you this as a friend: I dislike Paris. I've had nothing but bad luck over there and, frankly, I'd like never to see it again." Then, noting Amy's deepening frown, he added: "But I will sail there in two weeks to see Anna."

Amy's face brightened, and Ziegfeld began to walk back to his office, lighting his cigar and buttoning his jacket over his lavender shirt. He paused and called over his shoulder, "And if anyone tries to get you to say Anna and I are divorcing, tell them 'NO' so loudly they'll forget they ever asked you."

The Shuberts did not take no for an answer. Foreseeing that Ziegfeld's affair would most likely mean the end of Anna's professional relationship with him, the Shuberts leaped at the opportunity to steal his most iconic star. They sent A. Toxen Worm to Paris with instructions to offer Anna a theater bearing her name plus $30,000 a week for thirty weeks.[9] Anna refused the offer and promptly informed Ziegfeld of the Shuberts' coup attempt. She also told him that Worm was spreading the rumor that Ziegfeld planned to marry Lillian Lorraine. By reporting the Shuberts' actions to him, Anna not only made Ziegfeld jealous but also rekindled his interest in her, and his protective nature took over. Anna's friends had introduced her to dozens of eligible men in Paris, but she had refused all attention from them. She attempted to justify Ziegfeld's behavior by espousing the concept of experimental marriage, but given her fidelity to him and her unwillingness to see other men, that justification was clearly insincere.

After receiving the news about Worm's overtures, Ziegfeld sailed for Paris. The *New York Review* derided his latest attempt to win Anna back: "Mr. Ziegfeld's declarations of personal rectitude given out in Paris are laughable, indeed, in light of the fact that he even permitted the Other

Woman to see him off on the boat when he left American shores to explain all to dear Anna, who at the time was sojourning on the French Riviera."[10] The Shuberts had legitimate grounds for their cynicism: Ziegfeld had sailed for Paris with a contract for a third season tour of *Miss Innocence* in his pocket. It appeared that his visit to Anna was for professional purposes only. However, Ziegfeld did not seem overly eager to throw Anna back into work; he insisted to her and to reporters that he wanted her to have a long rest before beginning the next tour in late 1911. Upon arriving in Paris, Ziegfeld put all his effort into mending his marriage. Each time he saw Anna, he presented her with a gift. He spent every moment with her, dining out, attending the theater, and driving around the city. The couple was, by all accounts, reconciled, which was enough motivation for Anna to return to New York. Neither Ziegfeld nor Anna was ready to let go of the other yet—Lillian or no Lillian.

The *Follies of 1910* was both a tribute to Anna and a celebration of new and exciting talent. Ziegfeld still billed the chorus as the "Anna Held Girls." A second, equally obvious tribute to Anna was a skit entitled "The Comet and the Earth," which capitalized on the hoopla surrounding the 1910 appearance of Haley's comet. The lyrics of the song clearly paid homage to Anna: "Still she wears a smile of a tempting style, for her bright eyes won't behave."[11] As performer Eleanor St. Claire sang, a cinematographic picture of Anna's face was projected on the comet. Rather than advertising the sophisticated technology used in the skit, Ziegfeld allowed it to be a surprise for the audience.

However, the innovative use of a cinematographic projection did not generate as much talk as Ziegfeld's new discoveries: Bert Williams, Fanny Brice, Irving Berlin, and, of course, Lillian Lorraine. The *Follies of 1910*, despite its nostalgic tribute to Anna, simultaneously parodied the French influence in theater. Bert Williams, a black entertainer from the West Indies, was the opposite of French society, yet he was the principal actor in the skit that made fun of it. Bert's song, entitled "White Folks Call It Chanticleer but It's Just Plain Chicken to Me," showed him to be unimpressed by French culture and cuisine. This was, according to historian Ann Ommen van der Merwe, "a notable irony in light of Ziegfeld's attempts to capitalize on the French inspiration for his first *Follies*." Sadly, some critics interpreted the skit differently. Chicago journalist Frederick Hatton wrote that Bert "epitomizes the love of the colored race for chicken."[12]

In an age when minstrels replaced men and women of true black heritage onstage, Bert Williams stood out as a maverick, even if critics and audiences did not fully understand him. Bert had begun in vaudeville and had helped popularize the cakewalk, a dance that lent itself well to his trademark style of singing, speaking, improvising, and syncopating in the same number.[13] Bert may have played a stereotypical "shuffling coon" character, but according to cultural historian Mel Watkins, he made the character not a buffoon but "a living human being . . . someone that people could be sympathetic to. You laughed at him, but you also sympathized with his plight."[14] Though Bert was talented and had a mild-mannered personality, many of Ziegfeld's performers threatened to quit rather than appear in the same show as a black man. "Go if you want to," Ziegfeld told his less tolerant cast members, "I can replace every one of you—except the man you want me to fire."[15] Ziegfeld was right to believe that theatergoers would accept a black man in a Broadway show; Bert quickly became an audience favorite.

Ziegfeld's next new discovery was arguably his greatest for the *Follies of 1910*: Fanny Brice. She brought plenty of humor to the show but also created a new category of Ziegfeld girl reserved solely for her. Fanny's mobile features, eccentric gesticulations, and talent for impersonations and comic singing drew more applause than any parade of lovely girls. "It's very interesting to see Fanny Brice as a Ziegfeld star when you think that Ziegfeld's mantra for the American woman was beauty," historian Dwight Blocker Bowers observed. Ziegfeld knew she was one of a kind and could sing both sentimental ballads and comic tunes. "He got a two for one with Fanny Brice," Bowers concluded.[16]

Born Fania Borach in 1891 to a poor Jewish family on the Lower East Side of New York, Fanny spent much of her childhood playing hooky, sneaking into theater houses, and eavesdropping on her neighbors. By listening to their conversations, she learned to mimic their Polish or Russian accents.

In 1906 she moved to Brooklyn and worked as a song plugger. A young man named Irving Berlin was her accompanist, and the two friends often became "convulsed with laughter" when she sang an especially maudlin lyric.[17] For the next three years, Fanny toured the eastern burlesque circuit. Her hilarious dancing and spontaneity kept audiences entertained. "In those days . . . I never had a routine or knew what I was going to do until I hit the stage," she said.[18] By 1908, she was being billed as Fanny Brice, using

the surname of a family friend. This put an end to the constant mispronunciation of Borach, and Fanny also hoped it would lessen the likelihood
of being cast in solely ethnic roles.

Fanny's breakthrough came in 1909 when she won her first sizable role
in Max Speigal's *The College Girl*. Fanny had lied to Speigal, telling him she
had a specialty number. Panicked, she then went to Irving Berlin and
asked him to write her one. The song he created set the precedent for most
of her subsequent shows. Called "Sadie Salome," the song recounts the
perils of a Jewish girl who leaves home in the hope of becoming a famous
Salome dancer, only to find that audiences dislike her. The self-deprecating
lyrics read: "Oy! Such a sad disgrace / No one looks in your face / Sadie
Salome, go home!"[19]

Ziegfeld caught Fanny's Salome act and asked her to appear in the
Follies. "Fanny, at last someone has noticed your good looks!" was her first
thought, she later admitted.[20] Like Anna Held, Fanny already had an established name and persona when Ziegfeld discovered her. Still, Ziegfeld fabricated stories of how she had been "hawking newspapers beneath the
Brooklyn Bridge" when he first spotted her. Ziegfeld had been trying to
move away from such fictitious publicity, but when the opportunity arose,
he could not resist planting intriguing stories about his stars. According to
Ziegfeld biographer John Kendrick, "Since Brice was often known to embel-
lish a story for publicity's sake it's safe to assume she took little if any
offense."[21] Fanny also took little offense that her good looks went unappreciated and she had no glamorous costume to wear in the show. She was simply ecstatic to be on Broadway and under contract to the crème de la crème
of producers. Being a Ziegfeld star gave her a view into another world, one
of "ease and luxury and beautiful things and soft speaking voices."[22]

Fanny knew that clothing was an "emblem of success" on Broadway,
especially to Ziegfeld girls. Thus, she bought a complete wardrobe that
"loudly proclaimed her new status in the theater." On a dinner date with
Ziegfeld and Lillian Lorraine, she wore one of her new outfits—a sapphire
blue gown with a garish orange coat and an oversized blue hat covered in
fake vegetables and an ostrich plume. "The ensemble did little more than
make Ziegfeld lose his appetite," Nils Hanson wrote. "He finally asked
Lillian to show Fanny how to dress, giving her $250 for that purpose."[23]
Lillian, a fashion trendsetter onstage and off, taught Fanny well, and Fanny
became known for her chic wardrobe and fine taste in jewelry. The two
women also became friends and always roomed together during tours.

However elegant she may have been offstage, Fanny wore tacky clothing onstage to complement her awkward characters. In one of her numbers in the *Follies of 1910,* "Lovie Joe," she wore a boldly striped dress with a ruffled collar and oversized belt. She sang the "coon" song like a black singer, pronouncing "sure" like "sho" and "more" like "mo" while simultaneously retaining her Yiddish mannerisms. Audiences had never seen anything like her. One critic for the *Dramatic Mirror* credited her with lifting the show from a "plane of boredom."[24] Fanny's material, written by Irving Berlin, was the key factor in her ability to do so. Berlin was the personification of the American Dream that Ziegfeld glorified onstage. He, more than any other songwriter with whom Ziegfeld worked, symbolized the modern era the *Follies* sought to encapsulate.

Born Israel Behlin in Russia in 1888, Berlin and his family immigrated to America when he was a young boy. Like Anna, the Behlins left eastern Europe to escape the pogroms. Berlin first worked as a singing waiter at flophouses and saloons. He adopted the name Irving Berlin after his first song, "Marie from Sunny Italy," was published and his surname was misprinted. He went on to fame working as a Tin Pan Alley song plugger and writer. Tin Pan Alley was an actual location, not simply a style of music, yet its music had a distinct sound that reflected the area's liveliness and diversity. A large number of Jewish immigrants who had come to New York in the 1880s and 1890s earned their livings selling pianos and sheet music and buying songs. Eventually, the majority of them became concentrated on West Twenty-Eighth Street, between Broadway and Sixth Avenue. Journalist Monroe Rosenfeld wrote that the conglomeration of music coming from the windows sounded like the clatter of pots and pans—hence the name Tin Pan Alley. Henry Ford once declared that Tin Pan Alley ruined the good songs of the 1890s; this may have been due to the fact that Tin Pan Alley songs were greatly influenced by the music one might hear at the black clubs in Harlem or in New Orleans cafés. Not until Irving Berlin broke into popular American music did ragtime become acceptable to mainstream society.

"Organ grinder, minstrel music, ragtime, and Temple high-holiday tunes—Irving Berlin combined all," Broadway historian Phil Furia asserted. According to Furia, Berlin's most famous tune, "Alexander's Ragtime Band," made ragtime "okay" and "fun."[25] Just as Anna had made sex playful through her innocent yet suggestive songs, Berlin made ragtime something that all-American girls and boys could dance to, without their parents fearing the end of civilization. By the time his best-selling hit was published in 1911, Berlin had already been churning out songs for a while. In 1910 his "Ragtime Violin" was a popular tune that many vaude-villians, including future Ziegfeld star Eddie Cantor, performed. Cantor later wrote: "There have been other great song writers, but what makes Berlin tops is that no one else is such a perfectionist. He can turn out music like a one-man factory . . . he was born with a brass self-confidence."[26] But to Berlin, the only thing harder than becoming a success was staying one. Indeed, he claimed his struggles did not begin until he made it big with "Alexander's Ragtime Band."

The striking similarities between Berlin and Ziegfeld, despite their different upbringings, are interesting to note. Both men, though ambitious and confident up to a point, were Gloomy Guses at heart. Ziegfeld always assumed his shows would flop, while Berlin repeatedly feared that he would "reach for [his talent] and it w[ouldn't] be there."[27] Both men were admittedly deficient in areas that were seemingly essential to their chosen careers. Ziegfeld was tone-deaf to comedy, while Berlin could play in only one key: F. However, both men could disregard their personal tastes when necessary and adjust their styles to the "demands and needs of the moment and the popular mood."[28] Music historian Alec Wilder called Berlin's style "as difficult to define as the color of a chameleon."[29] The same could be said of the *Follies,* with their mixture of comedy, music, satire, and spectacle. Because Ziegfeld and Berlin were of the same mind-set, Ziegfeld repeatedly hired Berlin as his principal songwriter, and the composer became the most prolific contributor to the *Follies* over the next seventeen years.

Irving Berlin, Fanny Brice, and Bert Williams were, in the words of Ethan Mordden, "genius crazies who came from a world unlike your own."[30] Considering these phenomenal talents introduced in the *Follies of 1910,* it is ironic that the show received almost unanimously poor reviews. After its opening on June 20, 1910, at the Jardin de Paris rooftop, one critic used the word "stupid" very generously in his summation of the revue. He further stated that although the first two editions of the *Follies* had been "as fun as Coney Island to go to, that is all in the past."[31] The *Follies of 1910* may have confused critics due to its lack of cohesion. The first edition had used Pocahontas and John Smith and the second had used Adam and Eve as central links between specialties. The 1910 edition did away with the pretense of plot.

The Shuberts' *New York Review* led the bandwagon in bashing the show, calling it "revolting and bearing the stench more nauseating than the Chicago stockyards."[32] Not a little of the Shuberts' revulsion came from the fact that Ziegfeld had hired a black man to appear on the same stage as white female performers. However, most critics singled out newcomers Bert Williams and Fanny Brice for praise. Lillian, as usual, was complimented on her loveliness but disparaged for her inability to sing or act. Nevertheless, she thrilled theatergoers, particularly during a number in which a trolley attached to the roof carried her over the audience. She was in the midst of theater patrons again in her second number, "Swing Me High, Swing Me Low." Seated on a trellis of flowered swings with several other chorus girls, she sang the hit tune as she threw miniature bouquets to the audience. "Her hose must have cost $50!" one woman exclaimed as Lillian swung past. If Ziegfeld had been sitting next to her, he could have corrected her: the hose actually cost $275.[33]

Despite some unfortunate reviews, nothing seemed to diminish the public's interest in the *Follies*. One of the attributes that made the *Follies of 1910* popular despite critical scorn was its generous use of ragtime. The show may not have seemed cohesive, but the ragtime numbers were so predominant that they could have been named the show's unifying theme. In addition, the girls in the show enticed theatergoers to buy tickets.

The chorus girls' allure inadvertently served as a teaser to attract audiences to the *Follies'* tryouts in Atlantic City in mid-June, held at the Apollo Theatre. Lillian, not surprisingly, was the leader of the scandalous stunt. She and six other chorus girls pranced along the beach in front of the Deal Casino, a beach and pool club whose membership included the wealthiest and most proper families of Atlantic City. According to reports, Lillian's white bathing suit was "never intended for publication or general circulation." After she and the other "diving Venuses" emerged from the water, a crowd of gasping onlookers gathered on the sand. Ziegfeld's troupe was not forced to leave the beach, but they departed on their own. Ziegfeld was pleased with the scandal, as it caused ticket sales to soar. "The spectacle was too much for the male patrons. Bathing for the day was suspended. Hereafter, when Ziegfeld desires to wash his flock, he will either have to hire his own ocean or outfit his charges with bloomers or hoop skirts," *Green Book* drolly noted.[34]

Ziegfeld, satisfied that his show had been an audience pleaser if not a critic's darling, enthusiastically began preparations for the 1911 edition as well as for a new musical comedy. The latter would have been a perfect vehicle for Anna; if she had not been engaged in the seemingly endless tour of *Miss Innocence,* she might have filled the title role in *The Pink Lady,* yet another musical set in Paris. Despite audiences' slowly shifting interest toward musicals with American settings, most theatergoers still found European-themed shows enticing. Starring Hazel Dawn, *The Pink Lady* told the story of a girl who accidentally meets her ex-lover's fiancée and then masquerades as an antiques dealer to hide her true identity. The production was directed by Julian Mitchell, who was now a regular member of Ziegfeld's theatrical circle. The play included scenes reminiscent of the *Follies,* complete with beautiful women posing on steps like living statues. However, unlike the *Follies,* the show was notable for its "fun and songs" developing "logically out of its situations."[35] The musical ran from March 13 to December 11, 1911, in its first season and from August 16 to September 14, 1912, in its second season at the New Amsterdam Theatre—a total of 336 performances. *The Pink Lady*'s smashing success convinced Klaw and Erlanger to include Ziegfeld's name—which was now synonymous with prestige—in the title of the next *Follies.* Ziegfeld rechristened the new edition of his revue the *Ziegfeld Follies of 1911,* abandoning his superstition about the lucky number thirteen.

Ziegfeld was determined to make the *Ziegfeld Follies of 1911* worthy of his name. He reengaged audience favorites Fanny Brice, Bert Williams, and Lillian Lorraine, as well as Irving Berlin. He also presented new talents, including two players who had helped make *The Pink Lady* a hit: Leon Errol and Bessie McCoy. Leon Errol, an Australian comedian, became a regular in both the *Follies* and Ziegfeld's later book musical shows. His trademark was dancing in an eccentric, wobbly-kneed way. Bessie McCoy was also an adept comedienne and dancer. She was best known for her "Yama Yama Man" number, which she performed in a baggy satin clown suit, pointed hat, and gloves with frighteningly long white fingers. She embodied the "benign infantilism that remained voguish throughout the period."[36] Bessie also brought other new talent to Ziegfeld's attention, including one of the first twin sister acts on Broadway: the Dolly sisters. The Hungarian twins Rosie and Jenny were frequently escorted to various nightspots by millionaire financier Diamond Jim Brady. Bessie had performed with the twins in a show produced by Charles Dillingham called *The Echo* (1910), and she advised Ziegfeld to see the show during its 1911 revival. He was impressed by the twins' "tantalizing sparkle." Yet he told them matter-of-factly, "You can't do much, but you're cute."[37] He took extra delight in hiring them because they had initially been Shubert discoveries. Rosie and Jenny were featured in an act with Lillian Lorraine and gorgeous dancer Vera Maxwell in the catchy number "Be My Little Baby Bumble Bee."

As much as Ziegfeld believed that spectacle, dance, and song were superior to comedy, it was comedy that dominated the *Ziegfeld Follies of 1911*. The biggest hit of the show was a nonmusical number spoofing the travails of tourists trying to find their trains during construction of the new subway. Leon Errol played a harassed traveler, and Bert Williams was a lackadaisical porter. In the act, Leon and Bert were connected by a rope and lifted into the air on a steel girder hundreds of feet above street level. Leon accidentally knocked Bert's lunch pail down and, as consolation, promised him a nickel tip. When Leon later fell off the girder, Bert (insulted by the five-cent tip) did nothing to stop the rope from uncoiling. At the end, Bert looked into the audience and said, "There he goes. Now he's near the Metropolitan Tower. If he kin only grab that little gold ball on the top. . . . 'um, he muffed it."[38] Unfortunately, the other comic genius in the show, Fanny Brice, was not as popular; her material was weak and failed to gain much notice. *Variety* asserted that Fanny's routines as well as the majority of the musical offerings in the show had little life and were slow.[39]

But, as had been the case with so many of Ziegfeld's past productions, audiences did not agree with the critics and took pleasure in both the musical and the comedy routines. Other than "Be My Little Baby Bumble Bee," the most successful song was a comical Irving Berlin composition called "Woodman, Woodman, Spare That Tree," in which Bert Williams sang that his only refuge from his wife was an elm tree she was unable to climb. The score of the *Ziegfeld Follies of 1911* did not include any songs destined to be classics; however, the musical portion deserves acknowledgment because it introduced two songwriters who would become as integral to Ziegfeld's musicals as Berlin. The first, Gene Buck, was also a talent scout, production assistant, and sheet music artist. He was later known as Ziegfeld's "right hand man."[40] The second newcomer, Jerome Kern, cowrote one of Bessie McCoy's numbers, amusingly titled "I'm a Crazy Daffy-dil."

Like Berlin, Kern shared similarities with Ziegfeld. He was raised in an upper-middle-class family of German immigrants. Kern's father sent him to study at the Heidelberg Conservatory, after which the young composer made his name in British theater. By 1910, his songs were appearing in dozens of Broadway musicals. Like Ziegfeld, Kern wanted musicals to be independent of European style. "What I would like to see is an opportunity given to American talent to express itself. . . . [Let] Americans do the work to begin with," he said.[41] Kern's style fit perfectly with the increasingly American-themed *Follies*. The more popular musical numbers in the show were decidedly American, including Lillian Lorraine's song about the latest dance trend, "The Texas Tommy Swing." Another rousing tune, "New York (You're the Best Town in Europe)," depicted European culture as overdone and overrated.

The *Ziegfeld Follies of 1911* played for only eighty performances between June 26 and September 2, 1911. Still, despite its lack of critical acclaim, the revue went a long way in making Ziegfeld's name a force on Broadway. Indeed, the press no longer referred to Ziegfeld as "Miss Held's manager." Anna was now known as "Mrs. Florenz Ziegfeld, Jr."[42]

The war between French and American, traditional and modern, had become progressively more obvious in Ziegfeld's professional and personal lives since 1907. But the *Ziegfeld Follies of 1911* symbolized his permanent union with modernity and Americanism. Anna had been teetering in the balance for four years, and now she began to tumble. With another exhausting tour of *Miss Innocence* to finish and her relationship with Ziegfeld in jeopardy, there was little stability in her life. For Anna, 1911 began to turn into a replay of 1910.

"Flo still hasn't put much distance between himself and that Lorraine girl." "Flo dropped everything to dash to Lillian's side when he heard she was mixed up in a fatal shooting in Denver . . . and when he got there he found out the shooting wasn't because of her at all."[43] Such gossip rang in Anna's ears, and she had no reason to disbelieve it. Ziegfeld had reengaged Lillian for the *Ziegfeld Follies of 1911;* to Anna, this served as proof that his relationship with the young woman had never ceased.

The Shuberts' renewed attempts to woo Anna to their employ in the summer of 1911 brought Ziegfeld's attention back to his "wife." Though Anna informed Ziegfeld of the producers' overtures, she did not feel so loyal toward her "husband" this time. When she returned from her customary summer holiday in Europe, she told Ziegfeld, "I will accept the Shuberts' offer if you do not stay away from Lillian Lorraine."

"I'll stay away from her," Ziegfeld agreed. "But she will appear in the *Follies,* Annie. The audience likes her. They come to see her."

"As long as *you* don't go to see her," Anna said. She turned to leave the room, staring fixedly at her husband. They had grown to be such strangers that Anna had not recognized him upon her arrival in New York, in part because he had grown a mustache.

On the drive back to their hotel, Ziegfeld suggested they go out to dinner, and Anna slightly softened. They spent the evening on the Atlantic City boardwalk, enjoying fine food and wine. Afterward, Anna and Ziegfeld rode in a rolling wicker chair—the transportation of choice for the elite who visited the boardwalk. Ziegfeld, like a gentleman, held Anna's purse, but somehow during the ride he managed to drop it. It had contained $1,000, and Anna was understandably upset by the loss. Ziegfeld said nothing about it, but the next morning Anna found a new diamond bracelet on her dressing table and a list of interviews Ziegfeld had arranged for her, ensuring that her name would appear in every newspaper in the United States. He had no hoaxes or over-the-top publicity planned, only stories that would introduce readers to the real Anna.[44] Despite these well-meaning gestures, Anna hovered between trust and suspicion toward her husband.

Lillian hovered in a different way: between employment and unemployment. As much as Ziegfeld adored Lillian, Abe Erlanger disliked her. Erlanger argued that, more often than not, she had the smell of alcohol on her breath and displayed unprofessional behavior on the set (such as tardiness and slowness in changing costumes).[45] One of the many factors that fueled Erlanger's resentment of Lillian was a scandalous confrontation between her and Fanny Brice during a performance of the *Follies*. Fanny and Lillian had started out as friends; however, their relationship changed after Lillian stole Fanny's boyfriend, Fred Gresheimer (who was married at the time but in the process of divorcing). Lillian regularly saw Gresheimer on the side while living on Ziegfeld's dollar at the Ansonia. Fanny let Lillian know that Gresheimer belonged to her. What next ensued between the two women was a noisy, hair-pulling, gown-tearing fight that took place just behind the stage curtains during a show. Patrons in the front row were amused when they overheard the heated tussle, and they half assumed that it was a typical Ziegfeldian stunt. The Shuberts' *New York Review* was quick to print the story, perhaps in the hope of demeaning Ziegfeld's shows and knocking them off their altar of elegance. According to the paper, the fight began when Fanny stepped on the train of Lillian's dress as she was about to make an entrance. Lillian released a string of foul expletives that triggered the physical part of the argument. "When the scrimmage was ended, Miss Lorraine's raiment was in rags. Her face and her hair bore sundry marks of the conflict and she had reached a state of hysteria which made it necessary for her to be carried bodily to her dressing room," the writer melodramatically noted.[46]

Lillian, infuriated, dropped out of the show for two weeks but eventually returned to finish the season. Surprisingly, Ziegfeld did not chastise Fanny over the incident. However, at the end of the season she received no written offer for next year's show. Assuming that this meant she was dismissed, Fanny signed with the Shuberts. Ziegfeld was devastated. Five years later, when he asked her why she had left, she told him, "I thought you didn't want me. You never sent me another contract."

With an injured look, Ziegfeld replied, "It's understood that you'll be in every *Follies* unless I tell you otherwise. You don't need a contract with me."

Fanny, unlike Anna, Lillian, and countless other girls in Ziegfeld shows, did not know the unlikable side of the man. He never pursued her romantically, so their relationship was not complicated by the ups and downs of an emotional entanglement. "I owe everything to him," Fanny later declared. "To me, he's a god."[47]

Erlanger and Klaw certainly did not see Ziegfeld as a god. They were dismayed when he lost a great talent like Fanny to the Shuberts yet retained the less gifted and unreliable Lillian. Erlanger threatened to fire Lillian if Ziegfeld did not keep her under control. Rather than punish his temperamental star, Ziegfeld calmed Lillian's high-strung nerves by inviting her to his Canadian getaway. Accompanying them was Nanny Johnson and Ziegfeld's friend, fishing partner, and fellow Chicagoan Henry Siegel. Anna was still on tour during this time, making it relatively simple for Ziegfeld to slip away to the secluded camp with his mistress. But the trip was less a romantic getaway and more an innocent lark, as confirmed by Nanny Johnson. "All we did was swim, fish, play cards, indulge ourselves with some pretty tasty food . . . Lillian and I shared a cabin sparsely furnished with only two cots, two chairs, a table and one kerosene lamp. No matter what some people might have thought, Flo Ziegfeld never came near our cabin any night during that entire week."[48] Ziegfeld camped outside in a tent, and he tried to coax Lillian to rough it and sleep in a tent of her own. She was irritated by the mere suggestion that she expose herself to the spiders and wild animals that might be roaming about the campground. However, Lillian and Ziegfeld's tiff did not affect their plans for the second week of their vacation. As had become his custom over the past two years, Ziegfeld brought Lillian and Nanny to an Indiana resort called the French Lick Spa, where they spent the week taking mineral baths and riding on horseback. By this time, Ziegfeld was, according to author Lee Davis, "insanely in love with Lillian Lorraine . . . despite her erratic, irresponsible, and often senseless behavior."[49]

Though Lillian's critics and many historians have described her as a hedonistic, vulgar gold digger, she had many redeeming qualities that her detractors overlooked. Lillian was the first to admit that she was after money: "I have no problems with accepting expensive gifts from my gentleman friends," she once told reporters.[50] And those who worked with Lillian truly liked her, even if they envied her. *Follies* dancer Eleanor Dana O'Connell recalled: "Lillian never had any real appreciation for the value of money . . . in her glory days, Lillian had lots of money and she helped plenty of our people through some pretty tough times . . . I have to say she was generous to a fault."[51]

In matters of friendship, Lillian was earnest, and despite appearances, she was just as earnest in her serious romantic involvements. Ziegfeld's pursuit of Lillian made him seem like the archetypal lecherous producer, but Lillian did not perceive him that way. After Ziegfeld's death, she provided a candid reflection on her true feelings for him: "I've made a lot of bad choices with men in my life, but Flo Ziegfeld was the only man I can honestly say I both loved and respected. If we had married it probably wouldn't have lasted long, and that would have been mostly my fault. Flo was decent and caring in so many different ways and sometimes, I'm sorry to say, I just didn't fully appreciate him."[52]

That realization may not have come until later in Lillian's life, but at age twenty, she already had the foresight to know she should *not* marry Ziegfeld. She knew he was already thinking of her as the future Mrs. Ziegfeld. He never had a formal picture taken with any of his stars except for Lillian. When she was sitting for a publicity portrait in 1910, Ziegfeld suddenly said, "Hold on, Lillian, I want to have a shot of us together." According to Nanny Johnson, he did this to prove the sincerity of his intention to marry Lillian. She described the picture as resembling a wedding portrait, with Lillian sitting on a "gold gilt loveseat with Flo behind her, arms outstretched in an obviously protective . . . stance. The two of them looked for all the world like a blissfully happy married couple."[53]

Ziegfeld's previous denials of any intention to divorce Anna were hard to believe, given his gestures toward Lillian. Though he allegedly had affairs with a number of his female employees over the decades, Lillian, according to Ziegfeld's second wife, Billie Burke, was the only one he truly loved.

Whether or not Lillian reciprocated Ziegfeld's passion, he continued to worship her. He commissioned two seminude miniature portraits of Lillian that were painted and baked on ivory and placed in a Tiffany frame. He kept those miniature paintings in his desk for the rest of his life, and according to his secretary, Matilda Golden, "he would constantly take them out, look at them, and his eyes would fill with tears. Then he would say 'If only she had not drunk, had not married badly, had not . . . ' Then he would replace the paintings and grimly close the drawer."[54]

The behavior that brought tears to Ziegfeld's eyes had not yet fully manifested in 1911. However, the coming year ended any delusions Ziegfeld had about Lillian, as well as any delusions Anna and Ziegfeld still maintained about their marriage.

At the beginning of 1912, Ziegfeld's personal life may have been filled with uncertainties, but his professional life showed more promise. Anna was still participating in a profitable tour of *Miss Innocence,* which had moved from the East Coast to the West Coast, playing in cities such as San Francisco and Seattle. Ziegfeld made preparations for his next book musical, *Over the River,* as well as the *Ziegfeld Follies of 1912.* Unlike his recent shows, *Over the River* would not be a Klaw and Erlanger production. Ziegfeld, still eager to be independent of the Syndicate, had teamed with another independent producer, Charles Dillingham. The two men had first met in Chicago in 1889. When Dillingham relocated to New York in 1910, he bought the Hippodrome and Globe Theatres. Dillingham, like Ziegfeld, was adept at staging musicals that blended fantasy and modernity, but Dillingham rarely tested propriety. "Mr. Dillingham was a clean showman whose productions had tremendous appeal to children," Ziegfeld girl Marcelle Earle later explained.[55]

The first show Ziegfeld and Dillingham coproduced was not meant for children, but it contained nothing that would have been deemed inappropriate for them to see. *Over the River,* set to open on January 8, 1912, at the Globe Theatre, was "glorified vaudeville" and starred Eddie Foy, one of the biggest names in vaudeville. Foy's character must serve time in jail, but to avoid the shame, he tells his wife that he is going on a trip to Mexico.

Ziegfeld and Dillingham created interest in the show by advertising it as "real cabaret on the stage," plus the now expected gimmick of surprise guests planted in the audience. The "guests" were actresses impersonating title characters from the previous year's musicals: *The Red Widow* (a Cohan show) and *The Pink Lady*. The show also boasted an exciting and modern score that included "Turkey Trot to Tango" and "The Chop Stick Rag." Ziegfeld gave the latter song to Lillian Lorraine, who held a prominent spot in the cast.[56] Lillian had also secured a place in the *Ziegfeld Follies of 1912*.

Anna, in California just before *Over the River* opened, was not pleased to hear that Lillian dominated her husband's new productions. Anna had grown progressively disillusioned with acting and was set on leaving the theater altogether. During an interview she granted to the *San Francisco Call,* she threw darts at the ways of the American stage—and the American producer (a thinly veiled rebuke of Ziegfeld): "I cannot warn young girls too strongly against choosing the stage as a means of livelihood. It is dangerous, very dangerous. . . . Conditions behind the footlights, especially for the chorus and the showgirl, are horrible to think of. . . . The girls are absolutely at the mercy of the owner of the show. . . . Among the privileges [of the manager of the show] is the right . . . to prowl around behind the scenes as much as he pleases. . . . They never back any but a musical which employs large numbers of pretty girls. They are never found behind productions which 'star' male actors." She then made a comparison between France and America: "There [in Paris] pretty girls do not have to go on the stage to advertise their beauty. The French love beauty and Frenchmen are most gallant."

"Do you think there are any cures for the evils of the musical comedy stage?" the reporter asked at the end of Anna's interview.

"No," she said with firm resolution.[57]

Anna's sober tone in that interview was a far cry from the gay *Parisienne* she had been sixteen years before. Even her humor had become cynical. When the company of *Miss Innocence* moved to Seattle, a reporter told her some interesting facts about Washington, one of which was that a divorce could be granted in two minutes.

"Then a divorce for me!" Anna declared.

"But you have to live here for a year," the reporter clarified.

"That's too long for me," Anna said.[58]

Anna's desire for a divorce was solidified after her return to the

Ansonia Hotel in March 1912. Ziegfeld had not kept his distance from Lillian, as he had promised, but Anna had kept her word to stay away from the Shuberts and serve out her contract with Ziegfeld. On her first day home, Anna went for an afternoon drive with Ziegfeld and Liane, who was on vacation from school. No harsh words were exchanged during the ride, yet their feigned cordiality was more nerve-racking than raised voices or accusations. When they arrived back at the Ansonia, Ziegfeld offered to take Anna's poodle for a walk. Showing an uncharacteristic desire to spend time with her stepfather, Liane decided to join him. But Ziegfeld turned to Liane after only one block and told her: "I think it would be better if you went back and stayed with your mother. She must miss you terribly." A suspicious Liane returned to the hotel but remained in the lobby, watching the door. Ziegfeld entered a moment later and stepped into the elevator without noticing Liane, who was hiding in one of the lobby's alcoves. "Tenth floor, please," he told the operator.

While her mother was on tour, Liane had kept a close watch on Ziegfeld whenever she was home from school. The girl knew about his frequent trips to the tenth floor, and through a bit of sleuthing, she had discovered that this was where "that nasty woman" lived. Once the elevator doors had shut, Liane rushed to tell Anna what she had seen. Though doubtful that Ziegfeld would be so brazen, Anna went to the tenth floor with Liane and approached Lillian Lorraine's room. They heard laughter and saw Ziegfeld emerging from her doorway. He was holding the poodle's leash in one hand and touched Lillian's face with the other. Liane and Anna watched as he drew her in for a long kiss. "I'll be back later, darling," he said. When he turned, he found Anna behind him. She vehemently berated him, but Ziegfeld did not respond and left without a word. The entire record of this encounter comes from Liane's memoirs, which were written in the first person from Anna's point of view and are thus widely held to be fictional. However, it is true that Anna somehow discovered that Lillian was living two floors above her, at Ziegfeld's expense. He insisted that he kept Lillian there only to monitor her behavior and preserve the show's reputation. But the servants and employees of the Ansonia knew that his frequent visits to the Lorraine suite were not for professional purposes.

Immediately after her confrontation with Ziegfeld, Anna returned to their eighth-floor suite, packed her trunks, and booked passage to France. Allegedly, her last words were, "I'm leaving Flo to heaven and Lillian Lorraine!"

6

The Girl at the Top
of the Stairs

Anna Held was not the only woman Ziegfeld lost in the spring of 1912. During the run of *Over the River,* Lillian Lorraine disappeared. Ziegfeld discovered her whereabouts after seeing a bold headline announcing her marriage to Freddy Gresheimer. Upon reading the news, Ziegfeld could not contain the intense feelings he had for this "slip of a chorus girl." He burst into tears and cried, "She married someone!"[1] The *New York Review* poked fun at the producer's reaction in a melodramatic headline: "Ziegfeld Faints at News of His Star's Wedding."[2] The *Review* was no kinder to Lillian. Its writers emphasized her reputation as a gold digger and quoted her rapturous declaration that her new husband had "oodles and oodles" of money.[3] The article concluded with Lillian saying good-bye to the stage and hello to a honeymoon in Europe. What the impetuous Lillian did not know was that Gresheimer was the proverbial black sheep of his family and had countless debts to his name.

Ziegfeld's grief over losing Lillian lasted for days. For hours, he gazed despondently at a portrait of her on his mantel.[4] According to Fanny Brice, "He could not bear to be alone." Fanny kept Ziegfeld company as long as he needed it; she remained his friend even though she no longer worked for him. Ziegfeld's despair continued even after he discovered that, less than two weeks after the couple's elopement, Lillian had left Gresheimer. She told reporters that the marriage was a mistake and was incompatible with her professional career (which she had obviously decided not to abandon). No one knew whether the marriage would end in separation, divorce, or annulment. But Lillian made one thing clear: she wanted to return to Ziegfeld's employ. One afternoon, Lillian returned to the Globe

Theatre full of brazen confidence that she still had a spot in *Over the River*. Behaving as if nothing had happened, she approached Ziegfeld and told him she was ready for work.

"You've already been written out of the show," Ziegfeld told her. As she turned to leave, he stopped her and softly asked, "Are you divorced?"

"No," she told him. "But you and I are through."[5]

Ziegfeld was devastated and feared he had lost Lillian forever, so he decided to restore her place in the show. Rehiring her not only kept her in his life but also boosted ticket sales. A reporrter for the *New York Review* quipped that "without Lillian Lorraine to stare at, *Over the River* would be a hard sentence!"[6] The show was not a smash hit, but it ran for a respectable 120 performances.

Anna Held was not blind to the impact Lillian's rejection had on Ziegfeld. However, he was still sending Anna desperate messages in Europe, insisting that he had severed all emotional attachments to Lillian. Anna was no longer interested in his false denials. The Ziegfeld-Held union sank on the same day as the *Titanic*: April 14, 1912. Their marriage was never official, but they had been together for sixteen years—more than enough time for the state of New York to deem their relationship a common-law marriage. The words on most people's lips when they heard of the breakup were: "I told you so."[7] Ziegfeld resented such smugness and still believed he could win Anna back. Nevertheless, he did not object when she filed divorce papers.

Ziegfeld had apparently lost his hold over Anna's life. When she arrived in Paris, she was more upset over the death of her dog, General Marceau, than the death of her marriage. "I can get a new husband but not a new dog," she told reporters.[8] However, after she had been alone in Paris for several weeks, she showed signs of regretting her decision to leave Ziegfeld. "He looked so forlorn I might give him another chance," she told one reporter.[9] But she did not go back to him. Throughout the divorce proceedings, Anna and Ziegfeld remained on amicable terms. "Anna Held is a woman in a million," Ziegfeld told the press. Living independently and without a corset, Anna became more fully integrated into the modern age and made a great comeback in Paris and London music halls.

Ziegfeld fared as well as Anna professionally, if not personally. He began production on another book musical, *A Winsome Widow*. Ziegfeld again teamed with Charles Dillingham to produce the play at the Globe Theatre. The new musical was a satirical comedy about the president of the

Purity League and a widow who challenges his ability to maintain his wholesomeness. *A Winsome Widow* included many *Follies* stars, such as Leon Errol and the Dolly sisters. Also in the cast was a nineteen-year-old actress named Mae West, whom Ziegfeld and Anna had noticed months before in another production. Among the many composers for the show was the reliable Jerome Kern. *A Winsome Widow* enjoyed a healthy run from April 11 to September 7, 1912, and won the critics' approval, although one detractor called the show little more than a "series of vaudeville turns." Critics concluded that "what raised it . . . was Ziegfeld's impeccable flair."[10] The production number that received the most praise was set in an ice palace with a line of ice-skating beauties gliding through sunlight, sunset, and moonlight.

Because *A Winsome Widow* ran through the summer, Klaw and Erlanger pushed the *Ziegfeld Follies'* premiere date to the peak of Broadway's theater season. The men also promoted the *Follies* to an indoor venue called the Music Hall at the Moulin Rouge Theatre. At first, audiences were wary of paying full price for what they saw as light summer entertainment. But Ziegfeld had proved over the last five years that his revues were more than mere summer larks. Writer Harry B. Smith used the audience's ambivalence for comic value on opening night: "Before the curtain rose, people in the audience started an argument, the subject of dispute concerning the kind of entertainment those present expected and preferred. The disputants were actors in the cast placed in various parts of the auditorium. Harry Watson was a gallery god vociferously demanding the sort of show he liked. Charles Judels was a Frenchman who from his orchestra seat decried all American theatricals."[11]

Though he had made invaluable musical and comedic contributions to the *Follies* since the beginning, the *Ziegfeld Follies of 1912* was Smith's last. The friendship between Smith and Ziegfeld had soured after Ziegfeld failed to pay the writer one too many royalty checks. With Smith's exit, Gene Buck and his collaborator Dave Stamper became the leading voices of the *Follies*. As a writing team, they possessed "a view of the musical that comprehended Ziegfeld's vision and . . . suited Ziegfeld's unusual taste."[12]

The 1912 *Follies* won over audiences and critics alike. Reviewers were more accepting of the show's loose format. Like the *Ziegfeld Follies of 1911*, the 1912 edition did not use a makeshift plot with historical characters as its nucleus. The featured players who received the most acclaim included Leon Errol, Bert Williams, Lillian Lorraine, and the ladies of the chorus.

With each passing year, the chorus had grown in number, and its members had become more conspicuously beautiful. The best tribute to feminine beauty was a number entitled "Palace of Beauties." The audience gasped when the first girl entered, dressed in a harlequin costume made of black lace. Following the harlequin were women dressed as Venus, Carmen, Joan of Arc, ballerinas, and, as the climax, the "Twentieth Century Girl" (represented by Lillian Lorraine). She wore a bold lemon-colored dress with a bright orange cape and black headdress. Lillian's numbers were always among the best received, and the show's biggest hit song, "Row, Row, Row," was no exception. A critic for the *New York Times* called it Lillian's "best individual number" and lauded her "nice little lilt."[13] "Never before was so much beauty shown so much as in this latest of the Ziegfeld nonsensicalities," critic Channing Pollock wrote in his summation of the 1912 *Follies*. Another reviewer observed, "When the theatrical history of 1912 comes to be written, Flo Ziegfeld's contribution to it will be chiefly recalled on account of his success as a picker of feminine loveliness."[14]

More than any other *Follies* thus far, the 1912 edition came closest to encapsulating Ziegfeld's vision of the world as he thought it should be. As biographer Charles Higham explained: "He not only dreamed of creating a world of glamour and luxury far removed from his strait-laced home, but he wanted to fashion unparalleled luxury and beauty in the theater itself. His need for wealth was reflected in his need for theatrical riches. Money was simply a means to an end—an escape from reality."[15] With a divorce, a fickle mistress, and a fierce rivalry with powerful producers looming over him, Ziegfeld needed an escape from reality. But his work provided a diversion only when the curtain was up and he could see his ethereal visions before him. Once the curtain closed, real life returned.

Ziegfeld's personal and professional worlds collided halfway through the *Follies'* season. Buck and Stamper had written a new number for Lillian called "Daddy Has a Sweetheart and Mother Is Her Name," which followed two lovers from youth to old age. Ziegfeld was entranced with the idea and spent $7,000 preparing a scenic set for it. However, the song never made it into the show. On the day Lillian was supposed to rehearse the song in front of Abe Erlanger, she was tardier than usual and even slower in her costume changes. Erlanger rose from his seat in the auditorium and yelled, "Tell her she's through and the song as well!" Newspaper reporters claimed that Erlanger rejected the song because "it was not lively enough," but the real reason was Lillian's unprofessional behavior.[16] Buck recalled being stunned at this turn of events. Ziegfeld, who seldom argued with his Syndicate bosses, had grown more confident after his forays into independent producing with Dillingham. He fought for the song and for Lillian, but Erlanger could not be moved. Lillian lost her job, and Ziegfeld lost the $7,000 he had spent on the number—plus the opportunity to see Lillian every day.

Lillian spent no time weeping over her lost place in the *Follies*. She and Buck took "Daddy Has a Sweetheart" to William Hammerstein, who owned many prominent vaudeville establishments. She was a hit in her one-woman show and received the best reviews of her career. Erlanger read Lillian's notices with ire; he was aware of the money he was losing. Ziegfeld gloated over his boss's mistake, but some of his colleagues believed he was secretly relieved that Lillian had been discharged. He realized that his feelings for her had damaged both his own well-being and his union with Anna. Though Ziegfeld was, by most accounts, finished with Lillian, he still maintained her suite at the Ansonia, even if she no longer welcomed him as a guest. This arrangement did not last long, for Lillian moved around a great deal, mostly from one beau or party to the next.

The ongoing divorce proceedings did nothing to lighten Ziegfeld's mood. Despite Anna's inarguable grounds for divorce—gambling and infidelity—she had to resubmit testimony concerning Ziegfeld's affair with Lillian Lorraine to convince the judge to grant the divorce, which, he informed Anna, would not be finalized until early 1913. Anna was torn between feelings of relief and desolation. According to Richard Ziegfeld, when Anna initially left her husband, she fully believed "this would bring him back," but instead, "Ziegfeld let the divorce go through."[17] On the day the divorce was granted (January 9, 1913), Anna's lawyer whispered to her: "He'll never really let you go."[18] This seemed true, judging by Ziegfeld's immediate attempts to woo Anna all over again. "A reconciliation is entirely possible," he told reporters. He confidently explained that they would remarry and "begin right."[19]

Anna subtly reciprocated Ziegfeld's overtures. She sent both him and his parents Christmas cards and gave the following statement to the press: "I have the friendliest feeling in the world for him."[20] But she denied that she still loved him. Anna theorized that he was pursuing her for business motives, given that the Shuberts and other producers were also vying for her. She had no serious intention of remarrying. According to Anna's friends, her newfound freedom was less difficult to handle than she thought it would be. She managed her own career and her own finances with ease.

Ziegfeld, forced to accept that he had no future with Anna, again attempted to lose himself in his work. However, he found his attention split between his work and Lillian. He could not win Anna back, but he was convinced he still had a chance of forming a legitimate relationship with Lillian. His divorce was final, and he had a new *Follies* under way. He entered the new year with hopes of shedding what Anna had once called his "tawdry affairs" and beginning a new chapter in both his professional and personal lives.

The summer of 1913 began on a hopeful note: the *Follies* opened to an eager audience in June. The June premiere might have seemed like a demotion, given that critics and theatergoers did not view summer entertainment as noteworthy. However, Ziegfeld felt that the show's new location more than compensated for the fact that it would not open during the peak theater season. The *Follies* had found a new home at the greatest theater on Broadway: the New Amsterdam.

Built in 1902 on West Forty-Second Street, the New Amsterdam represented the first Art Nouveau architecture in New York City. The theater, with its Beaux-Arts façade and arched doorway embellished with intricate carvings, looked like a palace from the outside. The interior was no less palatial. Walking into the theater was like entering Versailles or Buckingham Palace. The auditorium could accommodate 1,702 people—more, if one counted the seating in the rooftop garden. Inside the auditorium were box seats protruding from the walls, bordered by jade terra-cotta balustrades. Hundreds of "plaster of Paris friezes and sculptures depicting Shakespearean and mythological figures as well as Hoffman's *Tales of the Vienna Woods*" graced the walls.[21] The New Amsterdam was an architectural feat of matchless splendor—an ideal venue for the shows of "unparalleled luxury and beauty" Ziegfeld planned to produce.

The Shuberts' rivalry with Ziegfeld intensified when they heard that the *Follies* had won a spot at the New Amsterdam Theatre. They knew the July opening of their own revue, the *Passing Show of 1913,* would be anticlimactic after the *Follies*' June premiere. The *Passing Show* mirrored the *Follies* in only one respect: it used a runway projected out into the audience for chorines to dance on. The rest of the show was glorified burlesque and relied on comedic satires of contemporary Broadway hits. Not a single hit song came from the Shuberts' show. The primary reason for the *Follies'* superiority was money. Ziegfeld gave his stars bigger salaries and spent more on productions, thus winning the best talents and creating the most impressive spectacles. Nona Otero, a *Follies* dancer, claimed that "the Shuberts were 'cheapskates' . . . they wanted quality but never wanted to pay for it."[22] Despite the Shuberts' ongoing competition with Ziegfeld and the Syndicate, the battle among the producers was waning in importance. As Ethan Mordden explained: "The theatre expanded and evolved beyond the grasp of even the most powerful combine. Indeed, old-timers had to run to keep up with newcomers these days."[23] The fact that both the Syndicate and the Shuberts held a looser grip on Broadway theaters gave Ziegfeld renewed hope of someday becoming an independent producer with a theater of his own.

Although Ziegfeld's productions were artistically superior to the Shuberts', the material in the 1913 *Follies* was not especially noteworthy. Critics found the 1913 edition to be weaker than its predecessor in part because it reverted to relying on a loose plot. In this case, the "plot" revolved around a group of Indians surveying what the crazy modern Americans were doing to the land that had once been home to the native tribes. The show had many shortcomings, but eighteen years later, Gilbert Seldes claimed the 1913 *Follies* was more significant than critics initially gave it credit for. "By 1913 we can catch sight of Florenz Ziegfeld in one of his finest manifestations," Seldes wrote. "Year after year, the *Follies* had gone well and Ziegfeld was becoming an authority on two subjects: the beauty of women and the art of dance. . . . By 1913, Ziegfeld was generally held responsible not only for such specific forms as the grizzly bear, the turkey trot, the glide, and the dip, but for the dancing mania as a whole."[24]

Ziegfeld showcased the "dancing mania" most notably with Leon Errol spoofing the turkey trot in a skit entitled "The Turkish Trot." The act concluded with the entire cast—and a real horse—dancing together. The show also spoofed Cubist painters, after-hours happenings at Rector's restaurant, and suffragettes. One song about female independence was a Buck-Stamper composition, "I Can Live without You," which had Elizabeth Brice (no relation to Fanny) singing of everything she could survive without, including sunshine, jewels, roses, and her lover. "Such a song was well-suited to the playful sexual dynamics and abundant female stereotypes of the *Follies*," historian Ann Ommen van der Merwe noted.[25]

Despite its outdated format, the show played for 108 performances, 20 more than the 1912 edition.

The *Follies* may have run even longer if Lillian Lorraine and Bert Williams had been in the cast. However, both performers had signed contracts to appear at the London Opera House. Lillian ultimately did not follow through, for two reasons: Ziegfeld and Gresheimer. She was not yet divorced, but the mercurial Lillian still kept company with Ziegfeld. Even though she had said they were through, her actions did not align with her words.

During the summer of 1913, mutual friends of Lillian and Ziegfeld arranged a private dinner party for them at the Park Hill Inn in Yonkers. Described as a "romantic, old world charm hideaway," the inn was the perfect spot for both professional and romantic reconciliation.[26] During the dinner, Lillian purportedly signed a contract to perform for the remainder of the season in the 1913 *Follies*. Ziegfeld discarded the contract two weeks later, however, after reading an unsettling item in *Variety*: Lillian and Gresheimer were reunited. Greisheimer demanded that she cut off contact with Ziegfeld, but Lillian did not allow any man to dictate what she could and could not do. July brought a swarm of splashy headlines about the Ziegfeld-Lorraine-Gresheimer triangle. According to one story, Lillian was seated in a taxicab parked outside Louis Martin's restaurant, speaking to Ziegfeld through the car's open window. Suddenly she screamed, "Oh Freddy, don't, don't!" Gresheimer approached Ziegfeld from behind, brandishing his walking stick. Ziegfeld avoided the cane but not Gresheimer's fist. "You know that woman is my wife, don't you?" Gresheimer exclaimed, as he struck Ziegfeld on the right side of the jaw. The stunned Ziegfeld later reported to the press: "After he hit me, Gresheimer jumped into a cab and drove away with Miss Lorraine. I had no chance to get at him and I have no idea what motivated his attack on me."[27]

The next day, Lillian's sympathies remained with Ziegfeld. She claimed that after attacking the producer, Gresheimer had throttled her in the cab as he directed the driver to take them to Coney Island. There, he kept her captive to prevent her from running to Ziegfeld, and he also pawned her $5,000 ring. "He left me there and I haven't seen him since," she said. "If I know Fred, he's probably down in Atlantic City and won't be back until he runs out of money." Lillian's story had little, if any, credibility. The same night she was supposedly held captive, eyewitnesses saw her participating in a turkey trot contest. After winning the dance contest, she announced to a reporter: "I feel invigorated enough now to go after my husband!"[28]

Lillian did indeed go after Gresheimer, but not for a reconciliation. On July 17, 1913, she had a warrant issued for his arrest. She charged her husband with stealing not only the $5,000 ring but also other pricey jewels. Writers for the *New York Review* had fun with the story, which gave them a perfect opportunity to malign their competitor's name. "That Ziegfeld should finally have been pummeled for his attentions to another man's wife does not in the least astonish those who have watched his career as a boulevardier . . . what may be news to all . . . is that the costly bauble [the ring] was a gift to Miss Lorraine from Ziegfeld." Incidentally, the ring was later recovered, and Lillian gave it to Nanny Johnson.[29]

Two days after putting out a warrant for her husband's arrest, Lillian filed for an annulment. To justify the annulment, she explained that Gresheimer had treated her cruelly and inhumanly and was constantly drunk. "I could not stand his actions any longer. I will be glad when the court relieves me of him," Lillian said.[30]

Less than six weeks after the Gresheimer incident, Ziegfeld again found himself at the center of a feud over Lillian. He attended the Tourell Ballroom in Long Beach on the night of August 27, 1913, expecting to have a pleasant evening of fine food and dancing. Whether he knew it or not, Lillian was there with another man, whom newspaper reports identified only as someone occupying "a high position in the vaudeville field."[31] Ziegfeld's presence at the ballroom had already attracted attention before he approached Lillian and her escort. New Yorkers knew him to be an accomplished dancer, and despite being forty-six years old, he behaved like the flaming youths of the Jazz Age immortalized by F. Scott Fitzgerald less than a decade later. According to Seldes: "His patronage of any public place brought so many followers that people would not believe in the purity of his motives and it was rumored that Louis Martin paid him a 'handsome sum' to bring patrons to his café. . . . For ten years the story went he had never seen the sun except one morning when he was a little late returning home. When Mayor Gaynor closed the cabarets at one a.m. in 1913, Charles Dillingham wired to Ziegfeld 'this will enable you to get an hour or two of rest each night.'"[32]

Ziegfeld was not thinking about getting any rest in the early-morning hours of August 28. Aware of Lillian's appetite for gifts from her gentlemen friends, Ziegfeld approached her partner and asked in a voice audible to everyone on the dance floor: "How much are you giving her for that dance? A hundred dollars?"

The man paused and replied, "I don't know you. People hearing you speak to me like that would think I am a friend of yours. If you have anything to say to me, come on outside after the dance." Once the dance had ended, the man approached Ziegfeld and, according to a reporter for the *New York Review,* "took the *Follies* manager's proboscis between his thumb and index finger and gave it a mighty twist which drew forth a flow of blood and a howl of pain which brought many other dancers to the scene." He warned, "If you ever dare to speak to me again I'll use my fists instead of my fingers!" He and Lillian then launched into another turkey trot. The reporters for the *New York Review* delighted in painting Ziegfeld as a weakling when it stated that, "according to records kept by a man who makes a specialty of Broadway brawls, Ziegfeld has yet to come out first in any street fight."[33]

Anna, who was fulfilling music hall engagements in France and England, read the humiliating headlines about her former husband. They convinced her to forget about the possibility of reconciling with him once and for all. Whether he was being rash and self-destructive as a reaction to their divorce or whether he was simply going through a midlife crisis, his tacky and vulgar actions were unforgivable. Anna did not want any part of his lifestyle or to be drawn back into the vortex of his affair with Lillian.[34]

The fact that the middle-aged Ziegfeld kept returning to Lillian time and again indicates his desperation and loneliness during this period of his life. His swings from aloof and withdrawn to hedonistic and impetuous suggest that he may have been suffering from depression, but he did not discuss this with anyone. He had difficulty maintaining both friendships and romantic relationships because he did not openly express his thoughts or feelings. His work was his life, and when he was not barreling full speed ahead into a show, when he was left with just himself, he sometimes found Florenz Ziegfeld Jr. to be unpleasant company. His addictions to gambling, work, and women were distractions to ward off his constant fear of failure. When he did achieve success, his first thought was not "I've made it" but rather, "This is temporary—what about the next show?" The same could be said for his relationships. He never allowed them to fully bloom.

By the end of 1913, Ziegfeld had had enough of his affair with Lillian. Its bloom had faded after five years. At first, Lillian's vulnerability had "evoked a protective instinct" in Ziegfeld. But after her repeatedly reckless behavior, she was no longer "the most beautiful girl in the world" to him. Instead, he crowned her "the dumbest girl in the world."[35] Though Lillian's marriage was officially dissolved in December 1913, Ziegfeld had no desire to pursue her. She reentered his life on a professional and occasionally personal level in the coming years, but they both agreed that their affair was over. The most obvious sign of Ziegfeld and Lillian's separation came when she signed with the Shuberts for a revue, *The Whirl of the World*. The show was a great success, and Lillian's career continued to soar after she tried her luck in film. She flourished in the relatively new medium between 1913 and 1916, primarily in a serial thriller entitled *Neal of the Navy*. As usual, writers for the *New York Review* took advantage of any opportunity to take jabs at Ziegfeld: "It must be with bitter envy that Ziegfeld views the immense success of Miss Lorraine . . . because she is doing far finer work than she ever did for him."[36]

The exits of Anna and Lillian from Ziegfeld's life marked a turning point in his career as well as in the American musical theater. Beginning in 1914, the American musical became fully modern and was fast approaching its golden age. Jerome Kern helped speed its maturation with his 1913 production *Oh, I Say!*, which was among the first of the "smaller, plot-driven musicals."[37] The shift away from European-themed shows was becoming more evident as rumblings of discord in Europe reverberated in the United States. The first event to win Americans' full attention was the assassination of Archduke Francis Ferdinand in Sarajevo in 1914. The *Titanic*'s tragic maiden voyage in April 1912 was a smaller though not insignificant sign that Europe was not indestructible. A strong distaste for the Germanic operetta swept over Broadway, and a storm of new American shows took its place. The production that could be called the mother of the modern musical was Irving Berlin's *Watch Your Step* (1914). It introduced the syncopated walk of Vernon and Irene Castle, two of the most sought-after young dancers on Broadway. Also included was a song that taught the fox-trot. Harry B. Smith, Ziegfeld's old associate, wrote the show's snappy dialogue. Though *Watch Your Step* was influential, its format was still a cross between a revue and a musical comedy. Nevertheless, critics called it as "ephemeral as art, but as permanent as a landmark, namely for its creation of a more graceful rhythm to American [music] and an entire score using only native musical speech."[38] American rhythm had all but replaced European music by the mid-1910s. Ragtime reigned over opera, and less than a decade later, jazz, which was "fast, noisy, and new," reigned over ragtime.[39]

New York City itself was maturing with the musical theater. The construction of new theaters like the New Amsterdam coincided with the rapid erection of now iconic New York skyscrapers. The Flatiron Building, the Woolworth Building, and the Metropolitan Life Tower were only a few products of the building boom. Fifth Avenue had been widened to make room for more automobiles, and a drive down the avenue in 1914 would have found the most elite shops, including Tiffany's, Gorham's, and Cartier's.

When Ziegfeld attended a New Year's Eve ball on December 31, 1913, at the Hotel Astor's Sixty Club, he was seeking a new life as solid as the Flatiron and Woolworth buildings. He had begun to feel the effects of his taxing relationship with Lillian, his sleepless nights, and his constant partying and gambling. He viewed mortality as the ultimate failure; his aversion to death was so severe that he refused to attend funerals and even had difficulty looking at clocks, which reminded him of the passage of time. What he needed was a lifestyle that did not hasten death—one that gave meaning to his life beyond the next show, the next game of poker, or the next girl. He needed someone who knew everything about him yet still accepted him.

As much as Ziegfeld desired a new lifestyle, he could not escape his old one so easily. Because neither Ziegfeld nor Lillian Lorraine had a date for the New Year's Eve masquerade ball, they decided to attend together. Ziegfeld arrived at Lillian's suite in his favorite costume: a tramp, complete with "blackened nose, a dead cigar stub in his mouth, and a bicycle."[40] His appearance infuriated Lillian, and they argued during the entire ride to the Hotel Astor. Once they arrived, Lillian left Ziegfeld, and he did not see her for the rest of the evening. Then a woman dressed as Empress Josephine with large, dark eyes and a shapely figure caught his eye. It was Anna Held. She had recently returned to New York for professional reasons. But Ziegfeld was not in the mood for another reminder of his past or for the awkward, obligatory small talk with his ex-wife. His mood only darkened when the Shuberts came through the door. He did not even notice the petite, blonde ballerina accompanying the brothers. She was fifteen-year-old Marilyn Miller, the Shuberts' charming new discovery. She would have been a perfect candidate for a featured spot in the *Follies*, but that evening, Ziegfeld was not focused on stealing talent. He receded into the background and was headed for the door when Gene Buck blocked his path and asked him where he thought he was going. Didn't he know his old friends William Brady, Sam Harris, and Irving Berlin were waiting for him inside?

"I think I'll absent myself from felicity for awhile," Ziegfeld dramatically said.

After making a crack about playing *Hamlet,* Buck asked Ziegfeld to reconsider.

"I just want to go somewhere quiet, somewhere I can think. And get rid of this damn costume," Ziegfeld told him. Buck convinced him to return to the Ansonia only long enough to change into a tuxedo and then return to the party.[41]

By the time Ziegfeld returned to the ball, it was two in the morning. Despite the late hour, new arrivals kept pouring into the Sixty Club. Ziegfeld lingered at the bottom of the staircase in his tuxedo, watching the festivities with ambivalence. As he glanced up the staircase at the newcomers, his eyes fell on "the most enchanting woman" he had ever seen.[42] The woman had just come from a dinner party at Sherry's Restaurant. Accompanying her was W. Somerset Maugham, the writer of the play in which she was currently starring, *The Land of Promise.* Her brilliant red hair and cornflower-blue eyes immediately caught Ziegfeld's attention, and he abandoned any thought of leaving. The young woman wore a pink, ankle-length gown with a tight bodice and a full skirt designed by the British couturier Lucile, Lady Duff Gordon. "If skirts had been short that year," she later told her daughter, "Daddy [Ziegfeld] would have never married me." The reason: the young woman's self-described "piano legs," which were quite dissimilar from those of the long-limbed beauties in the *Follies.*[43]

The woman in pink "sailed into that crush of hot and wilted dancers, fresh as a rose, her pink skirts floating gracefully about her, her cheeks glowing, her red curls tousled by the wind."[44] As she passed the quiet and dark Ziegfeld, she mistook him for an Italian. He moved toward her, hoping to ask for a dance, but there was already a lineup of men with the same request. Undeterred, Ziegfeld approached master of ceremonies and member of the Syndicate J. Fred Zimmerman, who was "marshalling the Paul Jones"—a popular dance of the era that required frequent partner changes.[45] "Who is that?" Ziegfeld asked Zimmerman, nodding toward the redhead.

"That's Billie Burke!" Zimmerman replied, astonished that Ziegfeld, a connoisseur of female beauty, did not know her.

"I want to dance with her for a long, long time and I'll never get the chance with that bunch of Stage Door Johnnies hanging around," Ziegfeld said.[46] He slipped Zimmerman some money to give to the conductor, along with instructions to continue playing the Paul Jones and blow his whistle for a change of partners only when it would enable Ziegfeld to "dance with that young lady in pink." The appropriately titled "The Girl I Left behind Me" was playing when Ziegfeld first took Billie in his arms. She smiled at him without recognition. His monosyllabic replies to her light conversation did nothing to diminish her belief that he was a foreigner.

"Isn't it odd the way the whistle always blows just when I've reached you?" she asked him after their third dance. Ziegfeld remained silent. Billie recalled that he touched her with his knee every few moments as a signal to turn, something she "rather liked." Billie was becoming as transfixed with this stranger as he was with her. She was oblivious of Anna Held's jealous eyes watching them from the sidelines. She also failed to notice Alf Hayman, an associate of her manager, Charles Frohman, glaring at Ziegfeld with disapproval. Somerset Maugham attempted to reclaim his partner several times, but he finally lost his patience. "This is really the most irritating American custom I have ever . . . ," he began. His complaint was cut short when a man dancing past Billie and Ziegfeld called out, "Why hello, Flo!" Billie stopped, hardly able to suppress a gasp. Only one man in New York was called Flo. She had never seen Ziegfeld or his photograph; she had assumed he was a "dour man with a beard."[47] Now Billie became aware of Anna's envious stare and Hayman's judgmental frown and understood the reasons for their unfriendly demeanors. Billie recalled: "I knew all about him. Everyone in New York knew about him. His reputation with women was extremely dangerous . . . I was, and I knew it instantly, desperately and foolishly falling in love with this strange man. I felt a sudden enveloping oneness with him. It seemed he had danced me into a glimmering world full of swirling emotion."[48]

Billie went home that evening wondering if Ziegfeld felt the same swirling emotion she did or if he was simply interested in her for business purposes. It is doubtful that Ziegfeld saw her only as a potential money-maker. Unlike Anna Held and Lillian Lorraine, who had needed his help to become Broadway stars, Billie was already an established star in both America and England. She was twenty-nine years old—hardly the child-like ingénue Lillian had been—and had a small fortune of her own.

Ziegfeld's attraction to Billie was largely due to the marked differences between her and Lillian and Anna. For one thing, Billie possessed a motherly instinct, which they lacked. In 1909, after her friend Mrs. Thomas

Watson died of pneumonia, she adopted the woman's daughter Cherry as a "companion and protégé."[49] Billie was a constant in the girl's life, providing her with a home as well as exciting travels in Europe, beautiful clothes, and opportunities to star alongside Billie onstage. She treated Cherry like a princess—a great lady—just as Billie had been treated for most of her life.[50] "She symbolized what a perfect lady should be, Victorian style," Ziegfeld's press agent, Bernard Sobel, said of Billie. "Her deportment was faultless. She curved her finger in the proper way. She uttered modish cries and shrieks, lifted her skirts simply. She sustained the illusion that a lady could do no wrong. She was an exquisite piece of bric-a-brac, dressed with all the perfection of a Dresden china figure."[51]

Such an old-fashioned woman does not sound like one who would attract Ziegfeld's attention. However, Billie was not as old-fashioned as she seemed. Sobel asserted that Billie sustained the *illusion* of a prim Victorian lady. In truth, she was a thoroughly modern woman who was not afraid to enjoy her fame and fortune. According to her biographer Grant Hayter-Menzies, Billie liked to "let her hair down offstage . . . and sometimes onstage."[52] Indeed, in one of Billie's most popular shows to date, *The Mind-the-Paint Girl* (1912), she sang such suggestive lyrics as: "Mind the paint! / Mind the paint! / A girl is not a sinner just because she's not a saint!"[53] Each night she stepped onstage wearing only a negligee, which always drew "deliciously shocked" comments from the audience.[54]

Her offstage life was as unpredictable and full of surprises as Billie herself. Like the coquettish girls she played onstage, Billie had "an unhappy penchant for constantly falling in love with somebody or the other. Not seriously in love, not marrying . . . in love, but nevertheless, in love."[55] Billie's whimsy was what attracted so many admirers, but it also kept them at a distance. Billie may have gone through innumerable beaux, but she still asked for her mother's approval before accepting a date with any man. Her lifestyle was more old-fashioned than modern. She lived in a quaint house in Yonkers with her mother, Blanche Beatty Burke, and in interviews she espoused traditional, innocent views on marriage. Billie declared that if she ever found a man she loved more than her art, she would leave the stage behind.[56] In 1913 Billie had not yet found such a man.

Ziegfeld knew he would have to prove his worthiness if he was going to uproot Billie from her well-settled life with Blanche and her status as a Frohman star. He had had ample practice convincing the public that his stars and his shows were unsurpassable. Could he do the same for himself?

Billie initially kept her distance from this "dangerous man," but with her growing restlessness, the distance between them shrank a little every day. Like Ziegfeld, she was hoping for a new life in 1914.

As had been the case with Anna Held and Lillian Lorraine, Billie Burke had climbed from a hand-to-mouth existence to the highest echelons of society. She was born Mary William Ethelbert Appleton Burke on August 7, 1884, in Washington, DC. However, she preferred to be called Billie, after her father, Billy Burke. She spent most of her youth in London as her father's circus variety show toured Europe. Billy had won fame as a clown in Barnum and Bailey's circus, but when he started his own touring company, it was not a financial success. Billie described living in near poverty during most of her childhood. "I had dreamed of Kings and Queens and Princelings," she later wrote of her arrival in London. "Instead there was merely the chill smudge of Waterloo Station and the crisp cackle of cockney voices."[57]

Billie was a shy and retiring child, but Blanche was determined that her daughter should go onstage. So Billie tried to get over her introversion to keep her ambitious mother happy. Blanche molded Billie into both the perfect, well-educated lady and the extroverted, confident actress. She sent Billie on grand tours of Europe and made sure her daughter hobnobbed with the crème de la crème of London society. At the same time, she arranged for Billie to make her stage debut in 1902 at a rowdy music hall, where she sang "My Little Canoe," a "coon" song. The girl's timidity onstage endeared her to the audience, and the majority of the music hall patrons called for encores. Shortly thereafter, Billie won a role over established actress Edna May in *The School Girl* (1903), a light romantic comedy typical of the early 1900s. In the show, Billie performed "My Little Canoe" to rave reviews.

Now that Billie had established herself as a true talent, more plays were forthcoming, and her family's financial troubles were over. Over the next few years, Billie rocketed to fame by playing parts that, like Anna Held's, required her to look beautiful, but little else. "I was amusing on stage because I had delightful costumes, because I had witty lines to say, written by the wittiest authors. . . . These were light, smart comedies," Billie commented. "I was an ingénue, dressed in high fashion (my clothes were very important; they were the main reason for my early successes)."[58] Billie's plays differed from Anna's in that they had often been penned by literary greats such as W. Somerset Maugham, James M. Barrie, and Sir Arthur Wing Pinero.

By 1904, Billie's picture was plastered on the windows of photography shops and drugstores; hairpieces and dress collars bearing her moniker became the trend among young girls. Her name became so well known that it entered the modern lexicon: as a verb, to "billieburke" meant to behave adorably;[59] as a noun, a "billieburke" was a one-piece nightgown, usually made of voile or satin with lace trim. Billie was also partly responsible for a more lasting addition to the English language. Because of her hairstyle—a careless pile atop her head with tendrils flapping about her neck—she was nicknamed the American Flapper. The term "flapper," meaning a lively teenage girl, had its roots in 1890s English slang; by 1912, the term was commonly used in England to describe impetuous or slightly immature young women in their late teens and twenties. Thus, Billie helped popularize the conception of the flapper more than a decade before the term became synonymous with girls of the Jazz Age.

Billie's public image as both an ingénue and an appealing woman extended to her personal life as well. Though she was nineteen when she made *The School Girl,* Billie remained under the close watch of Blanche. This did not keep the stage door Johnnies from lining up to see her, but Billie seemed to attract suitors of a higher caliber compared with most other actresses. One of her admirers was Captain Francis Stanley Carey, the Marquis of Anglesey. The adoration of men such as Carey, plus the magnificent gowns she wore onstage, convinced Billie of the benefits of being an actress. "I was a contented little thing," Billie wrote with a touch of regret. "I wish I could report that I was ambitious, battling for opportunity, trying to learn. But . . . nothing happened at this time of my life . . . to inspire me with the notion that I might one day become a great actress."[60]

Billie soon met a man who gave her that inspiration. One evening following a performance of *The Belle of Mayfair,* Billie was introduced to Sir Charles Hawtrey. One of London's most renowned humorists, Hawtrey gave comedy a finesse that put it on a par with high drama. Billie's comedic talent impressed him, and he asked her to costar with him in *Mr. George* (1907). The play, which one reviewer disparaged as being of the "lightest possible texture," was not a success; however, the same reviewer singled out Billie's performance as "delightfully well-played."[61] Billie commented, "[I was] a comedienne, at last."[62] She would have continued under Hawtrey's tutelage had it not been for Syndicate producer Charles Frohman's tantalizing offer to come to New York and star opposite John Drew at a salary of $500 a week. Billie was hesitant to leave Hawtrey, but he patted her hand and said, "You go to America and make a big hit there . . . I think you are going to be a very fine comedienne."[63]

Accepting Frohman's offer would mean a permanent move from London to New York, and the thought of returning to the country of her birth thrilled Billie. She accepted the role in *My Wife* (1907), Drew's play, and she also accepted Frohman as her manager. He became something of a father figure to Billie, especially after her own father's death in 1906. Frohman was the antithesis of Ziegfeld in terms of publicity tactics. To make Billie a star, he did not use "flashy press agent tricks."[64] Instead, he introduced her to the Broadway elite: Maude Adams (who originated the role of Peter Pan in America), the Barrymores, Mark Twain, the Astors, and the Goulds. Rather than planting exaggerated stories about his stars' personal lives in the newspapers, Frohman presented his stars as lofty idols who retained an air of mystery by ensuring that the public did not know too much (or too little) about them. Once Billie was in America, Frohman perpetuated her ingénue image by casting her in roles similar to those that had so enchanted theatergoers in London. Her characters had "comeliness, girlishness, and spriteliness," but more important, as one critic observed, they had "wholesomeness."[65]

According to an article published twenty years later, which may or may not be accurate, Ziegfeld was in the audience during a performance of *My Wife*. This seems unlikely, given that Ziegfeld did not recognize Billie at the Sixty Club six years later. Also, he was more apt to be looking to steal stars from the Shuberts, not from Frohman. In any case, press agent Bernard Sobel *was* present during a performance of Billie's show, and he apparently overheard a member of Frohman's staff complaining about the actress: "She wants the world with a fence around it . . . she's English and a snob of course . . . she sells at the theater though . . . and when she steps out on the stage, every eye in the audience follows her from the moment she enters until she exits."[66] Sobel agreed with the latter half of the statement, but not the former. He did not find Billie to be a snob, although he admitted that she could barge through a group of chorus girls like they were "dust of the earth"; the next moment, however, she might hand the doorman a whole dollar for bringing her a two-cent stamp.[67]

Another prominent member of the audience was not a professional associate of Billie's but an admirer and friend: Mark Twain. Twain was morbidly depressed at this point in his life due to the death of his wife and two of his daughters. However, when Twain was with Billie, "he was gay and amusing."[68] Billie became a regular dinner guest at Twain's home. Once, he leaned his head against hers and said, "Billie, we redheads have to stick together." Among Billie's other notable admirers were Enrico Caruso and two of the writers responsible for her best plays, James M. Barrie and W. Somerset Maugham. Billie liked all her suitors, but she did not love them. She was still waiting for her one true love, and she apparently preferred that he be an American: "Nobody can make love like the American man—once he gets started."[69]

Billie's glittering life continued both onstage and off. Following *My Wife,* she appeared in what was arguably her greatest hit, *Love Watches* (1908), which ran for a record 172 performances. Audiences loved Billie and her exquisite Lucile gowns. She learned from Frohman that "society is about five months behind the stage in the correctness of its apparel." Thus, Billie used a London dressmaker who traveled to Paris to identify trends; Billie would then appear in New York wearing styles a season before they became fashionable in America. Her gowns boasted simple, long, circular skirts that followed the outline of her graceful figure. According to fashion historian Marlis Schweitzer, Billie's lithe, "slim form represented a distinctly modern ideal."[70]

Love Watches was a bona fide triumph not only in fashion but also in prestige for Billie. The play made her such a star that girls wrote to her asking for beauty advice and society women sent their dressmakers to the theater to copy the gowns she wore. Billie, like Ziegfeld, believed in the importance of color to convey mood, and she defied convention when it came to expressing her art. "A red-haired girl can wear almost any color except a dull shade of brown," Billie asserted. "One of the fine arts in stage dressing is to adapt . . . the color of your costume to the . . . emotion that you are called upon to interpret . . . red denotes animation."[71] Though red-haired women were commonly advised to avoid pink and red, Billie stunned audiences by wearing a pink satin gown accented by red roses in *Love Watches.*

Though she enjoyed being a fashion plate, Billie was tired of being a "cream puff." She was almost thirty years old, yet Frohman still cast her as a young girl. "Billie Burke has yet to prove that enduring youth is part and parcel of her fibre," a writer for the *New York Times* commented in 1908. "Will Billie Burke at forty-seven to fifty-two retain the light-heartedness, the ingenuous charm of twenty-two? Who can say? Not Billie Burke."[72] In her personal life, Billie was diverging from her ingénue stage persona. She increased her independence in 1911 when she bought her own estate, Burkeley Crest. The home, located in Westchester County in the town of Hastings-on-Hudson, was just a little over twenty miles from New York City. Though her mother still lived with her, Billie had assumed the role of adult and breadwinner. She even convinced the stubborn Frohman to give her 10 percent of the gross of her plays. Now she needed roles that reflected her growing maturity; she did not want to fall into the same trap as Anna Held.

The timing could not have been better for Billie when she was cast as Lily Paradell in *The Mind-the-Paint Girl* in September 1912. Lily Paradell had substance and grit. The role demanded Billie's strong comedic talents, but it also required dramatic aptitude. The play was uniquely modern in terms of its unexpected plot twist. Lily, a chorus girl, is treated like a commodity by both her managers and her suitors. High society sees Lily as only one step up from a prostitute, but when a young lord becomes infatuated with her, Lily uses her charms and flirtatious games to dominate him. Audiences were not accustomed to seeing such a strong heroine onstage. More surprising was that Billie Burke—who seemed to be complacent in her rosy world of beaux and ravishing clothing—was playing this new type of heroine. Billie's role may have shown her growing maturity, but she knew that a great deal of her box-office appeal still came from her clothing. Lucile designed the most talked-about gown in the play, a dress made of "diaphanous layers of lace and chiffon over peach or flesh-pink silk linings" with "seductive leg-baring slits." The nude-colored material and high slits "broke down the visual barrier between body and clothes."[73] Though inspired by the empire waist style that had been popular in the early nineteenth century, the gown's coloring and revised design combined the classic and the modern. A blending of modern and classic was the precise formula Ziegfeld followed in his own shows, and Billie's use of that same formula only increased her appeal to him.

Despite critical raves for her performance as Lily, Billie's next dramatic role in a dreary Maugham play called *The Land of Promise* (1913) highlighted her limitations as a dramatic actress. She admitted that "the change of character was perhaps too sudden for me," but she was saddened by her failure in drama. "I had dreamed of myself as a new Rejane, but now she had disappeared behind a screen. I never saw her again," Billie later wrote.[74]

Frohman immediately cast her in another light comedy, entitled *Jerry* (1914).

As dissatisfied as Billie may have been, her audiences still idolized her and flocked to every show she starred in. As proof of her untarnished fame, the *San Francisco Chronicle* printed a poem in her honor during a 1914 tour of *Jerry*. Titled "Fluffing with Billie Burke," the piece did not reflect Billie's personal feelings, but it encapsulated the image she conveyed to audiences: "When you prance down the boulevard . . . assume a jaunty, graceful glide like roller skating modified—just walk like Billie Burke!"[75]

Had Ziegfeld finally found his ideal woman in Billie Burke? A writer for *Time* magazine later observed that half of Ziegfeld's girls were blonde, half brunette. The writer failed to acknowledge the third category into which Billie fell: redhead. Reporter Djuna Barnes recalled that, while trying to interview Ziegfeld, he talked distractedly of Billie and of nothing else. "My God," he breathed. "She's wonderful! More wonderful than anything that could be imagined of her—and so new, so new!"

"Yes," Barnes said. "But why so new?"

"To me," he answered almost inaudibly. "I used to think dark hair was pretty. Lord, but I was young."[76]

Billie changed Ziegfeld's life; she was the first woman who made him consider being a husband and lover first, a manager and producer second. However, as much as Ziegfeld and Billie wanted to change their lifestyles, neither could do so overnight.

"Ziegfeld was one of the most active men I've ever met. Multiple accomplishment was his meat," Sobel once said.[77] The prospect of making Billie his wife while simultaneously being the top producer on Broadway were accomplishments that Ziegfeld saw as well worth pursuing. Indeed, such goals gave him the vigor needed to see him through the most swiftly changing period of his life and his career.

PART 2

Billie and Flo ... and Marilyn, 1914–1923

She will leave you and then come back again,
A pretty girl is just like a pretty tune.
—Irving Berlin, "A Pretty Girl Is Like a Melody" (1919)

7

Taming an Incorrigible Bounder

Florenz Ziegfeld Jr. may have had doubts about the prospective success of every show he produced, but he showed no hesitation once he made up his mind to pursue a woman. Billie Burke, however, initially had some questions about Ziegfeld's intentions toward her. On January 1, 1914, only one day after their first meeting, those intentions became clear: he was interested in her not as a star but as a woman. Upon entering her dressing room after a matinee performance of *Jerry,* she found orchids, roses, and chrysanthemums from Ziegfeld filling every corner. Billie was flattered, but she still hesitated to pursue a relationship because of the possible threat to her career. Yet Billie found it difficult to keep Ziegfeld at a comfortable distance. Not two days later, she ran into the producer on Fifth Avenue. It was no coincidence that he happened to be passing her car at the precise moment her chauffeur was helping her from the backseat. Surveying her sable jacket and a chinchilla coat Billie carried over her arm, Ziegfeld stated, "I see you are the most extravagant person in the world, next to me."[1]

"And I hear that you give actors thousand dollar bills that you carry about in your pocket," Billie retorted.

"I did not mean to give an actor a thousand dollar bill. I thought it was one dollar."

"And how did you know it was not a one *million* dollar bill?"

"Because," Ziegfeld replied nonchalantly. "I always carry those in an *inside* pocket."[2]

Ziegfeld was correct in his estimation that Billie's extravagance paralleled his own. Billie seldom wore the same dress twice. She seemed to have "a gown for every hour," as Anna Held had sung years before in *The Parisian Model*. In 1908 a reporter from *Theatre* magazine asked Billie how many dresses she owned. Blanche Burke interrupted to say, "Billie always travels with twenty-two private trunks."[3]

One might assume that Billie's extravagance alienated her middle-class fans. However, Billie was an active and beloved member of the small community of Hastings-on-Hudson. She opened her home to reporters, allowing them to photograph and comment on her relatively mundane domestic life at Burkeley Crest. "By offering the public access to her personal life . . . Billie Burke encouraged the press's descriptions of her as a sincere, all-American girl," theater historian Marlis Schweitzer observed.[4] Domestic at heart, Billie also enjoyed being an informal hostess at the modest gatherings she held at her estate.

She invited Ziegfeld to one of these small parties. He did not particularly want to share Billie with a group of guests, yet he also knew she would not go out on a date with him without a chaperone. Blanche Burke initially accompanied her daughter on every outing with Ziegfeld, but before long, he had completely won over his prospective mother-in-law. Billie sometimes felt like he was courting her mother rather than her. She often came home to Burkeley Crest to find the two of them chatting amiably in the parlor. Blanche would be gushing over the gifts he had brought her, among them pink champagne, out-of-season fruits, and pâté de foie gras. The most unusual gift he presented to Billie and her mother was a cow. He reasoned that if they lived in the country, it was only natural that they should have one. Ziegfeld may have won Blanche's approval, but Billie was still torn.

Little did she know that Ziegfeld was in a similar state of emotional confusion. He was unaccustomed to being infatuated with a woman solely on a personal level. Journalist Djuna Barnes described Ziegfeld's unusual preoccupation with the red-headed actress: "Flo Ziegfeld sits down a minute and tries to forget her, but into the back of his mind where he is trying to think up something to get [his latest] play over creeps the elusive mist of Billie's hair."[5] Eddie Cantor aptly elaborated on Ziegfeld's mind-set during his courtship of Billie: "The proud Ziegfeld stayed home waiting for a call from Billie Burke . . . [he] paced the room, starting every moment, imagining he heard the phone ring. But it didn't . . . finally Zieggy swallowed his pride and called her." Billie explained that she seldom called him because his telephone line was constantly busy. "The same day Zieggy called up the telephone company and had them install a private wire with a peculiar tinkle to the bell different from the usual ring," Cantor revealed. "He sent the telephone number to Billie Burke with a note saying, 'I'm sorry you found the line busy. It will never happen again. I've installed a private line exclusively for you.'"[6] Billie was speechless and more flattered than ever, but she was still not ready to commit herself to Ziegfeld. Nevertheless, reporters began to bombard her with questions about the nature of their relationship. "Are you engaged?" one reporter from the *San Francisco Call* asked. "Ridiculous! Ridiculous!" Billie declared. "Why, he's old enough to be—oh! The whole thing is preposterous and I won't talk about it."[7]

Because Billie denied any romantic involvement with Ziegfeld, many, including Blanche, began to assume that his interest in her was only professional. Ever the stage mother, Blanche pointed out that Ziegfeld's business connections made him ideal husband material. He tickled Blanche's ambitious streak when he made it clear that he could "do things quicker" for Billie than Frohman could. Ziegfeld's charm weakened Billie's resolve, even if marriage could mean the end of her association with Frohman. "You learn, after awhile when you grow up, what an enormous difference there is between mere happiness and your career," she later observed.[8]

One major factor in Billie's decision to reciprocate Ziegfeld's affections was Frohman's vehement opposition to their courtship. Since childhood, Billie's mother and her employers had been making decisions for her. She was not about to let them dictate whom she married. One afternoon, Frohman and Alf Hayman dropped in at Billie's estate, hoping to find Ziegfeld on the premises. They wanted him to hear the ultimatum they were about to give Billie. Though Ziegfeld's absence from Burkeley Crest was disappointing, it did not stop them from stating their case: "Ruin your career. Mustn't marry. Drop you if you do. Bad man. Also, he can't produce plays," Frohman told her in his clipped manner of speech. Frohman also summoned Billie to his office to remind her how much he had done for her. He tried to gain her sympathy by lying prostrate on his sofa and groaning loudly as if he were in pain. Hayman bombarded her with warnings against Ziegfeld as well. "He told her things about Flo that he had read about Casanova. He made Zieggy out to be such a dashing Don Juan that Billie's curiosity and interest were promptly excited," Cantor remarked. "She probably saw herself taming and subduing this incorrigible bounder and sewing wings on his coat."[9]

Ziegfeld continued to ply Billie with candy and flowers; he sent her passionate telegrams and called her frequently on the telephone. Frohman intercepted each telegram and phone call. Finally, Ziegfeld used Billie's show manager as a go-between to pass notes and arrange meetings with her. Their most clandestine meeting place was a most unlikely locale: Grant's Tomb. There, Ziegfeld first uttered: "Marry me. Marry me now."[10]

Billie did not accept right away. But as Frohman's warnings continued, Billie began to realize how much she wanted to be with Ziegfeld. Still, she sent notes trying to dissuade him from pursuing her. Ziegfeld, in a rare handwritten letter (he usually sent telegrams), was uncharacteristically desperate when he replied to one of those discouraging notes. It was early April 1914 when Billie's stage manager surreptitiously handed her the letter. On its envelope, Ziegfeld had scrawled: "Miss Burke, *Answer.*" Billie did not have to worry about Frohman catching her, as he was away on business; however, he had left his hat in her dressing room as a reminder for her to stay unmarried. Slipping into her powder blue dressing room, Billie opened the letter:

> My darling Billy [*sic*] dear wont you talk to me? Must I suffer for what people who have their own interests [think]. . . . At least see me—I promise to go away to Europe at once if you really mean that's all you care—I love you Billy with all my heart and soul and a man who has gone through all I have knows when he has found the one woman in all the world—you said you loved me. Honey, is that all you care? For God sake stay in town and see me tonight because I will go crazy tonight—would you write me a note like that because someone made you? . . . Please darling don't listen to anybody—If you dont care allright. I will sail at once. If you do noone on earth shall keep us apart—please answer—Flo.[11]

The note proved to be the turning point in their courtship. After reading it, Billie rushed to Grant's Tomb and finally accepted Ziegfeld's proposal. She later reflected that even if she had known then "what tortures and frustrations were in store for me . . . because of this man, I should have kept right on falling in love."[12]

Ziegfeld disappeared from New York for twenty-four hours following Billie's acceptance, ensuring that she could not change her mind and tell him no. But she had no intention of going back on her word, especially after her mother's elated reaction to the news of their engagement. Ziegfeld and Billie arranged to elope between the matinee and evening performances of *Jerry*. Ziegfeld would have his limousine waiting outside the theater to take them to a ferry headed across the Hudson River to New Jersey, where the couple would be married. As soon as the curtain closed on the matinee of *Jerry* on April 11, 1914, Billie rushed to her dressing room to change. She deliberately ignored Frohman's hat sitting on her vanity table. Hastening outside and leaping into Ziegfeld's car, she was shocked to find a small wedding party with the groom in the limousine. Her new in-laws and Blanche all sang out "Surprise!" when she climbed inside.

"We're going to Long Beach with you," Ziegfeld's mother declared.

"We thought it would be such a good chance for us all to get acquainted," Professor Ziegfeld said, smiling.

"It looks so much nicer this way," Blanche concluded.[13]

With chaperones in tow on their madcap rush to the altar, Billie and Ziegfeld maintained the strange mixture of Victorian propriety and Jazz Age nonconformity that had characterized their courtship from the start. The forty-six-year-old impresario and the twenty-nine-year-old actress were officially wed in the cluttered back room of a parsonage in Hoboken. The minister, a befuddled little man, became more confused when he looked at the names on the register: Ethelbert Appleton Burke and Florence Ziegfeld. "Do you, Ethelbert . . . ," he said to Ziegfeld, "And you, Florence," he said to Billie. They burst into laughter, stopped him, and sorted out their respective names.

After the ceremony, "Florence" and "Ethelbert" took the ferry back to New York so Billie could make the evening performance of *Jerry*. The newlyweds then spent the night at the Ansonia and left early the next morning for a two-day honeymoon in Long Beach—chaperones still in tow. "I knew that my friends, all of them, disapproved of this marriage . . . but this did not seem to matter," Billie stated.[14] However, the marriage did matter very much to two people: Anna Held and Lillian Lorraine.

Until Ziegfeld married Billie, rumors of a reconciliation between him and Anna still lived. Anna told the press she would "not re-light a dead cigarette"; however, she also spoke of wishing to return to "Mr. Flo's management" and even went so far as to say, "When I see him again I feel that, after all, nothing has passed that cannot be forgotten!"[15] Anna's constantly conflicted feelings about Ziegfeld were puzzling, to put it mildly.

There were several reasons behind her swings in emotion. The first one was simple: her career. Since parting with Ziegfeld, Anna had been unable to gain access to the best and largest theaters and received none of the publicity to which she had grown accustomed under Ziegfeld's management. Causing Anna more worry was Liane's determination to try her luck as an actress. The girl's first attempt to prove her skill, in a two-act vaudeville skit at Hammerstein's Theatre, was an unmitigated disaster. One Chicago reviewer called her "a rather heavy, dull, clumsy young person with little talent."[16] Four months before marrying Billie, Ziegfeld was still showing interest in Anna's and Liane's endeavors—the second reason for Anna's failure to rule out a Held-Ziegfeld reunion. On December 1, 1913, Ziegfeld wired the following telegram to "Miss Lilly Carrera" (Lilly was Liane's nickname): "HOPE YOU MAKE A VERY BIG SUCCESS TONIGHT. SAW THE ACT THIS AFTERNOON. IT WAS VERY NICE. TRY NOT TO PITCH YOUR VOICE TOO HIGH. LITTLE MORE REPOSE IS ALL YOU NEED. CALL ME UP. FLO."[17]

Ziegfeld's well wishes to his former stepdaughter showed his growing maturity and a fatherly instinct he had not possessed in his younger years. Anna was not as tactful as Ziegfeld in her feedback on Liane's act. She bluntly told the girl she lacked the talent necessary to be a success. Still, Anna was appreciative of Ziegfeld's telegram to Liane, even if she did not agree with his encouraging words. Anna even contacted Ziegfeld and asked for help in her own career. Without hesitation, he arranged a fifteen-minute vaudeville act for which she was paid $3,000 a week. Ziegfeld also helped Anna deal with two lawsuits over contractual disputes. She had little difficulty paying for legal advice after Ziegfeld booked her act at the prestigious Palace Theatre.

Considering Ziegfeld's ongoing attention, Anna did not take reports of his and Billie's intensifying relationship seriously. Rather, she shrugged it off as just another business venture. So Anna was stunned to open the newspaper and read of their elopement. She had difficulty concealing her lingering ill will for Ziegfeld, which, in a happier mood, she had professed could be forgotten. When reporters showed up at her apartment to get her reaction to the marriage, she stated: "To be happy, a woman must look up to her husband . . . for fifteen years he [Ziegfeld] kept me in captivity. I knew nobody else . . . I have seen so many men whom I like better." However, she told the press she had no intention of remarrying, not even the men she liked better. When the mob of reporters left Anna's room, she turned to Liane and confided: "It is too bad for Miss Burke. Flo will make her very unhappy. She's throwing away her career. He could never produce a show suited to her. I wonder why she married him?"[18]

Anna then packed her bags for Europe and filed a suit against Ziegfeld for $3,000 in unpaid alimony. "The judgment [of the case] was placed in the hands of the sheriff but was returned 'wholly unsatisfied.' Unless Ziegfeld can give satisfactory excuse tomorrow he may be compelled to join the Alimony Club in the Ludlow State Jail," a reporter for the *New York Tribune* wrote.[19] Ziegfeld did not go to jail; Anna dropped the suit and went on with her life in her beloved France. In the coming years, she funneled all her energy into lifting the country's spirit as World War I engulfed Europe.

Lillian Lorraine, like Anna, did not take the news of Ziegfeld's marriage with "benign acceptance."[20] Lillian was as fickle as Anna when it came to her feelings about Ziegfeld, and she showed him that they were not through one evening when he and Billie were dining at the New Amsterdam Aerial Roof Garden. Dressed in a floor-length sable coat, Lillian approached their table. Both Ziegfeld and Billie could smell alcohol seeping from her pores. "I want to talk to you for a minute," Lillian said.

"It will have to wait until later. It's impossible now," Ziegfeld told her.

"NOW, or . . . ," Lillian began, her voice becoming shrill.

Ziegfeld turned to a disconcerted Billie and murmured, "Excuse me." He then led Lillian to the back of the restaurant. "What is it, Lillian? That's my wife, you understand that? I'm married."

"That never mattered before," Lillian laughed. "If you don't listen to me now I'll throw off this coat, and I'm warning you, I haven't anything under it." Ziegfeld, concealing his panic, took her arm and led her outside. He put her in a taxi and hoped the incident would not appear in the morning papers.

The truth of this story is debatable, given that Billie Burke later claimed she never met Lillian Lorraine. However, of all the Ziegfeld girls, Billie admitted that she was most jealous of Lillian because she believed that Ziegfeld had genuinely loved her. In contrast, Billie was not jealous of Anna because she felt that Ziegfeld had never been wholeheartedly in love with her.[21] Regardless of whether Ziegfeld truly loved Anna or Lillian, both women meant a great deal to him, and he continued to care about them. However, Billie was his primary focus.

As Billie and Ziegfeld settled into their new life together at the Ansonia Hotel, Billie gave the apartment a makeover to reflect the couple's fresh start. She erased Anna's lingering presence by removing the gilt-edged, Baroque décor and replacing it with cool Neoclassical hues. She also disposed of a "stack of photos of Lillian Lorraine ... wearing ... black stockings with lace front panels, black satin slippers with diamond studded bows, and skirts pulled up to her knees."[22] Ziegfeld made no effort to save these relics of his past. He delighted in watching Billie, dressed in casual attire and with a scarf tied around her red curls, transform the apartment. Though Billie put a considerable amount of work into redecorating, she did not see the Ansonia suite as a permanent home. It was merely a place to live when their professional obligations forced them to stay in New York rather than return to Burkeley Crest at night. Ziegfeld still considered the Ansonia his primary home—for now.

One morning as Billie was browsing through a stack of fabric swatches for new curtains, the doorbell buzzed. She found a messenger boy at the door, carrying a telegram from Frohman. It read: SENDING JERRY ON TOUR IMMEDIATELY. Frohman had not fired Billie for marrying her Casanova, but he had made it clear that after *Jerry*, their professional association would be over. In the meantime, he could keep Billie and Ziegfeld from enjoying each other's company. The tour would take place while Ziegfeld was deep in rehearsals for the June opening of the *Ziegfeld Follies of 1914*. Though she hated to leave her husband at such a crucial time, Billie had no reason to doubt his fidelity. She later reflected that "Flo ... felt most fully and most responsibly married" to her.[23]

In reality, the "most fully and most responsibly married" groom barely knew his bride, just as she barely knew him. Over the years, they grew to know each other and discovered that they shared many similarities but just as many differences. According to *Theatre* magazine, Billie, like Ziegfeld, "enjoyed the outdoors." However, she could not thrive on the hectic schedule that so invigorated her husband. She appreciated "the heart of quiet and the companionship of real people and things."[24] The couple's primary difference was their temperament. According to their daughter, Ziegfeld was a laconic man, "slow to anger, ice water calm in the midst of chaos." Ziegfeld's tendency to be withdrawn frustrated Billie (as it had Anna), who was "volatile, gay, a chatterbox with an explosive, although short-lived temper."[25] One day Billie strode into the sitting room wearing a lovely new outfit and waited for a compliment or acknowledgment from her husband, but he did not even glance up from his newspaper. Just as she was about to go into what she termed her "blazing red-headed fury,"

Ziegfeld, "without once taking his eyes from the page . . . began to comment on every detail of [her] costume, naming each color precisely."[26]

Billie eventually grew accustomed to Ziegfeld's infuriating aloofness, and she was able to bring out hidden elements of his character that he had thus far revealed to no one. "Flo Ziegfeld . . . was a highly seasoned personality for a young bride to begin to know," Billie stated, and "our first year together was very difficult."[27]

Before Billie went on tour with *Jerry*, she and Ziegfeld spent the first month of their marriage enjoying nothing but luxury and each other's company. Ziegfeld delighted in pampering her. He especially enjoyed rinsing her hair in quarts of champagne to enhance its copper hue. Billie delightedly licked any stray trickles from her face. Even the simplest gifts he gave to Billie were extravagant. On her birthday, Ziegfeld handed her a single red rose with two hundred-dollar bills wrapped around its stem. "That's all I've got," he said.[28]

Their daughter later observed that the word *budget* was not in her parents' vocabulary; rather, they brought out the peacock in each other. Ziegfeld, as everyone well knew, spared no expense when it came to his grooming. According to a 1931 article, Ziegfeld was planning "to spend a weekend on a farm in New Jersey," but he suddenly recalled "that there was no barber in attendance there, [so] he stopped at the Hotel Astor, took one of the barbers there, and placed him permanently on his payroll—all for a single Sunday morning shave."[29] At home, Ziegfeld employed a local barber, Jake Hoffman, to shave him. Ziegfeld spared even less expense when it came to his attire. Though he had once poked fun at a stage door Johnnie outside Billie's dressing room for "primping his mink," he bought a mink coat for himself soon after their marriage. Billie was not a great fan of this new coat and remarked that his clothes were "too gay." He took her criticism seriously and went "completely overboard" in trying to remedy his wardrobe's shortcomings.[30] He acquired an enormous collection of conservative hats and dark business suits and dozens of light suits for vacation wear. For all his extravagance, he disliked wearing formal clothing and complained about the discomfort of collars. Billie, like Ziegfeld, wore expensive attire in public but was fonder of casual clothing. Around the house or when greeting interviewers early in the morning, she wore not a diaphanous Lucile gown but a gray silk kimono with red silk facing.

Billie discovered Ziegfeld's dislike of overly formal clothes and occasions in the first summer of their marriage. After the Chicago run of the *Follies* tour, Billie suggested a celebration at Claridge's, a lavish restaurant in New York. She had not been able to frequent the establishment in the past because of Frohman's rule forbidding her to make appearances in such public places. "Who wants to go there? We go fishing tomorrow," Ziegfeld said. And so they went fishing at Ziegfeld's rustic Canadian camp. Although Billie disliked outdoor sports as much as Lillian Lorraine did, she had an appreciation for nature. She thought their trip romantic and "divinely ordained."[31]

However, Billie began to fret over how their relationship would proceed after they moved permanently from the Ansonia to Burkeley Crest. She had finally convinced her husband to make the estate their primary home, but Ziegfeld would not give up his suite at the Ansonia completely, since he would be spending a great deal of time in New York on business. The thought of living in the country made Ziegfeld nervous, and the forbidding iron gate in front of the mansion made him feel imprisoned. His trepidation about living in the country is puzzling, given that he enjoyed his Canadian camp and wide open spaces in general. His nervousness may have stemmed from the fact that Burkeley Crest was Billie's house. Though not a traditionalist in many senses, he may have felt that he was walking over his bride's threshold rather than carrying her over his own. Settling into the estate also meant settling into a traditional married life, something he had never had with Anna. Making the home even more traditional was the presence of a child—Billie's ward, Cherry Watson, when she was home from boarding school. Fortunately, seventeen-year-old Cherry and Ziegfeld seemed to be compatible.

Ziegfeld was not quick in acclimating to his new lifestyle as a country squire. He had the most difficulty adjusting to the parties Billie hosted. Because Ziegfeld was naturally shy, he spent more time observing than mingling with the guests. He felt especially uncomfortable in the company of the intelligentsia Billie invited to their home, including Arthur Wing Pinero and Somerset Maugham. Even though Ziegfeld had been schooled in the most highbrow of fashions by his father, his preference for middle-grade entertainment and his lack of interest in reading made him feel as if he had little to contribute to a conversation with great authors. Ziegfeld "sat through many of these occasions [literary parties] in grim silence. Occasionally, however, he would come up with something that made the guests laugh uproariously."

"All actresses are conceited," he said one night.

"But Uncle Flo, Auntie Billie isn't conceited!" Cherry exclaimed.

"Ah yes, but Billie isn't an actress," Ziegfeld told her.[32] The guests chuckled heartily. Ziegfeld had not meant the comment as an insult to Billie; rather, he was complimenting the genuine quality she brought to her acting.

Billie's naturalness made Burkeley Crest seem informal and comfortable, and gradually, Ziegfeld's doubts about living at the estate melted away. Billie did everything she could to make Burkeley Crest a refuge from the stresses of her husband's work. The estate had views worthy of Monet's paintbrush: rose gardens, lush trees, Japanese teahouses, bridges over streams, and seemingly endless space for Billie's three poodles, Tutti, Frutti, and Sonny, to frolic. "We had those comforting things now associated with the tax exempt past," Billie later wrote.[33] Among these "comforting things" were servants and breakfast in bed on most mornings. The Ziegfelds' breakfasts were unpretentious: scrambled eggs, bacon, butterless toast with marmalade, coffee, and orange juice. Billie and Ziegfeld had the same relationship with food as they had with clothes. They enjoyed simple, rustic meals, but they also spent hundreds of dollars on rare delicacies. A reporter at the *New Yorker* wrote that "Ziegfeld has had perfect freedom to develop his idiosyncrasies. He is luxurious, he takes pleasure in the excessive and the rare. Long before Miss Fanny Brice said 'Order me anything out of season' Ziegfeld had made the unseasonable his aim in diet, quail being a favorite delicacy."[34]

Billie attempted to meld the grand and the simple when she decided to try her hand at being a housewife. Her unexpected common sense, inherited from the matter-of-fact and businesslike Blanche Burke, was instrumental in her efforts to tend to her husband without the help of butlers and maids. Billie's attempts at housewifery charmed Ziegfeld. She stood for hours in the kitchen with her mother-in-law, Rosalie, testing all her husband's favorite family recipes. Ziegfeld's parents and Anna Held had been close, but Professor and Mrs. Ziegfeld favored Billie because they saw her as a steadying influence on their son. Nevertheless, Billie later remarked, "Mother Ziegfeld soon discovered . . . that Flo had married a frivolous actress who needed the assistance of a butler to brew a pot of tea."[35] Billie may have had difficulty with culinary matters, but she had little trouble nurturing Ziegfeld in other ways. She was exceedingly conscientious of her health and her figure, since she tended to become roly-poly if she did not adhere to her exercise regimen of dumbbells every morning and daily five-mile walks. She made it a point to include Ziegfeld in her current diet and exercise fads. At one time she was convinced that standing on one's head was a cure-all for every ailment from the common cold to anxiety. Patricia later remembered that her father stood on his head and chinned himself every morning, just as Billie had taught him. Billie also sought to foster his psychological well-being and encouraged him to chant, "Every day in every way I'm getting better and better."[36] This mantra came in most handy when he was awaiting reviews after a premiere.

Billie's efforts yielded positive results. Ziegfeld's shyness and nervousness receded in her company, and she got to know his whimsical and teasing side. His humor was not obvious, especially since his expression hardly changed, even when he was being funny. Once when Billie was performing in *Jerry*, she heard Ziegfeld in the wings, chuckling at certain lines or actions in the play. He found the second scene particularly amusing. "In this one I stood behind a screen, completely hidden from the audience, and tossed my pajamas to my sweetheart," Billie remembered. "'Now I don't think a nice girl would do that,' he [Ziegfeld] said drily."[37] Billie also caught a glimpse of his humor during a rainstorm. The windows of Burkeley Crest were still open when the sudden storm hit. Billie, calling to the servants, darted about the house closing all the windows. She stumbled upon Ziegfeld stretched out comfortably on a divan near a window. "Windy, ain't it?" he said.[38] In another example of Ziegfeld's humor, he brought home a little pet monkey for Billie and insisted on naming it Charles Frohman. "Flo never *nudged* you with his humor. He dropped it, flatly, leaving you never quite sure whether he was laughing at you or at himself," Billie explained.[39] The first month of Billie and Ziegfeld's marriage, though a time of adjustment, was one of sincere happiness.

At first, Ziegfeld was only too happy to join Billie wherever she was touring in *Jerry*. He never failed to arrive with a "jewel in his pocket which she knew he could not possibly afford."[40] However, she was not always sure that the expensive gifts were meant for her. Her first doubts about his fidelity occurred after she saw him leaving the hotel room of an attractive chorus girl. He insisted he had been visiting the girl for business purposes, and Billie was too busy with *Jerry* to ruminate about the veracity of his claim. She still believed he was "most fully and most responsibly" married to her. Difficulties arose only when Ziegfeld could no longer follow her on tour due to his obligations in New York.

Billie and Ziegfeld, as well as all of Europe and the United States, were entering a difficult period. In 1915 the United States was still struggling to remain neutral with regard to the war in Europe. The war became more real to Americans after a German U-boat attacked a British passenger liner, the *Lusitania*. More than a hundred American civilians were among the thousand-plus casualties. One of them was Charles Frohman. Billie was devastated by Frohman's death. The last communication between the manager and his former favorite star had been a terse telegram reading: SEND ME MY HAT. Billie heard of her old manager's death while touring with *Jerry* in California; she collapsed and was unable to perform. Ziegfeld, in New York, was not present to comfort her.

For the four months they had been married, Billie and Ziegfeld had been together for only four consecutive weeks. Frohman's untimely death changed Billie's perspective; the importance of her career shrank in comparison to spending time with the man she loved. Work was no longer enjoyable to her. Alf Hayman, Billie's new boss, did not have Frohman's smooth touch and did not pamper Billie. When her tour ended in Hollywood, producer Jesse L. Lasky offered her a film contract. Hayman wired her from New York to inform her that Frohman stars were not allowed to appear in motion pictures. Billie replied, "I am through. I am going to do a picture."[41]

Frohman's death and Billie's temporary exit from the stage had one positive outcome: Ziegfeld became Billie's manager. This allowed the two to remain close even when they were thousands of miles apart. Though he had not had business in mind when they married, becoming Billie's manager enabled Ziegfeld to find her roles that highlighted her most charming qualities. Additionally, he could now ensure that she received the treatment befitting a great star. Ziegfeld's first order of business was to demand that Billie's salary match what she had earned onstage: $10,000 a week. He also arranged for Billie, Blanche, and Cherry to live in a Santa Monica mansion during filming. The home came complete with a chauffeur, cook, and housemaid. The man who handled the particulars of Ziegfeld's arrangements was Thomas Ince, the owner of Triangle Pictures.

The first film role Ziegfeld secured for Billie through Ince melded her little-girl qualities with the more modern and daring ones she had put to such impressive use in *The Mind-the-Paint Girl*. Billie's first movie was *Peggy* (1916), set in a small Irish fishing village described by the title character (an American girl portrayed by Billie) as being synonymous with a "prayer meeting and long whiskers."[42] Peggy brings vivacity to the sleepy little village by doing such outlandish things as wearing pants and racing about in her automobile on the Sabbath. At first, Billie found it hard to adjust to filming scenes out of order. She was disconcerted saying "Good-bye" in one scene and "Hello" in the next, yet film work agreed with her. "I like it [acting in film] not only because of its novelty, but because of its educational value," Billie told *Day Book*. "How I wish I had known several years ago what I know now of pantomime! . . . Within these few weeks I have learned more about the language of the body than I could have learned in a lifetime on the legitimate stage."[43] The film built Billie's confidence in Ziegfeld's management skills and assuaged her financial worries. However, it did not bring her and her husband closer together.

Ziegfeld had little time or inclination to travel to the West Coast; he was far too absorbed with his producing responsibilities. His shows were his life, leaving little room to nurture personal relationships. When Ziegfeld was engaged in a production, according to Billie, he "went into one of two moods: either he was overcome with utter lethargy or he wanted to play vigorously and always expensively."[44] He could be gone for twelve to fifteen hours at a time, overseeing rehearsals. Throughout the day, he dictated up to fifty telegrams, most of which were "600 words long, full of criticism, encouragement, [and] unimportant ornament."[45]

Just as Ziegfeld had had to adjust to Billie's world at Burkeley Crest, Billie had to adjust to life as the wife of Broadway's greatest, most ambitious, and seemingly busiest producer. Billie did not resent the fact that she had sacrificed more for their marriage (her stage career) than her husband had; rather, she enthusiastically took on the role as her husband's primary confidante and cheerleader. She felt the need to work only when finances demanded it. She stood by Ziegfeld through his greatest failures and his greatest successes with a constancy he had never found in Anna Held or Lillian Lorraine. The question remained whether he was capable of being a constant in Billie's life.

8

Lively Productions

Ziegfeld spent increasingly more time at the Ansonia Hotel in New York City and less time at Burkeley Crest as he poured all his energy into lifting the *Follies* from their rut. By 1914, Ziegfeld's revue had become formulaic. After the June 1 opening of the *Ziegfeld Follies of 1914* at the New Amsterdam Theatre, critic Channing Pollock confirmed that the series was in danger: "Mr. Ziegfeld's worst fault is that he imitates himself. Every year's performance is pretty sure to contain an altered version of something that made a hit another year."[1] The 1914 edition indeed included many "altered versions" of previous successes. The nostalgic song "Underneath the Japanese Moon" harked back to "Shine On, Harvest Moon," and "When the Ragtime Army Goes Away to War" filled the now obligatory space saved for ragtime and patriotic numbers.

The costumes in the 1914 edition were more impressive than the routine musical offerings. According to Richard Ziegfeld, there were more costumes that year "due to Billie Burke's presence at the show's opening."[2] Given Billie's love of clothing and her reputation as a fashion trendsetter, Ziegfeld wanted to impress his wife with a show full of costumes that outdid those in previous *Follies*. The plethora of costumes in the 1914 edition prompted Ziegfeld to make one of his best-known statements: "Women glorify gowns and certain gowns can glorify certain girls."[3]

The biggest hits of the evening, however, were not the costumes but the comedians. Their success finally convinced Ziegfeld to put more effort into the show's humorous skits. He told reporters: "I hunt for chances of putting in a laugh or taking out a slow bit. I keep the show combed, brushed, polished, and groomed."[4] Bert Williams, who had returned to the Ziegfeld fold, added plenty of laughs to the show. In the skit that most tickled audiences, he played a single-handed poker game. Though Bert's skit was well received, Leon Errol got the most enthusiastic notices. His skit involved a group of dance students waiting for their instructor. The students had been told that when their professor returned, they were to copy his every move. When a drunken man (Errol) entered the studio, the students mistook him for the teacher and attempted to mimic his boozy movements. The audience at the premiere of the *Ziegfeld Follies of 1914* was in "semi-hysteria" watching the students imitate Leon's rubber-legged state of inebriation.[5] Another comedian that pleased audiences was vaudevillian Ed Wynn, known for his befuddled and eccentric caricatures. Comedy certainly helped enliven the *Follies of 1914*, but Ziegfeld knew it would take more than comedy to attract audiences and convince critics he was not merely imitating himself.

Gene Buck was one of the four creative talents who helped Ziegfeld find a way out of this rut. "Back in the '90s people liked to sing around the piano at home but now they want to dance. They want to be a part of whatever everyone's doing up on stage," Buck said. "And after the *Follies,* everyone's going to eat, drink, and dance at Rector's and Delmonico's. Why not have them eat, drink, and dance here?" This suggestion immediately piqued Ziegfeld's interest. "We'll make the rooftop a supper club," he said. "And we'll need a platform, a stage—one that revolves—get entertainers, girls, orchestra—everything we have in the *Follies* but less formal." Billie was a bit dubious when Ziegfeld told her about this new idea. "And you, I suppose, will walk around like a waiter with a napkin on your arm," she declared. "Why, it's the silliest thing I ever heard! The great Ziegfeld!"[6] Billie had not known Ziegfeld long enough to appreciate that his "silliest" ideas were often the most profitable.

Ziegfeld staged his first supper club entertainment, entitled the *Dance de Follies,* on the rooftop of the New Amsterdam Theatre. The club gave audiences the opportunity to drink fine alcohol and satisfy their cravings to dance to the music they loved in the *Follies.* Ziegfeld took much of his inspiration for the supper club from Rector's restaurant, which often had four different orchestras playing in succession, performing new songs from Tin Pan Alley and Broadway shows. Ziegfeld girl Doris Eaton provided a vivid description of Rector's: "The songs were always played in the nightclubs in an up-tempo style for one-step dancers, adding to the liveliness and high spirit of the place. . . . Rector's was always festive, gay, and crowded with beautiful people. . . . It was a celebration of having arrived in showbiz."[7] Rector's could accommodate 1,000 people, while the New Amsterdam's roof could hold only 760. But Ziegfeld recognized that his supper–dance–floor show combination was a recipe for success, regardless of seating capacity. To make his rooftop show as enticing as Rector's, Ziegfeld increased his already massive budget and hired additional beautiful showgirls. The *Dance de Follies* was worth the money. It was such a success that Ziegfeld expanded the show the following year and rechristened it the *Midnight Frolic*. Billie admitted that the success of her husband's seemingly silly idea taught her "a handsome lesson."[8]

Before Ziegfeld could expand the *Midnight Frolic*, the New Amsterdam roof had to be completely remodeled. Ziegfeld employed Joseph Urban, a Viennese architect, artist, and set designer, to make his vision into a reality. Urban thus became the second person to help Ziegfeld out of his rut. Those who knew Urban described him as a "fat, jolly, vastly amusing man whose many chins wobbled as he talked."[9] Ziegfeld and Buck had seen Urban's spectacular and innovative designs in a Broadway production called *Garden of Paradise* and had met him backstage. They later approached Urban at the Pabst café, where the artist dined each night. Ziegfeld offered him a job, but Urban was hesitant to accept. "I will not demean myself to work on a 'girlie' show," Urban told him. Ziegfeld set a $10,000 check on the table, and Urban's expression brightened. "I will never interfere with your work or ask you to lower your standards," Ziegfeld promised. "The essence of my shows is speed, something needs to be happening every minute, so there must be alternating 'scenes in one.' With your architectural background, I know you could do it. It is the high caliber of your work I want."[10] Ziegfeld's pitch, delivered in his "odd, whiny voice," worked.[11] The two men shook hands, and for once, Ziegfeld's check did not bounce. Urban became one of Ziegfeld's closest friends, and he was one of the few artists the producer was happy to have as a guest at Billie's dinner parties.

To Ziegfeld's satisfaction, Urban designed the New Amsterdam rooftop in an untraditional fashion. There was no stage per se, but the west end of the room was covered with background scenery. Patrons sat at tables situated around the dance floor, while performers entertained them in the center. After a few editions of the *Frolic* (there were usually two a year), Urban added a four-foot-high platform with wide steps. This allowed entertainers to gracefully descend to the dance floor after emerging from a glorious backdrop with a large circular opening. Rubber wheels underneath the platform made it a telescopic stage on which tableaux "could be presented . . . while other scenes and numbers unfolded on the stage or the dance floor."[12] The open floor plan allowed plenty of room for impromptu performances. Ziegfeld hired a man dressed as a waiter to surprise customers by "spontaneously" juggling as he walked between tables during the show. The highlight of the first *Frolic* centered around a suspended glass walkway that hung over the first row of tables. Under the walkway were red, white, and blue lights. When twenty-four chorines danced on the walkway, their images were reflected in the glass, making it look as if they were dancing on their heads. Blowers under the walkway made the girls' skirts billow upward. However, each girl wore ankle-length bloomers to maintain propriety.

In the interest of propriety, Ziegfeld established a cardinal rule that prohibited his young female employees from socializing with patrons. Ziegfeld insisted that the girls maintain a certain distance from the patrons, yet he still wanted the audience to feel involved in the show. In the first edition, girls ran out with balloons fastened to their gowns and headpieces, singing "I Want Someone to Make a Fuss over Me." As they walked about the platform, men's cigars sometimes touched and accidentally burst the balloons. To make the patrons feel even more involved, Ziegfeld put a wooden hammer at each place setting. If an audience member desired an encore, he was instructed to bang his hammer on the table. The *Midnight Frolic* became a testing ground for new talent; if patrons banged their hammers after a specific act, Ziegfeld knew he had found a possible addition to the *Follies*.

Staging the entire production was Ned Wayburn, the third person to bring new life to the *Follies*. The well-established director of musicals was "slope-shouldered, fat, bespectacled, always wearing a beret and a large floppy cardigan with his initials on the left lapel."[13] It was the first time Wayburn had worked for Ziegfeld, and his desire to prove that he was up to the task often made him seem callous. He was not as lenient as Ziegfeld and did not have the producer's "bedside manner."[14] Wayburn's iron hand frightened some of the less experienced showgirls. "Dumb clucks with two left feet had better learn their routine!" he yelled if a chorine tripped during a rehearsal.[15] Wayburn was especially adamant that the girls not make any mistakes while performing what came to be known as the "Ziegfeld walk." The walk required the girls to strut with their arms outstretched and their chins lifted in an aloof and detached manner that mesmerized audiences. The Ziegfeld walk was ultimately Wayburn's most lasting contribution to Ziegfeld's shows. To aid Wayburn, Julian Mitchell returned to Ziegfeld's employ after a brief parting of ways. Mitchell was as strict a taskmaster as Wayburn. The girls called Mitchell "the old bastard" behind his back, knowing full well he was deaf and could not hear them.[16]

Such backstage discord did not give Ziegfeld confidence in his new endeavor. "I'm nearly off my nut trying to get this roof show right—looks rotten. Can't find girls to sing songs in a cute way," he wrote to a friend.[17] However, his pessimism was once again for naught. After it opened on January 5, 1915, the *Frolic* was such a hit that Ziegfeld raised the admission price from $1 to $2 (in 2013 currency, an increase from $22 to $45). None of the patrons complained. Some paid even more than $2 to secure tables on the floor. Eddie Cantor later called the New Amsterdam roof "the supper club of the 400."[18] Will Rogers, who climbed to fame in the *Frolic,* described the venue as being "for folks with lots of money and plenty of insomnia.... There has never been anything to equal it since then."[19] Billie, upon hearing of the *Frolic's* success, wired Ziegfeld from Hollywood: "I tell you darling you are an artist standing alone. I am crazy for you to get more productions opening and make use of that clever brain of yours. How I should love to have been there."[20]

Ziegfeld's investment in the *Frolic* went far in making him an "artist standing alone." His rooftop supper club was an original concept; no one could say he was still merely imitating himself.

One afternoon in 1915, Billie convinced Ziegfeld to accompany her to a fashion show. Before she started filming *Peggy,* she desired a bit of leisure time to view the latest creations of her favorite designer, Lucile Duff Gordon. Lucile had relocated to New York and was more popular than ever—especially after she survived the sinking of the *Titanic* in 1912. In America, Lucile discovered that fashion shows were the ideal way to present to clients the swiftly changing clothing trends of the 1910s. The fashion world had changed since Anna Held had first come to New York; Paris was no longer the last word in the latest styles. During World War I, transporting gowns from Europe to America was difficult, and buying insurance against enemy submarines was so expensive that Parisian couturiers could send only a few dresses at a time. "Without the lead of Paris, New York was lost sartorially, for the American designers were not equal to the occasion, and were turning out some frightful garments," Lucile claimed. "So I became an institution, the established leader of the fashions in America."[21] Once she established her dress shop in New York, she could hardly keep up with the orders.

Ziegfeld, despite his passion for elaborate garments, was nonplussed at the idea of spending an entire afternoon watching Billie pick out gowns for the new season. Nevertheless, he agreed to accompany her. Donning his black mink-lined coat, he escorted Billie to one of their Rolls Royce automobiles, prepared to be thoroughly bored. Upon arriving at Lucile's, Billie sighed and fawned over the gorgeous gowns that best complemented her copper hair and effervescent personality. Lucile, among other things, was known for her "personality gowns," which she individualized based on a client's mood and character. Each dress had an amusing title of its own— the innocent "School Girl," the refined "Salut d'Amour," and the provocative "Red Mouth of a Venomous Flower" or "Incessant Soft Desire."[22] The most creative titles were the brainchildren of Lucile's sister, society novelist and future silent film scenarist Elinor Glyn.

Lucile best displayed the variously titled gowns in her "mannequin parades," in which "living mannequins" strutted against backdrops representative of parties, dances, and shopping trips. Lucile's fashion shows were like mini-productions, "using ramps, curtains, wings, limelight, and music."[23] The shows became such popular events that she eventually moved them to a theater with a 3,000-seat capacity. "To one of these parades came that maker of stars, Florenz Ziegfeld," Lucile recalled in her memoir. "He sat there in the stalls, a quiet man among the wives and daughters of the Four Hundred."[24]

At first, Ziegfeld was disinterested as he sat in a gilt-edged chair against the wall. But the moment Lucile's models entered, they grabbed his attention, and he completely forgot that he was supposed to be bored. One "mannequin" in particular caught his eye—a tall, regal, somewhat supercilious model named Rose Dolores (better known simply as Dolores). She slunk across the stage dressed in an Eastern brocade gown à la the Arabian Nights. Though the parade went on for three hours, Lucile noted that "Mr. Ziegfeld sat it all out to the end."[25] Billie, noting her husband's rapt attention, "sat back in her chair, on her lips a soft smile that her husband was too intent to notice."[26] Little did Ziegfeld know that Billie had had ulterior motives in bringing him to the fashion show. She knew Lucile's innovative styles and presentation perfectly complemented Ziegfeld's taste and his idea of showmanship.

After the living mannequin show, Ziegfeld hastened backstage and said to Lucile, "without preliminary": "I've got to have that scene of yours for my *Follies*. You can ask any terms you like for it . . . I'd especially like Dolores.

Living mannequins. That's what I've been trying to do since the beginning, and you've been doing it for years in London. I'd like you to be my principal designer for the *Follies*. And I'd like to use most of the models I've seen here tonight."[27] Lucile, wearing a masculine collar and tie with her tailored suit, turned her strong-featured face to Ziegfeld and informed him, "I do not sell my models. I devise productions to please myself." Before Ziegfeld could attempt to persuade her, Lucile suddenly smiled and said, "I would consider it greatly pleasing to myself to work in the *Follies*."[28] So Lucile became the fourth talent to help the *Follies* reach their highest standard.

The next five years (1915–1920) were crucial to the evolution of the Ziegfeld girl. As Lucile explained in her memoir: "That first little scene of mine [living mannequins] which Ziegfeld introduced into his *Follies* made theatrical history in one sense, for it introduced 'the show girl,' who was there simply to look beautiful and wear beautiful clothes, as opposed to the chorus girl, who was there to sing and dance and generally hold the show together."[29] According to Broadway historians Michael Kantor and Laurence Maslon, Ziegfeld's chorines were divided into four categories: the stars, the dancers, the Ziegfeld girls (most well represented by the strutting beauties in the *Frolic*), and the statuesque beauties of the tableaux.[30] The "living mannequins" constituted the final category of *Follies* girls (excluding the unique niche filled by Fanny Brice) and crystallized Ziegfeld's ambition to keep his showgirls on a celestial plane, untouchable by the audience. In 1915 *Day Book* quoted Ziegfeld as saying there was no earthly use for the old notion of a showgirl—a vacuous, tall, gorgeous clotheshorse. Ziegfeld had a democratic philosophy when it came to picking showgirls; they could be short or tall; blonde, brunette, or redhead; poor or rich. When choosing his chorus members, he paid special attention to their feet and hands. "You can tell a lot about a girl that way," he stated. What further attracted him to a potential chorine was, in Ziegfeld's words, "her personality, her brittleness—the number of grains of purport that she's able to percolate per second—and then of course—there's the coloring." Still very much a newlywed, he added: "Personally I like it [a young woman's coloring] very vivid—red."[31] But above all, a showgirl had to have "brains and common sense." Ziegfeld concluded that "the cocktail drinking, cigarette smoking makes no hit with me."[32] Press agent Bernard Sobel later wrote that "the *Follies* was really a university with Ziegfeld as the head." And in fact, many of the girls under Ziegfeld's employ were university graduates and "great readers."[33]

However selective Ziegfeld was, he could not completely avoid choosing some showgirls who, like Lillian Lorraine, were beautiful but had no common sense and were fond of the unsavory high life. Backstage, many of the girls argued over who had more jewelry or fur. Rivalries also arose over who attracted the longest line of men at the stage door. Ziegfeld did his best to dissuade such girls from seeking employment in the *Follies* by making the following statement:

> There is a prevalent impression that once a girl is enlisted under the Ziegfeld standard, her troubles are over and her hard work is ended. What a mistake! Let us hope that for many it does mean the end of trouble so far as earning a livelihood is concerned, that it means happy and comfortable home living honestly earned. But ... a Ziegfeld production is no place for a drone or an idler ... they [showgirls] ... put in ... hours ... in striving to come nearer to perfection in that which is expected of them to do before the footlights ... there is not one honest, wholesome walk of life from which they have not come. .... Maybe she is a chambermaid, but if she has the necessary talent and qualities a place awaits her in the Ziegfeld ranks.[34]

Ziegfeld had perfected his vision of the Ziegfeld girl and elevated her status; women all over the country sought to imitate her. No longer an impresario extraordinaire, he belonged in a category of his own: the Great Ziegfeld. His name, along with "*Follies* girl," entered the English lexicon as synonyms for the last word in glamour and taste.[35]

Largely due to Joseph Urban's sets, Ned Wayburn's dance direction, and Lucile's gowns, the 1915 edition of the *Follies* "affirmed beyond any doubt Ziegfeld's preeminence in the field of elaborate revues."[36] The show opened on June 21, 1915, at the New Amsterdam Theatre between the first *Midnight Frolic* in January and the second *Frolic* in August. Lucile insisted that her gowns be bathed in blue light, which had a great impact on Urban. His use of primarily blue tones became so much a part of his style that eventually a shade of blue was named for him. In the *Follies of 1915* Urban's use of blue flowed from scene to scene with seemingly effortless continuity. The most opulent and praised number of the show used simulated underwater effects at the "gates of Elysium." Water-spouting elephants guarded each side of the gate. As the water poured from their trunks, Aphrodite rose from the pool and signaled a group of mermaids to dance.

The most rousing numbers in the show played on the audience's patriotic spirit and glorified not only girls but also US cities and the American way of life. During "Hello Frisco," singers Bernard Granville and Ina Claire stood before a map of America with a line drawn between New York and San Francisco. The song paid homage to the first transcontinental telephone call accomplished that year. However, the theme of being separated from one's love was what most touched audiences. Billie Burke later asserted that Gene Buck had been inspired to write "Hello Frisco" after overhearing Ziegfeld on the telephone as he tried to get through to her numerous times while she was in San Francisco filming *Peggy*. A string of flag-waving spectacles followed the "Frisco" number. Among them was "If Girlies Could Be Soldiers," featuring chorines as "combatants for male affection." The number was consistent with Ziegfeld's past depictions of sexually aggressive, dominant women.

The *Follies of 1915* had as much top-notch comedy as spectacle and song. The most lauded comical numbers featured Bert Williams, Ed Wynn, and a newcomer to the Ziegfeld family and stock company, W. C. Fields. Williams kept audiences in stitches as a hall boy eavesdropping on the tenants of an apartment house. Wynn's number poked fun at the emerging film industry. In the skit, he played a film director telling everyone onstage where to go, including Leon Errol as a clumsy villain. Wynn also made a hit performing a monologue in which he told the audience what he would have done if he had been given an entire role in the show. But it was W. C. Fields who, according to Eddie Cantor, kept "audiences screaming without [saying] a word."[37] Fields's skit had no dialogue; it simply showed a man playing billiards with himself. Fields's trade was making people laugh, but offstage he was a misanthrope. He was overly fond of drink and once said his blood was so full of alcohol that doctors used it to sterilize their instruments. Ziegfeld had little tolerance for anyone who overindulged in alcohol, and he disliked Fields more than any other humorist he had ever hired, but he kept the cranky comedian under contract because audiences loved him.

On the heels of the *Follies* came another *Midnight Frolic*. The August edition introduced two more new members of the Ziegfeld flock. The first was Will Rogers, a soft-spoken Oklahoman cowboy with a talent for twirling the lasso. Gene Buck had seen Will's lariat act at another theater and immediately alerted Ziegfeld about the prospective new star. "He twirls a lariat and tells jokes. Do you really believe New York society would be interested in such an act?" Ziegfeld asked.

Will was the first person to agree that he was no sophisticate. He once stated: "I stayed in fourth grade so long I got to know more about McGuffey's Reader than Mr. McGuffey."[38] Buck seemed to be the only one who believed in Will and his potential audience appeal. "I've already hired him," he told Ziegfeld. "I guess New York society will have to like him," Ziegfeld grumbled. After he saw Will's act, he was still grumbling. "I'd like you to let him go today. He can't be in the show," Ziegfeld told Buck.

Confident that Buck would fire Will, Ziegfeld left town and returned a week later to find that the cowboy was still performing in the *Frolic*. In fact, Will had asked for a $50 a week raise and proposed a change in his act. "Mrs. Rogers doesn't like my jokes any more than the audience seems to. She says I oughta talk about what I read in the papers," Will had explained. "Comments of that sort could cause a lawsuit, but let's give it a chance," Buck decided. They gave it a chance, and Will's revised act proved to be an enormous success. Upon Ziegfeld's return, Buck assured him that if he watched the *Frolic* that night, any thought of firing the cowboy would leave his mind. Ziegfeld grudgingly agreed.

Will stood in the center of the lavish dance floor dressed in a cowboy outfit, languidly twirling his lasso. "The reason Mr. Z keeps me here is 'cause the people seem to, after seeing my act . . . drink more. . . . You know I am going to stick with this fellow. I am off all the shows that go in for art. I am for Ziegfeld and dames. . . . Somebody has to do something while the girls change clothes even if they don't have much to change." Walking closer to the tables and nodding at the cigars beside each patron's plate, Will continued: "We have the greatest indoor sport in the world called bursting of toy balloons. All you have to do is leave your wife at home and get a front table, light a good ten cent cigar, get a good bottle of wine. Of course the more wine you have the further you will reach for a balloon." Next he chose a controversial topic: politics. Will's target was secretary of state and three-time losing presidential candidate William Jennings Bryan. "Bryan is against every public issue that comes up—about the only thing he is pleased with is *himself* . . . God bless you is about the only thing *he says* for nothing."[39] The audience did not seem to take offense; they only laughed more heartily.

Though Ziegfeld did not crack a smile during Will's entire monologue, he raised the comedian's salary to $220 a week. Ziegfeld eventually admitted, "He's the only comic who doesn't make me want to hide in my office." Will Rogers became known as a twentieth-century Mark Twain for his clever and wry comments on politics and society. He always began his monologues with this line: "All I know is what I read in the papers." What made Will popular nationwide was his ability to connect with people of all classes. "He never looked up to the mighty or spoke down to the masses . . . to a troubled world he brought a little peace of mind with a little piece of rope," Eddie Cantor wrote.[40]

Although it seems unlikely that an unrefined ex-cowhand and a polished Broadway producer would have anything in common, there were some unexpected similarities. Will was born in 1879 in Oklahoma to a mother of Cherokee descent. He grew up on his family's ranch and spent his idle hours playing with his lasso and wishing he could join the cowboys rounding up cattle. That ranch was much like the one Ziegfeld had so enjoyed visiting during the summer of his sixteenth year. Will abandoned school in tenth grade to become a *real* cowboy, but that never happened; however, he did play one onstage. In 1902 and 1903 Will traveled in South Africa with Texas Jack's Wild West Show, where he did roping tricks and dubbed himself the "Cherokee Kid." That show was much like Buffalo Bill Cody's Wild West Show, which had so fascinated the young Ziegfeld. If men like Diamond Jim Brady and Joseph Urban appealed to Ziegfeld's desire for the decadent or elegant life, Will Rogers appealed to his underlying desire for a simple, rustic existence. "They appreciated the same things," Patricia Ziegfeld later said in an interview. "My father and Will were outdoor people."[41] Ziegfeld did not have nicknames for any of his stars except for Will, whom he called "Bill." Will always referred to his employer and friend as Mr. Ziegfeld, but he deliberately mispronounced it "Zigfield," knowing full well that the common mistake was one of Ziegfeld's pet peeves.

The second new member of the August *Midnight Frolic* was a chorus girl who, like Lillian Lorraine, gained fame not for her comedic, singing, or dancing abilities but for her stunning appearance. Olive Thomas was a twenty-one-year-old beauty with a heart-shaped face and a rosebud mouth. In a 1914 contest she had been heralded the most beautiful girl in New York City. Billie Burke described her as "one of those girls Flo rolled $20 gold pieces with on the roof. The girls always won."[42] Ziegfeld instantly became infatuated with Olive. He and Billie had been apart for nearly the entire first year of their marriage, but Billie did not consider that justification for infidelity. Ziegfeld loved Billie, but his obsession with beautiful women made her doubt his faithfulness. Based on his attentions to Olive, he clearly did not maintain the distance from his showgirls that he demanded between the girls and their patrons. No proof exists that he actually had an affair with Olive, but there is no doubt that he favored her over the other showgirls.

As attentive as Ziegfeld was to his favorite showgirls, not all of them saw him as a "wolf." Many thought of him as a benign father figure. Marcelle Earle described him as a "handsome well-groomed man with a certain air of suaveness and distinction about him." When she came to him with her troubles, he smiled at her in his "kindly" and "benevolent" way and called her "my dear little girl" in his "pleasant nasal twang."[43] Pearl and Doris Eaton, who were regular *Frolic* and *Follies* cast members, had similar experiences. Ziegfeld's first comment about Pearl was that "any girl with legs that beautiful ought to be in our show," but he kept his admiration at a platonic level. Doris recalled, "We all were aware of the rumors about his incessant sexual escapades with Ziegfeld Girls, but he never made a pass at any of us and we could not have been treated better."[44] If Ziegfeld had been merely a benevolent patriarch to all the girls, Billie would have had no need to worry. But Patricia Ziegfeld admitted that her father had little control over his attractions: "When you're in that position and women want jobs sometimes the temptation is too great."[45]

While finishing her work on *Peggy* in California, Billie received many wires from "well-meaning" friends informing her of her husband's conspicuous interest in Olive Thomas. The same well-meaning friends also recounted stories of Ziegfeld's yacht parties on the Hudson with no shortage of beautiful chorines in attendance. Thomas Ince offered Billie a contract with Triangle Studio, but because accepting the offer would have meant remaining in California for five years, she turned it down. Billie wanted to save her marriage.

Upon hearing the rumors of Ziegfeld's behavior in her absence, Billie's quick temper flared. She traveled to San Francisco and wired her husband, demanding that he join her. Adding to her anger was the careless way Ziegfeld handled their money. At the rate he was spending, he was putting her beloved Burkeley Crest at risk. The illusions she had about her husband came down one by one, and Billie emerged from what she called her "fantasia" to face the harsh truth. One afternoon Billie was notified that she had withdrawn $900 from her bank account, but she had done no such thing. When she confronted Ziegfeld about it, she discovered that he had used her money to cover debts and expenses for his most recent production. Billie was exasperated. "He deliberately spent more on a production than it could possibly return even as a smash hit with all seats sold out for a full season," she ruefully commented.[46]

As perturbed as Billie was over Ziegfeld's spending habits, her primary concern was his fidelity. Ziegfeld responded to Billie's demands and rushed to San Francisco to meet her. As was his custom, he pulled a diamond from his pocket as means of making amends. Anna Held may have been satisfied with this form of apology, but Billie threw the jewelry across the room. In a storm of "blazing, red-headed jealousy," Billie tore down curtains, smashed lamps and china, and flung herself to the floor in tears.[47] Ziegfeld sat expressionless and silent in an overstuffed chair. When Billie had expended all her energy, Ziegfeld finally spoke: "The trouble with you Billie is that when you accuse me, you pick the wrong girl."[48] Bewildered and hurt, Billie returned to New York alone, hoping that Ziegfeld would follow her and beg her not to leave him.

And in his own way, Ziegfeld did plead with Billie to stay with him. Using business as a peace offering, Ziegfeld endeavored to find her more work in the film industry. He knew that Billie was happiest when she was working, and based on *Peggy*'s positive reception when it premiered in January 1916, he felt that Billie's future lay in film. However, he knew that he and Billie could not live at opposite ends of the country. The film industry still thrived at a number of New York studios, and surely she could work at one of them.

Ziegfeld found Billie's next potential assignment sooner than he expected. When Max Annenberg, the circulation manager for the *Chicago Tribune,* came to Ziegfeld's room at the Ansonia for a drink, he caught sight of Billie's picture atop the piano. "I'd like to see her face in every movie theater in the country. The theater is too small for her. What would you say to $100,000 for thirty weeks' work in a new movie serial?" Annenberg asked. He was the first to combine newspaper marketing and circulation with the designing, casting, and producing of movies.

"That's far too little," Ziegfeld said. "$150,000."

"That's never been done! Not even Mary Pickford gets that much."

"$150,000," Ziegfeld repeated.

Annenberg did not argue a second time. Billie won the lead role in the film serial entitled *Gloria's Romance*. The twenty-part series featured a fantastical plot and Billie's portrayal of a young heiress who, after driving her car off the road and into the ocean, must find her way back to her Palm Beach estate. During the trek home, she encountered alligators and Indians, among other things. The film was set to open at Dillingham's Globe Theatre, with a live orchestra playing music composed and conducted by Billie and Ziegfeld's friend and associate Jerome Kern.

"Is there any chance for glamour?" Ziegfeld asked Annenberg during the serial's production. Annenberg assured him there was no lack of glamour in the film. Billie would appear in settings that included a society ball, a courtroom, and a sickbed, where she would be wearing invaluable jewels. "Billie is the best actress who ever lived," Ziegfeld stated. "She deserves the best."[49]

Billie was pleased with the role Ziegfeld had negotiated for her, but she had not forgotten their quarrel completely. To erase any lingering bad feelings, Ziegfeld acquired a private railroad car for her trips between shooting locations. Additionally, he purchased a Rolls Royce painted in her signature color of powder blue and had her initials engraved on its doors. He also secured the use of the Cartier gems she would be wearing in the film. He then obtained permission for her to live at Burkeley Crest and work short hours when shooting on Long Island. As a final grand gesture, Ziegfeld rented a Palm Beach mansion for Billie while she filmed in Florida. When Ziegfeld came to visit in Florida, Billie's wariness seemed to have disappeared. But they found that laughter rather than elaborate gifts was what truly reconciled them. Because of the way color translated to black-and-white film, Billie had to wear the strangest hues of makeup. Her face was green, her lips were purple, and she wore special eye makeup to prevent her blue eyes from photographing as white. Looking at herself with Ziegfeld in the mirror, her appearance sent her into such a fit of giggles that she could not compose herself enough to film a scene that required her to be carried to a couch after an illness. The set was closed for the rest of the day. Billie and Ziegfeld went home in the blue Rolls Royce, still giggling.[50]

Though it seemed that Ziegfeld and Billie were fully reconciled, Billie maintained a pretense of coolness upon her return to New York. She claimed they would remain Mr. and Mrs. Ziegfeld only because there was $150,000 in it for them. The pretense fell away after Ziegfeld came to Billie one afternoon and told her, in his laconic fashion, that everything had been straightened out (presumably between him and Olive Thomas) and they had nothing to worry about. Billie watched his face carefully but saw no "telltale quirks at the corner of his mouth" that appeared when he was "being cavalier with the truth."[51] The fact that he had redecorated the suite at the Ansonia with dozens of photos of Billie certainly bolstered her belief that her marriage was safe. Yet she realized that she "could not hope to remain Mrs. Ziegfeld and at the same time become a motion picture star."[52] The poor reception of *Gloria's Romance* at the box office dealt her a severe blow after the success of *Peggy*. The series failed not only because audiences found the films too fantastical but also because the serial format was losing popularity.

As a single woman, Billie's philosophy had been that she would leave the stage behind if she ever found a man she loved more than her art. So far, she had been unable to live that philosophy. At the start of her marriage, she had had to fulfill her obligations to Frohman; then Ziegfeld's debts had made it necessary for her to pursue work in films. Now, Ziegfeld's success with the *Frolics* and Billie's handsome salaries from her film work enabled her to dedicate herself to being a homemaker. Billie's first goal was to make Burkeley Crest reflect both her and Ziegfeld's tastes. At present, the estate reflected only her and her mother's weakness for anything in the French country style. But Billie wanted Burkeley Crest to be something special to both her and her husband; as a couple, they were "city bred but incurably romantic about the country."[53] When he was not on Broadway, Ziegfeld needed a place where he could escape from his role as impresario, often working eighteen- to twenty-hour days. According to Patricia Ziegfeld, once a production opened, her father went through a period of nausea and moodiness. Some employees claimed he "flew into unjustified rages" over some perceived betrayal, but he was "quick to forgive—and equally quick to confess his own faults."[54] Such uncharacteristic displays of temper were proof that Ziegfeld desperately needed to distance himself from work, and Burkeley Crest was the ideal place to do that. When Ziegfeld returned to the estate after a marathon of rehearsals, he would sigh, "To hell with it," and take to bed for two or three days. Billie, though temperamental herself, was different from the other women he had known; she was a steady presence in the midst of his chaotic work life. She remained strong and completely free of self-pity as he "swung from one mood extreme to the other."[55]

What finally made Ziegfeld see Burkeley Crest as his true home was the news that Billie was awaiting, as one newspaper writer put it, an "interesting event."[56] That "interesting event" turned out to be a baby. Ziegfeld was a doting father even before his child was born; he spent $500 on blue outfittings for the nursery at the Ansonia, just in case Billie and the baby ever needed to stay in the city. Blue was the color of choice not because he assumed he would have a son but because blue was Ziegfeld's favorite color and Billie's signature color onstage.

His impending fatherhood so elated Ziegfeld that he made it his mission to let the entire nation know the news. He arranged so many interviews and photo sessions for Billie that it was difficult to open a newspaper without seeing images of her fondling a palm branch in her solarium or sitting in her parlor wearing a loose yet glamorous gown. Reporters lapped up her thoughts on the avant-garde concept of prenatal influences. Billie told *Day Book* that to help her child be born joyous rather than hypersensitive, she "tried not [to] get annoyed," "enjoy[ed] simple things," and engaged in "plenty of outdoor exercise." One method Billie used to keep depression at bay was surrounding herself with "sunshiny" colors. "Dull, ugly colors affect me terribly," Billie told journalist Antoinette Donnelly.[57] As difficult as it was, she also tried not to fall into introspection that could fuel unhappy thoughts. She advised pregnant women to find some "engrossing work" to keep their minds occupied.[58]

Billie's engrossing work was making improvements to Burkeley Crest and encouraging Ziegfeld in his work. Now that she was "retired" from show business for the time being, Billie was able to attend her husband's shows and was in the audience almost every night. Billie caused quite a stir whenever she entered the New Amsterdam Theatre. According to Marcelle Earle, "a big fuss would herald the arrival of the famous redhead, scintillating star. The ushers (and all others concerned) would make sure she was comfortable for she was expecting."[59] During this period a new tradition began: the *Follies* could not start until Billie had taken her seat and nodded to the orchestra conductor.

Ziegfeld, assured that his marriage was intact, returned to work with renewed vigor. He entered another marathon of rehearsals for the *Ziegfeld Follies of 1916*, two new editions of the *Midnight Frolic*, and *The Century Girl*, a new show with a score by Irving Berlin. Ziegfeld's shows were like his babies, and they needed as much nurturing and guidance as a newborn. If he wanted his productions to be original, Ziegfeld knew he had to outdo himself each year, and 1916 was no exception.

Florenz Ziegfeld as a young man in Chicago, circa 1894. (Courtesy of Billy Rose Theatre Division, New York Public Library for the Performing Arts; Astor, Lenox, and Tilden Foundations)

Advertisement for Ziegfeld's first star, Eugen Sandow, 1894. (Courtesy of Library of Congress Prints and Photographs Division)

Eugen Sandow in a Grecian pose, 1894. (Courtesy of Library of Congress Prints and Photographs Division)

Ziegfeld's first wife, Anna Held, 1897. (Photo by W. M. Morrison; courtesy of Library of Congress Prints and Photographs Division)

Anna Held in one of her many elaborate gowns, 1897. (Photo by W. M. Morrison; courtesy of Library of Congress Prints and Photographs Division)

The Hotel Ansonia, where Ziegfeld kept a suite during most of his career on Broadway. (Courtesy of Library of Congress Prints and Photographs Division)

Ziegfeld's first chorines, billed as the Anna Held Girls, circa 1906. (Courtesy of Historical Ziegfeld Group)

Sheet music for Anna Held's hit song from *The Parisian Model,* circa 1907. (Courtesy of Historical Ziegfeld Group)

Nora Bayes and Jack Norworth performing their "Shine on, Harvest Moon" number in the *Follies of 1908.* (Courtesy of Historical Ziegfeld Group)

Lillian Lorraine in her airplane number for the *Follies of 1909*. (Courtesy of Library of Congress Prints and Photographs Division)

Fanny Brice, circa 1910. (Courtesy of Jerry Murbach)

Follies dancers Rosie and Jenny Dolly, circa 1912. (Courtesy of Jerry Murbach)

Front façade of the New Amsterdam Theatre, with advertisements for the *Ziegfeld Follies of 1925*. (Courtesy of Historical Ziegfeld Group)

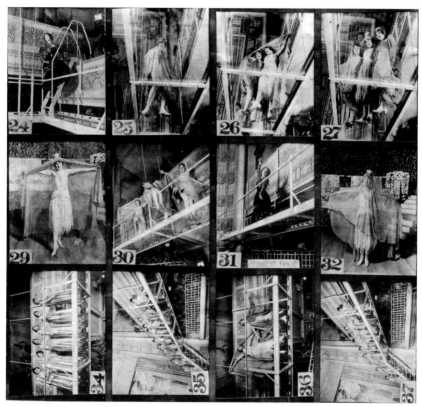

A variety of scenes from the 1915 *Midnight Frolic*. The top and bottom rows show the walkway suspended over the dining area of the rooftop garden. (Photo by White Studio; courtesy of Billy Rose Theatre Division, New York Public Library for the Performing Arts)

Billie Burke in one of her many Rolls Royces in the driveway of Burkeley Crest, circa 1914. (Courtesy of Library of Congress Prints and Photographs Division)

Olive Thomas when she worked for Ziegfeld, circa 1915. (Courtesy of Historical Ziegfeld Group)

Bert Williams, circa 1916.
(Courtesy of Jerry Murbach)

Ziegfeld and Billie enjoying
a ride in Palm Beach
during the filming of
Gloria's Romance (1916).
(Authors' collection)

Billie Burke in *Caesar's Wife* (1919). (Authors' collection)

Will Rogers, Ziegfeld's favorite comedian and best friend, circa 1916. (Courtesy of Library of Congress Prints and Photographs Division)

Billie Burke and Patricia in a photo from 1918. (*El Paso Herald,* June 4, 1918; courtesy of Library of Congress)

A souvenir program for *The Century Girl,* with a painting of Bessie McCoy by Raphael Kirchner, 1916. (Courtesy of Historical Ziegfeld Group)

From left: Justine Johnson, Bernard Granville, and Ina Claire in the patriotic *Ziegfeld Follies of 1916.* (Courtesy of Historical Ziegfeld Group)

Lillian Lorraine, Ziegfeld's mistress, on the cover of the sheet music for "Tackin' 'Em Down," 1918. (Courtesy of Performing Arts Encyclopedia— Musical Theater—The Library of Congress Celebrates the Songs of America)

A Raphael Kirchner painting of one of Ziegfeld's favorite chorines, Marcelle Earle, on the sheet music for "Ziegfeld Follies Rag," 1917. (Courtesy of Performing Arts Encyclopedia—Musical Theater—The Library of Congress Celebrates the Songs of America)

"Garden of My Dreams," from the *Ziegfeld Follies of 1918*. (Courtesy of Library of Congress Historic American Sheet Music 1850–1929 American Memory Collection)

A classic Alfred Cheney
Johnston shot of Ziegfeld girl
Alma Mamay, circa 1918.
(Courtesy of Jerry Murbach)

Dolores, the "living mannequin,"
in a fabulous Lucile creation,
circa 1918. (Courtesy of Jerry
Murbach)

MARION DAVIES
in "The Ziegfeld Follies"
Photograph by White, N. Y.

Marion Davies, mistress of Ziegfeld's benefactor William Randolph Hearst, in 1918, during her time as a Ziegfeld girl. (Courtesy of Historical Ziegfeld Group)

W. C. Fields, Ziegfeld's least
favorite comedian, circa 1918.
(Courtesy of Jerry Murbach)

A selection of scenes from the *Follies of 1919*. Marilyn Miller is riding the horse in
the top left photo, and Marcelle Earle is in the center of the top right photo.
(Photos by White Studio; courtesy of Billy Rose Theatre Division, New York
Public Library for the Performing Arts)

A typical Ben Ali Haggin tableau entitled "The Witching Hour" from a *Midnight Frolic,* circa 1920. (Courtesy of Historical Ziegfeld Group)

Irving Berlin, Ziegfeld's friend and songwriter for his shows, circa 1920. (Courtesy of Performing Arts Encyclopedia—Musical Theater—The Library of Congress Celebrates the Songs of America)

A selection of scenes from Ziegfeld's hit show *Sally* (1920), which featured Marilyn Miller, Leon Errol, and Dolores. (Photos by White Studio; courtesy of Billy Rose Theatre Division, New York Public Library for the Performing Arts)

Billie Burke (far left) at her desk in the sunny parlor of Burkeley Crest, circa 1922. (Courtesy of Hastings Historical Society)

Mary Eaton, Marilyn Miller's successor and the female lead in *Kid Boots,* circa 1920. (Courtesy of Jerry Murbach)

Billie, Patricia, and Ziegfeld with one of their dogs at Burkeley Crest, circa 1923.
(Courtesy of Hastings Historical Society)

Burkeley Crest, circa 1923. (Courtesy of Hastings Historical Society)

9

The Past Becomes Ashes

In 1916 every musical producer on Broadway was determined to outdo his competitors—primarily to see who could create the most American revue. As the United States drew closer to war, American composers worked harder than ever to crystallize the sound of American music. Irving Berlin had pioneered the American sound through ragtime, but two new composers—Cole Porter and George Gershwin—continued the quest to set America's voice to music. Porter made his debut in *See America First* (1916), while Gershwin got his start in the Shuberts' *Passing Show* (1916). Competing with the latter was the *Cohan Revue of 1916.* George M. Cohan had revolutionized musical theater by creating shows in which the music flowed naturally from the plot; he had now decided to try his hand at producing a revue. His show burlesqued prominent people and inventions of the time and even included "a generous tribute to Ziegfeld."[1] Theater historian Gerald Bordman noted that despite the contributions of exciting new talents like Porter and Gershwin, there was "a discernible drop in [the] quality" of musical shows in the 1916–1917 theater season.[2] This was not true, however, of Ziegfeld's productions. For this reason, he triumphed over his rivals and continued to hold the lead in both revues and musicals.

Beautiful girls and funny comedians, especially in Ziegfeld's phenomenal *Midnight Frolic,* helped the producer maintain his lofty place in the theater world. The best-received "girlie number" in Ziegfeld's new *Frolic,* which opened on January 24, 1916, was different from former ones: it ended with a laugh. In that number, a lingerie salesman showed the audience a series of drawings of women wearing less and less lingerie. Models dressed in wardrobes to match the drawings stepped onstage one by one. For the last picture, audience members leaned forward and held their breaths, wondering if Ziegfeld would actually allow full nudity onstage.

Then Will Rogers stepped forward dressed as a masked marvel. The audience heaved a sigh of relief and burst into laughter.

Following the premiere of the January *Frolic*, Ziegfeld and Billie enjoyed a short respite in Palm Beach before he had to hurry back to New York to begin preparations for his next show. *The Century Girl* (named after the Century Theatre, where it would play) had all the elements of a hit. The score was written by men from opposite ends of the American music spectrum: Irving Berlin and Victor Herbert. Herbert was the foremost composer in the field of operettas, including the enormous hits *Babes in Toyland* (1903) and *Naughty Marietta* (1910). Berlin's songs, in contrast, were driven by lyrics, which made them easy to integrate into the plot of a show. Costumes by Lucile, scenery by Joseph Urban, and comic relief from Leon Errol and Marie Dressler added to *The Century Girl's* appeal.

There was one hitch: the Century Theatre was located in Columbus Circle, quite a distance from Forty-Second Street and the theater district. To attract attention to the out-of-the-way locale, Ziegfeld hired an Austrian artist, Raphael Kirchner, to paint ten enormous portraits for the lobby, using Ziegfeld's showgirls as the models. Ziegfeld advertised that the artist's work alone was reason enough to attend the theater. Kirchner's breathtaking, colorful style blended realism with Art Nouveau and glorified the Ziegfeld girls to an extent not seen before. The drawings were printed in the show's program and were the first of many portrait series Ziegfeld commissioned from Kirchner. To further glorify the ladies of the chorus, Ziegfeld began an association with another accomplished artist, Alfred Cheney Johnston. Johnston, a society photographer with a degree from New York's National Academy of Design, took breathtaking black-and-white photographs of the Ziegfeld girls. Most of them were seminude but tastefully done in an ancient Greek style. Not all of Johnston's photos were suggestive; he took glamour portraits of Billie, as well as candid shots of Ziegfeld and his family.

Though Billie was not part of the show, *The Century Girl* was a sort of gift from Ziegfeld to his wife. The core theme of the production—the strength of women—was reflective of the era and women's growing role in society. Ziegfeld's previous shows had glorified only women's beauty and had exhibited their strength mainly through sexual aggression. *The Century Girl* celebrated their strength *and* their beauty—without the sex. The production showcased such heroines as Boadicea, Helen of Troy, Joan of Arc, and Empress Josephine. It reflected not only changes in women's roles but also changes in Ziegfeld's personal view of women. Anna Held and Lillian Lorraine, though great celebrities at their zeniths, did not possess the strength he had discovered in Billie. Her impending motherhood only increased her power in his eyes.

The *Ziegfeld Follies of 1916,* set to open on June 12, 1916, did not continue the heroine theme of *The Century Girl,* but a majority of the female performers showcased talents that had nothing to do with their appearance. Female humorists dominated the comedic portion of the revue. The most conspicuous new entry to Ziegfeld's chorus of glorified girls was Marion Davies, the future film star and mistress of William Randolph Hearst. Marion was a fine comedienne, but for the most part, she showed off her dancing ability in the *Follies.* Fanny Brice stole the show with three hilarious song-and-dance numbers: "Becky Is Back in the Ballet," about a clumsy Yiddish girl's futile attempts at a career in ballet; a spoof of the Russian dancer Nijinsky in her now famous "Dying Swan" ballet; and "I'm Bad," satirizing movie vamp Theda Bara. Though not as popular as Fanny Brice, Ina Claire provided much amusement as well, including a humorous but respectful imitation of Billie Burke. The 1916 *Follies* also had beautiful chorines aplenty in the customary ode to the Ziegfeld girl; "If You Were the Only Girl in the World," a Clifford Grey and Nat D. Ayer composition, went on to become one of the most popular tunes of the prewar and wartime eras.

The musical and comedic numbers that were not centered on women had a patriotic theme. One skit, "Recruitment," featured characters with silly names such as "Hazza Gun" and "Maybee Knot" and ended with a spectacle: a zeppelin rose above the stage, several airplanes flew over an enemy ship and sank it, and an Allied submarine rose triumphantly from the sea.

Following the patriotic bits were the specialty numbers, the most notable being Will Rogers in his *Follies* debut. "When we left Oklahoma, I promised my wife and kids that someday I'd make five hundred a week. That was our dream," Will confided to Ziegfeld. When Will received his first paycheck, it was for $500. Ziegfeld made no fuss when, a few months later, Will asked for $600. "I thought your dream was five hundred a week," he said. "It was," Will replied, "but since then we've had another child and he's kicking."[3] Ziegfeld not only raised Will's salary to $600 but also promised him $750 a week for his second year with the *Follies.* "My father and Will had a warm, comfortable, and rare relationship," Patricia Ziegfeld later observed. "They could ask anything of one another and it was as good as done. They had a rapport with one another and could talk about things they couldn't talk about with other people."[4]

Ziegfeld also had a special rapport with another member of his "stock company": Irving Berlin. Irving used Ziegfeld's love of Palm Beach as inspiration for one of the songs in the 1916 *Follies,* "In Florida among the Palms." Like Will Rogers, Irving became a close friend not only to Ziegfeld but also to Billie and was often a guest at Burkeley Crest dinner parties. Billie quickly observed the similarities between her husband and Irving. When he was not being a showman, Ziegfeld was "quiet, dignified, and reserved to the point of being almost ill-at-ease," whereas Billie described Irving as "shy and gentle."[5] The two men's "common shyness actually seemed to be a point of attraction."[6]

For a man who was naturally reserved, producing three shows simultaneously was a considerable strain. That strain began to manifest in Ziegfeld's behavior toward his staff. He would usually go out of his way to show courtesy and understanding, but now, his sudden fits of rage intensified. Constant spats between his office workers were among the main triggers for his temper, but Ziegfeld himself was sometimes the cause of squabbles at the office. He was late for appointments 99 percent of the time, leaving the secretaries to cover for him. Journalist Djuna Barnes described the Herculean task of actually making it past the front office staff and into the producer's office: "Getting at Ziegfeld is a task devoid of principle. You have to be a good liar, wholly daring, and willing to risk your mortal soul . . . the doorkeeper tells you that Mr. Ziegfeld is not there and never will [be] while you stay, and if you see Ziegfeld for himself he will still repeat that he is not there, and say it fearlessly."[7]

A look at Ziegfeld's desk would lead one to believe that he really was not in the office, for he loathed answering mail and often let letters sit unopened for months. He did not allow his secretary or any other well-meaning person to touch the mail or organize the piles of papers on his desk. His future secretary, Matilda Golden, asserted that he actually liked the clutter. During the last hectic and anxious weeks before an opening, Ziegfeld became especially overwhelmed and upset at his staff's "inability to bring order from chaos"—much of which he created himself. "Jesus, what kind of a place am I running here?" he would often exclaim.[8]

The *Ziegfeld Follies of 1916* was ultimately worth the stress. The revue ran for 112 performances, 8 more than the 1915 edition. The *Pittsburgh*

Press raved that the revue was the "greatest thing of its kind you've ever seen—just full of hits, from curtain to curtain—one number better than the next—and the whole thing a whirlwind success from start to finish."[9]

Ten days after the opening of the 1916 *Follies,* Ziegfeld experienced one of his bouts of nausea and fatigue. This spell, however, was more severe than previous ones—serious enough for reporters to print that he was suffering from nervous exhaustion. At this point in his career, he was financially stable and could limit himself to only one production per year. However, he could never turn down an opportunity that came his way; he took on new responsibilities simply because he welcomed the challenge. He had certainly risen to the challenge of winning the unofficial contest to produce the most patriotic revue of 1916. The spoofs on recruitment reflected Americans' eagerness to enter the war and become a world power. Ziegfeld girls symbolized all-American youth and beauty, and the diverse players of different colors and creeds proved that the American Dream was attainable for anybody. "Part of the Ziegfeldian surprise and delight lay in the all-American audience at the New Amsterdam enjoying but also being startled by new ethnic humor," Ethan Mordden observed. "This, Ziegfeld might have said, is how a nation like ours takes its entertainment, scanning the whole of its citizenry for unique attitudes and experiences."[10]

A new challenge—bigger than producing the most American revue and finding the best performers—now awaited Ziegfeld: fatherhood.

Ziegfeld had never changed his bachelor ways for Anna Held, but all of Broadway could see that he was now reconsidering his lifestyle as well as the material he chose for his shows. In 1916 Ziegfeld started to reshape the *Follies* into a higher-toned production, even if it meant the show lost a bit of its "heartiness." *New Yorker* journalist Gilbert Seldes ascribed this desire for a more refined, less raucous show to "the beneficial influence of Miss Burke."[11] Ziegfeld refused to produce a show that contained anything that might offend his wife or child. Billie's "beneficial influence" and their expected child were key factors in keeping "the structure of their [Billie's and Ziegfeld's] fabulous, fractious union" intact.[12] Continuing to make Burkeley Crest their shared home was another key factor in bringing the couple closer together. Up until their child's birth, however, Ziegfeld still spent weeks at a time at the Ansonia to oversee rehearsals.

The makeover of Burkeley Crest was still in progress when the baby arrived. Florenz Patricia Burke Ziegfeld was born in the suite at the Ansonia Hotel on October 23, 1916. She was pink-cheeked with red hair and blue eyes to match her mother's. Ziegfeld may have wanted to be more present in his family's life, but he was not the first to see Billie following their daughter's birth. After pacing the hall outside the suite for hours, he became impatient and took a taxi uptown to the Century Theatre. It was not publicly known, but Ziegfeld had a phobia of doctors, nurses, and blood. At the theater, while watching rehearsals for *The Century Girl*, Irving Berlin approached him and asked, "How's Billie?"

"I don't know. I had to leave," Ziegfeld replied.

"You can't walk out on your wife as she's having your baby," Berlin declared, gathering his hat and coat.[13] He had recently lost his own wife and was only too eager to substitute for Ziegfeld as a doting husband. He was Billie's first visitor after the arrival of baby Florenz, or Patricia, as her parents ultimately chose to call her. Berlin had brought a newspaper with him, and it contained an item about Lillian Lorraine. "What do you know? Lorraine got married," he told Billie.

"That's the last thing I want to hear about," she said, understandably exhausted and moody after giving birth. Berlin blushed, realizing his faux pas. Two days later, he more than compensated for his misstep by presenting Billie with a song composed especially for Patricia titled "You've Got Your Mother's Big Blue Eyes." "If you're half the lady that your mother is, I'll be proud of you," the first line rhapsodized.[14]

Despite Ziegfeld's poor start at being a family man, he eventually took on the role of father more wholeheartedly than anyone could have expected. "He was beside himself," biographer Charles Higham wrote. "And he called a bedroom conference as soon as it was possible, cooing over the crib of pink and white as Billie, in a heap of lilac scented pillows, spoke of every single thing the child had done in her fifteen days of life."[15] For a time, at least, thoughts of Lillian Lorraines and Olive Thomases receded in Ziegfeld's mind. With all sincerity, he told the press: "It is the titian, the red-headed girl who exercises the most catching influence."[16]

Given the happiness he was experiencing in his personal life, Ziegfeld's goal was to saturate his productions with the same emotion. The first show to receive this attention was the fall edition of the *Midnight Frolic*, which premiered on October 2, 1916. Exuberant comedian Eddie Cantor made his debut in this *Frolic*, which truly distinguished the production and made it even more reflective of Ziegfeld's high spirits. Like W. C. Fields and Will Rogers, Eddie added the American flavor that audiences craved.

Born in 1892, Eddie grew up in the ghetto on the Lower East Side of New York, the same area where Irving Berlin and Fanny Brice had spent their formative years. Eddie was orphaned at two years old and learned at an early age to use humor as a means of survival. Eddie's first forays into show business were amateur nights on vaudeville, where he always managed to avoid the "hook." He first presented himself as a Hebrew comic but then tried his luck with blackface, a more popular ethnic humor in the 1910s. He used the same material, but when he did it in blackface, audiences saw the routine as new. His material seemed even fresher because his blackface character was not the stereotypical minstrel. Wearing a pair of bone-rimmed glasses and a wasp-waisted coat, Eddie's character was flamboyant, slightly effeminate, and intellectual. In 1916 Eddie's agent, Max Hart, wired Eddie and said he wanted him to perform for Florenz Ziegfeld. Assuming that Hart had already secured a contract with the Great Glorifier, Eddie burst onto the New Amsterdam roof and declared, "Mr. Ziegfeld, I'm here!" Ziegfeld and Gene Buck were overseeing rehearsals, and the two men gave him blank looks. "I'm *Eddie Cantor!*" the comedian persisted. "Max Hart sent me." Buck and Ziegfeld nodded and decided to let the seemingly delusional young man continue. "What do you do?" Ziegfeld asked. Eddie replied, "Do I ask you what *you* do? You'll see, I'm wonderful!"[17] Ziegfeld managed to crack a smile, if only because of the boy's audacity.

For Eddie's debut in the *Midnight Frolic* he performed in his blackface persona. Before such luminaries as the Astors and Diamond Jim Brady, he announced that he was not a regular actor but a plumber from Hastings whom Mr. Ziegfeld had hired to fix his pipes at Burkeley Crest. "He heard me singing in the bathroom and thought this would be a good gag. So it doesn't matter if you applaud or not. Tomorrow I go back to plumbing," he told the audience. Eddie then called on Brady and Astor to assist him in the act by holding up some playing cards. As the men held up their cards, he launched into a comical song, "Oh how she could yicki hicki wicki wacki woo." The audience began to roar when they realized that the cards had nothing to do with the act. Leaving the stage, Brady asked, "What are we supposed to do with these cards?" Eddie replied, "Play with them dummy!"[18] This act got the most laughter in the entire show. Next, Eddie sang renditions of zany tunes while strumming aimlessly on a banjo. Pausing between songs, he stared innocently at the audience with his pop-eyes and said, "Two weeks ago, I couldn't play this thing at all." In his memorable closing lines, Eddie made a quip about his jailbird father, who didn't understand why he couldn't "take home samples" from his job at the bank. Eddie's street-smart humor, like Will Rogers's folksy monologues, was a treat for sophisticated New York audiences.

After Eddie's opening night, Ziegfeld sent him a cable reading, "ENJOYED YOUR ACT. YOU'LL BE HERE A LONG TIME." In fact, Eddie remained with Ziegfeld so long that Billie Burke later told him that of all the boys her husband had hired, he regarded only Eddie as a son. Their relationship often mirrored that of a father and son, complete with squabbles and clashes but also warmth and generosity. Theirs was "a peculiar love/hate relationship," Eddie's daughter Marilyn explained.[19]

Aside from Eddie Cantor's engaging acts, the October edition of the *Frolic* contained another interactive number called "Every Girl Is Fishing," in which chorus girls caught the outstretched sleeves of choice patrons with little hooks. There was no shortage of other "girl" songs. One featured women representing various dances, such as the polka, waltz, and tango. The most lavish number in the show spotlighted eight women symbolizing eight different countries as they walked one at a time into a magnificent golden melting pot. Once the eighth girl stepped inside, Olive Thomas emerged as the ultimate *Midnight Frolic* girl.

The fall *Frolic* marked Olive's last appearance in a Ziegfeld show. She left New York after marrying silent film actor Jack Pickford, Mary Pickford's brother. Tired of the "slow grind" of the *Follies,* Olive was among the first of Ziegfeld's stars to try her luck in Hollywood. When Olive broke the news to Ziegfeld, he collapsed into his desk chair and peered at her from behind his piles of unanswered letters. "You're insane for marrying . . . a movie career will ruin your talent," he told her. Olive raised her nose, picked up her sealskin coat, and left.

A month after the October *Frolic* opened, *The Century Girl* premiered on November 6, 1916. Reviewers wrote that the show "out-*Follies* the *Follies*" due to its abundance of beautiful, impish heroines; good old-fashioned vaudeville; and stunning sets. The most marvelous set of all became an iconic image of Ziegfeld productions: a celestial, winding staircase on which ravishing Ziegfeld girls descended.[20] The show was a smash hit despite competition from a Shubert production featuring the most unexpected of stars: Anna Held. Since 1914 Anna had re-created herself in vaudeville shows and in the war effort, visiting wounded French soldiers and donating her beloved Renault touring car to the French army. She returned to America and went on lecture tours to raise awareness of the suffering endured by the people of war-torn Europe. "Follow me!" became her catchphrase as she urged Americans to help the French defeat Germany. "But will I have enough talent to convince the people of the New World when I shout 'Follow me!'?" Anna mused.[21]

The Shuberts convinced Anna that they could help her succeed in her mission. She easily forgot her former animosity toward the brothers when they promised to erect a theater in her name. All she had to do was lend them her catchphrase as the launching point for a new musical. Anna had another, more personal reason for signing with the Shuberts. She had just seen newspaper reports of Patricia Ziegfeld's birth and could not help feeling jealous and a bit resentful of the fact that Ziegfeld was willing to be a true husband to Billie but not to her. She felt no obligation to be loyal to Ziegfeld, but she ultimately regretted her decision to sign with the Shuberts. It turned out that the play *Follow Me* was not designed as pro-France propaganda; instead, it was a typical "Anna Held show," complete with "eyes" songs and a naughty *Parisienne* as the main character. In an attempt to diminish the show's frivolity, Anna slipped in a message speech, encouraging America to enter the fight overseas.

Anna's enthusiasm dampened even more when she became ill and had to cancel many performances. On a number of occasions, Liane stepped in to fill her mother's role. She was billed not as Liane Carerra but as Anna Held Jr. Mother and daughter were somewhat closer since Anna and Ziegfeld's separation; still, their relationship remained superficial, and the letters they exchanged contained nothing deeper than comments on new gowns, touring schedules, or perfume scents. Anna, whose strength had never failed her before, was near despondency as she began to feel her age. "Why should I go on living, when my past is but ashes and my future is one of mourning?" she asked. "Little by little, the stage has robbed me of my bloom and strength. Soon I would be nothing but a puppet whose reputation they would exploit to make people smile and swell the box office receipts."[22] Despite her illness and feelings of futility, Anna's devotion to France drove her to appear in the majority of her shows.

Follow Me ran until February 3, 1917. The other actors saw Anna as something of a saint because, even when her illness worsened, she vowed to finish the play's run in a wheelchair if she had to, just so the rest of the company would continue to receive their pay. After the show's exhausting tour, Anna returned to New York and checked into the Savoy Hotel—the same suite Ziegfeld had reserved for her upon her arrival in America. Doctors examined the ailing actress and concluded that she had a rare blood condition, multiple myeloma. The insidious illness caused her bones to crumble and her body to waste away until she eventually weighed only seventy pounds. Rumors swirled that excessive dieting and overly tight corsets were to blame for her condition, but such gossip was completely unfounded. Ziegfeld, hearing of Anna's poor health, confided to Billie that, because of his phobia of death, he could not visit Anna. "Will you send her some things?" he quietly asked. "I'd be happy to," Billie replied. "Fresh eggs, vegetables, butter . . . and my own doctor if necessary."[23] Ziegfeld thanked her and slipped back into his office.

Ziegfeld could not visit Anna in person, but he acknowledged her through a characteristically over-the-top gesture. At Lillian Russell's suggestion, he staged a show about Joan of Arc entitled *Maid of Honor* in the Savoy Ballroom. There was exuberant cheering from the audience as Anna was wheeled in to watch the production and "La Marseillaise" played triumphantly behind her. After the final curtain, a tearful Anna telephoned Ziegfeld to thank him for the show. Actress Ina Claire recalled Ziegfeld's reaction to the phone call. Turning to her with tears in his eyes, he asked, "Why does that poor, good woman have to suffer so?"[24] Ziegfeld's feelings for Anna were clearly deeper than he had known, as were Anna's for Ziegfeld. She may have played the gay divorcée after their separation, but a statement she made after the final divorce decree revealed her true feelings: "Men easily recover from that disease [love], but it seems to last with a woman until it wrecks her life."[25]

In the last minutes of Anna's life, during fits of delirium, she called for him: "Flo! Flo!" According to one observer, Anna seemed to think that if Ziegfeld were at her bedside, she could revive the past and have a future. Anna's doctors had barred him from her room, believing that seeing him would upset her too much, and given his phobia, it is debatable whether he would have come in any case. Anna succumbed to myeloma on August 12, 1918, at age forty-five. Ziegfeld sent lilies of the valley and roses to her memorial service, but he did not attend. By his friends' accounts, he never attended a funeral. Anna's death—the death of his first glorified girl, the death of the beauty and grandeur with which he was now identified, the death of the first woman who had seen his potential and encouraged it—was something Ziegfeld could not endure.

Anna did not have the timelessness of Ziegfeld's current beauties. She was a symbol of Edwardian times; she conveyed the era's romanticized vision of a girl living in luxury whose only worries pertained to her beaux. Anna played a character women wished to be and men wished to have. According to biographer Ethan Mordden, Anna "expanded American art to comprehend other arts, thus to enrich it."[26] She helped Americans "comprehend" the can-can and burlesque dancers of the Left Bank not as bawdy but as sophisticated. A writer for the *New York Tribune* aptly summarized Anna's legacy: "A true artist was Anna Held in that role of the stage which she filled so gaily and popularly—a minor role and a frivolous one, yet done sincerely and well. Perhaps we all should have seen the significance of this touch of art. . . . However slender its substance, a true artistic gift, faithfully developed and expressed, necessarily presupposes a truth of soul and a courage of will beyond the ordinary."[27]

Following Anna's death, Ziegfeld rarely spoke of her, especially not in the presence of his family. In fact, Patricia did not learn of Anna's existence until she was almost ten years old. A little girl with whom she was playing at Burkeley Crest airily stated: "Your dad was married to an actress named Anna Held and everybody in the world knows about it except you." "Liar! Liar! Liar!" Patricia shouted at her. Billie tried to console her daughter, saying, "We didn't tell you, darling, because it really had nothing to do with you or even with Daddy and me for that matter and, it happened such a long time ago . . . it's over and forgotten darling. Daddy doesn't think about it anymore, and neither do I." Billie reached her hand out with a pleading smile, but Patricia looked at her "dumbly" before turning and leaving the room.[28]

Billie and Ziegfeld may have chosen not to acknowledge it, but Anna was part of their lives. She had helped Ziegfeld become the important man he was—a man capable of making fantasies come to life for audiences and even more so for his family.

10

The Ziegfelds' Xanadu

Was it a princess's mansion, a spectacular circus, a menagerie, an exotic garden, or an exclusive resort? In a sense, the twenty-acre Burkeley Crest estate was all these things rolled into one. Patricia captured the essence of the place in her memoir: "Burkeley Crest was, technically, a country estate, but it suffered from a severe case of split personality. It had some of the characteristics of a zoo and some of the characteristics of a medieval fief."[1]

Burkeley Crest might have buckled under the weight of its own grandeur. However, in 1917 the country was on the verge of an abundance of both necessary and fanciful consumer goods. Ziegfeld and Billie were ahead of their time, and years later they were accurately dubbed "the first couple of the Jazz Age."[2] According to Billie's biographer, Grant Hayter-Menzies, Ziegfeld was "the dreamer of big dreams," and Billie was his "glamorous sidekick." He called Burkeley Crest "a canvas for Flo to paint on as he wished, without a thought for backers' percentages or opinions of critics."[3] Though Ziegfeld and Billie reveled in the eccentricity of their kingdom, their home life was old-fashioned in some ways. They maintained a Victorian-style, multigenerational household. Blanche Burke had continued to live at Burkeley Crest after Billie's marriage. Ironically, the commonsensical Blanche had Ziegfeld's taste for overabundance. "She shared the conviction that if a thing were good, then more of the same was essential," Billie commented. Blanche had ordered the installation of several Japanese teahouses before Billie and Ziegfeld were married, and afterward she still insisted on building a teahouse "wherever there was a little clearing or wide space in the maze of shady woodland walks around the edges of the estate."[4] In addition to Billie, Ziegfeld, Blanche, and Patricia, there was a substantial household staff. (Cherry Watson, Billie's ward, had married and gone on to pursue her own career in the theater.)

The estate's grounds were inhabited by all manner of flora and fauna, and Ziegfeld was happy to be surrounded by nature. He was in his element when maintaining the garden. The Ziegfelds could have lived off the fruit of their land. Vegetable gardens, grapes, rhubarb, and several types of berries thrived at Burkeley Crest. However, the inedible fruits of the estate—flowers—were closest to Ziegfeld's heart. Flowers grew everywhere in both hothouses and outdoor plots. Daffodils lined the long driveway, rhododendrons and laurel bloomed throughout the estate's acres, and trellises of rambler roses shaded windows and teahouses. In addition to the flowers growing outdoors, Ziegfeld had the servants bring armloads of American Beauties from local nurseries each day and place them about the house. Biographer Charles Higham noted that Ziegfeld was "sublimely happy" while gardening, and "visitors to the house would see him moving about in a straw hat, carrying pruning shears and insect powders, terrorizing the gardeners as he learned about chicken raising, rose grafting, and cross pollinating. Billie often worked beside him, wearing pink or blue gingham and a white sunbonnet, trying to calm him as he subjected the staff to ruthless cross-examinations."[5] On one point he was adamant: a rose had to be discarded the moment its petals wilted. Given his fear of death, it is not surprising Ziegfeld could not tolerate fading blooms. Whenever Ziegfeld visited the local nurseries to select his plants, the residents of Hastings-on-Hudson flocked to town. They had good reason to hold their famous resident in good favor. Ziegfeld often hosted the Westchester County Children's Society Flower Show.

Though charitable to the local children, the child on whom Ziegfeld lavished the most gifts was his own daughter. He "poured a cornucopia of gifts upon Patricia: jewelry, fabulous clothes, flowers, animals, birds, and a vast collection of toys . . . and a diamond tiara."[6] His most conspicuous gift to Patricia was a playhouse. Although there was already a playhouse on the estate, its modest size and unkempt appearance "offended his sensibilities," so Ziegfeld replaced it with one that resembled Mount Vernon.[7] For his daughter's outdoor recreation, Ziegfeld commissioned Joseph Urban to design a swimming pool. It was large enough to accommodate a canoe, but it was impractical to try to row because the canoe would collide with the pool's centerpiece: a statue of a cherub holding a fish.

Partly for his daughter's pleasure and partly for his own, Ziegfeld also acquired a wide variety of pets. One of Ziegfeld's first presents to Billie during their courtship had been a cow. But a cow was quite ordinary compared with some of the other animals he brought home. The menagerie consisted largely of "out-of-work [animal] actors or circus performers" that Ziegfeld took pity on. Billie was an avid animal lover herself, but even she was overwhelmed by the family of buffalo that came to live with them. The buffalo did not come into Ziegfeld's possession by accident. He had been planning to produce a musical about the Wild West and had imported a pair of buffalo to use for the show's promotion. When the show never materialized, Ziegfeld brought the animals to Hastings-on-Hudson, where they produced one "hale, hearty, and mean offspring." Ziegfeld doted on the baby buffalo and cooed at it, but he was the only one who felt any affection for the beasts. In a 1994 letter to the Hastings Historical Society, Patricia explained the tension the animals caused in town: "Our paddock fence was not the sturdiest, and Mr. B[uffalo] could have easily pushed it over. . . . The buffalo created quite a stir in the village; the bellowing led to complaints, and neighbors worried they would escape. . . . At last the day came when the buffalo were going to go live elsewhere [a zoo in Pennsylvania] . . . we all stood along it [the driveway] applauding, waving and heaving a great sigh of relief."[8]

Ziegfeld quickly replaced the buffalo with another unconventional pet: a 300-pound baby elephant named Herman. Ziegfeld had acquired it at the suggestion of circus entrepreneur John Ringling. "Herman would be a perfect gift for your little girl," Ringling commented, nodding at the two-year-old animal. Patricia's sixth birthday was coming up, so Ziegfeld towed the boisterous Herman home in a trailer. Patricia delighted in riding on Herman's back and taking him for walks with the fifteen or so dogs roaming the estate, but he soon became as unruly as the buffalo. He often escaped from his stall and appeared at the kitchen door, asking for a snack. Once he found his way into the house, charged up the staircase, and got stuck between the banisters. Ziegfeld, unfazed by Herman's doings, said to Patricia, "You know he's not supposed to be in the house." Billie always took Herman's side when he became rowdy. "The poor thing must have been hungry," she would say in his defense.[9] The elephant and a trainer spent the summer at the estate, but when the weather became chilly, Herman rejoined Ringling's circus in Sarasota, Florida. At the time, Ringling was trying to unload more animals, including a tiger, two lion cubs, ten deer, two bears named Dempsey and Tunney, and a pair of white donkeys named Mr. and Mrs. Murphy. Despite the trouble with Herman and the buffalo, Ziegfeld transported the unwanted circus animals to Burkeley Crest, where they stayed until they grew up and "became dangerous nuisances," at which point "they departed for the [Central Park] zoo."[10] To show their appreciation, the owners of the zoo gave the Ziegfelds a cockatoo.

The cockatoo spurred Ziegfeld and Billie to add more birds to their menagerie: a bullfinch, canaries, partridges, pheasants, and parrots. Their two macaws, Harry and Lola, lived in a coop with a flock of pigeons that had been dyed pastel colors for their appearance in a *Follies* act. The parrots could recite the Lord's Prayer but were also known to imitate Billie's laugh or exclaim, "Aw, shut up!"[11] The Burkeley Crest menagerie also included rabbits in hutches and three beehives that provided the Ziegfelds with homegrown honey. Patricia most enjoyed Jacinto, a polo pony that had once belonged to the Prince of Wales. To keep the pony company were Ramsey, a small ram, and Bessie, a cow. Perhaps most beloved were the thirty cats on the premises. Billie was especially fond of the felines and once commented, "Like Lionel Barrymore, I prefer the company of cats." Though cats were her pet of choice, she also enjoyed the company of the numerous dogs she and Ziegfeld owned, including Pekingese, cocker spaniels, springer spaniels for hunting, and two Sealyham terriers named Isabelle and Ziggy. During thunderstorms, she would hide in her shoe closet with one of her dogs by her side.[12] Ziegfeld also acquired two "police" dogs that he appointed as guards for Patricia's room. The Ziegfelds reserved a plot of land as a pet cemetery, and whenever an animal passed away, the entire family mourned. As Patricia explained, "to us they were nearly human."[13]

While Ziegfeld's contributions to the household were on the bizarre and eccentric side, Billie's were purely domestic. They did not have as many servants as others in their position might have, for they enjoyed performing many household tasks themselves. Their staff included a butler, maid, cook, waitress, governess, gardener, and kennel man. Even though Billie did not cook or clean, she took on a great deal of responsibility for the daily running of the estate. She managed the household from her desk, set in front of a sunny window and "crammed with papers, lists of things to do, a ton of memorabilia, and framed photographs, cameos, leather stationery files, fan mail, and sheet music."[14] Like her husband, she had no talent for keeping her office area uncluttered. Much of the time she spent composing guest lists and menus for the monumental dinner parties held at Burkeley Crest. While Billie had breakfast in bed each morning, she and Deliah, the cook, would discuss the daily menus and plans for Sunday dinner. At first, when planning Sunday meals for guests, Billie would order only enough food for fewer than twenty people. But she soon learned that when Ziegfeld said he wanted a small dinner party, he meant forty to sixty guests. The dining room seated only eighteen; consequently, the Ziegfelds often entertained outdoors, where the staff prepared meals on a cast-iron stove complete with barbecue broilers and ovens.

Ziegfeld often usurped Billie's role as menu planner for their Sunday dinner parties. And once he took charge of the planning, the dinner bill could run up to four figures. "Something unusual," Ziegfeld would suggest for the menu. "And let's have terrapin. May be none here. I'll get 'em by plane. And better have some lamb and brook trout. Mrs. Ziegfeld would like a little of each." Sometimes their menus overlapped in the most inconvenient of ways. In one instance, both Billie and Ziegfeld ordered cakes for Irving Berlin's birthday. Billie's cake was pathetic compared with Ziegfeld's, which was "the size of a small skating rink and . . . decorated with the score of . . . Alexander's Ragtime Band."[15]

Attending a dinner party at the Ziegfelds' home was like visiting an amusement park, and the amusement was not restricted solely to the taste buds. Guests could wander the grounds and play horseshoes, croquet, or tennis. Indoors, they could explore the mansion's twenty-two rooms, play bridge, or view a new movie screened by a projectionist hired especially for such occasions. Sidney Boggis, the Ziegfelds' loyal if supercilious British valet and butler, would materialize at opportune moments to offer guests hors d'oeuvres and cocktails. The dignified Englishman often indulged in too many drinks himself, prompting Billie to insist that Ziegfeld keep the key to the liquor cabinet. "What's the difference?" Ziegfeld asked. "He might as well have the key. He drinks all the liquor anyway."[16] Despite Sidney's weakness, he remained a part of the Burkeley Crest family.

Burkeley Crest was not always all play and no work. Ziegfeld's work was so intertwined with his life that he could not help taking it home with him. Because Ziegfeld needed to be in touch with his office twenty-four hours a day, he had a phone installed in his bedroom and a telephone booth installed on the first floor under the stairs. Each telephone had two lines: one connected to his office, and a second one for outgoing calls. Another phone, tucked away inside the china cabinets, had no purpose except as a direct line to the garage. Whenever members of the family wished to go out, they could call the garage and have their cars driven directly to the front door.

The outside observer might say that the Ziegfelds were self-indulgent, cliquish, spoiled, and ignorant of the suffering and poverty outside the walls of their mansion. Those who knew the family would argue otherwise. Ziegfeld cared for his employees—both those at the New Amsterdam and those at Burkeley Crest. Whenever the family took a trip, Ziegfeld reserved private Pullman cars for the servants at the additional cost of $1,100. Once when Deliah became ill during a trip, Ziegfeld insisted that she take his private drawing room. Jake Hoffman, whom Ziegfeld had once hired as his private barber, was on the receiving end of an especially kind favor. After Jake's health took a downward turn and he closed his barbershop, Ziegfeld hired him to give him a daily shave and to take care of the chickens and ducks on the estate.[17] Whether screening films at Burkeley Crest or staging shows at the New Amsterdam, Billie recalled that "Flo's chief concern always was that every servant on the place found a comfortable seat to see the entire show. On opening night he reserved the front row of the . . . mezzanine for our staff and sent them to the theater in style, in special cars. . . . They understood and loved him and they spoiled him to the point where it was almost impossible for him to do anything for himself."[18]

The servants held Billie in equally high esteem. During the holiday season she presented each of them with a magnificent turkey and a hearty supply of candy. The townspeople of Hastings-on-Hudson also adored Billie, particularly the children. Every month she took the young people on picnics or trips to the Bronx Zoo in her five Rolls Royces. Alan Brock, who grew up in the town, recalled, "When she came out of the stationery store, a buzz of whispers filled the air, about her clothes, her red hair, her freckles, or her parasol. Laughing and chatting with everyone, she would summon the chauffeur and slip him a bill, and all of the kids followed him, like the Pied Piper, into Adam's Ice Cream Parlor."[19]

Both Ziegfeld and Billie believed in providing those around them with a taste of the luxury they themselves enjoyed. Ziegfeld's sense of identity was tied, "like vital organs shared by conjoined twins, to others' enjoyment of what he created."[20] Ziegfeld's wish to spread enjoyment had been the driving force behind his greatest productions, including his home. He tapped into this driving force as he prepared shows for the 1917 theater season because Americans needed beauty, laughter, and escapism more than ever: the country was at war.

War had become inevitable after the discovery of the now infamous Zimmermann note. In the note, German officials promised that if the

Mexican military allied with them, Germany would return the American territory that Mexico had lost decades earlier. Of course, Mexico would be able to reclaim the land only if Germany won the war. The American military learned of the note in January, and the United States entered the war three months later.

Ziegfeld was planning to a produce a show filled with even more patriotic zeal than the *Follies of 1916*. However, it was no easy task to create a show that would outshine the competing productions playing on Broadway in 1917. The best of the new musicals were those written by P. G. Wodehouse, Guy Bolton, and Jerome Kern. During the time he spent working in England, Kern had teamed with Wodehouse and Bolton. Wodehouse was a British humorist who had made his name writing light, upper-class stories, including the Jeeves and Wooster series. Bolton, also an Englishman, was a writer of farcical plays and a societal satirist; his writings had appeared in the American publication *The Smart Set*. The trio's best show to date was *Oh Boy!* which premiered on February 20, 1917, at New York's Princess Theatre. It was a romantic comedy of errors, typical of Wodehouse-Bolton-Kern productions, most of which centered on frivolous story lines held up by witty dialogue and rousing tunes that flowed naturally from the plot. *Oh Boy!* introduced the song "Till the Clouds Roll By." Ziegfeld set his sights on Bolton and Wodehouse, recognizing them as two of the most promising new talents on Broadway. Just as Gene Buck and Dave Stamper had modernized the *Follies,* Ziegfeld envisioned that Wodehouse and Bolton would further refine the series. He also saw them as potential writers of musical comedies he hoped to produce.

Because of his excessive ambition, Ziegfeld pushed himself to take on more projects than seemed humanly possible. With Charles Dillingham he coproduced a specialty midnight revue for the Cocoanut Grove (the rooftop entertainment venue at the Century Theatre) titled *Dance and Grow Thin* on January 18, the *Ziegfeld Follies of 1917* on June 12 at the New Amsterdam, *The Rescuing Angel* on October 8 at the Hudson Theatre, *Miss 1917* on November 5 at the Century Theatre, and the April and December editions of *Midnight Frolic* on the New Amsterdam roof. *Dance and Grow Thin* was comparable to the *Midnight Frolic,* except that it was longer. The show featured the music of Irving Berlin, costumes by Lucile, and scenery by Joseph Urban. Leon Errol, Lilyan Tashman, Gertrude Hoffman, and a new singing duo, Van and Schenck (who later earned fame singing "Ain't We Got Fun?"), performed in the revue. The most notable tune from the show, "For Me and My Gal," was penned not by Berlin but by George W. Meyer, E. Ray Goetz, and Edgar Leslie. The show ran until June with a healthy 117 performances.

Back at the New Amsterdam Theatre, Ziegfeld's spring edition of the *Midnight Frolic,* premiering on April 24, was even more pleasing to audiences than *Dance and Grow Thin.* It featured Will Rogers and included the now customary interactive routine. This time, girls ran about with small zeppelin-shaped balloons that patrons could burst with their cigarettes.

Ziegfeld had his hands full not only keeping his revues in order but also dealing with backstage drama and personal loss. He spent much time consoling Lillian Russell over the loss of their mutual friend and benefactor Diamond Jim Brady, who had died in April. (Brady left a large portion of his fortune to the former Ziegfeld specialty dancers the Dolly sisters.) Considering that he had lost one of his closest friends, Ziegfeld was in no mood to mediate disputes during rehearsals for the 1917 *Follies.* The conflict involved Jerome Kern, Victor Herbert, and ingénue Vivienne Segal. Segal's solo singing act immediately followed Bessie McCoy's on the program, which she saw as a great disadvantage (McCoy had returned to the *Follies* as the Yama Yama Girl). During rehearsals, Segal found herself torn between Kern and Herbert: Herbert insisted that she sing the show-stopping "Kiss Me Again," while Kern demanded that she sing his hit tune "They Didn't Believe Me." Notable is the fact that twenty-year-old George Gershwin began his association with Ziegfeld at this time, working as Kern's rehearsal pianist. According to Marcelle Earle, George arrived at each rehearsal wearing "an immaculate white shirt with rolled up sleeves. Gershwin would sit at the piano for hours, intent on the music and minding his own business."[21] However, Gershwin was forced into the fray during one rehearsal when, unsure which song to play, he chose "Kiss Me Again," causing another argument to erupt. Ziegfeld had to intervene to prevent the composers from using their fists to sort out their differences. "Let her sing what she wants to sing!" he shouted. Segal chose "Kiss Me Again," based on her belief that Kern's tune was too light to follow McCoy's dominating stage presence. Kern never forgave her.

Yet another temperamental artist was dance director Ned Wayburn. As usual, Wayburn's caustic behavior toward the chorus girls caused tension during rehearsals. Dancer Muriel Merrill recalled him shouting at the girls, "Walk a circle! I said a circle, not a pretzel! This is terrible." He then blew the whistle he always wore around his neck and shouted that he wanted certain girls out of the chorus and back on the ferry to Staten Island, where they came from.[22]

One would never suspect the existence of such backstage chaos when viewing the *Follies'* flawless execution. The curtain rose on a prospective son-in-law making a $10,000 wager that he could show his future father-in-law more New York sights in three hours than was ever written in the Arabian Nights. Joseph Urban created magical effects to show that New York was indeed more splendid than any setting in the Arabian Nights. He presented an astounding rooftop vision of the city and a scene of Lower Manhattan, complete with fruit-filled parapets. To illustrate Chinatown, Urban created a set simulating Chinese lacquer and featuring "fifty Ziegfeld beauties scampering up and down red and gold ladders against a black background."[23] The 1917 edition introduced new flesh-and-blood Venuses, including Dolores. Ziegfeld had not forgotten his fascination with Lucile's living mannequin number and put it to exquisite use in a patriotic tableau depicting Paul Revere riding a horse. The tableau was designed by Ben Ali Haggin, a Munich-trained artist. His tableaux became an attraction that rivaled Urban's settings.

Although the lush settings and tableaux dazzled audiences, theatergoers were most enthused by the show's jazzy numbers. Eddie Cantor, in his *Follies* debut, sang the biggest hits in the revue, "The Modern Maiden's Prayer" and "That's the Kind of a Baby for Me." The first song expressed many of the "modern maiden's" sentiments, including: "If my marriage proves to be phony, give me lots of alimony. This is the twentieth century maiden's prayer." The second song reflected women's growing wish for financial independence: "When I saw the check I thought it was a tent, but when the waiter came she simply signed her name—that's the kind of baby for me!" The song provided "a riotous finish to the act,"[24] and it was "good for as many as eleven or twelve encores."[25] "That's the Kind of a Baby for Me" was published with a widely circulated Raphael Kirchner portrait of Marcelle Earle on its cover, which boosted sales.

Eddie Cantor was on his way to becoming an even bigger draw than Marcelle or any other Ziegfeld beauty. His best skit in his first *Follies* paired him, in blackface, with Bert Williams. Eddie played Bert's effeminate son who is contemptuous of his father's philistine ways. "I have a very bad temper," Eddie's character declared when his father became fed up with his loftiness.

"And I'll show you where you got it from!" Bert retorted as he ran menacingly toward him.

"I think he intends to do me bodily harm!" Eddie said.

Bert later told Eddie that he counted the number of laughs each comedian received while onstage. For Eddie, Bert had counted only one laugh—one that started when he came onstage and did not stop until he stepped off.[26]

Will Rogers, Fanny Brice, and W. C. Fields furnished the rest of the program's comedy. Will, who was now Ziegfeld's "bosom friend," was not afraid to use his pal as the butt of jokes. The *Follies of 1917* divided the comedic numbers into "episodes" named after the featured star. Will's episode was humorously titled "The Episode of Will Rogers Sayings: He is liable to talk about anything or anybody."[27] In one of Will's sayings, he suggested that Ziegfeld was trying to get him to invest in future productions. "Before I would put a dollar into any show he produces, I'd get myself examined by a lunacy commission, yes I would," Will said with his down-home twang. Eyeing Ziegfeld in the audience, he continued to jest: "I understand that Billie Burke is going to have a theater of her own here in New York. It looks as though Billie has fallen for Flo's hokum because if it is true, it will be built with her own coin, and you can bet on that."[28] Most of the Ziegfeld company doubted that Will would be on the next payroll after such remarks. But rather than fire him, Ziegfeld gave Will a raise and offered him a permanent position in both the *Follies* and the *Frolic* if he wished.

Fanny Brice, who also had a standing offer of employment, did not disappoint her employer or her audiences. In her most hilarious number, "Egypt," she reprised her customary act as an awkward Yiddish girl attempting to be alluring. Brice portrayed Rebecca, an exotic dancer who was "Egyptian in everything but her nose."[29] Next, W. C. Fields amused audiences with his usual misanthropic persona. The show concluded with a patriotic finale composed by Victor Herbert. Its title evoked the same emotion as Anna Held's *Follow Me*: "Can't You Hear Your Country Calling?"

The *Ziegfeld Follies of 1917* enjoyed complimentary reviews and a healthy run of fifteen weeks. One reviewer noted that the sets were "unbelievably beautiful," as were the girls and the costumes they wore. Though the show's top-notch comedy contributed in no small way to its success, Ziegfeld still believed that "a balance between exhibited beauty and humor is so much theory."[30] The *Follies of 1917* outshone the previous edition's representations of American beauty, diversity, and progressiveness. Ziegfeld's name was now "so potent" on Broadway that it became a synonym for the last word in musical theater.[31]

The winter *Frolic*, which premiered on December 29, only added to Ziegfeld's lofty reputation on Broadway. He again hired Van and Schenck to perform and also engaged Frank Carter, a handsome crooner making his debut. The December *Frolic* almost failed to open when a fire destroyed all the costumes two days before the premiere, costing Ziegfeld a pretty penny. However, the producer often failed to pay the bills for his costumes, so the money he owed on the destroyed garments was simply added to his total debt. In August 1917 he still had an unpaid balance of $65,206.54 from the previous year's shows, but this had not stopped him from spending more than $100,000 on his new productions.

Despite the doubled cost for costumes, the December *Frolic* helped Ziegfeld pay off a significant amount of his debt. The show began with a presentation of lavishly dressed chorines vying for the prize of Most Beautiful Chorus Girl. The winner would have her salary doubled. A typical Ziegfeldian gimmick, it succeeded in wooing audiences. Ziegfeld may have pampered his girls more than any other producer, but he was not afraid to show his displeasure. One night he caught a *Frolic* showgirl, Lilyan Tashman, twirling her parasol behind her in an attempt to hide the fact that she was socializing with a patron. The next day Ziegfeld fired her and telegrammed Marcelle Earle, informing her that she would take Tashman's place. "*Teach* some of them a *lesson* around here," Ziegfeld told Marcelle with feeling.[32] Marcelle accepted the offer only after Ziegfeld agreed to give her a $10 a week raise to cover family costs, including her baby's milk and shoes. Now a father himself, Ziegfeld was happy to help a fellow parent.

Ziegfeld's wave of success with both the *Follies* and the *Frolic* in no way made him feel infallible. He knew that his next show could very well flop, and if that happened, his bank balance and, more important, his wife's confidence in him could be severely affected.

Billie was a supportive wife, but she found it increasingly difficult to grapple with Ziegfeld's frustrating tendency to withdraw when he was in the midst of producing a show. She later wrote that members of the household revolved like little moons around Ziegfeld's sun. Billie tried to make light of the isolation she felt when Ziegfeld devoted himself solely to his work: "I never . . . had any part in the management [of the shows], but heaven knows I heard enough about them each year. I used to share the excitement—and the worries. . . . What a lot of fun it was—and what a terrific lot of work, too!"[33] But fun was sorely lacking when it came to the constant rumors of Ziegfeld's flirtations with various chorus girls. Billie had believed Ziegfeld when he told her that their troubles concerning other women were over, but she was still unsure whether the rumors surrounding his affair with Olive Thomas had been true or false. Her uncertainty about her husband's fidelity made Billie "distracted and jittery."[34] Her initial reason for taking a hiatus from work had been to "hold onto her husband," yet she still felt as if she were losing him.[35] He may have showered gifts on her and Patricia, but no gift could replace attentive conversation and quality time spent together.

Billie loved being a mother and even told one reporter that she wished she had a dozen more babies because "that's how nice Patricia Florenz Ziegfeld is."[36] However, concern about her husband's mounting debts made her consider a return to the stage. Billie was well aware of Ziegfeld's penchant for over-the-top spending on a production. She was infuriated when she heard that, upon learning that Irish linen petticoats for *Follies* dancers were far more expensive than plain cotton ones, Ziegfeld shrugged and stated, "I know. But Irish linen does something to their walk—remember, they are Ziegfeld Girls!"[37]

Billie had to return to work not only for financial stability but also for her own mental health. Despite her devotion to her home and family, she found that she could not be truly happy unless she was involved in the theater in some capacity. In an interview she gave to *Photoplay* in 1917 she stated: "Please tell *Photoplay's* readers how important it is for a woman who has ever had a career to keep right on loving her work even though she's married. And by a career I don't mean, necessarily and exclusively, a celebrated career. I mean a woman who has done any useful thing well. . . . It might be baking an apple pie, it might be watching a business—just as well as it might be amusing an audience."[38]

Billie approached Ziegfeld about her possible return to the stage, hoping to gain his support, but it was difficult to catch his attention. He was in one of his lethargic, remote moods that customarily followed the opening of a show. He wanted only to be left alone and to read the daily paper. "The evenings at Burkeley Crest may be gay when company drops in, but frequently Mr. Ziegfeld 'puts on horrid black-rimmed spectacles and tucks his nose into a book of history or philosophy for a whole evening and insists on staying at home,'" Gilbert Seldes of the *New Yorker* observed.[39]

Billie decided the simplest way to dip her toe in the acting world again was to appear in a few quickly made silent films: *The Mysterious Miss Terry* (1917), *Arms and the Girl* (1917), and a screen adaptation of *The Land of Promise* (1917). All were shot at Famous Players Studio in New York. In a review of *The Mysterious Miss Terry*, the *Washington Times* critic called Billie the "woman of a thousand adjectives," including "winning, darling, soothing, and natural, cajoling, mischievous . . . a wonderful film star." As much as filmgoers adored Billie (from 1918 through 1922, her name never left the top-five list of box-office attractions), movies did not satisfy her loftier career ambitions, which involved the theater. In the meantime, she spent "a great deal more time at Burkeley Crest."[40] In her early career, she had written advice columns for young girls. Now she made fewer films per year and spent her spare time at home penning advice for young mothers. In 1918 a few of her suggestions included: "Don't put the baby in cold sheets" and "The baby's first need is fresh air."[41]

Billie was still anxious to return to the stage, and again she approached Ziegfeld about her plans. This time, she caught him in a more talkative mood. "Clare Kummer has a new comedy that I think may suit me," Billie told him. At first his face conveyed no reaction to her statement. Then he asked, "Do you have the script with you?" Billie presented him with the manuscript of *The Rescuing Angel*, the story of Angela, an indecisive girl who must choose between marrying for love and marrying for money to restore her father's fortune. Pushing his black spectacles up his nose, Ziegfeld read long into the night until he had finished the play. An impatient Billie waited for his verdict the next morning. After the maid served them their breakfast of grapefruit, toast, and soft-boiled eggs, Ziegfeld calmly said, "The play is worthless. I'm begging you not to do it. The character isn't what they expect from you. She's calculating to men and uses her charm to get what she wants from them."

None of Ziegfeld's arguments could dissuade Billie from pursuing the play. She signed with producer Arthur Hopkins for a thirty-week season at a weekly salary of $1,500 and 37.5 percent of the profits. Under the terms of her contract, she would earn no less than $45,000 for her work in the production.[42] Ziegfeld, despite his misgivings, coproduced the show. However, his influence was nonexistent, and the show contained none of the lavishness or artistic touches that were his trademark—his way of showing his disapproval. *The Rescuing Angel* opened on October 8, 1917, and limped along for three weeks before closing. The play's run was so short that Billie was not paid the $45,000 guaranteed in her contract, and Ziegfeld urged her to sue Hopkins for the remainder of her salary. Hopkins vehemently declared that the play's failure was Billie's fault because she had refused to perform in out-of-town tours. Ziegfeld came to his wife's defense by sending a letter to every newspaper in the country contradicting Hopkins's statement. He asserted that Billie's reason for refusing to tour was that Hopkins had vetoed any changes to the dismal script. Hopkins finally gave in to the Great Ziegfeld's demands and paid the remainder of Billie's salary: $34,500. Billie felt guilty about any stretching of the truth Ziegfeld might have done to win her the money, so she donated her settlement to the Red Cross.[43]

After this fiasco, Billie regretted not heeding Ziegfeld's warning against the play, but she was still determined to try her luck in another one. According to Bernard Sobel, Billie became increasingly conscientious as an artist and rivaled her husband in her meticulous attention to detail. She pored over scripts ten times, marking each phrase or inflection she deemed most important to ensure a perfect reading.[44]

As Billie searched for a new play, she and Ziegfeld invested their hopes in his next production, *Miss 1917*. The show, which opened at the Century Theatre on November 5, 1917, was a critical darling. Newspapers unanimously proclaimed it a triumphant, gorgeous, and charming work. The production boasted the talents of Marion Davies, Bessie McCoy, Van and Schenck, and Irene Castle. It seemed like the show could run for a year—or so Ziegfeld thought. Oddly, *Miss 1917* lasted a mere six weeks. Historians suggest that the reasons for the perplexing failure were the show's considerable length and its unfortunate location—the distant Century Theatre. Ziegfeld was reluctant to give up his partnership with the theater's owner, Charles Dillingham, but Century Amusement, the theater's parent company, was now bankrupt. Ziegfeld returned to Klaw and Erlanger for backing, but he found that Erlanger had recently split from his partner. That break gave Ziegfeld much more breathing room, and he began to "emerg[e] as the dominant partner."[45]

With a new, successful *Follies* and an equally lauded *Midnight Frolic* to his credit, Ziegfeld had not had an entirely bad year. And it looked as if 1918 would more than compensate for the missteps of the previous season, partly due to an exciting new star Billie had brought to his attention. She had become as astute as her husband when it came to choosing Ziegfeld girls. "I studied Ziegfeld girls, and I listened to what Flo . . . said about them," she later wrote. In April 1917 Billie had taken note of a petite, blonde ballerina during a performance of a Shubert-produced play entitled *Show of Wonders*. Billie had also become as ruthless as Ziegfeld when it came to poaching talent from rival producers—especially the Shuberts. Billie thought this ballerina was the most refreshing, delightful child she had ever seen. "Who is she?" Billie whispered to a friend in the audience. "Used to be known as 'Miss Sugarlump.' . . . Known now as Marilynn Miller," the friend replied.[46]

As the girl pranced gracefully in a number called the "Burmese Ballet," she projected a strong stage presence, despite her dainty stature. Nevertheless, Billie felt the dancer could use some advice in honing her fashion sense and her singing and dancing skills. After the show Billie rushed home to tell Ziegfeld about Marilynn Miller. Billie knew full well that, in the words of *Follies* chorine Doris Eaton, "discovering and developing unknown beauty and talent was the exciting challenge. It was his [Ziegfeld's] mania, molding, exploiting, and claiming as his own those rare, flawless visions."[47] But when Billie returned to Burkeley Crest, she was disappointed to find her husband in one of his "to hell with it" states. "You want me to look at a girl who can't dress, can't dance, and can't sing? For the *Follies?*" Ziegfeld asked. Neither Ziegfeld nor Billie remembered that Marilynn Miller had been a guest at the New Year's Ball where they had first met. "She makes the most enchanting effect," Billie continued. "A delightful thing *happens* when she comes on stage. Her smile . . ." She stopped, grasping for an adequate description of the dancer. "[She's] a confection of a girl."[48]

Ziegfeld folded his paper. "What's her name?" he asked.

"Marilynn Miller," Billie said. "Marilynn, spelled with two *n*'s."

"That would have to change. It'll confuse the audience—it'd look like a misprint and be bad for business," Ziegfeld said as he reopened his paper. Billie had piqued his interest, even if he gave the opposite impression.

No matter what turmoil Billie and Ziegfeld experienced in their marriage, theater remained their primary bond. Billie introduced Ziegfeld to Miss Sugarlump, just as she had introduced him to Lucile and her models, convinced that such talents would further his career. Billie knew that Ziegfeld was highly susceptible to the charms of other women, but she believed he would always return to her. Seeing Billie flit about in her care-free roles onscreen and onstage, one would not guess she was a realist. "She knew there was no changing Flo," Bernard Sobel commented. "[She had] a perspective as comprehensive as it was clear. She knows the world and can hold a cynical glass to inspect it [up] close."[49] Billie had to maintain both her realism and her faith, for if she allowed herself to be jealous of every Ziegfeld girl, her marriage would unravel.

Not long after Billie first mentioned Marilynn Miller, Ziegfeld went to see the girl perform. After the show he promptly began negotiations to buy out her contract. The Shuberts' *New York Review* printed a livid attack on their rival: "He's at it again, one of his favorite indoor sports, corralling talent that has been discovered by other managers."[50] Marilynn captured Ziegfeld's imagination immediately, just as Billie had known she would. However, she also sensed that the ballerina had caught more than her husband's professional attention. "I thought for awhile that Flo's career and my career would gallop successfully side by side and that at the same time we could be good parents. . . . Those were the fine days. They did not come all together," Billie stated. "They never came consecutively for me."[51]

11

The Greatest Victory Party America Has Ever Known

"She is the incarnation of freshness, of youth, of vitality.[1]" Marilyn was always smiling onstage and off. She seemed so happy and comet-like."[2] These statements could have been written by Ziegfeld himself as the definition of the perfect Ziegfeld girl. Marilyn (she reluctantly agreed to drop the second *n*) Miller's youth and charisma made her the ideal girl to move his productions into the modern era, which seemed to be made for Ziegfeld heroines. As the 1910s transitioned into the 1920s, women became the cultural focus. They achieved liberation not only by winning the right to vote but also by shedding their corsets, long curls, and ankle-length skirts. Anna Held had symbolized the naughty but nice European *Florodora* girl of the late Victorian era, and Billie Burke had symbolized the sophisticated yet naïve ingénue of the late Edwardian period. Marilyn was a symbol of both eras combined—a flirtatious and daring flapper who could be as charming as the girl next door.

Marilyn shared similarities with two of Ziegfeld's former loves, Anna Held and Lillian Lorraine. She led a hardscrabble life from the time she was an infant, and her story reads like a quintessential Mary Pickford melodrama. Born Mary Ellen Reynolds in 1898, she grew up like an orphan for the first four years of her life, even though both her parents were living. Her mother, Ada Reynolds, was too poor to buy clothes for her child, so she sent Marilyn to live off the charity of an aunt. After divorcing Marilyn's father, Ada married a vaudeville performer named Caro Miller. While visiting with four-year-old Marilyn at her aunt's house, Ada discovered that Marilyn could stand on the tips of her toes like a ballerina. This convinced Ada to add her youngest daughter to the family act that Caro Miller had formed with Marilyn's two siblings. At this point, Mary Ellen changed her name to Marilynn, combining her first name with her middle name, Lynn. Her stepfather drilled her mercilessly in her dance routines and hit her with a walking stick if her performance was unsatisfactory. She learned how to position herself so the red marks left by the stick would not show. From the time she was four until she reached her teens, Marilyn was the main attraction of the family's act, doing everything from dancing to celebrity imitations.

"I didn't choose to go on the stage," Marilyn revealed in an interview. "I was put on the stage because a living had to be earned. It's not a very pleasant childhood to remember."[3] Outside the stage doors of the "dusty old theaters" where her family performed, Marilyn and her sisters had to stick close together to ward off the seedy college boys and pimps who waited for them. A childhood so riddled with work and abuse might have left Marilyn bitter and hateful. However, these hardships gave her the determination to become successful so that she would never have to rely on men like Caro or the unsavory characters at the stage door. Her ambition was so great that she would sob in the wings if she was prohibited from going onstage due to child labor restrictions. Biographer Warren G. Harris wrote that she "gazed with longing toward her own particular heaven behind the footlights."[4]

Marilyn was fifteen when Lee Shubert approached her to appear in *The Passing Show*. Theatergoers were amazed at how the impish, five-foot-one-inch ballerina could dance so daintily and then convincingly spoof celebrities such as the burly, deep-voiced Bert Williams and the seemingly inimitable and eccentric Bessie McCoy. By 1916, she was the primary attraction in the Shuberts' new production, *The Show of Wonders*. One critic wrote that "to look at Marilyn Miller is to remember what a beautiful thing is youth at its youngest and prettiest."[5]

Given this description of Marilyn, it is little wonder that Ziegfeld agreed with Billie about Marilyn's potential. After examining her contract with the Shuberts, Ziegfeld claimed it was invalid. He pointed out that Caro Miller, who had signed the contract on Marilyn's behalf when she was still a minor, was no longer her legal guardian and had no power over her; therefore, the contract was worthless. The Shuberts were so angry at losing their greatest actress to Ziegfeld that they fired Caro Miller from his position as stage manager. Marilyn must have been glad to be free from her stepfather's control. She was not so happy, however, about Ziegfeld's insistence that she change the spelling of her name, but she acquiesced. How could she turn down an opportunity to work for the best producer on Broadway?

At nineteen years old, Marilyn had already lived the archetypal rags-to-riches story. Now it was time for her to enjoy the riches that only Florenz Ziegfeld could provide. However, if the fifty-year-old Ziegfeld thought she would let him play the part of benevolent sugar daddy, he was sorely mistaken. Marilyn had gotten away from her stepfather and was not about to become dependent on another older man. She was one of the few women who never reciprocated Ziegfeld's attentions. Whether he wanted to woo her romantically or solely on a professional level is debatable.

Billie believed that Ziegfeld loved Marilyn only as a "perfect actress." She tried not to succumb to jealousy but later admitted that she saw Marilyn, as she had seen Olive Thomas, as "a grave danger." Before her marriage, Billie had written in one of her advice columns: "Jealousy is a sure annihilator of happiness. . . . To be jealous of one's lover is to create discontent and suspicion. . . . Jealousy has always seemed to me to be such a mean, little characteristic . . . the greatest cause of unhappiness on this earth. . . . I should fight against it with all my strength."[6] One of Billie's best tools in fighting jealousy was to draw Ziegfeld's attention to her own career. Unlike Marilyn, Billie had no qualms about relying on him. After failing to heed his advice about the lackluster *Rescuing Angel,* she was determined to find a suitable play, with her husband's help. She followed Ziegfeld's suggestion to look for roles that would complement her best assets. And whether she wanted to admit it or not, that meant roles in light comedic plays with no shortage of ravishing costumes. She found a play that satisfied these requirements in the adaptation of an Alexandre Dumas story, *A Marriage of Convenience.* The play's producer and lead actor, Henry Miller, accommodated Billie's lavish taste in clothes and even went so far as to approve a $125 handkerchief. Miller was as ostentatious as Billie; one night when Ziegfeld saw Miller dressed in a waistcoat covered in gems, he asked, in a rare moment of humor, "Are you supposed to be Diamond Jim Brady?"[7]

A Marriage of Convenience was a period piece, atypical of Billie's greatest hits. Nevertheless, the play was a modest success and returned Billie to top standing on the stage. Billie's triumph in the show prompted Ziegfeld to take on the role of her manager again, and he promised to secure her the part of Lady Teazle in the upcoming production of *The School for Scandal.* However, as he became increasingly engrossed in the *Follies,* Billie's career fell by the wayside. She was not blind to the fact that her husband was so engrossed in this particular edition of the *Follies* partly because of two of its featured players: Marilyn Miller and, in a casting choice that sent shock waves through Broadway and the Ziegfeld home, Lillian Lorraine.

Why had Ziegfeld decided to rehire Lillian? She was not penniless, so his decision could not have been based on pity. Lillian had spent the last few years working in film, vaudeville, and, like Marilyn, the Shuberts' *Passing Show.* Ziegfeld did not need her professionally, but emotionally he needed to close the book on their relationship once and for all. He gave her a "test run" in the *Midnight Frolic* before deciding whether to include her in the cast of the *Follies of 1918.* The *Frolic,* which opened only a few weeks before the *Follies,* starred Lillian in a number entitled "Tipperary Mary." Lillian played a scrubwoman dressed in gingham and carrying an iron pail, and Abe Erlanger cynically commented that she would probably be too drunk to get up off her knees. Ziegfeld replied that he would simply have Lillian remain on her knees for the entire number if that were the case. Her act proved to be one of the most successful in the show, and Ziegfeld promptly included her in the *Follies.*

Another reason for Ziegfeld's decision to hire Lillian was that he wanted the 1918 edition of the *Follies,* set to open on June 18 at the New Amsterdam Theatre, to be an all-star cast of "established headliners and box office giants."[8] The onstage giants were Lillian, Will Rogers, Eddie Cantor, W. C. Fields, Frank Carter, Dolores, the Fairbanks twins (the Dolly sisters' successors, who had made their names in Biograph films and other Broadway shows), and Marilyn Miller. Backstage the giants included Joseph Urban, Ned Wayburn, Gene Buck, Dave Stamper, and Irving Berlin. An obvious name missing from this constellation of stars was Fanny Brice. Some believed she refused to be in the show because of unhealed rivalries between her and Lillian, but the true reason for her absence was that she was eager to go solo in a starring vehicle. With or without Fanny, the *Follies of 1918* had more box-office attractions than either the 1916 or 1917 edition.

Inspired by the recent victories of American and Allied troops in Europe, the 1918 *Follies* was, according to most critics, brazenly patriotic.

Ziegfeld even went so far as to include a bare-breasted Lady Liberty in one tableau (a loophole in censorship laws allowed girls to be nude onstage if they did not move). The opening number, "The Warring World," showed Kay Laurel as Lady Liberty atop a globe of the earth. As she looked down on doughboys fighting in the trenches, the sound of gunfire filled the theater. Many numbers showed women dressed in trousers and taking on masculine roles such as pilots and shipbuilders. But according to historian Ann Ommen van der Merwe, such gender role reversals were "more likely the result of *Follies* tradition than of Ziegfeld's desire to make a political statement about women . . . he was perfectly willing to portray women performing men's jobs as long as they appeared feminine while doing so."[9] One of the biggest hits of the show, however, had no female performers. It was a tune taken from an all-soldier revue Irving Berlin had written during his service in the army, *Yip Yip Yaphank.* The catchy song "Oh How I Hate to Get up in the Morning" more than satisfied the audience's desire for comedy: "Oh! how I hate to get up in the morning, / Oh! how I'd love to remain in bed; / . . . Someday I'm going to murder the bugler, / Someday they're going to find him dead; / I'll amputate his reveille, / and step upon it heavily, / And spend the rest of my life in bed."[10] Unlike *Yip Yip Yaphank,* the *Follies* did not include any real soldiers in the cast. However, Ziegfeld placed a notice on each theater seat explaining that the boys in the chorus were not slackers. All of them had been exempted from the draft for valid reasons.[11]

The show's closing song by Buck and Stamper was an anthem to the emerging popularity of jazz entitled "I Want to Learn to Jazz Dance." The tune introduced the word "shimmy," a dancing term that means to hold one's body stationary except for the shoulders, which move back and forth. The rehearsal pianist for the show was again George Gershwin, who represented modernity in the music world, just as Marilyn did in the world of acting and dance. "True music must repeat the thought and inspirations of the people and the time. My people are Americans and my time is today," Gershwin once stated.[12] The young composer exerted some influence over the syncopated rhythm of the *Follies* finale. He, like Irving Berlin, was a regular guest at Burkeley Crest. Billie recalled that he often dropped in before dinner and "play[ed] [the piano] without being asked and I would sit for hours listening . . . wholly conscious of the rare experience I was enjoying."[13] What the *Follies* and its music ultimately accomplished was to remind Americans what the boys overseas were defending—ingenuity, innovation, and unblemished youth.

Though Marilyn Miller was a more appropriate symbol of unblemished youth, Ziegfeld still saw Lillian Lorraine as the epitome of the girl soldiers kept in their hearts while fighting in the trenches. The fact that he gave her five of the twenty production numbers in the show, despite her "advanced" age of twenty-six, proved Ziegfeld's ongoing regard for Lillian. If Ziegfeld was seeking closure to his feelings for her, he likely came close to finding it when her conduct reminded him how unprofessional she could be. Lillian's presence helped sell tickets to the show, but she adversely affected the backstage atmosphere. According to Muriel Merrill, one of the twenty-four girls in the revue, Lillian was "constantly doing things to taunt Mr. Ziegfeld. One night . . . she came on stage with two of her front teeth blacked out—just to shock and annoy him. We all knew she could have married him at any time, but she wouldn't have any part of it."[14] Ziegfeld was in no way amused by her prank and, contrary to the showgirls' assumptions, had no intentions of marrying Lillian. Backstage he "raised hell" about her lack of professionalism.[15] Lillian's drinking problem had also become more conspicuous. Doris Eaton, a newcomer in the 1918 *Follies*, recalled that "in the 'Garden of My Dreams' number . . . she lost her footing and had to be helped back up by [costar] Frank Carter." A watchful stagehand had also helped the unsteady Lillian before the curtain went up but neglected to notice that her eight-inch-tall headdress was askew. Ziegfeld had been known to fire girls for twisting their hats or staining their costumes, yet he could not bring himself to fire Lillian for such a transgression.

Crooked headdress and drunkenness aside, the "Garden of My Dreams" number was, according to Robert Baral of the *Revue*, "the real song hit of the show."[16] Reviewers declared the Joseph Urban–designed set—a gorgeous Japanese garden complete with a miniature arched bridge and stunted cherry trees—a showstopper. Lillian, dressed in a kimono, stood atop the bridge as Frank Carter serenaded her. Lillian's next number was not as artistic, but its star power overrode any aesthetic deficiency. As Lillian sang "Any Old Time at All," four men—Will Rogers, W. C. Fields, Eddie Cantor, and Harry Kelly—crooned to her.

Though he could croon if need be, Will Rogers's monologues won him the most praise. Channing Pollock of *Green Book Magazine* called Will a "talking Thackeray" who spoke his mind on timely topics, mainly the war: "I hear Charley Chaplin is going to war. Now I can see the Kaiser hit with a custard pie square in the face! . . . The Republicans are jealous over the way the Democrats are running the war. I bet when peace is declared and the Republicans get in power, they'll start another war to show how much better they can run one." When not talking politics, Will made lighthearted but acerbic conversation directed at the audience: "The *Follies* give men an opportunity to come here with their new wives and see what their old wives are doing. If they come early they can see just where their alimony is going." At the conclusion of his monologue, Will "threatened" to write a book called "My Four Years with the *Follies,* or Prominent Men I've Met at the Stage Door."[17]

W. C. Fields and Eddie Cantor, along with fellow comics Harry Kelly and Gus Minton, provided the more riotous laughs in the show. In a now classic scene, Fields played a patent attorney, Cantor played his office boy, and Kelly and Minton portrayed crazy inventors. Their most outrageous invention was a chair that killed anyone who sat in it. Cantor's best work was showcased in a skit with Frank Carter entitled "The Aviator's Test." In that routine, Eddie underwent a strenuous and rather gymnastic physical examination that tested his ability to be a pilot. In one hilarious exchange, Frank asked, "Do you sleep well? Are you disturbed at night?"

"Yes I'm disturbed terribly," Eddie replied.

"What disturbs you?"

"My brother Morris. I sleep with him."

"How does he sleep?"

"Like this," Eddie said, putting his feet in Frank's lap. A furious Frank shoved them off.

"How long can a man live without brains?" Frank exclaimed.

"I don't know. How old are you?" Eddie responded in the final line.[18]

The skit was Eddie's most popular, but Ziegfeld initially vetoed it entirely. According to Eddie, he faced a crisis in the 1918 *Follies,* having resolved that "the old blackface must die."[19] The aviator scene with Carter was to be his stage debut sans blackface. At first, Ziegfeld evasively told Eddie he would consider the skit, but Eddie knew that "consider" meant "reject." Ziegfeld acquiesced only after Gene Buck reminded him that he had a tin ear for comedy. Biographer Charles Higham speculated that the producer's true motive for rejecting the skit was Eddie's complicity in arranging clandestine meetings between Frank Carter (Eddie's roommate) and Marilyn Miller. Ziegfeld may have felt betrayed by Eddie, who was aware of the producer's increasing fondness for Marilyn. But Eddie gave his boss an ultimatum: "Either the scene is in or I'm out altogether." Eddie noted that, "despite his hesitation, he [Ziegfeld] had the showmanship to let me experiment, gambling on the chance that audiences might not accept me in white face. In this regard, Ziegfeld is without exception the biggest sport in the business."[20] Ziegfeld's gamble paid off. Eddie continued to perform without blackface to much acclaim, and Marilyn and Frank continued their romance.

Despite the established stars she was competing with, Marilyn Miller was "undoubtedly the sensation of the show."[21] Her two solo dances, "Yankee Doodle" (which included a parade of girls waving international flags) and the fantasy-themed "A Dream," showcased patriotism as well as Marilyn's celestial style of dance. But the number that made the audience want to climb up onstage and carry Marilyn out on their shoulders was a lyrical spoof of Billie Burke. Marilyn even wore a silk dress in Billie's signature color, baby blue. The song, "Mine Was a Marriage of Convenience," alluded to Billie's current Broadway play but could also be taken as a cynical reference to her union with Ziegfeld. However, because the implication about the Ziegfelds' marriage was false, the song was viewed with humor rather than indignation, even by the couple themselves. *Harper's Bazaar* lauded Marilyn's overall performance with this observation: "Other girls can dance. Other girls can smile. But Marilyn Miller's the only girl who can do both at once—with her tongue in cheek, so to speak, and her hands tied behind her back, as it were . . . her work . . . is indescribably refreshing."[22]

The show's success exceeded that of any previous Ziegfeld production. However, that success came at a cost: Ziegfeld spent more than $10,000 on the *Follies of 1918*. He would have made more profits had it not been for ticket scalping, which had become an insidious problem on Broadway. Ziegfeld published full-page spreads in newspapers condemning the practice and vowing to stamp it out. He even offered a $1,000 reward to any person who provided proof that an employee of the theater was colluding with scalpers. The problem stretched into 1919, when the swindlers had people buy tickets from the New Amsterdam box office and then later resold them at inflated prices. Ticket scalping did nothing to diminish the 1918 show's merits—even though it diminished the profits. The *Follies of 1918* "went down in musical theater record books as one of the great extravaganzas of Broadway's Golden Age."[23] A critic for the *New York Times* wisely predicted that "the best *Follies* of them all will eventually grow out of the present show."[24]

The close of 1918 marked a new peak in Ziegfeld's career. He could have claimed he had more stars than there are in heaven (twenty years before MGM Studios made that statement). By winter, Ziegfeld was set to open a new musical comedy, *By Pigeon Post;* another *Midnight Frolic;* and an additional confection, the *Nine O'Clock Frolic.* History has all but forgotten *By Pigeon Post,* which folded on December 14, 1918, after only twenty-five performances at the George M. Cohan Theatre. Ziegfeld paid the show's failure little mind, however; the phenomenal popularity of his rooftop shows more than compensated for it. The *Nine O'Clock Frolic* and the *Midnight Frolic* offered no shortage of entertainment with featured players such as Fanny Brice, Bert Williams, and Lillian Lorraine. Lillian, as usual, created headaches for Ziegfeld. After the premieres of both rooftop shows, her name appeared in sensational headlines describing her incessant partying and her new suitors, one of whom was a "prominent broker."[25] When Lillian left Ziegfeld to perform in a new musical at the Central Theatre, *The Little Blue Devil,* he felt a temporary sense of relief. However, Ziegfeld could not shake his feelings of responsibility for her. One of the chorus girls in Lillian's new show recalled that one night, an inebriated Lillian fell in the gutter while trying to hail a cab. A friend called the Ziegfeld office, and he sent a member of his staff to pick her up.[26] Ziegfeld could have gone himself, but he had no interest in reentering her world of sordid affairs. Ziegfeld had finally gotten over his feelings for her; Lillian was like a wayward daughter to him now, not an object of passion.

As 1918 drew to a close, Ziegfeld began to see Marilyn Miller as another potential "wayward daughter." He perceived her unabashed pursuit of men, particularly Frank Carter, as the first sign of trouble. The more she refused Ziegfeld's attentions and "fatherly" warnings, the more appealing she became to him. And she knew it. If she kept playing her game of "hard to get," she could hasten her rise to stardom. Higham described Marilyn's charm as "ruthless . . . a glitter that made every man in the room turn around when she walked in."[27] This "ruthless charm" frustrated Ziegfeld to no end. He began to send her telegrams from his office, criticizing her for such small matters as crooked stockings. To counter his critiques, he ensured that she had a fresh costume for each performance, at a cost of $175 apiece.[28]

As preparations began for the 1919 *Follies,* Marilyn and Frank's love affair was no longer a rumor or a secret. Their relationship had become like the archetypal plotline of forbidden love, complete with disapproving parents (Caro and Ada Miller) and the jealous "other man" (Ziegfeld). Eddie Cantor continued to facilitate the couple's clandestine meetings, even if it meant his relationship with Ziegfeld became more precarious. Because she knew Eddie was a settled family man, Marilyn often told her parents that he had invited her to dine with him and his wife after rehearsals. Eddie would pick her up in his limousine, drop her off at Frank's apartment, go to a deli, order his customary snack—a bowl of corn flakes—and talk with friends until it was time to take her home. Marilyn and Frank were determined to marry, with or without parental approval or Ziegfeld's blessing.

Ironically, Ziegfeld's meddling in Marilyn's love life resembled Charles Frohman's interference in Ziegfeld and Billie's. Ziegfeld had fallen hopelessly in love with the image of Marilyn he presented onstage. Ethan Mordden explained that "Ziegfeld made her so tantalizing that he was sick with need; Pygmalion besotted with his creation."[29] Billie later wrote that her husband's infatuation with Marilyn did not surprise her, commenting that the actress was unmatched in "sheer slim provocative beauty."[30] Knowing that Marilyn was his most perfect star made Ziegfeld all the more vexed that she was willing to jeopardize her career for a man. At the time Ziegfeld learned of the couple's impending union, the *Follies of 1919* was only weeks away from opening. Ziegfeld believed that Marilyn's appeal to audiences would diminish if she did not seem "available," if only on a platonic level, to male audience members.

Ziegfeld knew the marriage was inevitable, but he was still devastated when he read in the paper one May morning that Marilyn and Frank had eloped in Maryland. During rehearsals later that morning, Frank came into the New Amsterdam, strolled across the stage, and smiled at Marilyn. Ziegfeld, seated in the auditorium and puffing on a cigar, fired Frank before rehearsals began. Hurt and enraged, Frank stalked from the theater. He lost little time in signing with the Shuberts for their new show, *See Saw*. Marilyn, as much as she loved Frank, remained in Ziegfeld's employ. She was not willing to sacrifice her starring role in the *Follies*.

Ziegfeld's frustration over Marilyn's actions was heightened by his realization that Lillian Lorraine was officially a lost cause. At the same time, he struggled to prove his devotion to Billie as he searched for her next play. On top of his personal headaches, he knew his next *Follies* had to surpass the previous edition. As he prepared for the 1919 theater season, Ziegfeld could certainly relate to Irving Berlin's lyrics: "Oh, how I hate to get up in the morning!"

After the whirlwind of activity in 1918, Ziegfeld took the first half of 1919 slowly. He produced no spring edition of the *Frolic*, funneling his energy into the *Follies* instead. Plus, he was still looking for a new vehicle for Billie. Given her fondness for W. Somerset Maugham, it was fitting that he chose Maugham's play *Caesar's Wife* as Billie's next project. The play was "more serious than anything Ziegfeld had heretofore produced," noted Richard Ziegfeld.[31] Set in an English colony in Cairo, Egypt, the play tells the story of Violet, the vivacious wife of a man twenty years her senior, who falls in love with his diplomatic secretary. Ziegfeld was in the midst of producing the 1919 *Follies*, which was still running at the time of the November 24 premiere of *Caesar's Wife*, but he managed to supervise his wife's new play as well. Although he was most adept at overseeing spectacles, his "scrupulously tasteful and discreet" attention to *Caesar's Wife* showed his competence at managing intimate dramas. And thanks to Joseph Urban's sets, the show did contain an element of spectacle; his rendering of the Nile basin had "a romantic suggestion of palms, dark green waters, and a dusky purple sky."[32]

As had been the case with Anna Held's venture into drama with *Mam'selle Napoleon* (1903), critics did not approve of Billie's turn as a dramatic actress. Maugham's play was well written and witty; however, Violet's continuous emotional upheaval, her lack of thought before speaking, and her judgmental attitude toward her female friends failed to garner sympathy from audiences or reviewers. Alexander Woollcott and Dorothy Parker, two members of the famed literary circle at the Algonquin Round Table, were especially unimpressed by Billie's performance on opening night at New York's Liberty Theatre. Woollcott called her a "decorative and girlish comedienne," and Parker described her acting as "an impression of Eva Tanguay."[33] (Eva Tanguay, the young, energetic singer-dancer from the *Follies of 1908*, was best known for singing "I Don't Care" with expressive gesticulations.) Parker's caustic comparison seemed to suggest that Billie was too old for the part and that she overdid her displays of emotion. Ziegfeld's reaction to Parker's review exhibited the type of chivalry and righteous indignation Billie missed whenever her husband's attentions strayed elsewhere. Storming into the offices of *Vanity Fair*, Ziegfeld threatened to withdraw all advertising from the magazine if Parker was not fired.

Vanity Fair promptly complied. Unfortunately, Ziegfeld's gesture gave the public the false impression that Billie was a spoiled actress whose husband ensured that she received only glowing reviews.

Billie once again redirected her energy toward Burkeley Crest and Patricia before returning to her fallback profession as a silent film star. While performing in *A Marriage of Convenience* and *Caesar's Wife*, Billie had still been a very devoted mother. Patricia wrote that "whenever Mother toured with a play, she took me along . . . she was determined not to leave me behind in the care of maids and nurses."[34] Billie did not have much spare time when she was touring, but she spent every free minute with her child. Patricia recalled the fun she and her mother had together and observed that Billie always seemed giddy, as if she had just drunk champagne. When both Ziegfeld's and Billie's shows were on tour, the family's routine meeting place was Atlantic City. When they traveled, their lifestyle remained as opulent as it was at Burkeley Crest. Billie never had fewer than forty pieces of luggage with her. Often she would bring along the dogs, a horse, and Patricia's polo pony, which had been a gift from Will Rogers.

"Would you like me to herd together the deer at home and bring them along too?" Ziegfeld teased Billie.

"Oh dear, if you'd only thought of it earlier," Billie sighed, grinning at her husband.[35]

While in Atlantic City, Billie and Patricia enjoyed playing with their dogs on the beach and scampering through the sand as if they "were exactly the same age."[36] Once when Billie overzealously tossed a piece of driftwood for the dogs to retrieve, two diamond and ruby rings flew off her finger and disappeared. The sight of Patricia and Billie on their hands and knees in search of the rings attracted a crowd. When the onlookers discovered that they were searching for jewels, they quickly spread the word. People were still digging in the sand for weeks afterward, hoping to find the gems. Patricia had just as much fun with her father. She and Ziegfeld would stroll along the boardwalk, sharing their amusement as they watched the vendors making taffy or explored a toothpaste manufacturing exhibit.

Such familial moments were too few. Billie was unhappy with Ziegfeld's long absences in New York and his insistence that he stay at the Ansonia during production of the *Follies*. Billie described herself as a "flickering star" at this time, in both her professional and marital lives.[37] However, the press did not see her as "flickering" at all. At the opening of the 1919 *Follies,* one journalist provided a vivid snapshot of Billie that confirmed she was as dazzling as ever: "The lovely Billie, who could have shown as a star in her own right by reason of her stage and screen successes, insisted on being present only in her official capacity as wife of the famous Flo. . . . From the interest which the audience took in her, I'm inclined to believe that not a few of its members felt that the winsome Billie, with her red-gold hair and blue, blue eyes, was a big feature of the evening's entertainment." The perceptive journalist chronicled her reaction to particularly amusing numbers in the show: "Isn't it screamingly funny?" exclaimed Billie, dabbing her eyes with her handkerchief. "And did you ever see prettier showgirls?" she went on proudly. "Or such lovely sets. Tell me honestly—what do you think is the prettiest thing you've seen here tonight?"

"You," the reporter brazenly stated before fleeing to his seat.[38]

"The 1919 *Follies* will be the greatest victory party New York has ever known," Ziegfeld had declared after reading about the armistice in the headlines of every newspaper on November 11, 1918. Victory ushered in a new era that did not yet have an identity. The new *Follies*, "sparked by a compelling blend of old-fashioned show biz traditions confronting the uncertainty of changing times," made the era's ambiguity fun rather than daunting.[39] The format of the 1919 *Follies*, which opened on June 16 at the New Amsterdam Theatre, remained the same, but its look and sound were modernized and refined. Joseph Urban's sets were more sophisticated and authentic than usual, the stars of the show were predominantly in their twenties, and for the first time in *Follies* history, the bulk of the score was penned by a single composer. Ziegfeld chose Irving Berlin for the task, but Gene Buck, Dave Stamper, and Victor Herbert contributed several songs as well.

The twenty-somethings in the cast included Marilyn Miller, the Fairbanks twins, Eddie Cantor, and several new singing talents: John Steel, Ray Dooley (a woman, despite her masculine name), and Eddie Dowling. Fourteen-year-old Doris Eaton was the youngest new member of the chorus. Fanny Brice, having failed at her attempts to go solo, planned to perform in the new *Follies* despite her pregnancy, and she even participated in rehearsals for several weeks; however, she had to drop out of the show a month before her child was due. Gilbert Seldes of the *New Yorker* elaborated on subsequent events: "Mr. Ziegfeld telegraphed her that he could not understand how anyone could be so unmindful of obligations under the equity contract as to get into such a condition."[40] Sending that ridiculous telegram apparently dissipated Ziegfeld's frustrations. He apologized to Fanny the next day and gave her a bit part as one of the now customary plants in the audience. He placed her in an aisle seat, "as if she was part of the audience, and turned her loose to make zany comments" during one of Marilyn's ballets, Billie recalled. "The effect was staggering. Audiences were exhausted between the double impacts of beauty and laughter."[41] Fanny was an ideal juxtaposition to Marilyn's elegance. Each night she changed her quips to retain the element of surprise that was ubiquitous in the *Follies of 1919*. Less than ideal was the absence of both W. C. Fields and Will Rogers from the cast. Fields was busy performing in the *Midnight Frolic,* and Samuel Goldwyn had lured Will to Hollywood with a film contract. Losing his "all-time favorite male performer" and best friend hurt Ziegfeld terribly.[42] He had already lost quite a few stars to Hollywood, including Mae Murray, Marion Davies, and Olive Thomas. Doris Eaton explained that this "exasperated Ziegfeld, who was a star maker without the power to hold his most famous creations."[43]

However, the comic talents of Eddie Cantor and Bert Williams more than made up for Will's absence. Irving Berlin's witty lyrics were the highlight of Eddie's skits. His most popular song in the show, "You'd Be Surprised," used subtle sexual overtones for comedy's sake. Berlin repeated the title several times in the tune, making each repetition carry "that punch of unexpectedness which plays so important a part in humor."[44] The lyrics still pack a punch today: "He's such a delicate thing but when he starts in to squeeze / You'd be surprised / He doesn't look very strong but when you sit on his knee / You'd be surprised."[45]

Eddie had honed his singing style by adding "special slurs and peculiar inflections" to his voice. This perfected style, along with his knowing eye rolls at the end of each stanza, explains why "You'd Be Surprised" was such a smashing success. The Prince of Wales was among those most amused by Eddie's antics. In fact, a reporter for *Variety* noted that the prince "never laughed more heartily in all his life." He specifically requested that Eddie sing a hit from the 1917 *Follies,* "That's the Kind of a Baby for Me." Before doing so, Eddie announced to the audience, "I've been asked not to mention the fact that a distinguished member of British royalty is with us tonight." He followed this statement by conspicuously gazing at the prince. "But I want him to know," Eddie continued, "that if he leaves New York without seeing the Bronx, he'll be sorry all his life!"[46] "Where's the

Bronx?" another distinguished audience member, Mrs. Vanderbilt, inquired before the orchestra struck up Eddie's song.

Another Berlin song, "Mandy," was also a big hit. Though the lyrics of "Mandy" were timeless, the song was executed in an old-fashioned minstrel style. Eddie Cantor and Bert Williams sang the tune, addressing the words to Marilyn Miller and Ray Dooley. The "Mandy" number was later re-created in two films, one of which starred Eddie, *Kid Millions* (1936). In 1954 Irving Berlin wrote the entire score for the holiday classic *White Christmas* and included "Mandy" in it. The number was not performed in blackface, of course, but the staging in the film was almost identical to the original staging in the 1919 *Follies*.

Though audiences and critics responded to Eddie Cantor's songs with great enthusiasm, the number that garnered the most praise for the comedian was not musical at all. Called "The Osteopath Scene," the skit was a physical comedy routine similar to "The Aviator's Test" of the previous year. According to Eddie, "The Osteopath Scene" transplanted "the idea of bodily punishment to a new and more fertile locale . . . it seems the audiences love to see somebody knocked and battered about to the point of insensibility so long as they feel he isn't really getting hurt."[47] Eddie's skits, whether they were slapstick or musical, were lighthearted. However, the topics of other humorous bits in the *Follies* were more serious and controversial.

At the close of 1919, Congress passed two constitutional amendments that greatly altered the American way of life: women won the vote, and Americans lost the luxury of drinking liquor. The Volstead Act, or Prohibition, did not take effect until January 1920, but Ziegfeld knew the *Frolic*'s days were numbered, enhanced as it was by boozy merriment. Ziegfeld gave liquor a grand send-off and even staged a "funeral" for the beloved nectar. The songs of mourning were a delightful mix of biting satire and upbeat humor. Eddie Cantor sang "You Don't Need the Wine to Have a Wonderful Time While They Still Make Beautiful Girls," and Bert Williams's rendition of "When the Moon Shines on the Moonshine" kept the audience in stitches. Marilyn was center stage for another act addressing Prohibition, "A Syncopated Cocktail." The Irving Berlin number featured girls parading in costumes representative of lemonade, sarsaparilla, and Coca-Cola.

The acts dealing with Prohibition may have been popular in their time, but what truly made the 1919 *Follies* go down in history were the numbers that celebrated beauty in ways that only Ziegfeld could imagine. One act, "Tulip Time in Holland," utilized a working windmill and a plethora of real tulips. In a circus ballet composed by Victor Herbert, audiences gasped as Marilyn Miller rode a live white horse across the stage. She then dismounted and flitted through an airy dance. However, one Irving Berlin number trumped all the others and epitomized the timeless female beauty that Ziegfeld strove to capture. The number in question? "A Pretty Girl Is Like a Melody." It anthropomorphized great classical musical pieces through a succession of gorgeous women. One girl dressed as Offenbach's "Barcarolle" from *Tales of Hoffmann,* while another was Puccini's "Un bel di vedremo" from *Madame Butterfly.* Ironically, "Pretty Girl," which became the *Follies'* theme song for years to come, had been a last-minute request. "I've got a set of six costumes and need a musical number for them," Ziegfeld explained to Berlin during a hasty meeting. "Just one more song, Irving, I need one more." The composer looked at photos of the costumes and later recalled: "I thought of an idea to have each girl represent a famous classical number. Pretty girls served as springboards for these old classics. It is interesting to note that the last thing I thought of was the song."[48]

Also noteworthy is that "Pretty Girl" was actually one of the least lavish numbers in the show. In the 1936 film *The Great Ziegfeld,* there are girls descending a magnificent revolving staircase. But as it was staged in 1919, the number was "a simple, exquisite presentation, the antithesis of flair and ostentation."[49] The curtain rose on a bare, dark stage with one man, crooner John Steel, alone in the spotlight singing: "A pretty girl is like a melody / That haunts you night and day, / Just like the strain of a haunting refrain, / She'll start up-on a marathon / And run around your brain. / . . . She will leave you and then come back again, / A pretty girl is just like a pretty tune."[50]

Between stanzas, more spotlights appeared, illuminating a new girl for each classical piece introduced in Berlin's composition. The lyrics of the song, like the number itself, were simple but as haunting as the girls they described. At first, when the number ended, there was a brief hush in the theater. According to Doris Eaton, "the audience initially seemed somewhat taken aback, still absorbing the loveliness in sound and sight and simplicity they had just experienced." Then the audience broke into applause that was "spontaneous and generous."[51] Although Marilyn did not appear in the act, the tune somehow became associated with her.

Audiences left the theater with the song playing in their ears, but Marilyn was the girl they pictured as the embodiment of the music. Ziegfeld's fears were unfounded—Marilyn's marriage had done nothing to diminish her audience appeal.

The 1919 *Follies* accomplished precisely what Ziegfeld hoped it would. The show was the greatest victory party America had ever seen, celebrating both the country's past and its bright if dizzyingly changing future. At the beginning of the 1919 theater season, Broadway producers had predicted that the shows released that year would represent the apex of theatrical achievement. If Ziegfeld's revue was any indication of what lay ahead for the season, the prescient producers had no reason to doubt themselves. Ziegfeld's brilliance had matured, and it was never more apparent than in the *Ziegfeld Follies of 1919*. Part of Ziegfeld's success was due to a technique that movie moguls would later adopt: gather a loyal, consistent stable of stars and a collection of first-rate backstage talent. In the 1930s MGM Studios became known for pampering its stars with homemade food in the commissary and custom-designed dressing rooms. Ziegfeld was like a one-man MGM; he truly believed that his stars were the best and thus deserved only the best. By infusing his show both with freshness, youth, and vitality and with nostalgia for the past, he had built the *Ziegfeld Follies* into the greatest institution on Broadway. As one reviewer put it, the *Follies of 1919* finally made Ziegfeld's name "known throughout the land."[52]

12

Dear Old Zieggy and Company

"A token of love and esteem presented to Florenz Ziegfeld Jr. by the members of his companies and executive staffs at the Follies Frolic Ball May 18, 1919."[1] So read the inscription on a fifteen-inch-high silver loving cup that Ziegfeld's dedicated employees gave to their boss. Despite Ziegfeld's perfectionism, his fits of temper, his jealousies and flirtations, he invoked fierce loyalty and affection from his staff. Many referred to him as "dear old Zieggy." Lucile (Lady Duff Gordon) had nothing but fondness for him and was seemingly never on the receiving end of his occasional rages. "I found him delightful to work with," she stated. "He is the most patient and the most considerate producer, never loses his temper no matter what happens, and treats every member of the chorus as politely as though she were a peeress in her own right."[2] Dancer Marcelle Earle went so far as to call him the father she never had.

Ziegfeld's employees held him in such high regard not only because of his consideration for them but also because of his accessibility. Although he preferred to communicate with his actors through telegrams, he did not hole himself up in an ivory tower during the workday. He was a ubiquitous but unobtrusive presence at most rehearsals. "I never heard him once shout out an order at rehearsals, although his quiet voice was always heard giving directions," Lucile recalled.[3] When he was not giving directions, he was often softly complaining, at which time his "quiet voice" became "high [and] nasal." Ziegfeld was so intent during rehearsals that Gilbert Seldes asserted: "If a bomb exploded under his chair he would likely ring for the messenger boy to ask the house manager what had happened."[4] His intensity did not intimidate the majority of his stars. Many of them, especially

Eddie Cantor and Fanny Brice, were comfortable enough to make jokes at his expense. They most delighted in mimicking his voice. Ziegfeld took no offense from such jokes and tolerated the stars' ribbing as he would his own child's teasing.

Ziegfeld was as generous with money as he was with his time and good humor. He purchased clothes for the children of the cleaning women at the New Amsterdam, paid for a tubercular chorus girl's hospital stay, and kept disabled and ailing employees on the payroll. "Most of the people who work for him consider him kind and deplore the ease with which he is victimized . . . he is approachable through the proper channels, but he lacks something of the easy, perhaps too easy, *camaraderie,* of the theater," Seldes noted.[5] True to Seldes's observation, Ziegfeld had little personal contact with the chorus girls and was often an unseen benefactor. According to Marcelle Earle, he "paid top salaries. . . . Most of the principals and chorus never had it so good. Once the obscure, unknown ones were tagged with the name of Ziegfeld, their prestige and fortune magically improved."[6] Ziegfeld often sent engraved platinum watches to the principals in his shows. His gifts to the chorus girls were less expensive: long-stemmed roses on opening nights and ice cream during the summer. The ice cream tradition came to an end when two chorus girls took their treats up to the balcony, quarreled, and soiled each other's costumes with the melting desserts. Ziegfeld had once sent a telegram to his company reading, "Anyone who soils her costume will be fired," so this was a serious offense.[7]

As considerate as Ziegfeld was toward his employees, he seldom invited them to his home. A few select staff members did receive coveted invitations to Ziegfeld's extravagant Sunday dinners: Jerome Kern, Irving Berlin, Ned Wayburn, Joseph Urban and his wife, and Ben Ali Haggin. Even Will Rogers, for whom he had "real love," and Eddie Cantor, for whom he had "the most affection," rarely came to dinner.[8] That Ziegfeld invited Berlin, Kern, and Urban is surprising, given that these men were on the second level of a hierarchy Ziegfeld had formed in his mind. As Richard Ziegfeld explained, "actors were at the apex, composers, set designers, authors, choreographers were on the next level, stage production people were near the bottom, and office staff were the lowest level."[9] One notable exception in Ziegfeld's hierarchy was W. C. Fields. Ziegfeld put the actor at the bottom due to his alcoholism and its effect on his work. Oddly, he did not hold Lillian Lorraine to the same standard. Richard

Ziegfeld attributed this double standard to Ziegfeld's parental relationships. From Professor Ziegfeld, he felt disapproval and a sense of competition, while from his mother, he felt only tenderness. Even though Ziegfeld got his musical training from his father, his mother had a larger influence on his career because she encouraged him to act on his ambitions. "When he [Ziegfeld] treated women with such respect and admiration, lavishing special attention on them, he was perhaps acting on his feelings towards his mother," Richard Ziegfeld asserted.[10]

Ziegfeld was not subtle about favoring his female stars. According to Billie Burke, each cast member received gold coins with his or her first salary check—but the checks for the men were $10, and the girls' were $20.[11] If a girl did not indulge in liquor and late-night parties, she was likely to receive an even fatter check. Unlike many producers, Ziegfeld did not forbid his female stars to marry or have children. He often became dismayed if a wedding or a pregnancy occurred at an inopportune time, but he was usually sympathetic to the girls who had families, for he found they tended to have the best work ethic. Ziegfeld was generally protective toward his female employees. Marion Davies recalled that he even insisted "that the stage door Johnnies had to be introduced properly."[12]

Ziegfeld's wariness when it came to stage door Johnnies—or any male, for that matter—may have been an extension of his feelings toward his disapproving father. However, a more important factor in his overall lack of enthusiasm for his male employees had to do with money. The majority of his male staff worked on the business end of things, and Ziegfeld had no warm feelings for anyone who reminded him of budget limitations. He perceived Joseph Urban and Irving Berlin as true artists, so they were excluded from Ziegfeld's general coldness toward men. In contrast, his old friend Harry B. Smith was a songwriter and could have been deemed an artist, but Ziegfeld did not place him at the same level as Urban and Berlin because Smith was pecuniary. Smith was the first of many male employees to sue Ziegfeld for withholding royalties.

Bernard Sobel, who acted as Ziegfeld's press agent, knew all too well the drawbacks of being on the lowest level of Ziegfeld's hierarchy. Patricia described Sobel's duties in her memoirs: "Daddy was forever sending Bernie telegrams and cables and calling him up at midnight with new ideas for publicity, some of them crazy. I don't know how Mr. Sobel stood the job, which included being a punching bag for Daddy when anything went wrong. He had the disposition of an angel and remained mild and smiling however violent Daddy's tirades got. In some ways he was like a doctor, on call at any hour, ready to restore confidence and sanity."[13] Sobel may have been a "punching bag," but he and Ziegfeld somehow became close friends. Sobel even stayed in contact with Billie years after Ziegfeld's death. Sobel was able to stand the job because Ziegfeld never failed to atone when he realized he had pushed his friend too far. Ziegfeld once sent Sobel a telegram contritely reading: "My dear Bernie, I would not hurt your feelings intentionally for the world. You ought to know that. Regards. Ziegfeld." Just to corroborate this message, Ziegfeld's valet, Sidney, wrote an addendum: "I know he means this. Sidney."[14]

Ziegfeld was hard on his employees only because he demanded the same perfection from them that he demanded from himself. However, like his employees, he fell short in many areas, especially organization. Sometimes he would scream that he needed to see a particular contract, and his staff would scramble to find it. But Ziegfeld was known for hiring stars without contracts, and even if a contract was eventually found, it was often just scribbled on a page torn from a notebook. In most cases, his secretary Matilda Golden (aka Goldie) unearthed the missing contracts from under the piles of papers and scattered elephant figurines on Ziegfeld's desk. Such slapdash contracts usually had no firm terms covering salary, touring agreements, or contract renewal, causing much annoyance among his stars. For instance, Fanny Brice once refused to tour unless she got a raise, and Ziegfeld hated "anyone who even hinted [at] not going on tour. He wanted his show the same in Cincinnati as it was on Broadway."[15] Near the end of every season, when actors' contracts expired, Ziegfeld sent "reams of telegrams . . . scolding and criticizing them so that anyone who was planning to ask for a raise would be glad to sign again on the old terms." Eddie Cantor was not so easily moved: "Once he [Ziegfeld] sent me a couple of stinging messages and I wired back my resignation. He wired immediately that he was only kidding but I didn't see the joke." To make amends, Ziegfeld raised Eddie's pay to $1,000 a week for twenty more weeks. "Then I did see the joke!" Eddie declared.[16]

As noted earlier, Ziegfeld's primary mode of communication had always been telegrams. Though he was present at most rehearsals, he became restless when opening night drew near and would often pace the lobby of the New Amsterdam. During final rehearsals, he would send the actors telegrams backstage rather than giving them directions in person. In his memoirs, Eddie Cantor categorized the typical Ziegfeld telegrams: If one began with "I don't want to annoy you . . . ," it was sure to be loaded with complaints. If one ended with "This closes the incident," the recipient was "sure to get daily telegrams on the same subject for the rest of the season beginning with, *There's no use crying over spilled milk but . . .*"[17] Ziegfeld's primary costumer, Lucile, received many demanding telegrams, but rather than be annoyed by them, she was invigorated by their seemingly impossible requests. She once received a note from Ziegfeld saying that he wanted sixty dresses for his new show within ten days. After a flurry of telephoning and activity, "in less than an hour the work [had] . . . begun."[18]

Such frenzy was normal in the Ziegfeld office. Sobel described the milieu: "Specialists from all departments . . . and numerous high pressure men kept coming in and out of the office all day long. Secretaries rushed back and forth . . . telephones rang continually. Messenger boys dodged in and out. Famous actors came for appointments, just as worshipful in their admiration of the glorifier as the scores of beautiful girls who crowded the waiting rooms . . . praying for a chance to get into his shows."[19] It sounded like a monkey house, and sometimes it was one—literally. Ziegfeld occasionally brought his pet monkey from Burkeley Crest, and it would sit at a typewriter, thoughtfully pecking at the keys. The Ziegfeld office had one sane inmate: his loyal secretary, Goldie. Biographer Charles Higham described Goldie (formerly a secretary at Fox Film Studios) as Ziegfeld's "conscience, custodian, and keeper of secrets of the Ziegfeld Empire."[20] She kept creditors away and brought order to the chaos. Goldie was not even fazed by the deplorable appearance of the office. Nothing about it reflected the beauty and opulence of Ziegfeld's work. Located in a building overlooking Forty-Second Street, the office had metal bars on the windows, "bilious green walls," and a lack of proper heating and ventilation.[21] Given the constant activity and the less than ideal conditions, it is no surprise that Ziegfeld worked best when attending to business from his bed at Burkeley Crest.

When Ziegfeld did arrive at the office late in the afternoon, his appearance usually brought a temporary lull to the mayhem. He often wore an eccentric outfit consisting of a huge beaver-lined coat and a $50 Stetson hat with a narrow brim and a slit in the middle of the crown. When he walked into a room, Ziegfeld girl Dana O'Connell said it was like the parting of the Red Sea: "He was not classically handsome, but he was a charmer and commanded attention."[22]

Though he was demanding, unpredictable, and incapable of running an office efficiently, Ziegfeld's reputation as the best employer on Broadway was unshakeable. He insisted that his "children" call him Flo, and he would sob whenever one of them left him. Doris Eaton concurred: "Those [girls] who were lucky enough to be selected were initially very shy in the presence of Ziegfeld, but they soon overcame their timidity and discovered that their famous boss was friendly and encouraging to all newcomers. Most of the time, Ziegfeld had a kind of softness about him in the way he treated the cast."[23] For this reason, the majority of Ziegfeld's employees stayed with him for as long as he produced shows.

Among Ziegfeld employees there was an unusual bond. They were less like costars and more like siblings. According to Eddie Cantor, "The Ziegfeld actors formed a happy household in those years [1917–1919]." Cantor, Will Rogers, and W. C. Fields referred to one another as the Three Musketeers; Fanny Brice was "the business advisor, the mother confessor, the doctor, the marriage counselor to everyone."[24] Bert Williams and Eddie Cantor were "Sonny" and "Pappy" onstage, and their offstage relationship was not much different. Eddie called Bert "a great and liberal teacher."[25] With a few exceptions (namely, Victor Herbert and Jerome Kern), Ziegfeld's composers had a similar camaraderie. Irving Berlin was a good sport and tolerated the high-spirited practical jokes played by the actors. Gene Buck was a favorite of all the girls and, according to Marcelle Earle, gave them two bits of advice time and time again: "If you can't say anything good about a person don't say anything at all" and "When you are shooting [meaning setting your sights on achieving something], aim for the King."[26] Victor Herbert was the perfect gentleman and always tipped his hat to each girl he passed backstage.

Squabbles occurred almost exclusively among the chorus girls. Marcelle Earle noted that "some of the newly glorified ones would ad lib to pad their parts and act temperamental. . . . How snobbish some girls could act as they affected the pretentious broad 'a' in speech, girls who never had it so good." Dance director Ned Wayburn had little patience for such girls, particularly those who came to work stinking of gin. "The people with the *brains* are sitting on *that* side of the footlights," he yelled, pointing to the orchestra. "Don't take yourselves too seriously. Some of you will wind up with a *tin cup* in your hands."[27] Wayburn was referring to the girls who, like Lillian Lorraine, loved alcohol and had a different escort each night.

Snobbishness was not limited to the ladies of the chorus. A number of the principals were, to quote Marcelle Earle, "swell-headed" or "H.A.P.s"— in theater slang, "half-assed principals." That was not the case with Will Rogers, who was known on- and offstage as a "plain, natural, homespun family man, chuck full of human warmth." One incident during a tour of Chicago proved him to be just as down-to-earth as he appeared in the *Follies* and *Frolic*. Will entered the dining car of the train on which the company was traveling, and two HAPs invited him to eat with them. "I'm agoin' to set with the gals over there," Will told the actors. As he settled down with Marcelle and her friend, he said, "Looks mighty good, what you gals are eatin'. I'll have the same." After sharing a meal with them, the cowboy picked up the check and said, "'Twas nice eatin' in such good company."[28]

Though Will Rogers associated with all ranks of Ziegfeld performers, he most often chose the company of the other two "musketeers," Eddie Cantor and W. C. Fields. This didn't change even after his buddies played an elaborate practical joke on him. Will often spoke of his boyhood in Oklahoma, and his reminiscences frequently included his pal Clay McGonigle, with whom he had had many adventures. Will apparently told these same stories a hundred times and always concluded by saying, "There is nothing in the world I own that I wouldn't willingly give half of to Clay."[29] Fields decided that it would be hilarious to forge a note from Clay McGonigle, telling Will that he would be in the audience of the *Follies* on a certain night. Will was "choked with emotion" upon receiving the note. On the night Clay was supposed to be in the theater, Will addressed a ten-minute monologue to his old pal. "Clay, do you remember Mrs. Hennigan's pies?" he asked, to the audience's confusion. "And Clay, do you remember when we were on that cattle boat?" At the show's intermission, Will eagerly searched the lobby for Clay. When Clay failed to appear, Will checked every hotel in New York. "Did I say anything that could've offended Clay?" Will miserably asked Eddie and Fields. Eddie felt terrible about the joke's effect on Will, but he predicted that if he told Will the truth, "He would've killed us."[30] When Will eventually discovered the joke, he found Eddie in the dining room of the Astor Hotel and slapped him on the neck so hard that the comedian almost fell into his soup. However, Will was not one to hold a grudge. He even went so far as to "kosher up" whenever he dined with Eddie. When he later underwent gallbladder surgery, he joked, "That's what I get for going to all those kosher restaurants with Eddie Cantor!"[31]

Eddie's adherence to Jewish dietary laws made him the next victim of a practical joke devised by Fields. On one occasion, boxer John L. Sullivan invited the "Three Musketeers" and Bert Williams out for dinner. Eddie was starving when he arrived at the restaurant, but course after course, he found only pork or shellfish on his plate. "I really don't have much of an appetite," Eddie said.

"Oh come on, you'll have some eggs," Sullivan said. Eddie agreed, but when the eggs arrived, they were covered in bacon.

Eddie soon surmised that he was the butt of a joke, but the prank ceased to be funny when he began to feel "hunger to [the] point of physical pain." Bert Williams, noting Eddie's rapidly paling complexion, took him aside and said, "Son, there's a package in my coat for you." Eddie went into the hall, looked inside Bert's pocket, and found a steak wrapped in a brown paper bag. "They've had a laugh," Bert said. "Now you have a steak." He then walked into the restaurant kitchen and broiled the steak himself.

Eddie was equally considerate of Bert. The actors shared a special bond not only because they performed so many acts together but also because they were both part of marginalized groups in society. Eddie rode with Bert in the servants' elevator at hotels, and he would not dine at any restaurant that refused to serve blacks. "My association with him was a joy and an education . . . [he was] an extremely human man full of fine sensibilities," Eddie concluded.[32]

Irving Berlin worked behind the scenes, but he was not immune to practical jokes. During the 1919 *Follies* tour through Atlantic City, Berlin was unexpectedly called back to New York. Eddie and Berlin's musical accompanist, Harry Akst, volunteered to pack the composer's bags for him. On a whim, they decided to include the wall hangings from the hotel in Berlin's baggage. Upon arriving in New York, Berlin received a sarcastic telegram from the hotel management "asking why he marched off with the pictures from their walls and why didn't he take the walls too?" A lengthy and heated correspondence ensued, but the dispute was never settled. Eddie wrote in his autobiography that "the pictures are probably still in Berlin's attic and undoubtedly he's never seen them."[33]

If Berlin had known that Eddie was behind the practical joke, he might have chosen to room with someone else during tours of the *Follies*. During stops in Atlantic City, the roommates spent many afternoons rolling down the boardwalk in the two-seat wicker chairs that were all the rage at the time. They discussed Berlin's latest tunes and how Eddie could best perform them. At Berlin's suggestion, Eddie sang "You'd Be Surprised" without his usual gimmick of running up and down the stage. "You don't have to get the song over, it'll get you over," Berlin said. So Eddie sang the song, rolling only his eyes, and then at the end he "ran like hell," to the amusement of the audience.[34] Berlin had an innate knowledge of what songs and arrangements would best suit each performer in the Ziegfeld fold. He had an especially keen intuition about what would work for Eddie Cantor and his other old friend, Fanny Brice.

Fanny mothered everyone in the Ziegfeld company, especially those who, like Eddie and Berlin, had come from the ghettos of New York. Fanny was the only female member of the Ziegfeld family who acted like "one of the boys." For all intents and purposes, she was the Fourth Musketeer. One evening she inadvertently played a joke on Eddie and Fields when she invited them to her apartment for her famous goulash and spaghetti. When the two men dove into their meals, their mouths began to foam. Somehow, the jar holding the grated cheese had been filled with soap flakes. Fanny flushed the spaghetti down the toilet and had to pay the next day to unclog the plumbing. Infuriated, she vowed to fire her maid, whom she blamed for the mix-up (she fired her maid almost every week for one reason or another but always rehired her the next day).

In addition to her talent for cooking (notwithstanding the soap and cheese fiasco), Fanny was an exceptional cardplayer. She treated each hand as if it were a world-shaking event. Eddie claimed that while Fanny was deciding which card to play, he had time to run several errands, and when he returned, she would still be pondering her decision. Fanny's quirks did not irritate Eddie. He felt he owed a great deal of his success to her. For Eddie's *Follies* debut back in 1917, Fanny had instructed Ned Wayburn to teach him a dance he could learn in an hour so that Eddie could be her partner in a minstrel number entitled "Just You and Me." At the end of the number, Fanny advised Eddie not to add tricks when he bowed to the audience. "You mustn't have the attitude that you're an interloper. You belong," she told him. Fanny made all those around her feel as if they belonged, from star attractions to chorus girls. She was nearly late for her curtain call one night because she was so busy letting the chorines try on her hats and giving clothes to girls "who didn't look smart enough." According to Eddie, among the actors in the *Follies* there was "a camaraderie I didn't know existed in show business . . . none of them was trying to steal the show. They were a family and they wanted *the family* to be a hit. They helped each other."[35]

By the end of the summer of 1919, however, the members of the Ziegfeld family found themselves embroiled in the most divisive strike in show business history. Principal players and chorines alike were faced with an almost impossible decision: betray one another or betray "dear old Zieggy."

> Over fair, over fair,
> We have been, we have been, over fair . . .
> So beware, have a care,
> Just be fair, on the square, everywhere,
> For we are striking, yes, we are striking,
> And we won't come back till the managers are fair.[36]

So sang the throng of 14,000 members of the Actors Equity Union as they marched up and down Broadway from August through September 1919. The song, a parody of George M. Cohan's "Over There," was a blatant attack on Cohan, who was the most outspoken producer against the union. He announced that if Equity won, he would leave show business and run an elevator instead. Eddie Cantor responded: "Somebody better tell Mr. Cohan that to run an elevator, he'd *have* to join a union."[37] Strike fever spread across the nation—175 occurred from coast to coast. The strikes increased in part due to socialist theories and the Bolshevik victory in Russia.

Ziegfeld shared Cohan's mind-set, even if he took a more diplomatic approach to the situation. He did not wish to alienate his greatest stars or his wife, for that matter, by condemning Actors Equity. Billie, though not a militant by anyone's standards, joined in the generally rebellious spirit of 1919. She lobbied in support of Liberty Bonds and against the use of animals for scientific research. Ziegfeld allegedly supported her views, but he "seemed content to lie back and let Billie do the work."[38] Politically, Ziegfeld was trying to walk a middle path. Although he was friendly with liberals such as Governor Jimmy Walker and Will Rogers, he also had to remain on good terms with his financial backers, all of whom were conservative. This put Ziegfeld in an awkward position; anything he did could offend one side or the other.

Ziegfeld saw no reason for his employees to strike, since he was the most generous employer on Broadway. Eddie Cantor thought differently. Being one of the most politically minded stars on Broadway, he was radical in his support of the union. His militancy proved infectious, and most of his colleagues followed him on the walkout from the New Amsterdam Theatre. Fanny Brice, Ed Wynn, Ray Dooley, Ziegfeld's old friend Lillian Russell, and Broadway's most popular jazz singer, Al Jolson, all joined the strike. Bert Williams came to work as usual on the day the strike began, in full makeup and costume. W. C. Fields, who was still playing in the *Frolic* and had not yet joined the strike, heard from Bert a few days later. "Do you know what happened to me the night of the strike, Pops?" Bert asked. "I went to the theater as usual, made up and dressed. Then I came out of my dressing room and found the stage deserted and dark, the big auditorium empty and the strike on. I knew nothing of it: I had not been told. You see, I just didn't belong."[39] Bert eventually joined Actors Equity, at Fields's urging.

Eddie Cantor temporarily abandoned the strike when Ziegfeld informed him that he was not a member of the Producing Managers Association, against which the actors were striking. However, five days later Eddie discovered that Ziegfeld had in fact joined the association, so he marched out again, ignoring Ziegfeld's follow-up telegram: "HOW COULD YOU DO THIS TO ME WHEN I'VE BEEN LIKE A FATHER TO YOU ALL THESE YEARS STOP WE NEVER HAD A DISPUTE ABOUT SALARY OR ANYTHING STOP." Eddie knew that Ziegfeld was not guilty of the abuses that had sparked the strike. But he felt the need to be in solidarity with his fellow performers who had suffered and, "in the process, elevate the profession as a whole."[40] Eddie responded to his boss's telegram with this explanation: "You misunderstand, Flo . . . there are producers not like you . . . you'll have to understand that this is not my doing something to you . . . we have to have rules; we have to have a standard."[41] Eddie was correct about the need for standards. Abuses were rampant in the theater world. Most actors received no salary for rehearsal time; they had to pay for their own costumes and provide their own transportation during tours. Managers had the power to dismiss any performer whose work they deemed inadequate, and there was no provision for appeal. Many producers used this power unfairly and fired performers over personal differences rather than professional ones.

As the strike dragged on for four long weeks, Ziegfeld faced the possibility of losing his exorbitant $182,000 investment in the *Follies of 1919*. Producers had predicted that 1919 would be the best season in Broadway history; instead, they suffered their biggest losses to date. Ziegfeld, determined to salvage the season, continued to show up at the vacant New Amsterdam Theatre throughout the strike's duration. Not everyone had deserted him. Among his principals, only Marilyn Miller remained. Marcelle Earle also continued to come to work. "The real Ziegfeld Girls were loyal to the Great Ziegfeld and didn't walk out despite pressure from the disgruntled ones. . . . Ziegfeld paid top salaries, why walk out on him?" Marcelle mused.[42]

The temporarily unemployed actors staged their own vaudeville revues on street corners to prevent patrons from going into any theaters associated with the Producing Managers Association. The strike grew in proportion once the musicians, stagehands, and electricians walked off the job to support the actors. Without backstage support to rely on, the producers agreed to recognize Actors Equity "as the legal bargaining agent for stage performers."[43] Producers ended most of the abuses at the center of the actors' protest. They now paid actors and chorus girls for rehearsals that lasted longer than four weeks. Managers still had a free hand in casting, but they could no longer fire an actor without cause. Eventually, Equity's win came to be seen as "a monument to the growing dignity and stability of the American theater."[44]

The *Follies* went on to enjoy a record run after the strike. Its healthy receipts were partly due to one battle Ziegfeld did win—against ticket scalpers. Ziegfeld had advocated for an ordinance against ticket speculation that had received the support of New York's district attorney. The ordinance passed, and although scalpers still existed, they became a much smaller problem. Ziegfeld sent a cable to the *New York Times* proclaiming his victory: "SPECULATORS DEFEATED FOLLIES PLAYED TO SEVENTY THOUSAND SIX HUNDRED AND EIGHTY TWO DOLLARS IN TWO WEEKS. . . . BIGGEST RECEIPTS IN THE HISTORY OF THE NEW AMSTERDAM."[45]

Ziegfeld was less enthusiastic about the success of Actors Equity—not because he objected to the actors' improved working conditions but because the strike's fallout had resulted in sorrow among his "family." First and foremost, Ziegfeld felt betrayed by his "children." Another sorrow was the separation of the "Three Musketeers." Will Rogers was in Hollywood, W. C. Fields remained in the *Follies*, and Eddie Cantor's career had fallen into a rut. Before the strike, Ziegfeld had promised Eddie a starring role in a book musical at an increased salary. However, when Eddie returned to work after the strike, Ziegfeld avoided the subject.

Even Marilyn Miller lost favor with Ziegfeld. Although he appreciated her admirable work ethic, he was hurt that she gave her loyalty to him only grudgingly. Marilyn often threatened to quit and emitted strings of obscenities at her boss. Her tirades seemed even more caustic when compared with the smiling, sprite-like girl onstage. Doris Eaton witnessed many of Marilyn's verbal outpourings and commented: "At times she treated him [Ziegfeld] so rudely and profanely (she could cuss with the best of the 'broads') that it appeared at times she had a strange hold over him."[46] That seemed to be true, for he never even considered firing her. Marilyn easily could have followed her husband's example and gone to work for the Shuberts, but she was not going to let any man destroy her, whether in her professional life or her private life. "She was ambitious and realistic in the way that genius performers have to be," biographer Ethan Mordden wrote. "Marilyn knew that her destiny was entwined with Ziegfeld's. . . . Ziegfeld seems to have known it, too, treating Marilyn with a deference he would never have shown to the other Girls in his employ."[47] Ziegfeld's "deference" included paying for Frank and Marilyn's honeymoon at the Astor Hotel. He may have done this as a sign of defeat or as a way to gain an advantage in his and Marilyn's tumultuous relationship. Marilyn cared little about his motives; she played Ziegfeld's game as well as the producer did himself. Whenever he gained the upper hand, she would immediately turn the tables on him. Marilyn's decision to keep working during the strike only gave her more power over Ziegfeld. Such manipulative behavior was entirely new to Ziegfeld. Anna Held, Lillian Lorraine, and Billie Burke had never played such games with him. Lillian had come close, but she had never made herself unattainable. Marilyn was precisely like the girls Ziegfeld presented in his shows—so elevated that they seemed touchable only in the imagination. Ziegfeld was fast discovering that what he presented in his shows was frustrating in real life.

Ziegfeld did not yield to Marilyn's manipulations. When the *Follies* reopened after the strike ended on September 10, 1919, Ziegfeld sent the show on a cross-country tour. This tactic was exactly what Frohman had done after Billie married Ziegfeld. But Marilyn had the last laugh: the tour schedules of the *Follies* and Frank's show coincided, allowing the couple ample time together. Ziegfeld seemed to be the only one in New York who was still against their marriage. A reporter for the *New York Tribune* called the union "the prettiest romance our stage has known in many a day." Marilyn and Frank were not only an attractive couple; they also provided mutual support for their respective careers. Frank spent much time trying to be a "jack of all trades," studying Shakespeare and Ibsen while maintaining his place in musical theater. "Don't specialize, except in matrimony," Frank stated. "Marilyn thought this was a noble sentiment for young actresses as well," the *Tribune* reporter noted.[48]

The couple was living proof that marriage was not a detriment but an asset to Marilyn's career. Her radiant happiness enthralled audiences but drove Ziegfeld mad. However, he managed to put business before his personal feelings. He temporarily banished Marilyn from his thoughts as he prepared that year's edition of the *Midnight Frolic*, the *Nine O'Clock Revue*, and a new endeavor, *Tonight at 8:10*. The *Frolic* starred Fanny Brice and W. C. Fields. Dolores, the former Lucile model, appeared in the climax of a number entitled "Dearest," in which she represented the perfect jewel at Cartier's. The most fun number, "Surprise Package," had audience members pull ribbons to unwrap an enormous candy box. Each patron went home with his or her own box of chocolates. The Shuberts, as usual, attempted to outdo Ziegfeld by opening their own version of the *Midnight Frolic* called the *Midnight Rounders*. They hoped this would prevent their chorines from accepting Ziegfeld's offers of employment, but they underestimated the sheer power of Ziegfeld's name. Three of the Shuberts' most beautiful former stars—Marilyn Miller, Gilda Gray, and Jessie Reed—all continued to wear the Ziegfeld banner in 1920, hindering the success of the *Midnight Rounders*. Adversely affecting both the *Midnight Rounders* and the *Midnight Frolic* was Prohibition. Authorities even accused Ziegfeld of being a bootlegger when the contents of a bag he was carrying while on tour clinked suspiciously. Inspectors discovered not bottles of liquor inside but Ziegfeld's cologne, which he fastidiously applied each day.

Tonight at 8:10 opened at the New Amsterdam Theatre two days before the national enforcement of Prohibition began on January 17, 1920. The variety show promised to be an innovative production with an all-star cast that included Marilyn Miller, Fanny Brice, Eddie Cantor, and W. C. Fields and a score by Irving Berlin. However, it had little chance of survival in the face of Prohibition. Authorities increasingly cracked down on venues that depended on liquor to give patrons maximum entertainment value, and *Tonight at 8:10* folded after only two nights. Ziegfeld spoke openly against Prohibition to a reporter for the *New York Tribune*: "It is a well known fact that anybody who wants a drink can get it . . . but my entertainment is a place where respectable people go. The police have seen fit to inspect drinks and otherwise degrade and humiliate tax-paying, liberty-loving Americans just as they have in cheap cabarets."[49] Despite his disdain for Prohibition, Ziegfeld wanted to ensure that the *Frolic* and *Revue* remained open. He issued a statement that he would install soda fountains in place of bars, but he did not believe in refusing service to customers who chose to indulge in liquor they brought with them. The *Midnight Frolic* and *Nine O'Clock Revue,* because they were already well-established productions, still attracted sizable crowds, despite the lack of alcohol. Nevertheless, Ziegfeld knew that the days of rooftop entertainment were nearing an end.

The *Nine O'Clock Revue,* which opened on March 8, 1920, on the New Amsterdam Theatre roof, marked Lillian Lorraine's last appearance in a Ziegfeld production. Fortunately, she left on a high note. Her most spectacular number was "Telephone," in which she wore a gown of georgette crepe with a skirt that seemed a mile long. Critics complimented her improved singing ability, and one reporter for the *Star Gazer* called her "indispensable."[50] In the spring of 1920, however, her name made headlines for all the wrong reasons. Tenants in the Manhattan apartment building where she lived complained about her midnight revelries and threatened to withhold their rent if she was not evicted. "Some of our tenants are even getting indigestion because of the racket . . . and there isn't a phonograph that could take a record of the conversations coming out of that apartment!" the landlord exclaimed at a court hearing. Lillian was issued a citation for being "a public nuisance" and had to pay a fine. She soon found new quarters, much to the relief of her neighbors.[51] Ziegfeld felt the same sense of relief when she severed her professional connections with him. He relished flamboyant publicity for his stars, but not sordid publicity. However, over the next three months, sordid publicity followed Ziegfeld.

Ziegfeld never intentionally ruined his stars' lives, but after his death, the "Ziegfeld curse" came to be associated with his glorified girls. By the 1940s, many former Ziegfeld beauties had suffered abusive marriages and alcoholism and had fallen into obscurity. Others experienced tragic losses or died prematurely by suicide or accident. However, a number of Ziegfeld girls felt the curse long before Ziegfeld's death, including Marilyn Miller.

On May 9, 1920, while the *Follies of 1919* was still on tour, Frank Carter was preparing to meet Marilyn at the show's next stop. He telephoned to let her know that he was on his way, and Marilyn begged him to drive carefully in the dark. On the road, Frank slammed on his brakes around a sharp curve; the car spun, tumbled down a steep hill, flipped over, and landed in a crushed heap. Frank was killed instantly. He was only twenty-eight years old. It has been alleged that Ziegfeld forced Marilyn to perform that night after learning of Frank's death and that she obediently did so, stating that she had never missed a show in her life and would not miss one now. In reality, Doris Eaton went onstage for Marilyn, and Ziegfeld gave the mourning actress an extended leave.

Marilyn did not stay away for long. Onstage, behind the footlights, had been the place she escaped to since childhood, and that escape was never more necessary than in the weeks following Frank's death. Marilyn threw herself into her work to keep from falling into an insurmountable depression. "I always lose myself when I dance," she stated. "I seem to be another, projected personality."[52] But no matter how carefree and girlish she appeared onstage, as soon as she stepped into her dressing room, the hard-edged bitterness, revealed in flashes of rage, took over. She funneled her anger toward Ziegfeld, blaming him for Frank's death. If Ziegfeld had not tried to keep them apart, Frank never would have signed with the Shuberts, he would not have been sent on tour, and he would not have wrecked the car. Marilyn's bitterness killed any traces of the elfin sprite Ziegfeld had fallen in love with. Nevertheless, he stepped in to act as her supporter and protector. He invited her to stay at Burkeley Crest to convalesce for two weeks while Billie was away on a trip. Whether he expected this to turn into something more intimate is unclear, but Marilyn was not taking any chances and declined the offer. Doris Eaton wrote: "In a bitchy way she made it clear that she did not find older men attractive, in particular the fifty-three-year-old Ziegfeld. Although it is widely known that she had many affairs throughout the rest of her life, I have personally always doubted that Ziegfeld was ever her lover."[53]

Marilyn may have declined Ziegfeld's offer of sanctuary, but she accepted his follow-up offer to send her to Europe, where she would study drama, art, elocution, singing, French, and even the philosophy of Delsarte. Ziegfeld was motivated by a desire to mold her into an even more perfect actress. Marilyn, however, took the trip not to please Ziegfeld but to honor Frank, who had predicted that 1920 would be her "banner year."[54] Marilyn drove herself mercilessly in her studies; she ignored the relentless, excruciating migraines resulting from a chronic sinus condition she had developed after an accident as a teenager. Ziegfeld had intended the trip to be primarily for relaxation; education was secondary. But Marilyn allowed herself only a momentary rest while staying at the Ritz Hotel in Paris. There, she received a sympathetic note from Ziegfeld's former infatuation, Olive Thomas, who had endured the same rigmarole with Ziegfeld over marriage versus career.

Olive was the second woman to fall victim to the Ziegfeld curse during the not-so-banner year of 1920. In September newspaper headlines across the country carried the blaring headline: "Olive Thomas Commits Suicide." Ziegfeld blamed Olive's husband, Jack Pickford, for her death. After all, she had committed suicide shortly after a bitter quarrel with him. The circumstances of Olive's death certainly cast Jack in a poor light. He claimed Olive had swallowed too many pills, but the coroner concluded that she had swallowed a bottle of mercury bichloride, a substance commonly used to treat syphilis, with which Jack was allegedly afflicted. Also, Jack was the primary beneficiary of Olive's new insurance policy, leading some to believe that he had killed her for her money. New evidence suggests that there were no traces of mercury bichloride in Olive's system, lending credence to Jack's story. In fact, Jack seemed genuinely affected by the loss of his wife. On his voyage across the Atlantic back to New York, he was wild with grief and tried to jump overboard, but a fellow passenger saved him.

During that same voyage, the Ziegfeld curse gained momentum when a third death occurred. Olive's friend Anna Daly, who was also a passenger on the ship, swallowed the drug veronal and died. Her suicide note read: "He doesn't love me anymore and I can't stand it and Olive is dead." The press identified "he" as a New Yorker who used to live in Chicago, which could have been a description of Ziegfeld. Reporters soon discovered that Ziegfeld had been seeing Daly for several months and had been sending her expensive gifts. Whether he was her lover or was simply trying to court her as a potential new star is unknown.[55] Marilyn did not attend the funerals of either Olive Thomas or Anna Daly. Like Ziegfeld, she avoided confrontations with mortality whenever possible.

Billie remained supportive of Ziegfeld during this storm of unpleasant publicity. She understood that reporters manufactured scandal whenever possible, and she refuted the accusations that her husband was an obvious "skirt chaser." Ziegfeld's reaction to Olive's death only confirmed Billie's trust in her husband's fidelity. He was devastated by her passing, feeling that he had lost a daughter rather than a mistress. He made all of Olive's

funeral arrangements; Irving Berlin was one of the ushers. The funeral created much hoopla, and the crowds were overwhelming. Gawking onlookers apparently trampled several women who had fainted. Though never a
great star, Olive Thomas became a bigger celebrity after her death largely
due to the mystery surrounding it. Legend has it that her restless spirit still
wanders the New Amsterdam Theatre. Janitors and night watchmen claim
they have seen her white, shrouded figure hovering in the halls.[56]

Ziegfeld kept himself busy with the *Follies of 1920,* which opened at
the New Amsterdam Theatre on June 22, 1920. During the run of the new
Follies, Ziegfeld also devoted himself to Billie and Patricia. Because Billie
was at home for most of this period, Ziegfeld's seemingly formless routine
acquired a semblance of comfortable order. He rose at eight, enjoyed a
shave from Jake Hoffman, and ate breakfast. Ziegfeld left for his office at
eleven o'clock, lunched at work, and ate dinner in the city between six and
eight. He retired to Burkeley Crest at ten o'clock when he had no show running. When a show was in production, he stayed at the Ansonia Hotel;
during these times, Billie would join Ziegfeld for dinner in New York and
then head back to Burkeley Crest while he concluded his work at the office.

"She was really marvelous for him and took wonderful care of him,"
Patricia said of her mother. "When they weren't working it was all play. . .
. She was the epitome of femininity."[57] The play Patricia referred to included
yearly retreats planned by Billie in an effort to prevent her husband's periods of nervous exhaustion. From January until Easter, Patricia and Billie
stayed at the Ziegfeld vacation home in Palm Beach. Ziegfeld joined them
for a few weeks but not for the entire season. To escape the New York heat
in the summer months, Ziegfeld chartered a yacht with all the amenities of
home and cruised around Sag Harbor, the Hamptons, and Rhode Island.
He employed no staff on the yacht except for the captain—a rare example
of "less is more" in the Ziegfelds' lifestyle. While on the houseboat, Ziegfeld
followed his natural rhythm of rising and retiring early. On vacation, Billie
and Ziegfeld enjoyed playing bridge. With Patricia, they played a game
along the lines of *Jeopardy!* called Guggenheim. Ziegfeld relished his soli-
tary time as well, which he spent whittling and canoeing.

Ziegfeld's short reprieve from work came to an end when the 1920
season began. He had great plans for the coming months, but they involved
riskier gambles than any game of poker at Palm Beach. Now that he had
perfected his revue, he was ready to move on to mastering book musicals.
He had produced musicals with Anna Held, but their thin plots had been

secondary to their music and specialty numbers, which had nothing to do with the story. Ziegfeld had the ambition, the necessary creative talent in his employ, and the perfect actress to help him realize his vision. The book musical he chose became what historians now call *the* show of the 1920s. Indeed, it fully realized the book musical's successor, the "new musical." This fresh form of musical ushered in an age of theater now dubbed the Cinderella era. Singer-actress Julie Andrews, as narrator of *Broadway: The American Musical* (2004), noted that only one star could fully reflect the new musical: "The living embodiment of the Jazz Age Cinderella was a petite beauty who could sing sweet but could dance hot: Marilyn Miller."[58]

The Actors Equity strike and a succession of deaths had disbanded the once happy Ziegfeld company. Ziegfeld could only hope that his new musical had the power to restore the optimism and camaraderie shattered by the events of 1920.

13

A New Normalcy

"America's present need is not heroics, but healing; not nostrums, but normalcy; not revolution, but restoration; not agitation, but adjustment . . . not submergence in internationality, but sustainment in triumphant nationality."[1] Thus spoke presidential candidate Warren G. Harding during his 1920 campaign. Harding's words won him 50 percent of the popular vote. Americans did indeed want a return to "normalcy" and "triumphant nationality." But what did normalcy mean in the theater? The musical had been changing for a generation, slowly maturing from a European form of entertainment into an American institution. The theater was creating a new normalcy that matched Harding's sentiments—and Ziegfeld was eager to make those sentiments tangible on the stage.

Ziegfeld was already acquainted with the writers responsible for creating the "new musical": P. G. Wodehouse, Guy Bolton, and Jerome Kern. Wodehouse and Kern set the precedent for all new musicals in *Leave It to Jane* (1917), *Irene* (1919), and *Mary* (1920). As indicated by the titles of these shows, the 1920s was a female-centric era. Women were the most obvious symbols of modernity, but they were not exactly a symbol of normalcy. Historian Ann Douglas described the change in the individual woman in the early 1920s: "Her hair is gone, her skirts are gone, her breasts are bound . . . much more skin, but kind of in different places . . . she's smoking, she's drinking, she had trashed the past and thrown it in the garbage can en route [to] a party at the speak easy—what would attract theater and musical comedy more than something changing that fast?"[2]

The shows that best reflected the overnight changes in society were Cinderella stories in which "the pluck and luck of the heroine triumphs at the end."[3] As narrator for *Broadway: The American Musical* (2004), singer-actress Julie Andrews expanded on the archetype: "She was almost always Irish, a good-hearted, poor orphan who used slangy banter to win the hand of her millionaire suitor."[4] Women in the audience could easily envision themselves as the humble, grassroots heroines. Anna Held's shows, and a number of Billie Burke's more sophisticated shows, had no place for the everyday working girl. In contrast, *Irene* had a dressmaker as its heroine, and *Leave It to Jane* featured a coed as its main character. The new musical at first rejected the old-fashioned method of creating "star vehicles," or shows tailored specifically to a certain star. Instead, the new musical favored an ensemble cast. But when Ziegfeld joined the ranks of new-musical producers, he mixed the notion of a star vehicle with that of an ensemble show.

Ziegfeld had begun shaping his Cinderella story in February 1920, during the family's annual vacation to Palm Beach, Florida. Palm Beach had become more popular during World War I due to the closing of casinos in war-torn Europe. It boasted Bradley's, a world-class gambling club; no shortage of liquor (even during Prohibition); and golfing, yachting, and fishing. Ziegfeld still relished gambling and lost thousands of dollars at Bradley's or at the horse races during his Palm Beach sojourns, but he felt he would be luckier in his next professional gamble. Along with Kern, Wodehouse, and Bolton, Ziegfeld chartered a yacht comically named *The Wench* for a trip through the Everglades. The trip was not purely business; plenty of Ziegfeld principals and chorus girls indulged in sunbathing, drinking, and dining on board. But between the partying, the trio of writers and Ziegfeld managed to come up with a show that was refreshingly innocent and simple in the midst of their Dionysian pleasures. Originally titled *The Little Thing*, the play was set at an actors' boardinghouse. It provided ample opportunity to showcase the vaudevillians and dancers used in the *Follies*, but Ziegfeld was dissatisfied. The show had to have a plot, and the plot's center had to be Marilyn Miller, not an entire group of entertainers.

"Who does Marilyn play?" Ziegfeld asked.

"Her name is Sally Rhinelander," Bolton replied. "Because she was an orphan found in a telephone booth with a Rhinelander number."

Sally Rhinelander evoked in Ziegfeld's mind *Sally in Our Alley*, a 1902 play about a sweet working-class girl. Based on what he had heard so far, the play seemed better suited as a George M. Cohan production, with little opportunity for grandiosity on a Ziegfeldian scale. As had been Ziegfeld's dominant concern when negotiating for *Gloria's Romance* back in 1916, he asked the writers: "Is there a chance for glamour?"

The writers continued to outline the plot: Sally's dream is to be a dancer, and an old woman living in the boardinghouse—a former dancer herself—helps Sally become one. Ziegfeld immediately perked up, his vivid imagination miles ahead of the three men beside him. By the time he began to speak, he had already dreamed up a full-fledged extravaganza. First, he changed the old woman into a man who could be played by one of the star comics from the *Follies*. Second, Sally's dreams would be realized not just in any show but by dancing in the *Ziegfeld Follies*. Third, she would endear herself to high society by masquerading as a princess. Fourth, she would win the heart of a high-society boy whose love for her only increased when her true identity was revealed. For the finale, the audience would see Sally glide over the stage, dancing an exquisite ballet on her opening night in the *Follies*. The finale, more than anything else, would give the show the Ziegfeld touch.

Ziegfeld may have been confident that his backers would support the show, but Kern, Wodehouse, and Bolton were not convinced that *Sally* was fresh enough to be a sure hit. The writers were most wary of Ziegfeld's princess-in-disguise idea. They likened it to the sort of fantastical, exotic plot twist typical of old musicals. But Ziegfeld's trademark had always been to present something new with a twist of something old. The show was a classic Cinderella story—a poor girl is freed from a life of drudgery by a wealthy Prince Charming—but Ziegfeld's idea for the ending made it fresh. He was not satisfied to conclude the show with a happily-ever-after marriage; instead, he envisioned the girl winning Prince Charming *and* a successful career. The show celebrated not only the American Dream but also the burgeoning identity of the modern woman. Marilyn Miller was an unthreatening example of modernity because she also embraced the old-fashioned normalcy Harding had promised to restore to America. "Marilyn Miller combined innocence with sexuality. She could convey that feeling of the big city, that sparkle of a star," drama critic Steve Nelson asserted. "She could be both sophisticated and the kind of rural archetype of the farm girl."[5]

Now that Ziegfeld had secured the perfect heroine for *Sally*, he poured his energy into the show's artistic aspects. The costumes included a gorgeous white fur ensemble designed by Lucile and rainbow-colored silk ballet gowns complete with sparkling wings, designed to make the dancing girls resemble butterflies. The butterfly costumes were put to good use in a ballet composed by Victor Herbert. Joseph Urban's sets included a lush estate like those one would see at Great Neck and an entire re-creation of the New York church where theater folk were married: the Little Church Around the Corner. But when Ziegfeld brought his plans for the show to Abe Erlanger, Erlanger was less than enthusiastic.

"You're out of your mind!" Ziegfeld raged. "This will be the greatest show of the season!"

As Ziegfeld fumed, Erlanger took notes of everything the show would entail. "It'll cost over $250,000," he said. "That's triple the amount of any show you've ever produced."

"I'll find the money myself," Ziegfeld said. And find the money he did—in his own bank account. Gone was the Florenz Ziegfeld who had always assumed his shows would flop; in his place was a self-assured, brazen man who had no doubt that *Sally* would be the greatest triumph of his career. But if he turned out to be wrong, Ziegfeld would be a pauper.[6]

Ziegfeld's prescience concerning *Sally* proved that he was ahead of his time. Historians mark the beginning of the golden age of the American musical as 1924, but the four years preceding it were an impressive prelude. "Critics reacted favorably to almost every musical put before them . . . but the critics were careful to separate the immediate entertainment value of a piece from any lasting artistic merit," Broadway chronicler Gerald Bordman explained.[7] Theatergoers of the 1920s reveled in what historians call "wonderful nonsense"—shows that did not rely on profound or memorable stories.[8] *Sally* supplied immediate entertainment, but its superior Jerome Kern score, universally appealing story, witty Wodehouse and Bolton repartee, sophisticated Victor Herbert ballet, gorgeous Lucile creations, and Joseph Urban settings gave it lasting merit. It was far more than "wonderful nonsense."

When the *Ziegfeld Follies* opened at the New Amsterdam Theatre on June 22, 1920, critics seemed to think that Ziegfeld had reserved the best of his chorines for *Sally*. Although the *Follies* maintained Ziegfeld's flawless production standards and constellation of unique performers, the beautiful girls—an essential aspect of the revue—were largely absent. More dominant in the show were headliners such as Fanny Brice, W. C. Fields, Van and Schenck, and Ray Dooley. Newcomers included Jack Donahue, an eccentric dancer, and former vaudeville musical comedian Charles Winninger. The score, written mostly by Irving Berlin, Gene Buck, and Dave Stamper, received little comment, as the songs were too similar to those in previous editions. The beginning of the show, however, was not imitative in the least, especially when an unexpected guest—a black kitten—made an appearance on opening night.

A journalist from the *New York Tribune* had fun recounting the story of the kitten, which had somehow made its way from the street and into the aisles of the New Amsterdam auditorium: "A white uniformed usher caught sight of the intruder. He gave chase and dived for her [the cat] as she neared the tenth row. He missed and landed in the lap of the occupant of the aisle seat." The kitten continued to make her way through the maze of legs until many audience members noticed the cat's presence and joined in the chase. Once caught and returned to Forty-Second Street, the cat found her way back into the theater a second time, at which point an usher recaptured the kitten and carried her farther away so that she would not return. The journalist thought the *Follies* was such a feast for the eyes that the kitten must have mistaken it for "a new sort of breakfast food" and thus could not be expected to behave "in accordance with the regulations of etiquette."[9]

After the hoopla surrounding the kitten subsided, theatergoers were in for another surprise. The opening scene of the *Follies* featured a group of chorus boys rather than girls, but much to the relief of the audience, the boys turned their chorus line into an object of comedy, stating, "We were sent out to avoid wasting the girls so early."[10]

Even though W. C. Fields was Ziegfeld's least favorite employee, he made the greatest hit in the show. His skit "The Family Ford" kept audiences laughing for days after they saw it. Fanny Brice played his wife, and Ray Dooley (in drag) portrayed their son. The skit involved Fields's attempts to keep his Ford in perfect condition and the inevitable damage inflicted on the vehicle: a blind man tapped his cane against the headlight and shattered it; a young man used the side of the car to light a match; when Fields finally started the motor, it died in a matter of seconds.

Absent from the cast was Marilyn Miller, who was still in Europe. In her place was Mary Eaton, Doris's older sister. Mary became a headliner after her performance in a satiric number called "Mary and Doug." The routine cleverly spoofed Mary Pickford and Douglas Fairbanks Sr.'s onscreen successes and offscreen love affair. Doris Eaton recalled that critics found Mary to be a satisfactory replacement for Marilyn, calling her "the prettiest girl in the *Follies*."[11] As a result, Ziegfeld decided that no one but Mary could be Marilyn's understudy in *Sally*.

Eddie Cantor had made a bet with Ziegfeld that he would *not* be in the

1920 *Follies,* but the comedian ultimately lost the bet. Audiences were delighted when Eddie made an impromptu appearance in a trio of numbers. After he had finished singing, Eddie dragged Ziegfeld onstage and urged him to share in the applause. The shy producer slipped away after less than a minute in the spotlight. Eddie's unexpected performance did not improve his and Ziegfeld's estranged father-son–type relationship. After the opening week of the show, Ziegfeld discovered that Eddie was reprising "The Osteopath Scene" from the 1919 *Follies* in a Shubert revue. At first, Ziegfeld did nothing about the plagiarism, until he heard everyone up and down Broadway raving about the skit. Ziegfeld sued and won. His victory was more of a blow to the Shuberts than to Eddie, however, since "The Osteopath Scene" was one of the brothers' main profit makers that season.

In the midst of the *Follies,* ongoing rivalries, and Prohibition, Ziegfeld managed to stage a *Midnight Frolic* in both the spring and fall of 1920. Fanny Brice and W. C. Fields appeared in the spring edition, but an oversized Ouija board stole the show. A blindfolded Indian princess carried the board around the room, using it to read the thoughts of the audience. The fall edition featured women dressed in sporty clothing appropriate for various pursuits, including polo, skating, tennis, and horseback riding. A juggling and acrobatic act juxtaposed a dignified tableau entitled "Le Trousseau." Ziegfeld did not expend much energy on either *Frolic* because of his involvement in *Sally,* but he knew that revues were still worthy of his attention and had not lost their appeal on Broadway.

The 1920s actually saw an increase in the number of revue-type shows. Nearly 120 of them opened over the course of the decade. The growing number of competing revues gave both established artists and new ones many more venues to showcase their talents. To Ziegfeld's chagrin, a host of new songwriters made their glorious debuts in shows other than the *Follies.* Teams such as the Gershwins, Richard Rodgers and Lorenz Hart, Buddy DeSylva and Lew Brown, and Arthur Freed and Nacio Herb Brown were among the voices of the increasingly youth-centered culture of the 1920s. A number of these songwriting teams wrote for new revues in direct competition with the *Follies.* The Gershwins became the staple writers for *George White's Scandals,* and Rodgers and Hart made their name in *The Garrick Gaieties.* The *Earl Carroll Vanities* shamelessly imitated the *Follies,* going so far as to place a sign over the stage door that read: "Through these portals pass the most beautiful girls in the world."[12] Even those closest to Ziegfeld, including Joseph Urban and Irving Berlin, strayed from the fold. Urban lent his talents to the *Scandals,* while Berlin joined with producer Sam Harris to build a theater of his own, the Music Box, where he staged revues to showcase his latest compositions.

Despite the new competition, Ziegfeld still held the title of Broadway's foremost producer. The Syndicate was more supportive than ever of Ziegfeld's productions (with the exception of *Sally*). In June 1920 the Syndicate board members elected F. S. Golding as director, ousting Marc Klaw from that position. This turn of events voided a lawsuit Klaw had filed against Ziegfeld and Erlanger for sums he claimed they owed him. Ziegfeld's triumphs continued when the board, which knew that his shows were the most profitable, awarded Ziegfeld the highest salary and 50 percent of the profits off the receipts of his productions; the partners drew only 25 percent.

However, even these victories did not prevent Ziegfeld's confidence in *Sally* from faltering. As a strange way of coping, he fell into his old pattern of staging stunts to draw publicity for his shows. One stunt involved a cow-milking contest between two showgirls. A second stunt used one of Ziegfeld's oldest tricks: a "plant" in the audience of the *Follies* tossed chorine Gilda Gray a $100,000 necklace. A third stunt was an elaborately engineered boat race on Central Park Lake involving numerous showgirls, including the Eatons. The sisters' boat capsized, and a brave policeman dove in to help the damsels in distress.[13]

Ziegfeld's insecurity manifested in other ways, and his behavior gradually became more eccentric. Charles Higham explained: "He constantly scrapped whole scenes and sets of costumes without warning . . . foolishly rather than with the inspiration of the past. He kept strands of colored ribbon in his pocket . . . he would fish one out and redo an entire show in that color."[14] His press agents began ghostwriting a prolific stream of articles with appealing titles such as "Behind the Scenes in Beautyland," which gave the impression that Ziegfeld was as inspired and in step with modernity as ever. These articles covered up the fact that Ziegfeld "hated the decade as much as he had loved the previous one—a sure sign that he was quite firmly middle-aged."[15]

Ziegfeld kept his disillusionment with the 1920s to himself as he continued to apply all his mental energy and financial savings to *Sally.* Marilyn put an equal amount of effort into the production. Upon returning from her travels, she spent twelve to eighteen hours a day being trained not only in dancing but also in singing and acting. As Billie Burke had warned Ziegfeld from the beginning, Marilyn's talent was limited in these areas. But Ziegfeld's hunches were seldom wrong, and he refused to believe that Marilyn could not be molded into the most sensational musical star of the decade.

During an early rehearsal, *Sally*'s musical director, Gus Salzer, had suggested that rather than singing her songs, Marilyn should simply talk them. But Marilyn knew she was capable of more. One day she went through the score, singing with a voice she had lacked months ago. Her delivery was clear, sweet, and haunting; listeners could hear no imperfections. "But how?" a shocked Salzer asked after Marilyn had completed her songs. "Why, we have a [Adelina] Patti here!" he added, referring to a well-known opera singer of the period.[16]

The excitement was palpable at the New Amsterdam Theatre as the show's premiere approached. Broadway-ites were already predicting that it would be the musical of the decade. Theatergoers knew that a show boasting the team of Ziegfeld and Miller could not fail. The talents of Leon Errol as the comic relief and Dolores as a settlement worker further boosted theatergoers' confidence in the production. Adding to the excitement was critics' and audiences' curiosity: could Ziegfeld still produce a straight musical comedy? After all, it had been more than a decade since *Miss Innocence* premiered, and at the time, critics had claimed that Ziegfeld was nothing without Anna Held. But *Sally* was proving that a show was nothing without the Ziegfeld name.

From the first moment the curtain rose on *Sally* on December 21, 1920, Ziegfeld's insecurities about the production disappeared. He knew he had been correct in plunging every cent he had into its production. The minute theatergoers saw Marilyn, they erupted into applause. The opening scene had her dressed as a ragamuffin, something Ziegfeld had initially opposed. But Gene Buck had convinced him that her transition from waif to elegant guest at a Long Island soiree would only enhance her glamour. Marilyn received unprecedented adulation following Herbert's "Butterfly Ballet," during which a mechanical platform rolled out over the orchestra pit, enabling the audience to watch her feet tap and spin. However, her greatest triumph came with "Look for the Silver Lining." With lyrics by Buddy DeSylva, one of the brightest new talents on Broadway, and music by Jerome Kern, the song was an ideal blend of old and new. It touched a country that was looking to regain the simple pleasures the Great War had taken away, and it truly communicated the themes of hopefulness and beauty that Ziegfeld was aiming for. "Our culture is a culture of optimism," theater historian John Lahr noted. "What the musical sells is optimism."[17] Few musicals are more optimistic than *Sally,* and even fewer songs are more optimistic than "Look for the Silver Lining": "Look for the silver lining / when'ere a cloud appears in the blue / remember somewhere the sun is shining / so always look for the silver lining / and try to find the sunny side of life."[18] At first, as Marilyn sang, she stared ahead, as if she were lost in her own private world; then she smiled directly at the audience, pulling them into her dream world. The audience demanded encore after encore of the refrain. At every performance, the audience reacted to the song with the same enthusiasm.

Though not as touching as "Look for the Silver Lining," Kern's other memorable song from the show, "Wild Rose" (with lyrics by Clifford Grey), provided the ideal contrast to the first tune's innocent, old-fashioned sentiment. Marilyn sang "Wild Rose" not as the piquant Sally but while masquerading as the alluring and sophisticated dancer Madame Nockerova: "I'm just a wild rose, / Not a prim and mild rose; / Tame me if you can, / I'm a rose to suit any man. / Some passion flower, / This is my hour, / Who'll get me no one knows, / I'm such a wild, wild rose."[19] After each chorus, Marilyn gave a blithe kick and a wink to the audience as a line of tuxedoed chorus boys surrounded her.

Marilyn's performance, enhanced by Kern's poignant melodies, made her the living embodiment of the American Dream, just as Ziegfeld had envisioned. One critic noted Marilyn's enhanced artistic skills and her more well-rounded characterization, which, sadly, she had achieved only after experiencing the loss of her husband. "She has come to dance with more than her former swiftness and with a new suppleness and abandon. Somewhere she has acquired a singing voice of resonance and body, together with a knack of twirling off comedy lines with a spirit of mischief. Somewhere, too, she had picked up a personality," the critic commented.[20]

As much praise as Marilyn received, Ziegfeld was the recipient of even greater accolades. The *World* called his show "nothing less than idealized musical comedy"; it went on to state that Ziegfeld knew "a little more than any of his competitors the secret of bringing beauty to his stage." The hard-to-please critic Alexander Woollcott asserted, "As you rush to the subway at ten minutes to midnight it is not of Urban nor of Jerome Kern, not of

Leon Errol nor even of Marilyn that you think first. You think of Mr. Ziegfeld. He is that kind of producer."[21]

Ziegfeld had hoped that the success of *Sally* would mend some of the broken relationships in his company, specifically between him and his star. But throughout the show's unprecedented run, Marilyn continued to heap all her suppressed frustration and anger on Ziegfeld. To Marilyn, his ongoing efforts to placate her smacked of bribery and seduction. Yet she did not refuse all his gestures. She enjoyed the satin and velvet dressing room he provided, and she relished becoming the first actress to receive 10 percent of a show's gross each week. She was now the highest-paid performer on Broadway, at a salary of $3,000 a week. Ziegfeld ensured that she had the best of everything at all times. While *Sally* was on tour in Boston after its New York premiere, he became fixated on having one of Marilyn's costumes cleaned. He sent a long wire to Marilyn about it, as well as similar wires to the wardrobe mistress, the stage manager, and the cleaner to whom the garment would be sent. As if this were not enough, he sent a messenger by train to Boston to see that this vital task had been completed. A colleague of Ziegfeld's remarked, "Ziegfeld spoiled the hell out of her. If Marilyn wanted the moon, he'd give it to her, plus Mars."[22]

To Marilyn, Ziegfeld remained not only the person responsible for Frank's death but also a dictator trying to mold her into whatever he wanted her to be. Marilyn had played hardball with her employer before *Sally,* but now she took her game to the next level. Marilyn knew that Ziegfeld wanted his favorites to be "chaste dollies" offstage, good girls who did nothing that might tarnish his name and thus decrease ticket sales.[23] So Marilyn set out to do everything she could to show New Yorkers that she was not the innocent orphan girl she portrayed onstage. Doris Eaton observed, "Marilyn became much more escapist and fun-seeking in her private life. Increasingly, she developed problems with alcohol and appeared to go from one relationship to another."[24] One of these "fun-seeking" jaunts involved a visit to the Plaza Hotel between performances of *Sally,* where she danced with forty Harvard boys who had invited her for tea.[25] If this did not raise eyebrows, her association with the wealthy Benjamin Kabatznick caused more than a few society ladies to cluck their tongues. Following an evening performance of *Sally,* Marilyn attended a party at Kabatznick's home that ended with a police raid. The officers hauled a naked showgirl off to jail; the drunk girl had stripped and auctioned herself off to the highest bidder. When the story splashed across the pages of newspapers the following morning, Marilyn vehemently declared that she had done nothing untoward at the party and denied that she was having an affair with Kabatznick. He was old and unattractive, she argued. Anyone who knew her knew that she preferred handsome young chorus boys.

Marilyn's escapades evoked scenes worthy of F. Scott Fitzgerald's pen, but her acquisition of an estate at Great Neck and the dizzying social life that came with it could have filled an entire Fitzgerald novel. With neighbors like Eddie Cantor, Lillian Russell, Groucho Marx, Ed Wynn, Vincent Astor, Solomon Guggenheim, and F. Scott Fitzgerald himself, there was rarely a dull weekend. In 1921 the Fourth of July party lasted well into the fifth. Marilyn's dog had run off, and she was frantic at the thought of it wandering about in the dark. Nearly every man present leaped to his feet to help search for the dog, but one man in particular won her favor. That man was Jack Pickford, hedonistic actor, playboy, husband of the late Olive Thomas, and a black name in Florenz Ziegfeld Jr.'s book.

Marilyn's attraction to Jack Pickford stemmed largely from the fact that he reminded her of Frank Carter. Like Frank, Jack was, in Marilyn's words, a "perpetual youngster" who was usually cast as "the Juvenile" in films or stage work. Jack's appeal also lay in his reputation as an alcoholic, a draft dodger, and a carrier of syphilis—someone Ziegfeld would certainly *not* want Marilyn to see. Only weeks after Jack and Marilyn met, they announced their engagement.

Marilyn and Jack's upcoming marriage was only one of many annoyances that plagued Ziegfeld in 1921. His new normalcy was not a return to serenity but an entrance into a hurricane.

The dawn of the Roaring Twenties brought upheaval and drama not only to Ziegfeld and Marilyn but also to Lillian Lorraine. After being evicted from her apartment, Lillian had taken up residence at the Walton Hotel. The same week, police impounded her car in Long Beach. Lillian's ill fortune continued after her new play, *Sonny* (1921), closed after only seven weeks.

More successful than both Lillian's show and the last *Follies* were Ziegfeld's two newest productions, February editions of the *Midnight Frolic* and the *Nine O'Clock Revue*. The *Midnight Frolic* was less inspired than its predecessors and borrowed heavily from the 1920 edition. The best new number involved two dozen beautiful Dutch girls dancing to headliner Eleanor Griffith's song "The Little Love Mill." In the number's climax, the Fairbanks twins danced before a realistic replica of a windmill designed by Joseph Urban. The *Nine O'Clock Revue* also featured the Fairbanks twins but no other big names. The finale was the highlight of the show, depicting a bevy of chorus girls playing winter sports at the swanky millionaires' playground Saint Moritz. The shows were still popular, but Prohibition had undeniably diminished their zest. Ziegfeld increasingly felt his age as midnight supper clubs became relics of the previous decade.

Lillian Lorraine, too, was becoming a memory of the 1910s. The 1920s had not treated her well thus far, and in February 1921 they literally crippled her. On the night of Lillian's twenty-ninth birthday, Nanny Johnson was awakened by a frantic call from one of Lillian's friends. "Lillian's just been rushed to the emergency room—come to Stern's Sanitarium, 365 West End Avenue, if you can," the friend said. Nanny and the rest of New York soon discovered what had happened to Lillian to make her truly worthy of the nickname "the broken butterfly." Lillian had just left a midnight supper club, the Fifty Fifty, on the arm of her latest beau and possible fiancé, Joe Welling. As they waited for a car, Lillian hugged her furs about her, shivering in the icy cold. When the car pulled up, she rushed to it, eager for warmth. Her heel slipped on the frozen sidewalk, and she fell hard on her back. She seemed all right at first, and the driver took her to her hotel (it is unclear whether Welling accompanied her). Once Lillian lay down, ready for sleep, radiating pain shot through her spine. Groping for the telephone, she called the hospital. The press jumped on the story and made it as lurid as possible: Lillian had fallen in the gutter after drinking all night. Lillian had fallen down the stairs of her apartment building after a bender. Her story became more sympathetic only when the press ran truthful stories based on the medical facts: Lillian had suffered severe fractures on the fourth and fifth cervical vertebrae and likely would never perform again.

Ziegfeld was not oblivious to the news about his former love. Lillian was the talk of the *Follies* girls backstage. Surprisingly, the curmudgeonly Ned Wayburn encouraged the other girls to visit Lillian. One of the chorines, Lucille Layton, was among the first to take his advice. But when she arrived at Lillian's hospital room, she found that another visitor was already there: Florenz Ziegfeld Jr. His visit was supposed to be a secret, as Ziegfeld and Billie's relationship was already precarious due to rumors about his conspicuous attentions to Marilyn Miller. The last thing Ziegfeld needed was gossip that he had rekindled his romance with Lillian. Though sympathetic to her, his visits had no romantic connotations. Nevertheless, Ziegfeld's eyes filled with tears during that visit, as they invariably did when he talked of or witnessed Lillian's dissipation. Before he left the hospital, he quietly paid her medical bills and incidentals but asked her not to contact him again—a request that Lillian ignored.

Although she recovered from her near paralysis and actually appeared in several more musical shows, Lillian never had sufficient work to support herself. She moved to Atlantic City, where she lived a pathetic and poverty-stricken existence. She never stopped haunting Ziegfeld, and he could never completely let her go. Ziegfeld's secretary would put through calls from a "Miss Mary Haddon," and it would be Lillian on the line, telling Ziegfeld her latest sob story. After a particularly long call in 1928, Ziegfeld crumpled in his chair and told his secretary, "If she calls again, say I'm out."[26] They never spoke again, although he continued to give Lillian a small allowance each month.

Lillian was arguably the most extreme victim of the Ziegfeld curse. She haunted Ziegfeld more than any of the other ill-fated women because he had failed to make her into a beloved star. He had been triumphant in doing so for Anna Held (who remained a national icon until her death in 1918), and he had turned Marilyn Miller into an even more beloved icon. If he had been able to do the same for Lillian, she might not have chosen the lifestyle that led to her downfall. He felt responsible for her failure, and failure was something that Ziegfeld was unaccustomed to in his stars and in himself.

"Best of them all," said one review.[27] "Much the same effect used . . . in the old days," said another.[28] These quotes reveal the dueling reactions to the June 21 opening of the *Ziegfeld Follies of 1921* at the Globe Theatre (*Sally* was still occupying the *Follies*' usual home at the New Amsterdam). The show may have lacked innovation, but it still had top-notch comedy, spectacle, and elements of surprise. A critic for the *New York Times* lamented how "a revue calling itself the *Follies of 1921* could demonstrate such scant inspiration in topical matters."[29] This reviewer was in the minority, however. The show did in fact address topical matters, including Prohibition and popular personalities such as the Barrymores, Jack Dempsey, and Marilyn Miller.

W. C. Fields was the main player in the Prohibition skit. He portrayed a minister who invited a magician to entertain his Sunday school class, but the magician's only trick was changing water into wine and vice versa. As the magician became increasingly drunk, the minister tipsily juggled tennis balls. When Prohibition agents appeared, they could find nothing but water. The prospect of defying Prohibition appealed to Ziegfeld, for he saw it as the ruination of his lucrative *Midnight Frolic.* However, there was no indication that he was amused by Fields's antics. When the audience laughed at his jokes, Ziegfeld murmured, "They don't mean it." Nevertheless, Fields's skits were the most popular. The best received was one in which Fanny Brice appeared as his wife and Raymond Hitchcock and Ray Dooley played "their two brats." The skit was similar to "The Family Ford" in the previous *Follies,* but this time it depicted a family trying to load their picnic supplies onto a train. After missing numerous trains due to their failed attempts, Fields threw down his hat and roared, "Next Sunday, when we go *out* we'll stay *home!*"[30]

Aside from the comedy of W. C. Fields, critics were most enthusiastic about the zany Fanny Brice. In addition to her straight comedic skits, Fanny sprinkled her humor into a number of songs. The most enduring comedic tune of the 1921 *Follies* was "Secondhand Rose." Out of character was Fanny's dramatic rendition of a French tune, *"Mon Homme"* (My Man). It was originally a risqué tune about a prostitute and her pimp, but Ziegfeld's songwriter, Channing Pollock, made it more palatable to American audiences by turning it into the lament of a woman who is still in love with her boyfriend, despite his infidelity and abuse. In a roundabout way, the song could have been viewed as a topical one. Audiences believed it referred to Fanny's husband, Nicky Arnstein, who was facing a prison sentence for his scandalous robbery of $5 million worth of bonds on Wall Street. Fanny sang a key lower than usual and without her well-known Yiddish inflections. She wore what was perhaps the simplest costume that ever graced Ziegfeld's stage: a ragged, dusty black dress and a scarf wrapped tightly around her shoulders. The backdrop was equally simple, consisting of a dark boulevard and a single streetlamp for Fanny to lean against. "My Man" proved to be the biggest surprise in the show, and critics called it the best song of the evening.

Although the show satisfied most critics and audiences, it did not satisfy Ziegfeld. He continued to tinker with the program, removing and changing acts frequently through its run. Historian Ann Ommen van der Merwe has suggested that the adjustments reveal a correlation between the Ziegfeld revue and its profitability: the editions that had more changes were "marked by less stability and less success."[31]

Nor was Ziegfeld satisfied with his newest edition of the *Midnight Frolic*. The fall *Frolic*, which opened on November 17, 1921, had much in its favor, including Will Rogers and Leon Errol as headliners. However, even these two big names did not attract as many theatergoers as previous editions had. Ziegfeld tried to remedy the problem by changing the *Frolic* into a road show; he called it the *Ziegfeld Frolic* to make it clear that the show was not a midnight rooftop entertainment dependent on alcohol for much of its enjoyment. The production opened on January 10, 1922, at the Garrick Theatre in Philadelphia and toured along the East Coast; however, it never reached New York. In an attempt to save the show, Ziegfeld added Will Rogers to the cast in February, but even he could not turn things around. The unsuccessful tour was the death knell for the *Frolic*, and Ziegfeld was not shy in expressing his indignation over its demise. He told a reporter for the *New York Tribune* that Prohibition was to blame and that "personal liberty is as extinct as the dodo." He went on to tell the reporter that he was considering Europe as a better venue for his entertainment: "London and Paris have for several years wanted me to transfer my midnight type of entertainment there. . . . I will confine my producing activities [in the United States] to productions like the 'Follies,' at least until some political parasite at Washington slips over another law that makes carrying opera glasses or staying out after eight o'clock a crime."[32]

Before he sailed for Europe (Billie and Patricia would remain at home), Ziegfeld prepared his next *Follies*. Even though his revue was in no danger from "political parasites," the *Frolic*'s failure had dampened Ziegfeld's enthusiasm. His depression and eccentricities became even more prominent than they had been during the production of *Sally*. His collection of elephant figurines grew, and he always carried a small one in his pocket. If someone happened to give him a statuette of an elephant with a down-turned trunk (considered bad luck), he became hysterical. Ziegfeld became equally distraught when W. C. Fields brought a dwarf to the office one day (Ziegfeld considered dwarfs bad luck as well). He slammed the door to his office and refused to come out until he was sure they had left.

Ziegfeld's pet monkey, Sally, could always be counted on to console him after too many bad omens had darkened his path. She was as much a good luck charm as an elephant with an upturned trunk. When she was not in Ziegfeld's office, Sally occupied a small cubicle backstage, using a cloth and a pail of water to wash the shelves and walls of her space; she also loved to cuddle stuffed animals. Sally even traveled with the *Follies* company to Palisades Amusement Park the following summer. When Sally became ill shortly after this jaunt, Ziegfeld spared no expense to save her life. He ordered numerous tanks of oxygen to help her recover from a near-fatal case of pneumonia.[33]

Ziegfeld managed to save Sally's life, but another death in his household hit him hard. When Blanche Burke passed away in February 1922, Ziegfeld felt as if he had lost his own mother. Ziegfeld was probably closer to Blanche than Billie was herself. "I am so grateful to him for making Mother's last days such happy days," Billie said. "He always made her birthday a sparkling thing. Hundreds of colored balloons would arrive for the parties he gave in her honor, and on several occasions he sent out a full orchestra from his roof to play for her."[34]

Ziegfeld, reminded of his own parents' mortality, began to visit them in Chicago more frequently. His father's kidneys were failing, and his mother was becoming increasingly feeble. Ziegfeld found it difficult to reconcile his parents' age with his vivid memories of them from his youth. He remembered his father as being warm and jolly beneath his stern Prussian exterior. According to Patricia, "When he [Professor Ziegfeld] hugged you, you knew you'd been hugged."[35] He spoke in a loud voice and played the piano at a similar volume, shaking the walls with the instrument's noise. Rosalie Ziegfeld's gentle, quiet demeanor was the opposite of her husband's. Whenever Ziegfeld visited, he would take his mother in his arms and carry her to the table at mealtimes. During an interview with Ziegfeld in New York, journalist Djuna Barnes recalled the producer evading her questions about his latest productions, shaking himself roughly, and putting his arms behind his head before finally speaking: "I'm homesick that's all. Homesick for Chicago."

"And your wife. Where is she?"

"I said I was homesick, didn't I?"[36]

Because Ziegfeld had become such a fixture in New York, it seemed as if he had lived there all his life. But clearly, he was not immune to the nostalgia of sentimental journeys to his hometown. Yet, as indicated by the latter half of his reply to Barnes, he could feel homesick even in New York, when work kept him away from Billie for too long. Billie and Patricia occasionally accompanied Ziegfeld on his trips to Chicago, but he most often went alone.

When not visiting them in person, Ziegfeld kept up a steady corre-spondence with his mother and father. A sampling of letters between Ziegfeld and his parents (in their still-broken English) reveals their inti-macy with the son who had once been such a wayward boy. Ziegfeld often sent his parents generous gifts, such as those to which Professor Ziegfeld refers in the following telegram (Ziegfeld Sr. was apparently as prolific a sender of telegrams as Ziegfeld Jr.):

Jan. 19, 1923 to Palm Beach
YOUR 500 CIGARETTES ARRIVED ON TIME WITH MANY THANKS DR
PATTON KEEPS ME OFTEN AT HOME WE TAKE SOME TIME HOUR
RIDE IN OUR AUTO BUT UNABLE TO TRAVEL JUST NOW MAMA AND I
SENT BEST LOVE FATHER[37]

Ziegfeld always kept abreast of his parents' health issues, and in the follow-ing note Professor Ziegfeld updates his son on his well-being and also subtly tells Florenz that he misses him:

Feb. 20th, 1923
Dear Flo,
    Dr. Patton was here yesterday and found that I need a little more kidney medicine. Received nice letter from Carl [Ziegfeld's brother]. . . . When do you come to Chicago? . . . you cannot afford to come hear [sic] during the cold-beastly weather.

Despite the obvious closeness between parents and son, it is interesting to note how formally the elder Ziegfelds sometimes signed their letters:

Feb 24, 1923
Dear Flo,
    Just a word that I go on with Patton's medicine for my kidneys. . . . I was terribly sick for medicine. I stopped it at once. Now takes . . . some pills which can do no harm. We send love to you dear good Flo You old father and mother Dr. and Mrs. F. Ziegfeld

Ziegfeld enjoyed his visits to "Dr. and Mrs. Ziegfeld," but he found more solace in time spent with his wife and daughter. Richard Ziegfeld commented that Ziegfeld "was probably not disingenuous when he told

Billie that nothing interested him but his family."[38] Billie was not convinced; almost every week she heard rumors of new affairs with actresses such as Billie Dove and Jessie Reed or a society woman from Palm Beach named Louisa Wanamaker Munn.

The lackluster reviews of Billie's 1917–1918 plays had been the impetus for her almost single-minded devotion to her daughter and her husband. However, she was disappointed that sacrificing her stage career had done nothing to quell Ziegfeld's dark superstitions or make him act more interested in his family than in his infatuations. Billie was a bit heartened when, in mid-1921, Ziegfeld made substantial efforts to show the sincerity of his familial devotion. He brought Billie a superb Booth Tarkington play, *The Intimate Strangers,* and told her it was the perfect "comeback" vehicle for her. His judgment was correct. The play, coproduced by Charles Dillingham and Abe Erlanger, opened on November 7, 1921, at Henry Miller Theatre. Finally Billie had the ideal role that allowed audiences to see her in an adult, sophisticated light. *Intimate Strangers* tells the story of Isobel, a woman who tests a middle-aged man's love for her by pretending to be older than she really is. The critics were kind to Billie. One reviewer, Lois Landis, perceptively commented, "The Billie Burke of the fascinating childishness and pink pajamas roles has disappeared forever. Marriage, motherhood . . . have created a lovely stranger."[39]

Billie's triumphant return to the stage did not diminish her presence in her family's life. There is no doubt that Billie loved her mother, but Blanche had been a daunting and often intimidating woman, and her death allowed Billie to revel in her new role as matriarch of Burkeley Crest. Billie once stated that Blanche had given up her own life to make one for Billie, and now Billie tried to do the same for Patricia. The five-year-old was a delicate child whose health needed constant attention. Billie was uncomfortable leaving her at home and even brought the girl on a tour of *Intimate Strangers* to be sure she received the best maternal and medical care possible. When her health allowed, Patricia also accompanied Billie to the theater during performances. One night, Patricia somehow managed to crawl into the fireplace on the set. In the middle of a scene, Billie looked down and saw her daughter's face staring up at her from the fireplace. Billie nearly fumbled her lines, and after the performance she sternly lectured Patricia, but she found it difficult to be truly angry at her daughter.

Billie was grateful to her husband for finding and producing *Intimate Strangers,* but by the spring of 1922, his interests were once again misdirected. Ziegfeld seemed to be consumed by getting his new *Follies* in order, following through with his plans to bring the *Frolic* to Europe, and vacationing in Palm Beach and New Brunswick. When Billie wrote to Ziegfeld while he vacationed, she seemed to feel guilty for mentioning domestic necessities that needed his attention. Her letters also reflected her increasing tendency toward thrift; gone were the days when she was the "most extravagant" woman Ziegfeld had ever met. The following letter from Billie was blunt, desperate, loving, and accusing all at once:

> My darling—I think you should know just where it's [their
> money] gone—and how it counts up— . . . I am afraid we will
> have to have some more in the bank. I have to pay the chauffeur
> by the week and . . . I prefer to pay by the hour. I haven't bought a
> thing. I have asked you about a few things for our sitting room
> here and the stairs carpet at home. I suppose I shouldn't have
> done it dear with all the bills out, but I bought 5000 New York
> Cities [stocks] for baby. . . . So awful. I want to save my salary
> and pay my debts too. Maybe my darling will help me out some
> way. You usually set me on my feet when I think all hope is gone.
> I worry so lately and some days it's so bad for me—my jobs have
> almost killed me. I am so run down. . . .
>
> Hope you are happy and you fish a lot. But dearest . . . you
> don't know how I suffer with you being so crazy about Louisa
> [Wanamaker Mann] and other people. You think I don't know
> she knows what a wonderful lover you are. She's not hanging
> around for something to eat. I know that. I try not to think of it,
> but I suffer inside just the same. I don't want any lovers but I do
> want my husband and I want all of him. And when you don't
> want me let's call it all off. No double crossing.
>
> My dearest love always, Bill.

Billie was clearly the realist Bernard Sobel had once described her as, but that did not make the 1920s any easier for her than it was for her husband.

Ziegfeld continued to feel outmoded; the 1920s was a period of many endings and few beginnings thus far. One of those endings was his close association with Lucile Duff Gordon, whose last show for him had been the 1920 *Follies*. Ethan Mordden summed it up: "Lucile was over; the old-time *Follies* were over . . . Lucile suited the old Ziegfeld, who microman-aged the outfits . . . intensely . . . Lucile was fabulous, but limited like the Empress Theodora."[40] Another ending came in March 1922 when Bert Williams died of pneumonia. W. C. Fields later stated that Bert was "the funniest man I ever saw—and the saddest man I ever knew."[41]

The one tangible beginning that gave the 1920s a silver lining was the ascent of Marilyn Miller in Ziegfeld's first new musical. But Marilyn con-tinued to shun him, and after *Sally,* she had no intentions of continuing to work for him. However, like Lillian Lorraine, she remained a part of his life if not a part of his work. Billie the realist was all too aware of her husband's obsession with Marilyn. She knew their marriage needed a fresh start, but this would be impossible if Ziegfeld continued to cling so fiercely to things and people he could never attain. Outwardly, Billie and Ziegfeld still appeared to be the first couple of the Jazz Age: successful, wealthy, and voguish.

"The Roaring Twenties were very pleasant," Billie drily wrote. "If you did not stop to think."[42]

14

The End of
the Glory Days

By summer of 1922, there were no signs that the Jazz Age was becoming more pleasant for Ziegfeld. Marilyn Miller had launched another attack on him, but this time, the fight was not a private duel. All of New York was aware of it.

The trigger for Marilyn's attack had taken place shortly before Ziegfeld left for Europe to make good on his promise to bring the *Frolic* to London and Paris. Marilyn had entered her satin and velvet dressing room to find a lengthy telegram from Ziegfeld lying on her vanity table. In it, he informed Marilyn that he would sue her for $5 million if she broke the terms of her contract by marrying during the run of *Sally.* Marilyn calmly set the note aside and phoned her attorney, who in turn called Ziegfeld and informed him that there was also a clause in the contract forbidding him to put on *Sally* without Marilyn.

Ziegfeld was not ready to admit defeat. As he had skillfully done so many times in the past, he planted outlandish stories in the press. But this time, the tales were not intended to make a star more appealing. Ziegfeld's goal was to make Jack Pickford as unappealing as possible. The first account to hit the papers told of Jack's dishonorable discharge from the navy. Apparently, Jack had paid a doctor $500 to ensure that he was exempt from combat duty until the war ended. Jack not only bribed the doctor himself but also recruited other men who were willing to pay to dodge the draft. In return for providing him with these new clients, the doctor gave Jack morphine and other prescription drugs. If this story did not make Jack into a villain, the second one surely did. Ziegfeld hired press agents to spread the rumor that Jack was responsible for Olive Thomas's death because he had introduced her to drugs. He also reiterated the theory that Olive had committed suicide because Jack had infected her with syphilis.

Although these reports sounded like the stuff of tabloid journals, Jack made no effort to deny them. Still, Marilyn refused to acknowledge any veracity in the stories. Instead, she retaliated by instigating a malicious smear campaign against Ziegfeld. "His attack on Jack is a perfect parallel to his attack on Frank Carter," Marilyn stated. "But in both cases, Ziegfeld wasted his spleen. . . . I [will marry] Jack in spite of the ravings and rantings of a regiment of Ziegfelds and [am] only too eager, too proud, and too happy to do so."[1]

Even in the midst of their caustic feud, Ziegfeld continued to send Marilyn bouquets and expensive pieces of jewelry, as if to remind her of what she would lose if she married Jack Pickford. His unrelenting, lavish attention caused even Ziegfeld's closest friends to wonder if he was having an affair with her. But Marilyn could not be wooed with grandeur. Shortly after her employer left for Europe, Marilyn launched a second attack that reached beyond Ziegfeld and touched the most important woman in his life: Billie Burke.

On the afternoon that an exhausted Billie returned home from a cross-country tour of *Intimate Strangers,* she was dismayed to find her tranquil Burkeley Crest buzzing like the floor of the New York Stock Exchange. Reporters swarmed the lawn and made a beeline for Billie as she emerged from her car. "What about the divorce?" they demanded, shoving one another aside and snapping photographs. "Did you see Miss Miller's statement?"[2]

Billie had not seen Marilyn's statement, and she had no idea whose divorce the reporters were referring to. However, she soon deduced that the alleged divorce was her own. Marilyn claimed that Ziegfeld's mission to destroy her engagement to Jack was fueled by her rejection of his romantic advances. She added: "I am paying the price for being good. . . . He [Ziegfeld] will say that his attentions were that of a manager who wished to please his star, but don't believe it. I was obliged to hold him at arm's length." She went on to describe how she made sure she was never alone in her dressing room; she always had her maid with her to help fend off Ziegfeld. "But he was too callous to take the hint. He was annoyingly persistent. I never saw his like, and I've been on the stage for most of my life!"[3] The climax of Marilyn's statement was the accusation that Ziegfeld had engaged in orgies with four or five chorus girls in his office. However, the charge was so outlandish that Billie gave it no credence. The statement that most deeply affected her was the claim that Ziegfeld wished to make Marilyn his wife. "She said he was desperately in love with her and would marry her if I would step aside," Billie later wrote. "She claimed that all that held him was Patricia."[4] "She waves that baby at him like George M. Cohan waves the flag!" Marilyn declared.[5]

Billie, having heard enough from the reporters, fled inside her home. Her red-headed anger was inflamed beyond endurance. She cabled Ziegfeld in London and demanded an explanation. Before she received a reply, the reporters outside insisted that she give them a statement. Billie's prim, "tea cozy hostess" persona all but vanished under her blinding rage at Marilyn's allegations. "As for this Miller person thinking she has a place in any but the professional and business thoughts of Mr. Ziegfeld! Well, the poor child's brain can't be functioning properly, that's all. She certainly flatters herself if she thinks for one moment Flo Ziegfeld wants to keep her from marrying that Pickford boy because *he* is in love with her," Billie exclaimed. Next she discredited Marilyn by alluding to her exploits with men like Kabatznick and his questionable friends. "Why doesn't Miss Miller tell the world the names of the very nice people, oh so very nice, who attended those parties at Great Neck?"[6]

Ziegfeld wasted no time replying to his wife's emotional telegram. The *New York Times* printed his response the following morning. Ziegfeld's words conflicted with his customary cool and aloof manner as much as Billie's effusions belied her usual ladylike and gay demeanor: "Billie darling, I am nearly insane. For God's sake cable me what it is all about. I am not afraid of the truth, and I swear to God there is nothing to which you can take exception. Wait until I am proven guilty. You and Patricia are all that mean anything to me. Be fair, dearest. Will sail on next boat."[7]

Ziegfeld's cable did little to comfort Billie. Before she had sufficient time to gather herself, the reporters were back at her door, prodding her with more questions and showing no concern for her fragile state. "When interviewed tonight, Miss Burke was pale and tired, and her eyes were red with weeping," a writer from the *New York Times* stated. "'No,' she faltered to the reporter when asked if she cared to deny the rumor that she would leave her husband. 'No, I won't deny it. I won't affirm or deny anything. I simply can't talk about it. It's all very, very personal. It's quite true that I sent my husband a cable, but the contents were for him alone. Won't you please say that Mrs. Ziegfeld says she hasn't anything to say.'"[8] The reporters relented for a while, during which time Billie was able to defuse her anger and look at the situation with a more rational, objective eye. "I made up my mind," she wrote. "I had to make it up in spite of newspaper stories and in spite of many advisers who at once set themselves up as domestic relations counselors. I decided I did not want a divorce."[9] Billie had barely reached this decision when the press was back at her door. "As for my husband, I can only say that I do not believe the accusations against him," she told the journalists. "Since our marriage eight years ago we have been very happy, and Flo has always been thoughtful and loving. But, whatever has happened, or is about to happen, I will live my life as I've always lived it. . . . You will understand that I can discuss Mr. Ziegfeld only to defend him against the charges that have been brought against him."[10]

Billie's defense of Ziegfeld was a direct contrast to Anna Held's reaction to his affair with Lillian Lorraine. Anna had initially turned a blind eye to the scandal, but she ultimately used it as grounds for divorce. Billie confronted the Marilyn Miller affair with her eyes wide open and reached her own conclusions about its authenticity. Her faith in Ziegfeld may have seemed naïve or even pathetic to cynical New Yorkers, but it was actually a sign of great strength and a selflessness one would not expect from an actress accustomed to a pampered existence. Billie put her daughter, her home, and her husband's career before her own feelings. Leaving Ziegfeld would have meant uprooting Patricia and destroying the home they had made together at Burkeley Crest. If she stayed with Ziegfeld and demanded that he fire Marilyn, he would have lost thousands of dollars on his investment in *Sally*. With stoicism, Billie faced the press and denied rumors of a tawdry love triangle, a divorce, and Marilyn's firing from *Sally* "at the special request of Miss Burke."[11]

Billie was relieved when, six days later on July 31, 1922, she read that Marilyn Miller and Jack Pickford had been married. They became husband and wife on the luxurious, sprawling grounds of Pickfair, home of the queen and king of Hollywood, Mary Pickford and Douglas Fairbanks. Now, as Mary Pickford's sister-in-law, Marilyn was America's "other sweetheart." With such strong ties to the influential Pickford and Fairbanks, Ziegfeld's importance diminished considerably in Marilyn's life. Indeed, her mother and sister-in-law were already grooming her for a screen test. But before Marilyn could make the transition from stage to screen, she had to grit her teeth until the end of the year, when her contract with Ziegfeld expired.

Billie may have decided to keep her marriage intact, but she did not allow Ziegfeld to emerge unscathed from the scandal. When he returned from London, Ziegfeld tried to woo Billie, as usual, with precious gifts. The first thing he did was to smile impishly and remove a $25,000 Tiffany's bracelet from his pocket. Billie grabbed the bracelet and threw it across the room. Patricia, in a moment of comic relief, caught the bracelet in midair and kept it for herself, although she occasionally let Billie borrow it. Billie's trust in Ziegfeld was precarious, to say the least. On one occasion, when he did not arrive home until the early hours of the morning, Billie, in her pajamas, confronted Ziegfeld as he bent over the icebox in search of a snack. When he was evasive as to his whereabouts, Billie grabbed a soup ladle and "belabored him about the head and shoulders with it." Ziegfeld was stunned for a moment but then began to laugh. He swept Billie into his arms and carried her upstairs. Billie momentarily forgave him and wrote in her memoir that Ziegfeld "rather liked being hit with a jealous soup ladle."[12]

Ziegfeld also used another familiar tactic to win back Billie's favor: publicity. Interviews with Ziegfeld during this period reveal that Billie held considerable power in the marriage. Ziegfeld stated: "Billie Burke's husband is too lucky to be jealous of anybody's attentions to Marilyn Miller. Billie Burke fascinates me more than ever. She is the most charming woman in the world, and Patricia is a wonder baby." Most notable is Ziegfeld's reference to himself as "Billie Burke's husband." Ironically, newspapers referred to Billie as "Mrs. Florenz Ziegfeld, Jr., who used to be Billie Burke."[13]

Whether Ziegfeld knew it or not, he was responsible for giving Billie the confidence she now possessed. She had learned how to stand up for herself, how to express her own wishes, and how to say no. In 1922 Billie was accepting film roles despite producer Alf Hayman's disapproval. Frohman may have been dead, but Billie was still associated with his old business manager and successor. Hayman wired her: "IF YOU SIGN UP WITH PICTURES BEFORE WE SEE YOU AGAIN WE WILL NOT CONTINUE WITH YOU FOR ANOTHER SEASON." Billie curtly responded: "ANYMORE IRATE TELEGRAMS FROM YOU AND I WILL SIGN IMMEDIATELY."[14]

Billie no longer took any nonsense, especially from men. Ziegfeld's "nonsense" had given her the grit she needed to take charge of her own life, but his confidence in her acting abilities and his insistence that she receive the best treatment possible also played a large part in her newfound self-respect. And Billie needed every ounce of self-confidence and strength she had. Though sincerely invested in proving that his wife and his marriage were first and foremost in his life, Ziegfeld kept Billie in a state of flux. He was constantly switching from aloof to attentive, neglectful to adoring. Billie found herself in limbo. She was not content to be simply "Mrs. Ziegfeld," but because of her family responsibilities, she could not return to being Billie Burke the carefree actress and fashion plate.

Billie and Ziegfeld settled back into their life at Burkeley Crest as best they could. They continued to put on the façade of the perfect society host and hostess at their Sunday dinner parties. As Billie and Ziegfeld tried to balance their marriage and careers, they found themselves both closer together and farther apart than ever before.

Ziegfeld's professional life was just as rocky as his personal one. The 1922 *Follies* had opened on June 5 in the midst of the Marilyn Miller drama. The new edition cost more than any previous one, yet it lacked the innovation one might expect from such an expensive production. Ziegfeld endeavored to make the show's primary draw beauty, but audiences were so oversaturated with beauty that they began "to accept it without making much ado about it."[15] The 1922 *Follies* was the first to use the slogan "Glorifying the American Girl," reflecting Ziegfeld's ongoing conviction that spectacle trumped the skits that usually drew the most applause. The show did indeed glorify more girls than ever. Mary Eaton appeared, as did a newly glorified girl, fifteen-year-old Barbara Stanwyck (using her birth name, Ruby Stevens); Stanwyck later toured in the 1923 *Follies*. More than eighty other chorines were featured in various visual feasts. "Frolicking Gods" had girls dressed as Greek statues come to life. "Lace Land," a Victor Herbert ballet, cost Ziegfeld $31,000, mostly because he demanded that the costumes be made of real lace and that genuine red roses be affixed to the costumes and replaced daily. The number was worth the cost. Audiences may have been blasé about Ziegfeld's spectacles, but a writer for the *New York Times* appreciated the ballet's "startling effect." The same writer claimed that although the *Follies* was still "the blue-blood of revues," the comedy in the new edition was "verbally rough" and in need of a few "elisions."[16]

Whatever the critics thought, the comedians were still audience favorites. In his solo act, "Yankee Philosophy," Will Rogers expounded on relevant political topics and engaged in his usual lighthearted banter. One can deduce the content of Will's act from an interview he gave to journalist Gladys Hall in his dressing room backstage. He spoke at length about *Follies* girls and his thoughts on the "new-fashioned" woman:

> There's a lot of talk nowadays about the old-fashioned woman and the new-fashioned woman. I don't know. I take folks as I find 'em, and there's something to be said for all . . . why these girls [in the *Follies*] have hearts as big as their hat boxes . . . just 'cause girls are beautiful they get panned. I don't get this association of beauty and evil. Most of the bad 'uns and criminals I've seen have been as ugly as blazes. Real beauties can afford to be good . . . Mrs. Rogers is never jealous [of Will's high regard for the chorines]. She knows there ain't any of these girls going to lose their heads over *me* . . . most of the *Follies* girls are home folks![17]

Will's other acts, including a spoof on disarmament and one on baseball, received equally warm receptions. Ziegfeld was both pleased and confused by the reaction to Will's acts: audiences and critics wanted originality from the *Follies,* yet they were most satisfied when favorite performers stuck to their familiar personas.

In the comedy department, the 1922 *Follies* also included what is now one of the best remembered songs of the series: "Oh, Mr. Gallagher and Mr. Shean." The act was later re-created in the 1941 Judy Garland film *Ziegfeld Girl.* Vaudeville performers Al Shean and Edward Gallagher wrote and sang the song. In one sample verse, the men discuss rising prices and Prohibition:

> SHEAN: Ev'rybody's making fun
> Of the way our country's run
> All the papers say
> We'll soon live European.

> GALLAGHER: Why Mister Shean,
> Why Mister Shean.
> On the day they took away
> Our old canteen,
> Cost of living went so high
> That it's cheaper now to die.

SHEAN: Positively, Mister Gallagher.

GALLAGHER: Absolutely, Mister Shean.[18]

Gallagher and Shean and Will Rogers were not the only cast members to address modern topics. If the *Ziegfeld Follies of 1922* lacked innovation, it at least embraced modernity. Many of the show's featured scenes were titled after Jazz Age symbols, including "Bootlegger," "Flapper," and "Movies." "It's Getting Dark on Old Broadway" alluded to the increasing popularity of black performers in mainstream theater and their introduction of the shimmy dance.

By the end of June, the *Follies of 1922* was in trouble. Will Rogers had dropped out of the cast and planned to return to Hollywood. According to Marcelle Earle, "the clouds of gloom blotted out the *Follies*' sunshine of happiness" after Will left. The entire company planned a going-away party for the cowboy-philosopher and held it onstage after his last performance. A feast was laid out on tables placed end-to-end across the stage, while "hot, jazzy dance music played. Everyone danced. Even the policeman left his beat to join in."[19] Marcelle recalled that Will did not join in the fun. He watched wistfully, knowing how much he would miss his "family" at the New Amsterdam. Another reason for his sadness was Ziegfeld's absence from the party. Ziegfeld loathed farewells as much as he did funerals. He also felt betrayed, as he always did when a member of his company left him. However, Ziegfeld sent Will a note that communicated his feelings: "My dear Will. . . . I have never had anyone appear in any of my attractions that was a greater joy to be associated with than you. . . . Give my love to your family and it is with regret that I must say 'au revoir' to my friend . . . [in his own hand, Ziegfeld added A REAL MAN]. Very Sincerely yours, Ziegfeld."[20]

Will was a hard act to replace. Ziegfeld added a new group of performers called the Tiller Girls to the chorus, which posed a threat to the existing Ziegfeld girls. Lucille Layton Zinman said that, until the Tiller Girls came along, chorines did not have to be trained dancers. But now their dancing had to be top-notch. Marcelle Earle recalled the grueling process the chorus girls went through under Ned Wayburn's zealous and unsmiling direction. The girls' morale was low, and many were not above cursing and griping out loud.

A bit of the show's pep returned when Eddie Cantor filled Will's place after a revised version of the *Follies of 1922* opened on June 25. At the time, Eddie was starring in the Shuberts' *Make It Snappy,* which was playing across the street from *Sally* at the Winter Garden Theatre. One critic stated that Eddie Cantor at $3.30 a seat was better entertainment value than Marilyn Miller and Leon Errol at $4.40. Eddie put an eye-catching advertisement in *Variety* reprinting the comment, knowing full well that Ziegfeld would see it.

"You know that book show I promised you?" Ziegfeld asked Eddie over the telephone on the morning after he read the advertisement.

"Yeah, the one you evaded every time I brought it up," Eddie replied.

"Well, how would you like to do one for me now?"

Eddie agreed, but he made it clear that he was returning to the *Follies* only because he wanted to do a book musical. Eddie may have looked like a cocker spaniel (his own words), but he would not come running back to Ziegfeld like a puppy. He had proved he could be successful under another producer. Backstage rifts aside, Eddie added much-needed exuberance to the show, singing such tunes as "Oh Gee, Oh Gosh, Oh Golly I'm in Love" and "My Girl Uses Mineralava" (a popular cosmetic beauty clay).

Despite its shortcomings, the *Follies* grossed $37,000 during its first weeks, enjoyed larger audiences than ever before, and ran longer than any other edition. Yet the show grossed $9,000 less than its production costs and, according to theater historians, marked the end of the series' glory days. Ziegfeld did everything he could to save the *Follies* from going extinct along with the *Frolic.* He reduced ticket prices in an attempt to retain his middle-class audience, but critic Robert Benchley grumbled that $4 was still too high for what the show offered. Ziegfeld's next idea was to dramatically changed the show's release strategy. Instead of being only a summer entertainment, the *Follies* would be a year-round attraction "with carefully timed changes designed to pique audiences' interest."[21] However, most of those changes involved removing topical matters and inserting numbers that were only slight modifications of successful ones from previous years.

Rather than solving the *Follies'* problems, Ziegfeld's ideas only created new ones. The reduction in ticket price amounted to a weekly loss of $5,000. Even so, Ziegfeld still insisted on fresh roses for the chorines' costumes each day. Doris Eaton commented, "Ziegfeld was truly a perfectionist, though some would say a foolish spendthrift."[22] Ziegfeld showed his first sign of thrift when he began to pay his New York showgirls less than the ones who went on tour with the *Follies.* He reasoned that the prestige of being a Ziegfeld girl was enough to justify the salary discrepancy. However, the touring girls' salaries were higher than any other chorines' on Broadway, thus negating any savings Ziegfeld may have hoped to achieve.

Even if the *Follies* had reached the end of its glory days, Ziegfeld was still known throughout the United States and Europe as the last word in musical theater. *Sally* continued to enjoy a successful run into 1923, but if Ziegfeld could not pull together another show to match it, he could lose his status on Broadway. He was not blind to the fact that the more intimate acts in his shows, and in nearly every show on Forty-Second Street, were gaining popularity. Ziegfeld's trademark was blending new trends with the tried and true, so he set out to find an intimate drawing-room comedy that he could infuse with music and dance. And he could think of no better way to reconcile with Billie Burke than to cast her in such an endeavor.

Ziegfeld secured for Billie the lead role in a Booth Tarkington play entitled *Rose Briar.* The play was to be staged at the Empire Theatre, the site of Billie's greatest past glories. The show's script, however, was not on par with Billie's previous successes such as *Love Watches* (1908) or *The Mind-the-Paint Girl* (1912). It was, in fact, a step backward for Billie. She was cast in the frivolous role of an heiress who loses her fortune and must perform as a cabaret star to earn a living. At the cabaret, an unhappily married man with a wealthy wife falls in love with her, leading both the man and his wife to consider divorce. Billie would be singing and dancing against backdrops by Joseph Urban and Ben Ali Haggin, and despite her limited abilities in these areas, she remained remarkably optimistic and hopeful as the play progressed through rehearsals. Ziegfeld tried to remain optimistic as well, not only for Billie's sake but also for the sake of his standing as a producer. He had a lot riding on *Rose Briar;* he had abandoned the idea of moving his rooftop entertainments to London and Paris and was still searching for an appropriate vehicle for Eddie Cantor. He might have pursued his exportation of the *Frolic* with more vigor, but he knew he had to be with his family or lose them. Still, Ziegfeld was often absent even when he was in the country; he was spending more and more time in Palm Beach. He said he wanted to be with Billie and Patricia, yet he failed to follow the old adage that "actions speak louder than words."

Ziegfeld's nerves were strained to their limit, and he felt every one of his fifty-five years. However, he did not forget to send Billie an elaborate telegram of congratulations on *Rose Briar*'s opening night—Christmas 1922. Reading his words, one can see shades of insincerity, as if he were rehearsing a speech for an audience. His language is flowery, but it lacks the warmth and intimacy Billie craved:

Dear Billie: Please extend my congratulations to the entire company and to yourself on the occasion of celebrating thirthieth [*sic*] anniversary of the Empire Theatre to-night. Also my regrets that illness makes it impossible for me to be present, but I am highly gratified that Miss Billie Burke, a former and famous Frohman star, is playing at the Empire on this auspicious occasion and had the honor of conducting this memorable celebration. The Empire Theatre has always stood for all that is lofty and dignified in the theatre, and a questionable play has never been produced on the Empire stage. In thirty years the public has shown its appreciation of the high standards of the Empire Theatre. This theatre will always stand I hope as a monument to the memory of that great and wonderful producing manager, Charles Frohman, and I am proud to see that Gilbert Miller, his successor, in charge of the destinies of the Empire is preserving those same high standards always associated with the name of Frohman. Tell David Belasco how sorry I am not to be there with him on the stage which is dedicated with his own play thirty years ago and give him my sincere regards and appreciation of the great work he has done since the time the Empire opened. I wish also to pay the highest tribute possible to the beauty, charm and talent of the celebrated star who is now appearing at the Empire Theatre in "ROSE BRIAR," but I am afraid if I get too enthusiastic in this telegram the others will think I am prejudiced in your favor. Once more my sincerest regards to every one and express my regret that I cannot be present with you all to-night. If I had known the Empire was going to have an anniversary I would not have come to Palm Beach until after it was over. Sincerely, Flo.[23]

If anything, the telegram sounds more narcissistic than heartfelt (note that he closes not with "love" but with "sincerely"). Also, the extent of his "illness" was questionable. Billie knew that her husband's idea of convalescing was enjoying Palm Beach soirees and society women at their vacation home. But Billie took his absence in stride, clinging to the fact that Ziegfeld had at least acknowledged her. She did not want to jeopardize the upswing their professional and personal lives seemed to be taking now that the Marilyn Miller scandal had cooled.

But after the reception of *Rose Briar,* neither Billie nor Ziegfeld could say that their careers were on the upswing. The show's dance sequences and Billie's performance of a Jerome Kern song, "Love and the Moon (Are Traitors They Say)," looked and sounded identical to those one would expect to see in the *Follies.* A critic for the *New York Times* commented that the show "just skirts the borders of the *Follies.*" Critics did not miss Billie's difficulties with her role, stating that her performance was not "truly drawn, and one never has a really clear conception of the girl."[24]

Billie could have used her husband's moral support in the face of such discouraging reviews. But while she was performing in *Rose Briar* in January and February 1923, he was more focused on moving on to his next projects. His mind teemed with ideas for Eddie Cantor's show and for the next *Follies.* He was also preoccupied with securing the necessary funds to produce both shows. The society ladies of Palm Beach were, as Ziegfeld had found in the past, excellent benefactresses. But business and funding dilemmas were not sufficient excuses to neglect his wife and daughter, and Billie was not afraid to tell him so. While Ziegfeld enjoyed the sun in Florida and Billie juggled rehearsals and a child in New York, their relationship was reduced to the exchange of telegrams and letters. Their correspondence reflected the unpredictability of their feelings for each other in the aftermath of the Marilyn Miller scandal. The letters were utilitarian one moment and desperate the next. Billie's words could be loving, accusing, placating, despondent, or ecstatic. In most of the letters, Billie's handwriting resembled a hasty scribble, indicating that she wrote them in states of high emotion. One letter expressed Billie's dissatisfaction with Ziegfeld's behavior and the loneliness his absence caused her:

> You always love me best when I am far away and New York is so far and so interesting but I am doing my damndest not to ask anything for anything you wouldn't want me to. I wish to God I had the same effect on you that others seem to have and that I seem to have on others. I suppose the fact that I love you is my salvation and my attraction. Men always want something they can't get. . . .

You do love me I guess but you love others so much too it makes me a little desperate at times and I think what's the use and then I remember I am somebody's mother too but oh God I could do with some loving. . . . . Gilbert's [Gilbert Miller, Frohman's successor at the Empire Theatre] telling a lovely story about you calling him up, his asking how you are. You saying in loud strong voice "I'm feeling fine"—Gilbert is so thrilled you'll be coming home soon. You in a small little voice—"Oh I am still kind of weak"!!! Dear old Palm Beach. It's broken up many a home. I hope we will survive it—but I wish to God you'd got it out of your system before I met you.[25]

The letter truly encapsulates the schizophrenic nature of their marriage. In the first half of the letter (quoted above), Billie is scolding; in the second half, she gives lively updates about the progress of her play and seems eager to have Ziegfeld produce another musical show for her in the spring: "I think the money would be in a musical play by Kern and your other friends as support but maybe we could do that later. You don't want to do another production this season, not an expensive one. Kern says 'Sally' is too wonderful . . . I hope it gets us out of debt. . . . The play never went so well as it did tonight."[26]

Next, Billie returns, if less vehemently, to a cajoling mood toward her husband. She mentions Patricia in the hope that this will awaken Ziegfeld's conscience and lead to his return:

Oh, if you want to feel your heart swell with pride you only have to look at that darling baby riding round . . . her little horse . . . I'll be glad when you get back. She needs a father so. A child misses so much with out the man's point of view on life—girls need their fathers almost more than boys I think—

You should give her some of your time as well as crowding her with just presents. She needs your companionship. You're always so busy at home with telephone etc it doesn't give either of you a chance. I am feeling better today but I am terribly nervous . . . I hope you are better.

Take care of yourself and I hope you get really strong . . . ever and always I hope you don't stay away too long.

Baby[27]

Without Ziegfeld, Billie found herself relying more on her circle of theater friends. She reveled in being their gracious hostess and felt no need to put on a façade because she truly enjoyed giving parties. Her reentrance into the theater world inspired her to give a reception for British dramatic actress Gladys Cooper. That party, in Billie's words, was "one of the most wonderful nights I have ever had." Her only source of unhappiness was Ziegfeld's absence. She wrote to him in Palm Beach:

> I am glad you are getting a little stronger. You know you don't have to keep on saying you are weak just so you won't have to come home. You can just stay down there . . . not much caring what we think—your new boat must be wonderful. Poor old Flo darling [if you didn't] have baby and me to take care of you could be so happy having all the things you want for yourself and you could enjoy them without having to fib or apologize for them. When it comes to what we want there is so much talk about what it costs. . . . [At the] party last night . . . [it was] nice to be made a fuss of and told pretty things but one never gets enough of this—I have never had enough from you. [Other people] seem to see things in me but [you are] strangely cold—but what's the use of quibbling.[28]

Ziegfeld did quibble. During his marriage to Anna Held, he had planted newspaper stories about his chivalrous actions to defend her name. Now he used a similar tactic, but he executed it in a far different manner. He used actual actions rather than false stories to prove that he was a devoted husband. But again, his actions reflected his narcissism—he wanted to make himself look good and did not consider what Billie truly wanted. Rather than spend time with her, he showered her with gifts. First, he tried to make her dressing room at the Empire Theatre a home away from home. During the holiday season, he sent her a miniature Christmas tree. Responding to the gift, Billie wired: "I WEPT WHEN I SAW MY DRESSING ROOM YOU ARE SUCH A STRANGE BOY AND CAN MAKE ME SO HAPPY AND YET SO MISERABLE."[29]

Billie was darkly humorous in a follow-up letter concerning Ziegfeld's generosity: "Thank you for what you did and my dressing room was a wonder. Everyone raved over it, it was just like you. I know I am going to have the most wonderful funeral."[30] However, she was not going to over-look her husband's reckless behavior simply because he had given her a lovely dressing room. As she often did in her letters, Billie paired searing words with pretty ones:

> I hear you are gambling which seems a folly. I wonder why you felt you had to lie to me about it. Do you think I really mind those things when I mind much more your not telling me the truth. . . . When you return I am trusting in your consideration for my feelings in the matter . . . I started to tell you what was going on here and all the pent up bitter feelings will come out. But I can't help it if they are old wounds and won't heal. Give all the lovely ladies [in Palm Beach] my dearest regards and a kick in the— . . . I am glad I do not listen to any of their drivel. . . . Hope the fish are coming pretty.
>
> Tear this up at once, Billie[31]

Billie seems to have written this note in a fit of temper and then had a change of heart (telling him to tear it up). However, gambling had been and continued to be a source of trouble for Ziegfeld's wives. And thanks to his gambling, there were unpaid debts that neither Billie nor Ziegfeld could escape. In one note, Billie informed him that she had been presented with two bills that threatened the Ziegfelds' standing in Hastings: an unpaid electric bill and a $1,200 hotel bill.

Financial matters showed no signs of improving as *Rose Briar* struggled to stay alive on Broadway. Billie wrote to Ziegfeld: "IF I COULD ONLY HEAR AT NIGHT A LITTLE OF WHAT THEY GIVE ME AT MY MATINEES I DONT MEAN JUST MONEY DARLING IT WOULD BE WONDERFUL HOPE YOUR [sic] NOT DISOURAGED [sic] AT BUSINESS BUT I AM AFRAID ITS BAD PLEASE MAY I HAVE ALL OF MY SALARY JUST A LITTLE LONGER."[32] A week later, Billie asked if Ziegfeld could possibly dig up "another five" from the bank, or she would have to draw on her salary.

Billie's frustrations with Ziegfeld's alternating attentiveness and aloofness were most evident when she wrote about her inability to find a temporary home in New York during her play's run. She said she felt like a hen scratching around for a place to roost with her chick. In the past, Ziegfeld had always secured the best lodging for his wives. Why he neglected to do so at this time can be attributed to both his nervous exhaustion and his increasing fascination with the beautiful people of Palm Beach. It was not until February 13, 1923, that Ziegfeld finally found Billie and Patricia acceptable lodgings. Billie wrote to him from her new apartment (its precise address is unknown): "I FEEL SO HAPPY THINK WE ARE AT LAST IN COMFORTABLE SURROUNDINGS YOUR FLOWERS WERE SO LOVELY. . . . DONT WORRY ABOUT ME NOW I AM HOUSED I CAN GET SOME REST . . . PLEASE DON'T FEEL YOU MUST COME HOME STAY ANOTHER MONTH AND BY THAT TIME YOU WILL WANT TO COME MAYBE BUT I DONT WANT IT BECAUSE YOU THINK YOU OUGHT TO . . . YOUR WIFE."[33]

The fact that Billie signed the telegram "your wife" rather than her customary "Bill" or "Baby" showed the coolness she felt toward her husband—lovely flowers or no lovely flowers. And giving him permission to stay in Palm Beach was a thinly veiled way of inducing guilt—or presenting him with a test she hoped he would pass. At first, Ziegfeld failed the test; he stayed in Palm Beach while Billie remained in the production of *Rose Briar* as it limped along. The show's failure was a severe blow to both Billie the actress and Billie the wife. She eventually took matters into her own hands and, with Gilbert Miller, began to search for an appropriate part for herself. She hoped Ziegfeld would step in and help her, but he was not as alacritous as usual. However, looking for her own part actually seemed to buoy her spirits: "I DO HOPE BOLTON AND KERN AND WORDHOUSE [*sic*] WILL HAVE AN INSPIRATION MY VOICE IS IMPROVING BUT I WANT TO BE FUNNY DO BEE [*sic*] GOOD AS YOU CAN I KNOW YOU LOVE A DARLING ALL MY LOVE BILL."[34]

Ziegfeld finally took action. Mention of the theater, which had long been their common bond, had succeeded in redirecting his attention toward Billie. He promised that he would find a play better suited to her talents. But Billie had other ideas. Strangely, she *wanted* to take the musical roles that were not her strong suit. Only she was privy to her real motives: did she hope to infatuate her husband, or did she sincerely want to conquer the art of musicals? She wrote to Ziegfeld: "NOTHING WOULD MAKE ME HAPPIER THAN MUSICAL PLAY AM SURE THAT'S WHERE THE MONEY IS BUT HAVE NO FAITH IN OLD FASHIONED PLAYS BEING USED. . . . BUSINESS SO BAD LETS DO A MUSICAL COMEDY IF [I] HAVE A FUNNY FACE WE MIGHT JUST AS WELL USE IT I THINK YOUR WRITERS COULD FIT ME AM TIRED AND HOMESICK FOR YOU TONIGHT DEVOTEDLY BABY."[35]

Billie became even lonelier and more homesick when Patricia left to visit Ziegfeld in Palm Beach in March 1923. After suffering many a flu and cold, Patricia was thrilled to, in Billie's words, "be with her daddy and have him all to herself" in a warm climate more conducive to her health. Billie wrote from New York: "I hope Baby is going to be well. I know she will be happy. She loves you so very much . . . I have no more love left here darling." Billie felt "like a lost sheep" without her daughter and husband. She declared, "There's nothing left in this old town and the only things I care for on earth are both in Palm Beach." As was Billie's pattern, she sent one emotional and raw message, followed by one apologizing for her previous "cross old wire." She wrote, "I bet you're some excited old Daddy. I wish I were in your place, only I could never wait that long to see her [Patricia]."[36]

During the run of *Rose Briar*, Billie began to suffer from nervous exhaustion, and her doctor diagnosed her with hyperthyroidism. She described herself as "blue and tired" and stated that "nothing goes right." In the following wire, Billie expresses her ongoing worries about debts, her health, and the lack of revenue from *Rose Briar*:

> I SAW MY DOCTOR TODAY AND HE FRIGHTENED ME RATHER ABOUT MYSELF ONLY A CONDITION BROUGHT ON BY WORRY AND REST WILL HELP IT I AM DOWN TO ONE HUNDRED AND EIGHTEEN AND CANT PUT ON ANY FLESH BUT THE BILLS FOR FIVE THOUSAND CAME IN SATURDAY THAT UPSET THEY MUST BE PAID BY DARLING IF YOU REALLY MEAN I CAN HAVE MY SIX WEEKS PAY IT WOULD TAKE AWAY ALL MY ANXIETY BUT I WOULD WANT IT NOW FOR I KNOW YOU WOULD FORGET BUT IF I CAN HAVE IT AND GET CLEANED UP MAYBE MY POOR NERVES WOULD CALM DOWN.

The anxious and overwhelmed Billie was finally able to reunite with Ziegfeld and Patricia after *Rose Briar* closed on March 10, 1923, after a disappointing eighty-eight performances. From the train station in New York, Billie sent an eager wire to her husband stating that she was so anxious to see him in Palm Beach she "felt like a bride." She added: "I AM GLAD YOU WANT US I AM MORE MISERABLE THAN I HAVE DARED TELL YOU LOVE. . . . I CAN NEVER THANK YOU FOR ALL YOU DID FOR ROSE BRIAR I ONLY HOPE I WILL PROVE TO YOU I AM A REAL STAR."[37]

Billie's desire to prove herself to her husband stemmed from his ongoing attentions to Marilyn Miller. Once the family returned from Palm Beach, Ziegfeld again oversaw the seemingly endless run of *Sally*. He had no solid plans for a follow-up show for Marilyn, and he sensed her restlessness. Fearing he was about to lose his most valuable asset, he sent her rubies and bottles of Chanel No. 5 to persuade her to stay under his employ. Billie now knew that Ziegfeld's interest in Marilyn was only professional. Still, she could not help worrying that her husband continued to pamper and appease the woman who had caused so much strife in their marriage.

Patricia's memoir provides a glimpse into Billie's unresolved feelings about Marilyn. One night, after much begging on Patricia's part, Ziegfeld agreed to take her to a performance of *Sally,* but Billie intervened. "It's much too long and complicated for someone of your age, dear," she told her seven-year-old daughter. "You'd be bored to tears."

"Are you intimating that *Sally* is dull?" Ziegfeld asked.

"No. Only that it's unsuitable for a young child."

"Beautiful music, marvelous scenery—what's unsuitable about that? Anyway, Patty will adore seeing Marilyn dance."

"Oh, of course, I almost forgot!" Billie exclaimed. "Marilyn *is* in the show, isn't she? Well, it might be a good idea for Patty to see her at that. Before it's too late I mean."

Ziegfeld sighed.

"Poor Marilyn. She used to be so lovely. I want you to remember when you see poor Miss Miller that she was once a graceful, pretty dancer," Billie told Patricia.

"All is now growing clear," Ziegfeld muttered.

"Is poor Miss Miller sick?" Patricia asked.

"Not sick exactly—you'll see," Billie said.

Patricia did see what Billie meant—all too clearly. She adored the show and thought Marilyn looked like a "thistledown angel." However, her illusions fell away when Ziegfeld took the awestruck girl backstage to meet Marilyn. Marilyn's response to Ziegfeld's knock at the door was, "Hello you lousy son of a bitch, you no good bastard." Ziegfeld attempted to quiet her, indicating that his daughter was with him. "You've talked about her to the point of nausea," Marilyn responded. "Hello," she said to the girl. She then launched into a complaint about her costume: "This piece of crap you call a costume" weighs a ton. "What are you planning to do about this fucking costume?" Marilyn yelled.

"We'll talk about it later," Ziegfeld said, herding Patricia away.

"No, now!" Marilyn screamed. She hurled a jar of cold cream that narrowly missed his head and shattered against the door.

Ziegfeld slammed the door shut behind him and wiped his forehead with a handkerchief. He then explained to Patricia that backstage was like the other side of a shiny Christmas tree star—the side with the price tag and tin showing through.

"I like the front side best," Patricia said, indicating the stage.

Once they arrived home, Ziegfeld and Patricia both felt a bit feverish. Billie placed her hands against Patricia's red cheeks and shook her head.

"Guess who we met?" Patricia asked. "Poor Marilyn Miller."

Billie could not help smiling. Ziegfeld went upstairs, relieved to be home "for a little peace and quiet."[38]

Judging by Marilyn's behavior, it is not surprising that she canceled her contract with Ziegfeld before *Sally* ended, despite all his attempts to woo her. Marilyn told the press that Ziegfeld had meddled once too often in her private life. Ziegfeld accepted Marilyn's comments gracefully, remarking, "If that statement is satisfaction to her, I am satisfied."[39]

Unemployed for the first time since she was five years old, Marilyn found herself at loose ends. She had not given up the idea of becoming a film star; indeed, its appeal only increased after the *New York Times* reported that Billie Burke had been voted "Queen of the Movies" at a gala event held in the Astor ballroom to raise money for the Association for Improving the Condition of the Poor. Billie's victory was interesting, given that she had no new film releases in 1922. Marion Davies and Constance Binney were the runners-up.[40] Marilyn was sure she could dethrone Billie in Hollywood just as she had on Broadway.

Ziegfeld also felt at loose ends with the loss of Marilyn—the girl who had brought his shows into the Jazz Age. Together, their names had equaled gold. However, as Alexander Woollcott had observed, audiences remembered not Marilyn but Ziegfeld as they rode the subway home from the theater. If Woollcott was right, Ziegfeld did not need Marilyn to remain a vital force. Once Marilyn was out of the picture, Ziegfeld realized how much he relied on the grounding influence of his wife and daughter. With them as his motivators, Ziegfeld was determined to make the remainder of the 1920s the most prolific and inspired phase of his career. Whether he realized it or not, Ziegfeld was his own greatest star.

PART 3

The Darkest Hour of Success, 1923–1932

Others find peace of mind in pretending.
Couldn't you?
Couldn't I? Couldn't we?
Only make believe.
—*Oscar Hammerstein II, "Only Make Believe" (1927)*

15

Little Boy Blue

Though the *Ziegfeld Follies* had made Ziegfeld his own greatest star on Broadway, he knew that his professional future lay in musical comedy. Nothing better convinced him of this fact than the critical reaction to his *Follies of 1923*, which opened at the New Amsterdam Theatre on October 20, 1923. One reviewer declared that the show was "smothered under general mediocrity."[1]

Like the 1922 edition, the *Follies of 1923* had little in the way of innovation. Ziegfeld did his best to please audiences, however, featuring favorites Fanny Brice and Eddie Cantor to liven up the show. On opening night, Eddie sat in the audience holding a wrench, hammer, and screwdriver. Before the overture began, he started banging loudly on his seat, trying to loosen it. An usher attempted to quiet the comedian, but Eddie declared, "Let me alone! I paid $22 for this seat and I'm taking it home!" Both Ziegfeld and the critics considered this bit the funniest in the entire show. Eddie Cantor also penned two skits himself. The first, entitled "South Sea Island," had Fanny Brice playing an awkward native, garishly adorned with shells and bangle bracelets. In his second skit, Eddie narrated famous moments in history as Fanny humorously brought them to life. The figures she portrayed included Pocahontas and Queen Isabella. The routines were certainly funny, but they harked back to both performers' earlier work. For instance, the first *Follies* had used John Smith and Pocahontas as its central characters.

The show contained one innovative number that proved Ziegfeld had not lost his magic touch: "Shadowgraph." It was an experiment in three-dimensional display, with shadows that leaped across the footlights. Members of the audience were given special glasses that allowed them to see the shadows. Because it was completely different from anything anyone had ever seen, "Shadowgraph" was the best-reviewed number in the show. Musical accompaniment by the Paul Whiteman Orchestra added to its superiority (Whiteman gained fame the following year when he conducted the most pioneering composition of the decade, George Gershwin's "Rhapsody in Blue"). The second-best number in the show, "Amateur Night," allowed each entertainer to showcase his or her unique talents. Fanny Brice parodied herself, performing the maudlin tune she had sung to win her first amateur contest. Critics called it the "wow" of the night.

The *Ziegfeld Follies of 1923* may have been, in the words of historian Gerald Bordman, an "obvious step down," but it ran for a healthy 233 performances.[2] However, its long run did not make up for the mediocre material, and Fanny Brice was not afraid to say so. Even though she was at the height of her success in 1923, she broke with Ziegfeld after that year's *Follies* not only because of the inferior material but also because he had failed to find her the starring vehicle he had allegedly promised her. She and Ziegfeld remained friends until his death, but she never returned to his employ.

The *Follies'* sagging material between 1922 and 1925 can be attributed to both Ziegfeld's increased focus on musical comedies and his tumultuous personal life. Before the opening of the 1923 *Follies,* Ziegfeld rushed to Chicago upon learning that his eighty-two-year-old father was dying of pneumonia. Shortly after he arrived, the professor died. The loss of his father affected Ziegfeld more strongly than he admitted. Though father and son had had their differences, Professor Ziegfeld had been a paramount influence in his son's life. The finesse of his business relationships and his fine taste in the arts were indelible legacies passed on to his son.

The producer's generally dark mood following his father's death colored his view of Eddie Cantor's prospective new show. Still, he knew he could not renege on the long-awaited project, having lost Fanny Brice for much the same reason. Ziegfeld's pessimism about the project was enhanced by the lack of a script—or even an idea for a script. The concept for Eddie's show finally came to life during a Sunday afternoon lunch in Pelham, New York. In attendance were Eddie, scriptwriter William Anthony McGuire (a heavy drinker), and songwriters Harry Tierney, Joe McCarthy, and Otto Harbach, who had recently penned the score for *Irene.* Ziegfeld had suggested the meeting in the hope that, together, the five of them could figure out something for a show. Eddie arrived at the meeting dressed in eccentric golf attire, complete with checkered knickers and a garish cap. The outrageous outfit inspired McGuire to suggest a show about a crooked golf caddy who bootlegs liquor on the side. The others were enthusiastic, and they arranged to have another meeting at the end of the week. McGuire's alcoholism made him notoriously unreliable, and he failed to appear at the second meeting. However, he miraculously produced a rough draft five days later.

"What? You really have a show? What's the idea of rushing me?" an astonished Ziegfeld asked when Eddie presented him with the script. Ziegfeld was impressed with the work, but Eddie knew his boss needed time to grow accustomed to the thought of any new production. Feeling that both he and the show were being rushed, Ziegfeld's gloomy outlook about its chances of success grew darker. Eddie, however, was known as the "apostle of pep," and he refused to give in to Ziegfeld's pessimism. He threw every ounce of energy in his small, wiry body into convincing the producer that his one-man show was worthy of the investment. Eddie did everything from putting golf balls on Ziegfeld's desk to hopping onto the producer's lap and pinching his cheek. The usually poker-faced Ziegfeld actually erupted into laughter, and he even contributed suggestions for the show: "How about this: the country club's physical therapy director can be played by a woman—a big, strong woman. Someone like Jobyna Howland. She'll give you a work over like the 'Osteopath Scene' but this time it'll include an electric chair," he explained with a macabre grin. Eddie later wrote that the show "contained every type of comedy for which I was best suited. The pattern of its comic scenes and their sequence were skillfully designed and have rarely been excelled. The shades of fun varied from light gags and wisecracks to human situations and from great physical hokum to delightful nonsense."[3]

The casting process for the show, entitled *Kid Boots,* began in the midst of Marilyn Miller's contract dispute with Ziegfeld. She had walked out of *Sally,* and Mary Eaton was doing a good job of filling her shoes. Because Mary had saved *Sally,* Ziegfeld had promised her a starring role in his next musical comedy, and *Kid Boots* presented an ideal opportunity. Mary portrayed the girl to whom Boots the caddy played Cupid in a romantic side story.

Eddie wrote in his memoirs that his and Mary's "association in the show was of the pleasantest."[4] However, Mary's sister Doris remembered things differently. She described Eddie as a "backstage tyrant" who never treated Mary as an equal or a professional and never socialized with her. "He never showed any personal warmth to her [Mary] or any of the Eatons," Doris said. She also asserted that Eddie did not even mention Mary's name in his memoirs, which is untrue.[5] Mary was also having troubles with Ziegfeld, and Doris recalled that the press was full of stories about their disagreement. Ziegfeld had included a clause in Mary's contract that prohibited her from marrying while working in his show. But when Mary discovered that the clause was not legally binding, she shrugged it off and happily took the $2,000 a week Ziegfeld offered her.[6]

Despite his own enthusiasm, Ziegfeld still had doubts about how audiences and critics would react to the show. Thus, to avoid potential embarrassment on Broadway, he opened the show in Detroit, where the audience response was overwhelmingly positive. After the first-act curtain, Ziegfeld, Eddie, and director Edward Royce joined hands backstage and did an impromptu dance of ring-around-the-rosy. Once the final curtain fell, an elated Ziegfeld went into Eddie's dressing room and kissed him. Ziegfeld decided to bring the show to New York without further hesitation. Calling the entire company together backstage, Ziegfeld solemnly stamped out his cigar and looked each actor in the eyes before stating, "Do not wire or phone anyone in New York. We don't want anyone to know what kind of a hit we have. It'll only make it harder to live up to expectations. Let's surprise them all. If a single telegram is sent to New York it will mean instant dismissal."

After the company dispersed, Ziegfeld immediately overruled himself and went first to the telegraph office and then to a phone booth to tell every critic he knew that *Kid Boots* was a smash. With a stern expression, he returned to the theater as if nothing had happened. He then called comics Harlan Dixon and Marie Callahan over to discuss their dance routine, which involved them rolling all over each other onstage. It had not been successful during rehearsal, and Ziegfeld wanted the dance to be perfect, especially now that he had told critics about his hit. Contrary to past experience, Ziegfeld proved that he had a sense of comedy—he showed the comedians how to do the dance himself. Eddie Cantor recalled that the producer "rolled all over the stage like a baggy pants clown until the routine was just as he wished it. Then he gravely dusted off his trousers and he and I went to a Chinese restaurant for supper."[7]

During dinner, Ziegfeld continued to mull over how to perfect the show. He peered at Eddie across the table until the comedian began to shift self-consciously in his seat. "You're funny, Eddie," he said. "Don't wear funny clothes."

"All right Mr. Ziegfeld," Eddie agreed. He was relieved. Eddie thought that somehow his boss knew that he had disobeyed Ziegfeld's gag order by calling his wife and indirectly communicating *Kid Boots*' success by telling her to go ahead and buy the expensive new coat she wanted.

Ziegfeld looked away from Eddie, took a pen from his pocket, and picked up his menu. After doing some lengthy mathematical calculations on the back of it, he chuckled. "If we sell out every performance, I'll only lose $1,200 a week!" he said.

Kid Boots opened at the Earl Carroll Theatre on December 31, 1923, and the audience was in stitches from beginning to end. In the first scene, Eddie's character, Boots, was introduced, and he gave a hilarious impression of being a tough guy despite his decidedly wimpy exterior. His fellow caddies replied "Yes, ma'am!" to everything he said, which infuriated Boots. He tore off his red necktie and cried, "Don't let this thing fool you! I'm a pretty tough guy, I am. When I have waffles for breakfast, I throw away the waffles and eat the irons!" He then lectured the caddies: "How often have I told you guys there's been complaints about golf balls being missing? Now I don't mind sneaking in a ball now and then but remember, a golf ball is never lost 'til it stops rolling. Remember, honesty is the best policy. You've either got to be honest, or I get half."

In a scene reminiscent of Eddie's famous osteopath skit, Boots tried to give Dr. Fitch, a physical therapist, a golf lesson. However, the doctor caught on to the fact that Boots had rigged the game when her ball always rolled crookedly. Later, Dr. Fitch took revenge by bringing Boots to an examining table and, as Eddie recalled, "ma[king] a handle of my hair and tr[ying] to see if my head was removable." At the conclusion, Boots staggered to an electric chair, the therapist turned the switch, and the scene blacked out.[8]

The music in the show delighted audiences as much as the jokes did. At the suggestion of Fanny Brice, Ziegfeld hired George Olson and his band, and they brought a modern, jazzy feel to the score. Ironically, the biggest hit of the show was penned by Harry Akst and not by the principal songwriters, Harbach and McCarthy. "Dinah" remained a standard for decades afterward, with its most famous rendition being sung by Bing Crosby.

On opening night, Ziegfeld and Billie planned to attend a New Year's Eve ball after the show's final curtain. Ziegfeld had left his tuxedo in Eddie's dressing room, and he took the opportunity to congratulate his star. "From now on, I'm not Mr. Ziegfeld," he told Eddie. "I'm Zieggy or Flo. I won't see you at midnight, Eddie, so happy new year." Eddie cried real tears, overwhelmed by Ziegfeld's kind words. Eddie had grown up without a father, and now he felt like he had one. Ziegfeld left Eddie with a "fine old wine bottle" before joining Billie at the ball.[9]

New York reviewers lavished as much love on Eddie as the producer did. *Time* magazine reported that *Kid Boots* was "the best musical of a five year period . . . Cantor is inordinately funny and Mary Eaton's fine flavor of respectability made an excellent foil for Cantor . . . the only objection that can be raised is the practical impossibility of getting tickets."[10] Ziegfeld was so pleased with the play and its reception that he made very few changes after opening night—a great rarity for the perfectionist producer. However, as if he could not be comfortable unless he changed *something*, Ziegfeld decided that all the costumes and scenery in act one needed to be altered, and $20,000 later, they were.

Although Ziegfeld was pleased with Eddie's performance, according to Patricia, he had to "constantly work on him [Cantor] to cool it."[11] "It" referred to Eddie's penchant for ad-libbing double entendres that were irrelevant to the show. Ziegfeld also had to "work on" Eddie's tendency to wear himself out doing benefit shows; in fact, he put a clause in Eddie's contract forbidding him to do so. One night, Ziegfeld attended a benefit with Billie and was surprised to find Eddie performing onstage. The comedian's eyes popped when he saw his boss sitting in the front row. He leaned across the stage and said in a stage whisper, "This isn't me you see up here!" Ziegfeld actually laughed and did not chastise his new favorite star for breaking his contract. The tense relationship they had endured since the 1919 Actors Equity strike had officially ended.

Kid Boots ran until February 1925, with box-office receipts totaling $1.75 million (almost $24 million in 2013 dollars). When it went on tour in 1926, the total gross amounted to $3 million.[12] While traveling with the show, Eddie received a twelve-page telegram from Ziegfeld that was a mangled mess of ideas, suggestions, and admonitions. Eddie was so confused that he sent only a single-word response: "YES." Ziegfeld shot back: "WHAT DO YOU MEAN YES DO YOU MEAN YES YOU WILL TAKE OUT THE SONG OR YES YOU WILL PUT IN THE LINES OR YES YOU WILL FIX THAT SCENE OR YES YOU HAVE TALKED TO THOSE ACTORS." Eddie, still confused, sent back a one-word answer: "NO."[13] After the thousandth performance of *Kid Boots,* Ziegfeld made up for his exhausting telegrams by presenting Eddie with a thin platinum pocket watch that Eddie's daughter, Marilyn, would keep in working order for more than seventy years.[14]

Eddie's phenomenal success in the play prompted Hollywood to come knocking at his door. Famous Players–Lasky produced a silent version of *Kid Boots* (released on October 4, 1926) with Eddie, Clara Bow, and Ziegfeld girl Billie Dove as the stars. Like Will Rogers, Eddie remained in Hollywood for a while, but he still had much more work to do for Ziegfeld before he permanently relocated to the West Coast. The movie version of *Kid Boots* could not re-create the magic of the Ziegfeld production. With no sound and no color, movies were not yet real competition for Ziegfeld.

Ziegfeld's confidence had returned. The *Follies* may have become outdated, but Ziegfeld now had two shows to his name that defined the Jazz Age: *Sally* and *Kid Boots.* With his confidence high, he next sought to produce a hit for his wife that was on a par with his two great musical comedy successes.

While *Kid Boots* was still in production, Ziegfeld thought he found the ideal show for his wife. Billie, however, was already pursuing a project she had found for herself: *The Swan,* by Gilbert Miller. Ziegfeld immediately cautioned her against it. Billie was torn: should she follow her own instincts or her husband's advice? Her faith in Ziegfeld was improving, but it was not strong enough for her to trust him completely as her manager. She could not ignore the fact that he had produced every one of her failed plays.

Bypassing Ziegfeld's objections, Billie vied for the lead role in *The Swan,* the story of a princess who is in love with a young tutor in her kingdom. Trouble ensues when her parents insist that she marry a prince to restore the family fortune. Billie did everything in her power to convince her husband of *The Swan*'s merit, mentioning it casually in a series of letters and telegrams to Ziegfeld while he was in Palm Beach. She was not afraid to use flattery as well as a sprinkling of guilt to sway her husband's opinion:

I don't know what about the Swan job. They are going to settle it tomorrow. I would like to make some more money this season. . . . Everyone says you're looking beautiful. It must be very gay there [in Palm Beach]. . . . I hope to talk to you before the day is over. It would help. . . . Take good care of yourself and remember I love you more than you ever think. I am ashamed to let you know how much because you don't love me the same. I'd like to kiss you so just on your shoulder where it's shiny and very brown.[15]

Next, she sent a telegram with a conspicuous note stamped on it from Western Union reading: "The sender of this message requests a reply. May we have it, please?"

GILBERT IS WAITING FOR YOUR DECISION ABOUT THE SWAN I AM AFRAID WE WILL LOSE THE EMPIRE [the Empire Theatre, where the play would be staged] IF YOU DON'T LET THEM KNOW THE PLAY LOOKS AWFULLY GOOD TO ME. . . .

THANKS FOR ALL YOU DO FOR ME I AM REALLY VERY RELIEVED YOU ARE SO GOOD TO ME I MUST BE DYING I AM SO HAPPY AT HAVING THE SWAN TO DO WE HAVE TO CONSENT TO TAKING IT ON THE ROAD IF SUCCESSFUL BUT PLEASE DO NOT OPPOSE THIS AS IT IS ONLY FAIR TO THE MANAGEMENT IT WOULD ONLY BE FOR A SHORT TIME IN ANY CASE PLEASE DO NOT OBJECT AS IT GIVES ME AN ENGAGEMENT FOR THE SPRING.[16]

Billie apparently did not receive the reply she wanted. Her next telegram, dated February 17, 1923, dripped with sarcasm and facetiousness: "IT WOULD BE MADNESS FOR YOU TO COME BACK TO THIS AWFUL COLD AND YOU ARENT HAPPY HOME ANY WAY SO PERHAPS ITS JUST AS WELL YES ITS TERRIBLE DEAR I AM OUT DANCING UNTIL SEVEN EVERY MORNING AT THE RENDEZVOUS CARRIED HOME BUT I WILL TRY TO MEND MY WAYS."[17]

By February 28, Ziegfeld must have sent her an acceptable reply, for Billie's next wire was full of affection: "MY DEAREST FOR THE FIRST TIME IN THE NINE YEARS THAT I HAVE LOVED YOU I FEEL YOU REALLY CARE ENOUGH TO HAVE MADE ME VERY VERY HAPPY I FEEL SUCH A LOAD TAKEN OFF MY POOR SKINNY SHOULDERS AND MY FAITH IN YOU HAS BEEN JUSTIFIED I DO LOVE YOU SO AND WHEN I THINK YOU DON'T CARE WHAT I AM GOING

THROUGH I JUST DON'T WANT TO LIVE I AM VERY HAPPY AND VERY VERY GRATEFUL . . . DEVOTEDLY BILLIE."[18]

However, Ziegfeld must have lied in his response, simply to placate her. When he returned home, he told her exactly what he thought of *The Swan*. "No, no good," he said, tossing aside the script. Billie had no patience for his dismissive attitude and flew into a rage, throwing china and crying over her foundering career. If he did not secure this role for her, all the tenderness and trust they had rebuilt over the past year would be for naught. No matter how unjustified Ziegfeld's objection might have seemed to Billie, it was his circuitous way of saving her career. Ziegfeld knew that Billie's work in *Intimate Strangers* had moved her beyond playing swooning ingénues. Her failure in *Rose Briar* had proved this. Because it was her hoydenish charm that had first attracted Ziegfeld to Billie, moving her away from roles that heightened her little-girl qualities was not easy for him. But Billie, at age thirty-seven, could no longer pass for the eighteen-year-old Princess Beatrice in *The Swan*. Ziegfeld was willing to cast Billie in the play, but as the princess's meddling mother—a character part. Billie, however, would accept nothing less than the role of leading lady.

The Swan opened in October 1923 and closed in June 1924—without Billie. Ironically, the actress who played the part of Princess Beatrice, Hilda Spong, was nine years older than Billie. The play's great success, according to a writer for the *New Yorker*, prompted "Miss Burke [to] refuse to speak to Mr. Ziegfeld for six weeks."[19] As a show of independence and perhaps to irritate her husband, Billie also joined Actors Equity in 1924. Ziegfeld was still searching for the right vehicle for Billie when *The Swan* closed, and he tried his best to smooth his wife's ruffled feathers. He chartered a houseboat for the entire family, hoping the excursion would also restore Billie's health. Her spirits were indeed buoyed not only by the luxurious onboard accommodations but also by Ziegfeld's insistence that he would find her a show bigger than *Kid Boots* and *The Swan* put together.

Ziegfeld finally chose Clare Kummer's *Annie Dear*, which satisfied Billie's wish to be funny and star in a musical comedy. In another respect, it seemed a strange choice, since Billie would be playing a girl barely out of her teens. But this may have been Ziegfeld's way of apologizing to her for dissuading her from taking a youthful role in *The Swan*. *Annie Dear* was based on one of Billie's silent pictures, *Good Gracious Annabelle* (1919). Billie played Annie, a girl who is betrothed to a man she deems uncouth, even though she has never met him. Unwilling to marry, she flees to a society home on Long Island and poses as a maid at the estate. When her fiancé comes to visit the estate, she does not recognize him and finds herself falling in love with him. Eventually, she discovers his identity, and the happy couple are married.

The play was reminiscent of *Sally*, using the formula of a girl ascending in society by means of disguise. But what truly made *Annie Dear* a signature Ziegfeld show was a fantasy ballet sequence in which Billie, dressed as Little Boy Blue, searched for gold at the end of a rainbow. The ballet was done in blues and grays to depict Little Boy Blue's encounters with cloud, rain, moon, and wind on his search for the gold. When Billie finally reached the treasure, the stage settings burst forth in myriad colors. The play also gave Billie the opportunity to wear a spectacular gown that resembled those worn by the Ziegfeld girls, complete with an enormous headdress and a ruffled, billowing skirt.

Annie Dear used a fair amount of wit to elevate its tired, farcical plot. The opening scene amused audiences with its depiction of theatergoers in line outside a ticket agency. Ziegfeld even allowed the playwright to poke fun at him in the scene: the theatergoers complained to one another that *Kid Boots* and the *Follies* were sold out. One character declared: "I know a friend of a friend of Flo who will see we see the show!" The characters then merrily marched off to see *Annie Dear*. Billie had many witty lines herself. In one scene, she referred to Rock Point, Long Island, as "the locale where all the fashionable robberies take place."[20]

When *Annie Dear* premiered on November 4, 1924, at the Times Square Theatre, Ziegfeld did not engage in his customary practice of pacing back and forth in the lobby until the final curtain. Instead, he watched Billie from a prominent balcony seat. Bernard Sobel recalled Ziegfeld's reaction to Billie's performance in the Little Boy Blue scene: "I heard a muffled sob and I looked up. I saw tears coursing down his cheeks."[21] Sobel speculated that Ziegfeld's weeping may have resulted from his fear that he had destroyed Billie's girlish innocence through his affairs and gambling. The show could be viewed as Ziegfeld's greatest gift to Billie, emphasizing beauty, youth, and grandeur. But Billie looked back on *Annie Dear* as a failure. She considered her performance in the "whopping big song numbers" inadequate, and she stated that the play would not "be set down as a milestone in the theater."[22] Adding to her sense of failure was the fact that reviewers once again focused on her lovely appearance rather than her acting abilities. Perhaps her feelings about the show would have been different if she had seen her husband's emotional reaction to her performance.

However moved he was by his wife's acting, Ziegfeld agreed with her: the show was no theatrical milestone. The music was inferior, and Ziegfeld's constant arguments with playwright Clare Kummer had prevented him from exercising his "traditional largess." Ziegfeld had suggested changes in the material to make the show more artistic, but Kummer had insisted on retaining the original material. Ziegfeld finally lost his patience; he "threw up his hands and closed the show on January 31, 1925 after 103 performances."[23] Billie again left the stage, unsure which direction to take in her career. Ziegfeld was choosing roles she did not want, yet the roles she did want no longer suited her. As her first mentor, Sir Charles Hawtrey, had prophesized, she could become "a very fine comedienne." But by 1924, Billie was not convinced of this. So far, her success had been based on her beauty, and once her looks began to fade, she thought she would have no future.

Despite its shortcomings, *Annie Dear* fared better than Marilyn Miller's new show, *Peter Pan*. The production opened on November 6, 1924, at the Knickerbocker Theatre, only two days after *Annie Dear* premiered. Ziegfeld had been cognizant of Marilyn's upcoming show and had knowingly set Billie up to compete with his ex-star. Ziegfeld's former partner, Charles Dillingham, was now Marilyn's manager, and he too joined in the competition. His advertisement for *Peter Pan* used the slogan "Glorifying Glorious Youth"—a blatant copy of Ziegfeld's "Glorifying the American Girl." But it was Ziegfeld who had reason to gloat after the opening of *Peter Pan*. Marilyn was the glorified girl incarnate, and audiences could not accept her in the title role of a young boy. Ziegfeld was the first to agree. His philosophy was that "five or six minutes of girls in drag is sexy fun. Three hours of it is irritating, a waste of woman."[24] Simply put, Billie's Little Boy Blue number was fun, whereas Marilyn's Peter Pan was just plain annoying. Ziegfeld had even more reason to gloat when he heard that Marilyn was regretting her marriage to Jack Pickford. Jack accompanied Marilyn to New York when she began work on *Peter Pan,* and he was often drunk. Marilyn began to wonder if she should have stayed with Ziegfeld. She never openly gave him credit, but she knew he had been responsible for making her famous in *Sally.*

Marilyn, Billie, Ziegfeld, and Dillingham all faced even greater competition from the young producing team of Alex A. Aarons and Vinton Freedley. The two men penned one of the biggest hits of 1924: *Lady Be Good*. The show boasted an exciting, modern score by George and Ira Gershwin that debuted the songs "Somebody Loves Me," "Fascinating Rhythm," and "The Man I Love." *Lady Be Good*'s dialogue was slangy and had a tempo as quick as the music's. The stylized Art Deco sets were equally modern. Fred and Adele Astaire, the most dazzling new dancers on Broadway, starred in the production. The show exemplified a seamless transition to the 1920s that Ziegfeld's shows (with the exception of *Kid Boots* and *Sally*) did not. It ran for 330 performances, compared with 96 for *Peter Pan* and 103 for *Annie Dear*.

With such competition, Ziegfeld was determined to produce shows that were just as fresh as *Lady Be Good*. However, he found it difficult to focus on finding such shows with an array of creditors, composers, and artists suing him for failing to pay them back rents or royalties. To complicate matters, Actors Equity was stirring up trouble again. This time, the dispute was over the closed-shop rule, which required employers to hire only members of the union and mandated that employees maintain their union membership to remain employed. Many prominent members of Actors Equity did not believe in the closed-shop rule, which forced Ziegfeld to close down touring productions of the *Follies* and *Sally*. Worried about his mounting financial losses, Ziegfeld scrambled to make the 1924 *Follies* pleasing to modern audiences and enough of a hit to relieve at least a portion of his financial burdens.

As early as August 1923, Ziegfeld had tried to lure Will Rogers back from Hollywood and moviemaking. He wrote to his friend: "It's time you were back. Please wire me back immediately after talking to your boss, Mrs. Rogers [of] your decision. . . . I would endeavor to get two great scenes for you . . . practically making you the star of the organization in the Follies. . . . There is no time to lose and I hope you realize that your pictures should come second to your public appearance. . . . I want you to come without fail, Bill. Answer quick."[25] What finally persuaded Will to rejoin the *Follies* was Ziegfeld's generosity toward Will's children, who were the center of the cowboy's life. At Christmas, Ziegfeld sent a mah-jongg set for Mary, a motorized scooter for Will Jr., and an enormous sailboat for Jimmy. Despite the year-round schedule Ziegfeld had implemented for the

Follies, it still opened in the summer, and on June 24, 1924, Will Rogers was in the cast.

Ziegfeld toyed with the idea of including a plot in the June edition of the *Follies,* but he shrewdly abandoned the notion before the premiere. The revue contained a large number of western-themed numbers, such as the songs "The Great Wide Open Spaces" and "I'd Like to Corral a Gal," a rope dance by the Tiller Girls, and Will Rogers's skits. Two of Will's skits, "A Couple of Senators" and "Investigating Investigations," were political satires. The latter act, as critic Eugene Lorton described it, had a politician as the chief witness in an investigation. The witness-politician "convulsed the audience for fifteen minutes with a monologue that begins nowhere and ends at the same place without completing a single connected sentence. As the chairman of the [investigating] committee, Will then tells the witness that his statement is the most lucid and comprehensive explanation that has ever been made."[26] After a musical interlude in the second act, Will performed his usual "Will Rogers Sayings." Among other things, he philosophized on the differences between a good *Follies* and a bad *Follies,* concluding that the difference amounted to $1.80.

The spring *Follies* tried to keep up with modern times with a number entitled "Jazzland," but it remained on the old-fashioned side, with mostly sentimental tunes such as "Lonely Little Melody" and a compilation of Victor Herbert songs that included "The March of the Toys" and "Kiss Me Again." Those numbers served as a tribute to the great composer, who had died in May 1924. According to Charles Higham, Ziegfeld was inadvertently responsible for the composer's death. Apparently, Ziegfeld's secretary told Herbert that Ziegfeld was not in his office when the composer came by to collect some unpaid royalties. But as Herbert was leaving, he saw a showgirl, hair tousled and lipstick smeared, exiting Ziegfeld's office. The composer's face became purple with rage, and he suffered a stroke a few minutes later.[27] The story sounds far-fetched and may not have happened at all. In any event, Herbert's death was a great blow to Ziegfeld.

As he began preparations for the new edition of the *Follies* (set to open in October 1924), Ziegfeld was again at the point of a nervous breakdown. He decided that unless he took a vacation, he would be of no use to anyone. Even at the idyllic Burkeley Crest, Ziegfeld could not escape the incessant ringing of the telephone, the Western Union boys continually knocking at the door, or the worries of producing musical comedies bigger and better than his greatest successes.

"The simple life," Ziegfeld sighed. "That's the ticket. Somewhere out there where the moose plunge down the lake and the trout leap out of the water and Freddie Zimmerman can't call me on the telephone."[28] Hoping to achieve this romantic vision of a spare, simple life, Ziegfeld took Billie and Patricia to his camp in New Brunswick, Canada. But, as in the past, Ziegfeld was not content with the ordinary. In the coming year, he created new fantasias for himself and his family that, though unadorned, were more enticing than any idealized visions he could create onstage.

16

Vacations from Reality

The New Brunswick camp had always worked its magic on Ziegfeld; there, he was not a harried producer but a simple family man. Patricia took after her father and thrived in the rustic environs. Billie, however, like Anna Held and Lillian Lorraine before her, suffered in silence at the Canadian retreat, particularly during the family's last trip there in the summer of 1923. She had little tolerance for the twelve-mile hike to camp or the lack of indoor plumbing. Nor did she relish the lack of privacy in the cabin, which consisted of one large room with beds on one side and a dining table and chairs on the other. The moment Billie stepped inside, she tied a handkerchief over her curls and set to cleaning and cheering the place up a bit. One of her first orders of business was to cover the bare wooden walls with bright Indian blankets she had bought for that purpose. She also demanded that everyone take a bath in the lake every day, even if the water was, according to her, "oomph degrees." Billie's discontent was nothing new. On a previous visit, she had sent a telegram to her mother reading: "WISH I WERE HOME AND IT WAS WINTER."[1]

Given Billie's dissatisfaction with the New Brunswick camp, Ziegfeld obtained a new one in 1924, before *Annie Dear* premiered and in the midst of the production of the year-round *Follies of 1924*. He took out a ninety-nine-year lease on a small island northwest of Quebec and christened it "Billie Burke Island." He called the grounds themselves "Camp Patricia." Ziegfeld's revised idea of roughing it was much less rustic, and he "more closely resembled a rajah on safari with carpets, ices, cooks, and distinguished guests."[2] The new camp contained six cabins with electricity and indoor plumbing; there were maids, a tutor for Patricia, and eight guides. There was also plenty of imported cheeses and fish from Hastings-on-Hudson. Ziegfeld proudly showed his wife and daughter around the grounds during their first trip there in the late summer of 1924.

Though the new camp was decidedly better than the old one (which Ziegfeld sold), Billie spoke up on one particular point. "I want it perfectly understood that there is to be absolutely no hunting within a one-mile limit of this camp. . . . I will not have this lovely place turned into an abattoir."[3] She and Ziegfeld argued over the point for two days. He grew even more frustrated when Billie put out a salt block that encouraged deer to venture inside the one-mile limit to enjoy the treat. In a letter, Patricia described her mother's reaction to hunting: "Mummy won't walk with us, she just sits in the canoe and cries when she hears us shooting."[4] After one unusually long debate over the subject, Billie mutely rose, grabbed a rifle, walked outside, and fired at a target Ziegfeld had posted for practice. She hit the bull's-eye. Ziegfeld, expert marksman that he was, stared at her in awe. For the rest of the Ziegfelds' years visiting the island, there was never a shortage of deer, moose, and bears wandering the grounds. Richard Ziegfeld observed, "Part of the sustaining force in the marriage may well have been the fact that Flo never quite knew what Billie would do next."[5]

Ziegfeld kept Billie guessing as well. Especially surprising was his habit of simply throwing his belongings in a paper bag when packing for the camp. He was equally lax about his appearance and even grew a beard. He took on the persona of a Canadian woodsman, "talking in monosyllables, [and] stalking through the woods as silent as a cat."[6] Ziegfeld and Patricia bonded at the camp, despite Ziegfeld's minimal speech. He cooked her elaborate breakfasts of tomatoes, eggs, corn, and baked beans. He also took her out in the canoe and taught her to swim, dive, and fish.

Even while living the simple life, Ziegfeld made a big fuss whenever guests were invited to the camp. One of the most frequent visitors was Dr. Jerome Wagner, a man twenty years Ziegfeld's junior, a favorite among theatrical circles, and a regular patron at the New Amsterdam since 1914. Ziegfeld even used Wagner as the "house doctor" for his cast members, despite the fact that he was not a general practitioner but a proctologist. Wagner was one of the rare people whose humor appealed to Ziegfeld— even the doctor's practical jokes, and even if the joke was on Ziegfeld.

Wagner played a whopper of a practical joke on his friend during one particular visit to Camp Patricia. Ziegfeld informed his valet, Sidney, that the Duke of Athole was going to be their guest. Little did Ziegfeld know that Wagner was planning to pose as the royal. Patricia recounted the event in her memoir: "We turned the place upside down. We met the duke and my father shook hands with him, and when he turned around to shake hands with someone else, my father kicked him in the butt. Everybody absolutely fell apart. It turned out that Daddy had recognized Wagner as an imposter. Sidney of course was dashed to think that he wasn't going to socialize with this wonderful Englishman he had been preparing for weeks to meet."[7]

"Doc," as his friends called him, was also a regular guest at the Sunday dinners at Burkeley Crest. Wagner was usually able to lift Ziegfeld's gloomy spirits, but on one occasion, he was in such a bereft state that even Doc was unable to cheer him. "Any morning now I expect to walk outside and see an abandoned automobile on the front lawn. Probably an old Model T, with chickens roosting in the clutch," Ziegfeld lamented. The reason for Ziegfeld's sarcastic pessimism and his vision of Burkeley Crest's decay was that Doc Wagner had been "reduced to eating his dinner tonight from a broken plate." To remedy the matter, Ziegfeld ordered a $38,000 set of china that had belonged to the czar of Russia. The new dinnerware was so immense that it did not fit on the Ziegfelds' generously sized dining table. Billie demanded he send it back, declaring that she now knew what the Russian Revolution had been about. Ziegfeld agreed but said, "I think I'll keep just one plate, though. For next Sunday, for Doc Wagner's dinner."[8] Ziegfeld would have to be satisfied with the $50,000 set of china he had imported from Paris in 1922—chips or no chips.

With renewed energy from his respite in Canada, Ziegfeld reentered the theater world to oversee production of *Annie Dear* and prepare the fall edition of the *Follies,* which opened on October 30, 1924. He hoped to employ Will Rogers, but as usual, Will was difficult to convince. In part, he was reluctant to commit because he wanted three matinees off so he could see the polo games. Ziegfeld responded: "You know Bill, there isn't anything I would not do for you, but you must realize . . . to give matinees without you in them *would be absolutely impossible.*" Ziegfeld finally agreed to have matinees on Friday and Monday instead of Saturday and Wednesday, "owing to your [Will's] great desire to see the Games . . . I agreed to do this, so you know [in] what high esteem I hold you."[9] Will returned to the *Follies,* but his presence did not bolster reviews as much as Ziegfeld had anticipated.

The fall edition of the *Follies* had little new material, with the exception of a new song, "Ever Lovin' Bee," and a comic skit by W. C. Fields called "The Back Porch." This skit was one of the best comedic bits in the show; consequently, Ziegfeld decided to include it in a new musical comedy he was reluctantly producing for Fields. Ziegfeld had agreed to produce the show only after Gene Buck bluntly told him: "If you want to pay your lawsuits, you'll star Fields in a show. He equals money."

Though the successes of *Sally* and *Kid Boots* had cast a sunnier light on Ziegfeld's view of the 1920s, the litigiousness of the decade constantly renewed his distaste for it. Ziegfeld lost more cases than he won, and most of them dragged on for years before being settled out of court. The most creative presentation of a lawsuit came from cartoonist Bert Green, whose work Ziegfeld had deemed unsatisfactory. Green consequently sued the producer for $25,000. Green's lawyers tried for weeks to serve Ziegfeld with papers, but they could not make it past Goldie or any other member of Ziegfeld's loyal staff. Finally, Green's lawyer devised a scheme. He emptied six bottles of Scotch whiskey, refilled them with water, wrapped them up, and took the package to Ziegfeld's office. Tommy Caldwell, Ziegfeld's attendant, heard the telltale clink of bottles in the package and allowed the lawyer into the producer's office. However, Goldie was suspicious and told him she would take the package and give it to Ziegfeld herself.

"It's from the captain of a ship and he instructed me to deliver it to Mr. Ziegfeld personally," the lawyer insisted.

"Well . . . all right," Goldie said.

A moment later the lawyer stood before Ziegfeld, who was as suspicious as Goldie. "What captain? What ship?" he demanded.

"Here's a note from the captain. It'll answer all your questions," the lawyer said, backing toward the door. Before Ziegfeld could unseal the letter, the lawyer had made a beeline out of the office.

"If Green's pictures were half as funny as the way he served them [the legal papers] to me, they'd be a riot," Ziegfeld declared.[10] Ziegfeld ultimately lost the suit.

Ziegfeld needed a hit, and in theory, *The Comic Supplement* had all the makings of one. The show starred W. C. Fields, used innovative color and staging, and featured gutsy satire on American politics. All the players looked like comic-strip characters come to life. Yellows, reds, and greens shone garishly against grays and blacks. By the end of the show's production, Ziegfeld admitted he liked its artistic aspects. The most memorable number had girls dressed as stenographers and waitresses climbing a real stairway set against windows. Their forms created a fascinating shadow play depicting how they spent their evenings. However, it seemed that Ziegfeld could not please audiences: his *Follies* were too old-fashioned, and *The Comic Supplement* was too avant-garde. The latter opened on January 9, 1925, at the Shubert Theatre in Newark, New Jersey, and won critical accolades for its sets and costumes, but the production never made it to New York. The play lost $40,000, nearly half of what it cost to produce. Abe Erlanger was still backing Ziegfeld's shows, but he now owned his own theater and was not greatly affected by the show's losses. Ziegfeld was increasingly irked that Erlanger was growing wealthy while he did most of the work and made less money. "If I only had my own theater everything would be different," Ziegfeld told Erlanger. "I lose up to 40% of any show's profit from rent alone."[11]

The fact that *The Comic Supplement* played at a Shubert-owned theater was a sure sign that the decades-old feud between the Syndicate and the Shuberts had cooled—at least temporarily. There were two reasons for this truce: the powerful producers were becoming more independent, and theater ownership was being consolidated. In 1923 Ziegfeld had showed his independence by resigning from the Producing Managers Association, mostly because of his dislike for the new head of the association, Joseph Leblang. Leblang openly preferred the Shuberts and discriminated against all non-Shubert theaters. Although the Shuberts denied this favoritism, it appeared to be real, for the brothers' theaters soon began to house the shows of ex-Syndicate managers.

Ziegfeld had neither the funds nor the power to house other producers' shows. He needed a new "angel," and fortunately, he found one in William Randolph Hearst. Hearst's long list of job titles included newspaper magnate, politician, and backer of films and theater productions. He became a frequent guest at Burkeley Crest and at the Ziegfelds' Palm Beach home. Ziegfeld had met Hearst through Charles Dillingham, who had been leasing the Cosmopolitan Theatre (at 5 Columbus Circle between West Fifty-Eighth and Fifty-Ninth Streets) from Hearst after failing at the Century Theatre. Ziegfeld set his sights on the Cosmopolitan, and after lengthy negotiations, Hearst granted him a lease on the theater. Hearst gave Ziegfeld complete control of the Cosmopolitan's shows and its inside decor. Ziegfeld hired Joseph Urban to redecorate the theater, and he completed the task beautifully; he painted sixteen canvas panels on the walls and hung Flemish tapestries from the balcony seats. Hearst had dual reasons—business and personal—for giving Ziegfeld such a free hand. Hearst had a special liking for Ziegfeld because Hearst had first spotted his future mistress and true love, Marion Davies, at the *Follies*. Also, the two men shared a love of art for art's sake. Thus, Hearst thought it would benefit both himself and Ziegfeld if he built a new theater near the Warwick Hotel (which he owned) at Fifty-Fourth Street and Sixth Avenue. The name of the proposed theater? The Ziegfeld. The men shook hands on the deal, and Ziegfeld delightedly commissioned Urban as the architect. "It'll be completed by 1926. In a little over a year, I'll have my own theater," Ziegfeld announced to anyone who would listen. During the construction of what promised to be the most spectacular showplace on Broadway, Ziegfeld continued to lease the Cosmopolitan and hold an interest in the New Amsterdam.[12]

With such bright professional prospects, Ziegfeld had reason to be jolly during the 1924 holiday season. As the *Follies* toured the country, he planned his usual Christmas gift to his mother: arranging for her to see his revue when it played in Chicago. But this year, Ziegfeld had a more elaborate gift in mind. While Mrs. Ziegfeld was enjoying the spectacle, stagehands secured the grandest tree available to erect in the parlor of her home and adorned it with hundreds of lights and decorations. Unfortunately, the feeble Mrs. Ziegfeld was unable to enjoy either of her son's gifts. According to stage manager Victor Kiraly, when Ziegfeld's sister led her mother downstairs to see the tree, the old woman "stood still, showing no sign of perception; she was stone-blind and sobbing, knowing full well that the annual surprise was no longer to be enjoyed by her."[13] Ziegfeld put aside his fears of illness and mortality and did everything he could to ensure that his ailing mother did not feel isolated. He and Patricia regularly traveled to Chicago to visit her.

Busy with family, friends, ongoing productions, and his new theater, Ziegfeld still found time to launch yet another project. W. C. Fields's show had not been a hit, but Ziegfeld had confidence that Leon Errol's new showcase, *Louie the 14th*, would be. In the play, which takes place in post–World War I France, Louis ends up as the fourteenth guest at a society dinner for the purpose of "soothing a superstitious host."[14] The show's composer, Sigmund Romberg, was the talk of Broadway after his show *The Student Prince* became the smash hit of 1924—even bigger than *Lady Be*

Good (Romberg's show played for 608 performances until May 1926). However, Ziegfeld was dissatisfied with Romberg's score for *Louie the 14th,* which he found too grating. He often wandered into the orchestra pit during rehearsals, shouting, "Take down that brass!" As he grew older, Ziegfeld's dislikes became more intense, and too much brass was one of his pet peeves.[15]

Louie the 14th should have been a hit. It boasted lovely costumes, a great star, beautiful girls (among them a young dancer named Louise Brooks), and lush settings. In the dinner scene, Ziegfeld hired a real chef to prepare the meal and serve the food on a table covered with a genuine gold cloth. The table settings were none other than the Imperial Russian china that had not fit in the dining room of Burkeley Crest. The production opened on March 3, 1925, but despite its artistic merits, it played to unenthusiastic audiences. It lasted on Broadway only until it began what Ziegfeld hoped would be a more lucrative fall tour. The site of the Cosmopolitan Theatre was a major factor in the show's failure. According to Ethan Mordden, its location eighteen blocks from the nexus of Broadway and Forty-Second Street might as well have been "in the suburbs."[16] The play's tour was equally dismal and ended abruptly after Leon Errol injured his ankle doing his trademark rubber-legged stunts. No one could replace him.

The lackluster year of 1925 showed no signs of brightening after the opening of the spring and summer editions of the *Follies* (premiering on March 10 and July 6, respectively). Both were officially called the *Ziegfeld Follies of 1925,* but they might as well have been called the *Ziegfeld Follies of 1924.* Rather than producing an all-new 1925 edition, Ziegfeld simply made a few changes. Louise Brooks performed a specialty dance with Lina Basquette, and Eddie Cantor spoofed *Lady Be Good* in a skit entitled "Eddie Be Good." Ziegfeld, as usual, tried to convince Will Rogers to appear in the show, sending him this lighthearted telegram: "DEAR BILL: I READ WITH INTEREST IN THE WORLD [a newspaper] THAT YOU HELD ME UP FOR YEARS. WELL, BILL, I AM WILLING TO BE HELD UP SOME MORE. WHEN WILL YOU START AGAIN? ZIEGFELD."[17] Will did not answer right away because there was one scene in the show he could not condone. In the second act, in a Ben Ali Haggin tableau set at an Eastern slave market, one girl exposed her breast. "Fix the nudity or I quit," Will told Ziegfeld.[18]

Nudity was not new to the *Follies,* but in the past, it was legal to show nude figures as long as they remained perfectly stationary. In the 1920s undressed women—even those who were as still as statues—were becoming a point of controversy. Though the decade was supposed to be "roaring," it was rather conservative in other ways, and the political climate had a lot of influence in the theater. Ziegfeld was willing to mold his shows to satisfy popular (and political) demands, and he became one of the most outspoken opponents of nudity onstage following the 1925 theater season. By June 1926, a year after the 1925 *Follies* closed, Ziegfeld appointed himself the leader in bringing Broadway "back to artistry and normalcy" rather than a producer whose shows pandered to "the vilest tastes of playgoers to force a box office stampede." He admitted that he had imported stage nudity from the Paris revues that had inspired the *Follies,* but "in the hands of less artistic producers," nudity had become coarse and exploitative. He was chivalrous in his statement as well, condemning the fact that many chorines had to do whatever their bosses told them to do if they wished to keep their jobs. As far back as 1921, Ziegfeld had made statements against distasteful or unnecessary nudity. "The primary object of wearing clothing is to adorn the wearer's form and not to reveal it," he had told one reporter in August 1921. He went on to attest that his costumers glorified girls through "beautiful presentation of feminine pulchritude."[19] Ziegfeld's sentiments so impressed John Summer, president of the New York Society for the Suppression of Vice, that he invited Ziegfeld to become a member in 1926.[20]

What had prompted Ziegfeld's sudden shift to modesty and normalcy? In large part, the answer lies in the fact that he was the father of a quickly maturing girl, and he had begun to feel more fatherly toward his younger chorines. Also, he valued Will Rogers's friendship and his opinions. Finally, Ziegfeld wished to maintain the favor of theatergoers, many of whom were liberated women who did not appreciate seeing their gender demeaned. Despite the fact that the *Follies* now reflected Will's moral code, the fall of 1925 marked his final appearance in any Ziegfeld show. He had forged a new career path as a sort of modern Mark Twain, giving witty lectures around the country. Ziegfeld hated losing any employee, but losing a best friend was even more unbearable. The showman had made a special arrangement with Western Union that allowed him to send 3 million words a year at a reduced rate, and he used a considerable amount of that allotment on Will, asking him to return to the *Follies*. At one point Will received so many telegrams from Ziegfeld about both business and personal matters that he quipped: "Keep this up. Am on my way to buy more Western Union stock."[21]

After mounting the summer edition of the decidedly more family-friendly *Follies*, Ziegfeld took his own family on another much-needed vacation. The Ziegfelds traveled with their customary trainload of trunks as they toured France and England. Their longest stop was in Deauville, for Patricia's health. During their trip, Billie carried several mysterious hatboxes that Patricia discovered were filled with paper covers. Neither Ziegfeld nor his daughter could guess their use. "For the seats," Billie explained. Ziegfeld gave her an exasperated smirk. "Now Flo, don't look like that. Europe is full of germs and I've made enough toilet seat covers so that we can each have our own supply." Once the family arrived at the Ritz in Paris, Billie's "germ mania" continued—this time over Patricia's milk. Ziegfeld tried to order a bottle, but Billie refused to let her daughter drink French milk. "Well, she can either drink champagne or we can locate a cow and milk it ourselves," Ziegfeld suggested.[22] Finally, the Ritz kitchen sent up powdered milk that, according to Patricia, tasted like cement.

After leaving germ-ridden Paris, the Ziegfelds went to the outskirts of London, where Ziegfeld's first star, Eugen Sandow, now lived. Ziegfeld and the aging bodybuilder spent hours reminiscing about the good old days. Patricia recalled that Sandow, who had been ill, received her and her parents in a brocade dressing gown. "He was still divinely handsome . . . but I was amazed to find him so short," she said.[23]

As usual, Ziegfeld could not keep business off his mind, even when on vacation. While staying at the Ritz in London, he announced that he wished to include British girls in his *Follies*. Five thousand girls swarmed to Piccadilly Square, vying for the producer's approval. Ziegfeld broke more than a few of their hearts by clarifying that they would have to audition in New York. Two girls defied his edict by masquerading as maids at the hotel. While tidying the Ziegfelds' room, they broke into an impromptu song and dance number. Ziegfeld was so impressed that he brought the girls back to America with him, but the union's closed-shop rule made it impossible for him to employ them.

Nevertheless, the producer was greatly rejuvenated by the trip. According to biographer Charles Higham, it had been almost like a second honeymoon for Ziegfeld and Billie. However, once he was back in New

York, Ziegfeld was faced with several unpleasant realities. One was a dispiriting review of the current edition of the *Follies*. A critic for *Bookman* magazine reported: "We kept sitting there a little angry at being given so much of the old stuff. . . . It was a good enough revue in its way, but when one thought of the good old days, it was nothing at all."[24] Another blow was the news of Eugen Sandow's death in October 1925. The strongman had died of a stroke after trying to lift an automobile from a muddy ditch.

Ziegfeld's spirits sagged further upon seeing Marilyn Miller shining under Charles Dillingham's management in *Sunny*, a shameless imitation of *Sally*. Its plot was another Cinderella story, this time with Marilyn as a poor circus performer who falls in love with a rich American while touring in England. As in *Sally*, the heroine marries the man of her dreams and gains both love and wealth in the end. In addition to its Ziegfeldian plot, *Sunny* used a number of former Ziegfeld employees, including Jerome Kern, Julian Mitchell, Otto Harbach (one of the lyricists for *Kid Boots*), and Jack Donahue. To add insult to injury, the show was staged at the New Amsterdam, which had housed so many Ziegfeld productions that many thought he owned the theater. *Sunny* exceeded *Sally's* phenomenal run and became the biggest hit ever performed at the New Amsterdam Theatre; it seemed as if it would keep going for years. Marilyn had reached her zenith—without Ziegfeld. And after *Sunny* broke all box-office records, Dillingham stated (according to Fred Astaire), "He [Ziegfeld] hates it when I get a hit! You know he's very jealous of me."[25]

Despite all the negative realities that bombarded Ziegfeld upon his return to New York, he miraculously maintained the enthusiasm he had found during his European vacation. However, there were no *Ziegfeld Follies of 1926*. The *Follies* had begun as a Klaw and Erlanger property, and now that the Syndicate was defunct, all its properties were entangled in lawsuits concerning realty and contracts. With ownership of the *Follies* up in the air, Ziegfeld was barred by law from producing the show. He circumvented this hurdle by renaming his next show the *Ziegfeld Revue*. It was slated to open in the summer of 1926. In the meantime, Ziegfeld, fed up with New York audiences and critics, retreated to Palm Beach to rethink the direction of his career.

Ziegfeld, now sixty years old, had reached the age when many men begin to think about retirement. What kept him so ambitious? Affairs with showgirls, Palm Beach soirees, and new Rolls Royces were simply perks of his success; they were not what he valued most, nor were they what kept him going at a pace that might kill a man twenty years his junior. His family was responsible for his vitality. As proof of their invigorating influence on him, one need only note how desolate Ziegfeld became during his long separations from Billie and Patricia. In a handwritten note to Patricia, penned while Ziegfeld was staying at the Hotel Washington in Washington, DC (presumably during a tour), he wrote:

> 6 AM
> My own Patricia,
>   It's 6 in the morning and Daddy cant sleep because he is away from his two babies. Soon I will be thorough [*sic*] and we 3 will go away and have a good time. Be sure and write to me.
>   Kisses, Daddy

At the top of the letter, Ziegfeld had doodled a drawing of a swan and three stick figures dancing together.[26]

The long separations from his daughter were not only because of Ziegfeld's career ambitions but also because of Patricia's health. For a while, she was a thin, sickly child with "acidosis ailments," and Billie spent many sleepless nights worrying over her daughter's failure to thrive. She followed one doctor's recommendation to feed the girl a bland, low-fat diet. When that regimen had no effect, she took a second doctor's advice to feed Patricia a rich diet full of butter, bacon, and cream. All of Patricia's doctors advised against taking her south to Palm Beach because she had become ill during past sojourns there. Patricia's inability to travel was upsetting to Ziegfeld; he desperately wanted to spend time with her and was positive that Palm Beach was not to blame for her past illnesses. Billie and Ziegfeld had been at odds over Palm Beach's benefits and drawbacks for years. In February 1923 Billie had written to her dismayed husband: "AM AFRAID YOU BLAME ME FOR NOT TAKING PATRICIA SOUTH BUT IT WAS ENTIRELY OUT OF MY HANDS WILCOX [Patricia's doctor] SAID EMPHATICALLY HE WOULD NOT TAKE THE RESPONSIBILITY BUT YOU CAN GO AGAINST HIM IF YOU WISH."[27] Ziegfeld had chosen not to defy the doctor—not yet, that is—and Billie tried to convince him that Patricia was blooming in wintry New York: "SHE NEVER LOOKED SO WELL OR WAS HAPPIER BEFORE THIS DOCTOR

SAYS SHE NEEDS HARDENING UP SHE WAS NEVER MORE ILL THAN SHE WAS PALM BEACH I DONT KNOW WHAT TO SAY SHE WOULD GET DOWN WHEN IT BEGAN TO GET HOTTEST AND THEN COME BACK TO THE COLD SHES GOT TO GET ON HER FEET AGAIN BEFORE SHE CAN DO ANYTHING."[28]

Even while apart, Ziegfeld and Patricia shared a special bond. Ziegfeld could attribute much of his theatrical success to his wife, but even more so, he valued his daughter's opinion. Patricia remembered him asking her thoughts about an actress's voice or a particular costume. According to Richard Ziegfeld, "He genuinely cared about her reaction . . . he also wanted an evaluation that was free of ulterior motives."[29] Patricia was his best cheerleader, and her little notes about his shows meant more than any notices from the *New York Times.* While he was producing *Kid Boots,* she sent him the following sweet letter: "dear daddy i wish kid boots is a great great success so we can go to Palm beach this winter to stay the rest of our live a great big hug with love and a million kisses from Patricia."[30]

Ziegfeld's relationship with Patricia reveals a side of him that was virtually unknown to the public and even to his closest friends. He would do anything for her. Ziegfeld had set aside a trust for Patricia, and he never touched that money, no matter how close he came to bankruptcy. Any traces of the self-serving showman and insincere charmer were almost nonexistent in her presence. However, his lavish gifts to Patricia were legendary. The Mount Vernon playhouse at the northwest corner of the Burkeley Crest property was one of the most ostentatious. The playhouse was fit for a star, and this was no coincidence, for it came from Hollywood. Ziegfeld had gone to visit William Randolph Hearst on the West Coast in 1923, and Hearst had invited him to watch Marion Davies perform a few scenes from her movie *Little Old New York.* The front of a Mount Vernon replica was part of a set for the film.

"What happens to that set once the film is completed?" Ziegfeld asked.

"It'll be scrapped, no doubt," Hearst replied.

Ziegfeld ordered that the replica be sent to Burkeley Crest, where he had carpenters put a back on it and create rooms. The spring 1974 edition of the *Hastings Historian* printed this description from Joan Berston, one of Patricia's playmates: "On entering its center door, one stood in a large room rising two stories. A steep staircase, with approximately 4-inch risers, led to the bedrooms on the second floor. To the left of the main room were the kitchen and dining rooms. The place was superbly furnished with miniature reproductions of colonial furniture."[31] In addition, the playhouse had a working fireplace, a kitchen, and a small electric stove that Patricia used to make fudge and cookies. The window boxes outside were filled with geraniums.

Throughout Patricia's childhood, her father showered her with gifts. For instance, when he learned of her passion for collecting butterflies, he sent her an impressive display of the insects pinned behind glass. Patricia, however, would have preferred to catch the butterflies herself, with her father's help. Billie often wrote to Ziegfeld and explained that gifts were no substitute for his presence: "I think Patricia is going to be the one to demand your coming home. She says she will give you a few weeks more but not many. Don't think I'm putting her up to it. She's not that kind of a kid."[32] As if to prove Billie's point, Patricia wrote a darkly humorous note threatening her father's life if he did not return home: "i have a gun to shoot you if you do not come home you wait and see. . . . i want to see you but i can not see you every time you call up over the telephone . . . love and kisses from Patricia."[33] As chiding as Patricia could be, she was also eager to please her father. Billie revealed to him in a wire: "BABY BUSY MAKING A VALENTINE FOR YOU BUT IT'S A SECRET SHE IS SO SWEET ABOUT IT."[34]

Patricia relished spending extended periods with her father at Burkeley Crest, Palm Beach, or Camp Patricia. Ziegfeld was not only her father but also her best pal. They both enjoyed a blend of the privileged good life and the rustic outdoor life. During their fishing trips, they shared huge hampers of sandwiches, salads, and cake—a towering yellow confection with chocolate frosting. After fishing, father and daughter would apply olive oil to their skin and sit out in the sun.

What kept Patricia and Ziegfeld bonded during his absences was their collusion, like two mischievous children, to get Patricia out of the hands of doctors and teachers and onto the glittering sands of Palm Beach. In the excerpts from the three letters that follow, Patricia demonstrated that she could be as stubborn as her parents once she made up her mind about something:

> dear daddy i am going to ask Dr. Wilcox if I may go you see it is nearly March. ah But it gets hot daddy and you know yourself too mummy wants to go down too and i want to go down there too.

But i really think it would be better for me on the boat than a house dont you think so?

dear daddy we are comeing down the 11th of march daddy. i am going to Buy a Bathing suit for myself i am going to get some thats not for Xmas for Palm Beach oh . . . i forgot to ask Dr. Wilcox that i wanted to go But i just can not wait two weeks longer . . . love and kisses from Patricia.

mr wilcox dosent approve of it daddy But we are comeing down now any way—but mummy is the one hard one to try to get down . . . but she will not come i will come and put her to Bed and when she wakes up she will find that she is in Palm Beach wont that be fun daddy . . . good night love from Patricia XXXX.[35]

Despite Patricia's ardent desire to go to Palm Beach, Billie heeded Dr. Wilcox's advice. During their time in New York without Ziegfeld, Billie took it upon herself to find a school for her daughter—one that suited a girl accustomed to living in a gilded realm. Patricia recalled in her memoir: "Mother and Daddy wanted me to be able to do all the things a cultivated lady was supposed to do—play a good game of tennis, walk across a ballroom correctly, know history and French and arithmetic, and recite the capitals of Europe. On the other hand, they also wanted to be able to take me along to Palm Beach or Canada or Atlantic City whenever they went. It was a challenge to the school system."[36] That was an understatement. Billie tutored her daughter as much as she could, although she had virtually no formal schooling herself. Billie was a lover of books and saturated Patricia with children's classics such as *Heidi* and *The Wind in the Willows*.[37] When Blanche was still alive, Patricia shared her grandma's penchant for reading the dictionary as a hobby and learning three new words every day. As Patricia grew older, Billie grew increasingly concerned about the girl's need for a more structured education, as well as her lack of socialization with other children.

As Billie determinedly scoured the New York school system for a niche for her child, she confided to her husband in a telegram: "MY HEART THROBS VISITING SCHOOLS SHE IS NO LONGER MY BABY."[38] Billie finally decided that the Lincoln School on 123rd Street in Manhattan would be the best fit; it was a predecessor to the "hippie" schools of the 1960s—less interested in the three Rs and more interested in "dabbling around in pots of paint or modeling lumpy objects of clay."[39] Patricia drolly wrote that as far as manners went, anything was acceptable as long as no one pulled a gun on anyone. Billie wrote to Ziegfeld about their daughter's schooling with much optimism:

JAN 18 1923 TO PALM BEACH

DID NOT WANT TO TELL YOU UNTIL IT WAS SETTLED PATRICIA PASSED HER TESTS YESTERDAY AND WAS ADMITTED TO THE LINCOLN SCHOOL SHE STARTED THIS MORNING IN THE FIRST GRADE HER MENTALITY WAS SUFFICIENT FOR HIGHER GRADE BUT THEY WANTED HER TO LOVE THE YOUNGER CHILDREN AS THAT IS WHAT SHE NEEDS MORE THAN LEARNING. . . . BABY IS HAPPIER THAN I HAVE SEEN HER. . . . HOPE YOU WILL [be] PLEASED I AM VERY HAPPY. . . . EVERYTHING SEEMS WORKING OUT WELL AM CRAZY [to] TELL YOU ABOUT THE SCHOOL ITS ALONG SUCH WONDERFUL LINES LOVE BILLIE[40]

Ziegfeld did not share his wife's enthusiasm. In his opinion, time spent in Palm Beach would be a better geographic, artistic, and social lesson for Patricia. Billie tried to convince him that Patricia needed other children as playmates. And in the following telegram, she told him of the doctor's latest recommendation: "FLO DEAREST I AM AFRAID DOCTOR DOES NOT APPROVE OF SUCH A CHANGE FOR BABY NOT ONLY DENYING HER THE BENEFIT OF HER SCHOOL AND HER ASSOCIATES BUT THE SEVERE CHANGE IN CLIMATE YOU DONT KNOW WHAT IT WAS FOR HER TO HAVE HER MIND OCCUPIED IT TOOK AWAY ALL THAT NERVOUSNESS."[41] Ziegfeld told Billie, in so many words, that the doctor was a humbug.

Despite Ziegfeld's doubts about the Lincoln School's merit, Patricia continued to attend. For Christmas, the students strung pitted dates and apples around the classrooms, and after a few weeks of being "thoroughly withered and coated with New York City grime," they were told to present the fruit to their parents as gifts. Ziegfeld was convinced this was the principal's way of "deliberately attempting to poison him."[42] What worried Ziegfeld even more was what he considered the poisoning of Patricia's mind. He was appalled at the poor example of a composition she presented to him:

A Poene
up in the trees birdies in leaves up in the mountain and in the trees
and that is the end of my poen by Patricia burke ziegfeld.[43]

When Ziegfeld expressed his dissatisfaction to the principal, she told him: "I think your daughter would be happier at another school."[44]

He replied, "Very well then. Patricia has always been happy traveling with her mother and me. A thousand dollars for two semesters should have given Patricia more than a trite poem about birdies in the mountains. Good day." He then enrolled her in the Halstead School in Yonkers, where she would attend in the fall after finishing the spring semester at Lincoln.

Billie had primary responsibility for the everyday disciplining of Patricia, but she still had room for fun and games. She had discovered a Welsh belief that catered to Ziegfeld's superstitious nature: if one uttered "Rabbits!" three times in succession on the first morning of each new month, one would be guaranteed good luck. The night before, Billie left notes on Ziegfeld's and Patricia's pillows with the word "Rabbits" written on it, to remind them. The next morning, Patricia and her father sat at the breakfast table, drinking the papaya juice Billie insisted they ingest every day. Then, after kissing Patricia good-bye, Ziegfeld walked across the lawn as she watched him through the window. Ziegfeld caught hold of a branch of the copper beech tree, chinned himself six times, and shouted "Rabbits! Rabbits! Rabbits!" at the top of his lungs. Patricia giggled and shouted the lucky words back to him from the kitchen as he stepped into his Rolls Royce and headed for New York.[45]

"Rabbits" did indeed bring them good luck. To father and daughter's delight, Patricia persuaded Billie to let her stay in Palm Beach for the summer before starting at Halstead in the fall. However, Billie was anxious about her decision to defy the doctor's orders:

MARCH 2 1923
BABY GETTING AWAY MONDAY WENT TO HER SCHOOL THIS MORNING AND THEY ARE BROKENHEARTED AT OUR TAKING HER AWAY THEY ARE VERY MUCH AFRAID IF SHE DOES NOT HAVE CHILDREN COMPANIONSHIP

SHE WILL DEVELOP SOME NERVOUS DISORDER THE PRINCIPAL DOES NOT THINK WE ARE DOING RIGHT BY HER SHE MUST BE BACK IN APRIL TO START AGAIN SUCH A DIFFERENCE SINCE SHE HAS STOPPED GOING TOO BAD THE WAY THINGS WENT THEY ADVISE HER BEING SENT TO SCHOOL AT PALM BEACH WHILE SHE IS THERE SHE MUST BE AWAY FROM GROWNUPS I HOPE YOU WILL UNDERSTAND LOVE BILL[46]

Billie ultimately did not regret her decision. Palm Beach's warm, welcoming climate finally had a beneficial effect on Patricia's health, and she became "ruddy and rugged, . . . [a] buxom little girl with red cropped hair."[47] Fortunately, Patricia found playmates her own age at the resort, most of whom were the offspring of Ziegfeld's wealthy benefactors. Among them were the Munn children, whom Patricia called "holy terrors," and socialite Evelyn Walsh Maclean's son Jock, with whom she enjoyed exploring Indian mounds. Jock's little sister played with them as well, all the while wearing an ermine coat that dragged behind her in the sand. Patricia, however, insisted that she preferred Captain Gray to friends her own age. Gray, a tall man in his thirties with a scar below his mouth, piloted the Ziegfelds' boat, the *Sally*. He seemed very romantic to Patricia and shared her love of fishing. He took her out on the boat when Ziegfeld and Billie were unavailable, and when Jock was busy, Gray accompanied her to the Indian mounds.

Ziegfeld could be just as much a pal to Patricia as her playmates or Captain Gray, but when he scolded her, it made her "just want to shrivel up."[48] One thing he could not abide was artificiality, which is ironic, considering that many a socialite at Palm Beach wore a perpetual facade. He strongly urged Patricia to refrain from having her hair permanently waved, wearing heels, or covering her face in excessive amounts of makeup. These were the same rules he applied to the girls he glorified onstage. Ziegfeld believed that a woman's beauty came naturally and that makeup could heighten her beauty but should not overpower it.

As far as her parents were concerned, Patricia was in no danger of entering the artificial life of show business and high society. As a very young child, she had concocted stories of the stage, but in her stories she was always a spectator rather than a performer. At age seven, she wrote the following story for her father: "there was a little girl that wished to know my mother she never saw my mother before on the stage and her name is

Alice Ziegfeld Jr. she is 6 years old she lives in new york city the number of the street west 63rd street and shes dying to see you soon in the play . . . the name of the play rose Briar She wants 2 sits [seats] for the play She is going to take a friend with her 2 sits [seats] dont forget Patricia."[49]

Several years later, twelve-year-old Patricia expressed a desire to become an actress after participating in a school recital. She "had a grand daydream" in which Ziegfeld came up to her after the recital and said, "Patricia Burke Ziegfeld, you are an actress! Someday your name will shine even more brightly from the marquees of Broadway than your mother's did." The recital itself was a small affair, with Patricia playing a woodpecker and most of the other girls wearing gypsy costumes. Patricia explained to her parents that the play had no title because her teacher, Miss Baird, thought "putting a title on a thing limits its freedom to ignite the minds of the onlookers."[50] Horrified at any bit of theater that was less than perfect (particularly if it involved his daughter), Ziegfeld commissioned his new costumer, Jack Harkrider, to design the outfits for the recital. Afterward, Miss Baird told Ziegfeld that the show had been such a success she wanted to make it semiannual. "Just like your very own *Follies!*" she gushed. At this news, Ziegfeld grew sober. He did not want the responsibility of supervising school recitals twice a year, and he did not want to steer Patricia toward the theater. Not surprisingly, Ziegfeld pulled Patricia from the school shortly after the end of the semester. An exasperated Billie suggested sending their daughter to an exclusive girls' school in Dobbs Ferry, New York, but Patricia flatly refused, claiming she had met snobby girls in Palm Beach who attended the institution. Instead, her parents hired private tutors for the remainder of Patricia's schooling, which seemed to suit her better than any school. Despite the doctors' warnings that Patricia would be damaged by the lack of companionship and socialization provided by the classroom atmosphere, she thrived in the sparkling whirl of her parents' world.

In the 1936 film *The Great Ziegfeld,* Billie deemed the small number of scenes devoted to the Ziegfelds' family life the most authentic. She was particularly taken by the film's depiction of Christmas Eve at Burkeley Crest. The scene showed the drawing room filled with extravagant gifts, including a miniature circus for Patricia that Ziegfeld promised to bring to life in his next *Follies* (many *Follies* had circus-themed acts). Billie admitted in later years that she did not like the film because it failed to capture

Ziegfeld the father and husband; it focused instead on his persona as an over-the-top showman. "I could not bear to see it," Billie confessed. "No movie and not anything I write now can recapture the gentle moments which were our real life together."[51]

Those gentle moments justified the title of Patricia's future memoir: *The Ziegfelds' Girl: Confessions of an Abnormally Happy Childhood.* She was a remarkably unaffected, cheerful little girl whose heart truly belonged to her daddy. And her daddy continued to pressure his wife and daughter to join him in Palm Beach whenever possible. Billie and Ziegfeld had made Burkeley Crest as well as Billie Burke Island and Camp Patricia into their own fantastical alternate realities. Ziegfeld saw no reason why Palm Beach could not be another one. "Palm Beach was the rich, full life," Patricia wrote. "Daddy felt instinctively, I think, that the Palm Beach intervals were sort of a lovely make-believe, something like spending the bleak winter months in an amusement park where there was sunshine every day and the sand was made of white sugar and the enormous sums of money they spent didn't matter because it was only stage money."[52]

An amusement park atmosphere was what Ziegfeld needed as he searched for direction in his career. But even an amusement park charges a high price for admission.

17

A Shot in the Arm

Initially, Palm Beach seemed like the ideal place for the Ziegfelds to escape from the demanding, tumultuous life of New York City. Ziegfeld saw it as Camp Patricia's regal sister, offering luxury rather than rusticity. However, Billie saw Palm Beach as a playground for uncouth, hedonistic heirs and heiresses. With its growing population of young people, Palm Beach was infused with the reckless spirit of "flaming youth" synonymous with the Jazz Age. Biographer Ethan Mordden described it as "a younger resort than most because it had no reputation to uphold. Elsewhere, divorce was hush-hush, a scandal; in Palm Beach it was what you had for breakfast . . . Palm Beach had no manners."[1]

Billie agreed to join Ziegfeld in Palm Beach each year only because of the newfound benefits to Patricia's health and because Ziegfeld gave her carte blanche to make their vacation home just as appealing as Burkeley Crest. Billie packed up her own linen and china from home and even brought along Sidney the valet and Deliah the cook. Ziegfeld did his part by having the family's pet lion cubs shipped to Florida. Surely the big cats' presence would give the Palm Beach community what Ziegfeld called "a shot in the arm."[2]

As a couple, Billie and Ziegfeld were like a shot in the arm to Palm Beach society, and their joint appeal seemed to help mend their shaky marriage. Unlike many show business people who vacationed in Palm Beach, the Ziegfelds' "moved easily into the inner circle of resort society," with no self-consciousness over the fact that they represented new money. If ever there was a place to flaunt one's wealth, Palm Beach was it. Unlike the low-key 400 families of New York, Palm Beach socialites flashed their riches as flagrantly as Lorelei Lee flashed her diamonds in *Gentlemen Prefer Blondes*. Heiress Barbara Hutton's home was the epitome of glitz. The mansion was designed to be a replica of Versailles, only grander, and

306

the grounds included a golf course. What set Billie and Ziegfeld apart was that anything they did, they did without ostentation. Patricia explained: "What they did was purely for their own pleasure and amusement, and as a result they pleased and amused everyone around them."[3]

The fact that the Palm Beach millionaires had become quite bored with one another further enhanced Billie and Ziegfeld's appeal. That boredom was, as Patricia explained, "the natural result of being forced to dine with the same people and listen to the same across-the-table talk while eating the same rich food night after night."[4] The after-dinner entertainment occasionally livened up the parties. Hostesses sometimes hired famous opera singers for private concerts at a fee of $10,000; other amusements included "fishing on a grand scale, safari by water comparable to big game hunting . . . treasure hunts, dances, and musicales."[5] When Billie and Ziegfeld gave parties, they strove to make them grander and more extraordinary than anything Palm Beach had ever seen. Just as he often did for their Sunday dinner parties at Burkeley Crest, Ziegfeld took over the job of host at their Palm Beach soirees. Theoretically, this could have been a relief to Billie; however, in one instance, Billie had reason to believe that her husband's "help" would result in their banishment from Palm Beach society.

Billie had already made all the arrangements for this particular dinner party, when Ziegfeld ordered the cook to change the entire menu—and neglected to tell his wife. Not until their high-society guests removed the silver covers from their plates did she discover her husband's deed. On the plates were not the caviar and rare fish she had ordered but cabbage, corned beef, and potatoes. "Mother took one look at the fifty pounds of Irish potatoes and gave a little shriek," Patricia remembered.[6] The girl could hardly stifle a giggle as she watched the guests' glasses fogging with cabbage steam. Billie held her breath, waiting for a reaction. To her relief, the guests burst into laughter and began to applaud. They proceeded to drink beer from the bottle and eat so many helpings of mashed potatoes, turnips, and corned beef that a number of the ladies' escorts had to assist them to their cars. Billie wrote, "Flo was right, as he always was; he cared little for convention, but he knew what people liked."[7]

Though Ziegfeld cared little for convention, he blithely fell into the usual Palm Beach routine. In the mornings, the men conducted business at their private offices or went to their brokers to get updates on their stocks. While the men attended to business, the women played cards or sunbathed and gossiped. Billie and Ziegfeld regrouped late in the morning to go for a swim and sip cocktails. Later, the men sojourned to Bradley's Casino, and after a nap in the late afternoon, families gathered for dinner. At night, while the rest of his family slept, Ziegfeld would return to the casino. Bradley's was the razor that slit the half-healed wounds in the Ziegfelds' marriage. The casino also revealed a side of her husband that Billie had not yet met: the social climber. The Ziegfelds' wealth paled beside that of the older, more established, sinfully rich millionaires. "Everyone had handfuls of money to spend, the world was a place created just for fun," Billie later wrote of Palm Beach. "And Flo Ziegfeld, of all people in the world in this peculiar era, was the best-equipped man for having that fun."[8] To multimillionaires such as Edward Munn and steel tycoon Leonard Replogle, fun meant gambling at Bradley's twice a day and dropping what would be, to Ziegfeld, an entire show's profits without batting an eye.

Though no fellow gambler or guest at the Ziegfelds' dinner table suspected it, Billie and Ziegfeld were in desperate need of money. Ziegfeld still had creditors knocking at his door; most of the unpaid debts were for costumes and sets he had haphazardly ordered and then rejected in the process of crafting his shows. In 1924 Ziegfeld owed $10,000 in rent for the New Amsterdam. Usually he was able to avoid declaring bankruptcy thanks to the revenue from his shows. But, as was the case with *Kid Boots,* a sellout every night could still result in a loss due to the sheer expense of running the show. Despite his professional woes, Ziegfeld did not scale back on his personal spending. Billie admitted their dinner parties were so expensive that "a large family could eat steak for a year" on what they cost.[9] Knowing that his bank account needed a boost if he wished to maintain such an extravagant lifestyle, Ziegfeld went after Palm Beach society with the same fervor he had pursued the most important women in his life. As Ziegfeld became more involved with the multimillionaires at the gambling tables, Billie discovered that her initial wariness of Palm Beach had been well founded.

Billie fell into a severe depression each time her husband drained their funds in an effort to impress Palm Beach society. She remembered Ziegfeld "sitting dour-faced and silent at the roulette wheel hours after everyone else had gone home, determined to break the bank, determined to be the best."[10] As his gambling addiction intensified, Ziegfeld began to slip off to

Bradley's during dinner parties, neglecting his guests. Billie, mortified, would bicycle over to the casino and plead with him to come home, but he would not take his eyes off the roulette table. "Please leave . . . return to your guests. I'll be home soon," he absently assured her. Billie would bicycle back home, sobbing, and then lie in bed all night waiting for her husband to return.

Irving Berlin, a frequent guest of the Ziegfelds' at Palm Beach, wrote Billie a satiric ballad called "The Gambler's Bride" in an attempt to make light of Ziegfeld's addiction. Those who heard the song roared with laughter; Palm Beach society saw gambling as a diversion not to be taken seriously. Billie, however, stormed at Ziegfeld, tore down curtains, and threw china each time he came home with empty pockets. But as usual, Ziegfeld found her tantrums attractive and continued to frequent Bradley's. Gambling (along with Lillian Lorraine) had been the undoing of Ziegfeld's marriage to Anna Held. Why would he make the same mistake with Billie? Eve Golden explained that "Billie Burke was willing to put up with a lot more crap from Ziegfeld than Anna was, probably because they had a daughter. They [Anna and Billie] were both tough women, but Billie was more invested in saving their marriage than Anna was."[11]

Ziegfeld never stopped living in the fantasy world of his *Follies,* where luxury and grandeur were a matter of course. In contrast, Billie had grown up and faced the reality that money could not magically be replenished. In a letter she sent to Ziegfeld back in the winter of 1923, while she was in New York and he was in Palm Beach, she was terse yet persuasive: "Thank God you haven't enough money to loaf all the time with those numbskulls—or you would never achieve any of these glorious things you have given the world."[12] Unfortunately, Billie's tough love did nothing to stop Ziegfeld's obsession. Patricia recalled that the issue of her father's gambling reached a climax in February 1924. Eavesdropping through the living room doors, she heard Billie "saying things like 'This must stop' and 'When will it all end' and 'Think of the child.'" Ziegfeld calmly replied that Billie was making a mountain out of a molehill. He then stalked from the room and went to Bradley's, not returning until dawn. When he arose at noon the next day, Ziegfeld found Billie and Patricia at the head of a line of household staff standing by the front door. They were all dressed in traveling clothes and surrounded by a trainload of luggage. "I have reserved rooms at the hotel . . . Goodbye," Billie said. "I'm taking Baby with me."[13]

Billie's drastic action finally got through to Ziegfeld. He recognized the extent to which his gambling was affecting his family, and he realized that his role as a father meant more to him than any sum of money he could win from a lucky hand of poker. Billie had made a home for him—the first true home of his adult life—and he did not want to lose it. Breaking from his customary aloofness, Ziegfeld dashed down the staircase, clasped Billie's arm, and begged her to talk the matter over with him for five minutes. "Is that too much to ask?" he implored. Billie, with an impassive expression on her face, curtly granted him the five minutes. After the allotted time had passed, Patricia heard the bedroom doorknob turn. Ziegfeld emerged, deflated and pale but once again his typical calm self. "The crisis is over," he said, and proceeded to tell the servants to unpack the piles of luggage flanking the hallway. Winking at Patricia, he said, "Your mother can't even run away from home without baggage for a world tour."[14]

Billie emerged from this crisis more determined than ever to keep her marriage intact. Her stoic exterior may have reinforced Ziegfeld's conviction that she was as resilient and independent as the women he glorified in his shows. But this second disaster had come too soon after the couple's first close shave with divorce. It left Billie feeling weak and bewildered. But for a time, at least, she felt secure. "Flo promised and I had no more trouble with him—*that year*," she later wrote.[15]

Ziegfeld's gambling and his attraction to other women did not disappear completely, but they noticeably diminished after 1923. Ziegfeld's attention to certain attractive society women—namely, Louisa Wanamaker Munn, Mrs. Paris Singer, and Barbara Hutton—was now based solely on how much money they could invest in his shows or their ability to connect him with other potential benefactors. Billie knew that Ziegfeld's love for her was strong, yet she could not help feeling insecure when she saw photographs of him enjoying other women's company. She tried to mold herself into what she thought was her husband's new ideal—a combination of a fast, flashy Palm Beach heiress and a Ziegfeld girl. Ziegfeld girls were perfect not only in face but also in figure, and Billie claimed she had a tendency to gain weight if she was not vigilant. But no matter how fit she became, Billie was convinced she looked like an old-fashioned, plump Gibson girl next to the chic heiresses and chorines.

Billie's growing concerns about her appearance manifested in increasingly rigorous beauty and exercise rituals. She received a weekly facial consisting of a verbena-based cream that resembled black molasses. Billie recalled, "I took care to awake first, before my husband popped an eye at me—the first thing a husband sees in the morning, whether he likes it or not, is *you*."[16] At Burkeley Crest, Billie had an Exercycle and a vibrating machine, but she was even more exercise-conscious in Palm Beach. According to Patricia, her mother "had boxing lessons each morning . . . and swimming and diving lessons . . . and tennis coaching."[17] On top of all that, Billie took daily five-mile walks and constantly experimented with her diet. She scanned the newspapers and clipped articles about "miracle foods" that increased longevity and vitality. One of her fad diets consisted only of stewed fruit, wild honey, and papaya juice. Eventually, she became a vegetarian; this is hardly a surprise, considering her love of animals and her hunting ban at Camp Patricia.

Despite Billie's dissatisfaction with her appearance, most of the Palm Beach set considered her, at age forty-one, the most beautiful woman at the resort. The rich women Ziegfeld courted were jealous of the fact that even when dressed in a sun-proof ensemble of knickers, a large hat, a long-sleeved blouse, and gloves, Billie retained an air of glamour. Patricia recalled, "Mother was beautiful under any circumstances, with her blue eyes, her pink-and-white complexion, her radiant smile, and her blazing red hair."[18] One incident concerning Billie's hair exemplified her fragile ego. It all started when Louisa Wanamaker Munn complimented Billie on her hair and told her never to bob it. Billie resented this comment from the recipient of so much of her husband's attention. It also sparked Billie's resentment toward her husband, who had repeatedly stated that hair was a woman's crowning glory. Not an hour after Munn's comment, Billie went to the hairdresser and requested a bob—a decision she regretted as soon as she saw her reflection in the mirror. Billie avoided going home as long as possible, and when she finally did—wearing a hat pulled down tightly over her head—Ziegfeld and Patricia were already eating dinner. Her distress only increased when Ziegfeld asked how she could stand wearing a hat when it was blistering hot outside and Patricia giggled at the strangeness of wearing a hat at the dinner table. Billie then burst into tears and tore it off. "There!" she said with tears running down her cheeks. "Look at me! It's horrid and I don't know what made me do it and if I were you I'd go ahead and divorce me, Flo, I really would." Patricia described Billie's bobbed curls as a "shining cap" that made her look like a "contrite little boy."[19]

"Do you know something?" Ziegfeld said after her outburst. "I like it."

Billie was utterly confused. Only weeks before, Ziegfeld had denounced bobbed hair in a newspaper column.

"I think you look absolutely beautiful," he assured her. "There's just one thing I wish you'd do." Billie nodded, smiling at him and drying her tears. "Start letting it grow again right away," he said. Billie could have burst into tears all over again. "I like it only in Florida," he explained. "It's a Palm Beach sort of thing, you know."

"It's a Palm Beach sort of thing." That short phrase told Billie that her husband wanted to keep her separate from Palm Beach society. Palm Beach represented none of the tasteful, subtle beauty Ziegfeld loved in Billie and fostered in his shows.

To make amends with his wife, Ziegfeld wrote a follow-up article to his previous one, this time praising the bob and denouncing the modern trend for women to have boyish figures. The article, published on April 19, 1925, and titled "Bobbed Hair Making American Girls Most Beautiful in the World," included a photo of Billie with a caption reading: "The charming and famous star who was one of the first devotees of bobbed hair."[20] But according to his press agent, Bernard Sobel, Ziegfeld "hedged and faltered" when trying to challenge the flapper profile. Ziegfeld claimed the ideal girl was five feet four inches tall and 130 pounds—almost identical to Billie's measurements, but far from those of a gamine flapper. "His success was built on curves . . . he could never sympathize with this unfeminine new fashion," Sobel commented.[21] Sobel concluded that it was pity Ziegfeld did not live to see the flapper profile fall out of fashion.

Ziegfeld's published statement to the effect that Billie remained his ideal woman boosted her confidence. Never again did she feel compelled to compete with a Ziegfeld girl or a Palm Beach socialite. Billie still disapproved of his flings, but she no longer took them seriously. In the following telegram, her tone is more mocking than accusing when she comments on her husband's rejection by his latest Palm Beach conquest: MORNING DARLING. . . . CANT IMAGINE YOUR FEELING BLUE DOWN THERE . . . ALTHO I HEAR YOU HAVE BEEN LEFT RATHER FLAT FOR ANOTHER HEAVY SWAIN CHEER UP DARLING. LOVE BILLIE.[22]

Ziegfeld received his fair share of rejections from Palm Beach heiresses, but he garnered enough support from their husbands to turn his latest ambition into a reality. He envisioned making Palm Beach a theatrical venue to rival or even outshine Broadway. His plan was to open a supper club at the resort that would provide entertainment similar to that in the *Midnight Frolic*. His benefactors gave him a free hand to make the club as magnificent as he wished, and Ziegfeld took full advantage of their generosity. Determined to make the supper club as cutting edge as the roof of the New Amsterdam, Ziegfeld called on Joseph Urban to transform the barn-like structure he had obtained. Urban designed a backdrop that depicted a moonlit Palm Beach night and turned the roof into a blue dome. The ceiling, done in arabesques using varying shades of black, gave patrons the feeling that they were sitting beneath a starry sky. Ziegfeld christened the spectacularly renovated building the Montmartre.

Once the building was complete, Ziegfeld immediately set to work on the club's first show, entitled *Palm Beach Nights* (rather than the *Ziegfeld Revue,* as he had originally planned). Eventually the title evolved into *No Foolin'*, after the show's hit song. *Palm Beach Nights,* like the *Midnight Frolic,* was a testing ground for acts that Ziegfeld might include in future editions of the *Follies.* He wanted to make *Palm Beach Nights* markedly different from the *Follies* of old, and the youth-oriented resort town was the perfect place to experiment. One of the key players in modernizing Ziegfeld's revue was a twenty-five-year-old designer named John Harkrider (who later designed the costumes for Patricia's school recital). He became as essential to Ziegfeld as Lucile had been in the prewar era. Lucile's gowns had been designed to rival a given show's headliner, but Ziegfeld now required costumes that blended naturally into the show. Ziegfeld had his own ideas about the costumes and scenes for *Palm Beach Nights,* and Harkrider seemed to understand what the producer wanted without explanation. The designer quickly assumed almost all artistic responsibility for the show, including lighting and choreography. Ned Wayburn, who was supposed to be the director, was not impressed. Wayburn and the majority of Ziegfeld's tried-and-true staff members resented this golden boy, who was allowed to spend more than $90,000 on costumes and $40,000 on sets.

"I need egret feathers ordered immediately," Harkrider told Ziegfeld one afternoon.

"I'd like to see the work you've done so far first," Ziegfeld said.

"I'm not having anyone rehearse in the costumes. Too much rehearsal will damage the feathers," Harkrider explained. Harkrider sounded like

Ziegfeld himself, so it was not surprising that he allowed the young man to order the feathers.

"This is the biggest gamble I've ever taken. You'd damn well better pay off," Ziegfeld told him.[23]

Harkrider did pay off. When he revealed the costumes, Ziegfeld was stunned. The headdresses, topped by twenty-eight-foot-tall plumes, caught the lavender and blue light of Urban's setting. Such costumes became Harkrider's signature, and his name became well known up and down Broadway. Though grateful for the opportunity Ziegfeld had given him, Harkrider seethed inside when the producer said of the completed number: "It's the best *I've* ever done."[24] Palm Beachers agreed. The press proclaimed the show "the most brilliant affair of the season to date." On opening night (January 12, 1926), tickets started at $200—a pittance for the millionaires who frequented the Montmartre. The curtain opened to show a silver globe hanging in the air. The globe then lowered to the stage, exploded, and revealed Ziegfeld girl Claire Luce in a glittery flapper gown. The other acts in the show, including the humorous ones, were not performed by Ziegfeld's roster of well-established stars. He employed many new talents, including a quartet called the Yacht Club Boys, dancer-singer Peggy Fears, singer Charles King, and future film star Paulette Goddard. The only familiar name in the cast was *Follies* regular Ray Dooley.

The show was different from the *Follies* not only because of its new costumer but also because of its lack of subtlety. Ziegfeld normally disliked obvious glamour and preferred to create elegant shows that were lavish but not gaudy. In Palm Beach, however, he showed his willingness to change with the times and cater to modern tastes, and audiences there lapped up the "showy but thin" production.[25] Despite appreciative audiences in Florida, the show made little impression on New Yorkers, even after Ziegfeld replaced the flashier acts with more artistic ones. The show opened on June 24 at the Globe Theatre, ran for only three months, and lost $30,000. Apparently, it was just a "Palm Beach sort of thing." The show's failure dealt Ziegfeld a severe blow. Making things worse was the fact that his valued associate Julian Mitchell had died of a stroke on opening night. Mitchell had returned to work for Ziegfeld and directed many of the numbers in *No Foolin'* during rehearsals.

Ziegfeld was again facing bankruptcy, and this time, he was almost saved by a miracle. Before the New York run of *No Foolin'*, he received news that a rich uncle, Siegfried Ziegfeld, had died and left him $2 million. However, the will stipulated that Ziegfeld would receive the money only if he did not marry; otherwise, the fortune would go to Siegfried's German relations. "The fortune with which my name has been connected is a mystery to me . . . I never heard of Siegfried Ziegfeld . . . I never heard of any Ziegfeld who made a fortune in the United States. But if he did and wishes to leave it to me, I can use it, because it certainly takes a lot of money to stage Broadway productions," Ziegfeld stated.[26] Needless to say, his marital status disqualified him from inheriting the money he needed so badly.

Undeterred by financial difficulties and judgmental New Yorkers, Ziegfeld plunged into his next professional venture, a book musical entitled *Betsy*. Like nearly all his shows, *Betsy* held great promise initially. Ziegfeld not only employed the dynamic young team of Richard Rodgers and Lorenz Hart to compose the score but also cast the popular vaudevillian Belle Baker as the lead. The show's simple plot revolved around a spinster whose siblings cannot marry until she finds a husband of her own. Rodgers and Hart, like most composers, found Ziegfeld a frustrating man to work for. When Ziegfeld invited the men to dinner at Burkeley Crest, they thought he intended to discuss *Betsy,* but Ziegfeld avoided the subject throughout the meal. Finally, after dessert, he seemed ready to get down to business. But once Rodgers and Hart were comfortably seated in the drawing room, they discovered the true reason behind their dinner invitation. According to Rodgers, Ziegfeld "simply instructed us to go to the piano and perform all the songs from *Betsy* for the amusement of his . . . daughter."[27]

Rodgers and Hart may have delighted Patricia with their compositions, but they knew New York critics would not be so easily impressed. They faced the daunting task of composing songs for a script that was little more than an outline. The show's scriptwriters, Irving Caesar and David Freedman, fought constantly with the composers. During one such dispute, Ziegfeld became so frustrated that he went "charging around the theater screaming like a wounded water buffalo."[28] Rodgers was even less impressed with Ziegfeld when the producer decided to include an Irving Berlin song called "Blue Skies" in the show, without asking Rodgers and Hart's opinion. On opening night (December 28, 1926) at the New Amsterdam Theatre, Ziegfeld also arranged to have a spotlight "pick out Irving Berlin seated in the front row" so that he could rise and take a bow.[29]

Rodgers admitted that Berlin's tune was superior to anything he and Hart had composed. Still, Ziegfeld's and the audience's preference for Berlin's tune crushed Rodgers, "particularly since Ziegfeld insisted he wouldn't think of doing the show with anyone else." He observed that Ziegfeld "could never be accused of having the human touch, at least not where men were concerned."[30] In his autobiography, Rodgers recalled a "blow up" when Ziegfeld said "some rotten things" that led Rodgers to declare that he was through with the "lousy show." The general manager "also made some cracks and I raised hell," he admitted. The next day, a contrite Ziegfeld sent the general manager to apologize to Rodgers. Ziegfeld and Rodgers came to an uneasy truce, and according to Rodgers, the next night "Z. and I were walking around rehearsals with our arms about each other's waists."[31] Rodgers conceded that Ziegfeld "did show consideration for girls." However, "even there his overriding ego or insecurity would occasionally take over." Rodgers recalled one instance in which Ziegfeld admonished a girl for a minor infraction and reduced her to tears in front of the entire company. Rodgers concluded that *Betsy* was "the worst experience of my career."[32]

The feeling of animosity between Ziegfeld and Rodgers was mutual. Ziegfeld had little trust for songwriters; in the past, he had often discovered that a song presented to him as new had actually been published before. Journalist Djuna Barnes recorded Ziegfeld's embittered attitude toward songwriters: "They will say anything, sing anything, and then go away and do as they please . . . the only way to get the best of a composer is to kill him and I can't do that—it's against the law. I don't see why."[33] It is unclear why Ziegfeld failed to establish a rapport with the majority of his composers and backstage staff (Joseph Urban, Irving Berlin, Gene Buck, and a few others excluded), but perhaps it was because Ziegfeld felt that they threatened his creative control. He was always willing to pass on the responsibility for carrying out his artistic visions to someone else, but when that person asked for credit where credit was due, Ziegfeld usually seemed taken aback and noncommittal. Call it narcissism, a God complex, success poisoning, or insecurity on his part, but Ziegfeld could never quite acknowledge that his staff had a hand in developing his magic touch. On other occasions, such as his recognition of Berlin at the premiere of *Betsy*, Ziegfeld proved he was capable of sharing the credit.

Berlin's "Blue Skies" was well received, but otherwise, most critics agreed that *Betsy* was "butchered . . . and a waste of time."[34] However, one reviewer from the *New York Times* admitted that the show had Ziegfeld's "customary opulence and unimpeachable taste."[35] Even so, *Betsy* ran for a mere thirty-nine performances. Despite his success with *Sally* and *Kid Boots,* most of Broadway still thought Ziegfeld was well past his glory days. His hated being considered a has-been and expressed that frustration through his uncharacteristically harsh behavior toward even the girls in the production.

The Great Ziegfeld's reign may have been over, but his work was far from done. At the dawn of 1927, Ziegfeld had two new productions planned, both of which would premiere at his very own theater on the corner of Sixth Avenue and Fifty-Fourth Street. At least one of those shows had to be a hit.

Ziegfeld hoped the opening of his theater would prove that he was on his way up—not down. Because his art was different from every other producer's, Ziegfeld wanted his theater to be different as well. He personally supervised its design and construction, employing Joseph Urban for most of the work. Historian Gerald Bordman called the end product "a masterpiece of art deco."[36] Hundreds of hidden bulbs lit up the curved front of the theater, giving it a celestial glow that complemented the moonlight over Broadway. Its oval-shaped interior resembled an ornately decorated Easter egg. A writer for the *New York Times* provided a thorough description of the $2.5 million theater: Upon entering a "hall of gold," one was overwhelmed by the interior's shimmering curtains, proscenium, carpets, chairs, and lights—a "setting of ineffable luxury." Murals set in gold ornamented the walls and were "delicately blended with the pastel shades of blue and green." At first glance, they looked "like a cubist version of anything at all," but eventually they came into focus as "quaint, lovely figures" from myth and fairy tale.[37]

The theater's second story was no less impressive. There, audiences found the entrance to a terrace where they could enjoy fresh air on stifling summer nights. The theater lobby and even the bathrooms were "spacious beyond anything New York had seen."[38] Joseph Urban's daughter, Gretel, recalled that Ziegfeld was very taken with the theater and told her, "Your father sure hit the jackpot this time." He then took a seat in the second row and swung his legs over the back of the seat in front of him with "a beatific smile on his face."[39]

Will Rogers, from his ranch in Beverly Hills, was among the first to congratulate Ziegfeld: "I SURE AM GLAD YOU ARE GOING TO HAVE YOUR OWN THEATRE . . . JUST THINK WHAT YOU WILL ACCOMPLISH WHEN THERE IS NO ARGUMENT OVER PERCENTAGE WITH ERLANGER . . . I FEEL THIS IS JUST THE STARTING FOR YOU OF A CHAIN . . . I HOPE YOU NEVER HAVE TO PUT IN MOVIE SCREEN . . . YOUR OLD HIRED HAND WILL."[40] Will later traveled to New York to act as the master of ceremonies at the theater's opening. He amused audiences with his thoughts on the location of the showplace: "Mr. Ziegfeld chose this corner because of the absence of saloons. Since the saloons have disappeared there have been many more theaters and this accounts for the fact that the entertainment is not as good as it was."[41]

As part of the ceremony, Billie and Patricia filled a large iron box with paraphernalia from the past: the previous day's newspapers; photos of Rosalie Ziegfeld, Billie, Patricia, and Eugen Sandow; a program from *Sally*; and a photo of Charles Frohman (included at Billie's insistence). Finally, Ziegfeld put in a brick from a Greek theater, representing the history of the stage from its glorious beginnings in Greece to its modern-day pinnacle in New York. Patricia then placed the box at the theater's cornerstone and cemented it. The festivities continued with a live band led by Vincent Lopez. The musicians played enthusiastically outside the theater, despite an abrasive north wind. Hearty men from WGBS Radio stood by, broadcasting the entire to-do. A crowd of 1,500 spectators and guests looked on. Among the crowd were Joseph Urban, Ned Wayburn, Marilyn Miller, and Gene Buck. Marilyn's unexpected presence was proof of her willingness to return to the Ziegfeld fold, despite their tumultuous past. And Ziegfeld had big plans for her, but first, he had to win her back.

Ziegfeld wanted his theater's inaugural show to be something unusual. The *Follies* would not suffice; he needed a show as big as *Sally* or *Kid Boots*. He found the property he was looking for in *Rio Rita*. The play, set in the Southwest, is the story of a Texas ranger who falls in love with a senorita (played, oddly enough, by Irish actress Ethelind Terry) in the midst of his quest to catch a ruthless bandit. Ethan Mordden described the show as being like two in one: one part romantic and strongly influenced by operetta, and the other part humorous and influenced by modern musical comedy. Curiously, the comedic part of the show focused on characters only loosely related to the romantic leads (most notably in scenes with the popular vaudeville duo Robert Woolsey and Bert Wheeler). The loose structure allowed for many spectacular numbers spotlighting Ziegfeld showgirls, including his latest discovery: the Albertina Rasch Dancers. The dance troupe was even more skilled and refined than the Tiller Girls, and their Harkrider costumes of scarlet, black, and gold added no end of glamour. Harkrider used his trademark feathered headdresses to create costumes for breathtaking Aztec goddesses, and for a chorus of Mexican men, he designed straw hats, with no two being alike. During scene changes, women of the chorus danced in vividly colored shawls and velvet dresses. *Rio Rita*'s scenery alone cost $50,000. Designed by Urban, the sets included a Mexican mesa, a gloomy underground chamber, a cabaret, a Mexican village set against snow-capped mountains, and a mansion complete with a courtyard. Mordden summarized the spectacular show as a "*Follies* with a storyline."[42]

The scriptwriters were Guy Bolton and Fred Thompson, and the musical writers were two of the contributors to *Kid Boots*, Joseph McCarthy and Harry Tierney. Bordman described the script as well crafted and the music as an inspired and merry blend of all song types. The most popular tunes—"The Kinkajou" and "Following the Sun Around"—had fox-trot rhythms. Two sweetly romantic songs proved to be favorites as well: "If You're in Love, You'll Waltz" and "You're Always in My Arms." Ziegfeld had promised Will Rogers that his shows would be family friendly, and even after Will's departure, he strived to make them so. The *American* heralded *Rio Rita* and its music as being "unblemished by vulgarity."[43]

The show's only questionable aspect involved two roosters used in one of the scenes. The Humane Society accused Ziegfeld of promoting cockfighting, but when he appeared before Magistrate Henry Goodman, Ziegfeld insisted that the birds wore leather pads on their spurs to prevent them from injuring each other.

"Are you familiar with chickens?" Goodman asked Ziegfeld.

"I have a poultry farm," Ziegfeld truthfully replied, alluding to his collection of chickens at Burkeley Crest.

"Do you give these birds the same attention as those on your farm?"

"I give them better attention," Ziegfeld said.[44]

The Humane Society dropped the charges against the producer, and *Rio Rita* went on without further incident.

Ziegfeld held a special show for Charles Lindbergh after the aviator completed the first transatlantic flight. Seating was limited, and the house was nearly sold out. The only seat that happened to be available was the one beside Lindbergh. Mrs. William Randolph Hearst desired that seat for herself. After all, her husband had funded the Ziegfeld Theatre. However, Ziegfeld would not hear of it. "That seat is for Patty," he said, referring to his daughter."Flo, it's Mrs. *Hearst*," Bernard Sobel told him. Ziegfeld scowled and, according to Sobel, acted like "a spoiled child, grudgingly handing me the ticket" for Mrs. Hearst.[45]

Mrs. Hearst thoroughly enjoyed the performance, as did the rest of New York theatergoers. *Rio Rita* had a triumphant premiere on February 2, 1927, and ticket sales topped $1 million in the first twenty-two weeks. The show ran for more than a year and racked up almost 500 performances. For once, Ziegfeld made a profit on a production—nearly a quarter of a million dollars. Billie convinced her husband to channel a portion of the profits into a savings account under her name, suspecting that he might gamble it all away. She was correct in her assumption. In celebration of his success, Ziegfeld went on a gambling binge at Bradley's and lost. Also at this time, Ziegfeld took another major gamble: he started playing the stock market. His attorney convinced him to invest more than $2 million in Chrysler, Eaton Axle, and Mexican Seaboard Oil.[46]

Complications ensued in May 1927 when *Rio Rita's* director, Edward Royce, sued Ziegfeld for breach of contract. He claimed the producer had not paid him the 1 percent of the show's profits plus the $1,000 a week salary he had been promised. Royce told every reporter he could find that Ziegfeld was broke after losing $100,000 in Palm Beach. "He's meddlesome and his knowledge of stagecraft is restricted to women and costumes, but nonetheless he thinks himself somewhat of a stage director and manager," Royce stated. Ziegfeld shot back, calling Royce a has-been and claiming that his excessive drinking had forced the producer to spend $7,000 to engage a new director. Ziegfeld denied having lost $100,000 in Florida (the exact amount he lost is uncertain), but what seemed to incense him most was being called broke. He listed his many holdings and ownership of the *Follies* and *Rio Rita*, Burkeley Crest, and a one-twelfth interest in the Famous Players–Lasky silent film *Ben Hur*.[47] After several months in court, Royce lost his lawsuit. Once again, it was apparent that Ziegfeld and his backstage employees, whether composers or directors, did not mix well.

Ziegfeld's triumph over Royce did not bring perfect harmony to his life. Although having his own theater seemed to bring him some luck, preparing a new *Follies* and a book musical simultaneously, as well as dealing with his gambling losses and legal battles, left Ziegfeld completely drained. He developed bronchitis and, between shows, returned to Burkeley Crest for sun-ray treatments (usually used to treat vitamin D deficiency, which Ziegfeld may have had, given that he spent most of his time in the theater or the office). One afternoon he forgot to wear the required dark glasses and, howling in pain, emerged from the room half blind and with blisters forming around his eyes. Fortunately, his eyesight was not permanently impaired, although he had to wear dark glasses for a time. Shortly thereafter he began coughing up blood and was forced to slow his pace, but it was hardly what most people would call restful. While recovering, he stayed in a suite at the Warwick Hotel across from his theater. He stubbornly went forward with plans for the next *Follies,* communicating with his staff solely through telegrams and phone calls. He had proved he was far from a has-been and was not going to stop his ascent now. "When I start to do a thing I don't stop until I finish it," Ziegfeld said.[48]

The new edition of the *Follies,* returning after an absence of nearly two years, promised to be as big a triumph as *Rio Rita.* The show was slated to open at the *Follies'* customary home at the New Amsterdam Theatre. Irving Berlin was happy to be back in the Ziegfeld fold as the revue's primary composer after the failure of his own series, the *Music Box Revue.* Also employed in the production were Eddie Cantor, Cliff "Ukulele Ike" Edwards, the Albertina Rasch Dancers, and singer and balletic dancer Ruth Etting, who, like Mary Eaton, served as a sort of stand-in for Marilyn Miller. To Ziegfeld, the *Follies'* grand return would not be complete without his favorite star, Will Rogers. Currently serving as the mayor of Beverly Hills and recovering from gallbladder surgery, Will was unlikely to accept Ziegfeld's offer, but this did not stop the producer from sending relentless telegrams to try to convince him. The first started out by expressing concern for Will's health:

I READ IN THE PAPERS YOU ARE SICK I ALWAYS WAS WORRIED ABOUT THE TERRIBLE LIFE YOU WERE LIVING IN DUMPS AND ON RAILROAD TRAINS NO HUMAN BEING CAN STAND THIS LIFE I HOPE HOWEVER IT IS NOTHING SERIOUS ALL WE HAVE THAT IS WORTHWHILE IS OUR HEALTH AND I HOPE YOU WILL REALIZE IT IN TIME AND GIVE UP BARNSTORMING AND COME TO NEW YORK GO IN THE FOLLIES

AUGUST FIRST AND GET YOURSELF A NICE COUNTRY PLACE WITH A
POLO FIELD AND REST FOR AT LEAST THREE OR FOUR MONTHS . . .
NOW MAKE ME VERY HAPPY AND SEND ME A WIRE THAT YOU WILL
OPEN WITH THE FOLLIES . . . I KNOW YOU REMEMBER THE DAY YOU
TOLD ME THAT IF YOU EVER GOT FOUR HUNDRED DOLLARS A WEEK
YOU WOULD BE SATISFIED . . . NOW LOOK AT YOUR DARN SALARY I
NEED SOME OF THE ROGERS LUCK IN THE NEXT FOLLIES AND YOU
HAVE TO GIVE IT TO ME IF ONLY FOR A MINUTE . . . LOVE FLO[49]

Will did not agree to return to the *Follies*, despite continual prodding from Ziegfeld. After a month, Ziegfeld began to mention other people who would like to see the comedian return. His frustration at Will's refusals is evident in the following telegram, which he failed to sign with his customary "Love Flo": "WE ALL SEND LOVE WERE REHEARSING THE FOLLIES AND EDDIE CANTOR AND THE REST OF US MISS YOU TERRIBLY ZIEGFELD."[50] Will wrote back: "I was very sorry to be out of the show, but I couldent [sic] help it . . . thank you boss. You are a good boss."[51]

The *Follies* opened without Will on August 16, 1927, and played until January 7, 1928, at which time it went on tour. By fall of 1928, Will had returned to Broadway in a musical called *Three Cheers*. Bearing no grudges, Ziegfeld sent him a complimentary telegram and, proving that he did indeed have a sense of humor, wrote: "BUT REMEMBER YOU ARE ONLY PINCH HITTING [in *Three Cheers*] YOU STILL BELONG TO ME SORRY I CANNOT BE THERE TONIGHT BUT I AM SENDING THE BOSS BILLIE LOVE FLO."[52]

Even without Will's help, the *Ziegfeld Follies of 1927* reclaimed the iconic revue's former glory. The show had not one hit song but four: "Shaking the Blues Away," "My Blue Heaven," "The Prisoner's Song," and "St. Louis Blues." Ruth Etting's performance of "Shaking the Blues Away" was the best jazz number thus far in the *Follies*. The tune perfectly encapsulated the 1920s notion that melancholia could be swept away with dance, and it was performed as an all-out spectacle with several different choruses, including the Jazzbow Girls, the Albertina Rasch Dancers, and the Banjo Ingénues. Also included in the show was an all-female orchestra, a 1920s craze that was later hilariously spoofed in the 1959 film *Some Like It Hot*. The new *Follies* had fewer girls serving as mere models for extravagant gowns and living tableaux; all the glorified women were animated and in constant motion. The omission of models posing as live paintings must have pained Ziegfeld, for bringing art to life was his passion. But he had given up fighting the things he hated about the 1920s. By embracing the decade and its trends, he increased his own success.

Ziegfeld knew that one secret to success had not changed over the decades: give the audience plenty of comedy. The show had no semblance of a plot, but Eddie Cantor, as the sole comic headliner, acted as its unifying element. Eddie penned most of his own material for the show. In one particularly humorous skit, "The Taxicab Scene," a pushy woman escorted the bashful Eddie home. When she became fed up with his lack of flirtation, she declared: "You're the coldest proposition!"

"I'm sorry," Eddie replied. "I'm sorry we're not the same temperature."

The woman eventually kicked Eddie out of the cab, shouting that he'd better walk the remaining ten miles home "or else agree to be mauled with affection."

"I guess I'll else," Eddie decided, slinking back to the cab.[53]

The next skit used another recipe for success Ziegfeld had learned from the earliest *Follies*: use topical events as the basis for comedy. Eddie was in his element impersonating the mayor of New York City, Jimmy Walker. The routine included two comical Irving Berlin songs, "Jimmy" and "My New York." In this act, Eddie had plenty of opportunity for impromptu additions. When Charles Lindbergh attended one performance, Eddie asked him: "Do you find air pockets too tight when flying over Scotland?" Another guest was a surgeon famous for operating on Jack Dempsey's nose. The doctor was the epitome of dignity, but Eddie noticed that after each skit, his collar became increasingly wilted from exuberant laughter, so Eddie threw him a new collar after each scene. Another object of an impromptu joke was a dog that began scratching itself with a hind paw during a skit entitled "The New York Dog Shop." Eddie likened the dog's scratching motion to strumming and dubbed the dog "Ukulele Ike." Unfortunately, the dog refused to repeat his performance the next night.

Juxtaposing Eddie's comedy routines was a string of sentimental songs, proving that Ziegfeld had not completely denounced the past for jazz's sake. Violins and harps replaced banjos and pianos as pairs of lovers sang sweet ballads such as "It All Belongs to Me," "When You Were Sweet Sixteen," and "The Prisoner's Song," a mournful tune sung by a jailed man who wishes to return to his girl. Eddie Cantor also sang "My Blue Heaven," glorifying family life. Although Berlin was the show's primary composer, both "The Prisoner's Song" and "My Blue Heaven" were written by others in 1924 (the former by Guy Massey and the latter by Walter Donaldson and George Whiting). After those soothing melodies, a stirring production number returned the audience to the Jazz Age. "It's Up to the Band" flooded the stage with gold—gold costumes, gold pianos, and a gold backdrop. Two staircases curved around either side of the stage, and chorus members descended the steps flanked by twelve pianos, each with a different girl seated at it.

In the second act, another jazz number, "Jungle Jingle," conspicuously portrayed jazz's wildness. Each girl in the routine was dressed as a different jungle animal. Claire Luce wore a gown made of ostrich feathers and entered the stage riding an ostrich. Press agent Bernard Sobel, at Ziegfeld's insistence, had planted a dozen stories in the papers about the live bird that carried Luce across the stage. When Ziegfeld dragged Sobel to Burkeley Crest with a new angle on the story, Sobel protested, "The papers won't touch another ostrich story from us, Mr. Ziegfeld. We've done everything with that bird except have it run for mayor of New York."

"This one will have them tearing up their front pages. Listen—ostrichnappers! . . . A gang of hoodlums sneaks backstage during a performance and tries to make off with the ostrich."

"Why? Why would anyone kidnap an ostrich?"

"For the feathers of course."

Ziegfeld suggested that Eddie Cantor could spot the thieves and yell "Police!" as he jumped on the bird's back—the ostrich's cue to prance onstage. Everyone would think it was part of the act. Patricia later wrote that, due to the many wild stories Ziegfeld had planted in the papers, editors came to see him as the boy who cried wolf. They did not believe the tale of the ostrich-nappers, but at least Ziegfeld had enjoyed inventing it.[54]

The 1927 *Follies'* booming business showed no signs of slowing down. It appeared that Ziegfeld would recoup the $289,000 he had spent on the production and then some. However, what could have been one of the longest running editions of the series came to an abrupt end after 167 performances. Eddie Cantor, the show's sole comic, had shouldered so much of the burden that he became utterly exhausted and was unable to continue. Eddie later wrote that the show took five years off his life. In addition, Eddie's wife had just given birth to their fifth daughter. When Ziegfeld jestingly questioned the harried new father's growing family, Eddie quipped, "It's for you, Flo. I'm raising my own Albertina Rasch ballet."[55]

All joking aside, Eddie could no longer shrug off his exhaustion. "If you're tired take a few days off," Ziegfeld wrote in response to Eddie's complaints of fatigue. Eddie knew he would need more than a few days, and he also knew that Ziegfeld had little patience for weakness or illness in himself or others. Ziegfeld was so incensed by Eddie's untimely exit that he brought the comedian before Actors Equity, and surprisingly, the union sided with the producer. Though Eddie said he was too ill to work, witnesses claimed they had seen him strolling about town. "If you've seen me around town, it's because I've been visiting a Park Avenue physician each day. I'm sick," Eddie declared. Ziegfeld was not convinced and told him, "I've always treated you like a son and you're acting like a naughty expensive child, trying to ruin me!" Ziegfeld stood to lose $35,000 if Eddie quit.[56]

Ziegfeld was brokenhearted and filled with shame when he learned that Eddie was truly ill with pleurisy. The comedian was hardly able to breathe, much less perform. During a sojourn to Billie Burke Island, Ziegfeld sent Eddie the following wire by way of apology: "CAUGHT A LITTLE BEAR AT SIX THIS MORNING SHALL I BRING HIM FOR YOUR KIDS LOVE AND KISSES YOUR FATHER FLO."[57] Ziegfeld urged Eddie to take a rest cure in Palm Springs. When Eddie regained his health and returned to New York, Ziegfeld welcomed him back "with open arms" and began to hunt for another starring vehicle for the comedian.[58]

The past year had been a tumultuous one for Ziegfeld. He had started the year convinced that he could never please New York critics and should relocate to Palm Beach indefinitely. But now that he had his own theater, a masterful revue, and a fresh musical comedy to his name, he had regained his status on Broadway. As 1927 neared its end, Ziegfeld found himself preoccupied not with a new musical for Eddie Cantor or another *Follies* but something entirely different. The new project was neither a comedy nor a drama; it fell into a category all its own. The name of that production was *Show Boat*.

18

Splendor and Intelligence

"Last night I heard the first act of *Show Boat*. . . . This is the best musical comedy I have ever been fortunate to get hold of; it looks wonderful . . . this is the opportunity of my life."[1] Ziegfeld wrote this on November 26, 1926, immediately after Jerome Kern and Oscar Hammerstein II presented their adaptation of Edna Ferber's novel to him. Though a common theatrical myth persists that Ziegfeld was hesitant to produce *Show Boat* because of its heavy themes and scant opportunities to present chorus girls, these words prove otherwise. Only two days later, the *New York Telegraph* already contained an item about his plans to produce the show.

Jerome Kern was the first to approach Edna Ferber with the idea that her 1926 novel be adapted into a musical comedy. The author was hesitant at first, but after Kern secured Hammerstein as his librettist, she became more enthusiastic. When Kern and Hammerstein completed the music for the first act, they presented their compositions to Ziegfeld. As noted by Broadway historian Miles Kreuger, "Who else would they bring them to? Ziegfeld was God, the greatest producer of his time, and he was the only man they felt had the vision, the power, and the influence to be able to put it on. Ziegfeld at once leapt to do it."[2] This last statement may have been true, but Ziegfeld had his concerns. "Hammerstein's libretto has not got a chance with the critics," he complained to Kern. "We cannot do a musical with all this sadness."[3] Ziegfeld recommended using the character of Captain Andy as comic relief, and Hammerstein acceded to this request. Despite his own problems with comedians and comedy, Ziegfeld had been observing audiences for more than thirty years, and he knew that humor always won them over.

Show Boat the musical and *Show Boat* the novel are entirely different in theme, although the spirit of the novel remains in the play. Usually a musical adds a light twist to a sad story, but with the exception of Captain

Andy's comedic quips, Hammerstein's treatment gave a dark twist to a light story. Ferber categorized her novel as a "frivolous, escapist book . . . *Show Boat* carries no message, it is just a romantic novel about a rather glamorous phase of American life . . . *Show Boat* . . . was just fun."[4] The adjectives Ferber used to describe her book—escapist, fun, romantic, glamorous—bring to mind a Ziegfeld show. However, Hammerstein was not trying to make *Show Boat* fit the mold of a typical Ziegfeld production. The composer was progressive in his political views and had an optimistic vision of a world without racial tension. Ferber was not an activist; in a 1928 article, when asked to describe her view of an ideal world, she made no mention of ending racial intolerance. The theme of racial prejudice in *Show Boat* was purely Hammerstein's brainchild.[5]

The story of *Show Boat* the musical begins in 1887, a time when traveling showboats were at their peak. The *Cotton Blossom* is one of the most popular floating theaters, as is its captain. Captain Andy opens the show with an enthusiastic spiel about the attractions the townspeople have in store for them—namely, the voluptuous singer Julie La Verne. Andy's wife, Parthy, is an irascible woman who serves as a hilarious contrast to the boisterous captain. Their daughter, Magnolia, is a sweet and unaffected girl who dreams of performing onstage. A handsome and notorious gambler, Gaylord Ravenal, falls in love with her, but they keep their feelings for each other private. The novel focuses mainly on Magnolia; however, the character of Julie is far more prominent in the play. Julie's story acts as a springboard for Hammerstein's agenda. For her entire life, Julie has kept the secret that she has a drop of Negro blood in her heritage, and now she is in love with a white man named Steve. Julie and Magnolia become friends and discuss their respective problems with the men they love. Gaylord has been told to move on due to his shady lifestyle, and Magnolia asks Joe, a black laborer on the levee, if he knows Gaylord's whereabouts. Joe responds that the only one who can answer her is "Ol' Man River." Then the sheriff boards the showboat and informs everyone that Julie is black and that she and Steve are guilty of miscegenation. Hammerstein added an effective scene in which Steve cuts Julie's finger, puts his lips to her blood, and declares, "I'm part Negro too." Steve and Julie leave the ship before any more chaos ensues, and Magnolia replaces Julie in the show. Gaylord, who failed to heed the demand that he move on, takes on Steve's roles; he renounces his bachelor lifestyle, and he and Magnolia marry. *Show Boat* depicts the plays performed by Magnolia, Gaylord, and the rest of the company, thus introducing the show-within-a-show concept, which was quite innovative in 1927. As an onstage audience watches the acts on the showboat, the actual audience in the Ziegfeld Theatre becomes involved in both Magnolia and Gaylord playing their roles on the showboat stage and the actors playing their roles on the Ziegfeld stage.

The play's next act opens at the Chicago World's Fair in 1893, a setting clearly influenced by Ziegfeld. Sandow and Little Egypt are even mentioned in the opening dialogue. Gaylord has deserted Magnolia and their young daughter, Kim, in favor of his old life as a gambler (one wonders whether Ziegfeld saw himself in the Gaylord character). Magnolia is the typical female heroine portrayed in Ferber's novels—independent and able to succeed without a man's help. Show business is Magnolia's ticket to independence (as it is for the heroines in *Sally* and *Betsy*). She looks for work in none other than the Trocadero, the nightclub opened by Ziegfeld and his father. The manager of the Trocadero is modeled after Ziegfeld himself, and Hammerstein pokes fun at Ziegfeld's reputation for producing lavish shows while simultaneously worrying about their financial losses. One line has the manager bemoan the cost of his "two thousand dollar production."[6]

Unbeknownst to Magnolia, Julie also works at the nightclub. Steve has left her, and the brokenhearted Julie is now an alcoholic. She knows her chance for stardom has passed, so she sacrifices her job in the hope that Magnolia might have a chance for a better future. Other than the racial theme, "the brilliant revisioning of Julie as the prima donna of the Trocadero Restaurant who sacrifices her job . . . [for] Magnolia" added the most depth and intensity to the show.[7] Magnolia is successful at the Trocadero, and she enrolls her daughter in a convent school. A brief scene shows Gaylord visiting Kim at the school and singing her the optimistic tune "Make Believe" as a sort of farewell. Magnolia and Kim ultimately return to the *Cotton Blossom*.

The story fast-forwards to 1927. Kim is now a young lady, following in her mother's footsteps as a performer on the *Cotton Blossom*. One day, a middle-aged man appears on the boat; it is none other than Gaylord. Magnolia, without any resentment for the pain he has caused her, takes his hand and leads him onboard. The ending is not true to the novel, but Hammerstein wanted the play to conclude "in a theatrically happy fash-

Patricia's playhouse, a miniature re-creation of Mount Vernon, on the grounds of Burkeley Crest, circa 1923. (Courtesy of Hastings Historical Society)

Billie Burke relaxing in the garden at Burkeley Crest with one of the Ziegfelds' many dogs, circa early 1920s. (Courtesy of Historical Ziegfeld Group)

Barbara Stanwyck photographed by Alfred Cheney Johnson circa 1923, during the time she danced in the *Follies*. (Courtesy of Historical Ziegfeld Group)

Eddie Cantor in his popular blackface persona, 1923. (Courtesy of Performing Arts Encyclopedia—Musical Theater—The Library of Congress Celebrates the Songs of America)

Mary Eaton and Eddie Cantor in *Kid Boots* (1923). (Photo by White Studio; courtesy of Billy Rose Theatre Division, New York Public Library for the Performing Arts)

Louise Brooks as a Ziegfeld girl, circa 1925. Although she appeared in only two of his shows, Ziegfeld had a portrait of her hung in his office. (Courtesy of Jerry Murbach)

Ziegfeld behind the cluttered desk in his office. Note the black spectacles in his hands, which Billie Burke once described as "horrid." (From *Theatre* magazine, 1926; courtesy of Historical Ziegfeld Group)

The fabulous façade of the Ziegfeld Theatre designed by Joseph Urban, circa 1927. (Courtesy of Library of Congress Prints and Photographs Division)

Ethelind Terry in *Rio Rita* (1927). (Courtesy of Historical Ziegfeld Group)

The Albertina Rasch Dancers in *Rio Rita* (1927). (Courtesy of Historical Ziegfeld Group)

Claire Luce being painted by artist Clarence Busch in the *Ziegfeld Follies of 1927*. The extravagant ostrich feather outfit was typical of costumer John Harkrider's style. (Courtesy of Historical Ziegfeld Group)

Oscar Hammerstein II, Ziegfeld, and Jerome Kern outside the Ziegfeld Theatre only hours before the premiere of *Show Boat,* December 1927. (Authors' collection)

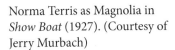

Norma Terris as Magnolia in *Show Boat* (1927). (Courtesy of Jerry Murbach)

Helen Morgan as Julie in *Show Boat* (1927). (Courtesy of Jerry Murbach)

The show-within-a-show scene in *Show Boat* (1927). Charles Winninger is playing the violin in the foreground, and Norma Terris on the stage at the left. (Photo by White Studio; courtesy of Billy Rose Theatre Division, New York Public Library for the Performing Arts)

Marilyn Miller in *Rosalie* (1928). (Courtesy of Jerry Murbach)

Ziegfeld, immaculately dressed, circa 1927. (Authors' collection)

Ziegfeld looking dapper with a mustache, circa 1928. (Courtesy of Hastings Historical Society)

Eddie Cantor (standing) and Ziegfeld in Ziegfeld's office, 1928. (Courtesy of Historical Ziegfeld Group)

A poster for the film *Glorifying the American Girl* (1929), starring Mary Eaton. (Courtesy of Historical Ziegfeld Group)

A scene from the film *Whoopee!* (1930). The elaborate Indian headdresses are true to those John Harkrider designed for the original show. (Courtesy of Historical Ziegfeld Group)

Ruth Etting in the nostalgic *Ziegfeld Follies of 1931.* (Courtesy of Jerry Murbach)

Ziegfeld with a group of his glorified girls, 1931. (Courtesy of Historical Ziegfeld Group)

Ziegfeld, Billie, and Patricia, circa 1931. (Courtesy of Historical Ziegfeld Group)

Fred Astaire and Marilyn Miller in *Smiles* (1931). (Courtesy of Historical Ziegfeld Group)

A program for *Hot-Cha!* (1932). Bert Lahr is surrounded by four glamour girls (counterclockwise from top): June MacCloy, Marjorie White, Lupe Velez, and June Knight. (Courtesy of Historical Ziegfeld Group)

HOT-CHA!

Cover of an album of recordings from Ziegfeld's short-lived 1932 radio program, *Follies of the Air*. The photograph of Ziegfeld is circa 1912. (Courtesy of Historical Ziegfeld Group)

Ziegfeld and Patricia, circa 1932. (Courtesy of Historical Ziegfeld Group)

Songwriters Jerome Kern
and George Gershwin in the
mid-1930s, when they both
moved to Hollywood.
(Courtesy of Library of
Congress Prints and
Photographs Division)

Will Rogers and Billie Burke in *Doubting Thomas* (1935). (Courtesy of Historical
Ziegfeld Group)

Elaborate advertisement for the film *The Great Ziegfeld* (1936) in *Variety* magazine, depicting a larger-than-life tableau. (Authors' collection)

Advertisement for the film *The Great Ziegfeld* (1936) in *Variety* magazine. This famous scene, based on "A Pretty Girl Is Like a Melody," shows a typical Ziegfeldian set—one with plenty of steps. (Authors' collection)

Left to right: Luise Rainer as Anna Held, William Powell as Ziegfeld, and Myrna Loy as Billie Burke in *The Great Ziegfeld* (1936). (Courtesy of Jerry Murbach)

Left to right: Paul Robeson, Irene Dunne, Hattie McDaniel, and Helen Morgan in the 1936 film version of *Show Boat*. (Courtesy of Jerry Murbach)

A scene from the film extravaganza *Ziegfeld Follies* (1946). Lucille Ball is pictured to the left. (Courtesy of Jerry Murbach)

Georges Guetary in the "Stairway to Paradise" number in *An American in Paris* (1951). The design of this number was heavily influenced by Ziegfeld's productions. (Courtesy of Jerry Murbach)

Barbra Streisand as Fanny
Brice and Walter Pidgeon
as Ziegfeld in the film
Funny Girl (1968).
(Courtesy of Historical
Ziegfeld Group)

The beautiful statue
marking Blanche
Burke's grave at
Kenisco Cemetery,
Valhalla, New York.
(Courtesy of
Historical Ziegfeld
Group)

ion."[8] The show ends with a rendition of "Ol' Man River," sung by Joe as an old man. By having Joe sing "Ol' Man River" in 1887 and again in 1927, the play shows "how the roots of the present reached back to the world of show boats and ultimately to the sources of American popular music in black music making."[9]

Though Julie is the one who possesses "Negro blood," Kim and Magnolia sing in a style more typical of black entertainers than Julie does, showing the influence of black music in white culture.[10] This was nothing new in Ziegfeld shows. Anna Held and Fanny Brice had imitated black singers, but Bert Williams is the best example of Ziegfeld's contribution to making black music—sung by a black singer—a part of mainstream entertainment. Had Williams still been alive, he would have been Ziegfeld's actor of choice for the part of Joe.

Another black entertainer, Paul Robeson, was the inspiration behind the lyrics for Jerome Kern's masterpiece "Ol' Man River." According to Kern, "the melody of 'Ol' Man River' was conceived immediately after" he first heard Robeson's deeply mournful, soulful singing style.[11] When writing the lyrics for Kern's music, Hammerstein decided they should have the same tidiness as the plot of the show. According to Hammerstein, the Ferber novel lacked "the tightness a play requires. I thought we lacked something to make it cohesive. . . . And the one focal influence I could find was the river."[12] Reading the poignant lyrics of "Ol' Man River," anyone—black or white—can relate to the singer's longing: "Ah gits weary / an' sick of tryin' / Ah'm tired of livin' / An' scared of dyin', / But ol' man river, / He jes' keeps rolling along."[13]

Ziegfeld, Hammerstein, and Kern could envision only Robeson in the part of Joe. However, Robeson was more interested in performing in bohemian Greenwich Village cafés and did not want to sacrifice his art for a commercial show. Ziegfeld shelved *Show Boat* in the hope that he might eventually convince Robeson, but as 1927 wore on and Robeson was still not amenable, Ziegfeld finally cast another talented black singer, Jules Bledsoe, as Joe.

Aside from Joe, the most important casting choice was for the character of Julie. The performer who won the role was Helen Morgan, a nightclub singer who had once been described as "the sad eyed crooner of blues songs who sang her way . . . right into the slightly alcoholic heart of Broadway."[14] Like Julie, Morgan had a drinking problem. She once made headlines when the police raided and closed her nightclub. Undeterred, she opened another club—which the police also raided. Journalists were quick to mention in their coverage of the raids that Morgan was the star of Ziegfeld's new show. Unlike the early days of his career, when he manufactured publicity to sell his shows, Ziegfeld now tried to avoid scandal. He announced to the press that Morgan was moving to Great Neck and renouncing her clubbing lifestyle in favor of country living. Nevertheless, Morgan's hedonism continued, and it proved to be a boon to ticket sales. Ultimately, however, audiences remembered Morgan not because of her life offstage but because of her wistful renditions of "Can't Help Lovin' that Man of Mine" and "Bill."

The show seemed to be well on its way, but in February 1927 it had to be postponed because Ziegfeld had again pushed himself to the point of illness. The *New York Times* reported that the play would not resume preproduction until September. In the interim, Ziegfeld would rest at Burkeley Crest to recover from his "severe attack of bronchitis and general exhaustion."[15] Meanwhile, rumors swirled that by the time production started again, Marilyn Miller would be back in the Ziegfeld fold and playing the leading role in *Show Boat*.

While Ziegfeld recovered, critics and would-be audiences had much more than Marilyn Miller and Helen Morgan to discuss. Because of its racial themes, *Show Boat* had become controversial. In the show's original opening, Hammerstein had written a scene in which black laborers sing: "Niggers all work on de Mississippi / Niggers all work while the white folks play."[16] Ultimately, Hammerstein changed the *n*-word to "darkies." More controversy revolved around the proposed intermixing of black men and white women onstage, which was unheard of in 1927. Although Jules Bledsoe was African American, the actress playing Joe's wife was a white woman in blackface (Tess Gardella, whose stage persona was Aunt Jemima). Ziegfeld broke new ground by hiring an all-black chorus and black actors for most of the parts that called for them; however, they were still separated from the white actors for the majority of the play. For instance, the blacks would be on a balcony while the whites were on the ground floor during any given number. Yet Ziegfeld gave his black performers the full star treatment. After his death, a reporter for an African American newspaper stated that the black race had lost "a friend" and that Ziegfeld had been responsible for making African American chorines "glorified beauties."[17] Billie Burke concurred, asserting that her husband "lavished more attention on them [the black actors], it often seemed to me, than he did on some of the others."[18]

Ziegfeld devoted equal attention to the casting of the white characters as he did to the black ones. He chose Edna May Oliver as Parthy, Captain Andy's horse-faced, busybody wife. Although Oliver was a dramatic actress, she pulled off her comedic lines well. In one scene she grows angry when Magnolia refuses to tell her how Gaylord makes his money. Parthy huffs: "How I hate not to know things!" Kreuger observed that this line "always brought down the house." Charles Winninger, a vaudevillian and *Follies* veteran, was cast as Parthy's husband, Andy, and he too brought down the house. In one show-within-a-show scene in which the leading cast member takes ill, Andy lowers the curtain and acts out for the audience how the play would have continued. He plays both the hero and the villain, "whacking himself in the jaw so hard that he knocks himself down." He then wrestles with himself on the floor, one moment insulting himself and the next speaking in a falsetto voice as the heroine begging for mercy. He ends by smashing a water pitcher on "the imaginary head of the villain" and states that he has succeeded in killing the "dirty rascal deader'n a doornail."[19]

For the supporting roles of Frank and Ellie (two actors on the showboat), Ziegfeld hired the husband-and-wife vaudeville team of Sammy White and Eva Puck. They had caused a sensation in Rodgers and Hart's *The Girl Friend* in 1926. Their *Show Boat* characters had a relationship similar to that of Fred and Adele Astaire: a comic, sibling-like bond full of slangy repartee.[20] According to *Variety*'s review for one of *Show Boat*'s earliest tryouts, Puck and White's comedy and dancing received the most enthusiastic applause. Their most popular number was "Life upon the Wicked Stage."

As for the role of Magnolia, the rumors were true: Ziegfeld wanted Marilyn Miller. However, she was still playing hard to get. Ziegfeld persisted in negotiating a new contract with her, but he had to wait until her obligations to Charles Dillingham had been fulfilled. Marilyn must have felt at least a twinge of jealousy when another actress was cast as Magnolia. The lucky lady was Norma Terris, a vaudeville comedienne who had worked with Hammerstein in 1922 and was also the wife of Ziegfeld's friend Doc Wagner. Like Marilyn, she had made her name by mimicking current dramatic and musical stars. Terris considered herself perfect for the role: both her grandfathers had worked on the Mississippi River, and she claimed that the plot of *Show Boat* was virtually her mother's life story.[21] Terris was the one who inserted imitations into the acts of the Magnolia and Kim characters (she portrayed both mother and daughter). Apparently, her impersonations were so popular that they continued for an hour before the show moved on.

For the role of Gaylord, Ziegfeld hired Howard Marsh, a Shubert-employed operetta star who had made his name in *The Student Prince* (1924). According to Edna Ferber, his voice had a "constipated quality" that did not bring to mind the charismatic Gaylord Ravenal.[22] However, the contrast between Marsh's trained voice and Terris's untrained one was an interesting experience, although some critics complained that it was interesting in a negative way.

After a year of casting and preparations, *Show Boat* finally went into production. Norma Terris recalled that Ziegfeld was present at every rehearsal. She described his "imposing figure" entering the theater and calling across the footlights, "What the hell's this? You're dragging around like a lot of corpses. . . . Any of you boys and girls too tired to go on, please get out and go home." Eddie Cantor, now fully recovered from his illness, often accompanied the cranky Ziegfeld to rehearsals. The comedian improved Ziegfeld's spirits, much to the relief of the cast. "I loved to be with him and he seemed to like having me," Eddie said. "He certainly knew he could always get an honest opinion [from me]."[23] Journalist Djuna Barnes also offered her opinion to Ziegfeld during a backstage visit. She told him she thought the show would be a success. "Well, that does not prevent me from suffering the tortures of the damned, does it?" Ziegfeld groaned in a soft monotone as he held his head in his hands. Barnes turned to Ziegfeld's press agent, Bernard Sobel, and asked, "Often like this?"

"Always," Sobel replied.

"That so, what's the reason?"

"Nobody knows."

"Isn't he ever cheerful?"

"Oh always," Sobel replied.

"But this is despair."

"Dear me no; that's temperament."[24]

Sobel's description of Ziegfeld as cheerful hardly seems accurate; his temper was far more evident. Ziegfeld's lack of patience during rehearsals was not surprising, given that many sessions lasted up to twenty hours. Years later, the November 27, 1939, issue of *Life* magazine featured artist Doris Lee's painting that vividly depicts a rehearsal of the show: Kern is frazzled at the piano, his hands going in both directions over the keys. Goldie, Ziegfeld's secretary, sits in the front row taking copious notes on a sheet of paper. Joseph Urban (whom Ziegfeld had employed to create the sets) sits back, critically surveying the set while holding a smoking cigar between two fingers. The scene director stands holding a script while Ziegfeld looms above them all with an upside-down pipe in one hand and pointing toward the stage with the other. He looks like a man with an important mission to accomplish. Much of Ziegfeld's impatience stemmed not from the actors but from the backstage artists. John Harkrider and Joseph Urban were constantly at odds. Ziegfeld seemed to be the only person happy with Harkrider's presence. Harkrider wanted everything Hammerstein had written to be revised, and he demanded that the scene painters color the sets to his specifications, thus overriding Urban's orders. Urban complained, "It is an insult. They [Hammerstein and Bernie McDonald, Urban's set builder] threaten to quit. I, too. After all these years, Flo, it is like we are droppings from a cow." Ziegfeld acted as a mediator and negotiated a compromise that "kept Harkrider out of everybody's hair. In return, Hammerstein agreed not to interfere with staging concerns."[25]

As much as Ziegfeld respected Urban's expertise, he wanted to go with his customary method of using bright lights and decadent costumes for the show. But, at the urging of Kern and Urban, he sacrificed his own taste and agreed to use authentic costumes and realistic sets. Hammerstein, Kern, and Ferber had all traveled to the South "to get a feel of the atmosphere."[26] Still, Ziegfeld could not put aside all his tastes and eccentricities. He insisted that the female performers wear silk stockings fresh from the refrigerator. What Ziegfeld hoped to accomplish with the cooled hosiery is up for debate, but perhaps he thought it would keep the cast members more alert and peppy under the hot stage lights.

By December 1927, the show was finally ready for out-of-town tryouts. Ziegfeld, as usual, was sure the show would fail. He remained convinced that a musical could not have real drama and still be a success. "I think that before we opened . . . he thought all that story stuff would be cut out,"

Hammerstein recalled. "What would remain would be pretty costumes and scenery and the tunes and the girls and the comedian."[27] At first, it seemed that Ziegfeld's dark predictions were correct. He moved from the lobby to the stairs to the balcony on opening night, with Goldie and Eddie following his every step. They all keenly noted that there was little applause, even after the show's big numbers. When the scene closest to Ziegfeld's heart, set at the 1893 World's Fair, failed to bring cheers, he broke into sobs. "They don't like it! Goddamn it, I knew they wouldn't!"[28] The final curtain fell, and still the audience did not applaud. "Well, now I've really done it," Ziegfeld muttered to Goldie. "No curtain calls. That means failure." Suddenly there was the sound of one person applauding, and then another and another until the entire audience was standing and cheering; it went on for five minutes. Ziegfeld puffed on his cigar with the trace of a smile on his lips. "I think it's going to be all right," he finally said.[29]

The *New York Times* did not review the show until a week after its New York opening at the Ziegfeld Theatre on December 27, 1927, but word of mouth proved to be enough for theatergoers. Ziegfeld arrived at his theater the morning after opening night to find a line wrapped around the block, waiting to buy tickets. When Brooks Atkinson of the *Times* finally did review the show, he heralded it as "one of those epochal works about which garrulous old men gabble for twenty-five hours after the scenery has rattled off to the storehouse."[30] *Show Boat* was one of the few Ziegfeld shows that was profitable. A year later, the show was still running and had made $2.5 million. Ziegfeld was now a multimillionaire.[31]

Ziegfeld had always been a risk taker. His biggest hits contained elements that could have alienated audiences if not done tastefully (e.g., sexuality, political satire, racial and class discrimination). But the "Ziegfeld touch," as Ziegfeld himself defined it, consisted of "splendor and intelligence." *Show Boat* pleased theatergoers because it respected their intelligence, yet it still included plenty of glamour, spectacle, and comedy. Historian and critic Hal Prince observed that the show was "seismic . . . that's for sure. The earth shook."[32]

When comparing *Show Boat* with the other popular musicals of the 1927–1928 theater season, one can see why it was so seismic. In *Good News,* the plot's main dilemma was whether the captain of the football team could pass his exams and thus be allowed to play in the big game. George Gershwin's *Funny Face* was a light romantic comedy about a shy bookkeeper who is discovered by a fashion photographer in Paris. Both productions boasted catchy tunes, witty dialogue, and excellent star attractions, but they did not match the scope and innovation of *Show Boat*. Indeed, no show ever would. Thomas Hischak, author of *The Oxford Companion to the American Musical*, called *Show Boat* "the first masterpiece and arguably still the finest musical play [in history]."[33]

Because *Show Boat* was unlike formulaic, star-driven Broadway shows, it could be revived again and again without losing any of its appeal to audiences. In the *Follies*, Ziegfeld had created an ideal American girl who could transcend time and changing definitions of beauty. With *Show Boat*, he created an ideal play that could also transcend time and tastes. Musician Michael Feinstein noted that "*Show Boat* didn't change musical theater overnight, or even over a decade. Through the rest of the twenties and into the thirties, stars were still the paramount consideration, followed by songs."[34] However, *Show Boat* paved the way for a new era of book musicals: sophisticated, fully realized works with meaningful plots and top-notch scores to accompany the story line. Though Ziegfeld did not produce another serious book musical and continued to invest in the escapist shows he preferred, *Show Boat* had cemented his reputation as Broadway's greatest producer.

"Suddenly the music could say something with an integrity that it hadn't quite said before," singer-actress Julie Andrews said of *Show Boat* in her narration of the 2004 documentary *Broadway: The American Musical*. "Thanks to Kern, thanks to Hammerstein, and thanks to the performers, but mostly thanks to Ziegfeld, who made it possible. But it was a hard act to follow."[35] It was indeed a hard act to follow, but Ziegfeld never stopped trying. Will Rogers observed of his friend: "His hardest opposition has been himself. If he had been new every year, and that particular show was his first, why each one would've been heralded as a masterpiece, but naturally they had to compete with each other."[36]

Ziegfeld's newfound financial security offered him the ideal opportunity to slow his pace and focus more on his wife and daughter. But Ziegfeld's competition with himself was a relentless battle. Billie continued to support his professional ambition, even though it forced her to become increasingly self-reliant.

"I was a part-time actress, a part-time artist, a part-time professional," Billie Burke wrote of her life.[37] Billie had called herself an actress and a professional for more than twenty years, but it was not until 1927 that she referred to herself as an artist. Billie stated, "[it] is supremely difficult for women to be artists" because "an artist is a person who devotes himself ruthlessly, even selfishly to his craft or skill, forgetting every other consideration."[38] Billie's refusal to neglect her roles as mother, wife, and hostess of Burkeley Crest delayed her reentrance into the theater or film (she had not made a picture since 1921) and kept her from reaching the same professional peak as her husband. She was proud of her accomplishments as wife and mother: these were her masterpieces. But Ziegfeld's newfound glory as the producer of *Show Boat* was contagious. Billie had been yearning to return to the stage, and at last she did. Her career also reached a milestone in 1927, though hers was of personal rather than historical significance.

Billie had become more independent in her personal life as Ziegfeld's professional obligations kept him away from home more frequently. She now intended to transfer that independence into her professional life and achieve success without Ziegfeld's help. Billie's choice to return to the stage was partly because the theater was simply in her blood and she did not feel whole when not involved in it. But another factor in her decision was the desire to prove to herself that she could manage her own career. She needed to know that she could support herself. Ziegfeld was a millionaire now, but Billie knew he could lose the profits of an entire show in one night of bad luck. Though he had cut back on his gambling, as he had promised, the fever had not left him completely. Billie reluctantly accepted Ziegfeld's weakness and no longer badgered him about it—as long as he always came home to her in the end.

By 1927, Billie was virtually her own manager and was ably choosing roles that best suited her. The show that marked the permanent exit of Billie Burke the ingénue and introduced Billie the modern sophisticate was *The Marquise*. For the first time in her career, Billie portrayed a woman her own age—a forty-two-year-old marquise and former actress. The story follows the marquise as she tries to thwart the wedding plans of her two grown children and pursue a marriage of her own with a former suitor. Noel Coward wrote the play, which in Billie's words, "means that it was smart."[39] As Billie observed, the play was quite intelligent and glittered with situational comedy and witty dialogue. When one character in the play states that he believes in self-sacrifice, the marquise replies: "You're wrong then. It's one of the most sterile forms of self-indulgence in the world."[40] *The Marquise* takes place in the eighteenth century at a chateau located a few hours from Paris. Its historical setting provided ample opportunity for Billie to wear breathtaking costumes; however, she hoped that this time her acting would garner more praise than her wardrobe. *The Marquise* turned out to be a bigger hit than any of the shows Ziegfeld had produced for her. Critics claimed that it brought the "intermittent" Billie back to a "still worshipping audience." They also noted that, by undertaking a mature role, Billie "performs a public service: those who feel middle age creeping on them will be vastly cheered at Miss Burke's portrait of forty-two."[41] *The Marquise* opened on November 14, 1927, during the run of the *Ziegfeld Follies of 1927,* and played for a respectable eighty performances.

Billie had little time to breathe between her comeback role and the production immediately following it. In May 1928, as Ziegfeld was busy managing *Show Boat* and three more upcoming musicals, Billie opened in another play that proved middle age did not have to be dull. Written by Harrison Owen, *The Happy Husband* cast Billie as a wife whose husband takes her for granted until she shoulders the guilt of a neighbor woman who has been caught having an affair with a dashing gentleman. The play may have had clever themes, but it glided over the deeper emotions Billie's character was supposed to feel as the silently suffering wife. Had the play been more skillfully written, Billie could have brought much more of herself to the role, drawing on her own feelings of being taken for granted by Ziegfeld. To Billie's dismay, reviewers mainly complimented her gorgeous costumes in the show. *The Happy Husband* opened on May 7, 1928, and closed in July after seventy-two performances.

After this disappointment, Billie had an increasingly difficult time finding leading roles that suited her. The best leading roles, particularly in comedies, were meant for younger actresses. The only meaty roles Billie could find were character parts, and she found the idea of becoming a supporting actress dispiriting, especially after her success in *The Marquise.* She had rejected a supporting role during her argument with Ziegfeld over *The Swan* (1923), and she was still averse to the idea. Billie was not ready to leave the stage again, so she decided to wait for another appropriate role to come her way.

During this time, Billie continued to be the one constant in Ziegfeld's life. In her role as Mrs. Ziegfeld and mistress of Burkeley Crest, she would never be a supporting player. Ziegfeld needed her constancy more than ever as he strove to maintain his reclaimed glory on Broadway.

During Ziegfeld's recuperation from bronchitis and exhaustion in the early stages of *Show Boat*'s production, he had taken a short sojourn to Palm Beach, where the real sun was much more conducive to his recovery than the sun-ray treatments at Burkeley Crest. The trip did not prove to be as restful as anticipated, however. While in Florida, he received a forty-two-page telegram from William Anthony McGuire, the writer of *Kid Boots*, outlining a fantastical plot for a new musical comedy.

Contrary to *Show Boat*, McGuire's play was in no danger of containing too much sadness. *Rosalie*'s themes were similar to those in *Sally* and *Sunny*, such as using disguise and mistaken identity as a means of wooing. Princess Rosalie, from the fictitious country of Romanza, is attending college in America, where she keeps her identity a secret. A West Point cadet trained in aviation (obviously modeled after Charles Lindbergh) visits Rosalie's campus, where they meet and fall in love. Matters become complicated when Rosalie's mother comes to visit, intending to take her daughter back to Romanza. Her mother would not approve of her romance with a commoner, but rather than lie to the cadet or abandon her family, Rosalie reveals her true identity. In the end, the couple is able to overcome the restrictions of social class and happily marry. *Rosalie* is different from other Cinderella-type shows, in that it breaks from the genre's popular formula. Rosalie is already wealthy and successful and, in an interesting reversal of goals, is willing to fall down the social ladder to find love.

The story did not impress Ziegfeld. He found it unremarkable and too similar to other popular musical comedies. However, the title won him over—Rosalie was his mother's name. The thought of telling the ailing matriarch that he was producing a show in her honor convinced him to accept McGuire's outline. Ziegfeld's sister, Louise, was so pleased that she convinced her wealthy, industrialist husband to help finance the production.[42] McGuire, aided by the more reliable Guy Bolton, completed the script for the show. Ziegfeld hired George and Ira Gershwin to compose the music and lyrics. Sigmund Romberg and P. G. Wodehouse assisted the Gershwin brothers with the musical score. Michael Feinstein, recalling his talks with Ira Gerswhin, stated: "Ziegfeld would demand that songs be produced in short order, even shorter than was the case with other musicals. Because Ziegfeld was so capricious in his song selection, songwriters had to overwrite more than usual, which is why George and Ira had help on the shows they did for him."[43]

Ziegfeld may have been initially unimpressed with the play, but one actress was not: Marilyn Miller. She loved both the show and its music. In February 1927 Ziegfeld officially announced that she had signed a new five-year contract with him. Charles Dillingham had agreed to release her from her contract with him, admitting that she did not have a strong enough singing voice to carry the sole musical production he intended to stage the following season: *Trilby.* "It was my suggestion that Miss Miller make the new arrangement for next season," Dillingham declared.[44] Ziegfeld was thrilled. Marilyn was still a big box-office draw; in a 1927 poll she had been named one of the most popular female actresses of the stage. Marilyn's presence in *Rosalie* gave Ziegfeld confidence that the show would be a worthy follow-up to *Show Boat.* As further security for the show's success, he engaged Jack Donahue to play the aviator's comic sidekick and Frank Morgan as Rosalie's hapless royal father.

Outwardly, Marilyn and Ziegfeld seemed to have forgotten their personal differences. Marilyn told the press she was "delighted again to place my theatrical future in his [Ziegfeld's] hands, as he is the greatest musical producer in the world."[45] Ziegfeld was equally genial toward Marilyn. In his announcement to the press regarding their reunion, he proclaimed her "unquestionably the outstanding musical comedy star of the world. It was only through misunderstanding that she left my management."[46] The "misunderstanding"—that is, Marilyn's marriage to Jack Pickford—was all but over. After Jack's return to Hollywood in September 1925, he had numerous affairs and his drug use increased. Rumors circulated that Ziegfeld had taken Marilyn back only after she agreed to divorce Jack, but those rumors were unfounded. Marilyn did not serve Jack with divorce papers until after she signed her new contract with Ziegfeld. Nevertheless, such gossip weakened Marilyn's image as a liberated woman not beholden to any man—especially Ziegfeld.

Despite Marilyn's kind words in interviews, her resentment of Ziegfeld had not softened over the years. And Ziegfeld certainly had no intention of rekindling a romance with her. Biographer Ethan Mordden aptly described their relationship as "lovers in art and business only."[47] Ziegfeld attempted to dispel the tension through humor, but Marilyn did not find him entertaining. Once Ziegfeld knocked on her dressing door and asked, tongue in cheek, "Will my Princess Rosalie deign to see me tonight?" Such gestures generally had one of two results: Marilyn would tell him to get lost, or she would order her maid to slam the door in his face.[48] Ziegfeld also tried to mend their relationship by asking Bernard Sobel to prepare a scrapbook filled with press clippings, photos, and sketches from Marilyn's shows. The book cost Ziegfeld $200 to create. When Marilyn discovered that it was a present from her employer, she tossed it under a pile of boxes and old clothes in her dressing room closet without even opening it.[49]

Marilyn had become markedly hardened since her first starring role in *Sally*. The flood of acclaim she had received for *Sunny* and the success she promised to bring to *Rosalie* did not restore the gay, ever-smiling girl her former costars recalled. The change in her personality may have been due to hubris or frustration at the lack of fulfillment in her personal life. Even before *Rosalie*, she had started to act like a diva. During preparations for *Sunny*, Hammerstein had played the entire score for her and described in painstaking detail the show's plot. Afterward, all Marilyn said was, "When do I do my tap specialty?"[50]

Audiences would never guess that Marilyn was anything but the sweetheart of Broadway when *Rosalie* opened on January 10, 1928, at the New Amsterdam Theatre. A writer for the *World* described Marilyn's entrance after an "unwarrantable absence" from the stage: "Violins tremble; trumpets blare. Fifty beautiful girls in simple peasant costumes . . . rush pell-mell onto the stage . . . squealing 'Here she comes!' Fifty hussars . . . kneel to express an emotion too strong for words. The lights swing to the gateway at the back and settle there. The house holds its breath. And on walks Marilyn Miller."[51]

Brooks Atkinson of the *New York Times* also had nothing but praise for Marilyn and the show. He lauded Marilyn's "brilliant charm and pleasing manners" that had endeared her to audiences for years. He gave a nod to Jack Donahue as well, who was now more "clown than hoofer" and, in Atkinson's opinion, the highlight of the show. Donahue kept audiences laughing uproariously by using jazz slang to refer to the royal family. At one point, he casually informed the queen that she might be a royal but she "is not so hot." Frank Morgan provided as many laughs as Donahue, particularly when he and the queen argue over his attachment to a ventriloquist's dummy he affectionately calls "Nappy" (short for Napoleon).

Atkinson also complimented the show's aesthetics. He called the peasant costumes made of satin and chiffon brilliant, the sparkle and glitter of the royal attire incomparable, and Urban's sets the epitome of glamour. Atkinson concluded his summary of *Rosalie* by drolly commenting that the show lacked nothing except costumes for the audience. Atkinson was not as impressed by the musical score.[52] However, *Rosalie* included two hit tunes: "Oh Gee! Oh Joy!" and the love song that is now considered a standard, "How Long Has This Been Going On?"

Rosalie proved highly pleasing to critics and audiences alike. Whereas *Sally* (1920) and *Sunny* (1925) had reflected the American Dream and the confidence of 1920s America, *Rosalie's* satiric portrayal of European monarchies in comparison to the United States' liberal, caste-free system was consistent with Ziegfeld's glorification of America. Historians have unfairly deemed *Rosalie* one of Ziegfeld's more forgettable productions. Granted, it could not compare with *Show Boat,* but it was a more than competent farcical snapshot of its time. The modern beat of George Gershwin's music and Ira Gershwin's slick lyrics represented the triumph of musical comedy over operetta, while Rosalie's marriage to an "average Joe" represented the triumph of democracy over monarchy.

Rosalie ran for a whopping 335 performances from January to October 1928. With *Show Boat* and *Rosalie* both selling out at the box office, Ziegfeld had proved that he was undeniably the last word in musical theater. But he could not focus on his accomplishments; he was already thinking about what innovative twist he could use in his next production to maintain the element of surprise that audiences expected from a Ziegfeld show.

19

Ziegfeld Laughs ... and Cries

Ziegfeld's boldness was at an all-time high in March 1928 when, only two months after *Rosalie* premiered, he chose to produce a show that, by all accounts, should have been a flop—an operetta. Ziegfeld had loathed this form of musical since he had worked as a boy at his father's conservatory, and he still disliked the genre. One would assume that audiences shared Ziegfeld's disdain. After all, hadn't much of *Rosalie* been about the triumph of musical comedy over operetta? But Ziegfeld saw staging an operetta as a prime opportunity to surprise audiences and give an outmoded genre a new twist. As he had proved with *Show Boat,* he was not afraid to put his own tastes aside for a worthwhile project. Consequently, he chose an operatic version of *The Three Musketeers* as his next project. The classic Alexandre Dumas tale was anything but creaky after William Anthony McGuire adapted it and P. G. Wodehouse and Clifford Grey wrote clever lyrics to Rudolf Friml's score. According to biographer Ethan Mordden, the show had "the least imposing score of all the famous twenties operettas."[1]

McGuire's worsening drinking problem severely hindered the show's momentum. The writer would often be found sleeping in alleys after all-night drinking sprees, so he was in no shape to keep up with Ziegfeld's demands. The producer had asked that the script for *The Three Musketeers* be completed so quickly that by the show's first rehearsal, McGuire had finished only half of it. To buy himself some time, McGuire screened the 1921 Douglas Fairbanks film version of *Musketeers* for the company while he ran upstairs to hurriedly pen the final act. The finished script was so tardy that when the play opened on March 13, 1928, at the Lyric Theatre, the actors had to read their lines from cue cards hidden in their palms. McGuire's behavior was consistently unprofessional, even when he was not drinking. When he strolled into Ziegfeld's office with a few pages of script he had managed to write, he would often give Goldie slimy kisses along her neck. One day she got fed up and pulled a knife on him. Rather than be offended, McGuire used this bit of drama as inspiration for a bedroom scene between D'Artagnan and Milady de Winter. McGuire was not the only unprofessional member of the *Three Musketeers* company. Rudolph Friml also had an immature side. At one conference involving Friml, Harkrider, McGuire, and Ziegfeld, Friml lunged at Goldie and pantomimed that he was raping her. Ziegfeld's face turned a purplish red as he stood up and bellowed: "Rudy, you leave that little girl alone. Don't ever do that again!"[2] Apparently, Ziegfeld was the only chivalrous male in the room, for the rest of them only laughed at Ziegfeld's outburst. Goldie's ongoing loyalty to Ziegfeld was amazing, given the harassment, the long hours, and the meager pay.

The actors in *Musketeers* also tested Ziegfeld's patience. As D'Artagnan, Ziegfeld hired Dennis King, a tenor he had considered for Ravenal in *Show Boat*. Vivienne Segal costarred as Constance Bonacieux. King resented that Segal's breathtaking Harkrider costumes and her charismatic stage presence stole every scene. Segal disliked King just as much. During a love scene, King pinched Segal so hard in her midsection that her voice quavered when she sang her high notes. Segal retaliated by giving King a harsh nudge with her elbow that knocked the wind out of him as he sang a high note. Segal escalated the feud when she placed a tack on King's seat that caused him such pain that an understudy had to take his place. Ziegfeld, like a stern father, threatened to bring both of them to Actors Equity to settle their dispute. Fearing the loss of their union cards and their jobs, the two gritted their teeth and tried their best to work together harmoniously.

Dennis King's charms may have been lost on Segal, but he left one girl completely infatuated: Patricia Ziegfeld. Patricia became enamored with the tenor the moment she saw him swashbuckling onstage. Billie banned her daughter from the show after she had attended five consecutive performances. But that did not take Patricia's mind off King. She wrote him a letter on pink stationery sprinkled with Billie's perfume, but she was so excited that she forgot to enclose it in the envelope. King received an empty envelope with only his name and Patricia's return address on it. He apparently sent Patricia a yellow rose corsage and a compassionate response, "with his sincerest regards." However, he did express his "bewilderment at receiving an empty envelope."[3] Patricia claimed the experience was so humiliating that the memory of it made her break into a cold sweat for years afterward.

As charismatic and dashing as they were, the actors in the show took a backseat to Joseph Urban's sets and John Harkrider's costumes. Brooks Atkinson began his review of *The Three Musketeers* by alluding to its gorgeousness: "Most of the world's romance and a good part of its beauty and color seem now to be concentrated upon Mr. Ziegfeld's *The Three Musketeers*." He also gave a nod to Ziegfeld, who "direct[ed] with a firm hand" and subordinated even beauty to the "blood-chilling, blood-heating romance" of the plot. The fact that the show's story dominated its visual appeal reflected that Ziegfeld was repeating the winning formula he had found with *Show Boat*.

Ziegfeld now had four simultaneous hits on his hands. During the week of March 13, 1928, one could step into virtually any theater on Broadway and find one of his shows running there: *Show Boat* played at the Ziegfeld Theatre, *Rosalie* played at the New Amsterdam, *Rio Rita* at the Majestic (it had been moved out of the Ziegfeld Theatre to make room for *Show Boat*), and *The Three Musketeers* at the Lyric. McGuire, who had often heard Ziegfeld bemoan the four "failures" he had on his hands, wired the producer a sarcastic cable: "Please accept my condolences in this, your darkest hour of success."[4]

Critic Percy Hammond, who had once decried the *Follies* as being obscene, deemed Ziegfeld's recent shows "pure and undefiled successes."[5] The editor of *Time* was so impressed with Ziegfeld's new wave of book musicals that he featured the producer on the magazine's cover. The writer of the accompanying article commented: "Probably the most spectacular feature of a successful theater season in Manhattan has been the gigantic and prolonged good fortune of that wise and prolific producer of plays, Florenz Ziegfeld. Without exception, no other producer has ever enjoyed such consistently large revenues from his theatrical ventures."[6] For the time being, Ziegfeld had no financial worries or pessimistic thoughts. The players in Ziegfeld's four hits, though temperamental, further boosted his newfound confidence. On May 18, 1928, the companies of Ziegfeld's four shows presented him with a bronze bust of himself, designed by Jean

DuBarry. The bust was placed between the two box-office windows at the Ziegfeld Theatre. Billie and several friends were present at the unveiling ceremony.[7]

To further celebrate Ziegfeld's prolific year, Billie had thrown him an extravagant party in Florida for his sixty-first birthday on March 21. She served only the most tasteful dishes: caviar, duck, chocolate mousse, and a Burkeley Crest special—angel food cake with coconut icing. The gathering itself was an elaborate costume party, and Billie had ordered costumes sent from each of Ziegfeld's biggest New York productions. Eight groups of friends exhibited the costumes in a pageant-like entrance at one of Palm Beach's most exclusive venues, which had been rented for the occasion. Even Patricia played a part in the spectacle, appearing as "Joan of Arc in a blue tunic and a suit of chain mail" in "an elaborate tableau a la Ben Ali Haggin."[8] Ziegfeld wore a costume that was not from any of his shows: a hobo. It was the same costume he had worn on the night of the New Year's ball where he first met Billie. His choice of such a sentimental costume and the fact that Billie had arranged such a grand party for her husband suggested that they were enjoying a long-awaited period of stability in their marriage.

Following the party, Doc Wagner ordered Ziegfeld to Camp Patricia and forbade him to make any phone calls or discuss anything concerning the theater through letters, telegrams, or conversations.[9] Palm Beach was a vacation spot in itself, but Camp Patricia would provide Ziegfeld with a serene, business-free environment that was more conducive to rest. Ziegfeld invited Wagner and a Palm Beach friend, Leonard Replogle, to accompany him. Canadian customs authorities dampened the men's spirits when they were caught crossing the border with liquor hidden in Replogle's private railway car. Replogle somehow managed to finagle his way out of the charge, but Wagner and Ziegfeld had to pay fines. Ziegfeld displayed his intermittent sense of humor when he gave Replogle a birthday cake the following year surrounded by half-empty brandy bottles with candles in their necks.[10] Though Ziegfeld enjoyed his respite in Canada, he was eager to return to New York and start work on his next show, an Eddie Cantor vehicle.

Because Ziegfeld was flush with money and had regained his health, he was undaunted by the prospect of producing another show while simultaneously overseeing the other three that were still playing on Broadway. The profits from his hits, compounded by the money he had received for selling the rights to most of his productions to Hollywood, had made him wealthier than ever before. He still did not consider films a serious threat, even after talkies came into vogue. He viewed filmmaking as just an easy way to make extra money. Even Will Rogers was unable to convince Ziegfeld that film was a viable medium. In an attempt to persuade Ziegfeld to come to California, Will wrote: "You'll knock 'em dead, Flo. You'll out-glorify all those glorifiers in Hollywood."[11]

Marilyn Miller saw potential in motion pictures and, without a second thought, left Ziegfeld to become a film star. Just as *Rosalie* was wrapping up its New York run in October 1928, First National Pictures offered her a contract. Marilyn's film debut was an adaptation of her first starring vehicle on Broadway: *Sally.* The film version was much abridged, but it featured the most beloved songs from the play plus a two-strip Technicolor sequence of the exhilarating "Wild Rose" number. Ziegfeld had released Marilyn from her contract without argument; he was sure she would return to him between pictures. He had also promised her a starring role in a show he planned to produce: *East Is West,* an adaptation of a 1918 comedy about a Chinese waif in love with an American. Ziegfeld intended to rename the show after the girl Marilyn would portray, Ming Toy. The production seemed all the more promising after Ziegfeld hired the Gershwins to compose the score.

Despite losing his greatest star (temporarily, he hoped), Ziegfeld's life in New York had never been so idyllic. He no longer felt out of place in the decade he had initially detested. Perhaps what kept him cheerier in the waning years of the 1920s was that most reminders of his rose-colored past—Rector's, Lillian Russell, Diamond Jim Brady, and Anna Held—were gone. Ziegfeld seldom spoke of his old friends, his decadent days in Europe, or the early days of Broadway. According to biographer Charles Higham, "his face darkened" if he came across reminders of his past, such as photographs of old friends or playbills from Anna Held productions. In 1928 Ziegfeld was far from being a Gloomy Gus, as his first wife had dubbed him. His associates and family now saw him grinning more often than frowning, and patrons at Dinty Moore's restaurant were astonished to hear him laugh out loud on occasion.[12]

A further boost to Ziegfeld's spirits was the phenomenal success of *Show Boat* not only in America but also in London. Producing the show on Drury Lane was a man with a quite unusual name: Sir Alfred Butt.

According to historian Todd Decker, Butt "produced . . . on a lavish scale that equaled that of Ziegfeld and the Shuberts."[13] Paul Robeson finally accepted the role of Joe in the London version of the show. Ziegfeld, in a gesture demonstrating that there were no hard feelings, sent the actor a warm telegram of congratulations.

"If the opening night is any indicator, the London run is going to be a long one," Jerome Kern told Ziegfeld from London. The run was indeed a long one: 350 performances. Ziegfeld was so impressed by the way Robeson drew audiences that he considered opening a second company of *Show Boat* on Broadway when the actor returned to New York. However, because Actors Equity had suspended Robeson due to contractual difficulties, Ziegfeld was forced to shelve the idea. The disappointed producer gave a statement to the press: "*Show Boat* would have given employment to 160 artists. I had already signed many principals, all of whom feel that Equity's suspension of Paul Robeson has worked them a great injury."[14]

Despite this setback, Ziegfeld remained chipper as he and McGuire made plans for the new Cantor show. At Eddie's suggestion, McGuire had taken a hit play about a hypochondriac, *The Nervous Wreck* (1923), and turned it into a musical comedy with a fittingly comic title: *Whoopee*. After a stay at the Battle Creek Sanitarium, Eddie claimed: "I felt completely qualified to play it [the lead role as a hypochondriac], I'd been rehearsing in doctors' offices and sanitariums for over a year."[15] The play tells the story of Henry, who goes to a dude ranch in California to improve his health. While there, Henry meets the beautiful Sally (played by Ruth Etting, who sang the hit tune "Shaking the Blues Away" in the 1927 *Follies*). Henry helps Sally avoid the romantic overtures of the local sheriff so that she can unite with the man she loves—a half-breed who, in the end, is discovered not to be part Indian at all. He had merely been raised by Indians after the death of his parents.

The comedic dialogue McGuire inserted between the love scenes helped ease Ziegfeld's doubts about the show. His main misgiving was that the leading part was too "straight" for Eddie, but McGuire gave the actor plenty of one-liners, such as the following exchange between the oblivious Henry and his nurse, who has fallen in love with him:

NURSE MARY: Oh, poor Henry. Let me hold your hand.
HENRY: It's not heavy. I can manage. Hold your own hand.[16]

Although McGuire had finished a fair amount of the script, Ziegfeld did not trust him to complete the rest of it in a timely manner. He was right: McGuire did not deliver a completed script in time for rehearsals—or even for opening night. Eddie recalled that "the rough draft that was supposed to take three weeks to write was not completed in ten weeks, and at each rehearsal the actors waited in suspense for their next scene."[17] Gus Kahn and Walter Donaldson, the songwriters for the show, kept the actors (and Ziegfeld) in just as much suspense. Ziegfeld's customary dislike of composers flared as the time for the play's Pittsburgh tryouts in the summer of 1928 approached. Most of the songs had been written, but Ruth Etting needed a song tailored for her. Ziegfeld sent the following livid message to Kahn and Donaldson, threatening to bring in Rodgers and Hart or Harry Tierney and Otto Harbach to finish the show: "I can't wait any longer. All night parties have been more important to you. I have not had one line delivered or a note since we have been here and I can't sacrifice Eddie Cantor or my production further. Same time members of my company are kept up all night. I prefer you both leave for New York and I will get your work done by others at your expense. Ziegfeld."[18] Kahn and Donaldson scrambled to defuse their boss's wrath and gave him "Love Me or Leave Me," a splendid torch song for Etting that ultimately became a showstopper.

McGuire, Donaldson, and Kahn may have had negative experiences with Ziegfeld, but the ever-dependable John Harkrider and Joseph Urban remained on his good side. Harkrider transformed Indian garb into eye-popping creations. What Harkrider described as the "topper" was a scene in which an apparently nude Indian princess rode in on a white horse; she wore a headdress of white feathers "draping from eight carved poles carried by eight warriors."[19] In reality, a skin-toned bodysuit with a sprinkling of diamonds around her breasts and hips gave the illusion of nudity. Urban's sets included a pink and silver finale (one of Ziegfeld's favorite color combinations). Ziegfeld ordered a cow delivered to the theater to add realism to the settings. Realism is exactly what he got. During one performance, the animal used the stage as a restroom. Eddie Cantor remedied the situation by grabbing a broom and shovel from the wings and dancing onstage to clean up. Eddie's ad-libbing garnered one of the biggest laughs in the show. "Keep that in," Ziegfeld told Goldie. "Make a note."[20] But the cow refused to repeat the performance, much to Ziegfeld's chagrin.

This was not the only time Eddie ad-libbed, even though he knew

Ziegfeld disapproved of excessive improvising onstage. That, he wrote, "was always an added incentive to me. I wanted to panic him as much as I wanted to panic the audience." One night during a September 1928 tryout of *Whoopee* in Pittsburgh, Eddie ad-libbed the following conversation with actor Spencer Charters:

"Have you had an operation?"

"Yes."

"Where?"

Charters pulled up his shirt, and Eddie followed suit. They compared scars.

"I paid a thousand dollars for this operation," Eddie said.

"I paid two thousand," Charters replied.

"Two thousand! Let's see it again . . . oh, no wonder. You got hemstitching. And a zipper!"

Eddie eyed Ziegfeld in the audience, but the producer's poker face remained immobile. Then, suddenly, Ziegfeld began to rock with laughter. After the show he came backstage, wiping the tears from his eyes. "Eddie, you ought to do more of that. It's the funniest thing in the show."[21]

The music in the show, though not improvised, was equally amusing to audiences. The title song, "Makin' Whoopee," became one of the biggest hits of the year. Its witty lyrics went on for numerous verses, each one building in comic value: "He doesn't make much money / Five thousand dollars per / Some judge who thinks he's funny / Says 'you'll pay six to her' / . . . You'd better keep her / You'll find it's cheaper than makin' whoopee."[22] One night in Pittsburgh, Eddie's successful delivery of the song was nothing short of miraculous, given that he had recovered from laryngitis only an hour earlier. As the clock ticked closer to showtime, a panicked Ziegfeld obtained the name of the best throat specialist in the city from Urban. "But he's still recovering from a near-fatal automobile accident now. He can't treat Eddie," Urban said.

"Well, he didn't die, did he?" Ziegfeld asked.

"No," Urban slowly replied.

Without another word, Ziegfeld wrote a $1,000 check with the doctor's name on it. He then enlisted two theater attendants to carry the doctor from his sickbed and into an ambulance he had borrowed from a local hospital. From the stretcher, the doctor painted Eddie's throat and gave him several other medications. Just in time, Eddie's voice returned.

Backstage, more troubles confronted Ziegfeld in the person of Ruth Etting's notorious husband, Martin Schneider. Known as the Gimp, he was a professional bodyguard and would often come to rehearsals, gun in tow. He would poke the weapon in people's ribs, tell them to "Put your hands up!" and laugh when their faces turned white. He was not afraid to scare Ziegfeld, either. He often cornered the producer in the back alley of the theater and suggested certain improvements in his wife's role. Ziegfeld told Schneider that Etting's role was as near perfection as it could be and he would not change it. The Gimp would walk away, muttering, "It wasn't a suggestion. It was a demand." Fortunately, he never made good on his threats.[23]

By the first week of December 1928, *Whoopee* was ready to open at the New Amsterdam Theatre. The audience loved every moment of the show, despite its hefty length. Eddie joked that "the audience came in at eight thirty and left two days later."[24] Ziegfeld eventually cut forty-five minutes from the play. Among the bits he tossed were some comedic lines uttered by Ethel Shutta, who played Nurse Mary. Shutta was the wife of bandleader George Olsen, whose band happened to be providing the music for *Whoopee*. When Shutta's part was cut from the finale, Olsen declared that he and his band would leave the show—which they did when Ziegfeld failed to restore Shutta's material. Ziegfeld then hired Gus Salzer and his band as replacements.

Despite the difficulties involved in pulling the show together, Ziegfeld never lost his commitment to the project. The setting held a special place in his heart, given his lifelong fondness for the Wild West. Critics were quick to notice that the western numbers, specifically those featuring Harkrider's elaborate Indian headdresses and Urban's complete re-creation of the Grand Canyon, were the most beautiful.

Whoopee proved to be even more profitable than *Show Boat*. Eddie called it his and Ziegfeld's "biggest joint success" financially.[25] Now, both the comedian and the producer were millionaires. One day while they were enjoying massages together, Ziegfeld and Eddie shared a father-son chat. "I was just thinking, Eddie, how lucky you are. You have a family, you have money. You have the biggest hit in New York, working for the biggest producer in the world. You've got everything," Ziegfeld said.

"No, Flo. I haven't got everything. Where's my Rolls Royce?" Eddie asked.

Ziegfeld laughed, and Eddie had no reason to think his boss had taken the comment seriously. But Ziegfeld remembered that when Eddie had first started working on the New Amsterdam roof, he used to stand downstairs before the show for the sheer pleasure of seeing patrons arrive in their Rolls Royces. After the Saturday matinee one week later, Ziegfeld invited Eddie to dinner at Dinty Moore's. The two men met in front of the New Amsterdam and began to stroll down the sidewalk. Eddie noticed a gleaming, pearl gray Rolls Royce parked along the curb. An orchid adorned the car's door handle, and attached to it was a small card. "Read it," Ziegfeld told him. Eddie read the card in a daze: "Eddie, now you have everything. Flo." A chauffeur opened the door for Eddie, and the elated comedian rode in the jump seat, waving to Ziegfeld as the car disappeared down the street.[26]

In December 1928 Ziegfeld's confidence and bank account were both at all-time highs. He felt ready to take another risk. Regardless of Prohibition and the waning popularity of rooftop entertainment, he decided to resurrect the *Midnight Frolic*. He spent $65,000 to refurbish the long-abandoned New Amsterdam roof and enthusiastically approved Urban's new designs for the walls and dome, which included butterflies and Ziegfeld's favorite animals, elephants. Harkrider would design the costumes, and Ziegfeld hired the Paul Whiteman Orchestra to provide the music. The star attraction of the new *Frolic*, which was basically an amalgam of numbers from Ziegfeld's book musicals, was Helen Morgan. Though audiences were appreciative, Ziegfeld was dissatisfied with the show's lack of fresh material. To remedy the situation, he closed the show and planned to reopen it in February.

The revised version was closer to the original *Frolic*, full of surprises and new talent. Dorothy Fields provided the song lyrics, and Sammy Lee of *Show Boat* directed the dance ensemble numbers. However, what made the reopening a true hit was Ziegfeld's new discovery, French singing star Maurice Chevalier, who debuted on February 18, 1929. His outrageous accent, ever-present smile, and charisma never failed to charm audiences. Each night, Chevalier came onstage carrying a walking stick and wearing a tuxedo. Instead of the customary top hat, he wore a straw boater tilted at a jaunty angle. He gave the *Frolic* a sophisticated and European flair that harked back to Ziegfeld's first rooftop venue in 1907, the Jardin de Paris, and his first musical star, Anna Held. The Frenchman's style of singing was novel to American audiences; it sounded as if he were not singing at all but carrying on a conversation. Unfortunately, Chevalier had to leave after only four weeks, as he had a contract to fulfill in Hollywood. He went on to find great fame in films such as *The Love Parade* (1929) and *Love Me Tonight* (1932) with operatic star Jeannette MacDonald.

With Chevalier gone, the *Frolic* folded on April 25, 1929. Ziegfeld did not attribute its closing solely to the loss of Chevalier. In a statement to the *New York Times*, he explained that although the patronage had consistently been good, the venue's operating expenses and the company's high salaries made it impossible to maintain the show's high quality. Ziegfeld gave one final reason behind the *Frolic*'s closing, which was nearly identical to the reason he had given years before: "The only way to make money with a nightclub is to sell liquor which I can't and won't do."[27]

But Ziegfeld was in no danger of losing his millionaire status because one show had closed. Successful film adaptations of *Kid Boots* (1926), *Show Boat* (1929), and *Sally* (1929) not only made him wealthier but also gave the entire country a taste of what theatergoers were already enjoying. Still, he held fast to the belief that audiences preferred beauty in the flesh. Ziegfeld made the following statement to the *New York Times* in March 1929: "No better way will be found to glorify beauty than the stage. . . . Movietones cannot exist successfully without the legitimate theatre. . . . The first movietone producer who helps the theatre is the one who will find himself with successful movietone productions."[28] In April 1929 Ziegfeld vehemently denounced Arthur Hammerstein (uncle of Oscar Hammerstein II), whom he saw as a danger to the legitimate theater. Hammerstein had announced that he planned to use "canned sound" in place of a real orchestra for his next musical show. Ziegfeld told the *New York Times*, "No real artist would ever think of singing with a mechanical instrument . . . everyone knows also that to individualize art in this manner will be absolutely impossible with a mechanical orchestra thundering along, regardless of how the actor feels and his reaction to the audience." Ziegfeld conceded that such a practice could be beneficial to the movie industry, but to intermix film production devices with theater would do "a great injustice to both" mediums.[29]

Ziegfeld dove into his next stage production with added gusto, more committed than ever to uphold the integrity of the theater. Entitled *Show*

Girl, the play was based on a novel by J. P. McAvoy and adapted for the stage especially for Ruby Keeler. Keeler had been a chorus girl in *Whoopee* before she temporarily left the stage to marry aging jazz singer Al Jolson. The play's story was typical: a girl is plucked from the chorus line and achieves fame and fortune on Broadway. To ensure that *Show Girl* would be as big a hit as *Whoopee,* Ziegfeld rounded up his usual creative team: Joseph Urban, William Anthony McGuire, John Harkrider, and the Albertina Rasch Ballet. For music, he employed *Whoopee's* songwriter Gus Kahn, as well as the Gershwins. "You must write a score in two weeks," Ziegfeld told George Gershwin. "Just dig down in the trunk and pull out a couple of hits."[30]

George and Ira Gershwin were baffled. They had already completed half the score for *Ming Toy,* the operetta planned for Marilyn Miller. "We were most enthusiastic about this project [*Ming Toy*]," Ira stated. But Ziegfeld, "in his hypnotically persuasive manner (always great charm until a contract was signed)," had decided to postpone the operetta and start *Show Girl.*[31] The Gershwins and Kahn wrote twenty-seven musical items for potential scenes in the show. McGuire, as usual, was slow in finishing the script; he would sit back and listen to George at the piano and say, "You never can tell. Maybe I'll get a good idea for a scene from one of the songs."[32] McGuire apparently found little inspiration. Ira quipped that *Show Girl* set a record for "sparseness of dialogue in a musical."[33]

Of the little dialogue in the show, the best of it was performed by a new comedian Ziegfeld had hired for a supporting part: Jimmy Durante. Ziegfeld had not cast such an unlikely comic personality in one of his shows since W. C. Fields had debuted in the *Follies* back in 1915. However, unlike Fields, Durante was a likeable man. According to Eddie Cantor, Durante would "want to give you a whole roast beef" if "you were to bring him in a sandwich."[34] Durante kept audiences laughing in every one of his scenes in *Show Girl.* His heavy Bronx accent aided his comedy, just as Fanny Brice's Yiddish accent had helped hers. His penchant for throwing out quips about current events or aiming impromptu jokes at well-known audience members was similar to the style of another Ziegfeld star, Will Rogers. But in contrast to Will's understated manner, Durante was all zaniness. Much of his humor centered around his homely appearance—mainly the size of his nose. When he came onstage, he would point at his "schnozz" and say, "Dere it is, folks, de real thing. It ain't gonna bite 'cha and any famous personages in the dump can come up and autygraph it."[35] In a statement to the *New York Times,* Ziegfeld said: "I think that Jimmy Durante is the greatest comedian I have ever had."[36]

Ziegfeld had just as many accolades for Ruby Keeler. "I personally thought that Ruby Keeler gave one of the greatest performances of a character . . . that I have seen in my thirty-five years experience," he said.[37] Ziegfeld was exaggerating his impressions of both Keeler and Durante; most of his closest friends and associates knew that Will Rogers was Ziegfeld's favorite comedian and Marilyn Miller his favorite musical star. The effusive comments to the press about his two new stars were intended mainly to increase ticket sales. However, his praise for Keeler was sincere, if overstated. He was so taken with the fresh-faced dancer that he ordered Urban to redecorate her dressing room at the Ziegfeld Theatre in white organdy. On opening night, July 2, 1929, Ziegfeld sent Keeler a box from Cartier's full of exquisite toiletries, as well as makeup and gold, crystal, and pearl jewelry. Ziegfeld asked Goldie to hide in Keeler's dressing room to witness her reaction to the gift. To Goldie's shock, Keeler did not even notice that the makeup set she was using was new. When Al Jolson came into the room, he pointed it out to her. Ziegfeld tried to gain the dancer's attention again by sending her $125 silk stockings from Paris. But Keeler's mother prevented the gift from reaching her daughter. Mrs. Keeler did not approve of Ziegfeld's overtures, which she assumed were romantic in nature. Though Ziegfeld was infatuated with Keeler, he never acted on his feelings for her. The gifts were merely his way of showing Keeler how well a Ziegfeld star was treated.[38]

Ziegfeld could be short with many performers, but he was always patient with Keeler. Still, even the great producer's words of encouragement did not prevent the young dancer from going numb with stage fright during the dress rehearsal for her most important number, a minstrel skit with "a hundred beautiful girls on steps that cover[ed] the entire stage."[39] Her song in the number was "Liza," but upon reaching the top of the staircase, she forgot every lyric to the Gershwins' song. Her husband, who was seated in the front row, began to sing the song to her. Smiling, Keeler's memory returned, and she danced down the staircase with perfect ease and rhythm. Ziegfeld asked Jolson to repeat his accompaniment for each performance during the show's first week. Critic Brooks Atkinson of the *New York Times* called it a "touching episode."[40]

Despite audiences' warm reception, reviews were mixed. Atkinson commented that "the task of blending materials that are episodic and individual make *Show Girl* the least notable of the recent Ziegfeld productions," and it lacked "the stately flow of the best Ziegfeld pageants." McAvoy's novel had used telegrams, letters, and satire on the greeting card business as a loose construction for his story, and McGuire was a bit too faithful to the book. Atkinson heralded Ruby Keeler as being "on her way to fame . . . a performer without pretensions or affectations," but he condemned her dialogue as banal. Atkinson singled out Durante for his "sizzling energy . . . raucous songs . . . and 'exubiance'" (Durante's mispronunciation of "exuberance"). Although Atkinson declared that the comedian's "spluttering, insane material does not melt gracefully into a musical comedy book," he conceded that Durante's "personality . . . batters its way through all barriers."[41]

The critics could find no fault with the show's aesthetics. As usual, Urban's opulent sets and Harkrider's costumes, which the girls wore "with enviable poise," proved that Ziegfeld was in no danger of losing his touch. Gershwin's music, however, was deemed less than first-rate. When paired with the feverish and screwball tunes penned by Durante himself, the score contained a less than "felicitous . . . combination."[42] Gershwin's music may have been criticized in 1929, but today, one of the numbers he composed for the show, the "American in Paris" ballet, is considered his greatest work after "Rhapsody in Blue." Ballerina Harriet Hoctor danced to the lively tune against a sparkling backdrop of the Eiffel Tower and the Paris skyline. Charles Higham stated that Ziegfeld exerted an "almost superhuman effort creating a glittering chiaroscuro of color and movement to this one number."[43] Despite all its faults, *Show Girl* played for 111 performances, and Atkinson concluded that "the summer was not likely to yield anything so handsome."[44]

Ziegfeld had once told Eddie Cantor to "not cry over spilt milk" when it came to problematic shows, but Ziegfeld seemed to be doing just that. After having four hits, the critics' reactions to *Show Girl* were disappointing. Ziegfeld poured the blame on the Gershwins and dictated long letters and telegrams to them. Like Rodgers and Hart, the brothers never received royalties for their work on the show.

The letdown of *Show Girl* softened Ziegfeld's attitude toward film. He decided to try in Hollywood what had failed on Broadway, thus becoming one of the first theater producers to bring his expertise to film. In the summer of 1929 Ziegfeld made a deal with Jesse L. Lasky at Paramount Pictures to supervise the production of a motion picture that would bring visions of the *Follies* to every movie screen in America. The plot of the film, appropriately titled *Glorifying the American Girl,* revolved around a chorus girl's rise to fame (almost identical to the plot of *Show Girl*). Signed to star in the musical was Mary Eaton, with specialty spots by Eddie Cantor and Helen Morgan. Even Ziegfeld and Billie made cameo appearances in a scene that depicted an opening-night audience crowding into the New Amsterdam. Like Marilyn Miller's *Sally* (also released in 1929), *Glorifying the American Girl* utilized two-strip Technicolor for the most spectacular musical scenes.

Ziegfeld took Patricia and Billie with him to Hollywood during the shooting of the film. The trip was a pleasant one, and it allowed the Ziegfelds to enjoy a warm reunion with Will Rogers, who was serving as the mayor of Beverly Hills. Patricia recalled that "Will and Aunt Betty [Mrs. Rogers] did everything they could to make us feel at home. We visited the ranch frequently. He [Will] let me have my own pony to ride whenever I felt so inclined—and that was about every day. He would visit us at the beach house we were renting and swim in the pool. He knew how to do all sorts of crazy dives."[45] Patricia enjoyed her playmates in Hollywood better than those in Palm Beach. The Rogers children had none of the pretensions of the Palm Beach set's offspring. Will Jr., Mary, and Jim were down-to-earth and straightforward like Patricia. Billie and Mrs. Rogers met for the first time that summer and remained close friends for the rest of their lives.

Though Ziegfeld enjoyed himself on Will's ranch and was beginning to see the appeal of West Coast life, he did not even consider relocating to California to devote himself to film. He was eager to return to the theater and begin preparations for two new shows. One was a Noel Coward operetta, *Bitter Sweet,* and the second was a whimsical comedic vehicle for Ed Wynn titled *Simple Simon.* The Coward show was Patricia's professed favorite of all her father's productions. Audiences in both London and New York shared her enthusiasm—even if Ziegfeld initially did not.[46] *Bitter Sweet* tells the story of the Marchioness of Shayne and the men she loved over the years. The show opens with her as an aged woman and then flashes back to 1875, depicting her love for her music teacher in Vienna and her subsequent career as an entertainer. Charles Higham called the show a "sugary romantic musical [that] was not Ziegfeld's kind of thing."[47] However, Billie had had luck with Coward plays in the past, and she encouraged her husband to produce the show. The score, with music and lyrics by Coward as well, was top-notch and included the song "If Love Were All." Despite the show's merits, Ziegfeld regretted accepting the project when he butted heads with Coward. "Where shall we insert a Ziegfeld girl number? My shows must have Ziegfeld girls," Ziegfeld told the refined Englishman.

"My plays are not spectacles. There's no room for a Ziegfeld girl number," Coward declared with a sniff.

"Very well. I shall do nothing to promote the play at all. It's up to you," Ziegfeld declared.

At tea with his friends that afternoon, Coward declared that Ziegfeld was "arrogant and high-handed." Ziegfeld complained to Gene Buck that Coward was "tired and effete."[48] The two men eventually came to speaking terms, but just barely.

By the time *Bitter Sweet* was ready for its Boston tryout in October 1929, Coward was already basking in praise from critics. Even Ziegfeld's "son," Eddie Cantor, stopped in the middle of a performance of *Whoopee* to introduce the playwright (who was in the audience) as "the greatest theatrical genius alive today."[49] One can only imagine how slighted Ziegfeld must have felt.

More upsetting to Ziegfeld was that Coward banned him from the backstage area during the Boston opening, declaring that the producer interfered too much. Ziegfeld temporarily put his frustration aside when he witnessed the show's enthusiastic reception in Boston. However, critics almost unanimously gave Coward full credit for its success. Ziegfeld's name did not even appear in reviews, unless one counted their mention of the Ziegfeld Theatre, where the show would premiere in New York on November 5, 1929. Ziegfeld had seldom been given enough credit for his multifaceted talents. He could guide a production, but he knew when his over-the-top ideas were unworkable and when to let his creative team take over. Biographer Ethan Mordden posed the question: "Did any[one] sense the contradiction of the man—that he had democratized show biz while remaining the pet of snobs? Did anyone . . . appreciate his menu of entertainments, whether *The Three Musketeers* or an Eddie Cantor goof-up?"[50]

In *Time* magazine's cover story on Ziegfeld's freakish string of successes in 1928, the writer had observed, "as he took his ease in a country manor, placid Zieggy did not reflect that almost every U.S. producer of gay, twin-kling dramatics had died without funds."[51] That statement took on an omi-nous truth when, ten days before *Bitter Sweet* was set to open in New York, the stock market crashed. Millionaires became paupers in a matter of min-utes. Ziegfeld was accustomed to losing and gaining exorbitant sums of money during his gambling sprees, but this financial upheaval was far worse than one night of bad luck at the gambling table. In the documen-tary *Broadway: The American Musical,* narrator Julie Andrews states that when the market crashed, "the bottom fell out of hilarity" in the theater world.[52] Who would be in the mood to watch light operettas or Eddie Cantor goof-ups now?

As the value of his stocks plummeted, Ziegfeld was going through his morning ritual at Burkeley Crest. He made his usual early telephone calls to half-asleep associates, completed his morning chin-ups on the lower limb of his favorite copper beech tree, and then left for New York. Allen M. Thomas, who lived in Hastings-on-Hudson from 1920 until 1966, wrote a vivid description of Ziegfeld as he left for work: "I remember see-ing him many a morning with his pearl gray homburg at just the right angle above his Jimmy Durante–type nose, gray suede gloves held ele-gantly folded on the silver head of his mahogany cane, riding . . . in a long Mercedes-Benz limousine with his chauffeur and footman (alias body-guard, I suspect) in inclement weather or his blue Hispano Suiza Cabriolet in fair weather."[53]

Ziegfeld's route took him through Yonkers, where he sometimes handed out tickets to his shows or, at Christmastime, $10 bills. On the morning of the stock market crash, Ziegfeld's dominant worry was testify-ing against a vendor he had sued over a $1,600 marquee sign he deemed inadequate. Such a petty argument became insignificant once Ziegfeld stepped outside the courtroom and heard newsboys on every corner yell-ing that $13 billion had been lost on Wall Street in one day. Ziegfeld lost $3 million. He could no longer afford to hand out even $1 bills to the resi-dents of Yonkers. Making matters worse was that Ziegfeld had noticed signs of distress on Wall Street during the summer but had decided not to sell his stocks. While at Camp Patricia, Ziegfeld's friend, financier E. F. Hutton, had wired him, urging him to sell. However, Hutton's and Ziegfeld's financial adviser, Paul Block, had convinced both men to keep their stocks.[54] "The market fluctuates," Block had told them.

Eddie Cantor ultimately lost everything in the crash. Will Rogers was one of Ziegfeld's only friends not to be hit hard by the Depression. Eddie had tried to convince Will to invest in the market with him, but Will did things his own way: "Don't gamble; take all your savings and buy some good stock and hold it till it goes up, then sell it," he said. "If it don't go up, don't buy it."[55]

It is easy to imagine the despair and anger felt by Ziegfeld and his colleagues, but at the time of their decision to hold on to their stock, they had had little reason to doubt their judgment. Eight theaters had opened on Broadway in 1927, and eleven new musicals had premiered in the summer months alone. Broadway experienced a feverish expansion, with a total of 270 plays of all genres reaching New York in the 1927–1928 season.[56] There was a seemingly endless array of new productions and fresh talent to dazzle audiences. But the same year the theater reached its pinnacle, talking pictures made their debut. Talkies were the first blow to the theater, which Broadway could have withstood had it not been for the second blow—the stock market crash.

Ironically, the first talking film to win a Best Picture Oscar was a Ziegfeldian tale of two showgirls climbing up the ranks of a Broadway musical. *The Broadway Melody* (1929) was set in New York, as were the majority of musicals made in Hollywood. "The films may have been made in Hollywood, but the subject matter always had to do with New York City," theater historian Miles Kreuger noted. "Because New York was the center of America and of course it was natural that Hollywood would be attracted to the world mythology of Broadway. . . . Broadway was the magic word. Anything could happen there. That's the Hollywood myth about Broadway and that's the myth Broadway had about itself."[57]

Anything could happen on Broadway, but after the crash, it seemed that nothing remained except the myth. New York City mayor Jimmy Walker implored movie studios to "show pictures that will reinstate courage in the hearts of people."[58] The same month *Bitter Sweet* opened, RKO Studios released a film version of *Rio Rita*. It was RKO's greatest success that year, but Ziegfeld did not benefit; he had sold the rights to the show, rather than entering into a profit participation deal with the studio. Like *Rio Rita*, Marilyn Miller's screen version of *Sally* was a hit with filmgoers. Ziegfeld hoped the film he had coproduced, *Glorifying the American Girl*, would be equally successful. However, upon its release in December 1929, he realized the futility of that wish. The film offered a glimpse into what the *Follies* were like, but its short running time (less than ninety minutes), uninspired screenplay, and choppy editing could not compare with Ziegfeld's theatrical productions.

Only three months after the release of *Glorifying the American Girl*, *Bitter Sweet* closed. Ziegfeld was convinced that he was finished; he felt hopeless and fell into a depression. Though often gloomy and pessimistic in the past, Ziegfeld had always believed that something better would come along, and each of his masterful productions proved his conviction. What had allowed Ziegfeld to prove himself in the past had been funding from faithful backers. But Charles Dillingham, one of his most reliable partners, had been hit as hard as Ziegfeld. Allegedly, Dillingham remarked to Ziegfeld after the crash, "Well, at least that finally makes us even."[59] Ziegfeld had no supporters now—except for Billie. She had proved her grit and resilience throughout her tumultuous marriage with Ziegfeld and in her own volatile career. The stock market crash was just another test of her strength and resourcefulness.

When Ziegfeld arrived home on Black Thursday (October 24, 1929), his weary, ashen face was nearly unrecognizable as that of the sophisticated, suave, meticulous producer extraordinaire who had left Burkeley Crest that morning. Billie always waited up for him, even if it meant having dinner at two o'clock in the morning. She was sitting in bed when Ziegfeld came in. She recalled that "his shoulders sagged and his step [was] uncertain" before he crumpled down beside her. She took his face in her hands and asked, "Well, poor old darling, what is it?" Ziegfeld openly sobbed and told her, "I'm through . . . for God's sake pray for me, I don't know how to pray."[60]

Billie hid it from her husband, but his dissolution left her in a state of utter fear and uncertainty. Nevertheless, Billie knew that "the next step was up to me, that I must find another play and get back to work, that I must help my husband."[61] Billie became all his former backers rolled into one, though on a much smaller scale. Long ago, her mother, Blanche, had advised Billie to keep a "nest egg" for her future. Though the young Billie had considered Blanche's advice to be overly frugal and abstract, she had listened to her mother and had been saving money for decades—away from the grasp of her gambling husband. "I hugged myself with the realization that I had half a million dollars, all from my . . . earnings. . . . I took comfort in the conviction that with that kind of money we were always safe, and my child's future was secure," Billie stated.[62]

They may have been secure, but it was only a temporary security. Billie's half a million dollars kept the family afloat for only a few months. After that, the hardships they had been staving off descended. Burkeley Crest had to be mortgaged, and it was only a matter of time before they would lose the estate and all their other properties forever. They dismissed the entire household staff except for their faithful butler, Sidney, and their cook, Deliah. Ziegfeld had no interest in new projects and spent his days wandering around the gardens. Billie was determined to hold on to their idyllic home for as long as possible, but the only way she could do that was to return to work. She took the first role offered to her in a drawing-room comedy entitled *Family Affairs*. The show opened on December 10, 1929, at Maxine Elliott's Theatre and folded after seven performances, doing little to help the family's finances.

As Billie searched for a better play, Ziegfeld returned to New York and what was left of his career. He learned that the Gershwins had sued him for unpaid royalties for *Show Girl*. However, the lawsuit was useless, as "the great showman was broke" and could not pay the composers even if they prevailed in court.[63] With much trepidation, Ziegfeld prepared for the opening of *Simple Simon*. It was an old-fashioned show in many respects, particularly its reliance on elements of fairy tale and fantasy to tell the story. The play revolved around Simon (portrayed by Ed Wynn), a newspaper shop owner on Coney Island who escapes his humdrum existence by dreaming of fantastic kingdoms. One reason for Ziegfeld's anxiety about the show was that he was still holding a grudge against Wynn for striking with Actors Equity in 1919. The music was especially problematic as well. Ziegfeld cut out song after song during tryouts and then put them back in or added new ones while the show toured. Still, nothing could enliven what turned out to be an ineffectual show with an insipid script. Rodgers and Hart, who supplied the music, must have regretted returning to Ziegfeld after their unpleasant experience on *Betsy* (1926). Once again, he failed to pay the composers royalties or a fee for their work.

Simple Simon opened on February 18, 1930, at the Ziegfeld Theatre. Brooks Atkinson of the *New York Times* tempered his negative review by acknowledging Wynn's talent and Ziegfeld's artistic edge. He wrote, "[Wynn] has become one of the two or three greatest comedians of the day." Atkinson was unimpressed with the script, calling it an ineffectual attempt to combine fairy tales with a satire on Puritanism. He agreed with Ziegfeld when it came to the work of Rodgers and Hart, declaring that Rodgers "echoes his style without improving it" and that Hart's lyrics were "more sprightly than the tunes that carry them." Despite the unimpressive score, one hit emerged from the show: "Ten Cents a Dance," sung by the inimitable Ruth Etting. Atkinson saved his kindest words for Ziegfeld, who needed them most. "What he has done Mr. Ziegfeld has done well," the critic stated. "When Mr. Ziegfeld gets his spectacles under way they are worthwhile."[64]

The show ran for a respectable 107 performances and probably could have gone on longer, but as usual, Ziegfeld's operating costs outweighed the box-office receipts. These insufficient profits were further compromised when President Hoover imposed a tax on theater tickets. Ziegfeld was an outspoken opponent of the tax and made the following statement to the *New York Times*: "The government does not tax admission to the motion picture houses, but it is still continuing to do so in the legitimate houses. A theatrical production generally gives eight performances a week, whereas the film houses give several every day. Naturally, their grosses are tremendous compared to those of the legitimate theatres. That is another reason why the picture industry can afford to pay munificent sums to all concerned in turning out its product. With conditions as they are at present, the legitimate theaters throughout the country should be taken into consideration."[65] The tax exempted only theater tickets that cost less than $3—an unheard of admission price for a Ziegfeld show. Ziegfeld hoped the president would make some adjustments to the law, but Hoover did not do so. The government would have lost $17 million if it had lifted the theater ticket tax, and the government needed the money as much as Ziegfeld and nearly every other American did.

Ziegfeld's confidence and boldness had crashed with the stock market. The Ziegfeld whom New Yorkers had seen laughing out loud in public disappeared as quickly as he had come. Ziegfeld considered changing his dim view of the film industry when up-and-coming Hollywood producer Samuel Goldwyn approached him with an interesting but problematic proposition. If Ziegfeld accepted Goldwyn's offer, it would mean compromising his artistic standards and his loyalty to the legitimate theater.

20

"I Can't Do This Anymore"

After twenty-three years of working to become the top producer on Broadway, Ziegfeld did not relish the prospect of doing it all over again in Hollywood. Will Rogers had claimed that Ziegfeld could "out-glorify all those glorifiers" in California; however, Ziegfeld's heart was not in film-making, and he knew he could not bring the integrity to movies that he brought to his beloved theater productions.

In contrast to Ziegfeld, Eddie Cantor was eager to work in Hollywood. Sam Goldwyn offered Eddie a contract to re-create his stage successes on screen. He had done well in Hollywood years before with the silent version of *Kid Boots* (1926), but talking pictures would give audiences the full Cantor experience. Eddie's enthusiasm was a major factor in convincing Ziegfeld to give the movies another chance.

Even though Ziegfeld's previous filmmaking endeavors, *Gloria's Romance* (1916) and *Glorifying the American Girl* (1929), had been disappointments, Hollywoodites still saw him as a potential asset to legitimizing the film industry. Goldwyn was particularly taken with Ziegfeld's productions; Cantor claimed that Goldwyn was "a little in awe of Ziegfeld."[1] After seeing *Whoopee* in the summer of 1929, Goldwyn lost little time in arranging a meeting with Ziegfeld. He envisioned re-creating all of Ziegfeld's stage successes on the screen. In June 1929 Goldwyn offered the producer $1 million a year to sign a fifty-fifty deal to create the Goldwyn-Ziegfeld Corporation. Cantor explained: "Goldwyn is all business. Nothing and no one matters except the picture he is making at the moment."[2] The same business style could be attributed to Ziegfeld, so the new partnership seemed like a perfect match. And after the stock market crash, the merger appeared to be a potential savior for Ziegfeld and his family.

The first Goldwyn-Ziegfeld project was a film version of the show that had so impressed Goldwyn: *Whoopee.* Choreographing the numbers in the film was an exciting new dance director, Busby Berkeley. Berkeley's precise and kaleidoscopic dance configurations were reminiscent of a military squadron, which was not surprising, given that Berkeley had worked as a drill instructor during World War I. Berkeley later gained acclaim for choreographing the best of the early film musicals, such as *42nd Street* (1933) and *Gold Diggers of 1933,* starring Ruby Keeler. However, Berkeley disliked Hollywood as much as Ziegfeld did and once declared: "They don't know how to make them [musicals] out there."[3] He agreed to do *Whoopee* only after learning that Cantor and Ziegfeld were on board. Because the film boasted the show's original star, dazzling sets and costumes, and innovative choreography, it seemed sure to capture Ziegfeld's artistry more accurately than *Glorifying the American Girl* had.

Hollywood offered Ziegfeld the ideal chance to increase not only his bank account but also his social circle. He rented a beach house in Santa Monica that had once been owned by the sister of Marion Davies. Ziegfeld, Billie, and Patricia were able to visit with Will and Betty Rogers, and they made many new acquaintances among Hollywood's elite. Ziegfeld bonded with Goldwyn and other moguls, including Irving Thalberg and Nick Schenck, while playing high-stakes bridge in a small cottage on Goldwyn's estate. Of all his new acquaintances, Ziegfeld was most impressed with Thalberg, who, at only thirty-one years of age, was already the head of production at MGM Studios. Thalberg had impeccable taste when it came to creating breathtaking visions onscreen. Ziegfeld sheepishly admitted that he had turned down Thalberg's wife, Norma Shearer, for a job years before.[4] Ziegfeld and Billie hosted a party for the Thalbergs as well as former Ziegfeld girl Paulette Goddard; the "It" girl, Clara Bow; MGM head Louis B. Mayer; popular actress Lilyan Tashman; and former silent film star Nita Naldi.[5] Outwardly, the Ziegfelds were still the golden couple of the Jazz Age, living in their own fantasia twenty-four hours a day. Inwardly, Billie and Ziegfeld knew they were putting on masks; Billie called their façade "a brave show but a travesty."[6]

Ziegfeld could not keep up the pretense for long. He spent endless, tedious hours with Goldwyn and William Conselman (who adapted

Whoopee's original script for the screen), discussing what to keep and what to eliminate from the stage show. Even though Ziegfeld and Goldwyn were friends, they seldom saw eye to eye when it came to making the film. "I want Lillian Roth, Adele Astaire, and Ruby Keeler as the girls in the picture," Ziegfeld stated. Goldwyn cast Eleanor Hunt and Ethel Shutta instead. (Recall that Ziegfeld had a dispute with Shutta's husband, George Olsen, during the stage production of *Whoopee,* in which she played the nurse.) Ziegfeld stated in no uncertain terms that Goldwyn knew nothing about casting: "One thing Hollywood has to learn is how to cast a production as Broadway casts a show. Nobody out there [Hollywood] knows a damn thing about casting . . . nearly everybody out on the coast used to work for me."[7]

Ziegfeld's opinion changed, however, when the ladies of the chorus were cast. Before arriving in Hollywood, he had preselected the chorus girls for the movie and brought them to California with him. The problem was that Goldwyn had already picked his own chorus girls for the film. To settle the matter, the two groups of chorines lined up side by side, and the girls were judged by "so-called independent experts" hired by Goldwyn. Goldwyn's girls won, and Ziegfeld admitted that perhaps Goldwyn knew something about casting after all. Ziegfeld even decided to take a number of Goldwyn's girls back with him to New York for his next show, whatever or whenever it might be.[8]

Ziegfeld may have eventually agreed with Goldwyn's casting choices, but he was dissatisfied with almost every other decision his new partner made. Goldwyn refused to release a film that, if it followed the original script, would run for three hours. Goldwyn took charge of the script and costumes. He even altered the film's title just enough to put his own stamp on it. *Whoopee* became *Whoopee!*

"They eliminated everything in it that was good and convinced me without any question of a doubt that they knew nothing about a musical show," Ziegfeld confided to his family. "There's no human way for me to get my conception of *Whoopee* on screen using the canned sound for songs that were a sensation onstage."[9] Of the sixteen Gus Kahn tunes in the Broadway show, only the title song, "Makin' Whoopee," remained. Goldwyn cut the original songs to avoid paying royalties, making Ziegfeld's irritation ironic, since he too avoided paying royalties whenever possible. One reason for the men's frequent clashes may have been that Ziegfeld saw in Goldwyn many of the most unlikable professional traits he saw in himself. Not surprisingly, Goldwyn was later dubbed "the Ziegfeld of motion pictures," and Cantor called him "the toughest man in the world to work for."[10]

One aspect of Goldwyn's character that Ziegfeld did not share was his frugality. "Daddy and Mr. Goldwyn would talk for hours about show business . . . they were worlds apart in their outlooks. Mr. Goldwyn had his eye on the penny, Daddy on the effect," Patricia recalled.[11] Though the two men were worlds apart, Goldwyn remained in awe of Ziegfeld and continued to work with him when other film studios refused to do so because of his reputation for overspending. Ziegfeld insisted on using the highly expensive process of two-strip Technicolor for the entire film, and Goldwyn agreed, resigned to the fact that the showman's standards for excellence would not be compromised.

Ziegfeld's experience in California—basking in the warm weather and working fewer hours than he had back east—made him consider dividing his time between Hollywood and New York. In large part due to Busby Berkeley, Ziegfeld had changed his mind and decided that he could indeed learn something from the film industry. Berkeley worked tirelessly to create musical numbers that could not be replicated onstage. He stated, "I introduced the big close-ups of beautiful girls. It had never been done before in musicals."[12] Ziegfeld realized that his artistic visions could reach a new level if released from the limitations of the stage. However, the idea of spending half the year in Hollywood became less attractive after his partnership with Goldwyn soured. When Ziegfeld demanded that the company name be changed to Ziegfeld-Goldwyn rather than Goldwyn-Ziegfeld, it became clear that the two men's egos were too large to take a backseat to anyone, and they had no real future together.[13] Goldwyn went so far as to ban Ziegfeld from the set of *Whoopee!* because of the producer's tendency to interfere. Though the men were partners in theory, Goldwyn wanted Ziegfeld's role to be merely an advisory one; in biographer Ethan Mordden's words, Goldwyn preferred that Ziegfeld do "as little advising as possible and be back on Broadway sooner than *that.*"[14]

At the preview for *Whoopee!* in San Diego during the late summer of 1930, Ziegfeld tried to convince Cantor to return to New York with him. "Wait till we see the picture, Flo," Eddie said. "If I squeeze your hand, we'll talk about another show." Ziegfeld waited throughout the ninety-three-minute film but felt no squeeze from Eddie. After the preview, Goldwyn patted his new star on the back; he knew he had a hit. *Whoopee!* cost $1.5 million to produce, but it made $2.3 million in profits and solved all of Cantor's money worries. Ziegfeld, impressed with both the finished film and the money it made, was willing to keep working with Goldwyn, despite their occasional clashes. After all, in the film's opening credits, he noted that his "partner" had allowed the Ziegfeld name to appear directly above the Goldwyn one. However, this was more of a benevolent farewell gesture from Goldwyn than an invitation to produce more films together. The Ziegfeld-Goldwyn Corporation never made another motion picture, and Goldwyn continued on an independent basis (Samuel Goldwyn Productions made many successful films until 1959, the most notable being Danny Kaye's musical comedies in the 1940s and 1950s and the 1946 World War II classic *The Best Years of Our Lives*). Because of his reputation for overspending, no other studios were willing to work with Ziegfeld.

With no more Hollywood offers forthcoming, Ziegfeld returned to familiar territory: Broadway. But what he found in New York made him doubt that the Broadway he knew still existed. The crash of 1929 had marked the end of the lighthearted revues and book musicals Ziegfeld had specialized in. More intimate, thoughtful revues with subdued, introspective material and "strident muckraking" had taken their place.[15] The only shows that Ziegfeld recognized now were revivals, which became surprisingly popular with a nation that seemed to be looking "both backward and forward."[16]

One revue that emerged unscathed from the crash was Earl Carroll's *Vanities*. While Ziegfeld was in Hollywood, Carroll had managed to book his show at the New Amsterdam Theatre, in which Ziegfeld still had a one-third interest. The *Vanities* were everything the *Follies* were not: bawdy, tasteless, and purposely shocking. The police even took notice of its impropriety, particularly one scene in which a man chases several girls and catches one just as the lights go out. A fan dance and a skit showing a window dresser changing a mannequin's clothes only added to the vulgarity. Ironically, the police did not object to the first-act finale that served as a protest against Prohibition. Carroll made minimal changes to appease the police, but his edits were not enough to satisfy Ziegfeld, who condemned Carroll's revue as "one of the filthiest things ever seen in New York." He informed anyone who would listen that he had had nothing to do with booking the *Vanities* at the New Amsterdam. A police raid during one performance resulted in Carroll, eight chorus girls, and one comedian being brought before a court in New York. A writer for the *New York Times* revealed that "business rivals" who were close friends of Ziegfeld were responsible for the raid. Carroll was livid and denounced Ziegfeld's "holier than thou" attitude and "poor sportsmanship." In a *New York Times* interview he stated: "Naturally Mr. Ziegfeld would not want a successful attraction of mine in a theatre in which he has a minor interest, and the box office receipts of the New Amsterdam Theatre, which were telegraphed to him nightly, were convincing proof that the 'Vanities' had broken all box office records before the raid. . . . His . . . attitude is ludicrous in view of the fact that he has openly admitted that he is the father of nudity in the American theatre."[17]

The *Vanities* played to packed houses following the scandal and ran well into the 1931 season. That same season, Carroll also experienced the wrath of the Shuberts, who accused him of pirating a number they had used in an earlier revue. Although the Shuberts had declared bankruptcy after the crash, they quickly recovered their biggest theater houses. They now operated on a smaller scale, but the percentage of working theaters they owned was bigger than ever.[18] Ziegfeld, once the greatest producer on Broadway, seemed to be the only one who was unable to regain his footing.

Ziegfeld needed a hit—badly. To the detriment of his health, he worked doggedly to create shows on par with his greatest hits. The sensation of Broadway's 1930 season was a Gershwin show, *Girl Crazy.* Like *Whoopee*, it was set in the Wild West. Its success could be attributed to a plethora of new talent, including Ethel Merman and Ginger Rogers, and cutting-edge music orchestrated by Benny Goodman, Gene Krupa, and Glenn Miller. Ziegfeld was determined to produce a worthy rival to *Girl Crazy*, and the first show on his agenda was *Tom, Dick, and Harry* (renamed *Smiles* by the time it went into production). The play was based on a story suggested by Noel Coward, with whom Ziegfeld was again on speaking terms, despite their differences during *Bitter Sweet*. Ziegfeld saw Coward's work as a perfect vehicle for Marilyn Miller. He was not concerned that critics had deemed Ethel Merman, the most exciting discovery of the season, "a direct contrast to her [predecessor], Marilyn Miller."[19] With her big voice and her lack of dainty features and movements, Merman was a "belter" who was more comparable to a vaudeville performer like Sophie Tucker. Yet she was exactly what audiences wanted.

Marilyn was not a new talent, but Ziegfeld balanced the past with the present by hiring two of the most popular young dancers on Broadway, Fred and Adele Astaire, as her costars. Ziegfeld had been trying to sign the Astaires for two years, but their manager, Alex Aarons, continually advised the brother and sister not to work with the producer. "I think you're sticking your neck out signing with Ziegfeld. He won't know what to do with you," Aarons told them. However, according to Fred Astaire, Ziegfeld held "a predominant place" in his and Adele's minds.[20] Fred had been enamored with Ziegfeld productions since seeing *The Soul Kiss* in 1908 (he claimed to have seen it twenty-eight times), which, according to Fred, contained "the first really great dancing I ever saw."[21] The Astaires received a cable from Ziegfeld reading: "DEAR FRED AND ADELE: I HAVE A WONDERFUL IDEA FOR YOU COSTARRING WITH MARILYN MILLER." Finally, Fred decided, "this seemed like the big one we were looking for." Ziegfeld returned to his Broadway office "aglow with plans and hopes for the show." "I don't see how it can miss," he told Fred.[22]

Smiles proved to be nothing to grin about. Fred Astaire wrote in his memoir: "I must say it was a devastating one [experience] for everyone involved. Nothing seemed right from the start."[23] The show began on a negative note due to Marilyn's objections over being relegated to a secondary role. She was still incensed at Ziegfeld for abandoning *Ming Toy*. Another problem was William Anthony McGuire, who failed week after week to deliver even the ghost of a script. "Can't you realize I must have it now?" Ziegfeld wrote frantically to McGuire, who was incoherent and in an alcoholic stupor. Ziegfeld finally dismissed him. He went through several more writers until he settled on Ring Lardner, who managed to piece together a script from what little McGuire had written.

Smiles suffered from an identity crisis: one minute it was a sophisticated, cutting-edge musical, and the next minute it was a throwback to the more sentimental shows of the early 1900s. Fred Astaire likened it to *The Belle of New York* (1897). *Smiles* tells the story of a French orphan (Marilyn) who is adopted by three American soldiers during World War I. The soldiers bring her to America, where she grows up and joins the Salvation Army. Despite her humble work, she is attracted to high society (represented by the Astaires). In the end, she decides to marry one of the soldiers who adopted her.

Unlike *Show Boat*, the songs in *Smiles* did not spring from the story line. Still, the Astaires offered debonair dance routines to accompany the slick songs, one of which was the Vincent Youmans tune "Say Young Man of Manhattan." The now famous routine featured Fred shooting down his competition of chorus men with the tip of his cane, using his tap shoes to imitate the rat-tat-tat of a gun. The skit was Fred's own invention. He claimed he worked it out at four o'clock in the morning in his Park Avenue apartment. When he told Adele about his vision the next morning, she replied, "Well hang onto it, baby. You're going to need it in this turkey."[24] The number was the only one that brought down the house. The skit was later reenacted to much acclaim in the film *Top Hat* (1935). Marilyn's songs and the romantic plotline, in contrast, seemed forced and unbelievable, especially to hardened, Depression-era audiences.

Ziegfeld grew increasingly disillusioned with the show and with Marilyn as she became more temperamental during rehearsals. She blamed the show's conductor, Paul Lannin, for her difficulties. His subpar conducting was why she failed to shine in the show, she argued. Youmans took Lannin's side and threatened to withdraw all his songs if Lannin was dismissed. Ziegfeld was forced to file a suit against Youmans to keep him from leaving the show without completing a score. To top everything off, Marilyn's work ethic had declined even further after her indulgent treatment in Hollywood. She spent much of her downtime engaging in practical jokes and pranks backstage, often at the encouragement of Adele Astaire. One prank involved Ziegfeld's long-suffering secretary, Goldie. Ziegfeld had frantically called Goldie at three o'clock in the morning, begging her to return to the office to find the telephone number of the show's costumer. Marilyn and Adele happened to be on the premises, despite the ungodly hour. As Goldie entered the office, they crouched in the darkness and grabbed her leg as she stumbled past them. Goldie screamed and turned on the light, to find Marilyn and Adele giggling on the floor.

Another amusing incident occurred during the show's tryout period. One night when the show was playing in Boston, Marilyn suggested to Fred Astaire that they take a ride over the Charles River Bridge toward Cambridge. As they crossed the bridge, Fred asked the driver to stop so he could look out over the water. Marilyn joined him, and they stood gazing at the river for several minutes. Then they heard a car drive up behind them. Someone grabbed Fred's coat collar, shook him "like a dicebox," and said, "You're not gonna do it, buddy." It took Fred and Marilyn quite a while to convince the two policemen that they were not planning to jump. Eventually, they "all became friends," and Fred invited the officers to attend a performance of *Smiles*. Fred ruefully noted that seeing the awful show was his way of getting even with the cops.[25] Though pranks and comic misunderstandings lightened the mood during tryouts and rehearsals, the cast was still convinced the show was a turkey—even if Ziegfeld disagreed.

Smiles opened on November 18, 1930, at the Ziegfeld Theatre, and its reception gave the producer every reason to believe that any misgivings about the show were unfounded. Marilyn and the Astaires received twelve standing ovations. Outside the theater, onlookers were equally enthusiastic. Police had to restrain the 10,000 fans and members of the press stalking the celebrities as they arrived in their limousines. The next morning Walter Winchell heralded *Smiles* as the "most colossal and most wonderful show" to ever be produced.[26] *Smiles* was worth every penny of the $22 ticket price, and Ziegfeld felt justified in paying Marilyn her weekly salary of $5,000.

However, the only reviewers who were smiling over the show were those employed by William Randolph Hearst. Hearst, who had funded the Ziegfeld Theatre, needed the show to be successful if he was to profit from his investment. A writer for *Time* described *Smiles* as "very pretty . . . very big" but had little else to say about it. The only aspects of the show that reviewers unanimously praised were its artistic detail and the Astaires' performance. Brooks Atkinson of the *New York Times* claimed that, "with them, dancing is [a] comedy of manners, very much in the current mode. Free of shop-trickery, they plunge into the midst of the frolic." Marilyn, too, garnered praise from Atkinson: "Her beauty has not dimmed and her formal smile is no less engaging . . . she dances lightly and sings pleasantly." Not all reviewers agreed, however. One critic remarked that Marilyn belonged to an older order of musical comedy in which star vehicles ruled, such as those Ziegfeld had produced for Anna Held decades before. Overall, Atkinson concluded that the show was a mere rough draft of a potential hit. "Doubtless Mr. Ziegfeld will keep on whipping his new production into shape, making the entertainment worthy of its beauty," he wrote. "But with such a heavy-handed book and such humorless dialogue it is difficult to believe *Smiles* will ever represent his best talent."[27]

Ziegfeld intended to whip his production into shape, but it became difficult when his health declined again. He experienced an attack of sciatica, a condition that causes pain or tingling in the leg brought on by compression of a spinal nerve root. This forced him to remain bedridden at Burkeley Crest. He then developed blinding headaches so severe that they affected his memory. Many of the cables and letters Ziegfeld sent from his bed were nonsensical and showed his deteriorating state of mind. He was known for feigning illness "to gain sympathy, to escape predators, or to avoid appearing in court on the innumerable lawsuits that threatened him," but there was nothing fake about his present state of health.[28]

Fred and Adele Astaire were worried when "Mr. Z" failed to appear at the theater, and they sent notes expressing their concern. Ziegfeld's reply was in no way incoherent, proving that he still had periods of lucidity: "Dear Fred: Don't worry—I'm feeling better—I'll fix the show! I could've fixed it in the first place, only there were too many cooks. Affectionately, Flo." However, Fred recalled that Ziegfeld "hardly got around to seeing us after that, much less to fix the show."[29]

Critics continued to batter the production; even Percy Hammond of the *New York Tribune,* who customarily gave Ziegfeld shows positive reviews, could not recommend *Smiles.* Ziegfeld wrote Hammond a strongly worded letter, chastising him for not recognizing *Smiles'* wholesomeness and charm. "Some people still accept a show without naked women, filth, and slime," Ziegfeld declared.[30] His words were consistent with his recent condemnation of Carroll's revue and his general attempt to make his shows family friendly. Still, Carroll's shows played to packed houses, while *Smiles* struggled to attract audiences during its two-month run.

The production so diminished Ziegfeld's funds that he was unable to pay the Astaires. They took the matter to court and eventually won a settlement. Even after the dispute, they had no hard feelings toward Ziegfeld. "We were fond of Flo and felt bad for him—as well as for ourselves," Fred wrote. He even accepted some of the blame for the show's failure: "He [Ziegfeld] tried very hard on that one, and I'm afraid I was no help at all. In fact, I was ashamed of my inadequate performance."[31] Fred need not have blamed himself, or anyone else in the production for that matter; the truth was that he and his sister were responsible for the show's running as long as it did. Reviewers had once given musicals some leniency, but by 1931, critical standards were more rigid. Neither critics nor audiences wanted to spend what little money they had on a show that was less than top-notch.

Further handicapping *Smiles* was Marilyn Miller's absence from the stage for several weeks. Her sinus troubles began to plague her once again, and the accompanying migraines only increased her despondency. Journalists ruthlessly speculated about the reason for her nonappearance, including the rumor that she was recovering from an abortion. None admitted the truth: she was having a nervous breakdown. Though ticket sales for *Smiles* nose-dived with her absence, they did not rebound when she returned. The show lost $300,000.

Smiles, which Fred Astaire called "an unprecedented, flashbulb flop . . . the kind of flop that made even the audience look bad," was a severe blow for everyone involved. After the show closed shortly after New Year's Day, Marilyn visited Fred and Adele's apartment and "practically collapsed in tears."[32] In 1922 Marilyn had declared that she would rather die than become a forgotten, gray-haired old woman. This sentiment was foremost in her mind in the weeks following the failure of both *Smiles* and her second film, *Sunny.* Marilyn was still a wealthy woman, however, despite her string of flops. She continued to receive a generous salary from her movie contract, but her money did little to relieve her despair. In her autobiography, former Ziegfeld dancer Doris Eaton aptly described what was at the root of Marilyn's depression and that of many actresses like her: "They [show people] work so hard to get there and succeed, and then when something happens and they no longer have the adulation and attention—indeed, when no one even notices them at all—it is a terrible blow. Ziegfeld filled his chorus with sixteen and seventeen year-old beauties, and most of them were out of show business by twenty. Many tried to marry quickly and to someone of great means and make life an endless party. But life is not that way, and the party often ended in sadness."[33]

Marilyn was in her early thirties; she had already had a considerably longer career than most Ziegfeld beauties. But she was not ready to quit, nor was she looking for another marriage to solve her problems. Ziegfeld offered her a part in a new *Follies* he was planning, but the idea remained abstract, given the absence of funding from his financially strapped backers. Marilyn refused his offer, and Ziegfeld discreetly disposed of her contract. Releasing her from his employ at this point was more an act of mercy than rejection, for all he could offer her were more shows from a bygone era of musical comedy. In addition, he could no longer afford her $5,000 a week salary.

Ziegfeld became invigorated with his plans to resurrect the *Follies*, although few others shared his excitement. Ruth Etting, Helen Morgan, and the Albertina Rasch Dancers were the only stars from the Ziegfeld fold to sign up for the project. Joseph Urban and Gene Buck, ever loyal, agreed to design the scenery and write the book. Ziegfeld envisioned the new *Follies* as a retrospective of the past that would prove the old-style musicals and revues still had a place on Broadway.

The failure of the Goldwyn-Ziegfeld merger in Hollywood, followed by the failure of *Smiles*, left Billie Burke desperate to earn money for her family. She knew Ziegfeld would not keep thrift in mind when planning the 1931 *Follies,* even though his only funding consisted of interests Abe Erlanger had left after his death in 1930. With a maturity necessitated by her reduced circumstances and her forty-six years, Billie accepted her first character part, in a play entitled *The Truth Game.* She later wrote that the play "came at a time when I felt more than ever that I needed to get back to the theater." She was cast as "a gay little lady" who attempts to turn every friendship into a profitable affair—a far cry from the innocent ingénue roles that had made her famous. Her character was manipulative and insincere, not unlike the gold diggers who populated Palm Beach. Billie drew on her real-life experiences with such women and made her role a hilarious satire. Audiences and critics loved *The Truth Game* (which opened on December 20, 1930, at the Ethel Barrymore Theatre), and Billie seemed to have found a new niche. But she continued to have misgivings about accepting character parts. "Oh, that sad and bewildering moment when you are no longer the cherished darling but must turn the corner and try to be funny!" Billie later wrote.[34]

The Truth Game also afforded Patricia an opportunity to return to the stage. Patricia had not caught the acting bug and had not appeared before an audience since her recital at the Halstead School for Girls. However, she found herself called to the stage while touring with Billie in Philadelphia in the spring of 1931. Billie met her daughter at the train station and looked her up and down a bit despairingly. She was a gangly girl of fourteen, dressed in Oxfords and a crookedly buttoned navy blue sweater. Nevertheless, Billie nodded to herself and said: "The girl who plays the maid in my play is ill. It's only a tiny part—hardly more than a line. But Ivor [Ivor Novello, Billie's leading man] and I thought it might be fun for you." Patricia balked at first. She reminded Billie that in her only previous stage appearance, as a woodpecker, she had merely flapped her arms without speaking at all. "You flapped beautifully," Billie assured her. Patricia finally agreed and began to get excited when Billie took her backstage to have her maid's uniform fitted. Patricia repeated her one line over and over again: "Please ma'am, may I have the keys to the stable? Sir Joshua's locked in and can't get out." When Billie informed Ziegfeld of their daughter's upcoming performance, he took the next train to Philadelphia and arrived in time for her debut. He summoned photographers and reporters and ordered a dozen red roses sent to Patricia backstage. She played the role for five performances and fumbled her lines (accidentally saying "Mother" instead of "ma'am") on more than one occasion, but Billie and Novello praised her nonetheless. Patricia later admitted she never "got inside" the character.[35]

"Well, would you like to make a career of acting, honey?" Ziegfeld asked her.

"I still like the front side best," Patricia told him, alluding to their conversation following the unpleasant meeting with Marilyn Miller backstage at the New Amsterdam Theatre in 1923.

Billie may not have gotten inside her character either, but she gave a good impression that she did. She was now fulfilling Sir Charles Hawtrey's prophecy: she would be a fine comedienne. When *The Truth Game* closed in March 1931, a triumphant Billie was on her way to developing a unique brand of screwball comedy that proved to be most popular with 1930s audiences. What was it that made Billie's comedy so special? The answer lay in her talent for uttering ridiculous lines and malapropisms with a perfect seriousness, temporarily convincing audiences of the logic in her nonsensical words. Once the nonsense dawned on them, they exploded with laughter.

The same season *The Truth Game* premiered, Billie landed another character role in a play entitled *The Vinegar Tree*. The production opened at the Belasco Theatre in Los Angeles in June 1931 (Billie was not in the original Broadway show, which had opened in November 1930). She was so successful in her role as a scatterbrained society matron that, after *The Vinegar Tree*, she was perpetually typecast in the same role. Critics lauded her, calling her "the queen of laughter" and inquiring "why she has not brought her rare talent for comedy to the public more often."[36] Billie put aside any thoughts of venturing into dramatic roles after her comedic talents garnered such admiration.

Billie and Ziegfeld broke their long-held vow not to be separated by work; they now found themselves on opposite sides of the country as Billie performed in California with the company of *The Vinegar Tree* and Ziegfeld remained in New York. "I violated my instinct, overriding my heart with what I argued were practical considerations when I went away from Flo," Billie reflected.[37] She hated leaving her husband when he needed her most, but their separation actually drew them closer together. Billie ordered Ziegfeld's staff to place freshly cut flowers in his office each morning while she was away, for she knew her husband could not abide wilt and decay. Ziegfeld arranged for a limousine to meet Billie at the train station in downtown Los Angeles. He also found her a luxurious house in Santa Monica that had been designed by MGM's set designer Cedric Gibbons. Finally, he ensured that Billie's dressing room was filled with flowers after her performances.

"It's all going to come out all right," Ziegfeld telegraphed Billie from New York. "I'm going to do another *Follies,* and everything will be fine."[38] Billie did not let on that she knew he was still putting on a façade. Nothing would ever be fine again.

At the beginning of 1931, Ziegfeld arrived at his theater to see no show's title emblazoned on its marquee. Snow covered the roof, and the windows were encrusted with ice. Ziegfeld solemnly entered his office. Dressed in his beaver-lined coat, he still looked as wealthy as he had been in his heyday. But when he sat down at his desk lined with elephant statuettes, he did not remove the coat. He could no longer afford coal for the furnace. "All I've worked for is crumbling before my eyes," he told Goldie. "I can't do this anymore."[39]

Even though Ziegfeld seemed defeated, he still worked to piece together all that was crumbling before his eyes. However, he made no effort to repair his mental state. He sat up at night writing long letters to his staff filled with complaints, many of which, according to Charles Higham, "were addressed to himself."[40] His illegible handwriting confused the letters' recipients and indicated that his psychological well-being had been damaged, perhaps irreparably.

At the office, all the staff members noticed signs of nervous strain in Ziegfeld. He walked in each morning impeccably dressed except for his shoes, which had obvious tears in the soles.

"Goldie, take out that straight line chorus formation. I detest straight line formations," he ordered.

"There're at least a dozen unopened envelopes on your desk, Mr. Ziegfeld. Perhaps I should . . ."

"No envelopes are to be touched," Ziegfeld retorted, throwing his coat over the ticking clock in his office. Eying the clock on Goldie's desk, he tossed his scarf over it. "I abhor a ticking clock," he muttered.

When Goldie brought in Ziegfeld's fresh flowers one day, he nearly broke into tears when he saw a red rose included in the bouquet. "Throw it out!" he ordered. Somehow, he had developed a phobia of red blooms, just as he had developed a phobia of clocks.[41] He needed no reminders that time was passing. According to historian Ann Ommen van der Merwe, Ziegfeld had "moved beyond any desire to adjust to current trends and simply reveled in nostalgia."[42]

Ziegfeld's new show was an ode to the *Follies* of the past; even the new entertainers he hired sang old tunes. The first act began in typical Ziegfeld style with a classic Gene Buck and Dave Stamper song, "Bring on the Follies Girls." The curtain parted to reveal a nude showgirl on a pedestal. Despite Ziegfeld's vehement condemnation of nudity onstage, this was his way of showing the proper way to present a naked woman: not as a crude member of a girlie show but as a Grecian statue. Next, as a balance to the more sentimental and nostalgic opening songs, there was a satire on the popular play *Grand Hotel* (1929), with Helen Morgan as the queen of the Russian ballet. Other characters in the play were spoofed as well, bearing such humorous names as Baron Al Capone and Cecil B. Goldwater of Hollywood. Later in the show came another skit, "Victim of the Talkies," that satirized actors whose voices transferred badly to film. These were the only topical sketches that were out of step with the show's overriding theme of nostalgia.

The most nostalgic number in the show, "Broadway Reverie," was a sentimental tribute to Broadway of yore. Many of the people and places it depicted were those dear to Ziegfeld. The first was Rector's, one of Ziegfeld's first haunts in New York. In that scene, Dorothy Dell, Ruth Etting, and the Collette Sisters sang torch songs that Brooks Atkinson condemned as "brabbling . . . music hall inbreeding."[43] Next in the reverie was the "Pink Lady Waltz," an allusion to Hazel Dawn. Then Ruth Etting sang "Shine on, Harvest Moon" as a tribute to Nora Bayes. Finally, Ziegfeld chorines dressed as the Nell Brinkley Girls paid homage to the 1908 *Follies*. Atkinson may have been unimpressed with the number, but most audience members and critics disagreed.

When the *Follies* opened on July 1, 1931, at the Ziegfeld Theatre, it attracted many attendees. Ziegfeld described their reaction to his revue: "Nine different things in the show stop the show cold, so the next person can't go on without repeated bow." Ziegfeld was so excited about the initial response that he wired Billie: "Darling, I would like to call you up every minute. . . . You never heard such applause in a theater." Among the most enthusiastic audience members were Irving Thalberg and Norma Shearer (Ziegfeld had gone to great lengths to secure seats for them). Ziegfeld noted, "The heat was terrific, yet we turned hundreds away at [the] matinee." He was already planning his next edition of the *Follies*, which he hoped would include old audience favorites. "When you see Will Rogers tell him I expect him to go on in the show in the fall," he wrote to Billie.[44] Gene Buck later told Billie that producing another *Follies* in the depths of the Depression and having it be a relative success "meant more than any venture Flo ever embarked upon."[45]

Ziegfeld's joy was diminished a bit by the reviews. Atkinson criticized "Broadway Reverie" but did his best to point out the show's merits: "Even in 1931, which is getting on to crisper things, Mr. Ziegfeld's suave style of showmanship wears well—the quiet amplitude of Mr. Urban's scenery, the luster of the lighting, the depth of the spectacles. And the girls: they more than hold their own. . . . Even without original ideas, the 1931 *Follies* is competent."[46] Ziegfeld considered competent only one step above inadequate; he wanted his shows to be nothing less than spectacular and beyond all expectations. Ommen van der Merwe has asserted that the 1931 *Follies* was actually the most quintessential of the series and established the Ziegfeld legacy: "Ziegfeld Girls, spectacular settings, sentimentality, and exotic flavor."[47]

Although most critiques were complimentary in their own way, they ultimately did nothing but remind Ziegfeld that he had become outmoded. *Time* magazine's review confirmed that the days gone by glorified in the *Follies* were just that—gone. The reviewer included both Ziegfeld and

Billie among the rubble of nostalgia, noting Ziegfeld's "slick gray hair . . . growing thinner as his piquant, forty-four year old second wife, Billie Burke, passes on to join his svelte first (Anna Held) in Broadway's legend of beauty." Ziegfeld "knows what nostalgia is," the reviewer continued, but his ideas of humor were "cheerfully dependable, not intoxicating." The writer concluded that the show followed the "old formula: really beautiful girls, the best tap and ballet dancing money can buy. . . . To all this he [Ziegfeld] added his priceless ingredient of nostalgia to make people say, 'Good old New York, good old Broadway, good old Follies.'"[48] The critique read almost like a eulogy, which was strangely appropriate, given that the show was essentially an overview of Ziegfeld's life work. After the first week of the *Follies'* run, attendance dropped notably. The show made barely enough money to recoup its production costs.

Following the show's premiere, Ziegfeld was eager to leave New York and visit Billie and Patricia in Hollywood. Billie saw little of him between stops on her West Coast tour of *The Vinegar Tree*, but Ziegfeld seemed more devoted to his family than ever. For once, he was not impatient to return to work. When he eventually had to go back to New York, he wrote to Billie that his only wish was "to have my little family together either out on the coast or here." He wired Billie: "I BELIEVE YOU SHOULD BOTH [Billie and Patricia] FIGURE ON A REST AT PALM SPRINGS I MAY GET A BREAK AND ABLE TO MEET YOU THERE PATTIE CAN THEN SEE MOTHER GETS PROPER FOOD I THINK THEY HAVE LITTLE BUNGALOWS THERE I HATE TO FACE NEW YORK ALL MY LOVE."[49]

Though Ziegfeld expressed concern that Billie was not eating properly, his utmost worry was for Patricia. Billie was still on the road, and Patricia was left behind in Hollywood with only a small staff to look after her. "Patty called up last night," Ziegfeld informed Billie in a letter. "Seems strange to leave her alone in Hollywood of all places." To make California more homelike for his daughter, Ziegfeld sent her Chloto, her favorite dog from Burkeley Crest: "CHLOTO WILL ARRIVE ON THE CHIEF SUNDAY FIVE OCLOCK CHAPERONED BY JAKE THE BARBERS SON ALL DINING ROOM STEWARDS HAVE BEEN NOTIFIED TO SUPPLY THE BEST OF FOOD AND ROOM CHLOTO WILL BE TAKEN OUT AT EVERY IMPORTANT STOP MANAGER OF THE RAILROAD WILL ESCORT HIM FROM THE DEPOT IN CHICAGO."[50]

The little dog made it safely to the West Coast, but Ziegfeld did not know how long it would be before he could reunite with his family. His separation from Billie and Patricia pained him greatly; his telegrams to them are filled with evidence of his suffering and his increasing dependence on them for his mental stability. In the following telegram to Patricia, he discusses trying his hand at filmmaking again so he might be closer to his "two babies": "WELL HERE I AM ALONE AND ITS LONESOME. . . . YOU KNOW DADDY IS GETTING OLD AND NEEDS REST BUT OUR EXPENSES ARE ALWAYS SO BIG . . . DADDY MUST TRY PICTURES. . . . DONT NEGLECT YOUR GOLF AND TENNIS AND FIRST THING I WANT YOU TO DO IS LEARN REALLY TO DANCE. . . . YOU MUST WRITE DADDY . . . LOVE AND KISSES TAKE CARE OF MOTHER."[51]

Ziegfeld, who hated to see his family live as anything but royalty, was desperate to reclaim his short-lived status as a millionaire producer. He threw himself into his work again, neglecting to consider that he, more than anyone in the family, needed care.

21

Going Home

"Show business has changed so much," a tired Ziegfeld confided to his daughter upon his return to Broadway in November 1931.[1] Judging by this statement, he still felt, as he had told Goldie months before, that he could not "do this [produce shows] anymore." However, due to his dwindling bank account, he had no choice but to keep on creating shows he hoped would be successful. Also, no matter how defeated he felt, he found it impossible to stop thinking about the theater and ideas for new shows that could restore his former glory.

An idea for a potential hit came to Ziegfeld via Lew Brown and Ray Henderson, who were writers for George White, a former *Follies* dancer and current producer of the popular revue series *Scandals*. Brown and Henderson had gained fame primarily through the songs they had composed, with B. G. DeSylva, for *Good News* (1927), including "The Best Things in Life Are Free" and "The Varsity Drag." The writing team had been in talks with White to produce a Bert Lahr vehicle, but when negotiations inexplicably broke down, Brown and Henderson approached Ziegfeld, who was only too happy to take on the show they presented. He had been holding a grudge against White since 1919, when the dancer left the *Follies* to start a rival revue. Ziegfeld, in a shrewd attempt to eliminate the competition, had offered White $2,000 a week to return to the *Follies*. White had sarcastically responded: "I'll pay you and Billie Burke three thousand dollars to go into the next *Scandals*."[2] White was everything Ziegfeld was not: vulgar, brash, and irreverent—a renegade fond of mayhem.

Ziegfeld knew he could do more with the Bert Lahr show than White could. *Hot-Cha!* was an irrational, fantastic comedy that may have been a success in the 1920s but only made Depression-era audiences roll their eyes. Lahr played a speakeasy waiter on the run in Mexico. Through a series of wacky misunderstandings, he becomes a bullfighter who miraculously triumphs in the ring. Ziegfeld could not understand why the script remained so problematic when he had such a reliable writing team working on it. Desperate, Ziegfeld turned to Lahr for advice. According to Lahr's son, his father cherished these "small moments of intimacy with Ziegfeld."[3] In the early 1930s, due to his poor health, Ziegfeld relied more than ever on telegrams and phone calls to communicate with his employees, so it was significant that he stepped out of his comfort zone to meet Lahr for coffee at Child's restaurant. As Lahr sipped his coffee, his hangdog face was more droopy than usual. "What can we do to fix this up?" he asked, waving the script at Ziegfeld. "I think we ought to bring in some new writers. This work Henderson and Brown have done is . . . lame." Why Ziegfeld asked for Lahr's advice is anyone's guess; he was deaf to the actor's suggestions and even seemed defensive about the show. "Keep the script the way it is," Ziegfeld told Lahr.[4]

New writers may have been the answer to saving *Hot-Cha!* from being a thin and imitative production. Brown and Henderson wrote jokes and songs intended to cheer Depression-era audiences. One tune, "It's Great to Be Alive," rhapsodized about flowers and twittering birds. Ziegfeld thought the song would bolster audiences' morale, just as "Look for the Silver Lining" had done more than a decade before. If the show's score did not resonate with audiences, surely the exciting new performers would. Lupe Velez, the free-living Mexican vamp of movie fame, was the leading lady. Charles "Buddy" Rogers, the affable singer-musician who was married to Mary Pickford, was the second male lead. Ziegfeld felt Rogers would attract a younger crowd, given that he had starred in *Wings* (1927), the first film to be awarded the Best Picture Oscar.

With such notable talents headlining the show, *Hot-Cha!* was by no means cheap to produce. Ziegfeld was in urgent need of backers. Eddie Cantor, who was once again a wealthy man due to his Hollywood success, lent his old boss $100,000, but this was not enough to cover all the show's costs. Ziegfeld grew so desperate that he turned to two notorious gangsters, Waxey Gordon and Dutch Schultz, for additional funding. During rehearsals, the bootleggers would bring in their cohorts and sit in the auditorium, smoking cigars and yelling out suggestions. "Why not call it *Laid in Mexico*?" Gordon called, followed by a round of laughter from his friends. The gangsters' interference enraged Ziegfeld, but he could do nothing to stop it. No one else would back him after his latest flops. He compromised his artistic taste by allowing *Laid in Mexico* to serve as the show's subtitle. Ethan Mordden wrote that critics "expressed reservations at the crass new tone on Broadway, redolent of the excesses of the late, degraded burlesque. . . . To keep up with the show business that had changed so much, he [Ziegfeld] had to accede to the more blatant pandering of the George White school."[5]

Acceding to the "George White school" caused Ziegfeld's already depressed psychological state to spiral downward. When three precious white jade elephants arrived at his office, he screamed at Goldie, "Do you want to ruin me?" He pointed an accusing finger at the elephants' downturned trunks. Goldie could not calm her boss until she showed him the smashed remains of the unlucky statues. Ziegfeld's eccentricities were likely exacerbated by his long separation from his family; Christmas 1931 was the first one he had spent apart from Billie since they were married. Billie, once again exhibiting her resilience and selflessness, sent her husband an encouraging telegram and hid the fact that she felt as fragile as he did: "JUST KEEP YOUR COURAGE AND LOVE US AND LOOK TO A HAPPIER FUTURE . . . SURELY OUR LOVE WILL HAVE SOME POWER TO HELP YOU OVER THESE BUMPS."[6]

However, no amount of love from Billie could make the production of *Hot-Cha!* run more smoothly. During a Pittsburgh tryout in February 1932, the entire company fell victim to a flu epidemic. Ziegfeld kept Goldie working day and night, despite her fever. With nurses and doctors at her side, she continued to take dictation from Ziegfeld, who seemed unconcerned that he might catch the illness himself. His insensitivity was not enough to make Goldie leave his employ, but other staff members were not so patient. Bernard Sobel, his reliable publicity man, had resigned after the last *Follies*. Ziegfeld tried to make amends with the following comical, apologetic telegram: "I FORGIVE YOU FOR LEAVING ME PERHAPS NEXT TIME YOUR WORD WILL BE GOOD I WILL TRY TO DO ALL MY OWN PRESS WORK HEREAFTER AS I HAVE NOTHING TO DO . . . I HOPE YOUR POOR NERVES WILL SOON GET RESTED AFTER YOU LEAVE ME I SUPPOSE YOU ARE ALREADY EATING NOTHING BUT MATZOTH PLEASE SEND ME SIX BOXES ON THE 6:40 TRAIN TONIGHT WHEN YOU MOVE TO YOUR ABIE'S IRISH ROSE QUARTERS IN THE BRONX GOOD LUCK MY POOR MISGUIDED BEST PRESS AGENT IN THE WORLD ZIEGFELD."[7] Despite Ziegfeld's persuasive telegram, Sobel did not return. Ziegfeld's ability to pay Sobel's salary was in question, and without a reliable paycheck, the agent was not willing to endure the stress that came with his job. Sobel stated: "Working for him [Ziegfeld] meant being on call twenty-four hours a day, every day of the week." Ziegfeld would sometimes call Sobel as early as five in the morning and talk "swiftly and endlessly. . . . I went nearly wild," the press agent declared. Sobel admitted that being in Ziegfeld's employ was a "glamorous occupation," but he also felt like the "glorifier's slave." He concluded that he loved, hated, and respected his boss, but he "could never quite convince" himself that he was Ziegfeld's "aide."[8]

Without Sobel, Ziegfeld piled more work on Goldie and himself. He ultimately came down with the flu, which hit him quite severely. Despite bone aches and violent stomach pains, he pressed on with his work from a special bed he had set up in his office.[9] Ziegfeld's wires to Billie during this period mentioned his deteriorating health and insufficient sleep (three hours a night), but somehow they remained optimistic overall. He stated that after the Pittsburgh tryout the notices for *Hot-Cha!* "were terrific"— an exaggeration for Billie's sake. According to Bert Lahr, Ziegfeld came to his dressing room after the show's first tryout with a wan smile on his face. Lahr recalled, "He never said 'Good show, Bert' or 'I think we have something.'" Instead, Ziegfeld spoke only to Lahr's valet about the actor's sequined matador costume: "Get a black bag for this outfit so the brocade doesn't tarnish."[10]

After three weeks touring on the road, and with expenses exceeding $90,000, Ziegfeld wrote to Billie: "How I ever got things this far and how I am alive handling this mob and temperamental authors, I don't know. I realize what is wrong and I only hope I have the strength to fix it. . . . I only wish you and Pattie were to be at the opening."[11] Billie, who was performing in a short-lived play entitled *Mad Hopes,* fretted over Ziegfeld's health and even considered leaving the production to be at his side. However, knowing that financial worries were contributing to his illness, she continued to work on the West Coast.

When it came time for the company of *Hot-Cha!* to return to New York, an ambulance took the still ailing Goldie and Ziegfeld to the train station. Ziegfeld's flu had turned into pneumonia. In the midst of planning the show's New York opening, Ziegfeld's condition worsened to such a degree that he was convinced he was dying. When John Harkrider came to visit him, Ziegfeld muttered three words to him over and over again: "All that beauty, Jack. All that beauty."[12]

Ziegfeld survived his illness, although it left him weaker than ever. His publicity campaign for *Hot-Cha!* was worth the effort, however; the play, which opened on March 8, 1932, at the Ziegfeld Theatre, became the season's fifth longest running musical (at 119 performances). Nevertheless, critics were lukewarm in their response to the production. Brooks Atkinson of the *New York Times* wrote that the show was "warm-cha in story and melody" and the libretto was "stodgy." The ladies of the chorus and Urban's "voluptuous and fiery" use of color were, as usual, singled out for their beauty, making the show "better to see than to hear." Bert Lahr received the most favorable reviews. Atkinson claimed that Lahr's "mugging merriment" made the $5.50 ticket price "worth a laughing playgoer's while." The production contained several signature Ziegfeld tricks. In his usual quest for authenticity, Ziegfeld had imported a bull from Mexico and "cautiously let [it] loose in a public square" for one of the matador scenes. The dance numbers were filled "with girls who tap-dance very smartly, and two pairs of exotic skirt-and-tight-pants dancers." A budding young tap dancer named Eleanor Powell entertained audiences with her footwork between acts one and two. Although the other costumes were designed by Charles LeMaire, John Harkrider was responsible for Powell's costume—shimmering gold pajamas with flowing, loose sleeves and attractively pleated pants. In his summation of *Hot-Cha!* Atkinson concluded that "Mr. Ziegfeld's mask and pageantry is up to his usual showman's standard."[13]

However, no amount of showmanship could convince the average playgoer to spend $5.50 for a ticket. Ziegfeld blamed Lahr for the show's meager box-office receipts, firing off wires to the comedian and telling him he had let the show down in the second act. However, he always signed the wires, "Love, Flo." Lahr, still unsatisfied with his lines, often ad-libbed onstage, and Ziegfeld, "like a petulant mother-in-law . . . scolded him for taking liberties with the script."[14] The producer who had once condoned Eddie Cantor's and Will Rogers's ad-libs now saw such improvisations as a sign that his actors found his producing ability subpar and lacked respect for his authority.

On May 25, 1932, Ziegfeld announced that the show would have to close. He printed a solemn notice in the *New York Times* reading: "It is with sincere regret that I am compelled to hereby give notice, in accordance with Equity contract conditions, that the 'Hot-Cha!' company closes next Saturday, May 28. The terrific running expenses make it impossible for the show to play at prices possible for the public to pay during these depressing times."[15] Two days later, Ziegfeld changed his mind, reduced ticket prices to $4.40, and announced that the company would take "a voluntary cut in salary."[16] Everyone but Buddy Rogers accepted the pay cut, so he was replaced by Art Jarrett. Despite these measures, the show played for only three more weeks. Ziegfeld's explanation was again the Depression: "I look upon the Depression primarily as a lack of confidence. In 'It's Great to Be Alive' we have the line 'there's just as many flowers, just as many trees.' It's all in people's minds to a great extent. But people have less money and try to spend it more carefully."[17]

Ziegfeld's words reflected that he was still a dreamer, holding on to idealistic illusions. But his acknowledgment that people had to spend their money more carefully proved that he was not unaware of reality. His own debts continued to mount, and he often had to flee his office by way of the fire escape or the cellar to avoid his creditors or the gangsters who had backed him.[18] Overall, he lost $115,000 on *Hot-Cha!* Ziegfeld's depression was not helped by the increased squabbling among his staff. Ziegfeld disliked the business end of the theater so much that he had given two men the same job. His two business managers, Dan Curry and Stanley Sharpe, were now one step away from a duel. "Sharpe is a family man, you know, Mr. Ziegfeld," Curry told his boss. "He needs money to keep that family going, and he does not feel he's paid enough. I have every reason to believe he's been stealing your funds." Ziegfeld approached Sharpe with the accusation, and he retorted: "Curry is a hopeless alcoholic. You mustn't believe anything he says."[19] Ziegfeld ultimately fired Sharpe after he sued the producer, who had not paid Sharpe's salary for three years. Sharpe had been so awed by Ziegfeld's artistry that he had not made a fuss—until now. Sharpe's lawsuit was added to the pile of cases already pending against Ziegfeld.

In addition, Goldie and the office telephone operator, Alice Poole, were constantly at odds. Alice enjoyed gossiping about scandals such as the Sharpe-Curry feud, and when Ziegfeld chided her about eavesdropping, she disconnected him in the middle of a sentence. As much as Alice annoyed him, Ziegfeld was even more irritated with his beloved Goldie. In the spring of 1932 she got married. He had never believed "the last virgin of Broadway," as he called her, would marry. But the harried secretary had finally decided to make a life for herself outside the Ziegfeld office.[20]

When Ziegfeld telephoned his wife about the madness at the office and the newest lawsuit, Billie threw herself into endless rages (conversations on which Alice gleefully eavesdropped). But the overworked Billie and the sickly, stressed Ziegfeld could not always console each other. Rumors abounded that Ziegfeld had found comfort and escape from his problems through the most peculiar avenues. To resurrect the young, virile man he had once been, Ziegfeld allegedly took hormone pills and staged wild orgiastic parties at Burkeley Crest. However, these stories must be taken with a fair amount of skepticism. Ziegfeld had never fully recovered from his bout with pneumonia, and he could hardly make it to the office each day, much less hold Bacchanalian feasts at home every night. The stories seem even more unlikely, given Ziegfeld's increasing reliance on and devotion to his family (in spite of Billie's rages).

Ziegfeld's mood, and Billie's, improved when he found a possible solution to his impending bankruptcy: a weekly spot on a CBS radio show sponsored by Chrysler Motors. He accepted the radio spot in March 1932, during the run of Hot-Cha! The job was a significant demotion, but it would bring the Follies to every household in America and keep Ziegfeld's name alive. Chrysler paid him a healthy $25,000 a week for the program, which Ziegfeld christened the Ziegfeld Follies of the Air. Still a perfectionist, he strove to give even his half-hour radio programs the Ziegfeld touch. Billie wrote that his radio shows set a standard "equal to his stage shows, and he recognized that radio was on its way to becoming the greatest medium of entertainment outside the theater."[21] The first show, which aired on April 3, 1932, featured Ziegfeld's latest discoveries, including comedian Jack Pearl and singers Jane Froman and Art Jarrett. He even convinced Will Rogers to participate in the program. The cowboy's presence meant more to Ziegfeld than all the other guests combined. During the first show, Will announced: "Every man that flies the ocean from now on will always be just an imitation of Lindbergh and every musical show that is produced is just an imitation of Zig-field."[22]

After his friend's warm introduction, Ziegfeld presented the rest of the stars. Listeners had the rare chance to hear his voice, which was invariably described as nasal or whiny. Billie argued that it was "large and resonant" but admitted that he sometimes used "a high nasal pitch for effect."[23]

However, at this point in his life, Ziegfeld's voice was thin, obviously aged, and weak; he sounded discouraged, despite his attempts to be cheerful. What had not changed with age was his distinct accent, evidenced by his pronunciation of the word "first" in the following sentence: "I wish to thank you for what I trust is your gracious acceptance of the foist of the Ziegfeld radio shows."[24]

After the first installment of the series, Ziegfeld moved away from spotlighting current stars and became fixated on making the show a retrospective of his theatrical past. His next guest star was Helen Morgan. With the show's master of ceremonies, Eddie Dowling, Ziegfeld reenacted a romanticized version of his first meeting with Morgan:

> ZIEGFELD: Remember the night, Eddie, when I dragged you through the rain up to a smoky little café . . . (male crooners begin to sing). . . .
> DOWLING: You didn't bring me up here in the rain to listen to four men. . . .
> ZIEGFELD: No, I brought you up here to hear a girl, and there she is. . . .
> DOWLING: She's sitting on the piano! Say that's a cute idear. . . .
> ZIEGFELD: Her name is Helen Morgan. Listen to her.

Morgan then launched into a torch song, "What a Life Trying to Live without You." At its conclusion, Ziegfeld told Dowling: "Go over and get her Eddie but don't tell her it's Ziegfeld or she'll want a lot of money."[25] Dowling brought Morgan to Ziegfeld's table, and she immediately recognized him from when she was a chorus girl in *Sally* (1920).

The rest of the programs followed in a similar vein. Fanny Brice guest starred, and Ziegfeld hoped to convince Billie to perform a duet of her star-making song, "My Little Canoe," with Will Rogers. By utilizing modern technology to keep the past alive, Ziegfeld stayed true to his method of melding the old with the new. However, one telegram he sent to Billie revealed that his faith in the formula was beginning to sag—even though he tried to hide it: "No matter how bad things are it's great to be alive and I don't know how I'm going to get through. Things in America are getting worse and worse but don't worry."[26]

Billie knew that her husband's hope was draining along with his vigor and health. She later wrote that until then, she "had never thought about the differences in our ages." However, reading between the lines in his telegrams, she realized how old he had become and that "all our hopes were dreams, and the dreams were gone."[27] In New York, Ziegfeld dismissed Doc Wagner's orders to take eight weeks' rest—no business—just as he ignored the piles of lawsuits and debts that bombarded him. His focus was, as always, the show, the next show, and the show after that.

Ziegfeld's next venture, like his radio program, was a revisiting of past glories. His new project may have been nostalgic, but it proved he was still a visionary. No producer up to that time had revived one of his own productions, but Ziegfeld did just that. He decided to bring his greatest success, *Show Boat,* back to Broadway. On a practical note, he still had all the costumes and sets in a warehouse, so the revival would be less expensive to produce. He managed to assemble most of the original cast (Norma Terris, Helen Morgan, Charles Winninger, Edna May Oliver, Tess Gardella, Sammy White, Eva Puck). However, Paul Robeson had agreed to play Joe, and Dennis King (D'Artagnan in *The Three Musketeers*) replaced Howard Marsh as Gaylord Ravenal. Tycoon A. C. Blumenthal, who had married ex–Ziegfeld girl Peggy Fears, helped fund the show and pay the actors' salaries. Ziegfeld set his publicity machine in motion to promote the show, using Robeson as the focal point. He utilized his radio program as a means of advertising. Morgan and Robeson guest-starred and sang a "miniature likeness of the show."[28]

Even in such a flurry of activity, Ziegfeld was lonely and pined for his family. In one wire to Patricia, he expressed his homesickness as well as his ongoing concern for Billie's career: "MY DARLING PATTY YOU DON'T KNOW HOW MUCH I WISH I COULD SEE YOU AND MOTHER TODAY IT HAS BEEN OVER SEVEN WEEKS NOW SINCE I'VE BEEN IN BED . . . I HOPE MOTHER GETS HARPO MARX IN HER SHOW IF FOR ONLY A FEW WEEKS THE TWO TOGETHER WOULD BE A SCREAM."[29] The show Ziegfeld was referring to was presumably *The Vinegar Tree* or perhaps the less successful *Mad Hopes*. There is no documentation that Marx ever appeared with Billie, although, as Ziegfeld said, the two certainly would have been "a scream."

Show Boat was slated to open at the Casino Theatre (formerly known as the Earl Carroll Theatre) on May 19, 1932. Ironically, Ziegfeld's old enemy Carroll had found himself in the same situation as Ziegfeld in mid-1931. Critics had deemed Carroll's revues too old-fashioned because of their reliance on showgirls and tired comedy. When Carroll could no longer meet his expenses, Ziegfeld swooped in, rented the theater, and renamed it the Casino, as homage to the original Casino Theatre where he had first seen Sandow perform. Audiences and critics greeted the revival with rapturous applause and enthusiastic reviews. Billie heard that the revival was "more beautiful than the original." Edna Ferber, author of the novel *Show Boat,* was in the audience on opening night and agreed with Billie's sentiments. After Robeson sang, Ferber recalled that the audience "shouted and cheered and behaved generally as I've never seen an audience behave in any theater in all my years of play going."[30] Robeson stood onstage for fifteen minutes of ovations and calls for encores.

The production may have seemed like a godsend to the money-strapped producer and his family. But no matter how enthusiastically the opening-night audience received the show, nothing could change the fact that there were simply not enough customers buying tickets. Those who could afford to pay had little desire to go out in the heat, which was unusually severe for May. Even with Blumenthal's help, Ziegfeld could not pay the company members their salaries. Paul Robeson did not stay for the show's entire run, and Dennis King refused to take a pay cut. Norma Terris, however, voluntarily returned half her salary to Ziegfeld. "Don't let him know where the money came from," Terris told Ziegfeld's business manager, Dan Curry.

The heat remained unrelenting throughout the summer, but the revival continued until October 1932. Once the show went on tour, Helen Morgan was among the few original cast members to stay. With business dropping off, Ziegfeld became more "broken in spirit and health" than ever before.[31] Returning home to an empty Burkeley Crest each weekend, he realized he could not justify maintaining the estate with him as its sole resident. Billie, who was still in California at the time, later wrote that she "could imagine him creeping up there [Burkeley Crest] on lonely weekends with no servants, with all the birds and the china and the animals gone. Many of these things were taken by persons who simply moved in on us and grabbed when our troubles came."[32] One night when Billie was listening to her husband's radio show, she noticed that his voice faltered at one point during the broadcast. It may have been imperceptible to the casual listener, but Billie caught "the weariness and sickness of it."[33] Immediately, she asked the producer of *The Vinegar Tree* to close the play while she traveled to New York to see to her husband. The producer graciously agreed, and Billie and Patricia packed their bags.

After months apart, Billie was shocked by how thin and stooped her husband had become. Sidney, Ziegfeld's loyal valet, explained to Billie in hushed tones the extent of Ziegfeld's decline. He was currently suffering from pleurisy and often drifted into rambling, incoherent monologues. Ziegfeld was convinced that several potential business deals would save him; these included a film contract with RKO for *Show Girl, Rosalie,* and *The Three Musketeers,* as well as a new show entitled the *Ziegfeld Vaudeville Revue.* Unfortunately, Dan Curry was unable to seal any of these deals. For Billie's sake, Ziegfeld kept up the pretense that he was healthy and everything would be all right. However, that ended one evening when he collapsed at a party for Will Rogers's daughter at the Pennsylvania Hotel. Buddy Rogers, who led the band there, helped Billie take Ziegfeld up to a room to recover.

Billie realized that Ziegfeld was not strong enough to continue his work in New York, so she arranged to close Burkeley Crest and secured reservations for the family to take a train back to Los Angeles. "Burkeley Crest had lost its charm," she observed. "It was still and sad, like a house long neglected, like a home where there is no more love."[34] The home that Billie had purchased with the fortune from her earliest successes had slipped through her fingers. A whole way of life made up of afternoon tea and scones, of caviar and angel food cake with coconut icing, of dinner parties for the Stotesburys and the Vanderbilts, had disappeared forever.

Patricia took the loss of her childhood home and way of life with surprising stoicism. She remained uncomplaining during the train ride to California. Her memories of the trip to Los Angeles reflected the family's drastically altered lifestyle: "This time there was no private car, no servants, no phone calls back to New York to check on box-office receipts."[35] The Ziegfelds tried to keep cool on the nightmarishly hot train by packing ice in their pillows. Ziegfeld was only half-conscious for most of the trip, but even in his incoherent state, he tried to attend to business, dictating telegrams and telling his family he needed to be back in New York by August for his radio program. In a more lucid moment, he found the energy to send two lengthy telegrams to his business manager, Dan Curry. Excerpts from the telegrams reveal Ziegfeld's desperation to solidify a deal that would restore his family's former way of life: THEY [director Bobby Connelly, his attorney, and RKO] HAVE ALL BEEN DOUBLE CROSSING EACH OTHER SO MUCH THAT NO ONE KNOWS WHERE THE PARTICULAR PRODUCTION

STANDS . . . I AM AN ASSET TO ALL AND THEY HAVE HAD ALL IVE MADE FOR YEARS NOW THEY MUST GIVE ME THE CHANCE . . . I SIGNED CONTRACT WITH RKO CALLING FOR A CASH PAYMENT TO ME FOR TWELVE THOUSAND FIVE HUNDRED . . . IT IS TWENTY FIVE HUNDRED LESS THAN THEY AGREED UPON BUT I CANNOT TAKE A CHANCE OF THEM NOT GOING THROUGH WITH IT." In part because of the many debts Ziegfeld had left unpaid in New York, he added: "DON'T LET ANYONE KNOW WHEN I LET YOU KNOW WHERE I AM. . . . I AM PUTTING A LOT ON YOUR SHOULDERS DAN."[36] The burden on Curry must have been too great; only moments before Ziegfeld sent his second telegram, Curry died of a heart attack.

Ziegfeld had to manage his own chaotic business dealings now, pleurisy or no pleurisy. Upon reaching Los Angeles, he sent more telegrams and made long-distance calls to New York, ensuring that *Show Boat* continued its tour and that the cast was being paid. "Baby, I know it's expensive, but I do love to telephone," he explained to Billie. Billie later wrote that she had never paid anything so gladly in her life, for Ziegfeld's telephone bill proved he was still the infuriating, lavish, yet charming man she knew and loved.

In late July, Ziegfeld had a full checkup at a Los Angeles hospital, and his doctors concluded that he was in serious but not critical condition. Billie initially settled him in their Santa Monica house, but Ziegfeld planned to regain his health at Will Rogers's ranch near Pacific Palisades. "I don't want to do anything until Will gets here. He'll know what to do," Ziegfeld told Billie. According to Patricia, Will was indispensable to the family. Once her husband was safe at Will's ranch, Billie took advantage of a tantalizing offer from George Cukor, one of the most well-regarded directors in Hollywood. He was currently preparing *A Bill of Divorcement*, an intense drama starring a newcomer to the screen, Katharine Hepburn, and a veteran of stage and screen, John Barrymore. He offered Billie the role of Katharine's mother and John's wife in the picture. Movie work meant no cross-country tours that would keep her away from her family, the chance to earn more money in less time, and the added perk of having old friends like Will Rogers and the Barrymores as neighbors.

Just as stability seemed to be within reach, Ziegfeld's pleurisy worsened. He was rushed to Cedars of Lebanon Hospital, where he received a series of mustard treatments. The agonizing procedures left Ziegfeld "sobbing helplessly like a child."[37] As he rested in bed, a telegram from Jimmy

Durante temporarily buoyed his spirits. "According to my secret opera-tives you're not sick," Durante wrote. "You're just in there writing a new Follies. Now listen, if I go in it, I want top billing and my dressing room must be perfumed daily. That's my ultimatum. If you need any help writing it, just move over. Here's to a speedy recovery. Best, Schnozzle."[38]

What brightened Ziegfeld's spirits even more than any well-meaning telegrams were Billie's constant visits. RKO Studio, where *A Bill of Divorcement* was being made, was only blocks from the hospital. Billie brought freshly cut flowers to her husband's room each morning (but no red roses). She made sure they were removed each evening before the pet-als wilted. Although Billie's workdays often lasted twelve hours, she was never too tired to visit her husband or listen to the ever-worsening news of his monetary state. Ziegfeld knew his finances were in ruins, but Billie did not tell him how severe the situation had become. His New York business office strongly suggested he declare bankruptcy. Western Union had cur-tailed his credit and had all the telephones removed from the Ziegfeld Theatre. On top of everything, New York tax officials were prepared to seize the company's assets. Billie kept the most unpleasant details to her-self, for Ziegfeld appeared to be rallying and had declared himself almost ready to take charge.

The strain of carrying this burden translated to Billie's scenes in *A Bill of Divorcement*. She played an overburdened woman who is torn between choosing a new life and a new husband or remaining as caretaker to her shell-shocked husband who has recently escaped from an asylum. The film was Billie's first talkie, and fortunately, her voice came across well. In com-parison to her later screwball comedy roles, her voice in *A Bill of Divorcement* sounded low and somber. Billie and Katharine Hepburn's scenes together, particularly one in which Billie describes her early mar-riage, are the most memorable and powerful in the film. "It was the feeling in the air, one did mad things," Billie's character tells her daughter (Hepburn), referring to the years preceding the Jazz Age. Billie could have uttered the very same words to describe her own former life.

On July 22, 1932, Billie was enjoying a ten-day break from filming *A Bill of Divorcement*. She spent the afternoon visiting Ziegfeld in the hospital, along with Will and Betty Rogers. After Will and Betty left for their ranch, Billie, Ziegfeld, and Patricia enjoyed a decadent feast of roast beef, asparagus, and champagne in celebration of Ziegfeld's improved spirits. "I'm leaving New York for good," Ziegfeld declared, sitting up in his hospital bed as he poured more champagne. "There's television, radio, and film here. I know it may be awhile before we recover from all these money problems, but I've got to get back in the fray."[39]

In the middle of dinner, Billie received a call from George Cukor. The director sheepishly requested that she come to the studio to do a screen test with a new actor, Walter Pidgeon, who was being considered for the role of her fiancé. Billie left the hospital, promising to return as soon as possible. "It was the happiest day we had had together for a long, long, time and my heart was light," Billie recalled.[40]

The costumers were fitting Billie into a frilly evening dress for the screen test when the call came from Ziegfeld's valet, Sidney, urging her to return to the hospital immediately. Cukor stopped the cameras and told Billie to go. She rushed to Cedars of Lebanon, still dressed in her costume. Upon seeing Sidney outside Ziegfeld's room, she slowed her steps. "Madam, it is too late. He just died in my arms, walking across the room. One short gasp was all . . . ," he began. Before he could finish his sentence, Billie's legs gave way beneath her. She awoke to find nurses hovering about, attempting to get her out of the dress into which the costumers had sewn her.

In the 1936 biopic *The Great Ziegfeld*, William Anthony McGuire wrote a more romantic and befitting death scene for his old boss. The film shows Ziegfeld ensconced in a luxurious suite on Broadway, speaking with Billings (a character based on Charles Dillingham). Both men are feigning that they were untouched by the stock market crash. After Billings departs, Ziegfeld falls into a dreamlike delirium, and images swirl about him, depicting ideas for his next show. "More steps," he murmurs, envisioning brilliant staircases with glorified girls posed on them. The film then shows Billie on tour in Los Angeles, calling Ziegfeld on the phone only moments before he dies. Although the death scene had little basis in reality, the words McGuire wrote were eerily similar to those Ziegfeld had spoken to Harkrider during the run of *Hot-Cha!*: "All that beauty."

Ziegfeld did not receive last rites. According to biographer Charles Higham, Ziegfeld had no belief in the afterlife, and "philosophy and religion were closed books to him."[41] However, given Ziegfeld's superstitions, he must have believed in some sort of otherworldly force. Patricia noted, "Daddy had a deep spiritual faith all his life but it was basically nonsectarian. . . . Mother and Daddy supported the local Episcopal Church. If there had been a Zen temple in Westchester County I would probably have been given a dose of Buddhism too."[42] Like the eclectic mix of comedy, glamour, jazz, ballads, ballet, and modern dance that defined his shows, Ziegfeld's faith had the same "anything goes" quality. However, his fear of mortality and the need to surround himself with symbols of good luck indicated a certain wariness about God and the afterlife. He may have committed many transgressions against his wives and against many composers, actors, and other colleagues, but in his last days, his openness and his sincere feelings for his family and closest friends revealed that he was not without conscience.

It would have been fitting if Ziegfeld's funeral were as big a production as his greatest shows were. But he had left no instructions as to what type of memorial service he wanted, and Billie was too distraught to decide. For days, her emotional state alternated between incessant crying and dreamlike paralysis. "Mother was tired," Patricia recalled. "The years of trouping, the strange hotel rooms, the long hours of rehearsal, the disappointments and failures and defeats all seemed to rise up in a great overwhelming wave."[43] The first wave came in the form of six lawsuits against the Burkeley Crest estate less than a month after Ziegfeld's death. Several years later, Billie was able to pay them off "with the few resources we [she and Patricia] could lay our hands on."[44]

Billie later wrote that when the family's troubles came, Patricia "was sturdy and comforting beyond her years. . . . She should have turned out a spoiled brat. She did not at all and I am still in awe of her."[45] According to biographer Grant Hayter-Menzies, "Patricia, a teenager, took over for her mother and in effect mothered her."[46] Inwardly, the brave and sturdy Patricia was experiencing intense grief. She became fixated on the fact that her father had not died where he had always been happiest: Burkeley Crest. "It wasn't until much later that I realized it didn't matter where he died, because, at the end, he was too tired to care anymore about anything," Patricia wrote in her memoir.[47]

Billie herself was almost too tired to care about anything, so she did not argue when Will Rogers took charge of planning Ziegfeld's funeral. He also paid his friend's hospital bills but insisted on remaining anonymous; even in death, he did not want to humiliate Ziegfeld. Will and his wife invited Billie and Patricia to stay at their ranch for two weeks while the funeral arrangements were being made. "Their love and the quiet of the hills was strengthening, but I could not for a long time shake off the illusion that if I could only run . . . far enough, somehow I would find Flo alive and waiting for me," Billie later wrote.[48]

Will seemed to be in complete control, but he was suffering just as much as Billie and Patricia. Eddie Cantor stated, "Will was as inconsolable as a child. He had lost someone whom he loved, a man whom he worshipped and, for weeks, he could not overcome the tragedy of the blow."[49] Will was, by all accounts, closer to Ziegfeld than any other man in the producer's life. Will represented the rustic, western lifestyle Ziegfeld so romanticized. He also served as a model of how to balance family, work, and finances. Although Will and Betty Rogers were at their friend's bedside during his last days, they chose to remember Ziegfeld in happier times. Betty Rogers wrote:

> I like to remember Mr. Ziegfeld and Will as they looked on one of their many horseback rides together . . . I watched the two men as they rode along side by side—Mr. Ziegfeld in a handsome pair of light-colored, winged chaps, sitting straight and erect, his gray hair sleek and glistening in the sun; Will carelessly sprawled in his saddle . . . his shaggy hair blowing awry in the wind. . . . There they were, the greatest producer of all time, and the vaudevillian with his rope who had pulled the *Follies* out of many a tight place. So different they were yet with so much in common. Each was grateful to the other. . . . They had been partners in making theatrical history.[50]

Will, in spite of his grief, was levelheaded enough to arrange a meeting with Eddie Cantor to finalize the funeral arrangements. Eddie was less successful at hiding his sadness. When he first heard of Ziegfeld's death, he was in such shock that he "sat stupefied at the telephone and cried as bitterly" as if he had lost his own father.[51] Together, Will and Eddie met with a local minister, the Reverend Franklin L. Gibson, to discuss Ziegfeld's memorial. At that point, Will's strength began to falter. Eddie recalled that "the great humorist's eyes were filled with tears and he kept floundering for words like a bewildered child."[52]

New York's WOR Radio held a memorial service for Ziegfeld on July

24, 1932. Bernard Sobel described the event as rather grotesque, an "informal theatrical performance, with the audience smoking cigarettes, consulting notes, chatting occasionally . . . from time to time newspaper and cameramen barged in."[53] The highlight of the program was Paul Robeson signing "Ol' Man River." Marilyn Miller was not there to sing "Look for the Silver Lining," but when she heard Robeson singing over the airwaves, she allegedly collapsed in tears.

In Los Angeles, Ziegfeld's funeral was held at Pierce Brothers Mortuary. It was as unremarkable as the radio station's memorial, but this was appropriate, given Ziegfeld's dislike of funerals and the attention they drew to the brutal reality of death. Will kept the ceremony low-key; he even made sure there were no newspaper announcements about the time and place of the service. "He wanted no public demonstration and no curiosity seekers. This was not the funeral of a theatrical potentate, but the passing of a man, loved by his friends," Cantor observed.[54] The chapel was very small and spare. The only evidence that the memorial was for the Great Glorifier was the plethora of beauties in attendance, including Marion Davies, Lilyan Tashman, Billie Dove, and Lina Basquette. Celebrities who had never met Ziegfeld, such as silent comedian Harold Lloyd, also came to pay their respects. Others he had known for a lifetime, such as Irving Thalberg, Norma Shearer, George M. Cohan, and William Randolph Hearst, found their way to the chapel as well. Rosalie Ziegfeld was not present. Ziegfeld's eighty-four-year-old mother was ailing and near death herself. She had already lost her other two sons, Carl (who died in 1921) and William (who died in 1927). Her doctors and Ziegfeld's sister, Louise, feared that it would only hasten her death to hear of Ziegfeld's passing. Rosalie died three months later, never knowing that her eldest son had gone before her. Louise died in 1940.

As the final guests filed into the chapel, crooner John Boles began to sing the spiritual "Goin' Home," with music based on Antonin Dvorak's 1893 Symphony no. 9. The lyrics by William Arms Fisher were written in 1922: "Going home, going home / I'm just going home / . . . Work all done, cares laid by / Going to fear no more. . . . / Nothing's lost, all's gain / No more fret nor pain / No more stumbling on the way / Going to roam no more. . . . / I'm just going home."[55] As Boles sang the last stanza of the song, the minister began to speak: "We are all gathered here today to remember a beloved father, husband, friend, and producer of plays, Mr.

Zig-field." Billie, Eddie, and Will looked at one another with thinly veiled horror. Will had mispronounced Ziegfeld's name in jest on many occasions, but to hear the minister repeatedly call him "Zig-field" was, according to Eddie, like a blow to the heart. To him, it represented "how little strangers knew or understood this man who had been largely responsible for spreading whatever little happiness there was still left. But it didn't matter—he [the minister] could tell us nothing we didn't already know about Zieggy."[56]

Due to her financial situation, Billie could not afford to have Ziegfeld's ashes spread over the roof of the New Amsterdam Theatre, as she knew he would have wished. Though it pained her, Billie had to settle on a crypt in what she called a "garish mausoleum" at Forest Lawn Memorial Park in Glendale.[57] "Only by little vases of fresh flowers twice a week, which we have never failed to provide can Pat and I pay our tributes to the man who loved beauty so passionately," she wrote.[58]

Shortly after Ziegfeld's death, Billie asked Will Rogers to write an article that would reveal the man behind the icon. Will obliged with a touching eulogy that he never delivered but that was published in hundreds of papers:

> He led us into what little fame we achieved. He remained our friend regardless of our usefulness to him as an entertainer. He brought beauty into the entertainment world . . . he left something on earth that hundreds of us will treasure till the curtain falls, and that was a "badge," a badge of which we were proud, never ashamed of, and wanted the world to read the lettering on it, "I worked for Ziegfeld." . . . The curtain has fallen for our boss, our master. . . . So good-bye Flo. Save a spot for me, for you will put on a show up there someday that will knock their eyes out.[59]

A final memorial was held for Ziegfeld almost a year later on April 21, 1933. The tribute took place at the Ziegfeld Theatre, which, in a cruel twist of irony, was being reopened as a movie house. The ceremony was a circus-like event with more than 1,000 fans and many former Ziegfeld stars in attendance. One undignified moment occurred when Gus Edwards called Lillian Lorraine to the stage to sing "By the Light of the Silvery Moon." She was wheeled up the aisle in a chair, as her old back injury had never completely healed. Lillian sang only a few notes before she became hysterical and had to be wheeled off the stage.[60]

The reopening of the Ziegfeld Theatre as movie house represented a new attitude on Broadway, one that was judgmental of the past and focused solely on modernity. Most of the new producers on Broadway possessed little appreciation of beauty, which had been Ziegfeld's trademark. He had seen each show and each girl as a unique, masterful work of art. Indeed, Billie once commented that he approached his shows like a painter. He wanted to make a profit, but for Ziegfeld, the drive to create a world where ugliness and want did not exist was stronger than the desire to earn money. Gene Buck observed:

> Florenz Ziegfeld was a real genius, a dreamer of dreams, an artist and one of the two or three greatest showmen America had ever produced. He brought distinction and credit to the musical comedy theatre and joy and happiness to millions of people for forty years. He helped thousands to fame and fortune by the magic of his talent and his imagination. There is really no one left to take his place. He had something that was all his own and it passed with his leave taking. His death has cast a shadow over the entire land of make believe.[61]

PART 4

The Legacy of Florenz Ziegfeld Jr., 1932–

He just keeps rollin,' he just keeps rollin' along.
—*Oscar Hammerstein II, "Ol' Man River" (1927)*

22

Going Hollywood

"Oh Goldie I loved him so. I don't think anyone knows what his going has meant to me. He was so wonderful. With all his faults, so wonderful."[1] So Billie Burke confided to Ziegfeld's loyal secretary, Goldie, only two weeks after his death. Ziegfeld's passing left a hole in the theater world that would not soon be filled, if ever. But the hole he left on Broadway was not as immense as the hole he left in his family. When Billie returned to work on *A Bill of Divorcement,* the makeup artist had difficulty dealing with the tears that relentlessly ruined her mascara.

Billie had more than one reason to cry after her husband's death. In addition to the half million dollars in debt Ziegfeld had left behind, the Bank of the United States sued Billie for $37,787, the amount outstanding on an old loan. Louis Levy, Ziegfeld's attorney, was able to dodge the suit by making Ziegfeld's financial records almost impossible to locate and by refusing to give the bank Billie's Santa Monica address. Goldie remained in charge of the Ziegfeld office until the New York district attorney seized every document in the files and the safe. There was not much to seize; the contents of the safe consisted of two $5 bills, three copies of sheet music, a large glass ruby, eleven rubber bands, a silk whip with a rhinestone handle, and a bronze elephant.[2] The items resembled those contained in the secret stash of a child.

In desperation, Billie asked Goldie if there was any equity in *Hot Cha!* and *The Three Musketeers* that had not yet been sold to Hollywood. "I have been working so hard at trying to make a little money for our keep," Billie wrote to the secretary. "I have neglected his [Ziegfeld's] affairs . . . his papers seem to have been scattered everywhere . . . did he have any accounts in any bank do you know?" The only account Goldie could locate, at the Citizen's Bank in White Plains, New York, held $2,773. So Billie started selling off the family's properties. The first to go was Camp Patricia, which was the only land in her name. The camp, which had been built for $80,000, was sold for a mere $2,500. "Oh how I hated to do that [sell Camp Patricia] . . . our dear old camp. I do think we could fight that [having the camp seized] only there is no money to fight anything," Billie lamented to Goldie.[3]

Producer Sam Goldwyn proved to be Billie's financial savior after Ziegfeld's death. Though the two men had not always been in harmony when it came to their business dealings, they had parted amicably, and Goldwyn still had high regard for Ziegfeld. "Billie, let me act as your agent and your clearinghouse," he proposed. "I will get you parts in pictures and look after you, and whether you are working or not, I will give you $300 a week so you won't have to worry."[4] Billie started to work for Goldwyn shortly after finishing a 1932 stage revival of *The Marquise* in California.

Goldwyn used Billie in only one of his own pictures (*Splendor*, 1935), but he willingly loaned her out to various other studios, including MGM and Hal Roach Studios. Billie's remarkable transition into film and her new life as a character actress resumed once she had recovered from her wave of exhaustion and catatonia. She again became the logical realist she had been throughout her marriage. "The wave couldn't knock her down completely," Patricia wrote. "She had one lifeline to hang onto—her work—and she clung to it with grim instinct. Mother was determined that she and I would go on, and that she would do her best to raise me to be the kind of young woman Daddy would be proud of."[5] As biographer Grant Hayter-Menzies explained, Billie was "concerned only with establishing a safe, comfortable home for her daughter . . . Billie didn't want Patricia to grow up too soon or become jaded by the world of show business and riches."[6] Billie later stated that becoming a widow in middle age was much more difficult than becoming a widow in youth because an older widow "needs emotional security and freedom from anxiety—she needs money. She needs physical health and comfort. She needs to be loved. She needs to believe in something . . . she needs to be useful."[7]

Her work made Billie feel useful, but it did not provide warmth and affection. Billie could have remarried, but she found it difficult "to adapt oneself to a whole new order of things. That is really why I did not marry again."[8] She was still desperately in love with Ziegfeld even decades after his death. He had left her and Patricia destitute; he had been unpredictable and often irresponsible. But by overcoming their seemingly insurmountable marital hardships, Billie and Ziegfeld had formed a deep bond that exceeded any other connection they had ever had. After Ziegfeld's death, Billie outwardly became a capable single mother. Inwardly, she described herself as a "small, bewildered comedienne" who, for the first time in her life, found herself virtually alone.[9] Billie described her emotions in her first memoir: "I still miss, not the exciting moments, not the security, not the big home, but the gentle touch of a dear hand, which it seems to me touched me only yesterday. . . . Having been protected for years, if not by wealth at any rate by a man who loved her, a woman senses—however she tried to hide it even from herself—a feeling of being neglected when it all ends. It isn't just the money . . . it's the lack of being *looked after*."[10]

One man was still looking after Billie: Sam Goldwyn. George Cukor and David O. Selznick had been so impressed with Billie's adeptness at drama in *A Bill of Divorcement* that they requested her for another Selznick drama. Goldwyn happily loaned her out for the film *Christopher Strong* (1933), in which Billie played a wife who suffers in silence as she watches her husband fall for a younger, more exciting woman (Katharine Hepburn), all the while believing that he will eventually return to her. As she had done in her first talking picture, Billie drew on personal experience to give a genuine and moving performance. Billie's first two films are not as well known as her later comedies, most notably the *Topper* series (1937–1941), so many modern viewers are unfamiliar with the depths of Billie's acting abilities. Fortunately, both *A Bill of Divorcement* and *Christopher Strong* are available on DVD and are frequently shown on the Turner Classic Movies channel.

It seemed as if Billie's first two films would establish her in Hollywood as a dramatic supporting actress. However, her next assignment, like her career-changing role in *The Vinegar Tree,* created the iconic character that generations of film viewers associate with Billie Burke: the scatterbrained society matron. The witty and sophisticated MGM dramedy *Dinner at Eight* (1933) encapsulates the lives of the rich during the Depression, just as *The Grapes of Wrath* (1940) encapsulates the lives of the poor. The film revolves around the planning of a dinner party, an event that was becoming a thing of the past even in 1933. Each character in the film is representative of the demise of a different area of society, whether in the entertainment world or the business world. At the heart of the film is Billie as Millicent Jordan, who is frantically attempting to plan a party with an even number of male and female guests. Mrs. Jordan represents the last vestige of the old, luxurious world of the Jazz Age, where something as inconsequential as a dinner party could be the most important thing in one's life. Oblivious to her husband's failing health and business and her daughter's affair with an aging actor, Mrs. Jordan delivers a heated speech to both of them in which she despairs over her seemingly insurmountable misfortunes: "I've had the most ghastly day anybody ever had! . . . They [the Ferncliffes, her guests of honor] call up at this hour, the miserable Cockneys, to say they've gone to Florida—Florida! And who can I get at this hour? Nobody! I've got eight people for dinner . . . eight people isn't a dinner! . . . I'm the one who ought to be in bed, I'm the one who's in trouble. You don't know what trouble is, either of you!"[11]

As the film unfolds and the characters' tragic personal lives are revealed, Mrs. Jordan emerges as the strongest member of the group. She immediately takes control and adapts to her degraded circumstances. With a comforting smile, she holds back tears as she tells her ailing husband, "But everyone's broke these days, darling. . . . We'll economize, that's what we'll do. I don't really need to go to the hairdresser on Thursday, and that box seat at the charity dinner on Saturday, we don't need that. . . . Everything will be all right, darling, you'll see."

As in *Christopher Strong* and *A Bill of Divorcement*, the strength of Billie's performance lay in the realism she brought to it. The roles of caretaker and manager are thrust on Mrs. Jordan, mirroring Billie's life with Ziegfeld in his declining years. *Dinner at Eight* helped Billie overcome her sorrow by poking fun at even the most tragic aspects of it. Hayter-Menzies observed that all the characters in the film seemed to be caricatures of the actors playing them; Billie was no exception. "Billie, who with Flo had lived a life of conspicuous consumption, has no trouble being convincing as the thriftless Millicent, even as the outmoded histrionics of her comedic acting style, full of the broad double takes and despairing hand-to-brow gestures of Victorian melodrama, perfectly meshes with all we would expect of Millicent Jordan." But this "melodrama" is only a façade; like the real Billie, there is a deeper side to the "silly women" she portrayed. Although they seem pampered and thoughtless, they are actually deeply emotional women. Menzies concluded, "These characters know pain and grief all too well, and in their manic activity are staving off confronting it."[12]

Billie's role in *Dinner at Eight* made her a bona fide member of the modern film world and established her as a comedienne of the highest caliber. She, along with actresses Jean Arthur and Carole Lombard and directors Leo McCarey and Howard Hawks, can be considered one of the pioneers of screwball comedy.

Over the next twenty years, Billie played Millicent Jordan, under different names, in dozens of films. Though no other film achieved the perfection of *Dinner at Eight,* her cumulative body of work left an indelible legacy. Billie's other notable roles included Mrs. Clara Topper in the *Topper* series and Mrs. Emily Kilbourne in *Merrily We Live* (1938). In 1939 Billie earned an Oscar nomination for best supporting actress for *Merrily We Live* but ultimately lost to Fay Bainter in *Jezebel* (1938). The same year, Billie won her most famous role as Glinda the Good Witch in *The Wizard of Oz* (1939). Billie later revealed that this role was her favorite, for it most reminded her of the glamorous, ethereal parts she had played in her early stage career. Also, the Glinda costume, with its high headdress, outlandish skirt, and sparkles, looked like a Harkrider creation. The producers had initially intended to cast Fanny Brice as a comical Good Witch and W. C. Fields as a curmudgeonly but good-hearted Wizard. However, Billie Burke as Glinda and Frank Morgan (another Ziegfeld alumnus) as the Wizard gave the film the heart and sentiment that have made it a perennial childhood favorite.

Billie's association with Ziegfeld made her show business royalty. Even though she was a character actress, the greatest leading ladies of the 1930s accepted Billie as one of them. Among her first friends on the MGM lot were Myrna Loy and Norma Shearer (who, like Billie, was a widow; she had lost her husband, Irving Thalberg, in 1936). "Movie stars have so much done for them, are hoisted to such uncontrollable heights, are bowed to as infallible by many, that it is a wonder indeed when any of them retains kindness," Billie stated. "Everybody has been kind to me here."[13] Billie's new social circle began to expand, and its core members included George Cukor, Katharine Hepburn, Dorothy Arzner (who had directed *Christopher Strong*), Ethel Barrymore, William Haines, Joan Crawford, and Elsa Lanchester, the eccentric English actress and wife of Charles Laughton.

American audiences now recognized Billie Burke as herself rather than as Mrs. Ziegfeld. However, during her first four years in Hollywood (1932–1936), her name and Ziegfeld's remained inextricably linked. Billie learned that the Shuberts wished to buy the rights to the title *Ziegfeld Follies of 1934*. Had Ziegfeld been alive, it would have been a major blow to see the Shuberts, his fiercest rivals, profiting from his name. However, Billie signed a contract allowing the Shuberts to produce one edition of the *Follies*, with the stipulation that the new *Follies* "be of the same character and quality as were the *Follies* produced by the late Florenz Ziegfeld." The contract entitled Billie to 3 percent of the gross, as well as credit as producer. "I was severely criticized at the time for my presumption in trying another *Follies*," Billie later wrote. "But I am sure that Flo would have wanted it like that; why wouldn't he have wanted his name and his show to benefit his wife and daughter when they needed help?"[14]

Under Billie's supervision, the *Follies of 1934* retained the same character as those Ziegfeld had produced. It opened on January 4, 1934, at the Winter Garden Theatre and showcased fresh talent. Songwriter E. Y. Harburg was among the bevy of writers hired for the show. Harburg made his name a few years later by penning the beloved tune "Over the Rainbow" for *The Wizard of Oz*. The musical numbers were staged by John Murray Anderson, who, with former Ziegfeld girl Doris Eaton, later opened a nationwide chain of dance studios. Choreographer Robert Alton went on to become one of Hollywood's top choreographers for musicals, including *Annie Get Your Gun* (1950) and *White Christmas* (1954). New discoveries included Eve Arden and Buddy and Vilma Ebsen, a brother and sister dance act (Buddy had been a member of a male ensemble in the Broadway production of *Whoopee*). The show proved to be such a success that Billie agreed to coproduce a 1936 version as well.

The 1936 edition, which premiered on January 30, 1936, at the Winter Garden Theatre, included established entertainers such as Bob Hope, Gypsy Rose Lee, Edgar Bergen, and Josephine Baker. Among the new featured talents were the gymnastic dancing sisters June and Cherry Preisser. Ira Gershwin wrote the lyrics for the songs in the 1936 revue, but he was the only Ziegfeld songwriter to contribute to the posthumous editions. The opening of the 1936 *Follies* was a "teaser," for the master of ceremonies insisted that the show would not feature girls. However, according to Vincente Minnelli, the show's art director, "A Ziegfeld show without girls would obviously have to go by another name." Minnelli was like Joseph

Urban and John Harkrider rolled into one. Minnelli's most notable contribution was a surrealistic ballet starring Harriet Hoctor. The number depicted three male dancers on a ramp tilted down toward the audience. Three other figures, dressed all in black, lay at an angle, suggesting the shadows of the three standing performers; they repeated the dancers' movements from their prone positions. "The number ended with the men who had cast shadows losing Harriet to the black silhouettes when they rise from the ground and spirit her away," Minnelli explained in his memoir.[15]

The costumes Minnelli created were as impressive as his scenic designs. He approached the *Follies* "in the spirit of fashion photography. Elegant, but with humor and style."[16] Josephine Baker, for example, wore a 100-pound gold mesh gown with a plum-colored ostrich cape. Elliott Norton of the *Boston Post* wrote that, thanks to Minnelli's artistic flair, the 1936 edition was "far and away the most beautiful of all." In fact, Norton made the audacious statement that Minnelli had "greater theatrical genius than the late Florenz Ziegfeld."[17] Most critics and theatergoers would have disagreed. Minnelli, however, earned the title of greatest musical film genius more than a decade later. He went on to direct Oscar-winning films such as *An American in Paris* (1951) and *Gigi* (1958).

Minnelli may have been the genius behind the artistry of the show, but Fanny Brice was the genius behind its comedy. She starred in both the 1934 and 1936 editions, making a triumphant return to the *Follies* after more than a decade's absence. Fanny first created her most famous character, Baby Snooks, in the 1934 *Follies*. Modeled after former child star Baby Peggy, Baby Snooks—a whiny brat whose goal was to make her parents' life difficult—was Fanny's first successful non-Yiddish character. With her long, skinny legs, Fanny looked hilarious in a baby-doll dress. The character became such a sensation that Fanny was engaged for a weekly radio show dedicated to Snooks. She later re-created the character in the Judy Garland musical *Everybody Sing* (1938), in which Fanny played Olga, a former Russian performer who is now the harassed maid of a madcap show business family. The final production number shows Olga quitting her job as a maid and choosing to act in a Broadway revue as Baby Snooks. The matriarch of the madcap family was played by none other than Billie Burke, giving audiences the rare opportunity to see two of Ziegfeld's favorite ladies together—and a chance to see the Baby Snooks routine in action.

Ziegfeld may have passed away, but his influence was still evident. The *Follies* continued to blend old favorites like Fanny Brice with exciting new performers. Furthermore, it proved that beauty and an abundance of talent, music, and comedy would never go out of style or be surpassed by virtual spectacles on film. Both editions of the new *Follies* mirrored Ziegfeld's shows in nearly every way, except that their costs did not exceed their profits. The modest profits Billie received from the shows caused the creditors to swarm and demand payment of Ziegfeld's debts. Using profits they had received from backing *Show Boat*, Ziegfeld's friends the Blumenthals paid the creditors that were hounding Billie.

Though her most pressing debts had been paid, Billie had no surplus with which to revive the still-shuttered Burkeley Crest. She was forced to say farewell to the last remnant of her life with Ziegfeld when, on April 29, 1940, everything at Burkeley Crest was auctioned off. The $250,000 house and the 295 objects in it sold for only $42,000. A $6,500 Hepplewhite dining room suite went for $475. A grand piano sold for a paltry $155. Ziegfeld's ornate walnut bed went for $31. The $4,000 Chinese wall hangings in Ziegfeld's bedroom netted only $50 each.[18]

Billie moved to a modest bungalow in Hollywood and continued to work in film while Patricia finished school. In 1937 Billie gave her daughter a twenty-first birthday party with as much Ziegfeld style as her finances allowed. All Patricia really wanted was for Hal Kemp's orchestra to play at the celebration. Billie "scraped the sugar bowl" to pay for the event, but she thought to herself: "A fine thing if Flo Ziegfeld's only daughter can't turn twenty-one and present herself to society with cascades of chrysanthemums and a first-rate band." Billie quipped that Ziegfeld would have liked the party, but he would have "considered nothing less than *two* bands" to play at the event.[19]

Shortly after the much-anticipated party, Patricia met her future husband, Bill Stephenson, at a college event where he worked as a dance instructor. When she told her mother about Bill, Billie said, "What a way to meet . . . two strangers at a dance."

"That's exactly the way you met Daddy," Patricia reminded her.[20]

"But that was in *New York*. This is California," Billie told her. Patricia found her mother's "amusing non sequitur" entertaining and continued to argue that her feelings for Bill were sincere. Nevertheless, Billie sent her daughter on a European tour for the summer and to New York for the winter, where Patricia could explore her interest in radio work. Though not a stage mother by any means, Billie admitted that she hoped "Ziegfeld's daughter may one day take her place as a producer. She has the flair, the quick recognition of talent, and the acumen."[21] However, Patricia still preferred the front side of the stage and never delved into producing or any other aspect of show business.

When she returned from her excursions, she was still in love with Bill, who was now an architect. Billie raised her hands "in a graceful gesture of defeat" and simply asked: "How many bridesmaids shall we have?" The wedding, held on June 11, 1939, was lavish, with an abundance of lace, satin, champagne, orange blossoms, lilies, and gilt chairs. Patricia concluded, "Daddy would have absolutely loved it."[22]

Ziegfeld also would have loved the unparalleled success of the next posthumous *Follies*. Seven years after the 1936 edition closed, the Shuberts secured Billie's permission to produce a *Ziegfeld Follies of 1943*. The most famous player in the show was Milton Berle; other notable performers included Arthur Treacher, Ilona Massey, and dancer Jack Cole, who would later be Marilyn Monroe's choreographer of choice. John Murray Anderson and Robert Alton again directed the musical numbers. The 1943 edition opened on April 1, 1943, at the Winter Garden Theatre and ran for 553 performances, longer than any *Follies* Ziegfeld had ever produced. The fast-paced show had lively sketches, catchy songs, and, of course, beautiful girls. In the midst of World War II, audiences were clamoring for lighthearted, escapist entertainment, and this is precisely what the 1943 *Follies* gave them. The final *Follies* premiered on March 1, 1957, at the Winter Garden Theatre, without Billie's supervision. The show paid homage to the *Follies* of old with tunes reminiscent of the original series, such as "Bring on the Girls" and "Miss Follies." The show ran for 123 performances and earned its featured star, Beatrice Lillie, a Tony nomination.

Judging by the popularity of the Ziegfeld name decades after his death, one would be hard-pressed to contradict a statement Billie made in 1948: "Although he was in difficulty at the time of his death, it is certain that, with his radio show, with the great properties he controlled, with the plans for new shows that he had and with Hollywood's realization that musical comedies were enormously profitable, Flo would have recovered and would have been a greater showman than ever."[23]

23

His Shows Must Go On

If Ziegfeld had lived, he likely would have moved to California and conquered Hollywood, just as he had Broadway. With the maturation of the film musical in the 1930s, studios were better equipped to create Ziegfeldian production numbers on the big screen. Had Ziegfeld recovered and relocated to the West Coast, he would have had access to the best creative talents in show business to help make his films as splendid as his theatrical productions. Hollywood in the 1930s was the location of choice for many of Ziegfeld's most gifted former employees. Eddie Cantor, Will Rogers, Fanny Brice, W. C. Fields, Irving Berlin, Jerome Kern, John Harkrider, George Gershwin, Marilyn Miller, and dozens of other lesser-known Ziegfeld talents had found their way into the world of film.

Fanny Brice, one of the first to go to Hollywood, declared: "I'm here to stay. This whole place is just like a playground. And after thirty years in show business, I'm about ready for a little playground. . . . All I want is to keep on acting and make people laugh and having people make me laugh."[1] Eddie Cantor, who starred in Goldwyn musicals throughout the early to mid-1930s, proved to be Fanny's closest friend in Hollywood. He wrote that his family and hers were "like one big family. Fanny would drop by every day to chat and raid the icebox. She hated to eat alone."[2]

Similarly, Will Rogers and Billie were like family. In Billie's fourth film, *Doubting Thomas* (1935), she was Will's leading lady. The delight they experienced playing opposite each other is almost palpable on the screen. Unfortunately, that was one of Will's last performances. An avid fan of aviation, Will joined well-known pilot Wiley Post in a plane bound for Alaska on August 15, 1935. During the flight, the engine failed and the plane crashed, killing them both. Will was fifty-six years old. Billie, like all of America, was gravely affected by Will's death. Unlike Ziegfeld, Will did not fear mortality and had even poked fun at it. One of his most famous sayings reads: "When I die, my epitaph, or whatever you call those signs on gravestones, is going to read: 'I joked about every prominent man of my time, but I never met a man I dident [sic] like.' I am so proud of that, I can hardly wait to die so it can be carved."[3]

Will, Ziegfeld's most beloved "hired hand" and friend, was the first of the Ziegfeld family of stars to pass away. Among the behind-the-scenes talent, Ziegfeld's steadfast scenic designer and friend Joseph Urban died in 1933, and his associate and competitor Charles Dillingham followed in 1934. Lucile Lady Duff Gordon, who had been Ziegfeld's go-to designer before Harkrider, died in 1935.

In the early 1930s, Marilyn Miller was still very much alive, but her popularity was waning. Her third film, *Her Majesty Love* (1931), in which she teamed with W. C. Fields, failed to gain a wide audience. However, when Moss Hart hired her to star in Irving Berlin's new revue, *As Thousands Cheer,* her celebrity was revived. She was the biggest hit in the show, singing what is now one of Berlin's best-known tunes, "Easter Parade." *Cheer* became the most popular production of the 1933–1934 Broadway season, playing for 400 performances. After the show closed, Marilyn decided to end her career on a high note and retire at the age of thirty-six. But she soon reconsidered when MGM producer Hunt Stromberg and director Robert Z. Leonard made her a tantalizing offer. They asked her to appear in a film that they and all the executives at MGM assumed would be the greatest musical ever made: a $2 million extravaganza re-creating the life and work of none other than Florenz Ziegfeld Jr.

The motion picture industry began its enormously popular trend of producing fictionalized musical biopics with *The Great Ziegfeld*. As early as the winter of 1933, Universal Studios had secured Billie Burke's permission to make a film about Ziegfeld's life. Shortly thereafter, William Anthony McGuire began work on the screenplay. However, by February 1935, McGuire was having "differences of opinion" with the studio—particularly when it came to his salary. Universal had invested almost $250,000 in the production and could not afford to give McGuire the higher pay he demanded. Ultimately, the entire project was "too costly" for Universal, which was feeling the negative effects of the Depression.[4]

Universal entered into negotiations with MGM to take over the project. MGM was the only studio that actually made a profit during the leanest years of the 1930s. The studio had even considered producing annual *Follies* on Broadway and then turning them into films. That idea never came to fruition, although the studio did buy the rights to the title *Ziegfeld Follies*. Ziegfeld's friend, Irving Thalberg, was still MGM's head of production at the time the studio acquired the rights to *The Great Ziegfeld*. MGM's films were considered the crème de la crème of the movie industry (largely due to Thalberg's expertise), making it the ideal studio to bring Ziegfeld's life to the silver screen. However, Louis B. Mayer believed in "confecting, not reflecting" reality. Consequently, the movie was whitewashed in many areas.

Nevertheless, the movie contained grains of authenticity due to the presence of several Ziegfeld alumni (aside from McGuire). Former Ziegfeld costume designer John Harkrider supervised the art direction; although he did not design the costumes for the film, Gilbert Adrian's work was on a par with any Harkrider creation. Musical numbers featuring Ziegfeld star Leon Errol and *Follies* dancers Gilda Gray and Ann Pennington were filmed but ultimately cut from the final version of the movie. In the acting department, Fanny Brice brought the most genuineness to the film by playing herself.

Marilyn Miller could have added more authenticity had she accepted MGM's offer to appear in the picture. She began negotiations with the studio, demanding $50,000 for her services and top billing alongside the principal stars. The studio could accept her salary demand but balked at giving her top billing. MGM then offered her $10,000 if she would allow another actress to portray her, but Marilyn threatened to sue if her name was even mentioned in the picture. Marilyn might be better remembered today if she had appeared in the film. The day before the movie's release on April 7, 1936, Marilyn died at age thirty-eight due to complications from surgery for her lifelong sinus condition. A flood of mourners attended her funeral. Strangely, *Time* magazine gave the still-popular actress only a one-line obituary. A writer for the *New York Telegram* offered a more fitting summation of Marilyn's legacy: "She gave Broadway all she could; we hope it made her happy, for she certainly gave great pleasure to others."[5] MGM honored Marilyn's wishes; McGuire changed her character's name to "Sally Manners," who appeared only briefly as a blonde ballerina in a Ziegfeld show.

The film contained more than a brief allusion to Lillian Lorraine. She was personified through a character named Audrey Dane, portrayed by

Virginia Bruce. In the film, Ziegfeld did not carry on an affair with the actress; rather, he resisted her flirtations and demanded that she quit drinking. The rest of the cast included Austrian actress Luise Rainier as Anna Held, Frank Morgan (who had been in Ziegfeld's 1928 production of *Rosalie*) as a Dillingham-like character named Jack Billings, Ray Bolger as a dancer modeled after Jack Donahue, and a Will Rogers look-alike, A. A. Trimble, as Ziegfeld's best friend. Surprisingly, Eddie Cantor was not in the cast, but he had other film and radio commitments at the time. Fanny Brice was the highlight of the movie. She was uproariously funny, especially in the scene when she meets Ziegfeld for the first time and mistakes him for a salesman of cheap fur coats. "Tell Mr. Ziegfeld I'm not in and if I was in, I wouldn't see him and if I did see him, tell him, I wouldn't buy a thing," she instructs her maid. After discovering that Ziegfeld is actually who he says he is, Fanny accepts his offer and quips: "If I can give Belasco four dollars for silk stockings made of cotton, I can give Ziegfeld a little more for a mink coat made of skunk."

The film, despite its impressive cast and crew, would have been more intriguing had it told Ziegfeld's true story. By leaving out his personal follies, the picture neglected major parts of his character. This was due in part to Billie Burke. "She was very protective of him [Ziegfeld] in the picture," Patricia recalled. "She was on his [William Anthony McGuire's] neck all the time to make sure he didn't besmirch him in any way."[6] Billie got little argument from Louis B. Mayer in her quest to keep the film free of tawdry affairs. Mayer was an avid proponent of the Breen office's film censorship code.

The studio's casting of William Powell in the lead role also contributed to the inaccurate, pristine portrayal of Ziegfeld. Powell's confident, outgoing persona contrasted sharply with Ziegfeld's retiring disposition and his preference to remain behind the scenes. Billie, in her statements to the press, was enthusiastic about Powell portraying her husband. However, she told reporter Barbara Rush in confidence that Powell was "nothing, absolutely nothing like Flo."[7] Powell's elegance matched Ziegfeld's, if nothing else. A critic for the *New York Times* noted that Powell gave an "attractive" and "flattering" performance as the producer.[8] MGM might have selected another actor to play Ziegfeld, but Universal had originally asked MGM to loan out Powell for the picture. When Universal sold the film rights to MGM, one of the stipulations was that Powell be allowed to appear in another picture for Universal, which had promised its exhibitors that it would release a movie starring the actor. That picture became Universal's classic screwball comedy *My Man Godfrey* (1936).[9]

Like Powell's Ziegfeld, Billie Burke's character was "nothing, absolutely nothing" like the true Billie. McGuire included none of her red-headed furies in the screenplay. Yet his portrayal of her steadfast support of and loyalty to Ziegfeld was true to life. For the part of Billie, MGM tested actresses Margaret Perry, who appeared in Mae West's *Go West Young Man* (1936), and Jean Chatburn, who was eventually cast as the grown-up Mary Lou, one of Professor Ziegfeld's pupils. In the end, the studio settled on Myrna Loy in October 1935. Billie admitted that the understated Loy was "lovely," but she did not look anything like Billie.[10] MGM chose Loy not for her looks but for her onscreen chemistry with Powell. The two actors were an immensely popular team in the *Thin Man* mystery films. Loy claimed that "Billie was on my conscience throughout the making of that picture." In a review of the film, a writer for the *New York Times* stated that Loy "is a stately Billie Burke, and somewhat lacking, we fear in Miss Burke's effervescence and gayety."[11]

Whether she approved of the casting choices or not, Billie still supervised McGuire's portrayal of the Ziegfeld character and the way the cinematographers and art department presented his showmanship. She was enthusiastic about MGM's initial choice of George Cukor as director, but ultimately the studio went with Robert Z. Leonard instead. The film included many original songs from Ziegfeld's shows, such as "A Pretty Girl Is Like a Melody" and "My Man," as well as Anna Held's early hits "Won't You Come and Play with Me?" and "It's Delightful to Be Married." Billie and Patricia researched the musical numbers to ensure their authenticity. Harkrider and Patricia helped choose the girls for the "Pretty Girl Is Like a Melody" number and advised Adrian about their wardrobe (Harkrider had a prolific film career until his death in 1982). The entire routine, set on a "giant twirling wedding cake," was filmed in one take.[12] MGM spent $220,000 for the "Pretty Girl" number alone—$40,000 more than Ziegfeld had spent on any of his shows.[13]

Though the film did an excellent job depicting the decadence of Ziegfeld's productions, according to biographer Grant Hayter-Menzies, it failed to show Ziegfeld the man as anything more than a spendthrift and a barker at the World's Fair. As he explained, "there was only so much time for exploring any deeper conflicts in his character or his marriage to Billie in a script that called for several re-enactments of *Follies* shows."[14] The center of a *New York Times* article observed that attempting to tell the story of Ziegfeld's life, the *Follies,* the *Midnight Frolic,* and his book shows in a three-hour film resulted in a "fragmentary" history that seemed "confused" at times. The writer noted that "the picture overcrowds its screen, [but] at least we must admit it is an impressive kaleidoscope; and probably nothing short of that could reflect the gaudy career of America's foremost showman."[15]

Overcrowded or fragmentary, the film was as successful as any great Ziegfeld production. Prior to the film's release on March 22, 1936, the public's interest had already been piqued, partly due to the premiere of the second posthumous *Follies* on Broadway in January 1936, and partly due to CBS radio's revival of the *Ziegfeld Follies of the Air.* The radio show, which aired at 8:00 p.m. on Saturdays from February 22 to June 6, 1936, was sponsored by Palmolive and recorded live from the Winter Garden Theatre. With the Ziegfeld name becoming ubiquitous on the stage, on the radio, and in film, it is no wonder that *The Great Ziegfeld* was a favorite at the box office. The film won the Best Picture Oscar and the Best Actress Oscar for Luise Rainer, whose flamboyant and dramatic portrayal of Anna Held was the most memorable in the movie. Anna actually had more screen time and was a more substantial character in the film than Billie.

According to Patricia, Billie was dissatisfied with the movie, despite her influence on its production. "Mother never felt it was the greatest picture," she stated. "She felt that they really didn't do complete justice to my father's life, but then they were trying to make a movie that would make money."[16] Make money it did; studio records show that its worldwide gross was $4,673,000. The picture's success should have benefited Billie, but any profits she received from the film only went to pay more debts.

Billie may not have been a great fan of the film, but *The Great Ziegfeld* (as well as the posthumous *Follies* and revived radio program) succeeded in boosting the public's interest in Ziegfeld shows. In 1936 Universal Studios made *Show Boat* into a full-length musical with Helen Morgan, Paul Robeson, and Irene Dunne heading the cast (Dunne had played Magnolia in the 1929 touring company). In 1937 MGM produced *Rosalie* with Eleanor Powell as the star (she had been a specialty dancer in *Hot-Cha!*) and Frank Morgan reprising his role as her father, the King of Romanza.

Hollywood producers were not only adapting Ziegfeld's shows for the screen; they were also using his formulas. Films such as *42nd Street* (1933) and *Presenting Lily Mars* (1943) utilized the Cinderella story found in *Sally, Show Girl,* and *Betsy.* A 1944 film, *Cover Girl,* used a Ziegfeld Cinderella plot twist reminiscent of *Rosalie*: a chorus girl rises to fame on Broadway but ultimately chooses to descend the social ladder for love's sake. A 1941 film called *Ziegfeld Girl* (McGuire wrote the scenario) had elements of the Cinderella story but deviated from Ziegfeld's formula by showing that not all such stories have happy endings. The film depicted three different types of Ziegfeld girls. Judy Garland portrayed the girl next door who goes from dancing and singing in a family vaudeville act to being a headliner in a Ziegfeld show. She is most reminiscent of Marilyn Miller. Hedy Lamarr played a Ziegfeld beauty who chooses family over career, much like one of Ziegfeld's favorite chorines, Marcelle Earle. Lana Turner portrayed a small-town girl who finds fame but then spends her time dating stage door Johnnies and overindulging in liquor. In one scene, a tipsy Turner even stumbles onstage and struggles to balance her head-dress, much like Lillian Lorraine decades before.

In 1944 producer Arthur Freed of MGM endeavored to produce not a Cinderella story but a film using Ziegfeld's revue formula. That film, titled *Ziegfeld Follies,* would not be released until 1946 because of the enormous amount of editing needed to cut its original 273-minute running time. Of the production numbers featured in the film, only one—Fanny Brice's "A Sweepstakes Ticket"—originated in a *Follies* (the 1936 edition). New sources note that the film was supposed to feature songs by former Ziegfeld employees Jerome Kern, Rudolf Friml, the Gershwins, and Victor Herbert. Songwriter Dave Stamper, who, along with Gene Buck, had penned most of the early *Follies,* was signed to work on the picture, "but the extent of his contribution to the final film has not been determined."[17] Only the Gershwins' song "The Babbitt and the Bromide" made the final cut. The film made up for its general lack of authenticity with dazzling visual effects and choreography. Director Vincente Minnelli and choreographer Robert Alton were largely responsible for the film's aesthetics. Other contributors to the movie were songwriters Hugh Martin and Ralph Blane (best known for "Have Yourself a Merry Little Christmas") and vocal arranger Kay Thompson (famous for authoring the *Eloise* children's book series).

The cast was just as impressive as the crew. Among the players were two former Ziegfeld stars, Fanny Brice and Fred Astaire, as well as MGM's brightest talents: Judy Garland, Gene Kelly, Keenan Wynn (son of Ed Wynn), Red Skelton, and Lucille Ball. Garland, Ball, and a number of other beauties, including Kathryn Grayson and Lucille Bremer, represented a new generation of Ziegfeld girls. According to journalist Adela Rogers St. John, Ziegfeld would have approved of the actresses (and, in fact, Billie Burke *had* personally approved of them). Rogers St. John observed: "There is a magic about the *Follies* which casts its light over the picture, that seems to transform the girls themselves."[18]

William Powell reprised his role as Ziegfeld and is depicted at the beginning in a red velvet smoking jacket, sitting among the clouds and stars in heaven. He gives a sentimental monologue as an introduction to the picture, concluding with a statement that was an accurate reflection of Ziegfeld's feelings in his declining years: "Children play with the dreams of tomorrow. And old men play with the memories of yesterday." He goes on to say: "What I would give to put on one last *Follies*. . . . I think I'd open with a pink number . . . and who better to introduce the whole thing than my old friend Fred Astaire." Astaire then enters the picture and makes an effective speech: "What can I say about Ziegfeld? Well, I can only say that as long as there's a song, a dance, and a musical show that is good, some-where around it is Ziegfeld. He never did care for villains, plots, and sto-ries. The *Follies* never had a story. The *Ziegfeld Follies* itself was the story of an era. It was gay, bright, beautiful, that's how Zieggy wanted it. And oh, I almost forgot—the girls . . . that's one of the most important parts of the *Follies*, you know." Astaire then launches into "Here's to the Girls," a pink production number featuring Cyd Charisse as well as a number of former Ziegfeld girls in the chorus.[19] As in Ziegfeld's *Sally* (1920), the film blends modern dance and ballet. The highlight is a ballet called "Limehouse Blues," featuring Astaire. Though aesthetically appealing and well made, *Ziegfeld Follies* suffers from uneven pacing. And with the exception of Fanny Brice's skit, its comedy is weak. Despite these flaws, the film made $2 million at the box office and proved that Ziegfeld was still the master of show business even after his death.

Hollywood producers borrowed not only Ziegfeld's formulas for his shows but also his techniques for large-scale production numbers. Although Goldwyn was sometimes called the Ziegfeld of Hollywood, Arthur Freed was a more appropriate holder of that title. He dominated the Hollywood musical the way Ziegfeld had dominated the Broadway musical. Freed made sure the songs in his films (with the exception of *Ziegfeld Follies*) blended seamlessly with the plot. He spared no expense, allowing his creative team to take risks and make their most fantastic visions into realities. He even brought an elaborate Technicolor remake of *Show Boat* to the screen in 1951. One of Freed's invaluable team members was Irving Berlin, who wrote the entire score for one of Freed's most profitable films, *Easter Parade* (1948). In that film, Freed used the living picture technique Ziegfeld had adopted from Lucile Gordon. In a number entitled "The Girl I Love Is on a Magazine Cover," a crooner reminiscent of John Steel serenades a succession of twelve "living mannequins" posing on larger-than-life covers of magazines such as *Harper's Bazaar* and *Ladies Home Companion*.

The same type of magazine-themed number had been used in an earlier film by Columbia Pictures, *Cover Girl* (1944). Though not a Freed production, it was on a par with any he supervised at the superior MGM Studios. Much of the film's artistry can be attributed to its star, Gene Kelly, who helped choreograph *Cover Girl's* most innovative musical numbers. Kelly was a pioneer among the creative talents in Freed's unit. He codirected and starred in one of Freed's most enduring films, *Singin' in the Rain* (1952), which also used the living mannequin technique. In a number celebrating the advent of talking pictures, a male singer serenades a series of women posing inside frames and modeling the latest fashions. The number, appropriately titled "Beautiful Girl," was penned by Freed himself.

The most artistic production numbers in Freed's films were the balletic sequences, most of which were executed by either Kelly or Vincente Minnelli. Ziegfeld is not usually associated with ballet, but according to Billie: "Flo has never been given proper credit for . . . [bringing] the loveliness of ballet into musical comedy."[20] Victor Herbert's "Butterfly Ballet," which Marilyn Miller danced in *Sally*, is among the earliest examples. In *Singin' in the Rain*, the iconic "Broadway Ballet" is reminiscent of the "Broadway Reverie" created by Ziegfeld in the *Follies of 1931*. The most famous ballet in any film is the finale of Best Picture winner *An American in Paris* (1951), directed by Minnelli. The ballet featured Kelly in a variety of surreal Parisian settings, including reenactments of Toulouse-Lautrec and Renoir paintings. The costumes by Irene Sharaff (who had also worked on the 1936 *Follies* and Freed's *Ziegfeld Follies*) were done in Harkrider style, with towering headdresses and diaphanous skirts. Gershwin provided the score for the ballet; his "American in Paris" had been the most successful part of Ziegfeld's musical comedy *Show Girl.* Though not balletic, another number in *An American in Paris* bore Ziegfeld's influence. In "I'll Build a Stairway to Paradise," Georges Guetary, a French entertainer similar to Maurice Chevalier, sings while ascending an illuminated staircase flanked by showgirls with feather headdresses strutting down the stairs using the "Ziegfeld walk."

The Ziegfeld name was still part of the American lexicon, thanks to producers like Freed who re-created his style on film. In the Freed-produced musical *Babes on Broadway* (1941), directed by Busby Berkeley, Ziegfeld's name was mentioned in the lyrics of a song that asks several impossible "what ifs" about New York: "What if Ziegfeld didn't have a goil?" In the same film, Mickey Rooney and Judy Garland launch into an impromptu dance around Judy's apartment, fancying themselves great musical stars. Rooney sings: "A dictionary's necessary but not for talking, / It's used for walking the Ziegfeld way!"[21] Garland takes a dictionary and walks with wobbly steps as she balances it on her head, attempting to strut like Dolores.

Ziegfeld was not just a name but an adjective. His name meant the top; it meant magic. However, in most of the films in which he is a crucial character, he is not shown onscreen at all. Rather, he is an invisible presence. In *Easter Parade,* for instance, Judy Garland and Fred Astaire audition for "Mr. Ziegfeld," but Ziegfeld is not shown in the audience watching their tryout. In all likelihood, he was supposed to be watching from the glass walls of his office high above the stage; he would then send a telegram downstairs, delivering his verdict on the act. At the close of the tryout, a man modeled after Gene Buck runs up to Garland and Astaire and jokes that they had better stop because, if they were any better, Ziegfeld would have to pay them more money. In other films, characters often allude to Ziegfeld, suggesting that they have exchanged words with the unseen producer. For example, Lana Turner states in *Ziegfeld Girl,* "Mr. Ziegfeld says, if I don't watch my figure, no one else will."[22]

The few times the Ziegfeld character appeared onscreen in a film, his presence usually served only to give the subject of a biopic a job. William Forrest portrayed Ziegfeld in three different films: *I'll See You in My Dreams* (1951), a pleasant film about the life of songwriter Gus Kahn; *The*

Story of Will Rogers (1952), a superior biopic with Will Rogers Jr. playing his father; and *The Eddie Cantor Story* (1953). Austrian actor Paul Henreid was miscast in his cameo as Ziegfeld in *Deep in My Heart* (1954), the story of composer Sigmund Romberg. In *The Helen Morgan Story* (1957), Ziegfeld was a bland presence as played by Walter Woolf King. In 1976 Paul Stewart portrayed Ziegfeld in *W. C. Fields and Me,* a romanticized look at the alcoholic comedian.

One film in which Ziegfeld was more than a one-dimensional character is *Funny Girl* (1968), the story of Fanny Brice. Walter Pidgeon was cast as Ziegfeld (eerily, Billie had been preparing to perform a screen test with Pidgeon on the day of her husband's death). He did not portray the producer as vibrantly as William Powell did, but his depiction was arguably the better one, for he did not make Ziegfeld into an outgoing and confident man. Admittedly, *Funny Girl* did not touch on the more complex aspects of Ziegfeld's character, but it showed him as a man (not an untouchable god) who could be both teasing and argumentative with his stars. Screenwriter Isobel Lennart penned a scene in which Fanny takes liberties by ad-libbing in an act. She and Ziegfeld exchange the following words:

> ZIEGFELD: Miss Brice, do I have to remind you this is my theatre?
> FANNY: So, what, nobody argues with the landlord?

Another humorous moment occurs when Fanny ad-libs again and Ziegfeld, fearing the worst, cries that he is ruined:

> FANNY: Flo! Flo, quit yelling or your ulcer will flare up.
> ZIEGFELD: That's funny coming from you. You gave me that ulcer![23]

Pidgeon re-created his role as Ziegfeld in the 1975 sequel to *Funny Girl* entitled *Funny Lady.*

Hollywood also produced biopics about the stars and composers Ziegfeld had helped make famous. Most of these films were not as well executed as *Funny Girl;* many did not even pretend to tell the true story of their subjects' lives. Two of the better biopics of the era were Freed productions: *Till the Clouds Roll By* (1946), about Jerome Kern, and *Words and Music* (1948), about Rodgers and Hart. Other films by less meticulous producers were *Shine on Harvest Moon* (1944), about Nora Bayes; *The Dolly*

Sisters (1945); *Rhapsody in Blue* (1945), about George Gershwin; and *Look for the Silver Lining* (1949), about Marilyn Miller.

In 1978, thirty-two years after *The Great Ziegfeld* won the Best Picture Oscar, television and film director Buzz Kulik decided to produce a TV miniseries that included the parts of Ziegfeld's life omitted by the MGM film. The three-hour *Ziegfeld: The Man and His Women* was, according to *New York Times* reviewer Hal Erikson, "ten times" less the film *The Great Ziegfeld* had been. The miniseries starred the overconfident Paul Shenar as Ziegfeld, "looking for all the world like a spoiled prep-schooler dressed up in his daddy's tuxedo." Although the movie attempted to depict every angle of Ziegfeld's public and private life, "the sense of beauty and grandeur, so vital to the success of the *Follies* . . . is totally missing." Part of the problem was the movie's peculiar structure. Each segment was narrated by an actress portraying one of the four most important women in Ziegfeld's life: Anna Held, Lillian Lorraine, Billie Burke, and Marilyn Miller. Erikson called Pamela Peardon's portrayal of Marilyn "shrill and unlikeable" and Samantha Eggar's performance as Billie "saintly to the point of tedium." In conclusion, Erikson stated that "*Ziegfeld: The Man and His Women* serves only one positive purpose—to whet the viewer's appetite for a cable TV revival of *The Great Ziegfeld*."[24] What the movie ultimately accomplished was to perpetuate Ziegfeld's reputation as little more than a squanderer and a skirt-chaser.

If film and television had not done Ziegfeld's legacy justice, perhaps the legitimate stage could. In 1971 composer Stephen Sondheim and writer James Goldman created *Follies,* a musical that told the story of a reunion of past performers in *Weismann's Follies* (based on the *Ziegfeld Follies*) in a decaying Broadway theater that is about to be razed. The play focused on the discontent of two former *Follies* girls and their husbands: Buddy and Sally Durant Plummer (the name Sally is an obvious homage to Marilyn Miller's *Sally*) and Benjamin and Phyllis Rogers Stone. The highlight of the production was when the ex-showgirls performed their old numbers accompanied by the ghosts of their younger selves. The show ran for 522 performances and was nominated for eleven Tony Awards. Although it did not tell the story of Ziegfeld's life per se or feature any songs from his shows, the production captured the sad fate of many of his employees and the Broadway he had helped create.

In 1988 British director Joe Layton produced a musical extravaganza focused directly on Ziegfeld. Entitled simply *Ziegfeld*, it opened at the London Palladium on April 26 and ran through October 1. The show was not so much a biographical musical as "a musical using all the hallmarks of a Ziegfeld revue—colorful costumes, beautiful girls, spectacular scenery and a melodious score from musical numbers by masters of the genre." What made the play interesting was the fact that every character in it— even Ziegfeld—broke out in song at some point. Ziegfeld, portrayed by Len Cariou, sang "I'm Always Chasing Rainbows" and "Makin' Whoopee." In another number, Ziegfeld and Anna Held sang "Who?" to each other, which is strange, given that "Who?" was originally sung by Marilyn Miller in Charles Dillingham's *Sunny* (1925). Billie Burke, Fanny Brice, and even Ziegfeld's secretary, Goldie, were among the characters in the show. Actress Louise Gold (as Fanny Brice) was the only performer to garner unanimously favorable reviews. According to London's *City Limits* publication, *Ziegfeld* was "deadly . . . a depressing hymn to meaningless expenditure."[25] In August, Chaim Topol was brought in to replace Cariou (Topol is best known for playing Tevye in *Fiddler on the Roof* [1971]). Despite revamps, reviewers continued to bash the show. Val Sampson of London's *Today* made the following comment: "The . . . cast are doubtless exhausted by working on a show that is so dreadful it has become a parody of a parody." Producer Harold Fielding had hoped the play would make it to America, but it died before it could be tested on Broadway audiences. It was listed in the *Guinness Book of World Records* (as of 1990) as the second greatest flop in theatrical history, with losses of around £3 million (the equivalent of more than $9 million in 2014).[26]

In 1991 the theater world again tried to pay proper homage to Ziegfeld with two new shows. Both productions featured Ziegfeld as an offstage presence whose influence was felt everywhere. *The Will Rogers Follies* opened at the legendary Palace vaudeville theater on May 1, 1991, and ran until September 1993, for a total of 981 performances. The production was more of a biography of Rogers than of Ziegfeld, but it was presented in the format of a typical Ziegfeld show. Each part of Will's life was depicted by a large-scale production number, one of the most notable being a scene in which Ziegfeld (whose voice, provided by Gregory Peck, interjected advice and opinions from behind the curtain) tells Will to hurry up and meet his girl. In reality, Will met his wife, Betty, at a train station, but the show created a more fantastical and romantic meeting by having her lowered from the moon. This was clearly an allusion to the many "moon" numbers in Ziegfeld's productions: "Shine on, Harvest Moon" (*Follies of 1908*), "By the Light of the Silvery Moon" (*Follies of 1909*), and "The Old Man in the Moon" (*Miss 1917*). Between the spectacles in the play, the Will Rogers character performed rope tricks and recited portions of his folksy monologues. Much of the play's success can be attributed to its lyricists, Betty Comden and Adolph Green, who were also responsible for the memorable tunes in Freed's *On the Town* (1949) and the clever screenplay for *Singin' in the Rain* (1952).

The second Ziegfeld-inspired show of 1991 had similarities to both Sondheim's *Follies* and the London flop *Ziegfeld*. The production, entitled *Ziegfeld: A Night at the Follies,* originated in London and focused on the stories of three showgirls. Lawrence Bommer of the *Chicago Reader* summarized the show as follows: "The cliche-loving plot, about three hopefuls who desert their boring boyfriends to become Ziegfeld stars, is the pretext for lavish production numbers and novelty songs. Of course the boyfriends pursue them to New York, where, thanks to dream sequences that double as *Follies* spectacles, the couples work out their conflicts."[27] Lou Cedrone of the *Baltimore Evening Sun* added that the lavish play, whose costumes alone cost $1 million, was like a "musical valentine to America's Greatest Showman."[28] Bommer found the show to be full of "cornball sentiment," but other reviewers, like Cedrone, saw the charm in its nostalgic and rousing production numbers featuring standards by Irving Berlin, Cole Porter, and Jerome Kern. The production toured nationally but never made it to Broadway.

Ziegfeld's influence on the entertainment world has not waned even in the twenty-first century. In honor of the hundredth anniversary of the *Ziegfeld Follies,* the New York City Center's *Encores!* devoted its entire season to productions paying homage to Ziegfeld and his brand of showmanship. The season opened with a revival of Sondheim's 1971 *Follies,* continued with an exact replication of Irving Berlin's 1932 play *Face the Music,* and concluded with a new show, *Stairway to Paradise*—a "revue in review" that included songs by Irving Berlin, Rodgers and Hart, the Gershwins, and Cole Porter, among others.

Jack Vietel, art director for the *Encores!* series, stated that the three tribute shows had "bravura show-biz pastiche numbers [that] sell love, optimism, romance and the art of burning the candle at both ends." He explained that a number of the songs in *Follies* "ponder the roads not taken and the dark forest in which all of us seemed to be wandering, direction-less," which was appropriate, given that in 2007 the country found itself "in a new round of soul-searching and self-doubt." William Goldman, brother of one of *Follies'* creators, once wrote that Broadway theater could be divided into two categories: "Shows that tell you a lie you want to believe and shows that tell you a truth you don't want to hear. The myths drive us relentlessly forward, and the hard truths make us stop and reconsider." According to Vietel, the 2007 season of *Encores!* endeavored to show Ziegfeld and his legacy from both points of view.[29] Ziegfeld himself pro-duced plays that presented both viewpoints; his *Follies* were often a mix-ture of both dreams and truth, as were his greatest book musicals such as *Sally* (1920) and *Show Boat* (1927). As such, the *Encores!* tribute to Ziegfeld was the most befitting reflection of the man thus far.

There is no sign that Ziegfeldian musicals are losing favor with mod-ern audiences. Indeed, they still dominate Broadway. A revival of *Show Boat* in 1994 ran for three years at the Gershwin Theatre. *The Phantom of the Opera* (1988), *The Lion King* (1997), and *Wicked* (2003) are only a few more examples of plot-driven musicals that can trace their roots to the foundations laid by Ziegfeld. Musicals are no longer a prevalent genre in film (with rare exceptions such as *Chicago* [2002], *The Artist* [2012], and *Les Miserables* [2012]), but it is only appropriate that Ziegfeld's legacy is more evident on Broadway. After all, Broadway is where his passion lay and where he became an icon.

24

Beauty Slain

Ziegfeld has been immortalized on both the stage and the screen thanks in part to the creative team that made his visions possible. He may have missed his chance to be a great showman in Hollywood, but many of the actors, musicians, and writers he knew and employed found greater opportunities in film than on the legitimate stage.

Eddie Cantor was among the most successful of the Ziegfeld stars. He appeared on radio, stage, and film even during the bleakest years of the Depression. On his radio show, which centered largely on his family, he invited guests into his "home," and one of the most welcome guests was Billie Burke. She recalled that "working with the comedian Flo used to call his son" was "always so much fun."[1] After slowing his pace in films during the late 1930s, Eddie turned his attention to philanthropy and helped Franklin D. Roosevelt found the March of Dimes in 1938. Before Eddie's death in 1964, Governor Pat Brown of California presented him with an award for his dedication and tireless service to the nation.

Preceding Cantor in death was his good friend Fanny Brice. Though her film career was short, she was a successful radio personality. During her last days, she seemed anything but ill. When Cantor visited her in the hospital, he found her "on the phone, placing bets all over the country" after discovering that a famous bookie was being treated in the neighboring room.[2] Fanny never collected on her bets; she died of a stroke on May 24, 1951, at the age of fifty-nine. Her funeral at Temple Israel in Hollywood was so well attended that the mourners spilled into the street. Fanny's memory has not faded over the decades, partly due to the success of *Funny Girl* (1968) and *Funny Lady* (1975).

Not all members of the Ziegfeld family were commemorated in film, but they still left indelible imprints in Hollywood. Jerome Kern, after a long decline in popularity, won the 1942 Academy Award for best song for

"The Last Time I Saw Paris." The song was from an Arthur Freed–produced film, *Lady Be Good,* based on the 1924 Gershwin show. Kern's home was the meeting place for ex–Tin Pan Alley composers, among them George Gershwin and Irving Berlin. According to a friend, Kern "was highly respected, but not content . . . George [Gershwin] would always usurp the piano [at dinner parties] and play his own music all night. Kern thought his own music was unappreciated."[3] Shortly after the filming of the Freed-produced biopic of Kern, *Till the Clouds Roll By* (1946), the composer collapsed on a sidewalk on Park Avenue. He had no identification with him and was taken to the Welfare Island Hospital—a great indignity for such a prominent artist. He died on November 11, 1945.

George and Ira Gershwin composed the scores for a number of films, including *Delicious* (1931), *Shall We Dance* (1937), and *A Damsel in Distress* (1937). Despite his vibrancy at parties and in the social whirl of Hollywood, George suffered a premature death. He began to experience fainting spells and complained that he smelled burning rubber. His doctors had written him off as a hysterical hypochondriac, but they were proved wrong when they discovered that George had a malignant brain tumor. He died at age thirty-nine in 1937. Ira had a prolific career following his brother's death, writing lyrics for such musicals as *Cover Girl* (1944), *The Barkleys of Broadway* (1949), and *A Star Is Born* (1954). He died in 1983.

Irving Berlin outlived virtually all the Ziegfeld alumni. He was the most popular songwriter in Hollywood for decades, writing what is now the United States' quasi–national anthem, "God Bless America," and one of the nation's most beloved holiday tunes, "White Christmas." The latter melody won an Oscar for best original song at the 1943 Academy Awards. After his long career in Hollywood, Berlin became reclusive, refusing to see even his closest friends. The telephone was his only link to the outside world. However, he came out of seclusion in 1988 when Carnegie Hall held a celebration of his hundredth birthday. When Berlin died the following year, he left behind a legacy of 1,500 songs.

Gene Buck, one of the *Follies'* first song- and scriptwriters, remained with Ziegfeld throughout his entire career. Buck had been relatively unaffected by the Depression. He was F. Scott Fitzgerald's neighbor at Great Neck, and according to Fitzgerald historian Matthew Bruccoli, he may have inspired the writer to pen *The Great Gatsby.* From 1925 to 1942, Buck was president of ASCAP (the American Society of Composers, Authors, and Publishers), an organization that another former Ziegfeld songwriter, Gus Edwards, had helped found in 1914. Buck died in 1947.

Ziegfeld's perennial writer and occasional nemesis William Anthony McGuire died in 1940 of uremia, a kidney condition brought on by alcoholism. McGuire wrote few screenplays after *The Great Ziegfeld,* the most notable being a biopic of Ziegfeld's old friend Lillian Russell and the scenario for *Ziegfeld Girl* (1941). McGuire did the majority of his Hollywood work prior to Ziegfeld's death. He also wrote the screenplays for many of Eddie Cantor's Goldwyn pictures, including *The Kid from Spain* (1932) and *Roman Scandals* (1933).

W. C. Fields, whose alcoholism also made him Ziegfeld's occasional nemesis, died of a stomach hemorrhage on Christmas Day 1946 (ironically, his most despised holiday). Fields had enjoyed a comeback due to Marilyn Miller's help in getting him into talking pictures. *The Bank Dick* (1940) and *My Little Chickadee* (1940) are among his best-remembered films. He is now considered one of the great comic geniuses, alongside Harold Lloyd, Charlie Chaplin, and Buster Keaton.

Lillian Lorraine died in complete obscurity in 1955. After Ziegfeld's death, she had no source of reliable income and was buried in a pauper's grave. When Lillian's former companion, Nanny Johnson, heard about Lillian's inappropriate burial, she and her friend Winnie Dunn obtained permission for the coffin to be moved to the Dunn family plot. After Lillian's death, biographer Nils Hanson discovered a song she had written with Harry Leighton. Its haunting, wistful lyrics reveal Lillian to be a deeper woman than the press and even Ziegfeld had assumed her to be: "I sat thinking last night of friendships / . . . I pictured my friend as I'd have him . . . / A steadfast friend, on whom to depend / Through life's battle of storm and strife. / The friendship of which I was dreaming / To one does so seldom come . . . Shall we ever find one . . . Yes! Someday I mean, if not we can dream . . . and I dream on."[4]

Although most tangible traces of Ziegfeld's memory have disappeared, a handful still exists. The first institution created in honor of his work, the Ziegfeld Club, was established in 1936 following the release of *The Great Ziegfeld.* The club's mission was to help indigent women of the theater. The organization championed such causes as Broadway Cares, Equity Fights

AIDS, and the Episcopal Actors Guild. Billie Burke officially sanctioned the club's creation and is listed as its first founding member, along with Bernard Sobel and the youngest of the Eaton sisters, Doris. Club members have allegedly swept all traces of Lillian Lorraine from their archives because of her crude behavior and alcoholism, which disgraced the reputation of the Ziegfeld girls. According to Nils Hanson, a past president of the Ziegfeld Club, whenever he mentioned Lillian's name in the presence of other members, the women grew silent. The club is less active today but still fundraises and now boasts an internet presence.

One woman with a prominent place in the archives of the Ziegfeld Club was Anna Held. However, Liane Carrera was not content to have her mother's photographs lost among those of the hundreds of other Ziegfeld girls in the club's files. In 1976 Liane opened a museum in San Jacinto, California, full of her mother's personal belongings and stage souvenirs. A few years after the museum opened, robbers stole all the displayed material. Liane died in 1988.

Doris Eaton Travis, the last living Ziegfeld girl and the last person personally employed by Ziegfeld, died in 2010 at age 106. Doris never forgot her days with Ziegfeld and had only positive memories of working in the *Follies*. "It [the *Follies*] was beauty, elegance, loveliness," she recalled in an interview with the *New York Times* in 2005, "beauty and elegance like a French painting of a woman's body."[5]

Doris had been among the first guests of honor at the New Amsterdam Theatre upon its restoration. The site of Ziegfeld's *Follies* and the majority of his greatest shows had fallen into disrepair. Disney Theatrical Productions bought the lease in 1993 and spent millions to revamp the old palace. In recent years the theater has housed musicals including *Mary Poppins* (2006) and *The Lion King* (1997).

Unfortunately, the greatest testament to Ziegfeld's memory, the Ziegfeld Theatre, was razed in 1966. Due to the Depression, Loew's, which had transformed the theater into a movie house in 1933, could no longer sustain it. Fanny Brice's second husband, producer Billy Rose, bought the theater in 1944 and leased it to NBC as a television studio from 1955 to 1963. The most famous programs broadcast from the Ziegfeld Theatre were the *Perry Como Show* and the televised Emmy Awards of 1959 and 1961. The Ziegfeld Theatre almost returned to its original purpose in 1963, when it reopened as a venue for Broadway shows. However, Rose ultimately lost interest in the theater and did not maintain it. The site is now home to the Alliance Bernstein building, a modern steel and glass sky-scraper much less pleasing to the eye than the artistic Ziegfeld Theatre.[6] Only a fragment of the Joseph Urban–designed façade remains: a glamor-ous stone carving of a woman's head that now resides in front of a private home at 52 East Eightieth Street in New York City.[7] The time capsule from the cornerstone of the theater was moved to the Billy Rose Theatre Division of the New York Public Library for the Performing Arts.

Three years after the demolition of the Ziegfeld Theatre, another Ziegfeld Theatre was built a few hundred feet from the original site. Although this new theater is a movie house, it reflects Ziegfeld's love of grandiosity and is one of the last lavish movie palaces in the United States. The interior is similar to the original Urban design, with lush red carpeting and gold trim on the seats, walls, and curtains.

Another building lost to posterity is the place where Ziegfeld grew up, the Chicago Musical College. The property on West Addams Street was auctioned in 1934 for a minuscule price. The college, however, is now a division of the Chicago College for Performing Arts at Roosevelt University.

The demolition of Burkeley Crest in 1941 was the greatest loss to the Ziegfeld legacy. There, the Great Ziegfeld could simply be Flo, husband and father, as well as a showman and host in a relaxed, unprofessional set-ting. French industrialist Dr. Jacques Gerard of the Gerard Machine Company bought the property, demolished the original home, and built a twenty-room French Baroque stucco mansion. During the time Billie and Ziegfeld lived at the estate, their presence in Hastings-on-Hudson had pulled the little town from obscurity. One former resident of Westchester County, Stephen Zebrock, recalled in an article written in 1941 for the *Hastings News:* "The names of Billie Burke and Florenz Ziegfeld of course went hand in hand every time anyone mentioned Hastings. It seemed as though no one could ever speak of our village without invariably adding, 'You know, that's where Billie Burke and Ziegfeld live.'"[8] The sole remnants of Burkeley Crest are the two majestic pillars that stood at the home's front gate.[9] The only relics of Burkeley Crest that Billie took with her to Hollywood were the bronze gate signs—reading "B" and "C"—that had been attached to the stone pillars. Grant Hayter-Menzies explained that Burkeley Crest was "a kind of lost dream to her, with its exotic menagerie and tennis courts and miniature Mount Vernon playhouse for Patricia, its flowers that Flo loved and the fact that Flo's influence was everywhere to be seen. The loss of Burkeley Crest was one which she never really faced and accepted."[10] Billie's sparsely furnished home in Hollywood bore no similarities to her former one.

One aspect of Billie's life that did not change was her focus on work and family. In the 1940s Billie found her new role as grandmother most rewarding. She was indulgent and loving, but she could also be strict and old-fashioned, insisting that her little granddaughters learn proper lady-like behavior. Patricia lived next door to her mother, which gave the grand-children ample time to spend with Billie, whom they lovingly called "Oma." Patricia named her eldest daughter after Ziegfeld without chang-ing the spelling of the name to the feminine form, Florence. She had two more daughters, Cecilia and Susan, and a son, William. Patricia did not want her family's theatrical past to make the children feel different from their peers, so the Stephenson brood was enrolled in Los Angeles public schools. "This [the Ziegfeld legacy] is part of my life and I accept it, and of course I'm proud of it but I don't make a point of it," Florenz Stephenson stated in 1959.[11]

In addition to spending time with her family, Billie indulged in new diet and exercise trends that kept her looking at least ten years younger than her actual age. She reduced her meat intake and ingested mainly veg-etables and fruits. On weekends she attended the Christian Science Church in Beverly Hills, along with fellow character actress Charlotte Greenwood.[12] However, no amount of activity could dispel her growing depression and loneliness. In 1947 she claimed to be "in a daze, to put it mildly."[13] Her lack of success in various professional ventures—a radio program called *The Billie Burke Show* (1943–1946), a return to Broadway in *Mrs. January and Mr. Ex* (1944), and a television series called *At Home with Billie Burke* (1951–1952)—did not help her depression. Throughout the late 1940s and 1950s Billie appeared in humble theater productions, made television appearances, and filled ever-smaller roles in unmemorable films such as *And Baby Makes Three* (1949) and *Small Town Girl* (1953). Billie knew the roles were beneath her talents as an actress and yearned for ones that pre-sented a challenge. "I could do better parts better," she wrote, "for those were the roles that I was trained in—the gay but intelligent, well-written, funny but believable roles that I had [on Broadway] . . . I should like to attempt to make those interesting young women grow up."[14]

In 1949 Billie found an ideal way to express herself when she penned her first memoir, *With a Feather on My Nose.* The book, written with the help of screenwriter and publicist Cameron Shipp, was a modest success, due in part to the candid account of her life with Ziegfeld. Ten years later she wrote a quasi-memoir (also with Shipp) called *With Powder on My Nose* that consisted mostly of advice on health and etiquette. Both books are charming and remain highly readable today.

Billie remained active until 1960, when she appeared in her last film, a John Ford western entitled *Sergeant Rutledge.* After this film, she admitted that "acting was not fun anymore."[15] She retired to her little home, surrounded by memories of the past. Her home office was an organized mess of memorabilia, including old posters from *The Mind-the-Paint Girl,* Ziegfeld's elephant figurines (all with their trunks held high), and the bronze bust of Ziegfeld that the companies of *Rio Rita, The Three Musketeers,* and *Rosalie* had presented to him. Billie spent much of the early 1960s tending to her orange tabby cat, Tommy, and her rose garden.

By 1965, Billie was showing signs of dementia and moved to a nursing home. In an interview from that time, she admitted, "I can't bear to watch most of my old movies. They depress me. Whenever I see one I turn it off. Mystery shows are my cup of tea these days."[16] In *With Powder on My Nose,* she had claimed that "age is something that doesn't matter unless you are a cheese." However, Billie now found that this was not true. Like Ziegfeld she did not wish to confront the passage of time and mortality. Until the day of her death, she fibbed about her age, claiming she had been born in 1886 when census records prove the date was 1884.

Billie died on May 16, 1970, of natural causes at the Rockwell Sanitorium in Los Angeles. At Patricia's request, George Cukor spoke at Billie's funeral. It was indeed the end of two eras, as Billie had represented the golden age of both theater and film. Billie Burke was truly a multifaceted woman of unexpected depth both onscreen and off. She had a temper to match her red hair; she had the courage and wit to see her through the most trying situations in her professional and personal lives. Helen Morgan had stated in 1946 that she supposed "the girls—and the stars—will be forgotten. Because everybody is forgotten in time."[17] But Billie escaped obscurity. Whether modern audiences know her name or not, they will certainly recognize her as the ageless Glinda, Witch of the North, a good fairy who, in Billie's words, "has only to wave her wand and the world is changed."[18]

Billie was buried in her family plot at the Kenisco Cemetery in Valhalla, New York. In 1974 Ziegfeld's remains were moved from Forest Lawn Memorial Park in Glendale, California, and he was laid to rest beside Billie. Patricia passed away in 2008 and was buried alongside her husband, William, and her parents. Before her death, Patricia readily spoke of her parents to biographers and participated in a number of documentaries and television specials. Biographer Grant Hayter-Menzies explained: "When I met her, in her 90s, she was as down-to-earth and charmingly frank as could be. I think that is a testament to both Flo's and Billie's parenting efforts."[19] Also down-to-earth are the family's gravestones, which are flat stone slabs with nothing but the dates of their births and deaths engraved on them. The only evidence of Ziegfeld's former glory is an elegant statue of a woman with a striking resemblance to Billie. The woman wears a diaphanous gown and sits with her hands clasped over her knees. Her head is turned, gazing wistfully into the distance. She seems to be looking both backward and forward. The statue officially marks Blanche Burke's grave, but over time, it has become a monument to Ziegfeld himself—a symbol of the hundreds of Galateas he molded and brought to life in his shows.

In Billie's first memoir she quoted Shakespeare's "Venus and Adonis" when describing her feelings after Ziegfeld's death; however, the quote could have served as an epitaph on the Great Glorifier's gravestone:

For he being dead, with him is beauty slain,
And, beauty dead, black chaos comes again

If Ziegfeld's life were to be summarized in one word, *beauty* would be the most appropriate. It is no coincidence that, when in a state of delirium, the only intelligible words he could utter were: "All that beauty . . . all that beauty."

Epilogue

"You Can't Ever Kill Magic"

Americans experienced Ziegfeld's death as both the end of an era and the close of an institution. Few experienced it as the passing of a man, a father, a husband, or a friend. Modern historians and playgoers still associate Ziegfeld's name with an institution—the *Follies*—but not many know his first name. Even fewer can describe his appearance. The fact that Ziegfeld remained largely unseen during his lifetime only heightened his status, then and now, as a legendary establishment rather than a human being. Biographer Charles Higham asserted: "Ziegfeld seems unreal to us because he never was real, probably not even to himself. He was a kind of ghost in an immense stage machine. . . . He simply lived a fantasy in a fantastic period. . . . His whole life was the theater and his private life an acted play. . . . He was utterly devoid of intellect which is one of the reasons why his character has remained somewhat mysterious . . . his driving force was one of demonic sensuality and a passion for vivid artifice."[1]

Those closest to Ziegfeld would argue against Higham's statement that he was utterly devoid of intellect. He was not a philosopher or a literary connoisseur, but he had his own brand of intelligence perfectly suited to his way of life. His intuition for what would please audiences was unparalleled. But that same intuition sometimes failed him in his personal life; more than once, he misjudged and displeased those closest to him. Ziegfeld was more than competent at compensating for his follies, however. Although he could be aloof and silent, he was alternately laconic and effusive in person. According to Bernard Sobel, Ziegfeld "talked slowly and smoothly, without giving the slightest indication of the inner forces which made him the greatest showman of his age," but in his more expressive moments, he spoke in "long unwieldy sentences that had power because they never came to an end until his thought was completed."[2] Even more

435

expressive than his words were Ziegfeld's actions. His grand gestures and lavish gifts were sometimes desperate attempts to woo or reconcile with a lover, a friend, or a star. But more often, his gestures were efforts to express appreciation and to make the receiver feel that, with him, there was no such word as *impossible*.

Ziegfeld's life was a game of trial and error—a relentless experiment to determine what earthlings enjoyed and how they would react to his other-worldly spectacles on- and offstage. Higham wrote that Ziegfeld's driving forces in these experiments were "demonic sensuality" and "vivid artifice." His obsession with beauty and his ruthless insistence on perfection from himself and all those around him may have seemed demonic. Yet his meticulous creation of gorgeousness was the very attribute that most pleased the earthlings—particularly females. "It wasn't just the girls in the shows that Ziegfeld glorified," Helen Morgan stated. "It was the American girl herself. He meant it. Women began to be conscious of beauty as they never had before. They imitated *Follies* girls and they saw it was a good idea to make the most of themselves."[3]

That the liberation of American women in the 1920s and the peak of Ziegfeld's career occurred simultaneously is no coincidence. Though his showgirls may have seemed objectified, their dominance in Ziegfeld's shows and their ability to use their beauty to their advantage gave them more power than any of the male characters. Ziegfeld preferred the company of women, even though his relationships with women were more tumultuous than those with men. With the exception of Will Rogers and Eddie Cantor, Ziegfeld had few male confidants who knew him well. His friends Joseph Urban and Gene Buck had only limited views of Ziegfeld's personality. They rarely saw the doting father, the devoted husband, or the benevolent employer.

Relating to others in a conventional fashion was not Ziegfeld's greatest strength. How he could withhold payment from songwriters and artists yet hand out $5 tips to doormen and bags of gold coins to scrubwomen is a cipher; how he could claim that Billie and Patricia were the only two people he cared about yet undermine their security through gambling and infidelity is another puzzle. Even after thorough examination, Florenz Ziegfeld remains enigmatic. Like any mortal, he went through many personae. He favored certain ones when the situation called for them and completely disregarded others when he outgrew them. Again, he remains a mystery because, even to himself, he was unreal and unknowable.

Ziegfeld's contradictions extended to the material in his shows. He strove to capture modernity, yet in every one of his productions, he favored the old-fashioned and the sentimental. Thus, the revue format he so loved was highly appropriate. In addition to being one of the oldest forms of theater, it had as many different facets as Ziegfeld's personality. In describing the world Ziegfeld created in both his revues and his book musicals, Sobel wrote: "The world of Ziegfeld glittered, glowed, and coruscated. Only the superlative was admissible, the finest fabrics, the most expert craftsmen, the quickest brains."[4]

If Higham's assertion—that Ziegfeld was not real even to himself—is true, then Ziegfeld lived his life in superlative, exaggerated terms to make himself significant in a world he often felt removed from. "In our age, there is no room for dreamers of this magnitude," Higham wrote of Ziegfeld. "He was a giant and he remains one. If in the last analysis he seems impossibly remote, it is because we cannot see quite that high."[5]

Yet, when historians look too high, they miss what is right in front of them. If one looks behind the "vivid artifice," one finds a man who rode horses with Will Rogers and preferred mashed potatoes and corned beef to caviar and squab. If one looks behind the man who had no belief in the afterlife, one sees a man constantly at war with his conceptions of morality and its spiritual ramifications—a man with multiple superstitions and the desire to make things right, whether through lavish gifts or shows that served as hymns to idealism and goodness. Though Ziegfeld feared mortality, he did not, contrary to popular belief, lack introspection or appreciation of the aging process. Rather, he saw it as an opportunity for innovation and self-exploration. "Keep your brain busy, your interests varied, stay out of the rut and you will find life fuller and richer when you are fifty," Ziegfeld said in 1928.[6] Despite his resistance to change in later life, Ziegfeld never fell into a rut, and in his constant drive to move forward, he kept Broadway from stagnating. Time and again he set precedents for new ways to stage shows, new themes to explore, and new musical styles. His way of doing business was to break old barriers without creating new ones.

Ziegfeld lived every moment as if acting on impulse, yet even in the midst of the seeming chaos, there was a perfect balance of beauty, mystery, comedy, and pathos. Each generation comes to know Florenz Ziegfeld's legacy in new ways—by attending a revival of *Show Boat,* listening to standard songs introduced in the *Follies,* patronizing a Las Vegas nightclub where showgirls strut in feathered headdresses down magnificent staircases, or simply seeing "Ziegfeld" flashing on the marquee of the New York City theater that still bears his name. In a sense, to become acquainted with Ziegfeld's work—his institution—*is* to become acquainted with the man. The magic he created was his best expression of himself, his greatest gift to those closest to him, and the most enduring legacy he left his country.

When Ziegfeld's colleagues and friends declared, "I can't believe he's dead," Will Rogers responded with a statement that has been verified with the passage of time: "He isn't [dead]. He never will be. He'll go on as long as there is a theater, and motion pictures, and music and dancing and laughter. You can't ever kill magic."[7]

Appendix

Shows Produced and Coproduced by Florenz Ziegfeld Jr.

Writers, composers, designers, stage directors, and opening and closing dates are provided whenever such information is available.

Broadway Shows

A Parlor Match (revival of a musical farce), by Charles Evans and William Hoey
September 21–October 31, 1896, Herald Square Theatre
Principals: Charles Evans, William Hoey, Anna Held, Virginia Aragon, Minnie French
Hit Song: "Won't You Come and Play with Me?" (by Alfred Plumpton)

La Poupee (original opera), coproduced by Oscar Hammerstein; based on the French *opera-comique* by Maurice Ordonneau, book adapted by Arthur Sturgess; music by Edmond Audran
October 21–29, 1897, Lyric Theatre
Principals: Anna Held, Frank Rushwood, G. W. Anson

Way Down East (original melodrama), coproduced by William Brady; based on a play by Lottie Blair Parker, adapted by Joseph Grismer
February 7–June 1898, Manhattan Theatre
Principals: Phoebe Davies, Odell Williams, Howard Kyle

A Gay Deceiver (original musical comedy), coproduced by William Brady; by Paul Wilstach and John Grismer
February 21–26, 1898, Harlem Opera House (tour)
Principals: M. A. Kennedy, W. G. Beach, Anna Held

The Turtle (original farce), based on the French comedy by Leon Gandillot, adapted by Joseph W. Herbert
September 3, 1898–January 28, 1899, Manhattan Theatre
April 23–29, 1899, Grand Opera House (tour)
Principals: W. J. Ferguson, Sadie Martinot, McKee Rankin

The French Maid (original musical comedy), coproduced by Charles Evans; by E. E. Rice; libretto by Captain Basil Hood; music by Walter Slaughter
September 26–October 1, 1898, Herald Square Theatre
Principals: Anna Held, Charles Bigelow, Eva Davenport

Mlle. Fifi (original farce), coproduced by William Brady; based on the French play by Dumanoir and Carre, adapted by Leo Ditrichstein and Joseph Grismer
February 1–April 22, 1899, Manhattan Theatre
April 24–29, 1899, Harlem Opera House (tour)
Principals: Anna Held, Rose Coghlan, Aubrey Boucicault

The Manicure (original musical farce), coproduced by William Brady; based on the French play by Sylvain and Artus, adapted by Joseph Grismer
April 24, 1899, Manhattan Theatre
Principals: Anna Held, Louise Thorndike Boucicault, James Colville

Papa's Wife (original musical), based on two French vaudevilles by Maurice Hennequin and Albert Millaud, adapted by Harry B. Smith; lyrics by Reginald DeKoven and Harry B. Smith, additional music and lyrics by William H. Penn, A. Baldwin Sloane, Herve, Frank Sloane, James O'Dea, and Glen MacDonough; scenic design by D. Frank Dodge and Richard Marston; costume design by Will R. Barnes
November 13, 1899–March 31, 1900, Manhattan Theatre
Principals: Anna Held, Charles Bigelow, Henry Bergman
Hit Song: "The Maiden with the Dreamy Eyes" (by DeKoven and Smith)

The Little Duchess (original musical comedy), by Harry B. Smith; music by Reginald DeKoven, lyrics by Harry B. Smith, additional music and lyrics by Julian Fane, Robert Cole, William Jerome, J. P. Harrington, Ellen Wright, A. Baldwin Sloane, J. Rosamond Johnson, and Leo LeBrunn; staged by George Marion; scenic design by Ernest Albert; costume design by Caroline Seidle, Will R. Barnes, and Archie Gunn
October 14, 1901–February 8, 1902, Casino Theatre
February 10–15, 1902, Harlem Opera House (tour)
April 21, 1902, Grand Opera House
Principals: Anna Held, Charles Bigelow, Sidney Barraclough

The Red Feather (original opera), by Charles Kline; music by Reginald DeKoven, lyrics by Charles Emerson Cook, additional music and lyrics by A. Baldwin Sloane, James T. Waldon, and A. Baldwin Sloane; scenic design by Ernest Albert; costume design by Caroline Seidle
November 9, 1903–January 2, 1904, Lyric Theatre
April 25, 1904, Grand Opera House
Principals: Grace Van Studdiford, George L. Tallman, Thomas Q. Seabrooke

Mam'selle Napoleon (original musical), based on the French play by Jean Richepin, adapted by Joseph W. Herbert; music by Gustav Luders, lyrics by Joseph W. Herbert; scenic design by Ernest Albert
December 8, 1903–January 16, 1904, Knickerbocker Theatre
Principals: Anna Held, Arthur Laurence, Frank Rushworth

Higgledy-Piggledy (original musical farce), coproduced by Joseph Weber; by Edgar Smith; music by Maurice Levi, lyrics by Edgar Smith; staged by George Marion; scenic design by John H. Young and Ernest Albert; costume design by Caroline Seidle
October 20, 1904–March 25, 1905, Weber Music Hall
August 26–September 9, 1905, Weber Music Hall
Principals: Anna Held, Joseph Weber, Marie Dressler, Charles Bigelow

The Parisian Model (original musical comedy), by Harry B. Smith; music by Max Hoffman Sr., additional music and lyrics by Vincent Bryan, P. H. Christine, Mr. Cobb, Gus Edwards, Herman Avery Wade, Vincent Scotto,

Harry B. Smith, Edward P. Moran, and Anna Held; staged by Julian
Mitchell; scenic design by Ernest Albert; costume design by Caroline
Seidle and Landloff, Paris
November 27, 1906–June 29, 1907, Broadway Theatre
January 6–25, 1908, Broadway Theatre
Principals: Anna Held, Charles Bigelow, Henry Leone
Hit Songs: "I Just Can't Make My Eyes Behave" (by Edwards and Smith),
"It's Delightful to Be Married" (by Christine, Held, and Scotto)

Follies of 1907 (original revue), by Harry B. Smith; music and lyrics by
Seymour Furth, E. Ray Goetz, Gus Edwards, Billy Gaston, Jean Schwartz,
Silvio Hein, Matt Woodward, Gertrude Hoffman, Vincent Bryan, Edgar
Selden, Will D. Cobb, Billy Gaston, William Jerome, Matt Woodward,
Martin Brown, Paul West, and Herbert Ingraham; staged by Julian
Mitchell, Herbert Gresham, and Joe Smith; scenic design by Peter V.
Griffin, T. Bernard McDonald, and John H. Young; costume design by W.
H. Matthews Jr. and Mme. E. S. Freisinger
July 8–September 14, 1907, Jardin de Paris (New York Theatre roof)
Principals: Nora Bayes, Emma Carus, Grace LaRue
Hit Song: "Come Down, Salomey Jane" (by Bryan and Goetz)

The Soul Kiss (original musical), by Harry B. Smith; music by Maurice
Levi, lyrics by Harry B. Smith, additional music and lyrics by Kenneth S.
Clark, Addison Burkhardt, Louis A. Hirsch, Matt Woodward, Jessie
Villars, Fleta Ian Brown, Lewis Gates, Cuthbert Clark, Clarence M.
Chapel, and Cecil Lean; staged by Herbert Gresham and Julian Mitchell;
scenic design by John H. Young, Ernest Albert, Frank E. Gates, and
Edward A. Morange; costume design by F. Richard Anderson, Pancaud of
Paris, and Wilhelm
January 28–May 23, 1908, New York Theatre
Principals: Adeline Genee, Cecil Lean, Florence Holbrook

Follies of 1908 (original revue), by Harry B. Smith; music by Maurice
Levi, additional music and lyrics by Albert Von Tilzer, Jack Norworth,
Nora Bayes, Melville Gideon, Edgar Selden, Jean Schwartz, and William
Jerome; staged by Julian Mitchell and Herbert Gresham; scenic design by
John H. Young; costume design by Alfredo Edel, F. Richard Anderson,

Mme. E. S. Freisinger, Hafleigh, and William H. Matthews
June 15–October 3, 1908, Jardin de Paris (New York Theatre roof)
Principals: Nora Bayes, Mademoiselle Daizie, Grace LaRue, Mae Murray, Jack Norworth
Hit Song: "Shine on, Harvest Moon" (by Bayes and Norworth)

Miss Innocence (original musical), by Harry B. Smith; music by Ludwig Englander, additional music and lyrics by Harry B. Smith, Egbert Van Alstyne, Harry Williams, Louis A. Hirsch, Addison Burkhardt, Nora Bayes, Jack Norworth, J. Rosamond Johnson, Bob Cole, Jean Schwartz, William Jerome, Vincent Bryan, Max Hoffman, and Gus Edwards; staged by Julian Mitchell; scenic design by Ernest Albert and John H. Young; costume design by Klaw and Erlanger's Costume Company
November 30, 1908–May 1, 1909, New York Theatre
September 27–October 9, 1909, New York Theatre
Principals: Anna Held, Charles Bigelow, Lillian Lorraine
Hit Songs: "I Wonder What's the Matter with My Eyes" (by Van Alstyne and Williams), "We Two in an Aeroplane" (by Van Alstyne and Williams), "Will You Be My Teddy Bear?" (by Bryan and Hoffman)

Follies of 1909 (original revue), by Harry B. Smith; music by Maurice Levi, additional lyrics and music by Harry B. Smith, Edward Madden, Gus Edwards, Jack Norworth, Nora Bayes, A. Seymour Brown, and Nat D. Ayer; staged by Julian Mitchell and Herbert Gresham
June 14–September 11, 1909, Jardin de Paris (New York Theatre roof)
Principals: Nora Bayes, Lillian Lorraine, Sophie Tucker, Eva Tanguay, Jack Norworth
Hit Songs: "By the Light of the Silvery Moon" (by Edwards), "Up, Up in My Aeroplane" (by Madden and Edwards)

Follies of 1910 (original revue), by Harry B. Smith; music and lyrics by Irving Berlin and Gus Edwards, additional music and lyrics by Will D. Cobb, Ballard MacDonald, Harry Carroll, Harry B. Smith, Will Marion Cook, Joe Jordan, Ford Dabney, James Henry Burriss, Chris Smith, Bert Williams, Alex Rogers, William Tracy, Lewis F. Muir, Vincent Bryan, Addison Burkhardt, Harry Von Tilzer, and Victor Hollander; staged by Julian Mitchell
June 20–September 3, 1910, Jardin de Paris (New York Theatre roof)

Principals: Fanny Brice, Lillian Lorraine, Vera Maxwell, Bert Williams
Hit Songs: "Lovie Joe" (by Cook and Jordan), "Swing Me High, Swing Me
Low" (by Hollander and MacDonald)

The Pink Lady (musical comedy), coproduced by Marc Klaw and Abe
Erlanger; based on the French play by Georges Berr and Marcel
Guillemaud, adapted by C. M. S. McLellan; music by Ivan Caryll, lyrics
by C. M. S. McLellan, additional music and lyrics by George Grossmith
Jr.; staged by Julian Mitchell and Herbert Gresham; scenic design by
Ernest Albert; costume design by F. Richard Anderson
March 13–December 11, 1911, New Amsterdam Theatre
August 16–September 14, 1912, New Amsterdam Theatre
Principals: Hazel Dawn, William Elliott, Alice Dovey

Ziegfeld Follies of 1911 (original revue), by George V. Hobart; music by
Maurice Levi and Raymond Hubbell, lyrics by George V. Hobart,
additional music and lyrics by Irving Berlin, Jerome Kern, James B.
Blyler, Sid Brown, Vincent Bryan, Henry Marshall, Stanley Murphy,
Raymond Peck, Channing Pollock, Rennold Wolf, Arthur Donnelly, Jean
C. Havez, Val Harris, Barney Fagan, and Bessie McCoy; staged by Julian
Mitchell; scenic design by Ernest Albert, Edward G. Unitt, and Joseph
Wickes; costume design by W. H. Matthews Jr.
June 26–September 2, 1911, Jardin de Paris (New York Theatre roof)
Principals: Fanny Brice, Dolly Sisters, Leon Errol, Lillian Lorraine, Bessie
McCoy, Bert Williams
Hit Song: "Be My Little Baby Bumble Bee" (by Blyler, Donnelly, and
Havez)

Over the River (original musical farce), coproduced by Charles
Dillingham; based on a play by H. A. Du Souchet, adapted by George V.
Hobart and H. A. Du Souchet; music by John Golden, lyrics by John
Golden, additional music and lyrics by Elsie Janis, Edward J. Griffin,
Charles Grant, William H. Penn, Jean Schwartz, Egbert Van Alstyne,
Charles Eggett, Henry B. Murtagh, Earl Carroll, Edward Clark, Harry
Williams, and William Jerome
January 8–April 20, 1912, Globe Theatre
Principals: Eddie Foy, Maud Lambert, Lillian Lorraine

A Winsome Widow (original musical comedy), based on "A Trip to Chinatown" by Charles H. Hoyt, adapted by Charles Hoyt; music by Raymond Hubbell, additional music and lyrics by John Golden, Jerome Kern, Nathaniel D. Ayer, Jean Schwartz, Stanley Murphy, Henry I. Marshall, Griffin and Murtagh, Robert B. Smith, William Jerome, and Franz Lehar; staged by Julian Mitchell; scenic design by Edward G. Unitt, Joseph Wickes, and Ernest Albert
April 11–September 7, 1912, Moulin Rouge Theatre
Principals: Harry Connor, Leon Errol, Elizabeth Brice, Dolly Sisters, Mae West

Ziegfeld Follies of 1912 (original revue), by Harry B. Smith; music by Raymond Hubbell, lyrics by Harry B. Smith, additional music and lyrics by William Jerome, James Monaco, A. Seymour Brown, Bert Grant, John E. Hazzard, Blanche Merrill, Leo Edwards, and Bert Williams; staged by Julian Mitchell; scenic design by Ernest Albert; costume design by Callot
October 21, 1912–January 4, 1913, Moulin Rouge Theatre
Principals: Leon Errol, Bernard Granville, Lillian Lorraine, Vera Maxwell, Bert Williams
Hit Song: "Row, Row, Row" (by Jerome and Monaco)

Ziegfeld Follies of 1913 (original revue), by George V. Hobart; music by Raymond Hubbell, additional music and lyrics by Gene Buck, Dave Stamper, Will D. Cobb, Harry Ruby, Earl Carroll, and Leo Edwards; staged by Julian Mitchell; scenic design by Ernest Albert, Frank E. Gates, Edward A. Morange, and John H. Young; costume design by Schneider & Anderson
June 16–September 6, 1913, New Amsterdam Theatre
Principals: Elizabeth Brice, Dolly Sisters, Leon Errol, Ann Pennington
Hit Song: "If a Table at Rector's Could Talk" (by Hubbell and Cobb)

Ziegfeld Follies of 1914 (original revue), by George V. Hobart; music by Raymond Hubbell, lyrics by George V. Hobart and Gene Buck, additional music and lyrics by Jean C. Havez, Bert Williams, Dave Stamper, A. Seymour Brown, J. Leubrie Hill, and Will Vodery; staged by Leon Errol; scenic design by William H. Matthews; costume design by Cora MacGeachy

June 1–September 5, 1914, New Amsterdam Theatre
Principals: Leon Errol, Ann Pennington, Bert Williams, Ed Wynn
Hit Song: "When the Ragtime Army Goes to War" (by Brown)

Ziegfeld Midnight Frolic (rooftop review), music and lyrics by Gene
Buck, Dave Stamper, and Louis A. Hirsch; staged by Ned Wayburn;
scenic design by Joseph Urban
January 5, 1915, New Amsterdam Theatre roof
Principals: Kay Laurell, Sybil Carmen, Ray Cox

Ziegfeld Follies of 1915 (original revue), by Channing Pollock, Rennold
Wolf, and Gene Buck; music by Louis A. Hirsh and Dave Stamper, lyrics
by Channing Pollock, Rennold Wolf, and Gene Buck, additional music
and lyrics by Charles Elbert, Irving Berlin, Seymour Furth, Bert
Williams, Ward Wesley, and Will Vodery; staged by Julian Mitchell and
Leon Errol; scenic design by Joseph Urban; costume design by Lucile
June 21–September 18, 1915, New Amsterdam Theatre
Principals: Ina Claire, Leon Errol, W. C. Fields, Mae Murray, Ann
Pennington, Olive Thomas, George White, Ed Wynn
Hit Songs: "Hello, Frisco," "Hold Me in Your Loving Arms" (both by
Buck and Hirsch)

Ziegfeld Midnight Frolic (rooftop revue), music and lyrics by Gene Buck,
Dave Stamper, and Louis A. Hirsch; staged by Ned Wayburn; scenic
design by Joseph Urban
August 23, 1915, New Amsterdam Theatre roof
Principals: Sybil Carmen, Allyn King, Will Rogers, Olive Thomas

Ziegfeld Midnight Frolic (rooftop revue), music and lyrics by Gene Buck
and Dave Stamper; staged by Ned Wayburn; scenic design by Joseph
Urban
January 24, 1916, New Amsterdam Theatre roof
Principals: Sybil Carmen, Dolly Sisters, Marion Harris, Will Rogers

Ziegfeld Follies of 1916 (original revue), by George V. Hobart and Gene
Buck; music by Louis A. Hirsch, Jerome Kern, Dave Stamper, and Irving
Berlin, lyrics by George V. Hobart and Gene Buck, additional music and

lyrics by Nat D. Ayer, Will Vodery, Harry Carroll, Franz Lehar, Leo Edwards, Clifford Grey, Alex Rogers, Ballard MacDonald, and Blanche Merrill; staged by Ned Wayburn, scenic design by Joseph Urban; costume design by Lucile, Cora MacGeachy, and Alice O'Neil
June 12–September 16, 1916, New Amsterdam Theatre
Principals: Fanny Brice, Ina Claire, Marion Davies, W. C. Fields, Bernard Granville, Ann Pennington, Will Rogers, Bert Williams
Hit Song: "If You Were the Only Girl in the World" (by Grey and Ayer)

Ziegfeld Midnight Frolic (rooftop revue), music and lyrics by Gene Buck and Dave Stamper; staged by Ned Wayburn
October 2, 1916, New Amsterdam Theatre roof
Principals: Peggy Brooks, Eddie Cantor, Olive Thomas, Sybil Carmen

The Century Girl (original revue), coproduced by Charles Dillingham; music by Victor Herbert and Irving Berlin, lyrics by Irving Berlin and Henry Blossom, additional music and lyrics by Helen Trix, L. Wolfe Gilbert, Carey Morgan, James Kendis, Harry B. Smith, and Elsie Janis; staged by Edward Royce and Leon Errol; scenic design by Joseph Urban; costume design by Lucile, Marie Cook, Raphael Kirchner, Cora MacGeachy, and William H. Matthews
November 6, 1916–April 28, 1917, Century Theatre
Principals: Leon Errol, Hazel Dawn, Marie Dressler, Vera Maxwell, Elsie Janis

Dance and Grow Thin (rooftop revue), coproduced by Charles Dillingham; by Raphael Kirchner, Marie Cook, and Alice O'Neil; music and lyrics by Irving Berlin and Blanche Merrill, additional music and lyrics by George W. Meyer, Edgar Leslie, and E. Ray Goetz; staged by Leon Errol; scenic design by Joseph Urban; costume design by Raphael Kirchner, Marie Cook, Alice O'Neil, Schneider & Anderson, Lucile, and Lichtenstein's
January 18–June 2, 1917, Cocoanut Grove Theatre (Century Theatre roof)
Principals: Will Archie, Van and Schenck, Gertrude Hoffman
Hit Song: "For Me and My Gal" (by Meyer, Leslie, and Goetz)

Ziegfeld Midnight Frolic (rooftop revue), music and lyrics by Gene Buck and Dave Stamper; staged by Ned Wayburn; scenic design by Joseph Urban

April 24, 1917, New Amsterdam Theatre roof
Principals: Sybil Carmen, Dane Claudius, Will Rogers, Ann Pennington

Ziegfeld Follies of 1917 (original revue), by Gene Buck and George V. Hobart; music by Raymond Hubbell and Dave Stamper, lyrics by Gene Buck and George V. Hobart, additional music and lyrics by Victor Herbert, James Hanley, J. C. Egan, Jerome Kern, Ring Lardner, J. Turner Layton, Les Copeland, Leo Edwards, Ballard MacDonald, Alfred Harriman, Henry Creamer, Rennold Wolf, and Blanche Merrill; staged by Ned Wayburn; scenic design by Joseph Urban; costume design by Lucile
June 12–September 16, 1917, New Amsterdam Theatre
Principals: Fanny Brice, Eddie Cantor, Walter Catlett, Dolores, Fairbanks Twins, W. C. Fields, Peggy Hopkins
Hit Song: "That's the Kind of a Baby for Me" (by Egan and Harriman)

The Rescuing Angel (original drama), coproduced by Arthur Hopkins; by Clare Kummer
October 8–November 3, 1917, Hudson Theatre
Principals: Billie Burke, Claude Gillingwater, Roland Young

Miss 1917 (original revue), coproduced by Charles Dillingham; by Guy Bolton and P. G. Wodehouse; music by Jerome Kern and Victor Herbert, additional music and lyrics by Benny Davis, Hugh Morton, Ren Shields, Harry B. Smith, Edgar Smith, Otto Harbach, James O'Dea, Henry Blossom, Stanley Murphy, Bob Cole, J. Rosamond Johnson, Joseph McCarthy, Gus Van, Joseph Schenck, C. Francis Reisner, Gustav Kerker, George Evans, John Stromberg, Karl Hoschna, Henry I. Marshall, Harry Tierney, Edward Hutchinson, and Billy Baskette; staged by Ned Wayburn; scenic design by Joseph Urban; costume design by Paul Chaflin, Dazian, Faibsey, Lucile, Cora MacGeachy, Phelps, Willy Pogany, and Max Weldy
November 5, 1917–January 12, 1918, Century Theatre
Principals: Lew Fields, Bessie McCoy, Elizabeth Brice, Van and Schenck, Irene Castle, Vivienne Segal, Marion Davies

Ziegfeld Midnight Frolic (rooftop revue), music and lyrics by Gene Buck, Dave Stamper, and Leslie Stuart; staged by Ned Wayburn; scenic design by Joseph Urban

December 29, 1917, New Amsterdam Theatre roof
Principals: Frank Carter, Van and Schenck, Will Rogers, Ann Pennington

Ziegfeld Midnight Frolic (rooftop revue), music and lyrics by Gene Buck and Dave Stamper; staged by Ned Wayburn; scenic design by Joseph Urban
April 24, 1918, New Amsterdam Theatre roof
Principals: Eddie Cantor, Frank Carter, Will Rogers

Ziegfeld Follies of 1918 (original revue), book and lyrics by Rennold Wolf and Gene Buck; music by Louis A. Hirsch and Dave Stamper, additional music and lyrics by Irving Berlin, Victor Jacobi, Buddy DeSylva, Harry Ruby, Sidney D. Mitchell, Edgar Leslie, Arthur Jackson, and Archie Gottler; staged by Ned Wayburn; scenic design by Joseph Urban; costume design by Schneider-Anderson Company
June 18–September 14, 1918, New Amsterdam Theatre
October 17, 1918, Globe Theatre
Principals: Eddie Cantor, Frank Carter, Will Rogers, Dolores, W. C. Fields, Lillian Lorraine, Marilyn Miller
Hit Song: "Oh! How I Hate to Get up in the Morning" (by Berlin, from *Yip Yip Yaphank*, 1918)

By Pigeon Post (original play), by Austin Page
November 25–December 14, 1918, George M. Cohan Theatre
Principals: Frank Kemble Cooper, Phoebe Foster, Peggy O'Neil

Ziegfeld Nine O'Clock Frolic (rooftop revue), music and lyrics by Gene Buck and Dave Stamper; staged by Ned Wayburn
December 9, 1918, New Amsterdam Theatre roof
Principals: Fanny Brice, Bessie McCoy, Lillian Lorraine, Bert Williams

Ziegfeld Midnight Frolic (rooftop revue), music and lyrics by Gene Buck and Dave Stamper; staged by Ned Wayburn; scenic design by Joseph Urban
December 24, 1918, New Amsterdam Theatre roof
Principals: Fanny Brice, Will Rogers, Lillian Lorraine

Ziegfeld Follies of 1919 (original revue), by Gene Buck, Dave Stamper, and Rennold Wolf; music and lyrics by Irving Berlin, additional music and lyrics by Gene Buck, Rennold Wolf, Dave Stamper, Joseph McCarthy, Harry Tierney, Victor Herbert, Joseph Tierney, Joe Young, Sam Lewis, Walter Donaldson, Eddie Cantor, Harry Ruby, Francis DeWitt, Robert Hood Bowers, Nat Vincent, Darle MacBoyle, and Marshall Walker; staged by Ned Wayburn; scenic design by Joseph Urban; costume design by Lucile and Mme. Francis
June 16–December 6, 1919 (performances suspended on August 12 due to Actors Equity strike; resumed on September 10), New Amsterdam Theatre
Principals: Marilyn Miller, Eddie Cantor, Bert Williams, John Steel, Johnny and Ray Dooley, Van and Schenck, Fairbanks Twins
Hit Songs: "Mandy," "You'd Be Surprised, "A Pretty Girl Is Like a Melody" (all by Berlin)

Ziegfeld Midnight Frolic (rooftop revue), music and lyrics by Gene Buck and Dave Stamper; staged by Ned Wayburn; scenic design by Joseph Urban
October 2, 1919, New Amsterdam Theatre roof
Principals: Fanny Brice, W. C. Fields, Allyn King, Doris Eaton

Caesar's Wife (original drama), by W. Somerset Maugham; scenic design by Joseph Urban
November 24, 1919–January 31, 1920, Liberty Theatre
Principals: Billie Burke, Norman Trevor, Ernest Glendenning

Tonight at 8:10 (rooftop revue), music and lyrics by Irving Berlin
January 15, 1920–January 17, 1920, New Amsterdam Theatre roof
Principals: Marilyn Miller, W. C. Fields, Eddie Cantor, Fanny Brice

Ziegfeld Nine O'Clock Revue (rooftop revue), music and lyrics by Gene Buck and Dave Stamper; staged by Ned Wayburn; scenic design by Joseph Urban
March 8–May 1920, New Amsterdam Theatre roof
Principals: Fanny Brice, Lillian Lorraine, Marcelle Earle, W. C. Fields

Ziegfeld Midnight Frolic (rooftop revue), music and lyrics by Gene Buck and Dave Stamper; staged by Ned Wayburn, scenic design by Joseph Urban; tableaux by Ben Ali Haggin

March 15, 1920, New Amsterdam Theatre roof
Principals: Fanny Brice, W. C. Fields, Lillian Lorraine

Ziegfeld Follies of 1920 (original revue), by Gene Buck; music and lyrics by Irving Berlin, Dave Stamper, Gene Buck, Joseph J. McCarthy, Harry Tierney, and Victor Herbert, additional music and lyrics by James Montgomery, Bert Kalmar, Harry Ruby, Gus Van, Joe Schenck, Eddie Cantor, Mac Emery, King Zany, George Fairman, Alex Gerber, Abner Silver, Jack Yellen, Abe Olman, Roger Lewis, and Ernie Erdman; staged by Edward Royce; scenic design by Joseph Urban; tableaux by Ben Ali Haggin; costume design by Lucile and Alice O'Neil
June 22–October 16, 1920, New Amsterdam Theatre
Principals: Fanny Brice, Jack Donahue, Ray Dooley, Doris and Mary Eaton, W. C. Fields, Van and Schenck, Charles Winninger
Hit Songs: "Girls of My Dreams," "Tell Me, Little Gypsy" (both by Berlin)

Ziegfeld Midnight Frolic (rooftop revue), music and lyrics by Ballard MacDonald and Harry Carroll; staged by Ned Wayburn; scenic design by Joseph Urban; tableaux by Ben Ali Haggin
September 2, 1920, New Amsterdam Theatre roof
Principals: John Steel, Annette Bade, William and Gordon Dooley

Sally (original musical comedy), by P. G. Wodehouse and Guy Bolton; music by Victor Herbert and Jerome Kern, lyrics by Clifford Grey and B. G. DeSylva; staged by Edward Royce; scenic design by Joseph Urban; costume design by Alice O'Neil
December 21, 1920–April 22, 1922, New Amsterdam Theatre
September 17–October 6, 1923, New Amsterdam Theatre
Principals: Marilyn Miller, Leon Errol, Dolores, Walter Catlett
Hit Songs: "Look for the Silver Lining" (by DeSylva and Kern), "Wild Rose" (by Grey and Kern)

Ziegfeld Nine O'Clock Frolic (rooftop revue), music and lyrics by Ballard MacDonald and Harry Carroll; staged by Edward Royce; scenic design by Joseph Urban
February 8–March 1921, New Amsterdam Theatre roof
Principals: Fairbanks Twins, Frank Farnum, Princess White Deer

APPENDIX

Ziegfeld Midnight Frolic (rooftop revue), music and lyrics by Ballard MacDonald and Harry Carroll; scenic design by Joseph Urban
February 9, 1921, New Amsterdam Theatre roof
Principals: Annette Bade, Fairbanks Twins, Herbert Hoey

Ziegfeld Follies of 1921 (original revue), by Channing Pollock, Willard Mack, and Ralph Spence; music by Victor Herbert, Rudolf Friml, and Dave Stamper, lyrics by Gene Buck and B. G. DeSylva, additional music and lyrics by Henry Creamer, J. Turner Layton, Grant Clarke, James Hanley, Channing Pollock, Blanche Merrill, Leo Edwards, Ballard MacDonald, Harry Carroll, Albert Willemetz, Jacques Charles, Gus Mueller, Buster Johnson, Andrew Sterling, Harry Von Tilzer, Edward P. Moran, Elsie White, Henry Busse, and Maurice Yvain; staged by Edward Royce; scenic design by Joseph Urban; costume design by James Reynolds
June 21–October 1, 1921, Globe Theatre
Principals: Fanny Brice, Ray Dooley, Mary Eaton, W. C. Fields, Van and Schenck
Hit Songs: "My Man" (by Pollock and Yvain), "Secondhand Rose" (by Clarke and Hanley)

The Intimate Strangers (original comedy), coproduced by Charles Dillingham and Abe Erlanger; by Booth Tarkington; staged by Ira Hards
November 7, 1921–January 21, 1922, Henry Miller Theatre
Principals: Billie Burke, Alfred Lunt, Elizabeth Patterson, Glenn Hunter

Ziegfeld Midnight Frolic (rooftop revue), music and lyrics by Gene Buck and Dave Stamper; staged by Leon Errol; scenic design by Joseph Urban
November 17, 1921–April 9, 1922, New Amsterdam Theatre roof
Principals: Will Rogers, Leon Errol, Kitty Kelly

Ziegfeld Frolic (original revue), by Ralph Spence and Will Rogers; music and lyrics by Gene Buck and Dave Stamper; staged by Leon Errol and Ned Wayburn
January 10–February 1922, opened at the Garrick Theatre in Philadelphia before touring
Principals: Will Rogers, Annette Bade, Hack McGowan, White Sisters

Ziegfeld Follies of 1922 (original revue), by Ring Lardner, Gene Buck, and Ralph Spence; music by Victor Herbert, Louis A. Hirsch, and Dave Stamper, lyrics by Ring Lardner, Gene Buck, and Ralph Spence, additional music and lyrics by Herbert Reynolds, James Hanley, Jimmie Duffy, Henry Creamer, J. Turner Layton, Ed Gallagher, and Al Shean; staged by Ned Wayburn; scenic design by Joseph Urban; tableaux by Ben Ali Haggin; costume design by Charles LeMaire, Evelyn Law, Ada Fields, James Reynolds, and Cora MacGeachy
June 5, 1922–June 23, 1923, New Amsterdam Theatre
Principals: Mary Eaton, Gallagher and Shean, Will Rogers, Tiller Girls, Ruby Stevens (Barbara Stanwyck), Eddie Cantor
Hit Song: "Oh! Mr. Gallagher and Mr. Shean" (by Gallagher and Shean)

Rose Briar (original comedy), by Booth Tarkington
December 25, 1922–March 10, 1923, Empire Theatre
Principals: Billie Burke, Frank Conroy, Julia Hoyt, Allen Dinehart

Ziegfeld Follies of 1922 (Summer Edition) (original revue), by Ralph Spence, Franklin Adams, Nate Salisbury, Emil Breitenfeld, and Eddie Cantor; music by Victor Herbert, Louis A. Hirsch, and Dave Stamper, lyrics by Gene Buck, additional music and lyrics by Charles Tobias, Eddie Cantor, Jean Schwartz, Ernest Breuer, Walter Donaldson, J. Turner Layton, Chic Johnson, Ole Olsen, Sam M. Lewis, Joe Young, Henry Creamer, and B. G. DeSylva; staged by Ned Wayburn; scenic design by Joseph Urban; tableaux by Ben Ali Haggin; costume design by Charles LeMaire, Ada Fields, Alice O'Neil, Ben Ali Haggin, and Cora McGeachy
June 25–September 15, 1923, New Amsterdam Theatre
Principals: Eddie Cantor, Ed Gallagher, Al Shean, Gilda Gray, Tiller Girls
Hit Song: "Oh! Gee! Oh! Gosh! Oh! Golly I'm in Love" (by Breuer, Johnson, and Olsen)

Ziegfeld Follies of 1923 (original revue), by Eddie Cantor and Gene Buck; music by Victor Herbert, Rudolf Friml, and Dave Stamper, lyrics by Gene Buck, additional music and lyrics by Joseph McCarthy, Harry Tierney, Bert Kalmar, Harry Ruby, Blanche Merrill, Leo Edwards, Gabriel Daray, Edgar Leslie, Benton Ley, Lee David, and Ambrose Thomas; staged by Ned Wayburn; scenic design by Joseph Urban; tableaux by Ben

Ali Haggin; costume design by Erté, Alice O'Neil, Evelyn McHorter, and James Reynolds
October 20, 1923–May 10, 1924, New Amsterdam Theatre
Principals: Fanny Brice, Eddie Cantor, Paul Whiteman's Orchestra, Lina Basquette

Kid Boots (original musical comedy), by William Anthony McGuire and Otto Harbach; music by Harry Tierney, lyrics by Joseph McCarthy; staged by Edward Royce; scenic design by Frank E. Gates, Edward Morange, and Herman Rossi; costume design by Evelyn McHorter, Henri Bendel Inc., Alice O'Neil, and Mme. Francis
December 31, 1923–August 31, 1925, Earl Carroll Theatre
September 1, 1924–February 21, 1925, Selwyn Theatre
Principals: Eddie Cantor, Mary Eaton, Harry Fender, Jobyna Howland, George Olsen and His Orchestra

Ziegfeld Follies of 1924 (original revue), by William Anthony McGuire and Will Rogers; music by Victor Herbert, Raymond Hubbell, Dave Stamper, Harry Tierney, and Dr. Albert Szirmai, lyrics by Gene Buck and Joseph McCarthy; staged by Julian Mitchell; scenic design by Frank E. Gates, Edward A. Morange, Ludwig Kainer, John Wenger, and H. Robert Law Studios; tableaux by Ben Ali Haggin; costume design by Charles LeMaire
June 24–October 25, 1924, New Amsterdam Theatre
Principals: Will Rogers, Vivienne Segal, Tiller Girls, George Olsen and His Orchestra
Hit Song: "Adoring You" (by McCarthy and Tierney)

Ziegfeld Follies of 1924 (Fall Edition) (original revue), by William Anthony McGuire and Will Rogers; music by Victor Herbert, Raymond Hubbell, Dave Stamper, and Harry Tierney, lyrics by Gene Buck and Joseph McCarthy, additional music and lyrics by Fred Mels, Leon Jessel, and Laurant Halet; staged by Julian Mitchell; scenic design by Frank E. Gates, Edward A. Morange, Ludwig Kainer, John Wenger, and H. Robert Law Studios; tableaux by Ben Ali Haggin; costume design by Charles LeMaire
October 30, 1924–March 7, 1925, New Amsterdam Theatre
Principals: Will Rogers, Vivienne Segal, Tiller Girls, George Olsen and

His Orchestra, Peggy Fears
Hit Song: "Lonely Little Melody" (by Buck and Stamper)
Annie Dear (original musical comedy), by Clare Kummer; music and
lyrics by Clare Kummer, additional music and lyrics by Sigmund
Romberg, Jean Schwartz, and Clifford Grey; staged by Edward Royce;
scenic design by Karl Koeck; costume design by Frances
November 4, 1924–January 31, 1925, Times Square Theatre
Principals: Billie Burke, Ernest Truex, Marion Green

The Comic Supplement (original musical comedy), by J. P. McEvoy;
music by Con Conrad and Henry Souvaine, lyrics by J. P. McEvoy; staged
by Julian Mitchell
January 9–February 1925, Shubert Theatre (Newark, New Jersey; the
show never played on Broadway)
Principals: W. C. Fields, Ray Dooley, Martha-Bryan Allen

Louie the 14th (original musical comedy), based on a German play by
Paul Frank and Julius Wilhelm, adapted by Arthur Wimperis; music by
Sigmund Romberg, lyrics by Arthur Wimperis; staged by Edward Royce;
scenic design by Gretl Urban; costume design by James Reynolds,
Frances, Schneider-Anderson Company, Eaves Costume Company, and
Milgrims
March 3–December 5, 1925, Cosmopolitan Theatre
Principals: Leon Errol, John T. Doyle, Ethel Shutta, Louise Brooks

Ziegfeld Follies of 1925 (Spring Edition) (original revue), by J. P. McEvoy,
Will Rogers, and W. C. Fields; music by Raymond Hubbell, Dave Stamper,
and Werner Janssen, lyrics by Gene Buck; staged by Julian Mitchell; scenic
design by Norman Bel Geddes and H. Robert Law Studios; costume design
by John Held Jr., Mabel Johnstone, and John E. Stone
March 10–September 19, 1925, New Amsterdam Theatre
Principals: W. C. Fields, Ray Dooley, Will Rogers, Vivienne Segal, Tiller
Girls

Ziegfeld Follies of 1925 (Summer Edition) (original revue), by J. P.
McEvoy, Will Rogers, W. C. Fields, and Gus Weinberg; music by
Raymond Hubbell, Dave Stamper, and Werner Janssen, lyrics by Gene

Buck, additional music and lyrics by Leo Daniderff; staged by Julian
Mitchell; scenic design by Norman Bel Geddes and H. Robert Law
Studios; tableaux by Ben Ali Haggin; costume design by John Held Jr.,
Mabel Johnstone, and John E. Stone
July 6–September 19, 1925, New Amsterdam Theatre
Principals: W. C. Fields, Ray Dooley, Ethel Shutta, Lina Basquette, Louise
Brooks, Will Rogers, Eddie Cantor

No Foolin' (original revue), by J. P. McEvoy and James Barton; music by
Rudolf Friml, lyrics by Gene Buck, Irving Caesar, and Ballard
MacDonald, additional music and lyrics by James Hanley; staged by Ben
Ali Haggin, Edward Royce, and Walter Wilson; scenic design by Joseph
Urban and John Wenger; costume design by John W. Harkrider
January 12, 1926, Montmartre (a dinner club–theater in Palm Beach,
Florida; originally titled *Palm Beach Nights*)
June 24–September 25, 1926, Globe Theatre
Principals: James Barton, Ray Dooley, Peggy Fears, Greta Nissen, Yacht
Club Boys, Claire Luce
Hit Songs: "No Foolin'" (by Buck and Hanley), "Florida, the Moon, and
You" (by Buck and Friml)

Betsy (original musical comedy), by William Anthony McGuire, Irving
Caesar, and David Freedman; music by Richard Rodgers, lyrics by Lorenz
Hart, additional music and lyrics by Irving Berlin, Irving Caesar, David
Freedman, and A. Segal; staged by William Anthony McGuire; scenic
design by Frank E. Gates, Edward A. Morange, Bergman Studios, and
Joseph Urban; costume design by Charles Le Maire
December 28, 1926–January 29, 1927, New Amsterdam Theatre
Principals: Belle Baker, Al Shean, Pauline Hoffman, Jimmy Hussey
Hit Song: "Blue Skies" (by Berlin)

Rio Rita (original musical comedy), by Guy Bolton and Fred Thompson;
music by Harry Tierney, lyrics by Joseph McCarthy; staged by John
Harwood, Sammy Lee, and Albertina Rasch; scenic design by Joseph
Urban; costume design by John W. Harkrider
February 2–December 25, 1927, Ziegfeld Theatre
December 26, 1927–March 11, 1928, Lyric Theatre

March 12–April 7, 1928, Majestic Theatre
Principals: Ethelind Terry, J. Harold Murray, Vincent Serrano, George
Baxter, Robert Woolsey, Bert Wheeler, Albertina Rasch Dancers
Hit Songs: "If You're in Love, You'll Waltz," "You're Always in My Arms,"
"Following the Sun Around," "The Kinkajou" (all by Tierney and
McCarthy)

Ziegfeld Follies of 1927 (original revue), by Harold Atteridge and Eddie
Cantor; music and lyrics by Irving Berlin, additional music and lyrics by
Bill Munro, Walter Donaldson, George Whiting, and Guy Massey; staged
by Sammy Lee, Zeke Colvan, and Albertina Rasch; scenic design by
Joseph Urban; costume design by John W. Harkrider
August 16, 1927–January 7, 1928, New Amsterdam Theatre
Principals: Eddie Cantor, Cliff "Ukulele Ike" Edwards, Ruth Etting, Claire
Luce, Albertina Rasch Dancers
Hit Songs: "Shaking the Blues Away," "It All Belongs to Me" (both by
Berlin), "The Prisoner's Song" (by Massey), "My Blue Heaven" (by
Donaldson and Whiting)

Show Boat (original musical comedy-drama), based on the novel by
Edna Ferber, adapted by Oscar Hammerstein II; music by Jerome Kern,
lyrics by Oscar Hammerstein II, additional music and lyrics by P. G.
Wodehouse, Joseph E. Howard, and Charles K. Harris; staged by Zeke
Colvan, Oscar Hammerstein II, and Sammy Lee; scenic design by Joseph
Urban; costume design by John W. Harkrider
December 27, 1927–May 4, 1929, Ziegfeld Theatre
Principals: Norma Terris, Helen Morgan, Howard Marsh, Charles
Winninger, Edna May Oliver, Eva Puck, Sammy White, Jules Bledsoe,
Tess Gardella
Hit Songs: "Ol' Man River," "Can't Help Lovin' that Man of Mine," "Make
Believe" (all by Hammerstein and Kern), "Bill" (by Hammerstein and
Wodehouse)

Rosalie (original musical comedy), by William Anthony McGuire and
Guy Bolton; music by George Gershwin and Sigmund Romberg, lyrics by
P. G. Wodehouse and Ira Gershwin; staged by Seymour Felix and William
Anthony McGuire; scenic design by Joseph Urban; costume design by

John W. Harkrider
January 10–October 27, 1928, New Amsterdam Theatre
Principals: Marilyn Miller, Jack Donahue, Frank Morgan, Bobbie Arnst
Hit Songs: "Oh Gee, Oh Joy" (by G. Gershwin, Romberg, Wodehouse,
and I. Gershwin), "How Long Has This Been Going On?" (by G. and I.
Gershwin)

The Three Musketeers (original dramatic operetta), based on the novel by
Alexandre Dumas, adapted by William Anthony McGuire; music by
Rudolf Friml, lyrics by Clifford Grey and P. G. Wodehouse; staged by
William Anthony McGuire, Albertina Rasch, and Richard Boleslavsky;
scenic design by Joseph Urban; costume design by John W. Harkrider
March 13–December 22, 1928, Lyric Theatre
Principals: Dennis King, Vivienne Segal, Lester Allen, Reginald Owen,
Harriet Hoctor, Albertina Rasch Dancers

Whoopee (original musical comedy), based on the play *The Nervous
Wreck* by Owen Davis, adapted by William Anthony McGuire; music by
Walter Donaldson, lyrics by Gus Kahn; staged by Seymour Felix and
William Anthony McGuire; scenic design by Joseph Urban; costume
design by John W. Harkrider
December 4, 1928–November 23, 1929, New Amsterdam Theatre
Principals: Eddie Cantor, Ruth Etting, Ethel Shutta, Paul Gregory, George
Olsen and His Orchestra
Hit Songs: "Makin' Whoopee," "Love Me or Leave Me" (both by
Donaldson and Kahn)

Ziegfeld Midnight Frolic (rooftop revue), music and lyrics by James
McHugh and Dorothy Fields; staged by Sammy Lee; scenic design by
Joseph Urban; costume design by John W. Harkrider and Charles Le
Maire
February 6–April 25, 1929, New Amsterdam Theatre roof
Principals: Maurice Chevalier, Helen Morgan, Lillian Roth, Paul
Whiteman and His Orchestra

Show Girl (original musical comedy), based on the novel by J. P. McEvoy,
adapted by William Anthony McGuire; music by George Gershwin, lyrics

by Ira Gershwin and Gus Kahn, additional music and lyrics by Thomas Malie, Sidney Skolsky, W. H. Farrell, Jimmy Durante, and J. Little; staged by William Anthony McGuire, Bobby Connolly, and Albertina Rasch; scenic design by Joseph Urban; costume design by John W. Harkrider
July 2–October 5, 1929, Ziegfeld Theatre
Principals: Ruby Keeler, Jimmy Durante, Ed Wynn, Frank McHugh, Eddie Foy Jr., Albertina Rasch Dancers
Hit Songs: "Liza" (by I. and G. Gershwin), "An American in Paris Ballet" (music by G. Gershwin)

Bitter Sweet (original operetta), by Noel Coward; music and lyrics by Noel Coward, additional music and lyrics by Henry J. Sayers; staged by Noel Coward; scenic and costume design by Gladys E. Calthrop
November 5, 1929–February 16, 1930, Ziegfeld Theatre
February 17–March 22, 1930, Shubert Theatre
Principals: Evelyn Laye, Gerald Nodin, Sylvia Leslie, Mireille
Hit Song: "If Love Were All" (by Coward)

Simple Simon (original musical comedy), by Ed Wynn and Guy Bolton; music by Richard Rodgers, lyrics by Lorenz Hart; staged by Seymour Felix and Zeke Colvan
February 18–June 14, 1930, Ziegfeld Theatre
Principals: Ed Wynn, Ruth Etting, Paul Stanton, Harriet Hoctor
Hit Song: "Ten Cents a Dance" (by Rodgers and Hart)

Smiles (original musical comedy), based on a story by Noel Coward, adapted by William Anthony McGuire; music by Vincent Youmans, lyrics by Clifford Grey and Harold Adamson, additional music and lyrics by Ring Lardner; staged by Ned Wayburn and William Anthony McGuire; scenic design by Joseph Urban; costume design by John W. Harkrider
November 18, 1930–January 10, 1931, Ziegfeld Theatre
Principals: Marilyn Miller, Fred and Adele Astaire, Eddie Foy Jr., Aber Twins
Hit Song: "Time on My Hands" (by Youmans, Grey, and Adamson)

Ziegfeld Follies of 1931 (original revue), by Mark Hellinger, J. P. Murray, and Gene Buck; music by Harry Revel, Ben Oakland, Dave Stamper,

Dimitri Tiomkin, Noel Coward, Nora Bayes, James Monaco, Chick Endor, Walter Donaldson, Jay Gorney, Hugo Riesenfeld, Ivan Caryll, Jack Norworth, Alfred Bryan, Mack Gordon, and Powell and Stevens, lyrics by Gene Buck, Walter Donaldson, Joseph McCarthy, Charles Farrell, Fred Fisher, Mack Gordon, J. P. Murray, Barry Trivers, E. Y. Harburg, Jack Norworth, and Noel Coward; staged by Gene Buck, Edward Clarke Lilley, Bobby Connolly, and Albertina Rasch; scenic design by Joseph Urban; costume design by John W. Harkrider
July 1–November 21, 1931, Ziegfeld Theatre
Principals: Ruth Etting, Gladys Glad, Helen Morgan, Buck and Bubbles, Albertina Rasch Dancers

Hot-Cha! (original musical comedy), based on a story by H. S. Kraft, adapted by Mark Hellinger, H. S. Kraft, Ray Henderson, and Lew Brown; music by Ray Henderson, lyrics by Lew Brown; staged by Edgar McGregor, Edward Clarke Lilley, and Bobby Connolly; scenic design by Joseph Urban; costume design by Charles LeMaire
March 8–June 18, 1932, Ziegfeld Theatre
Principals: Bert Lahr, Lupe Velez, Buddy Rogers, Eleanor Powell

Show Boat (revival), based on the novel by Edna Ferber, adapted by Oscar Hammerstein II; music by Jerome Kern, lyrics by Oscar Hammerstein II, additional music and lyrics by P. G. Wodehouse, Joseph E. Howard, and Charles K. Harris; staged by Oscar Hammerstein II and Sammy Lee; scenic design by Joseph Urban; costume design by John W. Harkrider
May 19–October 22, 1932, Casino Theatre
Principals: Norma Terris, Helen Morgan, Dennis King, Charles Winninger, Edna May Oliver, Eva Puck, Sammy White, Paul Robeson, Tess Gardella

Posthumous *Follies*

Ziegfeld Follies of 1934 (original revue), produced by Billie Burke and Lee Shubert; by H. I. Philips, Fred Allen, David Freedman, and Harry Turgend; music by Vernon Duke, Samuel Pokrass, Billy Hill, H. I. Phillips, Fred Allen, Harry Tugend, Ballard MacDonald, lyrics by E. Y.

Harburg, additional music and lyrics by Billy Rose, Edward Heyman, Joseph Meyer, Richard Myers, Dana Suesse, Peter DeRose, Robert Dolan, Ernest Hartman, and James Hanley; staged by Bobby Connolly, John Murray Anderson, Edward C. Lilley, and Robert Alton; scenic design by Watson Barrett and Albert R. Johnson; costume design by Russell Patterson, Raoul Pène Du Bois, Charles Le Maire, Billy Livingston, and Kiviette
January 4–June 9, 1934, Winter Garden Theatre
Principals: Eve Arden, Fanny Brice, Vilma and Buddy Ebsen, Jane Froman, Cherry and June Preisser

Ziegfeld Follies of 1936 (original revue), produced by Billie Burke and Lee and J. J. Shubert; by David Freeman; music by Vernon Duke, lyrics by Ira Gershwin, additional music and lyrics by Conrad Salinger, Joe Burke, Tot Seymour, Walter Kent, Richard Jerome, Edwin Gilbert, Edward Heyman, Vee Lawnhurst, Edgar Burke, and Harold Spina; staged by Robert Alton, John Murray Anderson, George Balanchine, Edward Clarke Lilley, and Edward D. Dowling; scenic design by Vincente Minnelli; costume design by Vincente Minnelli, Jane Quinn, Billi Livingston, and Raoul Pène Du Bois
January 30–May 10, 1936, Winter Garden Theatre
September 14–December 19, 1936, Winter Garden Theatre
Principals: Fanny Brice, Eve Arden, Josephine Baker, Edgar Bergen, Harriet Hoctor, Bob Hope, Cherry and June Preisser

Ziegfeld Follies of 1943 (original revue), produced by Lee and J. J. Shubert, Alfred Bloomingdale, and Lou Walters, by arrangement with Billie Burke; by Lester Lee, Jerry Seelen, Bud Pearson, Les White, Joseph Erens, Charles Sherman, Harry Young, Lester Lawrence, Baldwin Bergersen, Ray Golden, Sid Kuller, William K. Wells, and Harold J. Rome; music by Ray Henderson, lyrics by Jack Yellen, additional music and lyrics by Dan White and Buddy Burston; staged by John Murray Anderson, Robert Alton, Arthur Pierson, and Fred De Cordova; scenic design by Watson Barratt; costume design by Miles White
April 1, 1943–January 25, 1944, Winter Garden Theatre
January 25–July 22, 1944, Imperial Theatre
Principals: Christine Ayers, Bill and Cora Baird, Milton Berle, Jack Cole, Arthur Treacher

Ziegfeld Follies of 1957 (original revue), produced by Mark Kroll and Charles Conaway; by Arnie Rosen, Coleman Jacoby, David Rogers, Alan Jeffreys, and Maxwell Grant; music and lyrics by Jack Lawrence, Richard Myers, Herman Hupfeld, Howard Dietz, Sammy Fain, David Rogers, Colin Romoff, Dean Fuller, Marshall Barer, Carolyn Leigh, Philip Springer, Tony Velone, Larry Spier, and Uhpio Minucci, additional music and lyrics by Dee Libbey and Sid Wayne; staged by Rene Weigert, Beatrice Lillie, John Kennedy, and Frank Wagner; scenic and costume design by Raoul Pène Du Bois
March 1–June 15, 1957, Winter Garden Theatre
Principals: Beatrice Lillie, Billy DeWolfe, Tony Franco, Harold Lange

Films

Glorifying the American Girl (original musical), coproduced by Monta Bell; produced and distributed by Paramount–Famous Players Lasky Studios; screenplay by J. P. McEvoy and Millard Webb; music and lyrics by Irving Berlin, Walter Donaldson, Larry Spier, and Frank Tours; directed by Millard Webb; costumes and scenic design by John W. Harkrider
Released on December 7, 1929
Principals: Mary Eaton, Eddie Cantor, Helen Morgan, Rudy Vallee

Whoopee! (musical adaptation), coproduced by Samuel Goldwyn; produced by Samuel Goldwyn Company, distributed by United Artists; based on the play *The Nervous Wreck* by Owen Davis and the musical comedy *Whoopee* by William Anthony McGuire; screenplay by William Conselman and William Anthony McGuire; music by Walter Donaldson and Gus Kahn; musical numbers staged by Busby Berkeley; directed by Thornton Freeland; costume design by John W. Harkrider
Released on September 30, 1930
Principals: Eddie Cantor, Ethel Shutta, Paul Gregory, Eleanor Hunt

Radio Programs

The Ziegfeld Follies of the Air, produced by CBS Radio; sponsored by Chrysler Motors (1932) and Palmolive (1936); hosted by Eddie Dowling and Florenz Ziegfeld Jr.; music orchestrated by Al Goodman

April 3–24, 1932, 8:30 p.m.
June 1–July 26, 1932, 10:30 p.m.
February 22–June 6, 1936, 8:00 p.m. (recorded live from the Winter Garden Theatre)
Selected Guest Stars: Fanny Brice, Helen Morgan, Will Rogers, Jack Pearl, Jane Froman

Notes

Introduction

1. Billie Burke, *With a Feather on My Nose* (New York: Appleton Century Crofts, 1949), 147.

2. Bernard Sobel, *Broadway Heartbeat: Memoirs of a Press Agent* (New York: Hermitage House, 1953), 106.

3. Burke, *With a Feather on My Nose,* 160.

4. "The Theatre: New Plays in Manhattan," *Time,* January 15, 1934.

5. The Professor, "The Follies of Florenz Ziegfeld," *New Yorker,* March 14, 1925.

6. Richard Rodgers, *Musical Stages: An Autobiography* (Cambridge, MA: Harvard University Press, 2002), 96; Sobel, *Broadway Heartbeat,* 136.

7. Eddie Cantor and David Freedman, *The Great Glorifier* (New York: Alfred H. King, 1934), 116.

8. The Professor, "Follies of Florenz Ziegfeld."

9. William E. Leuchtenburg, *The Perils of Prosperity,* 2nd ed. (Chicago: University of Chicago Press, 1993), 198.

10. Burke, *With a Feather on My Nose,* 242.

11. Sobel, *Broadway Heartbeat,* 136.

12. Adela Rogers St. Johns, "The Girls Who Glorified Ziegfeld," *Milwaukee Sentinel,* July 14, 1946.

13. The Professor, "Follies of Florenz Ziegfeld."

14. Sobel, *Broadway Heartbeat,* 198.

15. Ibid., 199.

16. Charles Higham, *Ziegfeld* (Chicago: Regnery, 1972), 164.

17. Richard Ziegfeld and Paulette Ziegfeld, *The Ziegfeld Touch: The Life and Times of Florenz Ziegfeld, Jr.* (New York: Henry Abrams, 1993), 182.

18. Ibid.

19. Eddie Cantor, *Take My Life* (Lanham, MD: Cooper Square Press, 2000), 193.

20. Ziegfeld and Ziegfeld, *Ziegfeld Touch,* 122.

1. The Showman, the Strongman, and the Girl with the Eyes

1. Djuna Barnes, *I Could Never Be Lonely without a Husband* (London: Virago Press, 1985), 69.

2. Patricia Ziegfeld, *The Ziegfelds' Girl: Confessions of an Abnormally Happy Childhood* (New York: Little Brown, 1964), 33.

3. Ethan Mordden, *Ziegfeld: The Man Who Invented Show Business* (New York: St. Martin's Press, 2008), 12.

4. Quoted in John Kendrick, "History of the Musical, Burlesque," *Musicals 101,* 1997, http://www.musicals101.com/burlesque.htm (accessed September 30, 2012).

5. Quoted in Irving Cutler, *The Jews of Chicago* (Champaign: University of Illinois Press, 2008), 56–57.

6. Ziegfeld and Ziegfeld, *Ziegfeld Touch,* 17.

7. Ibid., 16.

8. Ziegfeld, *Ziegfelds' Girl,* 33.

9. Gilbert Seldes, "The Glorifier I–II," *New Yorker,* July 25–August 1, 1931.

10. Ziegfeld, *Ziegfelds' Girl,* 33.

11. Quoted in Ziegfeld and Ziegfeld, *Ziegfeld Touch,* 18.

12. Seldes, "The Glorifier I–II."

13. Ibid.

14. Ziegfeld, *Ziegfelds' Girl,* 34.

15. Mordden, *Ziegfeld,* 18.

16. Ziegfeld, *Ziegfelds' Girl,* 35.

17. Mordden, *Ziegfeld,* 25.

18. Ziegfeld, *Ziegfelds' Girl,* 36.

19. Linda Mizejewski, *Ziegfeld Girl: Image and Icon in Culture and Cinema* (Durham, NC: Duke University Press, 1999), 14.

20. Josh Buck, "Sandow: No Folly with Ziegfeld's First Glorification," *Iron Game History* 5, no. 1 (May 1998).

21. Ziegfeld and Ziegfeld, *Ziegfeld Touch,* 24.

22. Ibid., 21.

23. Ziegfeld, *Ziegfelds' Girl,* 36.

24. Buck, "Sandow."

25. Quoted in Ziegfeld and Ziegfeld, *Ziegfeld Touch,* 24.

26. Buck, "Sandow."

27. Ibid.

28. Quoted in Ziegfeld and Ziegfeld, *Ziegfeld Touch,* 28.

29. Robert Ruise, "Broadway 101," *Talkin' Broadway,* 1999, http://www.talkinbroadway.com/bway101/1.html (accessed October 1, 2012).

30. Quoted in Mordden, *Ziegfeld,* 33.

31. Quoted in John Kendrick, "Florenz Ziegfeld: A Brief Biography," *Ziegfeld 101,* 2002, http://www.musicals101.com/ziegbio.htm (accessed October 3, 2012).

32. Higham, *Ziegfeld,* 21.

33. John Kendrick, "Broadway in the Gay '90s," *Musicals 101,* http://www .musicals101.com/burlesque.htm (accessed September 30, 2012).

34. Lee Allyn Davis, *Scandals and Follies: The Rise and Fall of the Great Broadway Revue* (Montclair, NJ: Limelight Editions, 2000), 14.

35. Cantor, *Take My Life,* 120.

36. John Kendrick, "Anna Held," *Ziegfeld 101,* http://www.musicals101.com/ ziegheld.htm (accessed August 22, 2012).

37. Higham, *Ziegfeld,* 26.

38. Liane Carrera, *Anna Held and Flo Ziegfeld* (Pompano Beach: Exposition Press of Florida, 1979), 69.

39. Ibid., 72.

40. Kendrick, "Anna Held."

41. "Anna Held, Began as Chorus Girl," *New York Times,* June 13, 1909.

42. Ibid.

43. Kendrick, "Anna Held."

44. Eve Golden, *Anna Held and the Birth of Ziegfeld's Broadway* (Lexington: University Press of Kentucky, 2000), 17.

45. "Mlle. Anna Held Arrives," *New York Times,* September 16, 1896.

46. Golden, *Anna Held,* 17.

47. Ibid., 33.

48. Ibid., 27.

49. "Mlle. Anna Held Arrives."

50. Golden, *Anna Held,* 26.

51. Quoted in Michael Kantor and Laurence Maslon, *Broadway: The American Musical* (New York: Bulfinch, 2004), 13.

52. Ibid., 14.

53. "Anna Held to Be Married," *New York Times,* January 17, 1897.

54. Charles Evans, "The Importation of Anna Held," *San Francisco Call,* March 3, 1907.

55. Ibid.

56. Kendrick, "Anna Held."

57. Mordden, *Ziegfeld,* 42.

58. Kendrick, "Anna Held."

59. Eve Golden, e-mail interview with the authors, November 11, 2012.

60. Quoted in Kendrick, "Anna Held."

2. Gloomy Gus and the Petit Bourgeois

1. Carrera, *Anna Held and Flo Ziegfeld,* 41–42.

2. Randolph Carter, *The World of Flo Ziegfeld* (New York: Praeger, 1974), 23.

3. "Uses Milk in Baths; Anna Held Sued by a Milkman Who Cannot Get His Money," *New York Times*, October 10, 1896.

4. Charles Evans, "The Importation of Anna Held," *San Francisco Call*, March 3, 1907.

5. Mordden, *Ziegfeld*, 44.

6. Higham, *Ziegfeld*, 35.

7. Carrera, *Anna Held and Flo Ziegfeld*, 74.

8. Higham, *Ziegfeld*, 29.

9. Burke, *With a Feather on My Nose*, 147.

10. Marjorie Farnsworth, *The Ziegfeld Follies* (New York: Bonanza Books, 1956), 28.

11. Golden, *Anna Held*, 122.

12. Ibid., 45.

13. "Hammerstein's Olympia," *New York Times*, November 9, 1897.

14. Golden, *Anna Held*, 35.

15. Higham, *Ziegfeld*, 48.

16. Golden, *Anna Held*, 40.

17. "The Gay Deceiver," *San Francisco Call*, March 29, 1898.

18. Golden, *Anna Held*, 43.

19. "Anna Held Arrested," *New York Times*, October 28, 1898.

20. *Smithsonian*, November 2012, 18.

21. Mordden, *Ziegfeld*, 57.

22. "The Augustin Daly Sale," *New York Times*, March 22, 1900.

23. Higham, *Ziegfeld*, 51.

24. Cantor, *Take My Life*, 117.

25. Mordden, *Ziegfeld*, 59.

26. Golden, *Anna Held*, 48.

27. Quoted in Gerald Bordman, *American Musical Theatre: A Chronicle* (New York: Oxford University Press, 2001), 193.

28. Cantor, *Take My Life*, 255.

29. Golden, *Anna Held*, 49.

30. Cantor, *Take My Life*, 244.

31. Golden, *Anna Held*, 51.

32. Seldes, "The Glorifier I–II."

33. Mordden, *Ziegfeld*, 61.

34. Ibid., 110.

35. Ibid., 61.

36. "*Zaza* in New York," *Morning Herald* (Baltimore), January 11, 1899.

37. Golden, *Anna Held*, 59.

38. Ibid., 62.

39. Mordden, *Ziegfeld*, 62.

40. "*The Little Duchess*," *New York Times*, October 15, 1901.

41. Eddie Cantor, *My Life Is in Your Hands* (Lanham, MD: Cooper Square Press, 2000), 119.

42. "*The Little Duchess*."

43. Guisard, "Anna Held Is Longing to Appear in Something Serious," *San Francisco Call*, February 15, 1903.

44. Sobel, *Broadway Heartbeat*, 138.

45. Nils Hanson, *Lillian Lorraine: The Life and Times of a Ziegfeld Diva* (Jefferson, NC: McFarland, 2012), 53.

46. Guisard, "Anna Held Is Longing."

47. Ibid.

48. Golden, *Anna Held*, 132.

49. Cantor, *My Life Is in Your Hands*, 67.

50. Barnes, *I Could Never Be Lonely*, 72.

51. Seldes, "The Glorifier I–II."

52. Quoted in Mordden, *Ziegfeld*, 72.

53. Quoted in Golden, *Anna Held*, 78.

54. "Ziegfeld: The Man and His Women," *Eugene (OR) Register-Guard*, May 20, 1978.

55. Seldes, "The Glorifier I–II."

56. Guisard, "Anna Held Is Longing."

57. Golden, *Anna Held*, 82.

58. David J. Framberger and Joan R. Olshansky, "National Register of Historic Places Registration: Ansonia Hotel" (New York State Office of Parks, Recreation and Historic Preservation, July 1979).

59. Hanson, *Lillian Lorraine*, 56.

60. Mordden, *Ziegfeld*, 76.

61. Quoted in Golden, *Anna Held*, 85.

62. "Weber Ziegfeld Opening," *New York Times*, October 11, 1904.

63. "Here's a War of Theater Stars," *New York Evening World*, January 17, 1905.

64. Ibid.

65. "$500 Prize," *New York Sun*, February 28, 1905.

66. "Notes of the Stage," *New York Tribune*, February 16, 1905.

67. Seldes, "The Glorifier I–II."

68. "Fair Actress Is a Lucky Gambler," *Los Angeles Herald*, June 18, 1905.

3. "It's Delightful to Be Married"

1. Mordden, *Ziegfeld*, 83.

2. Carrera, *Anna Held and Flo Ziegfeld*, 85.

3. Stephen Whitfield, *In Search of Jewish American Culture* (Waltham, MA: Brandeis University Press, 1999), 43.

4. Mordden, *Ziegfeld*, 82.

5. "Marc Klaw a Big Winner," *New York Times,* March 29, 1908.

6. Golden, *Anna Held,* 93.

7. Mordden, *Ziegfeld*, 85.

8. Ziegfeld and Ziegfeld, *Ziegfeld Touch,* 38.

9. Gus Edwards, "I Just Can't Make My Eyes Behave" (1906), in John Kendrick, "Anna Held—Part II," *Ziegfeld 101,* http://www.musicals101.com/ziegheld2.htm (accessed September 13, 2012).

10. Anna Held, "It's Delightful to Be Married" (1906), in Kendrick, "Anna Held—Part II."

11. Mordden, *Ziegfeld*, 86.

12. Kendrick, "Anna Held—Part II."

13. Quoted in Kantor and Maslon, *Broadway,* 21.

14. Quoted in Golden, *Anna Held,* 96.

15. Quoted in Mordden, *Ziegfeld*, 88.

16. "Give My Regards to Broadway," episode 1 of *Broadway: The American Musical* (Arlington, VA: PBS, 2004), DVD.

17. Mordden, *Ziegfeld*, 90.

18. Ziegfeld and Ziegfeld, *Ziegfeld Touch,* 109.

19. Carrera, *Anna Held and Flo Ziegfeld,* 92.

20. Ibid., 93.

21. Ibid., 104.

22. Golden, *Anna Held,* 101.

23. Ziegfeld and Ziegfeld, *Ziegfeld Touch,* 39.

24. Carrera, *Anna Held and Flo Ziegfeld,* 92.

25. Ann Ommen van der Merwe, *The Ziegfeld Follies: A History in Song* (Lanham, MD: Scarecrow Press, 2009), 30.

26. Quoted in Golden, *Anna Held,* 199.

27. Ibid., 109.

28. "Anna Held Song Sung in Church," *New York Tribune,* June 27, 1907.

29. Carrera, *Anna Held and Flo Ziegfeld,* 112.

30. Burke, *With a Feather on My Nose,* 144.

31. Mordden, *Ziegfeld*, 92.

32. Farnsworth, *Ziegfeld Follies,* 31.

33. Hanson, *Lillian Lorraine,* 27.

4. A Maelstrom of Mirth

1. Mordden, *Ziegfeld*, 92.

2. Quoted in Bordman, *American Musical Theatre,* 270.

3. Hanson, *Lillian Lorraine,* 28.

4. "Give My Regards to Broadway" (DVD).

5. Ibid.

6. Farnsworth, *Ziegfeld Follies,* 31.

7. Mordden, *Ziegfeld,* 96.

8. John Kendrick, "Sample Scene: *The Follies of 1907,* Act Two: Scene II," *Ziegfeld 101,* http://www.musicals101.com/ziegfollscene.htm (accessed September 13, 2012).

9. Farnsworth, *Ziegfeld Follies,* 32.

10. *Ziegfeld on Film* (Hollywood, CA: Turner Entertainment, 2004), DVD.

11. Mordden, *Ziegfeld,* 94.

12. Seldes, "The Glorifier I–II."

13. Mordden, *Ziegfeld,* 95.

14. Quoted in "The Theatre: New Plays in Manhattan," *Time,* January 15, 1934.

15. Cantor, *My Life Is in Your Hands,* 11.

16. Higham, *Ziegfeld,* 66.

17. Hanson, *Lillian Lorraine,* 28

18. *Ziegfeld on Film* (DVD).

19. Cantor and Freedman, *Great Glorifier,* 78.

20. Hanson, *Lillian Lorraine,* 28.

21. Quoted in Kantor and Maslon, *Broadway,* 36.

22. Bordman, *American Musical Theatre,* 237.

23. Mordden, *Ziegfeld,* 216.

24. Golden, *Anna Held,* 120.

25. Ibid., 119.

26. Mordden, *Ziegfeld,* 100.

27. Bordman, *American Musical Theatre,* 258.

28. Hanson, *Lillian Lorraine,* 19.

29. Ibid., 7, 17.

30. Ibid., 12.

31. Ibid., 15.

32. Bordman, *American Musical Theatre,* 283.

33. Mordden, *Ziegfeld,* 99.

34. Jack Norworth, "Shine on, Harvest Moon" (1908), http://en.wikipedia.org/wiki/Shine_On,_Harvest_Moon (accessed December 25, 2013).

35. Seldes, "The Glorifier I–II."

36. John Kendrick, "Florenz Ziegfeld," *Ziegfeld 101,* http://www.musicals101.com/ziegbi02.htm (accessed October 3, 2012).

37. Mordden, *Ziegfeld,* 103.

38. Golden, *Anna Held,* 125.

39. "Showgirls' Baseball Cup," *New York Times,* March 4, 1909.

40. Gus Edwards, "By the Light of the Silvery Moon" (1909), http://en.wikipedia.org/wiki/By_the_Light_of_the_Silvery_Moon_(song) (accessed December 26, 2013).

41. Hanson, *Lillian Lorraine,* 25.

42. Golden, *Anna Held,* 138.

43. Ibid., 106–7.

44. Ibid., 132.

45. Ibid., 133.

46. Ibid., 135.

47. "Lew Fields Indignant," *New York Times,* June 12, 1909.

48. "She Drew the Line at Wearing Tights," *New York Times,* April 28, 1910.

49. Ziegfeld and Ziegfeld, *Ziegfeld Touch,* 47.

50. Seldes, "The Glorifier I–II."

51. "She Drew the Line at Wearing Tights."

52. Hanson, *Lillian Lorraine,* 33.

53. Quoted in Ommen van der Merwe, *Ziegfeld Follies,* 24.

54. Ibid., 30.

55. Ibid., 27.

56. Ibid., 30.

57. "Theatre: Ziggy," *Time,* May 14, 1928.

58. Burke, *With a Feather on My Nose,* 153.

59. Cantor and Freedman, *Great Glorifier,* 78.

5. Entrances and Exits

1. Ziegfeld and Ziegfeld, *Ziegfeld Touch,* 48.

2. Burke, *With a Feather on My Nose,* 48.

3. Hanson, *Lillian Lorraine,* 50.

4. Ibid., 51.

5. Ibid., 52.

6. Golden, *Anna Held,* 145.

7. Ibid., 147.

8. Ibid., 146.

9. Ibid.

10. Hanson, *Lillian Lorraine,* 36.

11. Ommen van der Merwe, *Ziegfeld Follies,* 41.

12. Ibid., 47.

13. Ibid., 49.

14. Quoted in Kantor and Maslon, *Broadway,* 40.

15. "Give My Regards to Broadway" (DVD).

16. Ibid.

17. Barbara Grossman, *Funny Woman: The Life and Times of Fanny Brice* (Bloomington: Indiana University Press, 1992), 14.

18. Ibid., 20.

19. Irving Berlin, "Sadie Salome Go Home," *LyricsTime,* 2002, http://www .lyricstime.com/irving-berlin-sadie-salome-go-home-lyrics.html (accessed December 28, 2013).

20. "How Fanny Brice Climbed from Road Shows to Follies," *Milwaukee Journal,* May 12, 1938.

21. Kendrick, "Florenz Ziegfeld."

22. Grossman, *Funny Woman,* 38.

23. Hanson, *Lillian Lorraine,* 39.

24. Grossman, *Funny Woman,* 47.

25. "Give My Regards to Broadway" (DVD).

26. Cantor, *Take My Life,* 71.

27. Benjamin Sears, *The Irving Berlin Reader* (New York: Oxford University Press, 2012), 15.

28. Jeffrey Magee, *Irving Berlin's Musical Theater* (New York: Oxford University Press, 2012), 11.

29. Alec Wilder, *American Popular Song* (New York: Oxford University Press, 1975), 93.

30. Mordden, *Ziegfeld,* 115.

31. Hanson, *Lillian Lorraine,* 42.

32. Ibid.

33. Ibid., 43.

34. Ibid., 41.

35. Bordman, *American Musical Theatre,* 308.

36. Ibid., 283.

37. Gary Chapman, *The Delectable Dollies: The Dolly Sisters, Icons of the Jazz Age* (Gloucestershire, UK: History Press, 2007), 22.

38. Bordman, *American Musical Theatre,* 312.

39. Chapman, *Delectable Dollies,* 23.

40. Marcelle Earle, *Midnight Frolic: A Ziegfeld Girl's True Story* (Basking Ridge, NJ: Twin Oaks Publishing, 1999), 151.

41. Quoted in Kantor and Maslon, *Broadway,* 47.

42. Golden, *Anna Held,* 132–33.

43. Ibid., 151.

44. Ibid., 152–53.

45. Ziegfeld and Ziegfeld, *Ziegfeld Touch*, 51.

46. Hanson, *Lillian Lorraine*, 64.

47. Grossman, *Funny Woman*, 38.

48. Hanson, *Lillian Lorraine*, 60.

49. Ibid., 63.

50. Ibid., 86.

51. Ibid., 91.

52. Ibid., 172.

53. Ibid., 60.

54. Ibid., 164.

55. Earle, *Midnight Frolic*, 214.

56. Bordman, *American Musical Theatre*, 318.

57. "An Expert's Condemnation of Musical Comedy," *San Francisco Call*, December 24, 1911.

58. Golden, *Anna Held*, 156.

6. The Girl at the Top of the Stairs

1. Higham, *Ziegfeld*, 84.

2. Hanson, *Lillian Lorraine*, 75.

3. Ibid., 76.

4. Ibid.

5. Higham, *Ziegfeld*, 84.

6. Hanson, *Lillian Lorraine*, 76.

7. "Anna Held Seeks Divorce," *New York Tribune*, April 15, 1912.

8. Golden, *Anna Held*, 158.

9. Ibid.

10. Bordman, *American Musical Theatre*, 321.

11. Ibid., 325.

12. Mordden, *Ziegfeld*, 128.

13. Quoted in Ommen van der Merwe, *Ziegfeld Follies*, 60.

14. Ibid., 58–59.

15. Higham, *Ziegfeld*, 86.

16. "Well-Known Theatrical Manager Compels Lillian Lorraine to Take Her Best Song out of Show," *Dubuque (IA) Telegraph-Herald*, February 18, 1913.

17. *Ziegfeld on Film* (DVD).

18. Golden, *Anna Held*, 160.

19. Ibid., 161.

20. Ibid.

21. Hanson, *Lillian Lorraine*, 132.

22. Ibid., 80.

23. Mordden, *Ziegfeld,* 129.

24. Seldes, "The Glorifier I–II."

25. Ommen van der Merwe, *Ziegfeld Follies,* 71.

26. Ibid., 80.

27. Ibid., 83.

28. Ibid.

29. Ibid., 84.

30. "Actress Wants Marriage Annulled," *San Jose (CA) Evening Tribune,* July 19, 1913.

31. Hanson, *Lillian Lorraine,* 86.

32. Seldes, "The Glorifier I–II."

33. Hanson, *Lillian Lorraine,* 87.

34. Golden, *Anna Held,* 163.

35. Ziegfeld and Ziegfeld, *Ziegfeld Touch,* 46.

36. Hanson, *Lillian Lorraine,* 82.

37. Golden, *Anna Held,* 165.

38. Bordman, *American Musical Theatre,* 348.

39. Ibid., 343.

40. Ziegfeld, *Ziegfelds' Girl,* 5.

41. Ibid., 6.

42. Ibid., 7.

43. Ibid., 8.

44. Ibid.

45. Burke, *With a Feather on My Nose,* 118.

46. Ziegfeld, *Ziegfelds' Girl,* 10.

47. Burke, *With a Feather on My Nose,* 119.

48. Ibid., 120.

49. Ziegfeld and Ziegfeld, *Ziegfeld Touch,* 55.

50. Grant Hayter-Menzies, *Mrs. Ziegfeld: The Public and Private Lives of Billie Burke* (Jefferson, NC: McFarland, 2009), 43.

51. Sobel, *Broadway Heartbeat,* 111.

52. Hayter-Menzies, *Mrs. Ziegfeld,* 68.

53. Ibid., 57.

54. Ibid., 58.

55. Ziegfeld, *Ziegfelds' Girl,* 16.

56. Ibid., 48.

57. Burke, *With a Feather on My Nose,* 11.

58. Billie Burke, *With Powder on My Nose* (New York: Coward-McCann, 1959), 19.

59. Burke, *With a Feather on My Nose,* 37.

60. Ibid., 75.

61. Paul Thompson, "London's Notable Plays," *Burr McIntosh Monthly*, May 1907.

62. Burke, *With a Feather on My Nose*, 42.

63. Ibid., 47.

64. Ziegfeld and Ziegfeld, *Ziegfeld Touch*, 55.

65. Leonard Berlandstein, Michele Majer, Marlis Schweitzer, and Sheila Stowell, *Staging Fashion, 1880–1920: Jane Hading, Lily Elsie, Billie Burke* (New York: Bard Graduate Center for Studies in the Decorative Arts, Design, and Culture, 2012), 76.

66. Sobel, *Broadway Heartbeat*, 110.

67. Ibid., 111.

68. Burke, *With a Feather on My Nose*, 69–70.

69. Hayter-Menzies, *Mrs. Ziegfeld*, 65.

70. Berlandstein et al., *Staging Fashion*, 80.

71. Ibid., 84.

72. "Many Novelties for Playgoers This Week," *New York Times*, September 20, 1908.

73. Berlandstein et al., *Staging Fashion*, 157.

74. Burke, *With a Feather on My Nose*, 123.

75. Ziegfeld, *Ziegfelds' Girl*, 20.

76. Barnes, *I Could Never Be Lonely*, 71.

77. Sobel, *Broadway Heartbeat*, 103.

7. Taming an Incorrigible Bounder

1. Ziegfeld, *Ziegfelds' Girl*, 15.

2. Ziegfeld and Ziegfeld, *Ziegfeld Touch*, 45.

3. "A Sunday Morning Chat with Billie Burke," *Theatre*, January 1908, 304.

4. Berlandstein et al., *Staging Fashion*, 168.

5. Barnes, *I Could Never Be Lonely*, 69.

6. Cantor and Freedman, *Great Glorifier*, 73–74.

7. "Score One for the Sixty Club!" *San Francisco Call*, April 12 , 1914.

8. Burke, *With a Feather on My Nose*, 123.

9. Cantor and Freedman, *Great Glorifier*, 73.

10. Burke, *With a Feather on My Nose*, 123.

11. Ziegfeld and Ziegfeld, *Ziegfeld Touch*, 54.

12. Burke, *With a Feather on My Nose*, 20.

13. Ziegfeld, *Ziegfelds' Girl*, 25.

14. Burke, *With a Feather on My Nose*, 134.

15. Golden, *Anna Held*, 175.

16. Ibid., 172.

17. Series III: Liane Carrera Papers 1908–1913, b. 2, f. 8, Anna Held Museum Papers, Billy Rose Theatre Division, New York Public Library for the Performing Arts, New York, NY.

18. Golden, *Anna Held,* 179.

19. "Anna Held Sues Flo for Alimony," *New York Tribune,* June 9, 1914.

20. Hanson, *Lillian Lorraine,* 97.

21. Golden, *Anna Held,* 179.

22. Ziegfeld, *Ziegfelds' Girl,* 4.

23. Burke, *With a Feather on My Nose,* 135.

24. Berlandstein et al., *Staging Fashion,* 167.

25. Ziegfeld, *Ziegfelds' Girl,* 19.

26. Burke, *With a Feather on My Nose,* 147.

27. Ibid., 160.

28. Ibid., 163.

29. Seldes, "The Glorifier I–II."

30. Hayter-Menzies, *Mrs. Ziegfeld,* 74.

31. Burke, *With a Feather on My Nose,* 163.

32. Higham, *Ziegfeld,* 96.

33. Burke, *With Powder on My Nose,* 33.

34. Seldes, "The Glorifier I–II."

35. Burke, *With a Feather on My Nose,* 162.

36. Ziegfeld, *Ziegfelds' Girl,* 140.

37. Burke, *With a Feather on My Nose,* 146.

38. Ibid., 151.

39. Ibid., 160.

40. Hayter-Menzies, *Mrs. Ziegfeld,* 76.

41. Ibid., 80.

42. Ibid., 84.

43. "Billie Burke Was Nervous When She Entered Movies," *Day Book,* December 14, 1915.

44. Burke, *With a Feather on My Nose,* 152.

45. Seldes, "The Glorifier I–II."

8. Lively Productions

1. Quoted in Ommen van der Merwe, *Ziegfeld Follies,* 72.

2. Ziegfeld and Ziegfeld, *Ziegfeld Touch,* 59.

3. "On This Day," *New York Times,* July 23, 1932.

4. Ziegfeld and Ziegfeld, *Ziegfeld Touch,* 59.

5. Ommen van der Merwe, *Ziegfeld Follies,* 74.

6. Burke, *With a Feather on My Nose,* 169.

7. Doris Eaton Travis, *The Days We Danced: The Story of My Theatrical Family from Ziegfeld to Arthur Murray and Beyond* (Norman: University of Oklahoma Press, 2003), 77.

8. Burke, *With a Feather on My Nose,* 169.

9. Higham, *Ziegfeld,* 102.

10. Ziegfeld and Ziegfeld, *Ziegfeld Touch,* 72.

11. Higham, *Ziegfeld,* 103.

12. Ziegfeld and Ziegfeld, *Ziegfeld Touch,* 63.

13. Higham, *Ziegfeld,* 105.

14. Earle, *Midnight Frolic,* 170.

15. Ibid., 171.

16. Ibid., 156.

17. Ziegfeld and Ziegfeld, *Ziegfeld Touch,* 64.

18. Ibid., 71.

19. Will Rogers, *The Autobiography of Will Rogers,* ed. Donald Day (Chicago: Peoples Book Club, 1949), 38.

20. Ziegfeld and Ziegfeld, *Ziegfeld Touch,* 164.

21. Lucile Duff Gordon, *Discretions and Indiscretions* (New York: Frederick Stokes, 1932), 242–43.

22. Berlandstein et al., *Staging Fashion,* 68.

23. Ibid., 64.

24. Gordon, *Discretions and Indiscretions,* 244.

25. Ibid.

26. Farnsworth, *Ziegfeld Follies,* 97.

27. Gordon, *Discretions and Indiscretions,* 244.

28. Ibid., 245.

29. Ibid.

30. "Give My Regards to Broadway" (DVD).

31. Quoted in Barnes, *I Could Never Be Lonely,* 73.

32. "Brains and Common Sense, They Make the Perfect Chorus Girl—Says Ziegfeld," *Day Book,* August 18, 1916.

33. Sobel, *Broadway Heartbeat,* 137–38.

34. Kendrick, *Ziegfeld 101.*

35. Burke, *With a Feather on My Nose,* 177.

36. Bordman, *American Musical Theatre,* 353.

37. Cantor, *Take My Life,* 139.

38. Ibid., 105.

39. Arthur Frank Wertheim, *Will Rogers: At the Ziegfeld Follies* (Norman: University of Oklahoma Press, 1992), 33.

40. Cantor, *Take My Life*, 141.

41. Wertheim, *Will Rogers*, 230.

42. Burke, *With a Feather on My Nose*, 172.

43. Earle, *Midnight Frolic*, 154.

44. Travis, *Days We Danced*, 62.

45. *Ziegfeld on Film* (DVD).

46. Burke, *With a Feather on My Nose*, 163.

47. Higham, *Ziegfeld*, 114.

48. Burke, *With a Feather on My Nose*, 173.

49. Higham, *Ziegfeld*, 115–16.

50. Ibid., 116.

51. Burke, *With a Feather on My Nose*, 171.

52. Ibid., 173.

53. Ziegfeld, *Ziegfelds' Girl*, 19.

54. Seldes, "The Glorifier I–II."

55. Ziegfeld and Ziegfeld, *Ziegfeld Touch*, 61.

56. Ziegfeld, *Ziegfelds' Girl*, 26.

57. Antoinette Donnelly, "Billie Burke's Philosophy of Life Reflected in Her Sunshiny Surroundings," *Ogden (UT) Standard*, February 26, 1916.

58. Billie Burke, "How I Will Bring up Baby," *Day Book*, January 9, 1917.

59. Earle, *Midnight Frolic*, 181.

9. The Past Becomes Ashes

1. Bordman, *American Musical Theatre*, 360.

2. Ibid.

3. Cantor, *My Life Is in Your Hands*, 108.

4. Wertheim, *Will Rogers*, 230–31.

5. Burke, *With a Feather on My Nose*, 186.

6. Ziegfeld and Ziegfeld, *Ziegfeld Touch*, 98.

7. Barnes, *I Could Never Be Lonely*, 69.

8. Ibid., 110.

9. "Follies of 1916," *Pittsburgh Press*, September 8, 1916.

10. Mordden, *Ziegfeld*, 150.

11. Seldes, "The Glorifier I–II."

12. Hayter-Menzies, *Mrs. Ziegfeld*, 88–89.

13. Ibid., 87.

14. Ibid.

15. Higham, *Ziegfeld*, 119.

16. Ziegfeld, *Ziegfelds' Girl*, 148.

17. Cantor, *My Life Is in Your Hands,* 153.

18. Ibid., 154.

19. Ziegfeld and Ziegfeld, *Ziegfeld Touch,* 76.

20. Mordden, *Ziegfeld,* 161.

21. Golden, *Anna Held,* 200.

22. Mordden, *Ziegfeld,* 158–59.

23. Burke, *With a Feather on My Nose,* 145.

24. Higham, *Ziegfeld,* 128.

25. Golden, *Anna Held,* 166.

26. Mordden, *Ziegfeld,* 178.

27. "Gay Death," *New York Tribune,* May 28, 1918.

28. Ziegfeld, *Ziegfelds' Girl,* 32.

10. The Ziegfelds' Xanadu

1. Ziegfeld, *Ziegfelds' Girl,* 46.

2. Ziegfeld and Ziegfeld, *Ziegfeld Touch,* 57.

3. Hayter-Menzies, *Mrs. Ziegfeld,* 93.

4. Ziegfeld, *Ziegfelds' Girl,* 48.

5. Higham, *Ziegfeld,* 96.

6. Ibid., 123.

7. Ziegfeld, *Ziegfelds' Girl,* 49.

8. Kate Kelly, "Billie Burke and Florenz Ziegfeld," Westchester County Historical Society, April 20, 2013, http://www.westchesterhistory.com/index.php/exhibits/people?display=burke_Ziegfeld.

9. Ziegfeld, *Ziegfelds' Girl,* 70.

10. Burke, *With a Feather on My Nose,* 179.

11. Kelly, "Billie Burke and Florenz Ziegfeld."

12. Ziegfeld and Ziegfeld, *Ziegfeld Touch,* 106.

13. Ziegfeld, *Ziegfelds' Girl,* 64–70.

14. Mordden, *Ziegfeld,* 210.

15. Burke, *With a Feather on My Nose,* 183.

16. Ziegfeld, *Ziegfelds' Girl,* 56.

17. Kelly, "Billie Burke and Florenz Ziegfeld."

18. Burke, *With a Feather on My Nose,* 184.

19. Quoted in Carter, *World of Flo Ziegfeld,* 101.

20. Hayter-Menzies, *Mrs. Ziegfeld,* 92.

21. Earle, *Midnight Frolic,* 236.

22. Ziegfeld and Ziegfeld, *Ziegfeld Touch,* 277.

23. Bordman, *American Musical Theatre,* 369.

24. Ommen van der Merwe, *Ziegfeld Follies,* 110.

25. Cantor, *My Life Is in Your Hands,* 125.

26. Ibid., 160.

27. Earle, *Midnight Frolic,* 205.

28. Quoted in Hanson, *Lillian Lorraine,* 120.

29. Ziegfeld and Ziegfeld, *Ziegfeld Touch,* 245.

30. Seldes, "The Glorifier I–II."

31. Bordman, *American Musical Theatre,* 369.

32. Earle, *Midnight Frolic,* 224.

33. Burke, *With a Feather on My Nose,* 203.

34. Farnsworth, *Ziegfeld Follies,* 8.

35. Burke, *With a Feather on My Nose,* 210.

36. "Motherhood Is an Inspiration to a Career," *El Paso (TX) Herald,* June 4, 1918.

37. John Kendrick, "Ziegfeld Quotations," *Ziegfeld 101,* http://www.musicals101 .com/ziegbi02.htm (accessed September 13, 2012).

38. "All Feminine Except the 'Billie,'" *Photoplay,* December 1917.

39. Seldes, "The Glorifier I–II."

40. Burke, *With a Feather on My Nose,* 200.

41. *Chronicling America* Digitized Newspaper Archives, circa 1916, Library of Congress, http://chroniclingamerica.loc.gov/ (accessed February 13, 2013).

42. Higham, *Ziegfeld,* 125.

43. Ibid.

44. Sobel, *Broadway Heartbeat,* 111.

45. Ziegfeld and Ziegfeld, *Ziegfeld Touch,* 83.

46. Burke, *With a Feather on My Nose,* 175.

47. Travis, *Days We Danced,* 85.

48. Burke, *With a Feather on My Nose,* 156.

49. Sobel, *Broadway Heartbeat,* 113.

50. Hanson, *Lillian Lorraine,* 126.

51. Burke, *With a Feather on My Nose,* 191–93.

11. The Greatest Victory Party America Has Ever Known

1. Warren G. Harris, *The Other Marilyn* (Westminster, MD: Arbor House, 1985), 66.

2. Sobel, *Broadway Heartbeat,* 120.

3. Harris, *The Other Marilyn,* 25.

4. Ibid., 26.

5. Ibid., 47.

6. *Chronicling America* Digitized Newspaper Archives, circa 1914, Library of Congress, http://chroniclingamerica.loc.gov/ (accessed February 13, 2013).

7. Hayter-Menzies, *Mrs. Ziegfeld*, 96.

8. Hanson, *Lillian Lorraine*, 125.

9. Ommen van der Merwe, *Ziegfeld Follies*, 116.

10. Irving Berlin, "Oh How I Hate to Get up in the Morning" (1918), *LyricsMode .com*, http://www.lyricsmode.com/lyrics/i/irving_berlin/oh_how_i_hate_to_get_up_in_the_morning.html (accessed January 16, 2014).

11. Travis, *Days We Danced*, 62.

12. "George Gershwin Quotes," *brainyquote.com*, http://www.brainyquote.com/quotes/authors/g/george_gershwin.html (accessed August 7, 2013).

13. Burke, *With a Feather on My Nose*, 187.

14. Quoted in Hanson, *Lillian Lorraine*, 135.

15. Ziegfeld and Ziegfeld, *Ziegfeld Touch*, 83.

16. Quoted in Hanson, *Lillian Lorraine*, 136.

17. Wertheim, *Will Rogers*, 86–87.

18. Cantor, *My Life Is in Your Hands*, 190.

19. Ibid., 186.

20. Ibid., 190.

21. Higham, *Ziegfeld*, 126.

22. Harris, *The Other Marilyn*, 60.

23. Hanson, *Lillian Lorraine*, 127.

24. "Newest 'Follies' Is Bold and Bountiful," *New York Times*, June 19, 1918.

25. Hanson, *Lillian Lorraine*, 143.

26. Ibid., 144.

27. Higham, *Ziegfeld*, 125.

28. Harris, *The Other Marilyn*, 58.

29. Mordden, *Ziegfeld*, 186.

30. Burke, *With a Feather on My Nose*, 193.

31. Ziegfeld and Ziegfeld, *Ziegfeld Touch*, 90.

32. Higham, *Ziegfeld*, 135.

33. Quoted in Hayter-Menzies, *Mrs. Ziegfeld*, 99.

34. Ziegfeld, *Ziegfelds' Girl*, 177.

35. Ibid., 189.

36. Ibid., 188.

37. Hayter-Menzies, *Mrs. Ziegfeld*, 101.

38. "Billie Burke Album," *Historical Ziegfeld Group*, http://historicalzg.piwigo .com/index?/search/296 (accessed August 10, 2013).

39. Kantor and Maslon, *Broadway*, 52.

40. Seldes, "The Glorifier I–II."

41. Burke, *With a Feather on My Nose,* 196.

42. Travis, *Days We Danced,* 79.

43. Ibid.

44. Ommen van der Merwe, *Ziegfeld Follies,* 121.

45. Irving Berlin, "You'd Be Surprised" (1919), *Song Lyrics,* http://www
.songlyrics.com/berlin-irving/you-d-be-surprised-lyrics/ (accessed January 18, 2014).

46. Mordden, *Ziegfeld,* 179.

47. Cantor, *My Life Is in Your Hands,* 187.

48. Sears, *Irving Berlin Reader,* 193.

49. Travis, *Days We Danced,* 78.

50. Irving Berlin, "A Pretty Girl Is Like a Melody" (1919), *Song Lyrics,* http://
www.songlyrics.com/berlin-irving/pretty-girl-is-like-a-melody-a-lyrics/ (accessed
January 18, 2014).

51. Travis, *Days We Danced,* 79.

52. Mordden, *Ziegfeld,* 179.

12. Dear Old Zieggy and Company

1. Ziegfeld and Ziegfeld, *Ziegfeld Touch,* 86.

2. Gordon, *Discretions and Indiscretions,* 245.

3. Ibid.

4. Seldes, "The Glorifier I–II."

5. Ibid.

6. Earle, *Midnight Frolic,* 249.

7. Burke, *With a Feather on My Nose,* 158.

8. Ibid., 159.

9. Ziegfeld and Ziegfeld, *Ziegfeld Touch,* 137.

10. Ibid.

11. Burke, *With a Feather on My Nose,* 159.

12. Marion Davies, *The Times We Had: Life with William Randolph Hearst* (New
York: Ballantine Books, 1985), 9.

13. Ziegfeld, *Ziegfelds' Girl,* 192–93.

14. Ziegfeld and Ziegfeld, *Ziegfeld Touch,* 160.

15. Cantor, *My Life Is in Your Hands,* 46.

16. Cantor, *Take My Life,* 131.

17. Ibid.

18. Gordon, *Discretions and Indiscretions,* 251.

19. Sobel, *Broadway Heartbeat,* 102.

20. Higham, *Ziegfeld,* 211.

21. Ibid., 215.

22. Hanson, *Lillian Lorraine*, 105.

23. Travis, *Days We Danced*, 71.

24. Cantor, *Take My Life*, 47.

25. Cantor, *My Life Is in Your Hands*, 159.

26. Earle, *Midnight Frolic*, 254.

27. Ibid., 245.

28. Ibid., 270.

29. Cantor, *Take My Life*, 107.

30. Ibid.

31. Ibid., 108.

32. Cantor, *My Life Is in Your Hands*, 160–62.

33. Cantor, *Take My Life*, 200.

34. Ibid., 73.

35. Cantor, *My Life Is in Your Hands*, 44.

36. Kantor and Maslon, *Broadway*, 58.

37. Ibid.

38. Ziegfeld and Ziegfeld, *Ziegfeld Touch*, 91.

39. Kantor and Maslon, *Broadway*, 55.

40. Cantor, *My Life Is in Your Hands*, 209.

41. Ziegfeld and Ziegfeld, *Ziegfeld Touch*, 90.

42. Earle, *Midnight Frolic*, 249.

43. Kantor and Maslon, *Broadway*, 58.

44. Cantor, *My Life Is in Your Hands*, 211.

45. Higham, *Ziegfeld*, 133.

46. Travis, *Days We Danced*, 74.

47. Mordden, *Ziegfeld*, 186.

48. "Be Jack of All Trades on the Stage, Not Master of One," *New York Tribune*, November 16, 1919.

49. "Ziegfeld to Close Frolic while Dry Act Remains Law," *New York Tribune*, May 19, 1921.

50. Hanson, *Lillian Lorraine*, 145.

51. Ibid., 146.

52. Harris, *The Other Marilyn*, 80.

53. Travis, *Days We Danced*, 74.

54. Harris, *The Other Marilyn*, 73.

55. Higham, *Ziegfeld*, 140.

56. Hanson, *Lillian Lorraine*, 101.

57. *Ziegfeld on Film* (DVD).

58. "Give My Regards to Broadway" (DVD).

13. A New Normalcy

1. "Return to Normalcy," *TeachingAmericanHistory.org,* http://teachingamericanhistory .org/library/document/return-to-normalcy/ (accessed August 15, 2013).

2. Quoted in Kantor and Maslon, *Broadway,* 82.

3. Ibid.

4. "Give My Regards to Broadway" (DVD).

5. Ibid.

6. Higham, *Ziegfeld,* 138.

7. Bordman, *American Musical Theatre,* 409.

8. Give My Regards to Broadway" (DVD).

9. "Ziegfeld Follies Rejects Mascot; Black Kitten Not Needed to Bewitch Public," *New York Tribune,* June 27, 1920.

10. Ommen van der Merwe, *Ziegfeld Follies,* 139.

11. Travis, *Days We Danced,* 85.

12. Ibid., 80.

13. Higham, *Ziegfeld,* 154.

14. Ibid., 153.

15. Ibid.

16. Harris, *The Other Marilyn,* 77.

17. "Give My Regards to Broadway" (DVD).

18. B. G. DeSylva, "Look for the Silver Lining" (1919), *Sing365.com,* http:// www.sing365.com/music/lyric.nsf/Look-for-the-Silver-Lining-lyrics-Judy- Garland/AA876D8228AACF3C48256C06000D896E (accessed January 24, 2014).

19. Clifford Grey, "Wild Rose" (1920), *Todd's Jerome Kern Lyric Page,* http:// www.thepeaches.com/music/composers/kern/WildRose.htm (accessed January 24, 2014).

20. Quoted in Harris, *The Other Marilyn,* 81.

21. Quoted in Mordden, *Ziegfeld,* 196.

22. Harris, *The Other Marilyn,* 100.

23. Mordden, *Ziegfeld,* 162.

24. Travis, *Days We Danced,* 74.

25. Harris, *The Other Marilyn,* 88.

26. Higham, *Ziegfeld,* 180.

27. Quoted in Bordman, *American Musical Theatre,* 410.

28. Quoted in Ommen van der Merwe, *Ziegfeld Follies,* 143.

29. Ibid., 144.

30. Earle, *Midnight Frolic,* 264.

31. Ommen van der Merwe, *Ziegfeld Follies,* 152.

32. "Ziegfeld to Close Frolic while Dry Act Remains Law," *New York Tribune,* May 19, 1921.

33. Earle, *Midnight Frolic,* 280.

34. Ziegfeld and Ziegfeld, *Ziegfeld Touch,* 102.

35. Ibid., 105.

36. Barnes, *I Could Never Be Lonely,* 75.

37. Series I: Florenz Ziegfeld Papers 1920–1924, b. 1, f. 13, Anna Held Museum Papers, Billy Rose Theatre Division, New York Public Library for the Performing Arts, New York, NY.

38. Ziegfeld and Ziegfeld, *Ziegfeld Touch,* 103.

39. Hayter-Menzies, *Mrs. Ziegfeld,* 102.

40. Mordden, *Ziegfeld,* 229.

41. Cary D. Wintz, *Encyclopedia of the Harlem Renaissance* (New York: Routledge, 2004), 1210.

42. Hayter-Menzies, *Mrs. Ziegfeld,* 105.

14. The End of the Glory Days

1. Harris, *The Other Marilyn,* 99.

2. Burke, *With a Feather on My Nose,* 209.

3. Harris, *The Other Marilyn,* 100.

4. Burke, *With a Feather on My Nose,* 209.

5. Hayter-Menzies, *Mrs. Ziegfeld,* 104.

6. Harris, *The Other Marilyn,* 101.

7. "Ziegfeld Cables Denial of Charges," *New York Times,* July 24, 1922.

8. Ibid.

9. Burke, *With a Feather on My Nose,* 209.

10. "Ziegfeld Cables Denial of Charges."

11. "Won't Leave Ziegfeld, Billie Burke Declares," *New York Times,* July 25, 1922.

12. Burke, *With a Feather on My Nose,* 211.

13. Harris, *The Other Marilyn,* 102.

14. Mordden, *Ziegfeld,* 205.

15. "New 'Follies' Is Prodigal," *New York Times,* June 6, 1922.

16. Ibid.

17. Ibid.

18. Ed Shean, "Mr. Gallagher and Mr. Shean" (1922), *Musicals 101,* http://www.musicals101.com/lygallagher.htm (accessed January 26, 2014).

19. Earle, *Midnight Frolic,* 279.

20. Ziegfeld and Ziegfeld, *Ziegfeld Touch,* 113.

21. Ommen van der Merwe, *Ziegfeld Follies*, 171.

22. Travis, *Days We Danced*, 96.

23. Series I: Florenz Ziegfeld Papers 1920–1924, b. 1, f. 12, Anna Held Museum Papers, Billy Rose Theatre Division, New York Public Library for the Performing Arts, New York, NY.

24. "Billie Burke in 'Rose Briar,'" *New York Times*, December 26, 1922.

25. Series I: Florenz Ziegfeld Papers 1920–1924, b. 1, f. 3.

26. Ibid.

27. Ibid.

28. Ibid.

29. Series I: Florenz Ziegfeld Papers 1920–1924, b. 1, f. 2.

30. Series I: Florenz Ziegfeld Papers 1920–1924, b. 1, f. 3.

31. Ibid.

32. Series I: Florenz Ziegfeld Papers 1920–1924, b. 1, f. 2.

33. Ibid.

34. Ibid.

35. Ibid.

36. Ibid.

37. Ibid.

38. Ziegfeld, *Ziegfelds' Girl*, 183–86.

39. Harris, *The Other Marilyn*, 119.

40. "Billie Burke Voted Queen of Movies," *New York Times*, May 10, 1922.

15. Little Boy Blue

1. Ommen van der Merwe, *Ziegfeld Follies*, 180.

2. Bordman, *American Musical Theatre*, 429.

3. Cantor, *My Life Is in Your Hands*, 246.

4. Ibid., 237.

5. Travis, *Days We Danced*, 118.

6. Ibid., 117.

7. Cantor, *Take My Life*, 129.

8. Cantor, *My Life Is in Your Hands*, 252.

9. Cantor, *Take My Life*, 129.

10. Quoted in Travis, *Days We Danced*, 120.

11. Ziegfeld and Ziegfeld, *Ziegfeld Touch*, 114.

12. Cantor, *My Life Is in Your Hands*, 259.

13. Mordden, *Ziegfeld*, 216.

14. Ziegfeld and Ziegfeld, *Ziegfeld Touch*, 114.

15. Series I: Florenz Ziegfeld Papers 1920–1924, b. 1, f. 2, Anna Held Museum

Papers, Billy Rose Theatre Division, New York Public Library for the Performing Arts, New York, NY.

16. Series I: Florenz Ziegfeld Papers 1920–1924, b. 1, f. 3.

17. Ibid.

18. Ibid.

19. Seldes, "The Glorifier I–II."

20. Mordden, *Ziegfeld*, 219.

21. Quoted in Hayter-Menzies, *Mrs. Ziegfeld*, 111.

22. Burke, *With a Feather on My Nose*, 201.

23. Bordman, *American Musical Theatre*, 444.

24. Mordden, *Ziegfeld*, 219.

25. Ziegfeld and Ziegfeld, *Ziegfeld Touch*, 117.

26. Quoted in Wertheim, *Will Rogers*, 209.

27. Higham, *Ziegfeld*, 152.

28. Ziegfeld, *Ziegfelds' Girl*, 95.

16. Vacations from Reality

1. Ziegfeld and Ziegfeld, *Ziegfeld Touch*, 118.

2. Burke, *With a Feather on My Nose*, 185.

3. Mordden, *Ziegfeld*, 207.

4. Quoted in Burke, *With a Feather on My Nose*, 190.

5. Ziegfeld and Ziegfeld, *Ziegfeld Touch*, 115.

6. Ziegfeld, *Ziegfelds' Girl*, 106.

7. Ibid., 118.

8. Ibid., 63.

9. Wertheim, *Will Rogers*, 213.

10. "Whiskey Ruse Used in Ziegfeld Suit," *New York Times*, August 16, 1924.

11. Ziegfeld and Ziegfeld, *Ziegfeld Touch*, 120.

12. Ibid.

13. Ibid., 119.

14. Mordden, *Ziegfeld*, 221.

15. Higham, *Ziegfeld*, 164.

16. Mordden, *Ziegfeld*, 223.

17. Wertheim, *Will Rogers*, 119.

18. Ziegfeld and Ziegfeld, *Ziegfeld Touch*, 121.

19. "Ziegfeld on Modesty in Dress," *Dubuque (IA) Telegraph-Herald*, August 28, 1921.

20. "Stage Nudity 'Disgust' Flo," *St. Petersburg (FL) Evening Independent*, June 26, 1926.

21. Wertheim, *Will Rogers*, 214.

22. Ziegfeld, *Ziegfelds' Girl,* 164.

23. Ibid., 174.

24. Quoted in Ommen van der Merwe, *Ziegfeld Follies,* 181.

25. Fred Astaire, *Steps in Time* (New York: It Books, 2008), 73.

26. Ziegfeld and Ziegfeld, *Ziegfeld Touch,* 103.

27. Series I: Florenz Ziegfeld Papers 1920–1924, b. 1, f. 2, Anna Held Museum Papers, Billy Rose Theatre Division, New York Public Library for the Performing Arts, New York, NY.

28. Ibid.

29. Ziegfeld and Ziegfeld, *Ziegfeld Touch,* 103.

30. Series I: Florenz Ziegfeld Papers 1920–1924, b. 1, f. 14.

31. Stephen Zebrock, "Billie Burke and Burkeley Crest," Hastings Historical Society, September 14, 2009, http://hastingshistoricalsociety.blogspot.com/2009/09/billie-burke-and-burkeley-crest.html (accessed March 3, 2013).

32. Series I: Florenz Ziegfeld Papers 1920–1924, b. 1, f. 2.

33. Series I: Florenz Ziegfeld Papers 1920–1924, b. 1, f. 14.

34. Series I: Florenz Ziegfeld Papers 1920–1924, b. 1, f. 2.

35. Series I: Florenz Ziegfeld Papers 1920–1924, b. 1, f. 14.

36. Ziegfeld, *Ziegfelds' Girl,* 79.

37. Ibid., 78.

38. Series I: Florenz Ziegfeld Papers 1920–1924, b. 1, f. 2.

39. Ziegfeld, *Ziegfelds' Girl,* 79.

40. Series I: Florenz Ziegfeld Papers 1920–1924, b. 1, f. 2.

41. Ibid.

42. Ziegfeld, *Ziegfelds' Girl,* 79, 80.

43. Ibid., 83.

44. Ziegfeld and Ziegfeld, *Ziegfeld Touch,* 109.

45. Ziegfeld, *Ziegfelds' Girl,* 156.

46. Series I: Florenz Ziegfeld Papers 1920–1924, b. 1, f. 3.

47. Burke, *With a Feather on My Nose,* 212.

48. Ziegfeld and Ziegfeld, *Ziegfeld Touch,* 109.

49. Ziegfeld, *Ziegfelds' Girl,* 85.

50. Ibid., 87.

51. Hayter-Menzies, *Mrs. Ziegfeld,* 160.

52. Ziegfeld, *Ziegfelds' Girl,* 111.

17. A Shot in the Arm

1. Mordden, *Ziegfeld,* 207–8.

2. Ziegfeld, *Ziegfelds' Girl,* 120.

3. Ibid.

4. Ibid.

5. Burke, *With a Feather on My Nose*, 213.

6. Ziegfeld, *Ziegfelds' Girl*, 124.

7. Burke, *With a Feather on My Nose*, 184.

8. Ibid., 212.

9. Ibid., 214.

10. Ibid., 215.

11. Eve Golden, e-mail interview with the authors, November 11, 2012.

12. Ziegfeld and Ziegfeld, *Ziegfeld Touch*, 115.

13. Ziegfeld, *Ziegfelds' Girl*, 118.

14. Ibid., 119.

15. Burke, *With a Feather on My Nose*, 216.

16. Burke, *With Powder on My Nose*, 33.

17. Ziegfeld, *Ziegfelds' Girl*, 115.

18. Ibid., 131.

19. Ibid., 133.

20. Florenz Ziegfeld Jr., "Bobbed Hair Making American Girls Most Beautiful in the World," *Milwaukee Sentinel*, April 19, 1925.

21. Sobel, *Broadway Heartbeat*, 108.

22. Series I: Florenz Ziegfeld Papers 1920–1924, b. 1, f. 3, Anna Held Museum Papers, Billy Rose Theatre Division, New York Public Library for the Performing Arts, New York, NY.

23. Ziegfeld and Ziegfeld, *Ziegfeld Touch*, 130.

24. Ibid.

25. Mordden, *Ziegfeld*, 230.

26. "Berlin Hears Fortune Is Lost to Ziegfeld," *New York Times*, May 9, 1926.

27. Quoted in Ziegfeld and Ziegfeld, *Ziegfeld Touch*, 136.

28. Ibid.

29. Sears, *Irving Berlin Reader*, 84.

30. Ziegfeld and Ziegfeld, *Ziegfeld Touch*, 136.

31. Rodgers, *Musical Stages*, 94.

32. Mordden, *Ziegfeld*, 232.

33. Barnes, *I Could Never Be Lonely*, 72.

34. Bordman, *American Musical Theatre*, 433.

35. "*Betsy* Presented; Elaborately Staged," *New York Times*, December 29, 1926.

36. Bordman, *American Musical Theatre*, 472.

37. "Ziegfeld Theater Will Open Tonight," *New York Times*, February 1, 1927.

38. Bordman, *American Musical Theatre*, 472.

39. Ziegfeld and Ziegfeld, *Ziegfeld Touch*, 139.

40. Wertheim, *Will Rogers*, 217–18.

41. Ibid., 217.

42. Mordden, *Ziegfeld*, 239.

43. Bordman, *American Musical Theatre*, 472.

44. "Ziegfeld Not Cock Fighter," *New York Times*, May 8, 1927.

45. Sobel, *Broadway Heartbeat*, 182.

46. Ziegfeld and Ziegfeld, *Ziegfeld Touch*, 142.

47. "Ziegfeld and Royce in Court Battle," *New York Times*, May 28, 1927.

48. Wertheim, *Will Rogers*, 13.

49. Ibid., 219.

50. Ibid., 220.

51. Ibid., 221.

52. Ibid.

53. Cantor, *Take My Life*, 282.

54. Ziegfeld, *Ziegfelds' Girl*, 193–94.

55. Cantor, *Take My Life*, 283.

56. Ibid., 281.

57. Ziegfeld and Ziegfeld, *Ziegfeld Touch*, 142.

58. Cantor, *My Life Is in Your Hands*, 134.

18. Splendor and Intelligence

1. Miles Kreuger, Show Boat: *The Story of a Classic American Musical* (New York: Oxford University Press, 1978), 20.

2. "Give My Regards to Broadway" (DVD).

3. Kreuger, Show Boat, 26.

4. Quoted in Todd Decker, Show Boat: *Performing Race in an American Musical* (New York: Oxford University Press, 2012), 27.

5. Ibid.

6. Mordden, *Ziegfeld*, 244.

7. Decker, Show Boat, 57.

8. Bordman, *American Musical Theatre*, 484.

9. Decker, Show Boat, 51.

10. Ibid., 52.

11. Ibid., 39.

12. Quoted in Kantor and Maslon, *Broadway*, 118.

13. Oscar Hammerstein II, "Ol' Man River" (1927), *StLyrics*, http://www.stlyrics.com/lyrics/showboat/olmanriver.htm (accessed February 6, 2014).

14. Decker, Show Boat, 64.

15. "*Show Boat* Postponed," *New York Times*, February 7, 1927.

16. Decker, Show Boat, 101.

17. Ibid., 121–22.

18. Burke, *With a Feather on My Nose*, 242.

19. Kreuger, Show Boat, 37.

20. Decker, Show Boat, 79.

21. Ibid., 81.

22. Ziegfeld and Ziegfeld, *Ziegfeld Touch*, 145.

23. Ibid.

24. Barnes, *I Could Never Be Lonely*, 73.

25. Ziegfeld and Ziegfeld, *Ziegfeld Touch*, 144.

26. Cantor, *My Life Is in Your Hands*, 132.

27. Quoted in Kantor and Maslon, *Broadway*, 112.

28. Higham, *Ziegfeld*, 184.

29. Cantor, *My Life Is in Your Hands*, 133.

30. Kreuger, Show Boat, 53.

31. Ziegfeld and Ziegfeld, *Ziegfeld Touch*, 232.

32. "Give My Regards to Broadway" (DVD).

33. Quoted in Decker, Show Boat, ix.

34. Michael Feinstein, *The Gershwins and Me* (New York: Simon and Schuster, 2012), 72.

35. "Give My Regards to Broadway" (DVD).

36. Wertheim, *Will Rogers*, 226.

37. Burke, *With a Feather on My Nose*, 206.

38. Ibid., 207.

39. Ibid., 218.

40. Hayter-Menzies, *Mrs. Ziegfeld*, 116.

41. "Billie Burke Lovely in Coward's 'Marquise,'" *New York Times*, November 15, 1927.

42. Higham, *Ziegfeld*, 186.

43. Feinstein, *The Gershwins and Me*, 55.

44. Quoted in Astaire, *Steps in Time*, 73.

45. "Rejoins Ziegfeld as Star; Marilyn Miller Signs a Five-Year Contract," *New York Times*, February 22, 1927.

46. Ibid.

47. Mordden, *Ziegfeld*, 258.

48. Harris, *The Other Marilyn*, 151.

49. Ibid.

50. Quoted in Kantor and Maslon, *Broadway*, 83.

51. Quoted in Bordman, *American Musical Theatre*, 486.

52. Brooks Atkinson, "The Play: Marilyn Miller Returning," *New York Times*, January 11, 1928.

19. Ziegfeld Laughs . . . and Cries

1. Mordden, *Ziegfeld,* 258.

2. Higham, *Ziegfeld ,* 191.

3. Ibid., 197.

4. Quoted in Cantor, *My Life Is in Your Hands,* 134.

5. Quoted in Carter, *World of Flo Ziegfeld,* 147–48.

6. "Ziggy," *Time,* May 14, 1928.

7. "Bust of Ziegfeld Unveiled," *New York Times,* May 18, 1928.

8. Ziegfeld, *Ziegfelds' Girl,* 125.

9. Ziegfeld and Ziegfeld, *Ziegfeld Touch,* 149.

10. Ibid., 150.

11. Ibid., 201.

12. Higham, *Ziegfeld,* 196.

13. Decker, Show Boat, 126.

14. Ibid., 130.

15. Cantor, *My Life Is in Your Hands,* 134.

16. *Whoopee!* (1930; Hollywood, CA: Samuel Goldwyn Company, 1992), video.

17. Cantor, *My Life Is in Your Hands,* 134.

18. Ellen Donaldson, "My Memories of *Whoopee,*" October 31, 1997, *Theatre under the Stars,* http://www.alscher.priv.at/whoopee/TUTS98/DonaldsonArticle .html (accessed April 25, 2014).

19. Ziegfeld and Ziegfeld, *Ziegfeld Touch,* 150.

20. Higham, *Ziegfeld,* 195.

21. Cantor, *My Life Is in Your Hands,* 135.

22. Gus Kahn, "Makin' Whoopee" (1928), *Song Lyrics,* http://www.songlyrics .com/eddie-cantor/makin-whoopee-lyrics (accessed February 9, 2014).

23. Higham, *Ziegfeld,* 195.

24. Cantor, *My Life Is in Your Hands,* 135.

25. Ibid., 137.

26. Ibid., 136.

27. "Ziegfeld to Close 'Midnight Frolic,'" *New York Times,* April 21, 1929.

28. "Ziegfeld 'Not Worried,'" *New York Times,* March 25, 1929.

29. "Ziegfeld Attacks Hammerstein's Plan," *New York Times,* April 4, 1929.

30. Edward Jablonski, *Gershwin* (New York: Doubleday, 1987), 189.

31. Ibid.

32. Ibid., 190.

33. Ibid., 191.

34. Cantor, *Take My Life,* 54.

35. Ibid., 56.

36. Ziegfeld and Ziegfeld, *Ziegfeld Touch,* 153.

37. Ibid.

38. Higham, *Ziegfeld,* 199.

39. Jablonski, *Gershwin,* 191.

40. Brooks Atkinson, "The Play," *New York Times,* July 3, 1929.

41. Ibid.

42. Ibid.

43. Higham, *Ziegfeld,* 197.

44. Atkinson, "The Play."

45. Quoted in Wertheim, *Will Rogers,* 231.

46. Ziegfeld, *Ziegfelds' Girl,* 195.

47. Higham, *Ziegfeld,* 200.

48. Ibid.

49. Mordden, *Ziegfeld,* 271.

50. Ibid., 272.

51. "Ziggy," *Time,* May 14, 1928.

52. "Give My Regards to Broadway" (DVD).

53. Zebrock, "Billie Burke and Burkeley Crest."

54. Ziegfeld and Ziegfeld, *Ziegfeld Touch,* 154.

55. "Will Rogers Quotes," *brainyquote.com,* http://www.brainyquote.com/quotes/quotes/w/willrogers161236.htm (accessed January 5, 2013).

56. Bordman, *American Musical Theatre,* 476.

57. "Give My Regards to Broadway" (DVD).

58. Quoted in Kantor and Maslon, *Broadway,* 130.

59. Higham, *Ziegfeld,* 202.

60. Burke, *With Powder on My Nose,* 46.

61. Burke, *With a Feather on My Nose,* 222.

62. Ibid., 121.

63. Jablonski, *Gershwin,* 192.

64. Brooks Atkinson, "'Simple Simon' Wynn's Field Day," *New York Times,* February 19, 1930.

65. "Asks Hoover's Aid in Repealing Tax," *New York Times,* December 8, 1929.

20. "I Can't Do This Anymore"

1. Cantor, *My Life Is in Your Hands,* 154.

2. Ibid., 152.

3. Jeffrey Spivak, *Buzz: The Life and Art of Busby Berkeley* (Lexington: University Press of Kentucky, 2010), 46.

4. Higham, *Ziegfeld,* 205.

5. Ziegfeld and Ziegfeld, *Ziegfeld Touch,* 157.

6. Hayter-Menzies, *Mrs. Ziegfeld,* 126.

7. Higham, *Ziegfeld,* 205.

8. Michael Freeland, *The Goldwyn Touch* (New York: Harrap, 1986), 115.

9. Higham, *Ziegfeld,* 207.

10. Cantor, *Take My Life,* 152.

11. Ziegfeld and Ziegfeld, *Ziegfeld Touch,* 157.

12. Spivak, *Buzz,* 51.

13. Carter, *World of Flo Ziegfeld,* 153.

14. Mordden, *Ziegfeld,* 277.

15. Bordman, *American Musical Theatre,* 502.

16. Ibid., 511.

17. "Carroll Retorts to Ziegfeld Attack," *New York Times,* July 13, 1930.

18. Bordman, *American Musical Theatre,* 511.

19. Ibid., 513.

20. Astaire, *Steps in Time,* 159.

21. Ibid., 18.

22. Ibid., 159–60.

23. Ibid., 161.

24. Ibid., 164.

25. Ibid., 162.

26. Quoted in Harris, *The Other Marilyn,* 176.

27. Brooks Atkinson, "Smiling at the Ziegfeld," *New York Times,* November 19, 1930.

28. Higham, *Ziegfeld,* 207.

29. Astaire, *Steps in Time,* 163.

30. Mordden, *Ziegfeld,* 281.

31. Astaire, *Steps in Time,* 164.

32. Ibid., 163.

33. Travis, *Days We Danced,* 136.

34. Burke, *With a Feather on My Nose,* 118.

35. Ziegfeld, *Ziegfelds' Girl,* 200.

36. Hayter-Menzies, *Mrs. Ziegfeld,* 129.

37. Ibid., 131.

38. Burke, *With a Feather on My Nose,* 226.

39. Ziegfeld and Ziegfeld, *Ziegfeld Touch,* 159, 155.

40. Higham, *Ziegfeld,* 210.

41. Ibid., 210–11.

42. Ommen van der Merwe, *Ziegfeld Follies,* 201.

43. Ibid., 203.

44. Burke, *With a Feather on My Nose*, 230.

45. Ziegfeld and Ziegfeld, *Ziegfeld Touch*, 161.

46. Brooks Atkinson, "Follies for 1931," *New York Times*, July 2, 1931.

47. Ommen van der Merwe, *Ziegfeld Follies*, 209.

48. "Theater: Good Old Follies," *Time*, July 13, 1931.

49. Burke, *With a Feather on My Nose*, 231.

50. Ibid., 227.

51. Ziegfeld and Ziegfeld, *Ziegfeld Touch*, 162.

21. Going Home

1. Mordden, *Ziegfeld*, 285.

2. John Lahr, *Notes on a Cowardly Lion* (New York: Alfred A. Knopf, 1969), 123.

3. Ibid., 128.

4. Higham, *Ziegfeld*, 212.

5. Mordden, *Ziegfeld*, 288.

6. Ibid., 231.

7. Burke, *With a Feather on My Nose*, 204.

8. Sobel, *Broadway Heartbeat*, 102–3.

9. Higham, *Ziegfeld*, 213–14.

10. Lahr, *Notes on a Cowardly Lion*, 129.

11. Ziegfeld and Ziegfeld, *Ziegfeld Touch*, 162.

12. Ibid., 163.

13. Brooks Atkinson, "Bert Lahr Gamboling Belligerently through a Ziegfeld Musical Show Set in Mexico," *New York Times*, March 9, 1932.

14. Lahr, *Notes on a Cowardly Lion*, 130.

15. "Ziegfeld's 'Hot-Cha' to End Its Run," *New York Times*, May 25, 1932.

16. "Hot-Cha! to Continue at Lower Ticket Rate," *New York Times*, May 27, 1932.

17. William E. Leuchtenburg, *The Perils of Prosperity*, 2nd ed. (Chicago: University of Chicago Press, 1993), 86.

18. Carter, *World of Flo Ziegfeld*, 154.

19. Ziegfeld and Ziegfeld, *Ziegfeld Touch*, 162.

20. Higham, *Ziegfeld*, 217.

21. Burke, *With a Feather on My Nose*, 233.

22. Ziegfeld and Ziegfeld, *Ziegfeld Touch*, 164.

23. Burke, *With a Feather on My Nose*, 152.

24. Ziegfeld and Ziegfeld, *Ziegfeld Touch*, 164.

25. "Ziegfeld Follies of the Air," April 10, 1932, *OTRCat: Old Time Radio Catalog*, http://www.otrcat.com/ziegfeld-follies-of-the-air-p-49069.html (accessed April 26, 2014).

26. Burke, *With a Feather on My Nose,* 232.

27. Ibid., 226.

28. Decker, Show Boat, 140.

29. Ziegfeld and Ziegfeld, *Ziegfeld Touch,* 165.

30. Decker, Show Boat, 140.

31. Kreuger, Show Boat, 99.

32. Burke, *With a Feather on My Nose,* 226.

33. Ibid., 234.

34. Ibid., 235.

35. Ziegfeld, *Ziegfelds' Girl,* 204.

36. Higham, *Ziegfeld,* 219–20.

37. Ibid., 222.

38. Ziegfeld and Ziegfeld, *Ziegfeld Touch,* 167.

39. Ibid.

40. Burke, *With a Feather on My Nose,* 239.

41. Higham, *Ziegfeld,* 233.

42. Ziegfeld, *Ziegfelds' Girl,* 155.

43. Ibid., 204.

44. Burke, *With a Feather on My Nose,* 243.

45. Ibid., 248.

46. Grant Hayter-Menzies, "The Real Glinda: A Conversation with Grant Hayter-Menzies," *The Wizard's Wireless,* January 20, 2009, http://www.frodelius.com/wirelesstelegraph/hayter-menzies.html (accessed December 8, 2013).

47. Ziegfeld, *Ziegfelds' Girl,* 204.

48. Burke, *With a Feather on My Nose,* 240.

49. Quoted in Wertheim, *Will Rogers,* 234.

50. Ibid., 232.

51. Ibid.

52. Ibid., 233.

53. Sobel, *Broadway Heartbeat,* 197.

54. Quoted in Wertheim, *Will Rogers,* 233.

55. William Arms Fisher, "Goin' Home" (1922), *Lyrics Mode,* http://www.lyricsmode.com/lyrics/r/religious_music/goin_home.html (accessed April 26, 2014).

56. Wertheim, *Will Rogers,* 233–34.

57. Higham, *Ziegfeld,* 223.

58. Burke, *With a Feather on My Nose,* 241.

59. Wertheim, *Will Rogers,* 234–35.

60. Higham, *Ziegfeld,* 225.

61. Gene Buck, "Florenz Ziegfeld: A Tribute from a Friend," *New York Times,* July 21, 1932.

22. Going Hollywood

1. Higham, *Ziegfeld*, 224.
2. Carter, *World of Flo Ziegfeld*, 127.
3. Higham, *Ziegfeld*, 224.
4. Burke, *With a Feather on My Nose*, 249.
5. Ziegfeld, *Ziegfelds' Girl*, 204.
6. Hayter-Menzies, "The Real Glinda."
7. Burke, *With Powder on My Nose*, 74.
8. Ibid., 76.
9. Hayter-Menzies, *Mrs. Ziegfeld*, 142.
10. Burke, *With a Feather on My Nose*, 249.
11. *Dinner at Eight* (1933; Hollywood, CA: MGM, 1997), video.
12. Hayter-Menzies, *Mrs. Ziegfeld*, 151.
13. Burke, *With a Feather on My Nose*, 254.
14. Ibid., 250.
15. Vincente Minnelli, *I Remember It Well* (New York: Doubleday, 1974), 77.
16. Ibid.
17. Ibid., 79–80.
18. Higham, *Ziegfeld*, 226.
19. Burke, *With a Feather on My Nose*, 255.
20. Ziegfeld, *Ziegfelds' Girl*, 205.
21. Burke, *With a Feather on My Nose*, 250.
22. Ziegfeld, *Ziegfelds' Girl*, 207.
23. Burke, *With a Feather on My Nose*, 250.

23. His Shows Must Go On

1. "Fanny Brice Recalls Old Days When She Began Stage Career Now for an Extended Period," *Evening Independent* (St. Petersburg, FL), March 1, 1938.
2. Cantor, *Take My Life*, 42.
3. "Will Rogers Quotes," *WikiQuote*, http://en.wikiquote.org/wiki/Will_Rogers (accessed February 24, 2014).
4. "The Great Ziegfeld," *AFI Catalog of Feature Films*, http://www.afi.com/members/catalog/DetailView.aspx?s=&Movie=8351 (accessed April 27, 2014).
5. Harris, *The Other Marilyn*, 219.
6. Hayter-Menzies, *Mrs. Ziegfeld*, 162.
7. Ibid.
8. "'The Great Ziegfeld,' Metro's Lavish Biography of a Showman Opens at the Astor," *New York Times*, April 9, 1936.

9. "The Great Ziegfeld," *AFI Catalog.*

10. Hayter-Menzies, *Mrs. Ziegfeld,* 161.

11. "'The Great Ziegfeld,' Metro's Lavish Biography."

12. Hayter-Menzies, *Mrs. Ziegfeld,* 162.

13. "The Great Ziegfeld," *AFI Catalog.*

14. Hayter-Menzies, *Mrs. Ziegfeld,* 161.

15. "'The Great Ziegfeld,' Metro's Lavish Biography."

16. Ziegfeld, *Ziegfelds' Girl,* 204.

17. "Ziegfeld Follies," *AFI Catalog of Feature Films,* http://www.afi.com/members/catalog/DetailView.aspx?s=&Movie=25060 (accessed April 27, 2014).

18. Rogers St. John, "The Girls Who Glorified Ziegfeld."

19. *Ziegfeld Follies* (1946; Hollywood, CA: MGM, 2006), DVD.

20. Burke, *With a Feather on My Nose,* 242.

21. Ralph Freed, "How About You?" (1942), *Leo's Lyrics,* http://www.leoslyrics.com/judy-garland-and-mickey-rooney/how-about-you-lyrics/ (accessed February 25, 2014).

22. *Ziegfeld Girl* (1941; Hollywood, CA: MGM, 2004), DVD.

23. *Funny Girl* (1968; Hollywood, CA: Columbia Pictures, 2001), DVD.

24. Hal Erikson, "*Ziegfeld: The Man and His Women,*" *New York Times,* http://www.nytimes.com/movies/movie/130081/Ziegfeld-The-Man-and-His-Women/overview (accessed April 28, 2014).

25. "Ziegfeld," *The Guide to Musical Theatre,* http://www.guidetomusicaltheatre.com/shows_z/ziegfeld.htm (accessed April 28, 2014).

26. "Follies," *Louise Gold Site,* 2013, http://www.qsulis.demon.co.uk/Website_Louise_Gold/Follies.htm (accessed April 28, 2014).

27. Lawrence Bommer, "Ziegfeld, a Night at the Follies," *Chicago Reader,* June 17, 1993, http://www.chicagoreader.com/chicago/puttin-on-the-ritzziegfeld-a-night-at-the-follies/Content?oid=882196 (accessed April 29, 2014).

28. Lou Cedrone, "*Ziegfeld* Offers Music and Glitter at a Good Pace," *Baltimore Evening Sun,* April 4, 1991, http://articles.baltimoresun.com/1991–04–04/features/1991094186_1_follies-ziegfeld-catherine-hart (accessed April 29, 2014).

29. Jack Vietel, "Ziegfeld, the *Follies, Follies,* and Encore!" *Playbill,* February 9, 2007, http://www.playbill.com/features/article/105650-Ziegfeld-The-Follies-Follies-and-Encores-2007 (accessed April 29, 2014).

24. Beauty Slain

1. Burke, *With a Feather on My Nose,* 257.

2. Cantor, *Take My Life,* 50.

3. Ted Chapin and Herbert Keyser, *Geniuses of the American Musical Theatre:*

The Composers and Lyricists (Milwaukee: Applause Theatre and Cinema Books, 2009), 130.

4. Hanson, *Lillian Lorraine*, 196.

5. Douglas Martin, "Doris E. Travis, Last of the Ziegfeld Girls, Dies at 106," *New York Times*, May 12, 2010.

6. "Ziegfeld Theater Will Be Razed for a Skyscraper," *New York Times*, August 5, 1966.

7. Christopher Gray, "An Architect's Evocative Legacy of Fantasy and Drama," *New York Times*, November 14, 2004.

8. Zebrock, "Billie Burke and Burkeley Crest."

9. Kelly, "Billie Burke and Florenz Ziegfeld."

10. Hayter-Menzies, "The Real Glinda."

11. Ralph Olive, "Grandchild of Theatrical Family Plans Career in Education," *Eugene (OR) Register-Guard*, October 2, 1959.

12. Burke, *With a Feather on My Nose*, 204.

13. Ibid., 187.

14. Ibid., 253.

15. Hayter-Menzies, *Mrs. Ziegfeld*, 203.

16. James Robert Parish and Ronald Bowers, *The MGM Stock Company: The Golden Era* (New Rochelle, NY: Arlington House, 1973), 99.

17. Rogers St. John, "The Girls Who Glorified Ziegfeld."

18. Hayter-Menzies, *Mrs. Ziegfeld*, 169.

19. Hayter-Menzies, "The Real Glinda."

Epilogue

1. Higham, *Ziegfeld*, 233.

2. Sobel, *Broadway Heartbeat*, 101.

3. Quoted in Rogers St. John, "The Girls Who Glorified Ziegfeld."

4. Sobel, *Broadway Heartbeat*, 102.

5. Higham, *Ziegfeld*, 233–35.

6. "Florenz Ziegfeld," *Rochester (NY) Evening Journal*, August 24, 1928.

7. Quoted in Rogers St. John, "The Girls Who Glorified Ziegfeld."

Selected Bibliography

Literature

Astaire, Fred. *Steps in Time*. New York: It Books, 2008.

Barnes, Djuna. *I Could Never Be Lonely without a Husband*. London: Virago Press, 1985.

Berlandstein, Leonard, Michele Majer, Marlis Schweitzer, and Sheila Stowell. *Staging Fashion, 1880–1920: Jane Hading, Lily Elsie, Billie Burke*. New York: Bard Graduate Center for Studies in the Decorative Arts, Design, and Culture, 2012.

Bordman, Gerald. *American Musical Theatre: A Chronicle*. New York: Oxford University Press, 2001.

Burke, Billie. *With a Feather on My Nose*. New York: Appleton Century Crofts, 1949.

———. *With Powder on My Nose*. New York: Coward-McCann, 1959.

Cantor, Eddie. *My Life Is in Your Hands*. Lanham, MD: Cooper Square Press, 2000.

———. *Take My Life*. Lanham, MD: Cooper Square Press, 2000.

Cantor, Eddie, and David Freedman. *The Great Glorifier*. New York: Alfred H. King, 1934.

Carrera, Liane. *Anna Held and Flo Ziegfeld*. Pompano Beach: Exposition Press of Florida, 1979.

Carter, Randolph. *The World of Flo Ziegfeld*. New York: Praeger, 1974.

Chapman, Gary. *The Delectable Dollies: The Dolly Sisters, Icons of the Jazz Age*. Gloucestershire, UK: History Press, 2007.

Decker, Todd. Show Boat: *Performing Race in an American Musical*. New York: Oxford University Press, 2012.

Earle, Marcelle. *Midnight Frolic: A Ziegfeld Girl's True Story*. Basking Ridge, NJ: Twin Oaks Publishing, 1999.

Farnsworth, Marjorie. *The Ziegfeld Follies*. New York: Bonanza Books, 1956.

Feinstein, Michael. *The Gershwins and Me*. New York: Simon and Schuster, 2012.

Freeland, Michael. *The Goldwyn Touch*. New York: Harrap, 1986.

Golden, Eve. *Anna Held and the Birth of Ziegfeld's Broadway*. Lexington: University Press of Kentucky, 2000.

Gordon, Lucile Duff. *Discretions and Indiscretions*. New York: Frederick Stokes, 1932.

Grossman, Barbara. *Funny Woman: The Life and Times of Fanny Brice*. Bloomington: Indiana University Press, 1992.

Hanson, Nils. *Lillian Lorraine: The Life and Times of a Ziegfeld Diva*. Jefferson, NC: McFarland, 2012.

Harris, Warren G. *The Other Marilyn*. Westminster, MD: Arbor House, 1985.

Hayter-Menzies, Grant. *Mrs. Ziegfeld: The Public and Private Lives of Billie Burke*. Jefferson, NC: McFarland, 2009.

Higham, Charles. *Ziegfeld*. Chicago: Regnery, 1972.

Jablonski, Edward. *Gershwin*. New York: Doubleday, 1987.

Kantor, Michael, and Laurence Maslon. *Broadway: The American Musical*. New York: Bulfinch, 2004.

Kreuger, Miles. Show Boat: *The Story of a Classic American Musical*. New York: Oxford University Press, 1978.

Lahr, John. *Notes on a Cowardly Lion*. New York: Alfred A. Knopf, 1969.

Mordden, Ethan. *Ziegfeld: The Man Who Invented Show Business*. New York: St. Martin's Press, 2008.

Ommen van der Merwe, Ann. *The Ziegfeld Follies: A History in Song*. Lanham, MD: Scarecrow Press, 2009.

Rogers, Will. *The Autobiography of Will Rogers*. Edited by Donald Day. Chicago: Peoples Book Club, 1949.

Sears, Benjamin. *The Irving Berlin Reader*. New York: Oxford University Press, 2012.

Sobel, Bernard. *Broadway Heartbeat: Memoirs of a Press Agent*. New York: Hermitage House, 1953.

Spivak, Jeffrey. *Buzz: The Life and Art of Busby Berkeley*. Lexington: University Press of Kentucky, 2010.

Travis, Doris Eaton. *The Days We Danced: The Story of My Theatrical Family from Ziegfeld to Arthur Murray and Beyond*. Norman: University of Oklahoma Press, 2003.

Wertheim, Arthur Frank. *Will Rogers: At the Ziegfeld Follies*. Norman: University of Oklahoma Press, 1992.

Ziegfeld, Patricia. *The Ziegfelds' Girl: Confessions of an Abnormally Happy Childhood*. New York: Little Brown, 1964.

Ziegfeld, Richard, and Paulette Ziegfeld. *The Ziegfeld Touch: The Life and Times of Florenz Ziegfeld, Jr.* New York: Henry Abrams, 1993.

Films

Dinner at Eight. Dir.: George Cukor. Perf.: Jean Harlow, John Barrymore, Billie Burke. 1933. Hollywood, CA: MGM, 1997. Video.

Funny Girl. Dir.: William Wyler. Perf.: Barbra Streisand, Omar Sharif, Kay Medford. 1968. Hollywood, CA: Columbia Pictures, 2001. DVD.

"Give My Regards to Broadway." *Broadway: The American Musical,* episode 1. Arlington, VA: PBS, 2004. DVD.

The Great Ziegfeld. Dir.: Robert Z. Leonard. Perf: William Powell, Myrna Loy, Luise Rainer. 1936. Hollywood, CA, 2004. DVD.

Show Boat. Dir.: James Whale. Perf: Irene Dunne, Allan Jones, Charles Winninger. 1936. Hollywood, CA: Universal Studios, 1990. Video.

Whoopee! Dir.: Thornton Freeland. Perf: Eddie Cantor, Ethel Shutta, Paul Gregory. 1930. Hollywood, CA: Samuel Goldwyn Studios, 1992. Video.

Ziegfeld on Film. Dir.: Peter Fitzgerald. Perf: Patricia Ziegfeld, Luise Rainer, Richard Ziegfeld. Hollywood, CA: Turner Entertainment, 2004. DVD.

Websites

"Billie Burke and Burkeley Crest." Hastings Historical Society. September 14, 2009. http://hastingshistoricalsociety.blogspot.com/2009/09 billie-burke-and-burkeley-crest.html.

"Florenz Ziegfeld and the Ziegfeld Follies." *The Parlor Songs Academy.* 2004. http://parlorsongs.com/issues/2004–1/thismonth/feature.php.

Internet Broadway Database. 2001. www.ibdb.com.

Kelly, Kate. "Billie Burke and Florenz Ziegfeld." Westchester County Historical Society. http://www.westchesterhistory.com/index.php/exhibits/people?display=burke_ziegfeld.

Kendrick, John. *Musicals 101.* 1997. http://www.musicals101.com/index.html.

———. *Ziegfeld 101.* 2002. http://www.musicals101.com/ziegfeld.htm.

Index

Screen Classics

Screen Classics is a series of critical biographies, film histories, and analytical studies focusing on neglected filmmakers and important screen artists and subjects, from the era of silent cinema to the golden age of Hollywood to the international generation of today. Books in the Screen Classics series are intended for scholars and general readers alike. The contributing authors are established figures in their respective fields. This series also serves the purpose of advancing scholarship on film personalities and themes with ties to Kentucky.

Series Editor
Patrick McGilligan

Books in the Series